# THEORY OF AUTOMATA and FORMAL LANGUAGES

# THEORY OF AUTOMATA AND FORMAL LANGUAGES

**AMIT KUMAR**
(Associate Professor)
Rakshpal Bahadur Management Institute (RBMI)

**Khanna Book Publishing Co. (P) Ltd.**
**Delhi**

ISBN : 978-93-80016-0-85

**First Edition, 2010**

*Published by:*
**Khanna Book Publishing Co. (P) Ltd.**
4C/4344, Ansari Road, Darya Ganj, New Delhi-110 002
Phone: 011-23244447, 23244448
E-mail: contact@khannabooks.com
Website: www.khannabooks.com

*Regd. Off:* 1694-95, 1st Floor, Nai Sarak, Delhi-110006 (India)
Phone: 011-23283211, 23256658
Fax: 011-23256658

*Laser Typesetting by:*
M/s Shree Shyam Computers, Delhi

*Printed in India*
Z.N. Printers, Delhi

# PREFACE

It gives me great pleasure in presenting the first edition of the book ***"Theory of Automata and Formal Languages"*** to my esteemed readers; it is a unique book valuable for beginners, intermediate and advance users.

## AN INVALUABLE AND IDEAL TEXT FOR

Undergraduate and postgraduate students of computer science at various levels. It is also an ideal reference book for professional students. Other than providing useful guidance to the students in various professional and competitive examinations, this book should serve as core textbook for the students of

- M-Tech, B-Tech. (CS & IT/EE), BE
- MCA, M.Sc (CS & IT)
- B. Sc (IT), BCA

## Distinguishing Features

Some of the most distinguishing features are:

- The book covers the three major theories of computer science-Automata Theory, Languages and Computability
- Each chapter provides a step-wise development of the subject matter under reference.
- ***More than 300*** solved examples on occasions, deliberately very simple examples are given to highlight the theoretical aspects of automata so that the concepts do not get submerged in complicated numerical examples.
- Special emphasis has been given on the topics like ***Finite State Machine*** and ***Turing Machine*** to make them as simple as possible to be within the understanding of the students.
- A step-by-step solution of ***DFA & NFA*** approach that is used in almost all DFA & NFA examples in Chapter 03 (Finite State Machine).

- Apart from simple language and lucid presentation, the emphasis is also on making the subject interesting by including interesting examples from day to day life and work environment.

With these features in view, I am sure that the book will be found useful by the students and teachers as well for whom it is primarily written.

In spite of all efforts, some errors might be there, I shall be grateful to our readers if the same are brought to our notice. Suggestions and comments for further improvement of the book will be gratefully acknowledged.

**AMIT GUPTA**

ACKNOWLEDGMENTS

First and foremost, I would like to thank the Almighty God who gave me inspiration to take up this task.

I would like to acknowledge my deep sense of gratitude to **Mrs. Veena Mathur**, Founder and Chairperson of Rakshpal Bahadur Group of Institutes, Bareilly & Gr. Noida, and **Er. Naveen Mathur,** Managing Director of RBMI Group for their benevolent support, suggestions and guidance.

I am thankful to Director General **Dr. Manish Sharma & Director Dr. Neraj Saxena** for their benevolent support, suggestions and guidance.

I wish to express my gratitude to **Dr. Ravindra Singh, Dr. K. B. Johari, Dr. Anoop Beri, Mr. Rajesh Verma, Mr. Vineet Agarwal, Er. Hemant Yadav, Mr. Umesh Pal Singh, Mr. Udit Agarwal, Mr. Navin Johari, Mr. Puspendra Singh, Mr. Prasant Gupta & Mr. Dhanish Tandon.**

I would like to acknowledge my sincere thanks to our learned professors and authors of a number of excellent books on the subject, and inquisitive students who motivated me to understand the subject better and present it in an engaging manner.

Most important, I want to thank you, the reader, for considering the thoughts, tools and techniques I lay out in these pages.

**Mr. Punit Khanna and Mr. Mukul Seth**, the publisher of this book, deserves special appreciation for the pain they have taken in bringing out this book in such an excellent form.

Finally, thanks to everyone at Khanna Publication who has played a role in getting this book onto the shelves.

**AMIT GUPTA**

***Decdicated to My Parents, Wife Sapna & little daughter Anya***

**Without their love and patience, I would never have had the time or strength to write.**

# REQUEST TO READERS

I request the readers to send their valuable suggestions for any modification or addition by way of text, examples. These would be gratefully acknowledged in the edition. The communication to author could be mailed to **amit123bly@gmail.com** and **amitgupta@rbmionline.com** with subject ***"Suggestions of Automata."***

***Amit Gupta***

# LIST OF REVIEWERS

The authors and the publishers gratefully acknowledge all he reviewers for their praise as well as constructive of the book. Here is a brief list.

| | |
|---|---|
| Dr. A. K. Sharma | RTU, Jodhpur |
| Surya Sharma | NIET, Gr. Noida |
| Rajesh Verma | RBMI, Bareilly |
| Prasant Gupta | FIT, Meerut |

# HOW THIS BOOK IS ORGANIZED

Welcome to **"Theory of Automata & Formal Languages".** This book is an outcome of long teaching experience of the subject. It includes the fundamental concepts, illustrative examples and application to various automata problems. These illustrated examples have been selected carefully on each topic and sufficient numbers of unsolved questions are provided which aim at sharpening the skill of the students.

The chapter of the book could be classified to include conventional as well as unconventional statistical topics as follows:

- **Mathematical Preliminaries** (Chapter-01)
- **Formal Languages** (Chapter-02)
- **Finite State Machine** (Chapter-03)
- **Regular Expression & Regular Grammars** (Chapter-04)
- **Context-Free Grammar** (Chapter-05)
- **Push-Down Automata** (Chapter-06)
- **Turing Machines** (Chapter-07)
- **Decidability & Indecisiveness (Undecidability)** (Chapter-08)
- **Theory of Recursive Function & Intractability** (Chapter-09)
- **Porpositions & Predicates** (Chapter-10)

## Appendix

**Appendix A –** Model Papers

**Appendix B –** Various University Papers

# CONTENT

CHAPTER

# 1

# MATHEMATICAL PRELIMINARIES

## 1.1 INTRODUCTION

This chapter contains some of the mathematical background that will be needed for our study of automata and formal languages. We will however give only a brief survey of mathematical difinitions and terminology which can be found in any standard text on discrete mathematics.

## 1.2 SETS AND ELEMENTS

Any well defined collection, class or list of distinct objects is called a set. The objects in a set can be numbers, people, letters, rivers, conutries etc. The phrase "well defined" signifies that we can decide with certainty whether a particular object belongs or does not belong to the set. A set is any collection at distinct and distinguisble objects.

The objects in a set are called the elements or members at the set.

---

The theory at sets was originated by the German mathematician George Canton.

---

**Examples of set**

→ The set of numbers 4, 6, 8, 10, 12.

→ The set of letters a, e, i, o, u.

→ The set of citizens of India.

→ The set of Indian students who have gone abroad.

**Notation.** Sets are usually denoted by capital letters or upper case letters A, B, C, X, Y, Z..... and the elements in a set are denoted by lower case letters a, b, c, x, y, z...

## 1.3 REPRESENTATION OF SETS

There are two ways of writing down a set, tabular form and set buider form.

*(i)* **Tabular form or Roaster form of a set:** In this form all the numbers of the set are listed. These members are separated by commas an enclosed in braces {}.

For example, if the elements of a set $A$ are 2, 5, 7, 8, 11, 13 then it can be written in tabular form as $A = \{2, 5, 7, 8, 11, 13\}$. Representation of the set in this way is known as tabular form of a set.

*(ii)* **Set-builder form of a set:** In this form a set is defined by starting the properties which are satisfied by its elements. Here the rule governing the membership of the set is stated.

For example, a set of all ever positive integers in written in set-builter form as

$$B = \{x : x \text{ is even positive integer}\}$$

or $$B = \{x : x \text{ is even positive integer}\}$$

and this read "$B$" is a set of numbers $x$ such that $x$ is an even positive integer.

**Example 1.1:** Write the following in tabular form

($a$) $A = \{x : x$ is a prime number less than is$\}$

($b$) $B = \{x : x$ is a letter in the word "induction"$\}$

($c$) $C = \{x : x \in N, 3 < x < 12\}$

**Solution:** $A = \{2, 3, 4, 5, 7, 11, 13\}$

$B = \{$i, n, d, u, c, t, l, o, n$\}$

$C = \{4, 5, 6, 7, 8, 9, 10, 11\}$

## 1.4 TYPES OF SETS

1. **Finite and Infinite sets:** A set is called finite if it has n distinct elements where $n \in N$. Such a set consists af a specific number of different elements. Otherwise a set is infinite.

   Some examples are

   → $A = \{2, 4, 6,...\}$ is an infinite set.

   → $B = \{x : x$ is an Indian$\}$ is a finite set.

2. **Null set or Void set or Empty set:** A set which contain no element is called a null set. It is denoted by the symbol $\phi$ or [].

   Some example are

   → The set of integers between $\frac{9}{4}$ and $\frac{11}{4}$.

   → The set of married bachelors

   → The set of persons of age greater than 150 years

3. **Singleton set:** A set containing only one element is called a singleton set, *e.g.*, $A = \{5\}$ an $B = \{0\}$ are both singleton sets.

4. **Subsets:** If every member in a set $A$ is also a member of set $B$, then $A$ is said to be a subset of $B$.

   We write this relation as $A \subset B$ and read "$A$ is contained in $B$".

5. **Superset:** If $A$ is a subset of $B$, then B is said to be the superset of A. This relation is written as $B \supset A$ which reads "$B$ contains $A$ or $B$ is superset of $A$".

6. If $B$ is a subset of $A$ and $B$ is not equal to $A$ then $B$ is said to be a proper subset of $A$.

7. **Disjoin sets:** If no elements of $A$ is a member of $B$ and on element of $B$ is a member of $A$, then $A$ and $B$ are said to be disjoint sets.

8. **Universal set:** The set of which all sets under investigation are subsets is called Universal set. The Universal set is generally denoted by $U$.

   Some examples are

   → All the person in the world constitute the universal set for the purpose of population studies.

   → In the study of plane geometry. All the points in the plane constitute a Universal set.

9. **Power set:** The set containing all the subsets of a given set $A$ as its element is called a power set of $A$ and is denoted by $2^A$ or $P(A)$.

   $$P(S) = \{T : T \subseteq S\}, \phi \text{ and } s \text{ both } \in P(s)$$

   some example is,

   → If $A = \{3, 4\}$, then all the subsets of $A$ are $\{3, 4\}$, $\{3\}$, $\{4\}$, $\phi$

   Hence its power set is $2^A = [\{3\}, \{4\}, \{3, 4\}, \phi]$

   Total number of elements $= 2^2 = 4$

**(10) Multiset:** Multiset are sets where an element can occur as a member more than once *e.g.*,

$$A = \{a, a, a, b, b, c, c\} = B = \{a, a, a, a, a, b, b, b\}$$

are multiset.

The multisets $A$ and $B$ can also be written as

$$A = \{4.a, 2.b, 2.c\} \text{ and } B = \{6.a, 2.b, 1.b\}$$

## 1.5 SET OPERATIONS

Like the processes of addition, subtraction, multiplication and division in the number systems, there are certain fundamental operations on sets which are described below:

1. **Union of sets:** The Union of two sets $A$ and $B$ is the set of all elements which belong to $A$ or to $B$ or to both $A$ and $B$. The union of $A$ and $B$ is denoted by $A \cup B$ and is read "$A$ union $B$".

   The union of $A$ and $B$ can also be written as

   $$A \cup B = \{x : x \in A \text{ or } x \in B\}$$

---

1. $A \cup B$ and $B \cup A$ are the same set.

   *i.e,* $A \cup B = B \cup A$.

2. $A$ as well $B$ as is always a subset of $A \cup B$

   *i.e,* $A \subset (A \cup B)$ and $B \subset (A \cup B)$

3. The set $(A \cup B)$ is also written as $A + B$ (set theoretic sum).

---

**Example:** If A = {1, 2, 3, 4} and $B$ = {5, 2, 4, 6} the $A \cup B$ = {1, 2, 3, 4, 5, 6}.

The easy way to write the union of two sets is first to write all the element of any one of the two sets and then include those elements of the other set that are not contained in the first one.

$$A \cup \phi = \phi \cup A = A,$$

Hence $\phi$ is an identity element for the operation of union.

2. **Intersection of sets:** The intersection of two sets $A$ and $B$ is the set of elements which belong to $A$ as well as to $B$ and it is denoted by $A \cap B$.

It is the set of all elements which are common to $A$ and $B$.

The intersection of $A$ and $B$ is also written as

$$(A \cap B) = \{x : x \in A \text{ and } X \in B\}$$

$A \cap B$ is also written as $AB$ and is called the set theoretic product.

---

1. By definition $(A \cap B) \subset A$ and $(A \cap B) \subset B$.
2. If $A$ and $B$ are disjoint sets, then $A \cap B = \phi$.
3. $A \cap B = \phi \cap A = \phi$
4. $A \cap U = U \cap A = A$

---

Hence $U$ (universal set) is an identity for the operation of intersection of sets.

**Examples of Intersection of sets:**

(*i*) If $A$ = {3, 4, 6, 8} and $B$ = {2, 6, 8, 4} then $A \cap B$ = {4, 6, 8}

(*ii*) If $A = \{x|x = 3n, n$ is positive integer

and $B = \{x|x = 2n, n$ is positive integer}

then $A \cap B = \{x|x = 6n, n$ is positive integer},

(*iii*) If $A$ = {p, q, r, s, t} and $B$ = {a, b, c, d} then $A \cap B = \varnothing$

The operation of union and intersection can also be defined for three or more sets in a similar manner.

Thus$A \cup B \cup C = \{x|x \in A \text{ or } x \in B \text{ or } x \in C\}$

and$A \cap B \cap C = \{x|x \in A \text{ and } x \in B \text{ and } x \in C\}$

In general $A_1 \cup A_2 \ldots U A_n$ is denoted by $\bigcup_{K=1}^{n} A_k$ and $A_1 \cap A_2 \cap \ldots \cap A_n$ is denoted by $\bigcap_{K=1}^{n} A_k$

3. **Difference of Sets:** The difference of two sets $A$ and $B$ is the set of elements which belong to set $A$ but do not belong to set $B$. This is denoted by $A - B$ or $A \sim B$ or $A \backslash B$ and is read "$A$ difference $B$ or $A$ minus $B$". $A - B$ can be written as

$$A - B = \{x | x \in A, x \notin B\}$$

It is also called the complement of $B$ with respect to $A$.

$$A - \phi = A, \phi - A = \phi, A - \cup = \phi$$

It is evident by the definition of difference of two sets that:

(*i*) $(A - B) \subset A$.

(*ii*) The sets $(A - B)$, $A \cap B$ and $B - A$ are mutually disjoint sets.

**Example of difference of two sets:**

(*i*) If $A = \{1, 3, 5, 7, 9\}$, and $B = \{3, 4, 5, 8\}$

then $A - B = \{1, 7, 9\}$

(*ii*) If $A = \{x | x \text{ is a real number}\}$

and $B = \{x | x \text{ is a rational number}\}$

then $A - B = \{x | x \text{ is a real number}\}$

4. **Complement of a Set:** The complement of a set $A$ is the set of elements which do not belong to $A$. It is, therefore, the difference of the universal set and the set $A$. The complement of a set $A$ is denoted by $A'$ or $A^c$.

$$A' = \{x : x \in U, x \notin A\}$$

**Example of complement of a set:**

(*i*) If $P = \{x | x \text{ is odd natural number}\}$

and $U = \{x | x \text{ is natural number}\}$

then $A' = \{x | x \text{ is even natural number}\}$

(*ii*) If $U = \{1, 2, 3, ..., 9, 10\}$

and $A = \{2, 4, 6, 8, 10\}$

then $A' = \cup - A$

$= \{x | x \in \cup, x \notin A\}$

$= \{1, 3, 5, 7, 9\}$

(*iii*) If $\cup = \{x | x \text{ is a letter of English language}\}$

and $A = \{u, v, w, x, y, z\}$

then $A' = \{a, b, c, ..., s, t\}$

**Some properties associated with complement of a set:**

(a) $A \cup A' = \cup$

(b) $A \cap A' = \phi$

(c) $\cup' = \phi$ and $\phi' = \cup$

(d) $(A')' = A$

(e) $A - B = A \cap B'$.

**[Proof.** $A - B = \{x | x \in A, x \notin B\}$

$= \{x | x \in A, x \in B'\}$

$= A \cap B']$.

5. **Symmetric difference of two sets:** Symmetric difference of two sets $A$ and $B$ is given by

$$A \oplus B \text{ or } A \,\Delta\, B = (A - B) \cup (B - A)$$

$$A \oplus B = \{x : x \in A \text{ or } x \in B, \text{ but not both}\}$$

Similarly,

$$B \oplus A \text{ or } B \,\Delta\, A = (B - A) \cup (A - B),$$

Hence, $A \oplus B = B \oplus A$

It is the set of all elements that belong to $A$ or to $B$ but not to both $A$ and $B$.

## 1.6 ALGEBRA OF SETS: DUALITY

**Laws of Algebra of Sets:**

(That are satisfied by the operations of Union, Intersection and Complement)

**Idempotent laws**

1. (*a*) $A \cup A = A$

(*b*) $A \cap A = A$

**Associative laws**

2. (*a*) $A \cup A \cup C = A \cup (B \cup C)$

(*b*) $(A \cup B) \cap C = A \cap (B \cap C)$

**Commutative laws**

3. (*a*) $(A \cup B) = B \cup A$

(*b*) $(A \cap B) = B \cap A$

**Distributive laws**

4. (*a*) $A \cup (B \cap C) = (A \cup B) \cap (A \cup C)$

(*b*) $A \cap (B \cup C) = (A \cap B) \cup (A \cap C)$

**Identity laws**

5. (*a*) $A \cup \phi = A$

(*b*) $A \cap U = A$

6. (*a*) $A \cup U = U$

(*b*) $A \cup \phi = \phi$

**Involution law**

7. $(A')' = A$

**Complement laws**

8. (*a*) $A \cup A' = U$

   (*b*) $A \cap A' = \phi$

9. (*a*) $U' = \phi$

   (*b*) $\phi' = U$

**De Morgan's law**

10. (*a*) $(A \cup B)' = A' \cap B'$

    (*b*) $(A \cap B)' = A' \cup B'$

11. (*a*) $A - (B \cup C) = (A - B) \cap (B - C)$

    (*b*) $A - (B \cap C) = (A - B) \cup (A - C)$

If $E$ is any identity of algebra of sets, then the dual E* of E is the expression obtained by replacing each occurrence of $\cup$, $\cap$ $U$ and $\phi$ in $E$ by $\cap$, $\cup$, $\phi$ and $U$ respectively [All *b's* are duals of *a's*] known as principle of *DUALITY*.

## 1.7 OTHER IMPORTANT RESULTS IN SET THEORY

1. Number of elements belonging to $A$ or $B$ or both $= n(A \cup B)$
2. Number or elements not belonging to either of the two $= n(A \cup B)'$
3. Number or elements belonging to both $A$ and $B = n(A \cap B)'$
4. $n(A \cup B) = n(A) + n(B) - n(A \cup B)$

   $= n(A) + n(B)$, if $n(A \cup B) = \phi$
5. $n(A - B) = n(A) - n(A \cap B) =$ number of elements belonging of $A$ only
6. $n(B - A) = n(B) - n(A \cap B) =$ number of elements belonging of $B$ only
7. $n(A \cup B) = n(A - B) + n(B - A) + n(A \cap B)$.
8. $n(A' \cup B') = n(A') + n(B') - n(A' \cap B')$

   $n(S) - n(A \cap B) = n(B' - A) + n(A' - B) - n(A' \cap B')$
9. $n(A' \cap B') = n(S) - n(A \cup B)$ [Neither belong to $A$ nor to $B$ *i.e.*, belonging to neither of the two.]
10. $\phi^c = U$
11. $U^c = \phi$
12. $A \cup A^c = U$
13. $A \cap A^c = \phi$
14. (*a*) $A \cup B = \phi \Leftrightarrow A = \phi$ and $B = \phi$

    (*b*) $A - B = \phi \Leftrightarrow A \subseteq B$

    (*c*) $A - B = A \cap B^c$

## 1.8 RELATION

If $A$ and $B$ are two non empty sets then the set of ordered pairs $(x, y)$ such that $x \in A$ and $y \in B$ and the first coordinate of every ordered pair of the set is related to the second coordinate according to a given relation, then the set of ordered pairs is called a relation from $A$ to $B$.

Thus the relation $R$ from A $S$ to $B$ is a subset of $A \times B$.

Symbolically if $R$ is a relation from $A$ to $B$ then

$$R = \{(x, y)\} : x \in A, y \in B \text{ and } xRy\}$$

$xRy$ means that $x$ is related to y according to the relation defined.

For example,

if $\quad A = \{2, 3, 4\}$ and $B = \{P, q\}$ then

$$A \times B = \{(2, p), (2, q), (3, p), (4, p), (4, q)\}.$$

Now any subset of $A \times B$ can be a relation

Thus $R = \{(2, p), (3, q), (4, p)\}$ is a relation from $A$ to $B$.

## 1.9 DIFFERENT METHOD OF REPRESENTATION OF A RELATIONS

There are five main methods to represent a relation $R$ from a set $A$ to set $B$.

### (i) Roaster Method

In this method all the elements (order pairs) of the relation are enclosed within braces.

for example, let $\quad A = \{1, 2, 3\}$ and $B = \{x, y, z\}$

then, $\quad R = \{(1, y), (1, z), (3, y)\}$

### (ii) Matrix Method

A rectangular array is formed whose rows are labeled with the elements of set $A$ and whose columns are labeled with the elements of set $B$. If an element $x \in A$ is $R$ related to the element $y \in B$, than a is written against $x$ in the column of $y$(*i.e.*, in the cell $(x, y)$). If $x \in A$ is not related to $y \in B$, then a 0 is written in the cell $(x, y)$. The array is called the matrix of the relation or relation matrix $M$.

$$M(x, y) = \begin{cases} 1 & if \quad xRy \\ 0 & if \quad xRy \end{cases}$$

For example, the relation $R = \{(1, y), (1, z), (3, y)\}$ from the set $A = \{1, 2, 4\}$, to set $B = \{x, y, z\}$ can be represented in matrix from as follows:

$$\begin{array}{c} \\ 1 \\ 2 \\ 3 \end{array}\begin{pmatrix} x & y & z \\ 0 & 1 & 1 \\ 0 & 0 & 0 \\ 0 & 1 & 0 \end{pmatrix}$$

## (iii) Arrow Diagram

The elements of sets $A$ and $B$ are written in two disjoint plane figures (circuit, rectangles, discs *etc*) and then arrows are drawn from $x \in A$ to $y \in B$ if $x$ is $R$-related to $y$.

For example, the same relation $R = \{(1, x), (1, z), (3, y)\}$

From set $A = \{1, 2, 3\}$ to set $B = \{x, y, z\}$ has been represented below by arrow diagram.

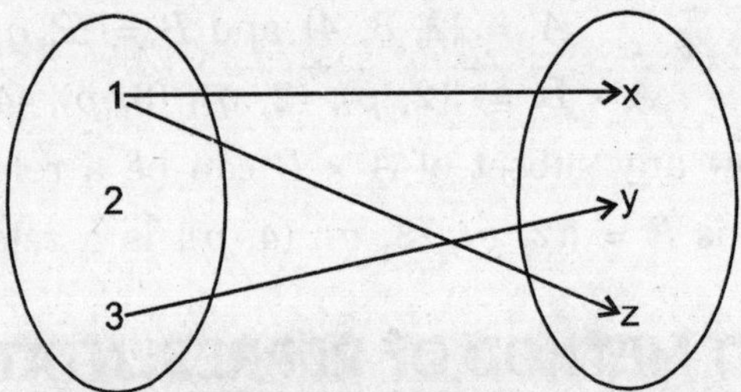


*Fig. 1.1*

## (iv) Digraph of a Relation on sets

When a relation is from a finite set A to itself then it can be represented by a digraph also.

First the elements of the set $A$ are written down.

Then arrows are drawn from each element $x$ to each element $y(x, y, \in A)$ whenever $x$ is $R$ related to $y$.

For example, let the set $A = \{4, 5, 6, 7\}$ and the relation R on A = {(4, 5), (5, 5), (6, 5), (6, 7), (7, 4), (7, 6)} this relation can be represented by a digraph as shown below.

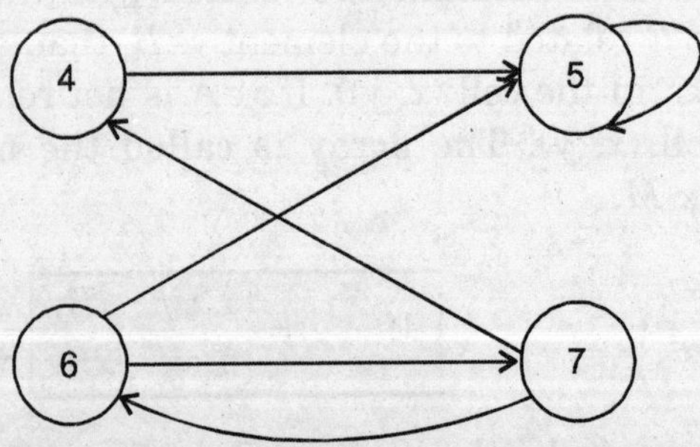


*Fig. 1.2*

### (v) Set Builder Form

In this method the rule that associates the first and second coordinates of each ordered pair is given *e.g.*

Relation from $A$ to $B$ given by

$$R = \{(x, y) : x \in A \text{ and } y \in B, x < y\}$$

where, $A = \{1, 2, 4\}, B = \{2, 3, 5\}$

## 1.10 FUNCTION

Suppose $A$ and $B$ are two non empty sets of reals numbers. A rule that associates to every elements $x \in A$ a unique element $y \in B$ is called a function or mapping from the set $A$ to the set $B$. Rule is denoted by $f$ and we write

$$\boxed{f : A \rightarrow B}$$

and read, "$f$ is a function from $A$ to $B$"

Set $A$ is called Domain of $f$.

Set $B$ is called Co-domain of $f$.

and $f(x) = \{f(x) : x \in A\}$ is called range of $f$

from $A$ to $B$ or $R = \{(y) : y \in B \text{ and } y = f(x), \forall x \in A\}$ is called range of $f$.

$x$ is called independent variable

$y$ is called dependent variable.

In fact $R$ is the image set of f from $A$ to $B$ if $x \in A$ and the rule $f$ associates $x$ to an unique element $y \in B$ such that $y = f(a)$, then $y$ is called $f$-image of $x$ and $x$ is called pre-image of $y$ in $A$. Now let us discuss various types of functions:

### 1.10.1 One-to-One Function

A function $f : A \rightarrow B$ is said to be one-to-one if for each pair of distinct elements of $A$, their $f$-images (in $B$) are also distinct.

It means that $f : A \rightarrow B$ is one-to-one, if for $x_1, x_2 \in A$, $(x_1 \neq x_2) \Rightarrow f(x_1) \neq f(x_2)$ in $B$.

for example, $A = \{a, b, c, d, e\}$,

$B = \{1, 2, 3, 4, 5\}$

and function $f$ is defined as follows:

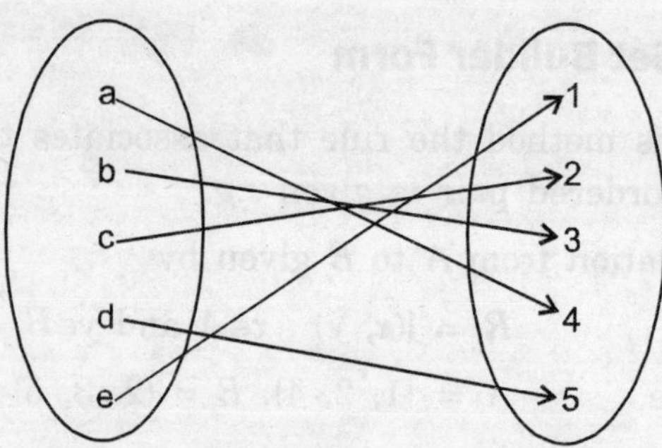


*Fig. 1.3 One to one function*

Here $f$ is said to be one to one function.

### 1.10.2 Many One Function

A function is many one it two or more elements in $A$ have the same image in $B$.

For example: The function $\{-2, 2, 3, 4\} \rightarrow \{4, 9, 16\}$ defined by $f(x) = x^2$ is many one because two different elements in $A$ $(1 - e, -2, 2)$ have same image in $B$.

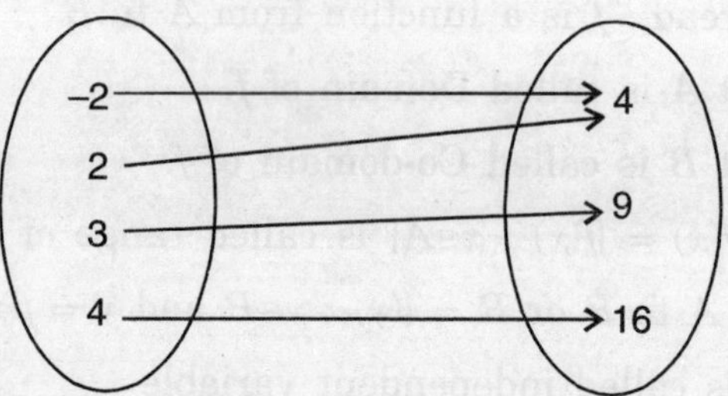


*Fig. 1.4 Many one function*

## 1.11 GRAPHS

A graph $G$ consists of two things,

(*i*) A set $V = V(G)$ whose elements are called vertices, points, or nodes of $G$.

(*ii*) A set $E = E(G)$ of unordered pairs of distinct vertices called edges of $G$.

We denote such a graph by $G(V, E)$.

For example: Given Fig. Represents the graph $G(V, E)$ where:

(*i*) $V$ consists of vertices A, B, C, D

(*ii*) $E$ consists of edges

$$e_1 = \{A, B\} \qquad e_4 = \{A, C\}$$

$$e_2 = \{B, C\} \qquad e_5 = \{B, D\}$$

$$e_3 = \{A, B\}$$

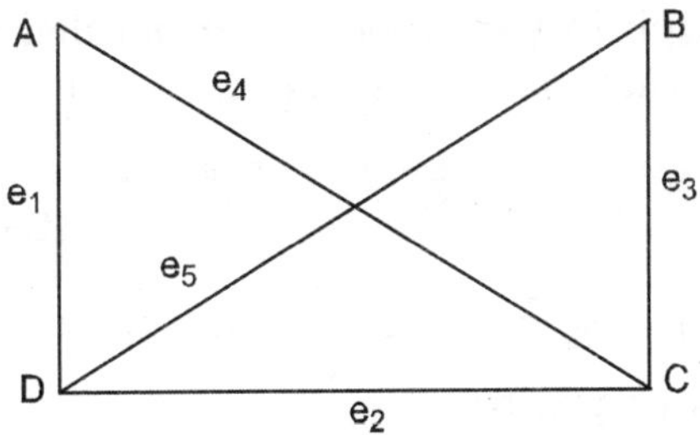


*Fig. 1.5*

### 1.11.1 Simple Graph and Multigraph

A simple graph is one for which there is no more than one edge between a pair of vertices. Any graph, which contains some parallel edges, is called a multigraph. The graph shown is Fig. 1.6(*b*) and (*c*) are multigraph while Fig. 1.6(*a*) is a simple graph.

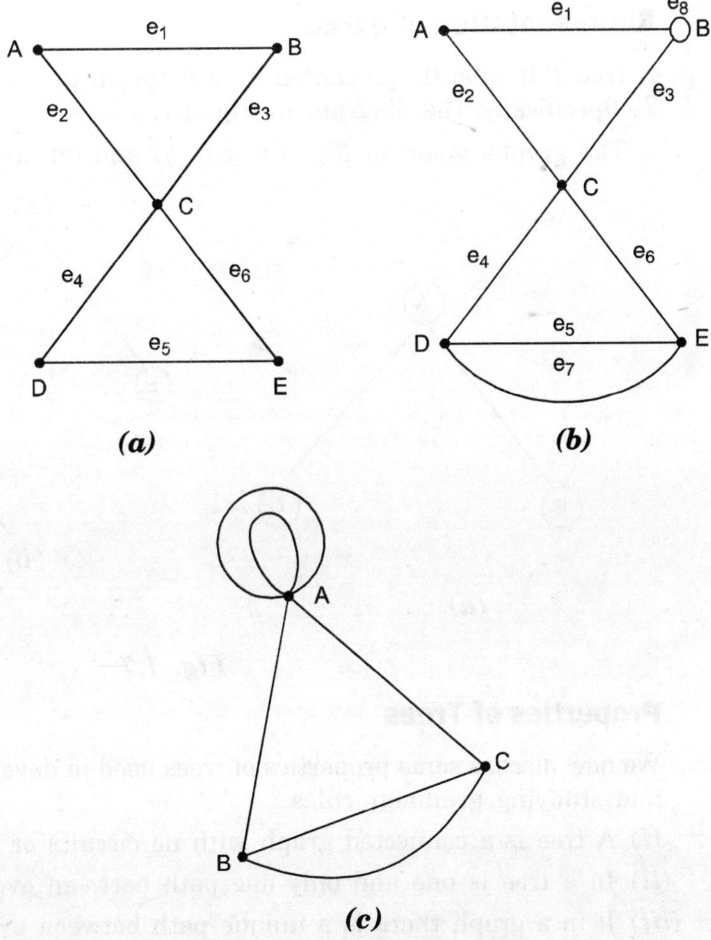


*Fig. 1.6*

A graph in which loops and parallel edges are allowed, is called a pseudo graph graph shown is Fig. 1.6 (c) is a pseudo graph.

## 1.12 TREES

A tree $T$ is defined as a finite set of elements called nodes, such that:

→ $T$ is empty, or

→ $T$ contains a distinguished node $R$, called the root of $T$, and the remaining nodes of $T$ form an orderd pair of disjoint trees $T_1$ and $T_2$.

If $T$ does contain, a root $R$, then the two trees $T_1$ and $T_2$ are called, reprectively, the left and right subtrees of $R$. If $T_1$ is non empty, then its root is called the left successor of $R$: similarly, if $T_2$ is nonempty, then its root is called the right successor of $R$.

A graph is called a tree if it is connected and has no circuits.

### Representation of a tree

A tree $T$ frequently presented by a diagram in the plane called a picture of $T$. Specifically, the diagram in Fig. 1.7.

The graphs given in Fig. 1.6 (*a*), (*b*) and (*c*) are not trees.

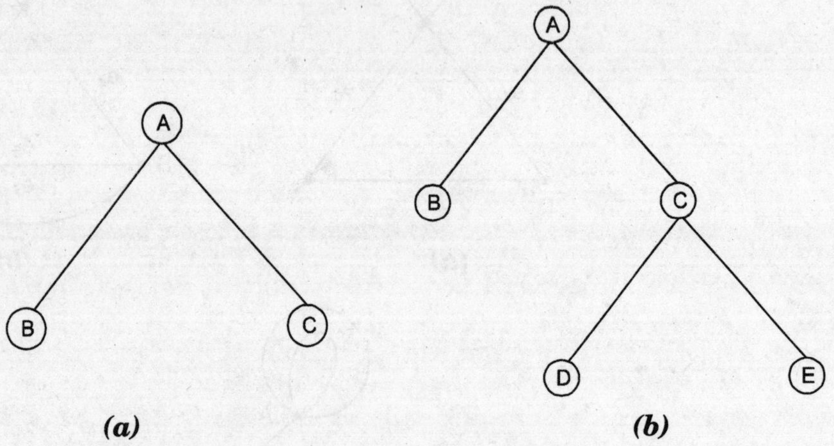


*Fig. 1.7*

### Properties of Trees

We now discuss some properties of trees used in developing transition systems and studying grammar rules

(*i*) A tree is a connected graph with no circuits or loops.

(*ii*) In a tree is one and only one path between every pair of vertices.

(*iii*) If in a graph there is a unique path between every pair of vertices than the graph is a tree.

(*iv*) A tree with $n$ vertices has $n - 1$ edges.

(*v*) If a connected graph with $n$ vertices has $n - 1$ edges then it is a tree.

(*vi*) If a graph with no circuits has $n$ vertices and $n - 1$ edges then it is a tree.

## 1.13 MATHEMATICAL INDUCTION

Let $P(n)$ be a mathematical statement or porposition, then $P(n)$ is true for all positive integers $n$, if.

(*i*) $P(1)$ is true

(*ii*) Whenever $P(m)$ is true for some positive integer $m \geq 1$, then $P(m+1)$ is true which means that

$$P(m) \Rightarrow P(m+1) \text{ is a tautology}$$

---

Instead of $P(1)$ we may take $P(n_0)$ where $n_0$ is the smallest positive integer $n_0 = 0$ (in some ases)

(*i*) is called the basic step

(*ii*) is called the inductive step

---

$P(m)$ is true for some +ve integer $m$ is called inductive Hypothesis.

**Example 1.2:** $P(n)$ is the statement "$n^3 + n$ is divisible by 3", then find $P(3)$ and $P(5)$ and verify if these two statements are true or not.

**Solution:** $P(n)$ : $n^3 + n$ is divisible by 3.

$P(3)$ : $3^3 + 3$ *i.e.*, 30 is divisible by 3.

This statement is true.

$P(5)$ : $5^3 + 5$ i.e., 130 is divisible by 3.

This statement is not true

**Example 1.3:** $P(n)$ is the statement "$3^n > n$, prove that whenever $P(n)$ is true $P(n+1)$ is also true

**Solution:** The statement $P(n)$ is true

*i.e.*, $$3^n > n \quad ...(1)$$

We have to prove that then statement $P(n+1)$ is also true

$$3^{n+1} > (n + 1) \quad ...(2)$$

On multiplying both the sides of (1) by 3, we have

$$3.3^n > 3n$$

$$\Rightarrow \quad 3^{n+1} > n + 2x$$

$$\Rightarrow \quad 3^{n+1} > n + 1$$

which proves (2)

Therefore $P(n+1)$ is also true.

## 1.14 PIGEON HOLE PRINCIPLE

If $n$ pigeon holes are occupied by $K_{n+1}$ or more pigeon, where $K$ is a positive integer, then at least one hole is occupied by $K + 1$ or more pigeons.

It means that if n pigeon holes are occupied by $n + 1$ pigeons, then at least one hole is occupied by more than one pigeon.

**Example 1.4:** Find the minimum number of students in a class so that three of then are born in the same month.

**Solution:** Here $n = 12$ (months) which represents the number of pigeon holes.

$$K + 1 = 3 \quad \text{or} \quad K = 2$$

Hence the minimum number of pigeons

$$= K_{n+1} = 25 \text{ students}$$

**Example 1.5:** What shall be the minimum number of worlds that must begin with the same alphabet at 27 english words.

**Solution:** Here, $K_{n+1} = 27$ and $n = 26$ number of alphabets

Therefore, $K = 1$ and $K + 1 = 2$

Hence at least 2 words must begin with the same alphabet.

# EXERCISE

## (A) Objective Type Questions

1. If $X \subseteq \overline{Y \cup Z}$ and $Y \subseteq \overline{Y \cup Z}$, then

   (*a*) $X \subseteq Y$ (*b*) $Y = \phi$

   (*c*) $Y \subseteq X$ (*d*) $Y = \phi$

2. $(X \cap Y \cap Z) \cup (\overline{X} \cap Y \cap Z) \cup \overline{Y} \cup \overline{Z} =$

   (*a*) $\phi$ (*b*) $U$

   (*c*) $X \cup Y \cup Z$ (*d*) $X \cap Y \cap Z$

3. If $X = \{x | x \in N \text{ and } x < 0\}$, then

   (*a*) $X = \overline{N}$ (*b*) $X = U$

   (*c*) $X = \phi$ (*d*) $X = N$

4. If $A = \{x | x \text{ is a multiple of } 4\}$ and $B = \{x | x \text{ is a multiple of } 8\}$, then

   (*a*) $A \cup B = B$ (*b*) $A \cap B = A$

   (*c*) $A \cap B = \phi$ (*d*) None

5. If $A$ has $n$ elements, then $P(A)$ has.........elements.

   (*a*) $n^2$ (*b*) $2^n$

   (*c*) $2^{n+1}$ (*d*) $2^{n+1}$

6. For any nonempty sets $X$ and $Y$, which one of the following is true:

   (*a*) any subset of $X \times Y$ is an equivalence relation

   (*b*) any subset $X \times Y$ is a relation from $X$ into $Y$

   (*c*) any subset of $X \times Y$ is a relation from $X$ into $Y$

   (*d*) any subset of $X \times Y$ is also a subset of $X \cup Y$.

7. Let $G = \langle V, E \rangle$ be a graph and $v \in V$. Let there are '*l*' loops at v and '*e*' edges are incident with v, then degree of v is

(*a*) $l + e$ (*b*) $2l + e$

(*c*) $2(l + e)$ (*d*) $2e$

**8.** If $G$ is an Euler graph, then the total number of vertices of odd degree is

(*a*) zero (*b*) two

(*c*) zero or two (*d*) none

**9.** If any graph $G = \langle V,E \rangle$ the total number of vertices having odd degree is

(*a*) $2\ |E|$ (*b*) even

(*c*) odd (*d*) $|E|$

**10.** The total number or edges in any tree with $n$ vertices is

(*a*) $\frac{n(n-1)}{2}$ (*b*) $\frac{n}{2}$

(*c*) $n$ (*d*) $n - 1$

**11.** The sum of the degree of $n$ vertices of a tree is equal to

(*a*) $n - 1$ (*b*) $2n - 1$

(*c*) $2n - 2$ (*d*) $2n$

**12.** How many subgraphs does $K_3$, the complete graph on 3 vertices, have?

(*a*) 15 (*b*) 17

(*c*) 19 (*d*) 11

**13.** How many subgraph does the complete graph $K_n$ have?

(*a*) $\sum_{r=1}^{n} \binom{n}{r}$ (*b*) $\sum_{r=1}^{n} 2^{\binom{n}{r}}$

(*c*) $\sum_{r=1}^{n} \binom{n}{r} 2^{\binom{r}{2}}$ (*d*) $\sum_{r=1}^{n} \binom{n}{r} 2^{\binom{n}{2}}$

**14.** The graph having multiset of degree equal to {1, 2, 2, 3, 3, 3} is

(*a*) simple (*b*) multi-graph

(*c*) pseudograph (*d*) none of the above

**15.** How many different Hamiltonian cycles does $K_n$ have?

(*a*) $n!$ (*b*) $(n - 1)!$

(*c*) $\binom{n}{2}$ (*d*) None of these

**16.** Which of the graphs shown in the Figure below is isomorphic to the others?

(*a*) $G_1$ and $G_2$ (*b*) $G_2$ and $G_4$

(*c*) $G_3$ and $G_4$ (*d*) None

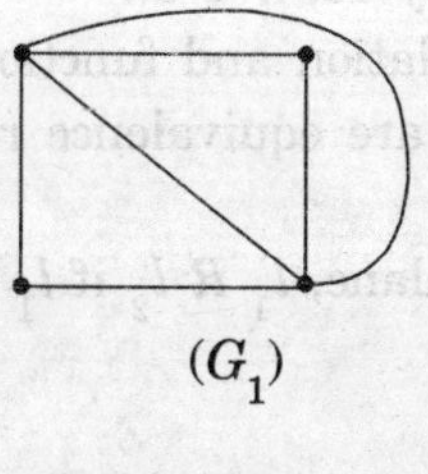

($G_1$) 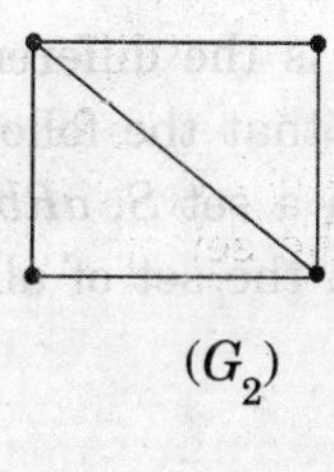 ($G_2$)

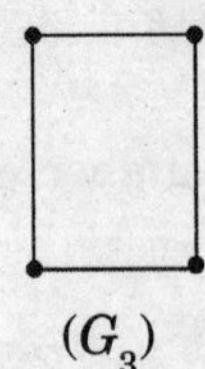

$(G_3)$

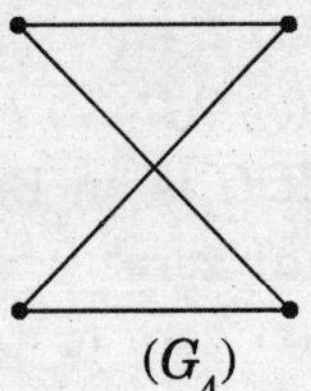

$(G_4)$

**17.** The number of components in a disconnected graph having $n$ vertices is

(a) two (b) at least two

(c) at most $n$ (d) none of these

**18.** The chromatic number of a graph that contains a cycle of length $2n$ is

(a) 2 (b) 3

(c) $\geq 2$ (d) $\geq 3$

**19.** The chromatic number of a tree having at least two vertices is

(a) 2 (b) 3

(c) 4 (d) $\geq 2$

**20.** The spanning tree of a graph $G$ is

(a) a spanning subgraph of $G$

(b) a spanning connected subgraph of $G$

(c) a spanning subgraph of $G$ which is also a tree

(d) none of these

## ANSWERS

| | | | | |
|---|---|---|---|---|
| **1.** (b) | **2.** (b) | **3.** (c) | **4.** (b) | **5.** (b) |
| **6.** (b) | **7.** (b) | **8.** (c) | **9.** (b) | **10.** (d) |
| **11.** (c) | **12.** (b) | **13.** (c) | **14.** (b) | **15.** (b) |
| **16.** (c) | **17.** (b) | **18.** (c) | **19.** (a) | **20.** (c) |

## (B) Problems

**1.** Determine the domain and range of the relation

$$\{(x, y), x^2 + y^2 = 25, x \text{ and } y \text{ are integers}\}.$$

**2.** If there are 13 boys in a class, then find the minimum number of boys born in the same months.

**3.** Find the minimum number of persons having the same birthday among a group of 367 persons.

**4.** Show that $n^3 + 2n$ is divisible by 3.

**5.** Show that $3^n < n$ where $n$ is positive integer > 6.

**6.** Show that $10^{2n-1} + 1$ is divisible by 11, $n \in N$.

**7.** What is the difference between relation and function 9.

**8.** Show that the following relations are equivalence relation:

(a) on a set $S$, $aRb$ if $a > b$.

(b) on the set of all lines in the plane, $l_1 \; R \; l_2$ if $l_1$ is parallel to $l_2$.

❑❑❑

CHAPTER

# 2

# FORMAL LANGUAGES

## 2.1 INTRODUCTION

The theory of formal languages is an area with a number of application in Computer Science. The word "formal" refers to the fact that all the rules for the languages are explicitly stated in terms of what strings at symbols can occur.

In this chapter we introduce the concepts of grammars and formal languages and discus Chomsky classification of languages. We also study the inclusion relation between the four classes of languages.

## 2.2 LANGUAGE

The word "language" means expressing views, thought, sentimens etc. in general but language can be definded in various other aspects also like,

For Professional, A language is a form of word used in communicating something that may be manner, style of expression etc.

For Computer, A language is any of various system of previously defined set of symbols (letters or alphabet) and rules for their manipulation. The set of alphabet is denoted by (sigma) Σ.

For example;

All the small letters (alphabet or symbols) of English language are denoted by

$$\Sigma = \{a, b, c, \ldots.., y, z\}$$

This set of letters is used to form a word in the compute language. Each word has its own specific meaning but it is not necessary that each word gives the specific meaning according to the English Language.

*For example;* Let the words be pen, computer, five, apple.

All these words are set of letters in Σ and have defined meaning by definition of computer language as well as English language. But when you use the word odg, ggod and ddog, these words have no meaning by definition of English Language but have meaning by Computer language.

In this book language means computer language.

### Alphabet, Word and Language

An **alphabet** or vocabulary Σ is a finite non empty set of elements called symbols or letters. A **word** or **string** ω on a non empty set Σ of symbols is a finite sequence of the element of Σ.

For example, the sequences

$w_1$ = aababb and $w_2$ = *abbcaabb* are word on Σ

we generally write $a^2$ for aa and $a^3$ for aaa thus $w_1 = a^2\ bab^2$ and $w_2 = ab^2ca^2b^2$.

The empty sequence of letters is denoted by ∈. It is called **empty word***. For empty word, we can use both symbols ∈. And Δ as they have same meaning. But in this book, we have used only ∈ for representing the empty string/word.

The set of all words on the alphabet Σ is denoted by Σ*.

A **Language** *L* over an alphabet Σ is a collection of word on Σ. As Σ* denotes the set of all words on $\Sigma_r$ the language *L* is a subset of Σ*.

*For example,* let Σ = {*a*} then a language of non empty string (or word) of letters (alphabet or character) is *L* = {*a, aa, aaa* ...)

or we could write this in an alternate form

$$L = \{a^n : n = 1, 2, 3, ...\}$$

*For example,* let Σ = {0, 1, 2, 3, 4, 5, 6, 7, 8, 9}

Then the language *L* can be defined by the set of words (strings)

*L* = {any finite string of letters that does not start with the letter zero}

This language loos like the set of all positive integers written in base 10 *i.e.,*

*L* = {1, 2, 3, 4, 5, 6, 7, 8, 9, 10, 11, 12, 13, 14, 15, ...}

*For example,* let Σ = {*a, b*}

Then the language *L* can defined by the set of words

*L* = {any nonempty finite string of *a* and *b*}

This language loos like the following set of string (word)

*L* = {*a, b, aa, ab, ba, bb, aaa, aab, abb, bab, ...*}

## Length of World or String

The length of string can be defined by the total number of characters (letters) in the given string.

*For example,* let the language *w* = *aaaa*

The length (*w*) = |*W*| = 4

or length (*aaaa*) = 4

If any language that includes the empty string *w* = ∈, then length (∈) = 0.

## Concatenation of word

The concatenation of two words $w_1$ and $w_2$, written as $w_1w_2$ is the word obtained by writing down the letters or characters of $w_1$ followed by the letters of $w_2$.

For example if $w_1$ = *aababbb* and $w_2$ = *aaabaa* the concantenation of $w_1$, $w_2$ is given by

* For empty word, we can use both symbols ∈ and Δ as they have same meaning. But in this book, we have used only ∈ for representing the empty string/word.

$$w_1w_2 = aababbbaaabaa = a^2bab^3a^3ba^2$$

1. The concatenation operation for words on the alphabet Σ is **associative.** The empty word ∈ is an identity element for the operation of concatenation.
2. The operation is not necessarily commutative.

## Closure or Kleen Closure or Kleen Star

The Kleen Clousser of an alphabet Σ is defined as a language in which any string of letters from Σ is a word including null string. It is denoted by $\Sigma^*$.

For example

if $\Sigma = \{a\}$ , then

$\Sigma^* = \{\in, a, aa, aaa, ...\}$

if $\Sigma = \{a, b\}$, then

if $\Sigma^* = \{\in, a, b, ab, ba, aa, bb, ...\}$ = {any string of $a$ and $b$}

if $\Sigma = \{a, bb\}$ then

$\Sigma^* = \{\in, a, bb, abb, aa, aabb, bba, bbaa, ...\}$

This string *aabaaabb* is not in $\Sigma^*$ because single $b$ will not come in any string of $\Sigma^*$.

**Example 2.1:** *Show that the string aabbaabba is in* $\Sigma^*$ *where* $\Sigma = \{aa, bb\}$.

**Solution:** Factorize the given string in the form of given input alphabet *i.e.*, ($aa$) ($bb$) ($aa$) ($bb$) ($a$). In the above factorization form of a given string, the last factor is only ($a$) which is not possible in the Kleen Closure of Σ *i.e.*, $\Sigma^*$.

**Example 2.2:** *Show that the string aabbbaabb is in* $\Sigma^*$ *where* $\Sigma = \{aa, bb\}$.

**Solution:** Factorize the given string the form of given input alphabet *i.e.*, ($aa$) ($bb$) ($bb$) ($aa$) ($bb$). In the above factorization form of the given string, all the factors are in the form of the given alphabet, so that the given string is in $\Sigma^*$.

**Example 2.3:** *Show that the Kleen star of* $\Sigma_1$ *and* $\Sigma_2$ *are all strings of a's and b's where* $\Sigma_1 = \{a, b, ab\}$ *and* $\Sigma_2 = \{a, b, bb\}$.

**Solution:** Since the sub string of $\Sigma_1$ and $\Sigma_2$ both have *a's* and *b's*. So the Kleen star of $\Sigma_1$ and $\Sigma_2$ is all strings of *a's* and *b's*.

If $S$ is a set of words, then $S^*$ is the set of all finite strings formed by concatenating words from $S$, where any/word may be used as after as we like, and where the null strings is also included.

For example, let $S = \{a, ab\}$ then

$S^*$ = {∈, any word obtained by composition at a and $b$ as after we like.}

= {∈, all strings of $a's$ and $b's$ except those that

start with $b$ and those contain two or more consecutive $b's$.}

$$= \{\in, a, aa, ab, aaa, aaab, aba, aaabb, ...\}$$

**Example 2.4:** Given $L = \{a^n b^{n+1}: n \geq 0\}$. is it true that $L = L^*$ for the given language $L$?

**Solution:** We know $L^* = L^0 \; U \; L^1 \; U \; L^2 \; U \; L^3 \; ......$

and $L^+ = L^1 \; U \; L^2 \; U \; L^2 \; U \; L^3 \; U \; L^4 \; ......$

Now, for given $L = \{a^n \; b^{n+1} : n \geq 1\}$, we have

$$L^0 = a^0 b^1 = b$$

$$L^1 = a^1 \; b^2 = ab^2$$

$$L^2 = a^2 \; b^3 = a^2 b^3......$$

Therefore, we have $L^* = L^0 \; U \; L^1 \; U \; L^2......$

$$= b \; U \; ab^2 \; U \; a^2 b^3......$$

Hence $\boxed{L = L^*}$

## Complement of a Language

The complement of a language is defined with respect of $\Sigma^*$; that is, the complement of $L$ is

$$\boxed{\bar{L} = \Sigma^* - L}$$

*For example,* let $\Sigma = \{a\}$ and the language $L$ is

$$L = \{\text{Any nonempty string of even length of } a's\}$$

This language looks like the following set of string (word)

$$L = \{aa, aaaa, aaaaaa, ...\}$$

The complement of language $L$ is

$$\bar{L} = \Sigma^* - L$$

*i.e.,* $= \{\in, aa, aaa, aaaaa, ...\}$

$$\bar{L} = \{\text{any strings of od length of } a's\}$$

*For example,* let $= \Sigma = \{a, b\}$ and $L = \{$only one string length of $a$ and $b\}$

Then the complement of $L$ is

$\bar{L} = \{$All string of $a$ and $b$ excepting one string length of $a$ and $b\}$

*i.e.,* $\bar{L} = \{\in, ab, ba, aa, bb, aab, ...\}$

## Union of Languages

The union of languages $L_1$ and $L_2$ is represented by

$$\boxed{L_1 + L_2}$$

*For example*, let $L_1$ = {*abaa*} and $L_2$ = {*aabb*} the union of language $L_1$ and $L_2$ is represented as

$$L = \{abaa + aabb\}$$

### Concatenation of Languages

The concatenation of language $L_1$ and $L_2$ is represented by

$$L_1L_2 = \{xy | x \in L_1, y \in L_2\}$$

It denotes the set of all word that are formed by concatenation of a word $x$ from $L_1$ with a word $y$ from $L_2$

*For example*, if $L_1$ = {*a*, *ab*} and $L_2$ = {*aa*, *bb*, *abb*}, then

$$L_1L_2 = \{aaa, abb, aabb, abaa, abbb, ababb\}$$

The concatenation of a language is also associative

## 2.3 RECURSIVE DEFINITION

A recursive definition of language is given by the following rules :

**Rule 1 :** Specify some basic objects in the set

**Rule 2 :** Give rules for constructing more objects in the set from the ones we already know.

**Rule 3 :** Declare that no objects those constructed in this way are allowed in the set.

**Example 2.5:** *Find the recursive definition for the set of positive even integer.*

**Solution:** By definition of recursive definition the set of even positive integers is defined as follows.

**Rule 1 :** 2 is in even.

**Rule 2 :** If $x$ is even, then so is $x + 2$.

**Rule :** The only elements in the set of positive even integers are those that can be produced from the two rules mentioned above.

**Example 2.6:** *Give the recursive definition of a polynomial.*

**Solution:** By the definition of recursive definition the polynomial is defined as follows.

**Rule 1 :** Any number is in polynomial.

**Rule 2 :** The variable $x$ is in polynomial.

**Rule 3 :** It $p$ and $q$ are in polynomial, then so are $p + q$, $p - q$, $(p)$ and $pq$.

The polynomial $pq$ represents a concatenation of alphabet letters $p$ and $q$.

Following sequence of applications of these rules can show that $5x^2 + 3x - 7$ is in polynomial.

By rule 1 : 5 is in polynomial

By rule 2 : $x$ is in polynomial

By rule 3 : $(5)(x)$ is in polynomial *i.e.*, $5x$

By rule 3 : $(5x)(x)$ is in polynomial *i.e.*, $5x^2$

By rule 1 : 3 is in polynomial

By rule 3 : $(3)(x)$ is in polynomial *i.e.*, $3x$

By rule 3 : $5x^2 + 3x$ is in polynomial

By rule 1 : –7 is in polynomial

By rule 3 : $5x^2 + 3x$ is in polynomial

**Example 2.7:** *Given a reclusive definitions for the language of odd palindrome over alphabet* $\Sigma = \{a, b\}$.

**Solution:** By recursive definition, the language of odd palindrome can be defined by the following rules.

**Rule 1 :** $a$ and $b$ are in palindrome

**Rule 2 :** If $x$ is in palindrome, then so are axa and bxb.

Some sequence of applications of these rules can show that *aabbbaa* is in odd palindrome.

By rule 1 : $b$ is in odd palindrome

By rule 2 : $b(b)b$ is in palindrome *i.e.*, *bbb*

By rule 2 : $a(bbb)a$ is in odd palindrome *i.e.*, *abbba*

By rule 2 : $a(abbba)a$ is in odd palindrome *i.e.*, *aabbbaa*

## 2.4 REGULAR EXPRESSION

The representation of language by another method *i.e.*, in algebraic fashion is called a regular expression.

The set of regular expression is defined by the following rules

1. ∈ and f are regular expression.
2. Any terminal symbol of input alphabet S is a regular expression. It is denoted by $\{a\}$.
3. If $R_1$ and $R_2$ are regular expression then

   (*a*) The union $R_1$ and $R_2$ is also a regular expression. It is denot by $R_1 + R_2$.

   (*b*) The concatenation of $R_1$ and $R_2$ is also a regular expression. It is denoted by $R_1R_2$.
4. The Kleen star (iteration) of a regular expression $R$, is also a regular expression. It is written as $R^*$.

5. If $R$ is a regular expression, then $(R)$ is also a regular expression.

*For example,* let us consider the language defined by the regular expression

$$(a + b)^* a(a + b)^*$$

This expression represents the following language.

→ The expression $(a + b)^*$ represents the set of all strings of $a$ and $b$ of any order and of any length including Î.

→ The expression $(a + b)^* a$ represents the set of all strings of $a$ and $b$ of any order and of any length ending with $a$.

→ The expression $(a + b)^* a(a + b)^*$ represents the set of all strings of $a$ and $b$ of any order and of any length that have at least one a in the string.

*i.e.,* $(\in)a(bba)$ or $(bba)a(ba)$ or $(bba)a(\in)$ or $(bba)a(abb)$ so on

or (any string of $a$ and $b$ of any order of any length) $(a)$ (any string of $a$ and $b$ of any order of any length)

*For example*, let us consider the language defined by the regular expression

$$(a + b)^* a(a + b)^*a\ (a + b)^*$$

This expression represent the following language.

→ The expression $(a + b)$ represents the set of all strings of $a$ and $b$ of any order and of any length including $\in$.

→ The expression $(a + b)^*a$ represents the set of all strings of $a$ and $b$ of any order and of any length ending with $a$.

→ The expression $(a + b)^* a\ (a + b)^*$ represents the set of all strings of $a$ and $b$ of any order and of any length that have at least one a in the string.

→ The expression $(a + b)^*a\ (a + b)^*a$ represents the set of all strings of $a$ and $b$ of any order and of any length that have at least two $a$ in the string but ending with $a$.

→ The expression $(a + b)^*a\ (a + b)^*a\ (a + b)^*$ represents the set of all strings of $a$ and $b$ of any order and of any length that have at least two $a$ in the string.

or (any string of $a$ and $b$ of any order and of any length) $(a)$ (any string of $a$ and $b$ of any order and of any length) $(a)$ (any string of $a$ and $b$ of any order and of any length).

*For example*, let us consider the language defined by the regular expression

$$(a + b)^* (aa + bb)\ (a + b)^*$$

This expression represent the following language

(any string of $a$ and $b$ of any order and of any length) (double letters of $a$ and $b$) (any string of $a$ and $b$ of any order and of any length).

## 2.5 PRODUCT SET

If $R_1$ and $R_2$ are regular expression then product set of regular expressions is defined as $R_1$ and $R_2$ where

$R_1R_2$ = {all combination of a string from $R_1$ concatenated with a string from $R_2$ in that order}

*For example* if $R_1 = \{a, aa, aaa\}$ and $R_2 = \{b, bb, bbb\}$.

Then $R_1R_2 = \{ab, abb, abbb, aab, aabb, aabbb, aaab, aaabb, aaabbb\}$.

*For example,* if $R_1 = \{a, aa, aaa\}$ and $R_2 = \{x, xx\}$

Then $R_1\ R_2 = \{ax, axx, aax, aaxx, aaax, aaaxx\}$

*For example,* if $R_1 = \{\in, a, aa\}$ and $R_2 = \{\in, x, xx, xxx, xxxx, ...\}$

Then $R_1R_2 = \{\in, x, xx, xxx, xxxx, ..., a, ax, axx, axxx, axxxx, ... aa, aax, aaxx, aaxxx, aaaxxxx, ...\}$.

## 2.6 GRAMMAR

Grammar is basically a set of rules, which gives us some meaningful language, like English Grammar is defined by some set of rules which gives us meaningful language *i.e.*, English language, is used by particular communities in proper manner.

*For Example*, while writing any sentence (or language) in English language definitely we have to follow some set of rules which are defined in English Grammar, and are accepted by a particular community.

*i.e.*, Suppose a sentence (or language) is

Anuj and Vikas (<Subject>) ran up the hill (<Predicate>)

In this sentence the basic description of sentence is as follows :

1. <sentence> → <subject> <predicate>
2. <subject> → <noun phrase>
3. <subject> → <noun> <conjunction> <noun>
4. <conjuntion> → and
5. <noun> → Anuj
   <noun> → Vikas
6. <predicate> → <verb> <prepositional phrase>
7. <verb> → ran
8. <prepositional phrase> → <preposition> <article> <noun>
9. <preposition> → up
10. <article> → the
11. <noun> hill

It means this sentence contains subject predicate which are defined by English grammar. In a similar way grammars are defined by computer languages. It means that when you are writing any language in the form of computer language then that language definitely follows some st of rules.

In terms of computer language, grammar is defined mathematically.

The final sentence only contains terminals, although both variables and terminals appears in its construction by the production.

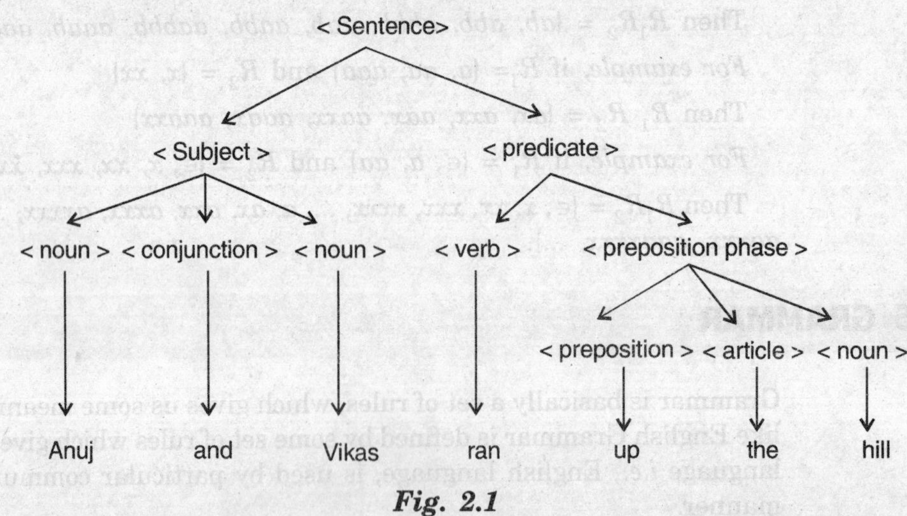


*Fig. 2.1*

### Terminal and Non-Terminal Symbol

The elements of the alphabet or vocabular (set of symbols used to derive member of the language) in a grammar that can not be replaced by other symbols are called terminal and the elements of the alphabet or vocabulary that can be replaced by other symbols are called non-terminal or variable.

In above example the set of terminal is {Anuj, and, Vikas, ran, up, the, hill} and the set of non-terminal is {<sentence>, <subject>, <predicate>, <noun>, <noun phrase>, <conjuntion>, <verb>, <prepositional phrase>, < prepositions>, <article>}

## 2.7 MATHEMATICAL MODEL OF A GRAMMAR

A grammar (or formal grammar) G consist of four tuples $(V, \Sigma, P, S)$ where,

- $V$ is a finite set whose elements are called non terminals or variables.
- $\Sigma$ is a finite set whose elements are called non terminals.
- $P$ is a finite set of production rules whose productions are in the form of $\alpha \to \beta$, where $\alpha$ and $\beta$ are strings on $V \cup \Sigma$ but $\alpha$ contain at least one symbol form $V$.
- $S$ is a starting symbol and $S \in V$.

The production rules of grammar are heart of a grammar, *i.e.*, when you are able to define production rules of grammar, the we can define a grammar. The following facts about the production rules are to be observed :

(*i*) If a production rule is in the form of $S \rightarrow \alpha\beta$, then you can replace $S$ by ab but not ab by $S$.

(*ii*) If a production rule is in the form of $S \rightarrow \alpha\beta$ then it is not necessary that $\alpha\beta \rightarrow S$ is a production.

**Notations:**

(*i*) If $A$ is any set, then $A^*$ is a set of all string over $A$ and $A^+$ is defined by $[A^* - [\in]$ or $AA^*]$.

(*ii*) $A, B, C, \ldots\ldots, A_1, A_2, \ldots\ldots$(*i.e.*, capital letters) denotes the variables or non-terminal symbols.

(*iii*) $a, b, c, \ldots\ldots x, y, z + -, *, /$ (*i.e.*, small letters and operators) denotes the terminal symbol.

**Example 2.8:** *Consider the grammar* $G = (\{S, A\}, \{a, b\}, P, S)$ *where P consists of following production rules*

$$S \rightarrow aAb$$
$$A \rightarrow aAb$$
$$A \rightarrow ab$$

*Find the language of the given grammar G.*

**Solution:** To find a language for a given grammar we have to find what is a minimum length of string to show lower string length and what is maximum length of strings to show upper string length. To find the maximum length of string see what particulars partners of strings are coming recursively.

In this example, the starting symbol is $S$, so we have to start with starting symbol $S$ as follows :

$$S \rightarrow aAb$$

In this production rule only $A$ is a non-terminal symbol on right hand side, so for finding the minimum length of string, replace $A$ by terminal symbols *i.e.*, use the production rule $A \rightarrow ab$ (or $A$ is replaced by $ab$). So the new production rule is $S \rightarrow aabb$, which gives the minimum length of string, since no non-terminal symbol is contained in the right side of the production $S \rightarrow aabb$.

For maximum length of string use the given production rules recursively, as explained below :

$$A \rightarrow \quad aAb$$

*i.e.*, $A$ is replaced by $aAb$, so

$$S \to aaAbb$$

Again use the same production rule

$$A \to aAb$$

So $\quad A \to aaaAbbb$

Using this production rules repeatedly, you get

$$S \to aaaAbbb \qquad \textit{i.e., } a^3Ab^3$$
$$\to aaaaAbbbb \qquad \textit{i.e., } a^4ab^4$$
$$\to a^5Ab^5$$
$$\to \ldots\ldots$$
$$\to \ldots\ldots$$
$$\to \ldots\ldots$$
$$\to a^nAb^n \qquad \text{Where } n \geq 1$$
$$\to a^{n+1}b^{n+1} \qquad \text{by } A \to ab$$

So the language generated by this grammar is

$$L(G) = a^{n+1}b^{n+1}/n \geq 1$$

or

$$\boxed{L(G) = a^nb^n/n \geq 2}$$

Here when you put the value of $n = 1$ (*i.e.*, the lowest value) you get the string of minimum length.

**Example 1.9:** Given grammar $G$ to represent language $L(R)$ with words consisting of

(*a*) Equal number of *a's* and *b's*

(*b*) Palindromes

(*c*) Palindromes of odd length

(*d*) Without consecutive occurrence of *b's*

(*e*) At least two *a's*

(*f*) At least one occurrence of '*aaa*'

(*g*) Palindromes of even length

**Solution:** (*a*) $S \to aB/bA$

$A \to a/as/bAA$

$S \to b/bs/aBB$

(*b*) $S \to \in/a/b/asa/bsb$

(*c*) $S \to a/b$

$S \to asa/bsb$

(*d*) $S \to as/bA/a/b/\in$

$A \rightarrow as/a/\in$

(e) $S \rightarrow Aa\ Aa\ A$

$A \rightarrow aA/bA/a/b/\in$

(f) $S \rightarrow ABA$

$B \rightarrow aaa$

$A \rightarrow aA/aA/bA/\in$

(g) $S \rightarrow \in/asa/bsb$

**Example 2.10:** $L = L_1\ UL_2$

$$L = \{a^n\ b^n\ c^m\ ;\ n \geq 1,\ m\ ^3\ 0\}$$

**Solution:** $L = L_1\ UL_2$

where $L_1 = \{a^n\ b^n\ ;\ n \geq 1\}$

$L_2 = \{a^n\ b^n\ c^m\ ;\ m \geq 0\ n \geq 1\}$

$L_1 : S \rightarrow A$ $\qquad$ $L_2 : S \rightarrow SC$

$A \rightarrow ab/aAb$

We define $P$ as

$$S \rightarrow SC/A$$

$$A \rightarrow ab/aAb$$

**Example 2.11:** *Consider the grammar*

$$G = (\{S,\ A,\ B\},\ \{a,\ b\}\ P,\ S\}$$

*where P consists of following production rules*

$$S \rightarrow aaB$$

$$A \rightarrow aaBa$$

$$B \rightarrow bbAa$$

$$A \rightarrow \in$$

*Find all the language of the given grammar G.*

**Solution:** Since the string contains the starting symbol $S$, so find language for $S$.

$S \rightarrow aaB$

$S \rightarrow aa(bbAa)$ by production rule $B \rightarrow bbAa$

$S \rightarrow aa(bb\in a)$ by production rule $A \rightarrow \in$

$S \rightarrow aabba$ is string of minimum length.

For string of maximum length.

If you see the production rules for every non terminal $B$, $bbAa$ wil come and for every $A$, either $\in$ will come or $aaBa$ will come. For finding maximum string length always use production rules which contains a non terminal symbols as shown below :

$S \to aaB$
$S \to aa(bbAa)$
$S \to aabbAa$ by production rule $A \to aaBb$
$\to aa\ bb\ (aaBb)a$
$\to aa(bbaa)^1\ B(ba)^1$
$\to aabbaa(bbAa)\ ba$ by production rule $B \to bbAa$
$\to aabbaabbAaba$
$\to aabbaabb(aaBb)aba$ by production rule $R \to aaBb$
$\to aabbaabbaaBaba$
$\to aa(bbaa)^2\ B(ba)^2$
$\to aa(bbaa)^3\ B(ba)^3$
$\to$ ....................
$\to$ ....................
$\to$ ....................
$\to aa(bbaa)^n\ B(ba)^n n \geq 0$
$\to aa(bbaa)^n bbAa(ba)^n$ by production rule $B \to bbAa$
$\to aa(bbaa)^n bba(ba)^n$ by $A \to \in$

Hence language generated by this grammar is

$$L(G) = aa(bbaa)^n bba(ba)^n \quad n \geq 0.$$

## 2.8 CHOMSKY CLASSIFICATION OF GRAMMAR

Grammars are classified according to the kinds of production which are allowed. The Chomsky's hierarchy is a classification of the grammars which generates formal languages. This hierarchy was described by ***Noam Chomsky*** in 1956.

Chomsky had suggested four dipperent closses of grammars as follows:

| Grammar | Language | Automation |
|---|---|---|
| Type–0 | Unrestricted grammar | Turing Machine |
| Type–1 | Context–Sensitive | Linear Bounded |
| Type–2 | Context–free | Push–down Automata |
| Type–3 | Regular | Finite State |

The grammar can be distinguished only through their production rules.

## 1. Unrestricted (or Type 0) Grammar

An unrestricted grammar $G$ consist of four tuples

$$G = (V, S, P, S)$$

where

$V$ is a finite set whose elements are called terminals or variables.

$\Sigma$ is a finite set whose elements are called terminals.

$P$ is a finite set of production rules whose productions are in the form of $\phi A\psi \to \phi w\psi$, where $\phi, w, \psi \in (V \cup \Sigma)^*$ and $A \in V \cup \{S\}$

$S$ is a starting symbol and $S \in V$.

**Or**

A grammar is called a unrestricted Grammar if it contains a contracting production rules.

### Contracting Production

A production rules, which is in the form of $w_{i+1} \to w_i$. That is $w_i$ produce shorter length than $w_{i+1}$. Such rule is called contracting production.

*For example,* $bC \to b$

Here $w_{i+1} = bC$ and length of $w_{i+1}$ (*i.e.*, $|w_{i+1}|$) = 2

and $w_i = b$ and length of $|w_i|$ (*i.e.*, $|w_i|$) = 1, which represents shorter length than $|w_{i+1}|$

### Contracting Grammar

A grammar containing at least one contracting production is called contracting grammar. Only type 0 grammar is contracting grammar.

*For example,* consider a grammar $G = (\{S, A\}, \{a\}, P, S)$

Where $P$ consists of following production rules

$$S \to aA$$

$$aA \to aaA$$

$$aA \to a$$

This grammar contains a contacting production rule (*i.e.*, $a \to a$) for a language ($L = a^n \mid n > 0$). So the given grammar is an Unrestricted (or Type 0) Grammar.

## 2. Context Sensitive (or Type 1) Grammar

A Contact Sensitive grammar $G$ consist of four tuples

$$G = (V, \Sigma, P, S)$$

where,

$V$ is a finite set whose elements are called non terminals or variables.

$\Sigma$ is a finite set whose elements are called terminals.

$P$ is a finite set of production rules whose all productions are in the forms of $\phi A\psi \to \phi w\psi$, $w \neq \in$ and only $S \to \in$ possible if $S$ is a starting symbol but $S$ should not appear on right hand side of any production rule, where $\phi$, $\psi$ $\in (V \cup \Sigma)^*$, we $(V \cup \Sigma)^*$ and $A \in V \cup \{S\}$

$S$is a starting symbol and $S \in V$.

**Or**

A context sensitive grammar is a grammar in which each production contains a non-contracting production rules.

### Non-Contracting Production

A production $\alpha \to \beta$ satisfying $|\alpha| \leq |\beta|$ is known as non-contracting production.

*For example,* $w_1 \to w_2 \to w_3 \to \ldots\ldots \to w_n$

$|w_1| \leq |w_2| \leq w_3| \leq \ldots\ldots \leq |w_n|$ are non decreasing in a length is called context sensitive grammar.

**Example 2.12:** *Consider a grammar* $G = (V, \Sigma, P, S)$ *where*

$$V = \{A, B, C\}$$

$$\Sigma = \{a, b, c\}$$

*and P as follows* $S \to aSBC \mid aBC \quad CB \to BC \quad cC \to cc$

$aB \to ab \quad bB \to bb \quad bC \to bc$

*Final all the language of the given grammar G.*

**Solution:** Since the string contains the starting symbol $S$, so find the language for $S$

$S \to aBC$

$S \to abC$ by production rule $aB \to ab$

$S \to abc$ by production rule $bC \to bc$

$S \to abc$ is string of minimum length

For string of maximum length

If you see the production rules for starting symbol $S$, $S$ will be recursively replaced by string $aSBC$ and finally $S$ will terminate with string $aBC$ as shown below :

$S \to aSBC$

$S \to aaSBC\ BC$ by production rule $S \to aSBC$

$\to aaSBBCC$ by production rule $CB \to BC$

$\to a^2S\ B^2C^2$

$S \to aa\ aSBC\ BBCC$ by production rule $S \to aSBC$

$S \rightarrow aaasBBCBCC$ by production rule $CB \rightarrow BC$

$S \rightarrow aaaSBBBCCC$ by production rule $CB \rightarrow BC$

$\rightarrow a^3SB^3C^3$

$\rightarrow$ ...............

$\rightarrow$ ..............

$S \rightarrow a^{n-1} SB^{n-1} C^{n-1}$

$S \rightarrow a^nB^nC^n$ by production rule $S \rightarrow aBC$

$S \rightarrow a^{n-1} aBB^{n-1}C^n$

$S \rightarrow a^{n-1}abB^{n-1} C^n$ by production rule $aB \rightarrow ab$

$S \rightarrow a^nbB^{n-1}C^n$

$S \rightarrow a^nbbB^{n-2}C^n$ by production rule $bB \rightarrow bb$

$S \rightarrow a^nbbB^{n-3}C^n$ by production rule $bB \rightarrow bb$

$S \rightarrow a^nb^2bB^{n-3}C^n$

$S \rightarrow a^nb^3bB^{n-4}C^n$ by production rule $bB \rightarrow bb$

$S \rightarrow a^nb^4bB^{n-5}C^n$

$\rightarrow$ ..............

$\rightarrow$ .............

$S \rightarrow a^nb^{n-1}bCC^{n-1}$ by production rule $bB \rightarrow bb$

$S \rightarrow a^nb^{n-1}bcC^{n-1}$ by production rule $bC \rightarrow bc$

$S \rightarrow a^nb^ncCC^{n-2}$

$S \rightarrow a^nb^nccCC^{n-3}$ by production rule $cC \rightarrow cc$

$S \rightarrow a^nb^nc^2cCC^{n-4}$

$S \rightarrow a^nb^ncccCC^{n-4}$ by production rule $cC \rightarrow cc$

$S \rightarrow a^nb^nc^3cCC^{n-5}$ by production rule $cC \rightarrow cc$

$\rightarrow$ ...........

$\rightarrow$ ...........

$sS \rightarrow a^nb^nc^{n-2}cc$ by production rule $cC \rightarrow cc$

$S \rightarrow a^nb^nc^n$

Hence language generated by this grammar is

$$L(G) = \{a^nb^nc^n | n \geq 1\}$$

*For example*, consider a grammar $G = (V, \Sigma, P, S)$

where $V = \{A, B, C, D\}$

$\Sigma = \{a, b, c, d\}$

and $P$ as follows :

$S \rightarrow aSBCD|$ $DB \rightarrow BD$ $DC \rightarrow CD$ $CD \rightarrow BC$ $aB \rightarrow ab$
$bB \rightarrow bb$ $bc \rightarrow bc$ $cC \rightarrow cc$ $cD \rightarrow cd$ $dD \rightarrow dd$

Again in this grammar all production rules are non-contracting rules. So given grammar is a context sensitive (or Type 1) grammar and the language generated by this grammar is $a^n b^n c^n d^n \mid n \geq 1$. That is

$$L(G) = \{a^n b^n c^n d^m | n \geq 1\}$$

*For example,* consider a grammar $G = (V, \Sigma, P, S)$

where $V = \{A, B\}$
$\Sigma = \{a, b\}$

and $P$ as follows

$S \rightarrow aSBAA|aBAA$ $AB \rightarrow Ba$ $aB \rightarrow ab$
$bB \rightarrow bb$ $bA \rightarrow ba$
$aA \rightarrow aa$

Again in this grammar all production rules are non-contracting rules. so given grammar is a context sensitive (or Type 1) grammar and the language generated by this grammar is $a^n b^n a^{2n} | n \geq 1$. That is

$$L(G) = \{a^n b^n a^{2n} | n \geq 1\}$$

*For example*, consider a grammar $G = (\{S, A\}, \{a\}, P, S\}$

Where $P$ consists of following production rules

$S \rightarrow aA$
$aA \rightarrow aaA$
$aA \rightarrow aa$

All the production rules of this grammar contain non-contacting production rules for a language ($L = a^n | n \geq 1$ or $n \geq 2$). So the given grammar is a context sensitive (or Type 1) grammar.

## 3. Context Free (or Type 2) Grammar (CFG)

A context free grammar $G$ consist of four tuples

$$G = (V, \Sigma, P, S)$$

where

$V$ is a finite set whose elements are called non-terminals or variables.

$\Sigma$ is a finite set whose elements are called terminals.

$P$ is a finite set of production rules whose all productions are in the form of $A \rightarrow w$ and $w \neq \in$, where $A \in V \cup \{S\}$ and $w \in (V \cup \Sigma)^*$

$S$ is a starting symbol and $S \in V$.

or In a production $\phi A\psi \rightarrow \phi w\psi$, the string, $\phi$ & $\psi$ both are required to be empty. Thus the possibility of replacing a non-terminal letter in a sequential form is independent of adjacent symbols *i.e.* It is independent of the context.

---

The grammar may also contain a production rule $S \rightarrow \epsilon$, if $S$ is starting symbol and left hand side of production rule always contain a single non-terminal symbol.

---

**Example 2.13:** *Consider a grammar* $G = (V, \Sigma, P, S)$ *where*

$$V = \{A, B, C\}$$

$$\Sigma = \{a, b, c, d\}$$

*and P as follows* $S \rightarrow aSd \mid aAd$

$$A \rightarrow bAd \mid bBd$$

$$B \rightarrow cBd \mid cd$$

*Find all the language of the given grammar G.*

**Solution :** Since the string contains the starting symbols $S$, so find the language for $S$.

$S \rightarrow aAd$

$S \rightarrow abBdd$ by production rule $A \rightarrow bBd$

$S \rightarrow abcddd$ by production rule $B \rightarrow cd$

$S \rightarrow abcddd$ is string of minimum length.

For string of maximum length

If you see the production rules for starting symbol $S$, $S$ will be recursively replaced by string $aSd$ and finally $S$ will terminate with string $aAd$. Again by the production rules for symbol $A$, $A$ will be recursively replaced by string $bAd$ and finally $A$ will terminate with string $bBd$ and again by the production rules for symbol $B$, $B$ will be recursively replaced by string $cBd$ and finally $B$ will terminate with string $cd$, shown below

$S \rightarrow aSd$

$S \rightarrow aaSdd$ by production rule $S \rightarrow aSd$

$\rightarrow aaaSddd$ by production rule $S \rightarrow aSd$

$\rightarrow a^3Sd^3$

$\rightarrow$ ...........

$\rightarrow$ ..........

$\rightarrow a^{n-1}Sd^{n-1}$ by production rule $S \rightarrow aSd$

$S \rightarrow a^nAd^n$ by production rule $S \rightarrow aAd$

$S \to a^nbAdd^n$ by production rule $A \to bAd$

$S \to a^nbbAddd^n$ by production rule $A \to bAd$

$S \to a^nbbbAdddd^n$ by production rule $A \to bAd$

$\to a^nb^3Ad^3d^n$

$\to$ ..........

$\to$ ..........

$S \to a^nb^{m-1}\ Ad^{m-1}\ a^n$ by production rule $A \to bAd$

$S \to a^nb^mBd^md^m$ by production rule $A \to bBd$

$S \to a^nb^mcBdd^md^n$ by production rule $B \to cBd$

$S \to a^nb^mccBddd^md^m$ by production rule $B \to cBd$

$S \to a^nb^mcccBdddd^md^n$ by production rule $B \to cBd$

$S \to a^nb^mc^3Bd^3d^md^n$

$\to$ .........

$\to$ .........

$S \to a^nb^mc^{k-1}Bd^{k-1}d^md^n$by production rule $B \to cBd$

$S \to a^nb^mc^kd^kd^md^n$ by production rule $B \to cd$

Hence language generated by this grammar is

$$L(G) = \{a^nb^mc^kd^kd^md^n \mid n,\ m,\ k \geq 1\}$$

$$L(G) = \{a^nb^mc^kd^l \mid n,\ m,\ k \geq 1 \text{ and } 1 = n + m + k\}$$

*For example,* consider a grammar $G = (\{S, A\}, \{a\}, P, S)$

where $P$ consists of following production rules

$$S \to A$$
$$A \to aaA$$
$$A \to a$$

All the production rules of this grammar contain in the left hand side only one non-terminal symbol. So this grammar is a context free (or Type 2) grammar and the language generated by this grammar is $a^{2n+1} \mid n \geq 0$. That is

$$L(\text{G}) = \{a^{2n+1} \mid n \geq 0\}$$

*For example*, consider a grammar $G = (\{S, A\}, \{a,\ b\}\ P,\ S)$,

where $P$ consists of following production rules

$$S \to A$$
$$A \to aAb$$
$$A \to ab$$

All the production rules of this grammar contain in the left hand side only one non-terminal symbol. So this grammar is a context free grammar (or Type 2) and the language generated by this grammar is $a^n b^n \mid n \geq 1$. That is

$$L(G) = \{a^n b^n \mid n \geq 1\}$$

*For example,* consider a grammar $G = (\{S\}, \{a, b\}, P, S)$,

where $P$ consists of following production rules

$$S \to aSb \mid A \mid B$$
$$A \to aA \mid a$$
$$B \to Bb \mid b$$

All the production rules of this grammar contain in the left hand side only one non-terminal symbol. So this grammar is a context free (or Type 2) grammar and the language generated by this grammar is $a^n b^m \mid n \neq m$. That is

$$L(G) = \{a^n b^m \mid n \neq m\}$$

## 4. Regular (or Type 3) Grammar

A regular grammar $G$ consist of four tuples

$$G = (V, \Sigma, P, S)$$

where $V$ is a finite set whose elements are called non terminals or variables.

$\Sigma$ is a finite set whose elements are called terminals.

$P$ is a finite set of production rules in which all the productions rules are in the following form

A production rule in the form of

$$A \to aB \qquad A \in (V \cup S)$$
$$A \to a \qquad B \in V$$
$$a \in \Sigma$$

is called a **right linear production.**

A production rule in the form of

$$A \to Ba \qquad A \in (V \cup S)$$
$$A \to a \qquad B \in V$$
$$a \in \Sigma$$

is called **left linear production.**

$S$ is a starting symbol and $S \in V$

*For example,* consider a grammar $G = (\{S, A\}, \{a\}, P, S)$

Where $P$ consists of following production rules

$$S \to aA$$
$$A \to aA$$
$$A \to a$$

This grammar contains production rules in the form of right linear production. So this grammar is a regular Grammar (or Type 3) and the language generated by this grammar is $a^n$ for all value of $n$ greater than one.

*i.e.,* $L(G) = \{a^n \mid n > 1 \text{ or } n \geq 2\}$

*For example,* consider a grammar $G = (\{S, A\}, \{a\}, P, S)$

Where $P$ consists of following production rules

$$A \to Aa$$
$$A \to Aa$$
$$A \to a$$

This grammar contains production rules in the form of left linear production. So the grammar is a regular Grammar (or Type 3) and the language generated by this grammar is $a^n$ for all value of $n$ greater than one.

*i.e.,* $L(G) = \{a^n \mid n > 1 \text{ or } n \ ^3\ 2\}$

*For example*, consider a grammar $G = (\{S, A, B\}, \{0, 1\}, P, S)$

Where $P$ consists of following production rules

| $G_1$: | | $G_2$: | |
|---|---|---|---|
| | $S \to 1B$ | | $S \to B1$ |
| | $S \to 1$ | | $S \to 1$ |
| | $A \to 1B$ | | $A \to B1$ |
| | $B \to 0A$ | | $B \to A0$ |
| | $A \to 1$ | | $A \to 1$ |

The grammar $G_1$ contains production rules in the form of right linear production and the grammar $G_2$ contains production rules in the form of left linear. So these production rules give regular (ro Type 3) Grammar and the language generated by these grammars are ($10^*$ 1 and $1(01)^*$ corresponding to the grammar $G_1$ and $G_2$ respectively. *i.e.,*

$$L(G_1) = (10)^*\, 1$$

and

$$L(G_2) = 1(01)^*$$

Regular grammars are a highly restricted subclass of context free grammars in which the right hand side of production rules may contain at most a single non terminal symbols.

**The brief representation of different kind of grammar are**

| Type | Format of production |
|---|---|
| 0 | $\phi A\psi \to \phi w\psi$ and $w$ may be $\in$ |
| 1. | $\phi Ay \to fwy$ and $w \neq \in$<br>$A \in V \cup \{S\}$<br>$S \to \in$ if $S$ is a starting symbol but $S$ should not appear on right hand side of any production |
| 2. | $S \to w$ and $w \neq \in$<br>$S \to \in$ |
| 3. | $A \to aB$, $A \to a$, $S \to \in$ — Right linear<br>$S \to Ba$, $A \to a$, $S \to \in$ — Left linear |

$\phi, \psi \in (V \cup \Sigma)^*$

$w \in (V \cup \Sigma)^*$

$B \in V$

$a \in \Sigma$

Here $\phi$, $\psi$ are strings and $S$ is a starting symbol

The heart part of the grammar is the production rules only. That is, if you are able to design a production rule of a language then you can write a grammar for that particular language.

## 2.9 CHOMSKY HIERARCHY

As explained above there are four different types of grammar. If you see the production rules of all types of grammars, you will find some relations among them the following relations exists among them. Each language family of type $i$ is a proper subset of the family of type $(i - 1)$.

That is

Type 1 $\subseteq$ Type 0, Type 2 $\subseteq$ Type 1, Type 3 $\subseteq$ Type 2

Graphically it shows in figure below :

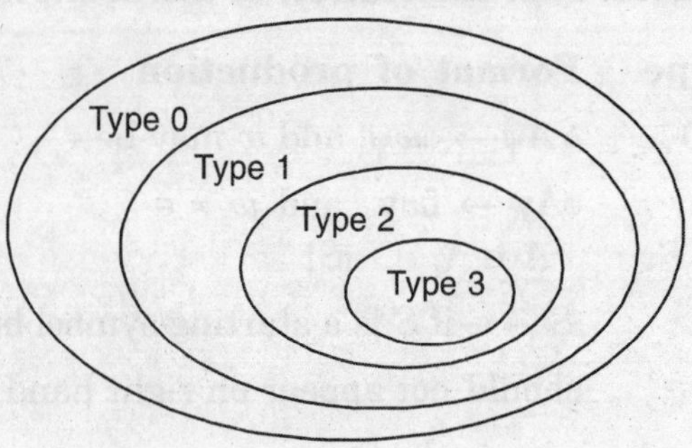


*Fig. 2.2*

## 2.10 LANGUAGES AND THEIR RELATED AUTOMATA

The following table shows the different type of languages, grammer and their automata.

| Language | Grammar | Machine | Example |
|---|---|---|---|
| Regular language | Regular Grammar → Right Linear Grammar → Left Linear Grammar | Deterministic or Non-deterministic finite-state acceptor | a* |
| Context-free language | Context-free Grammar | Non-deterministic Pushdown automaton | $a^n b^n$ |
| Recursively enumer able language | Unrestristed Grammar | Turing Machine | Any Computable function |
| Context-Sensitive language | Context-Sensitive Grammar | Linear-bounded Automaton | $a^n b^n c^n$ |

The following figure describes the types of languages and their corresponding automata. We known the function performed by finite automaton will also be performed by PDA, the function performed by push down automaton will also be performed by linear bounded automaton (LBA), and the function performed by linear bounded automaton will also be performed by a Turing Machine.

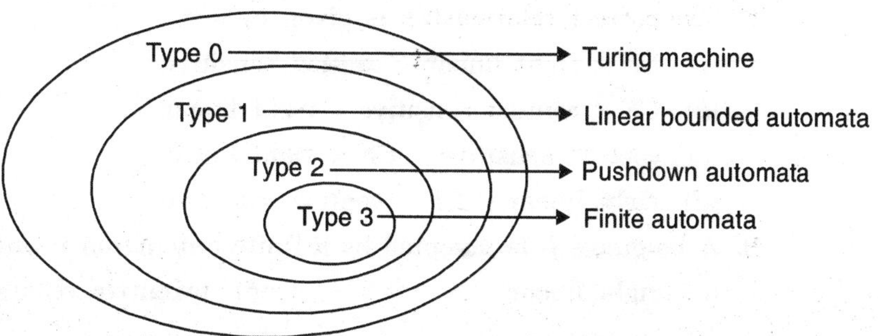


***Fig. 2.3***

# EXERCISE

## (A) Objective Type Questions

**1.** A grammar is context-sensitive if all production of the form $x > y$ are such that

(*a*) $\{|x| = |y|$ (*b*) $|x| \leq |y|$

(*c*) $|x| < |y|$ (*d*) $|x| > |y|$

**2.** Which of the following language is regular?

(*a*) $a^n b^n$ (*b*) $a^n b^n c^n$

(*c*) $a^n b^n$ (*d*) phi

**3.** Which of the following language is context free?

(*a*) $a^n b^n c^n$ (*b*) $a^n b^n$

(*c*) $a$ (*d*) $a^n b^i : n = j^2$

**4.** Type 2 grammar is also called

(*a*) context-sentence (*b*) regular

(*c*) context-free (*d*) none of these

**5.** Find language generated by the following grammar $S \to 0S1 \mid 0A1\ A \to 1A0 \mid 10$

(*a*) $\{0^n 1^n 0^n \mid n > 1\}$ (*b*) $\{1^m 0^n \mid m, n \geq 1\}$

(*c*) $\{0^n 1^m 0^m 1^n \mid m, n \geq 1\}$ (*d*) None of the above

**6.** Chomsky Hierarchy is representation of

(*a*) Grammars (*b*) Machines

(*c*) Parsers (*d*) None of these

**7.** Which of the following can be generated by : $S \to aS \mid bA,\ a \to d \mid ccA$

(*a*) *bccddd* (*b*) *abbbd*

(*c*) *aabccd* (*d*) *ababccd*

**8.** The correct relationship is given by

(*a*) *CF* < right linear < context sensitive

(*b*) *CF* < context sensitive < right linear

(*c*) context sensitive < *CF* < right linear

(*d*) right linear < *CF* < context sensitive

**9.** A language *L* is accepted by a finite automaton if and only if

(*a*) right linear (*b*) primitive recursive

(*c*) context sensitive (*d*) recursive

**10.** A grammar $G = (V, T, S, P)$ is right linear if

(*a*) $A \rightarrow xB \mid x$ ; $A, B \in V$ and $x \in T^*$

(*b*) *CF* < context sensitive < right linear

(*c*) $A \rightarrow xB \mid x$ ; $A, B \in V$ and $x \in T^*$

(*d*) None of these

**11.** Consider the grammar : $S \rightarrow aAB \mid abc$, $A \rightarrow aa \mid eB \rightarrow b$ then equivalent representation is

(*a*) $S \rightarrow aAB \mid abc$, $A \rightarrow aa$, $B \rightarrow b$

(*b*) $S \rightarrow aaaB \mid abc$, $A \rightarrow aa$, $B \rightarrow b$

(*c*) $S \rightarrow aaaB \mid aB \mid abc$ $A \rightarrow aa$, $B \rightarrow b$

(*d*) $S \rightarrow aB \mid abc$, $A \rightarrow aa$, $B \rightarrow b$

**12.** Language generated by the grammar : $S \rightarrow 0A \mid 1s \mid 0 \mid 1$, $a \rightarrow 1A \mid 1S \mid 1$ is

(*a*) all strings of 0'*s* and 1's

(*b*) all strings of 0'*s* and 1'*s* that does no contain 2 consecutive 0'*s*

(*c*) all strings of 0'*s* and 1'*s* that does no contain 2 consecutive 1'*s*

(*d*) all strings of 0'*s* and 1'*s* that neither contain 2 consecutive 0'*s* nor contains two consecutive 0'*s*

**13.** What is the highest type number to the grammar given by these production rules:

(*a*) Zero (*b*) One

(*c*) Two (*d*) Three

**14.** What is the highest type number to grammar given by these production rules:

(*a*) Zero (*b*) One

(*c*) Two (*d*) Three

**15.** A production of the form A → *a or A* → *aB* represents which type of grammar?

(*a*) Zero (*b*) One

(*c*) Two (*d*) Three

## ANSWERS

| 1. (*b*) | 2. (*d*) | 3. (*b*) | 4. (*c*) | 5. (*c*) |
|---|---|---|---|---|
| 6. (*b*) | 7. (*d*) | 8. (*b*) | 9. (*c*) | 10. (*c*) |
| 11. (*b*) | 12. (*d*) | 13. (*b*) | 14. (*c*) | 15. (*c*) |

## (B) Problems

1. Define a recursive definition for a calculator.
2. Define a recursive definition for arithmetic expression.
3. Define a recursive definition for a even palindrome over $\Sigma = \{a, b\}$.
4. Define a recursive definition for a odd palindrome over input alphabet $\Sigma = \{a, b, c\}$.
5. Define a recursive definition for the power set of 2 and 3.
6. Find a context free language for the following grammar whose production rules are given below :

(*a*) $S \to aA \mid aaA \mid \in$

$A \to aAb \mid B \mid$

$A \to Bb \mid \in$

(*b*) $S \to aSb \mid aA \mid Bb$

$A \to aA \mid \in$

$B \to Bb \mid \in$

(*c*) $S \to aSbb \mid aA \mid Bbb$

$A \to aA \mid \in$

$B \to Bb \mid \in$

(*d*) $S \to aSbb \mid aSbbb \mid abb \mid abbb$

(*e*) $S \to aSb \mid bSa \mid aA \mid Bb$

$A \to aA \mid \in$

$B \to Bb \mid \in$

(*f*) $S \to aSc \mid aAc$

$A \to bAc \mid bc$

(*g*) $S \to AB$

$A \to aA \mid \in$

$B \to bBc \mid Cc$

$C \to Cc \mid \in$

(*h*) $S \to aSc \mid A \mid \in$

$A \to aAb \mid \in$

(i) $S \rightarrow SS \mid aSb \mid bSa \mid aSa \mid bSb \mid \in$

**Hints:**

(a) $L(G) = a^n b^m : n \leq m + 2$

(b) $L(G) = a^n b^m : n \neq m$

(c) $L(G) = a^n b^m : n \neq 2m$

(d) $L(G) = a^n b^m : 2n \leq m \leq 3n$ and $n \geq 1$

(e) $L(G) = w : n_n(w) \neq n_b(w)$

(f) $L(G) = \{a^n b^m c^k \mid n, m \geq 1 \text{ and } k = n + m\}$

(g) $L(G) = \{a^n b^m c^k \mid n \geq 1 \text{ and } m \leq k\}$

(h) $L(G) = \{a^n b^m c^k \mid m, k \geq 0 \text{ and } n = m + k\}$

or $L(G) = \{a^n b^m c^k \mid k = |n - m|\}$

or $L(G) = \{a^n b^m c^k \mid n = k + m \text{ and } m = k + n\}$

(i) $L(G) = \{w \mid w \in \{a, b\}\}^*$

**7.** Find a Context-Sensitive language for the following grammar whose production rules are given below

(a) $S \rightarrow aSBC \mid aDC \quad CB \rightarrow BC$

$aB \rightarrow ab$

$dB \rightarrow bb \quad bC \rightarrow bc \quad cC \rightarrow cc$

$D \rightarrow bDC \mid bC$

(b) $S \rightarrow aSC \mid aAC \quad DC \rightarrow CD$

$A \rightarrow bAD \mid bD \quad bC \rightarrow bc$

$cC \rightarrow cc \quad cD \rightarrow cd \quad dD \rightarrow dd$

**Hints:**

(a) $L(G) = \{a^n b^m c^k : m = k \text{ and } m \geq n\}$

(b) $L(G) = \{a^n b^m c^n d^m : n \geq 1, m \geq 1\}$

❑❑❑

CHAPTER

# 3

# FINITE STATE MACHINE

## 3.1 INTRODUCTION

Theory of computation is a subject that deals with different mathematical models of machines and the relationship between Machine, Grammars and Languages. It is one of the important subject which has its wide applications in almost all fields of human nature, specialy in computers. Some of its important application areas are Compiler Design, Netural Networks and Parallel Computing.

In the chapter we will learn the finite state system. The finite state system consists of finite automata which can be deterministic or non deterministic in nature we will learn to design the deterministic finite automata as well as non deterministic finite automata. This chapter covers the conversion of non deterministic finite automata to deterministic finite automata. Then we will discuss the finite automata with output using Moore and Mealy machine.

## 3.2 FINITE STATE MACHINE

The finite state machine represents a mathematical model of a system with certain input. The model finally gives certain output. The input when is given to the machine it is processed by various states, these states are called as intermediate states.

The very good example of finite state machine is a control mechanism of ***elevator***. This mechanism only remembers the current floor number pressed, it does not remember all the previously pressed numbers.

The finite state system is a very good design tool for the programs such as text editors and lexical analysers (which is used in complers).

Finite state machine has only a finite, constant amount of memory (state). It can be Conceptualised as a directed graph. There is a finite number of states and each state has transitions to zero or more states. There is a input string that determines which transition is followed.

### 3.2.1 Finite Automata

The finite automation is a mathematical representation of finited state machine with discrete input and discrete outputs. The system is a control unit, which can be any one of a finite number of internal states and which can change states in some defined manner. The Fig. 3.1 shows a general representation of an automaton. The input is a string over a given alphabet written on an input file; which the automata can read but not change. The input file divided into set of cells where each cell contains one symbol at a time and also read the input file left to right one symbol at a time. It also detects the end of the input string by using specific symbol (*i.e.* write end marker). The output is also a string of some form. It may have a temporary storage device, consisting of an unlimited number of cells, each cell containing a single symbol from an alphabet (cell can contain same or different symbols).

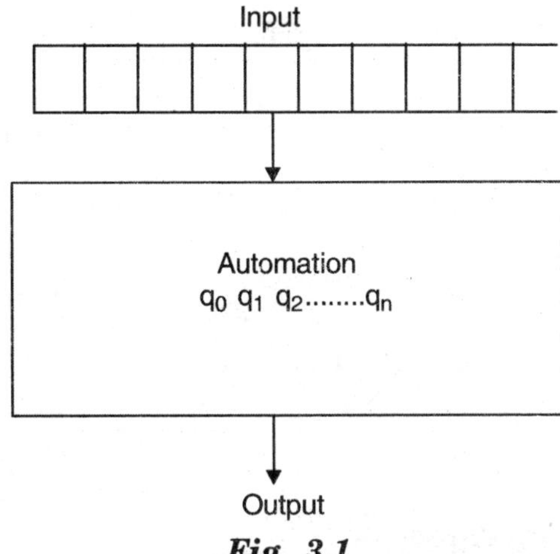


***Fig. 3.1***

An automaton is used to operate discrete timeframe. At any given time, the system is in some internal state and the input ins scanning a particular symbol on the input file. The internal state of the system at the next time step is determined by the next state or transition input symbol and the information currently in the temporary storage. During the transition from one state to next state the output may be produced or the information in the temporary storage changed depending upon the designed machine. The transition from one state to another state is called **move.**

## 3.2.2 Formal Definition of FA

A finite automata is a collection of 5 – types

$$(Q, \Sigma, S, q_0, F)$$

where, $Q$ is a finite set of states, which is non empty.

$\Sigma$ is input alphabet, indicates input set

$q_0$ in $Q$ is the initial state

$F$ is a set of final states

$\delta$ is a transition function or a function defined for going to next state.

### Transition Diagram

The *FA* is associated wiith a directed graph called a transition graph or transition diagram. The vertices of this graph corresponds to the states.

For example, A transition diagram for the input *aabb* as follows–

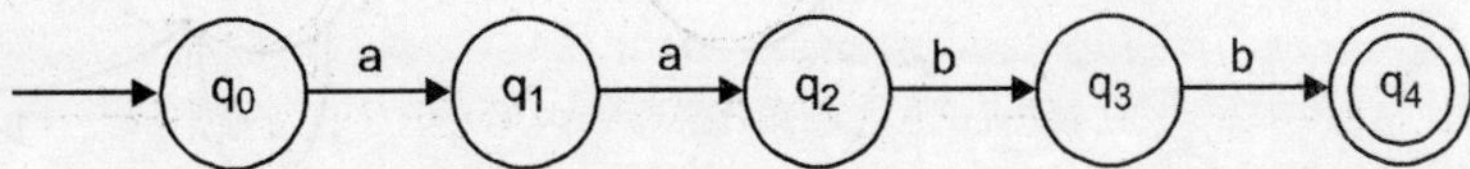


***Fig. 3.2***

where,

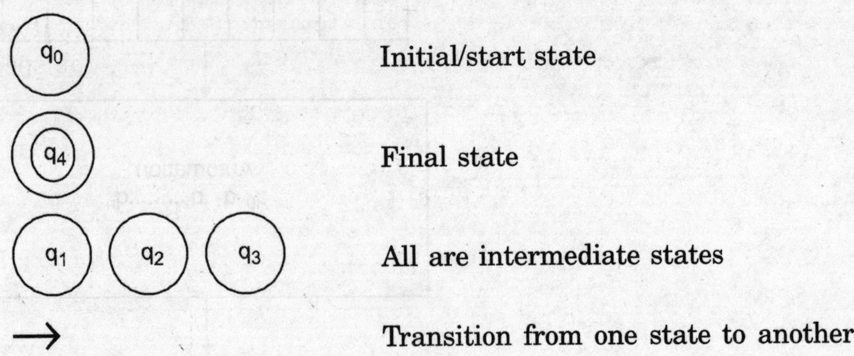


Initial/start state

Final state

All are intermediate states

Transition from one state to another

### Mapping Function

The FSM has two forms fo mapping functions

→ Machine Function

→ State Function

The machine function is a function which denotes, with certain input what will be the output from current state. It can be written as

$$S \times I = O$$

where, $S$ is current state, $I$ is the output $O$ is the output.

The state function is a function which denotes with certain input from current state what will be the next state. It can be written as –

$$S \times I = O$$

where $S_1$ indicates the next state.

Thus at any stage the machine will act as either on arrival of an input symbol it will change the state using state function or it will give output using machine function.

**Example 3.1:** Design finite automata which accepts only those strings which start with 1 and ends with 0.

**Solution:** The finite automata will have a start $q_0$ from which only the edge with input 1 will go to next state.

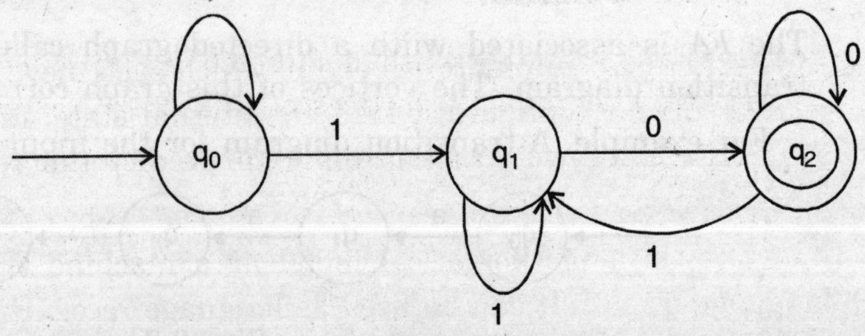


*Fig. 3.3*

In state $q_1$ if we read 1 we will be in $q_1$ state but if we read 0 at state $q_1$ we will reach $q_2$ which is a final state. In state $q_2$ if we read either 0 or 1 we will go to state $q_2$ or $q_1$ respectively. Note that the special care is taken for 0, if the input ends with 0 it will be in final state.

**Example 3.2:** Design *FA* to accept the string that always ends with 00.

**Solution:** The *FA* will have a start state $q_0$ from which only the edge with input 0 will go to next state: if we read 1 we will be in the $q_0$.

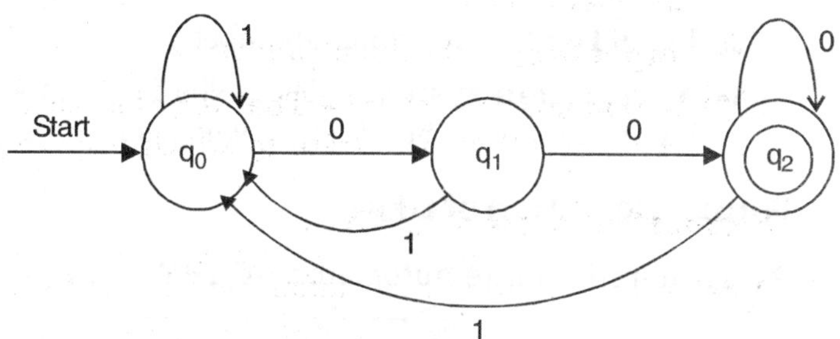


***Fig. 3.4***

If the input is 01001100 it will be processed as

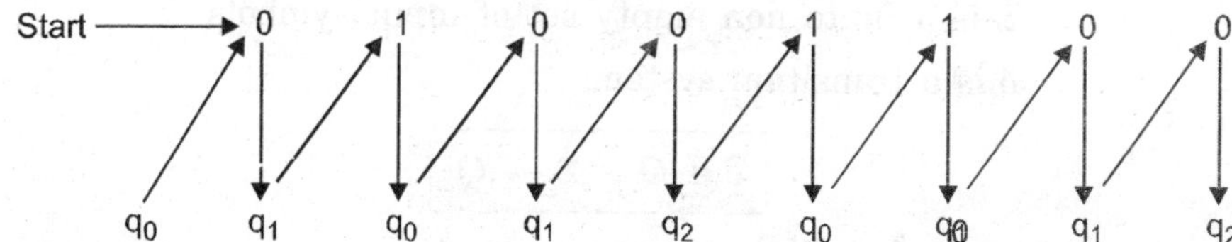


The $q_2$ is a final state, hence the input is accepted.

### 3.2.3 Types of Automaton

There are two types of automaton

(1) Deterministic Automaton

(2) Non-deterministic Automaton

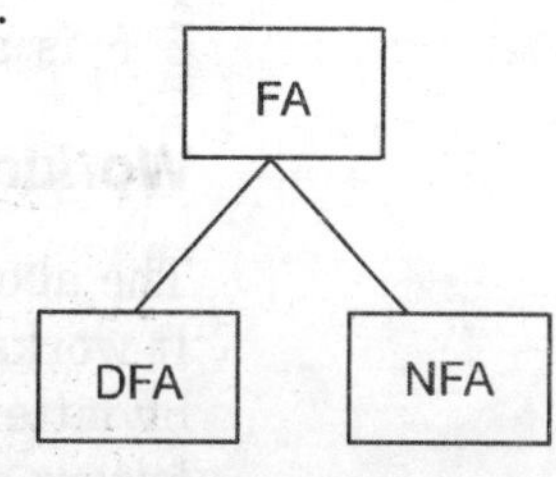


***Fig. 3.5***

## 3.3 DETERMINISTIC FINITE AUTOMATION (DFA)

A deterministic automaton is one in which each move is uniqually determined by the current configuration. If the internal state, input and contents of the storage are known, it is possible to predict the future behaviour at the automaton.

A DFA is a mathematical motel at a machine that accepts a particular language over Σ. It can be used as language recognizer, that is why it is also called an **Acceptor.**

The term deterministic means that one reading the input symbols the automaton changes its current state to some other state or may remain in the same state.

A DFA consists at following three things.

(1) **A finite set of states** – One of which is designed as the initial state, called the starting state and some (may be none) of which are designed as final states.

(2) **InputTape** – An input alphabet Σ.

(3) **A transition system** – That tells for each state and each letter of the input alphabet, the state to which to go next.

### Formal Definition of DFA

A deterministic finite automaton (or DFA or FA) is defined by the quintuple

$$M = (Q, \Sigma, S, q_0, F)$$

where

$Q$ is a finite non empty set of states

Σ is a finite non empty set of input symbols

δ is a transition system

$$\delta \in Q \times \Sigma \to Q$$

$q_0$ is an initial state and $q_0 \in Q$

$F$ is a set at accepting states (of final states) and $F \subseteq Q$

### Working of DFA

The above definition describes the composition of a DFA but not how it works. It works by being presented with an input string of letters that it reads letter by letter starting at the left most letter. Beginning at the starting state, the letters determine a sequence of states. The sequence of states ends when the last input letter has been read and if the last state is an accepting (or final) state then state string is accepted by a DFA otherwise rejected.

### Transition System

A transition system can be represented in any one of the following three ways:

**(*i*) Transition Graph**

A transition graph is a finite directed labeled graph in which each vertex (or node) represents a state and the directed edges indicates the transition of the state and the edges are labelled with the input alphabet.

A transition graph is shown in Fig. 3.6. In the Fig. 3.6 the initial is represented by a ring (or circle) with an arrow pointing towards it, final state by two concentric (or circle) and the other states are represented by just a ring (or circle). The edges are labeled by input.

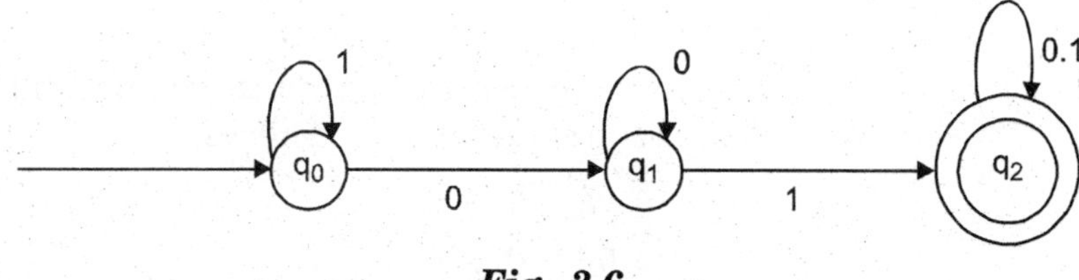


***Fig. 3.6***

For example, in the Fig. 3.6 state $q_0$ is an initial state, $q_2$ is a final state and $q_1$ is another state, and the transition performed by these states are follows

From state $q_0$ and input 0, go to the next state $q_1$

From state $q_0$ and input 1, go to the next state $q_0$

From state $q_1$ and input 0, go to the next state $q_1$

From state $q_1$ and input 1, go to the next state $q_2$

From state $q_2$ and input 0, go to the next state $q_2$

From state $q_2$ and input 1, go to the next state $q_2$

or

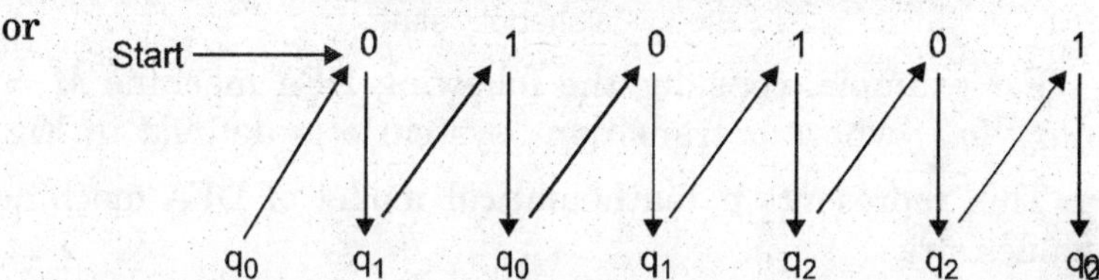


The $q_2$ is a final state, hence the input is accepted

A transition diagram may contain more than one inital state.

### (2) Transition Table

A DFA may be conveniently represented by a *transition table*. The transition table of Fig. 3.6 is represented in table-1

**Table 1. Input alphabets**

| States | 0 | 1 |
|---|---|---|
| $\rightarrow q_0$ | $q_1$ | $q_0$ |
| $q_1$ | $q_1$ | $q_2$ |
| ($q_2$) | $q_2$ | $q_2$ |

The table represents the transition graph of δ *i.e.*, to find the value of present state $q$ and input alphabet $x$ we have to look at the row labeled $q$ and the column labeled $x$. The initial state is marked by an → and final states are marked by single rings (or circle).

**(3) Transition Function**

A DFA may be also represented by a transition function. The transition function of Fig. 3.6 can be represented as follows;

$$\delta\ (q_0,\ 0) = q_1$$

$$\delta\ (q_0,\ 0) = q_0$$

$$\delta\ (q_1,\ 0) = q_1$$

$$\delta\ (q_1,\ 0) = q_2$$

$$\delta\ (q_2,\ 0) = q_2$$

$$\delta\ (q_2,\ 0) = q_2$$

Here the first argument of transition function δ represents the present (current) state and second argument represents the input letter and the right hand side represents the next state.

*For example,* $\delta\ (q_0, 0) = q_1$

$q_0$ → Present state; 0 → Input alphabet; $q_1$ → Next state

For example, consider the following DFA machine $M = (\{q_0, q_1, q_2\}, \{0, 1\}\ \delta\ q_0, \{q_2\})$ where *a* transition system δ is defined in Fig. 3.6.

This represents *a* mathematical model of DFA machine where the tuples values are

$Q = (q_0, q_1, q_2)$

$\Sigma = (0, 1)$

δ is shown in Fig. 3.6

$q_0$ is an initial state

$q_2$ is a final state

## Language of a DFA

To each DFA machine $M$ we associate *a* language $L(M) \in \Sigma'$. to see whether *a* word WEL($M$), we put *a* marker in the initial state and after reading a symbol move forward the marker along the edge marked with this symbol. If we each the accepting state at the end of the word $w$, then $w \in L(M)$, otherwise $w \notin L(M)$

In the above example we have $0 \notin L(M)$, $101 \in L(M)$ and $1101 \in L(M)$. Indeed we have, $L(M) = \{W \mid W\}$ contains the substring 01

To be more precise we give a formal definition of $L$ ($M$). First we define the entered transition function

$$\delta \in Q \times \Sigma' \rightarrow Q$$

Intuitively, $(q, w) = q'$ if starting from state $q$ we end up in state $q'$ when reading the word $w$ formally, $\delta$ is defined by following rules.

| | |
|---|---|
| **Rule 1** | $\delta\{q, \in\} = q$ |
| **Rule 2** | $\delta\{q. xw\} = \delta\{\delta(q, x), w\}$ |

Here $xw$ stands for $a$ non empty word whose first symbol is $x$ and the rest is $w$

For example,

If $\quad xw = 010$ then this entails that

$x = 0$ and $w = 10$. $w$ may be empty

*i.e.,* $\quad xw = 0$ entails $x = 0$ and $w = \in$

As an example we calculate

$\delta(q_0, 101) = 92$

Using $\delta$ we may now define formally

$$L(M) = \{w \mid \delta(q_0, w) \in F\}$$

Hence we have that $101 \in L(M)$ because

$\delta(q_0, 101) = q_2$ and $q_2 \in F$ as shown below

$$\begin{aligned}
&\downarrow\\
&\delta(q_0, 101)\\
&= \delta(\delta(q_0, 1), 01) \text{ by rule 2}\\
&\downarrow\\
&= \delta(q_0, 01)\\
&= \delta(\delta(q_0, 0), 1) \text{ by rule 2}\\
&\downarrow\\
&= \delta(q_1, 1)\\
&= \delta(\delta(q_1, 1), \in) \text{ by rule 2}\\
&= \delta(q_2, \in)\\
&= q_2 \text{ by rule 1}
\end{aligned}$$

## 3.4 ACCEPTABILITY OF A LANGUAGE BY A FINITE AUTOMATON

A language (string) $w$ is accepted by $a$ finite automation $M = (Q, \Sigma, \delta, q_0, F)$ if $\delta(q_0, w) = \delta$ for some $q \in F$.

**Example 3.3:** Consider the following DFA machine $M = (\{q_0, q_1, q_2\}, \{0, 1\}, \delta, q_0, \{q_1\})$ where $a$ transition graph is shown in Fig. 3.7.

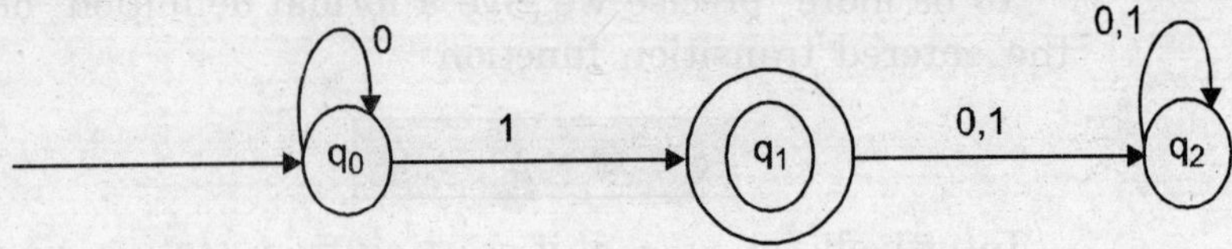


*Fig. 3.7*

Check if the string 00001 is accepted by DFA. Also find the sequence of states.

**Solution:** The given language is $\delta(q_0,\ 00001)$

$$= \delta(\delta(q_0,\ 0),\ 0001$$

$$\downarrow$$

$= \delta(q_0,\ 0001)$ from transition graph i.e., $\delta(q_0,\ 0) = q_0$

$= \delta(\delta(q_0,\ 0),\ 001)$ by rule 2

$$\downarrow$$

$$= \delta(q_0,\ 001)$$

$= \delta(\delta(q_0,\ 0),\ 01)$ by rule 2

$$\downarrow$$

$$= \delta(q_0,\ 01)$$

$= \delta(\delta(q_0,\ 0),\ 1)$ by rule 2

$$\downarrow$$

$$= \delta(q_0,\ 1)$$

$= \delta(\delta(q_0,\ 1),\ \in)$ by rule 2

$$= \delta(q_1,\ \in)$$

$= q_1$ by rule 1

$$q_1 \in F$$

Hence the string is accepted by DFA machine.

The sequence of states corresponding to the input symbol is given by

$$\longrightarrow q_0 \xrightarrow{0} q_0 \xrightarrow{0} q_0 \xrightarrow{0} q_0 \xrightarrow{0} q_0 \xrightarrow{1} q_1$$

**Example 3.4:** Find the sequence of states corresponding to the input symbol 0000111 for the transition digraph shown in Fig. 3.7

**Solution:** The sequence of states of input symbol 0000111 corresponding to the given transition digraph is given below.

$$\longrightarrow q_0 \xrightarrow{0} q_0 \xrightarrow{0} q_0 \xrightarrow{0} q_0 \xrightarrow{0} q_0 \xrightarrow{1} q_1 \xrightarrow{1} q_2 \xrightarrow{1} q_2$$

Since $q_2$ is not a final states, so the language 0000111 is not accepted by a DFA machine

This DFA machine accepts all set of strings (or words) of the form $\{O^n 1 \mid n \geq 0$ or $0^*1\}$

**Example 3.5:** Consider the following DFA machine M = $\{q_0, q_1, q_2, q_3, q_4, q_5, q_6\}$, {a, b}, δ, $q_0$, $\{q_5,\}$) where a transition graph is shown in Fig. 3.8.

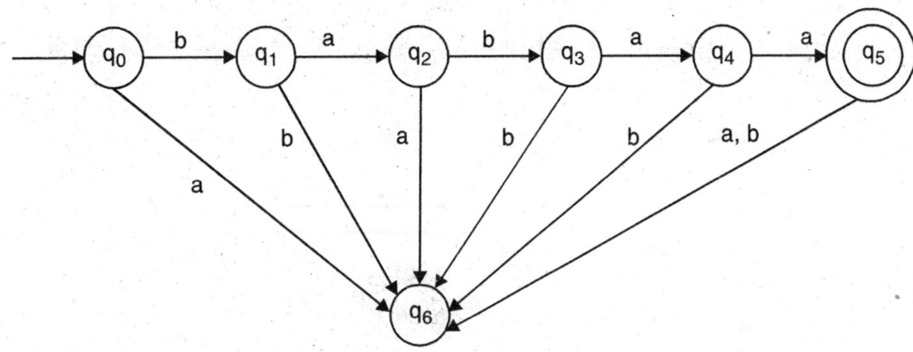


***Fig. 3.8***

Check if the string babaa is by DFA. Also find the sequence of states.

**Solution:** The given language is $\delta(q_0, \text{babaa})$

$= \delta(\delta(q_0, b), abaa)$ by rule 2

$= \delta(q_1, abaa)$ from transition graph *i.e.,* $\delta(q_0, b) = q_1$

$= \delta(\delta(q_1, a), baa)$ by rule 2

$= \delta(q_2, baa)$

$= \delta(\delta(q_2, b), aa)$ by rule 2

$= \delta(q_3, aa)$

$= \delta(\delta(q_3, a), a)$ by rule 2

$= \delta(q_4, a)$

$= \delta(\delta(q_5, a), \in)$ by rule 2

$= \delta(q_5, \in)$

$= q_5$ by rule 1

$q_5 \in F$

Hence the string is accepted by DFA machine.

The sequence of states corresponding to the input symbol is given by

$$\rightarrow q_0 \xrightarrow{b} q_1 \xrightarrow{a} q_2 \xrightarrow{b} q_3 \xrightarrow{a} q_4 \xrightarrow{a} q_5$$

This machine accepts only one string *i.e,* babaa, no other string is accepted by this DFA machine because if you change the string (or word), the sequence of state will reach on non final state.

**Example 3.6:** Verify which at the strings are acceptable by DFA of

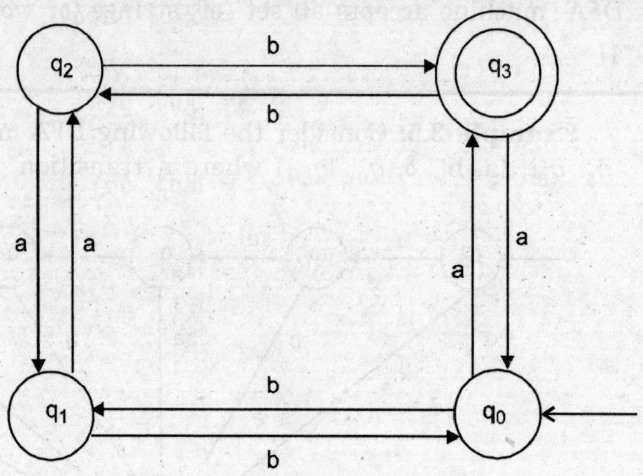


*Fig. 3.9*

(*a*) *abababb*

(*b*) *abbaba*

**Solution:** (*a*) The given language is $\delta(q_0, abababb)$

We have $x\omega = abababb$

$$x = a, \quad \omega = bababb$$

$$\delta(q_0, abababb) = \delta(q_3, bababb)$$
$$= \delta(q_2, ababb)$$
$$= \delta(q_1, babb)$$
$$= \delta(q_0, abb)$$
$$= \delta(q_3, bb)$$
$$= \delta(q_2, b)$$
$$= \delta(q_2, \in)$$
$$= q_3 \quad \text{[by rule 1]}$$

Since $q_3$ is the final state, the string *abababb* is accepted by the DFA.

(*b*) We have $x\omega = abbaba$

$$x = a \quad \omega = bbaba$$

The given language is $\delta(q_0, abbaba)$

$$\delta(q_0, abbaba) = \delta(q_3, bbaba)$$

$$\downarrow$$
$$= \delta(q_2,\ baba)$$
$$\downarrow$$
$$= \delta(q_3,\ aba)$$
$$\downarrow$$
$$= \delta(q_0,\ ba)$$
$$\downarrow$$
$$= \delta(q_1,\ a)$$
$$= \delta(q_2,\ \in)$$
$$= q_2$$

Since $q_2$ is non accepting state, the string *abbaba* is not accepted by DFA.

**Example 3.7:** For the finite state machine described by transation table

| States | 0 | 1 |
|---|---|---|
| $\rightarrow (q_0)$ | $q_2$ | $q_1$ |
| $q_1$ | $q_3$ | $q_0$ |
| $q_2$ | $q_0$ | $q_3$ |
| $q_3$ | $q_1$ | $q_3$ |

Find the string 101101 are accepted by DFA machine.

**Solution:** The given language is $\delta(q_0,\ 101101)$

$$\delta(q_0,\ 101101) = \delta(q_1,\ 01101)$$
$$\downarrow$$
$$= \delta(q_3,\ 11101)$$
$$\downarrow$$
$$= \delta(q_2,\ 101)$$
$$\downarrow$$
$$= \delta(q_3,\ 01)$$
$$\downarrow$$
$$= \delta(q_1,\ 1)$$
$$= \delta(q_0,\ \in)$$
$$= q_0 \quad \text{[by rule 2]}$$

Hence

$$q_0 \xrightarrow{1} q_1 \xrightarrow{0} q_3 \xrightarrow{1} q_2 \xrightarrow{1} q_3 \xrightarrow{0} q_1 \xrightarrow{1} q_0$$

Since $q_0$ is a final state, so the following string 101101 is accepty by a DFA machine.

## 3.5 SOME BASIC CONCEPT TO DESIGN A DFA

To design a DFA machine you have to find your logic but here we try to give some examples to develop your logic for DFA machine. As you know that the heart of DFA machine is transition system. It means when you are able to design a transition system for any problem, you are able to design a DFA machine.

**Example 3.8:** Find a DFA machine that accepts all the language (or string) of *a's* including ∈ over input alphabet $\Sigma = \{ a \}$

**Solution:** The language contains only a of any length including ∈ *i.e.*, the set of language looks as follows {∈, a, aa, aa, aaaa,...............}. To design a DFA machine use the following steps

**Step 1 :** Let us consider an initial state *i.e.*, $q_0$.

**Step 2 :** The language contains empty string (*i.e.*, ∈), so the initial and final state must be the same state.

**Step 3 :** Since the input symbol is a, then on initial state $q_0$ (or present state $q_0$) and on input symbol *a* the state will not change *i.e.*, $q_0$, which is a final state and transition diagram is as shown in Fig. 3.10.

***Fig. 3.10***

This transition digraph contain all five tuples value of a DFA machine *i.e.*, $(Q, \Sigma, \delta, q_0, F)$. So *a* DFA machine is $(\{q_0\}, \{a\}, \delta q_0, \{q_0\})$ where δ is shown in Fig. 3.10.

**Example 3.9:** Find a DFA machine that accepts all the language (or string) of *a's* and *b's* of any order and of any length including ∈ over input alphabet $\Sigma = \{a, b\}$.

**Solution:** The language contains *a* and *b* of any order and of any length including ∈ *i.e.,* the set of language looks like as follows: (∈, *a*, *b*, *aa*, *bb*, *ab*, *ba*, *aaa*, *abb*, *aab*, *bbb*, *baa*, *bba*, *aba*, *bab*,............}. To design a DFA machine use the following steps.

**Step 1 :** Let us consider an initial state *i.e.*, $q_0$.

**Step 2 :** The language contains empty string (*i.e.*, ∈), so the initial and final state must be the same state.

**Step 3:** Since the input symbols are *a* and *b*, then on initial state $q_2$ (or present state $q_0$) and on input symbol *a* and *b* the state will not change *i.e*, $q_2$, which is a final state and transition diagram is shown in Fig. 3.11.

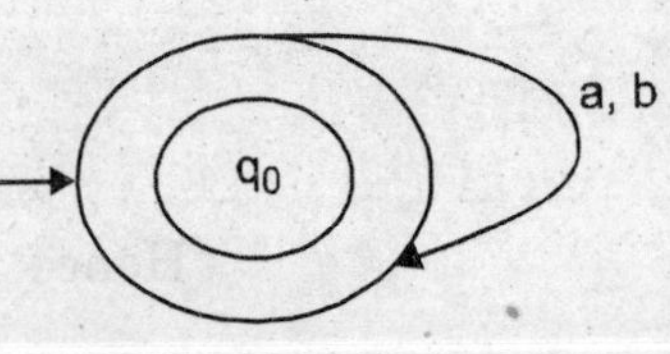

***Fig. 3.11***

This transition digraph contain all five tuples value of a DFA machine i.e., $(Q, \Sigma, \delta, q_0, F)$.

So a DFA machine is $(\{q_0\}, \{ab\}, \delta, q_0, \{q_0\}$ where δ is shown in Fig. 3.11.

**Example 3.10:** Find a DFA machine that accept all language (or strings) that have exactly one 0 over input alphabet $\Sigma = \{0, 1\}$.

**Solution:** The language contains exactly one letter of 0 and the other letters may be only 1's of any order and of any length either before 0 or after 0 or before and after both including $\in$. So the set of language look likes as follows {0, 10, 01, 110, 011, 101,...}. To design a DFA machine use the following steps.

**Step 1 :** Let us consider an initial state i.e., $q_0$.

**Step 2 :** Since the first input symbol is either 0 or 1, then on initial state $q_0$ (Or present state $q_0$) and on input symbol 0 consider the next state *i.e.,* $q_1$ and on initial state $q_0$ (or present state $q_0$) and on input symbol 1 the state will not change.

**Step 3:** On state $q_1$ the input symbol may be anyone *i.e.,* either 0 or 1. If input symbol is 1 then the next state will not change *i.e.,* $q_1$ which is a final state.

**Step 4 :** On final state $q_1$ if input symbol is 0 the string will not be accepted by DFA as the string to be accepted contains one 0 only.

The transition digraph is shown in Fig. 3,12.

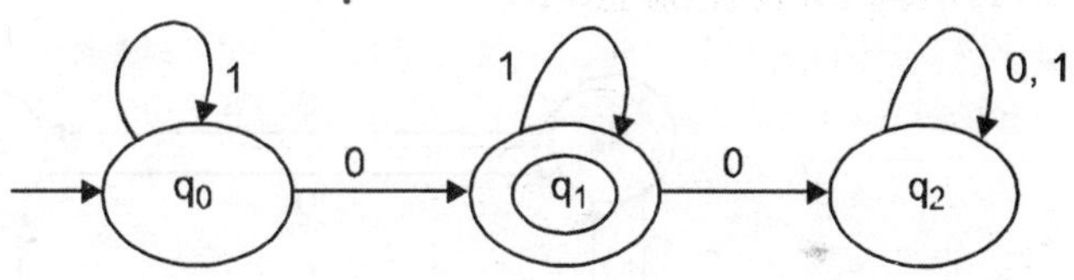


***Fig. 3.12***

**Example 3.11:** Find a DFA machine that accept all strings beginning with 0 over input alphabet $\Sigma = \{0, 1\}$

**Solution:** The language begins with letter 0 and the other letters may be of any order of 0's and 1's and of any length including $\in$. So the set of language look like as follows {0, 00, 01, 000, 011, 010, 001, 000, 0001, ..........}. To design a DFA mchine use the following steps.

**Step 1 :** Let us consider an initial state *i.e.,* $q_0$.

**Step 2 :** Since the first input symbol is 0 then on initial state $q_0$ (or present state $q_0$) and on input symbol 0 consider the next state *i.e.,* $q_1$.

**Step 3 :** On state $q_1$ the input symbol may be any one *i.e.,* either 0 or 1. If input symbol is either 0 or 1 the next state will not change *i.e.,* $q_1$. It is a final state.

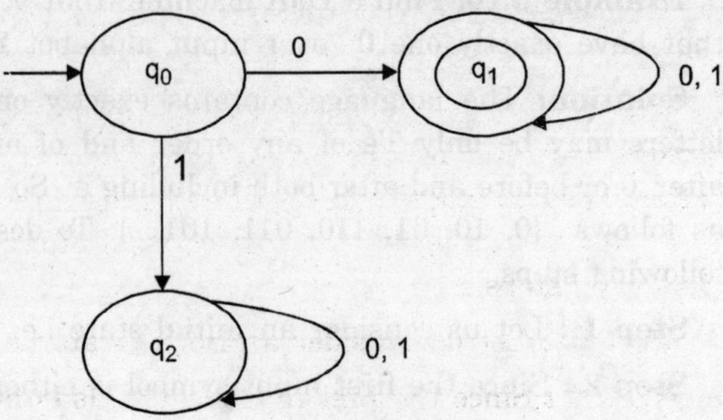


*Fig. 3.13*

**Step 4 :** On initial state $q_0$ if input symbol is 1 the string will be rejected by DFA. The transition digraph is shown in Fig. 3.13.

**Example 3.12:** Design DFA which accepts even number of 0's and even numeber of 1's. ***[UPTU B. Tech (Co) 2005, MCA. 2003 MDU B.Tech 2005]***

**Solution:** Clearly we can have four possible state (Odd, Odd), (Odd, Even) (Even, odd) (Even, Even)

Let us donote these states by $q_0$, $q_1$, $q_2$, $q_3$. The transition graph of the required DFA thus is given as:

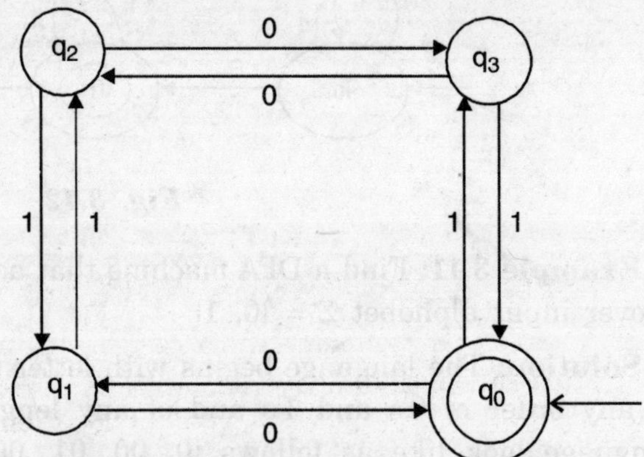


*Fig. 3.14*

If the input is 10111000 it will be processed as

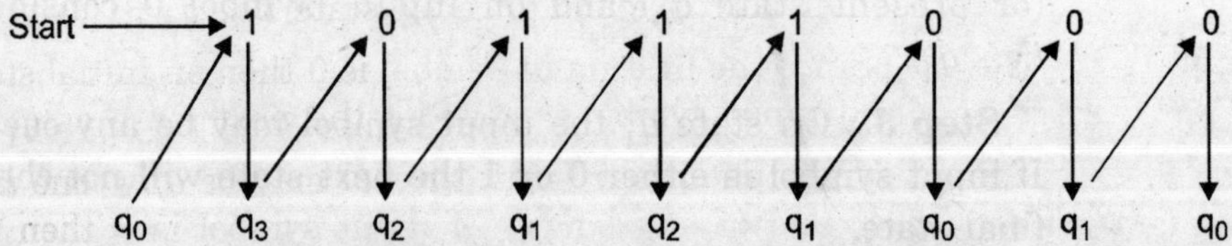


The $q_0$ is a final state, hence the input is accepted.

The transition table can be as follows–

| States | 0 | 1 |
|---|---|---|
| $\rightarrow$ ($q_0$) | $q_1$ | $q_3$ |
| $q_1$ | $q_0$ | $q_2$ |
| $q_2$ | $q_3$ | $q_1$ |
| $q_3$ | $q_2$ | $q_0$ |

**Example 3.13:** Construct a DFA accepting al strings over {0,1} ending in 01.

**Solution:**

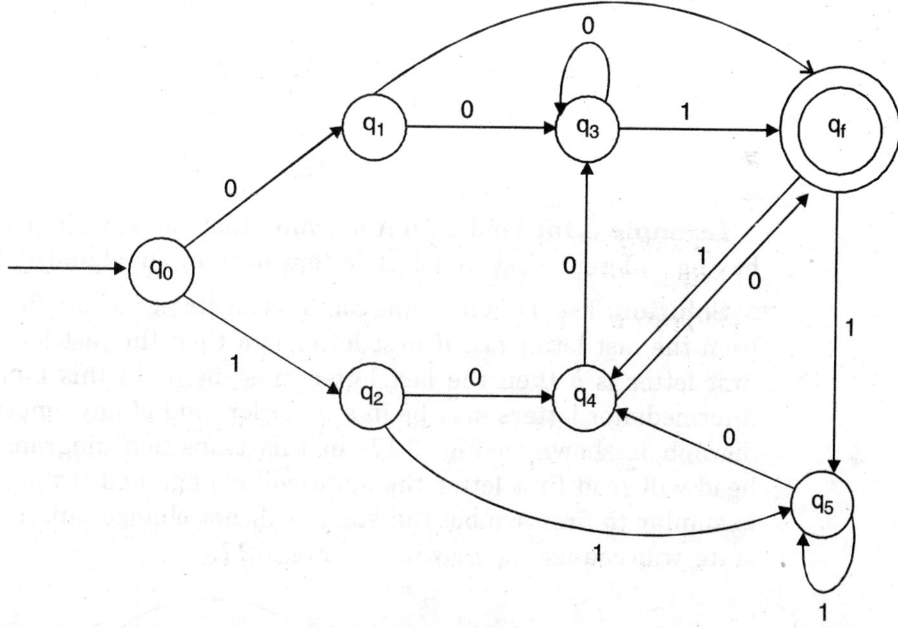


***Fig. 3.15***

**Example 3.14:** Find a DFA machine for the language $L$ = {0 $w$ 0: $w \in$ {0, 1)*}.

**Solution:** The language contains first and last letter as 0 and intermediate letters may be of any order of 0's and 1's and of any length including $\in$ *i.e.,* the set of language look likes as follows {00, 000, 010, 0000, 0010, 01000, 0110,...}. To design a DFA machine use the following steps

**Step 1 :** Let us consider an initial state *i.e.,* $q_0$

**Step 2 :** Since the first input symbol is 0 then on initial state $q_0$ (or present state $q_0$) and input symbol 0 consider the next state as $q_1$.

**Step 3 :** On state $q_1$ the input symbol may be any one *i.e.* either 0 or 1 of any order and of any length. If input symbol is 0 then the next state is $q_2$ which is a final state and if input symbol is 1 the next state is $q_1$ because 1 may be of any length.

**Step 4 :** On state $q_2$ if input symbol is 0 then the next state will not change *i.e.,* $q_2$ but if input symbol is 1 then the next state is $q_1$.

**Step 5 :** On initial state $q_0$ if input symbol is 1 the string will not be accepted by DFA.

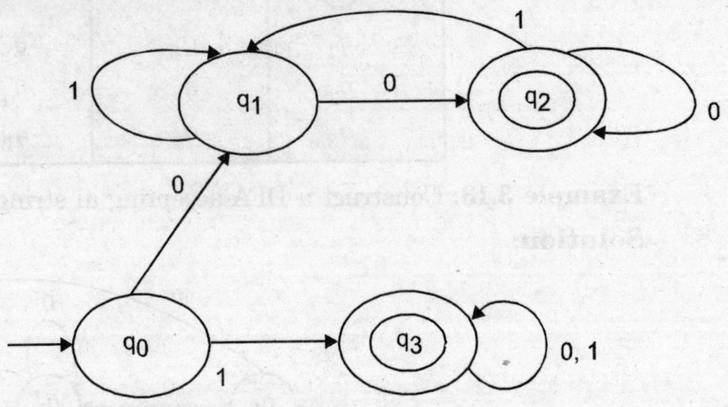


*Fig. 3.16*

**Example 3.15:** Find a DFA machine that accept all strings (or language) having different first and last letters over input alphabet $\Sigma = \{a, b\}$

**Solution:** The DFA machine contains all strings whose first letter is different from the last letter *i.e.,* if first letter is a then the last letter must be $b$ or if first letter is $b$ then the last letter must be $a$. In this language (or strings) intermediator letters may be in any order and of any lengths. The transition digraph is shown in Fig. 3.17. In this transition diagram if the read/write head will read first letter the state will change and if the if the next symbol is similar to first symbol the state will not change but if it is different the state will change as shown in Fig. 3.17.

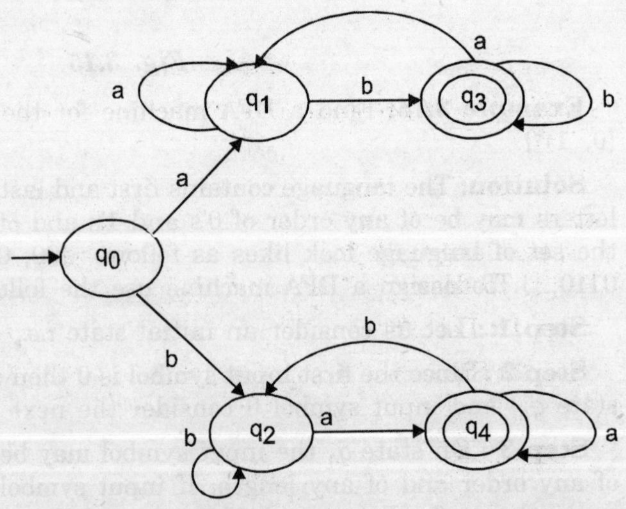


*Fig. 3.17*

**Example 3.16:** Find a DFA mahine that accepts an even number of either 0's or 1's or both 0's and 1's over input symbol Σ = {0, 1).

**Solution:** The heart part (*i.e.,* transition system) of DFA machine is shown in Fig. 3.18.

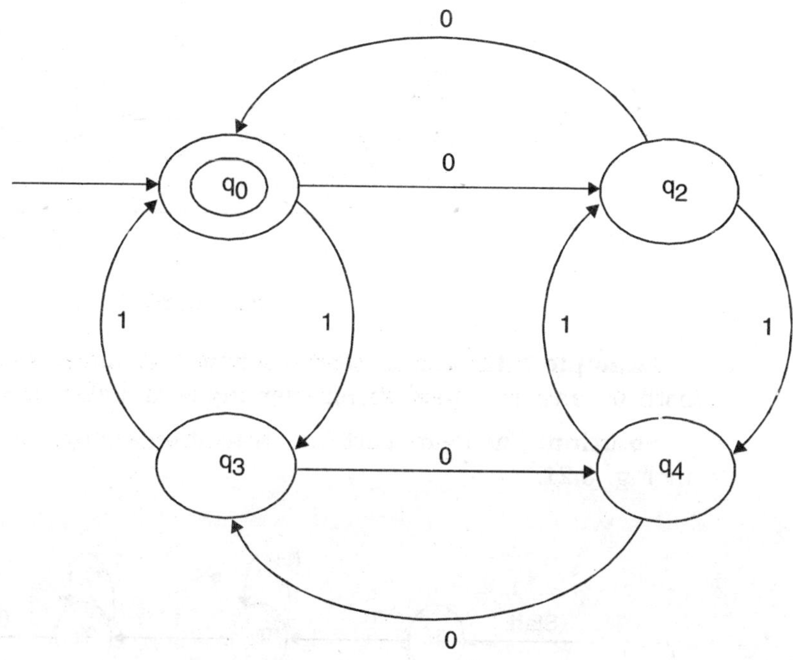


***Fig. 3.18***

**Example 3.17:** Find a DFA machine that accepts the language which has a sub-string 0101 over input alphabet Σ = {0, 1}

**Solution:** The heart part (*i.e.,* transition system) of DFA machine is shown in Fig. 3.19

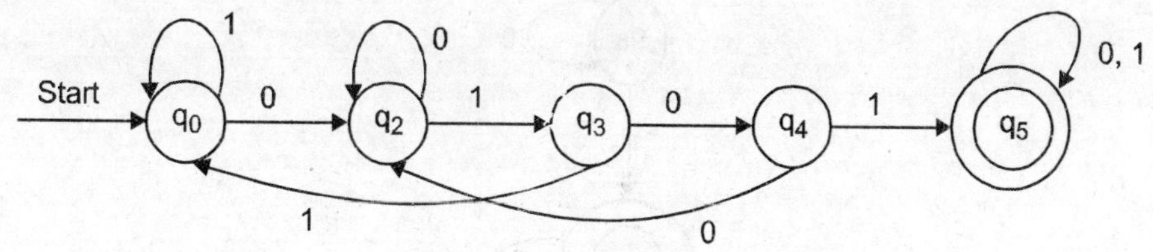


***Fig. 3.19***

**Example 3.18:** Find a DFA machine that accepts the language which has either odd number of 0's or even number of 1's but not both together over input alphabet Σ = {0, 1}

**Solution:** The heart part (*i.e.,* transition system) of DFA machine is shown in Fig. 3.20.

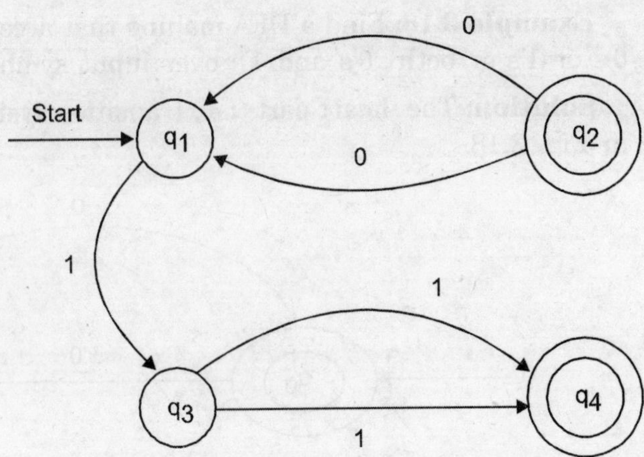


*Fig. 3.20*

**Example 3.19:** Find a DFA machine that accepts the language which has both 01 and 10 as substring over input alphabet $\Sigma = \{0, 1\}$

**Solution:** The heart part (*i.e.*, transition system) of DFA machine is shown in Fig. 3.21.

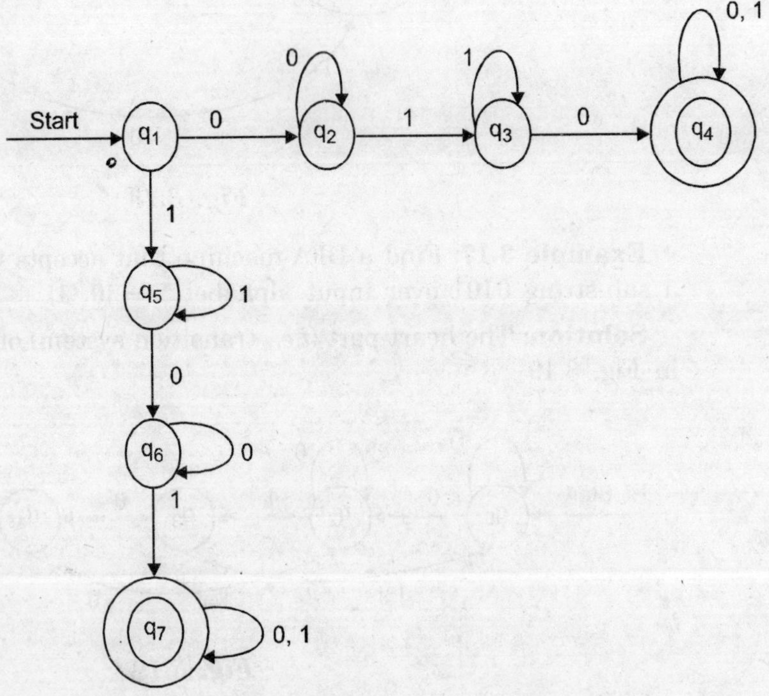


*Fig. 3.21*

**Example 320:** Find a DFA machine that accept the language which has neither 00 nor 11 as a substring over input alphabet $\Sigma = \{0, 1\}$

**Solution:** The heart part (*i.e.*, transition system) of DFA machine is shown in Fig. 3.22.

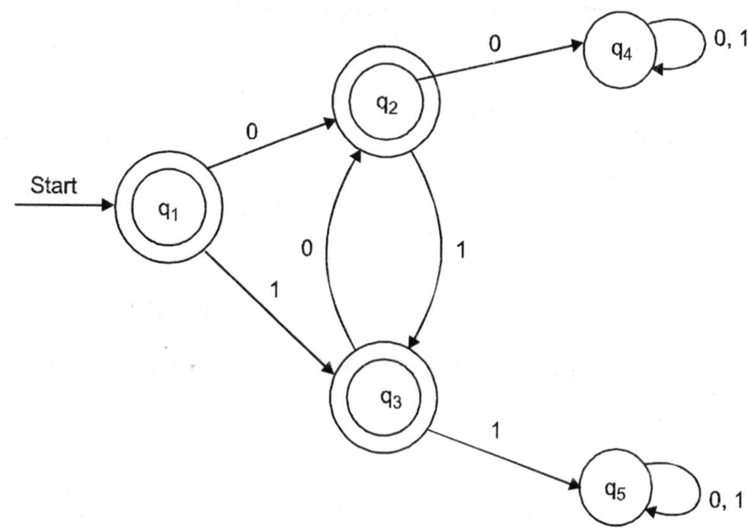


***Fig. 3.22***

**Example 3.21:** Design a DFA machine that accept all strings with no more than five *a's* over input symbol $\Sigma = \{a, b\}$.

**Solution.** The transition diagram of DFA machine δ is shown in Fig. 3.23.

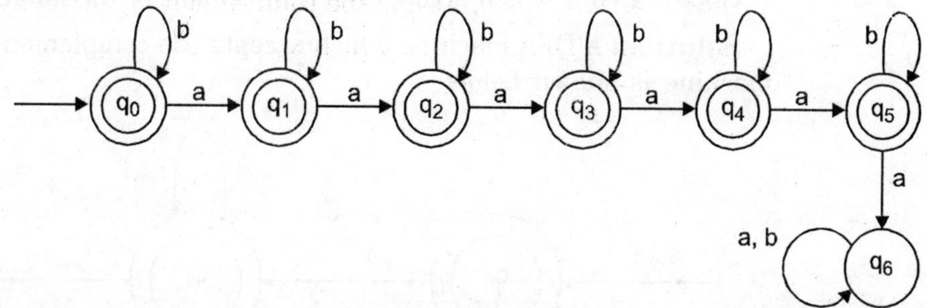


***Fig. 3.23***

**Example 3.22:** Design a DFA machine that all strings with at most three *b's* over input symbol $\Sigma = \{a, b\}$.

**Solution:** The transition system of DFA machine d si shown Fig. 3.24.

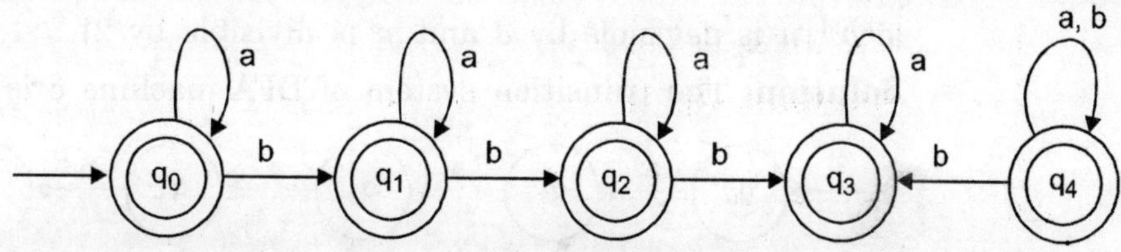


***Fig. 3.24***

**Example 3.23:** Design a DFA machine that accepts all language (or strings) where the number of 1's is multiple of 5 over the alphabet $\Sigma = \{0, 1\}$:

**Solution:** The transition system of DFA machine d is shown Fig. 3.25

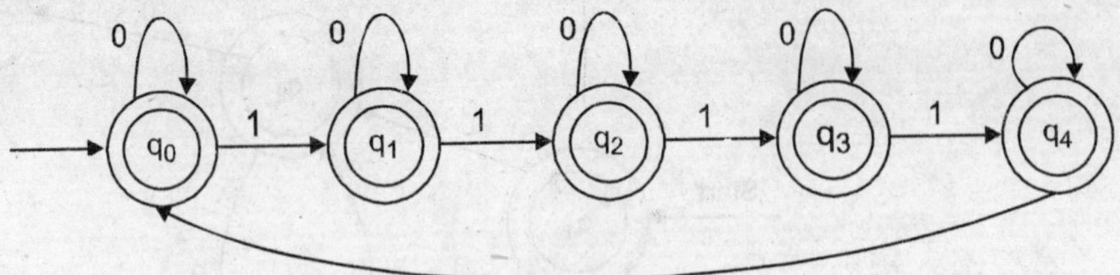


*Fig. 3.25*

**Example 3.24:** Consider the following automata (DFA) *M*.

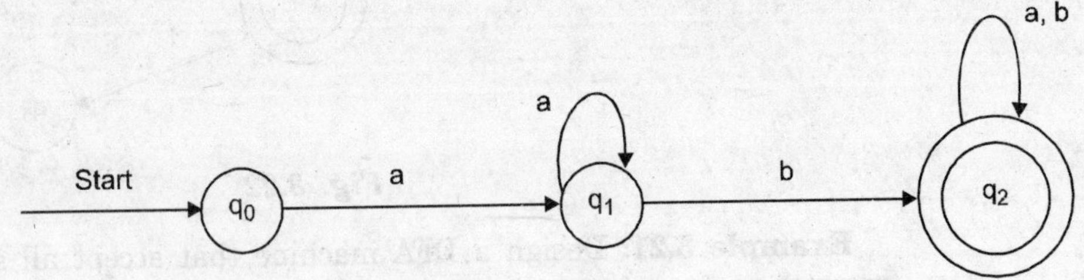


*Fig. 3.26*

Obtain a DFA which accepts the complement of the language accepted by M.

**Solution:** A DFA machine which accepts the complement of the above DFA machine is shown below

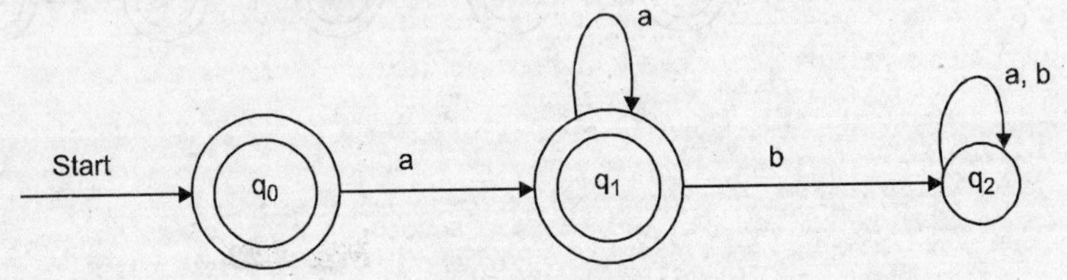


*Fig. 3.27*

**Example 3.25:** Construct a DFA recognizing the following language (or strings):

$\{a^n b^m \mid n$ is devisible by 3 and $m$ is divisible by 2]

**Solution:** The transition system of DFA machine δ is shown below

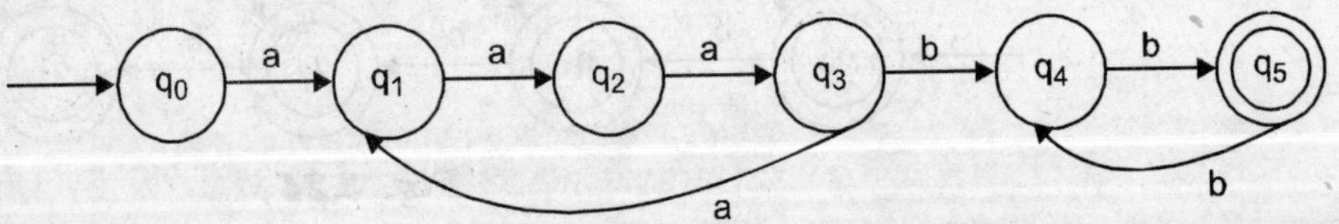


*Fig. 3.28*

**Example 3.26:** Design a DFA mchine that accept the all language (or strings) which are divisible by 3 over the input alphabet Σ = }0, 1, 2, 3, 4, 5, 6, 7, 8, 9}

**Solution:** The transition table of a DFA mchine δ is shown below

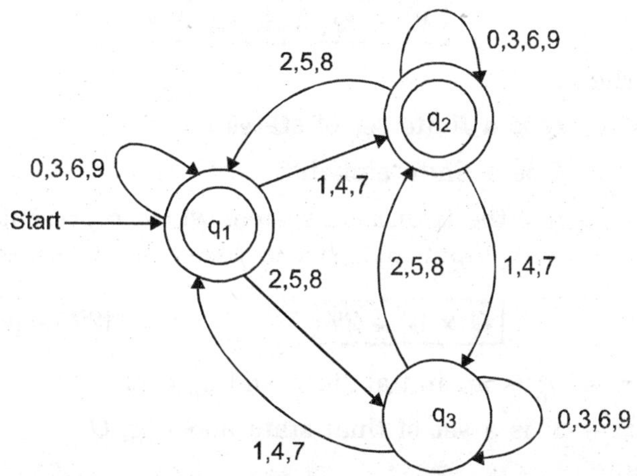


***Fig. 3.29***

**Example 3.27:** Design a DFA machine that accept the all language (or strings) which are divisible by 3 over the input alphabet Σ = {0, 1}

**Solution:** The transition table of a DFA machine δ is shown below

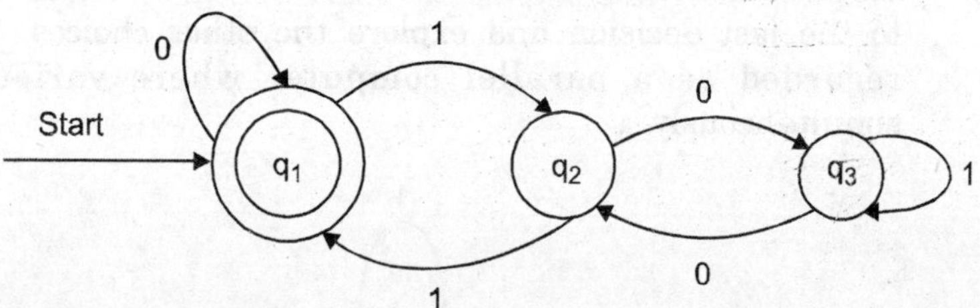


***Fig. 3.30***

## 3.6 NON-DETERMINISTIC FINITE AUTOMATA (NFA)

We shall now studya more converient device to desin a DFA, known as non-deterministic finite automaton (NFA). A NFA consists of a variable that can only take on a finite number of different states;

→ A head which the input tape will be read from left to right,

→ A transition system that forms the contrals of the automation;

→ An initial state and one or various final state

## Formal Definition of NFA

A formal definitionof Non-deterministic finite automata (NFA or NDFA) is as follows–

A NFA is defined the same way as DFA, *i.e.,* by the quintuple

$$M = (Q, \Sigma, \delta, q_0, F)$$

where,

→ $Q$ is a finite set of states

→ $\Sigma$ is a finite alphabet

→ $\delta$ is the transition system which represents a mappling between states with input alphabet to power set of states *i.e.,*

$$Q \times S \rightarrow 2^Q \qquad [2^Q \text{ is power of } Q]$$

→ $q_0$ is an initial state and $q_0 \in Q$

→ $F$ is a set of final state and $F \subseteq Q$

## Working of NFA

The idea of introducing the concept of NFA to simplify method of designing an DFA. There are various problems and situations when we do not know what would be the next move or exactly next state?

In case various moves are possible we start with one and follow it until the becomes the right choice? It choice does not come out to be right, we retreat to the last decision and explore the other choices. Thus, the NFA may be regarded as a parallel computer where various processes can run simultaneously.

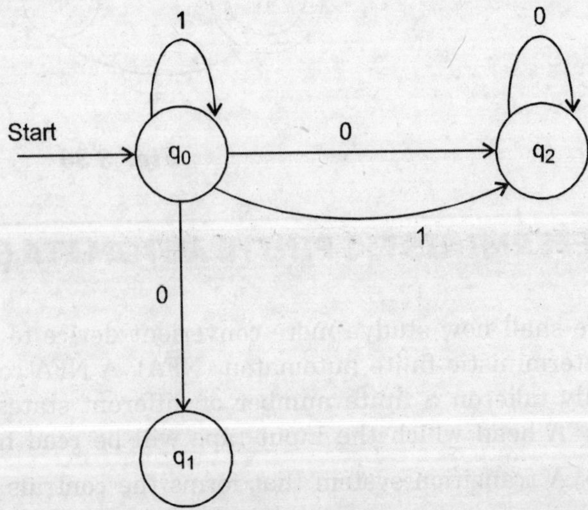


***Fig. 3.31***

In fig. 3.31 NFA shows from $q_0$ for input 0 there are two next state $q_1$ and $q_2$. Similarly, from $q_0$ for input 1 the next states are $q_0$ and $q_2$.

Thus it is not fixed or determined that with a particular input where to go next.

## Difference between NFA and DFA

In DFA, for a given state, on a given input we reach to a deterministic and unique state.On the other hand, in NFA we may lead to more than one states for given input. The DFA is a subset of NFA. We need to convert NFA to DFA in the design of compiler.

(I) In NFA, we can have various possible "next states" for a given pair of current state and input symbol

(II) A state can change into next state without having any input symbol *i.e.,* empty string moves are possible and

(III) The set δ (*s, a*) (*a* ∈ Sm *S* ∈ *S*) may be empty *i.e.,* there may not be any transition defined for the specific pair of inut symbol and current state.

---

The only difference between the DFA and NFA is in the transition system δ. For DFA, the outcome is a state which is an element of *Q′* for NFA, the outcome is a subset of *Q*.

---

**Example 3.28:** Consider the following NFA mchine $M = (\{q_0, q_1, q_2\}, \{0, 1\}$ $\delta, q_0, \{q_1\}$ where a transition graph is shown in Fig. 3.32.

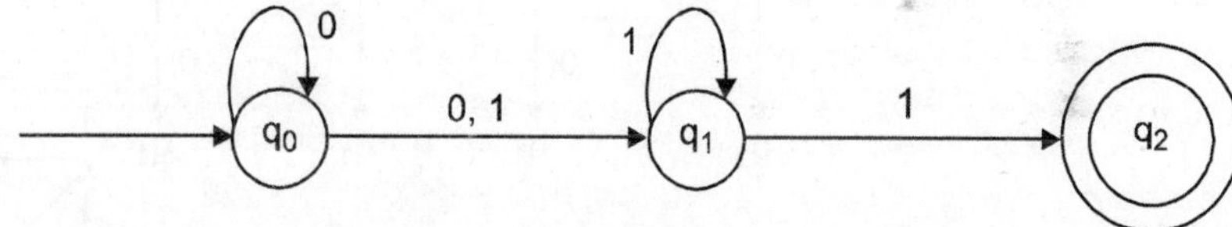


***Fig. 3.32***

Check the string 00001 is accepted by NFA. Also find the sequence of states.

---

Since the present state $q_0$ contains the next states $q_0$ and $q_1$ on input symbol 0. Hence the transition system is a transition system of NFA. All the transition diagram is a NFA.

---

**Solution:** The given language is $\delta(q_0, 00001)$

$= \delta(\delta(q_0, 0), 0001)$ by rule 2

$= \delta(q_0, q_1\}, 0001)$ from transition graph i.e., $\delta(q_0, 0)$

$= \delta(\delta(q_0, q_1), 001$ by rule 2

$= \delta((\delta\ (q_0, 0) \cup \delta(q, 0)), 001)$

$= \delta((\delta\ (q_0, q_1) \cup \phi), 001)$
$= \delta(q_0, q_1) \cup \phi\}, 001)$
$= \delta(\delta(q_0, q_1), 001)$
$= \delta(q_0, q_1)\ 0), 01)$ by rule 2
$= \delta(\delta(q_0, 0), \cup \delta(q_1, 0)), 01)$
$= \delta(q_0, q_1) \cup \phi\}, 01)$
$= \delta(\delta(q_0, q_1), 01)$
$= \delta((\delta\ (q_0, q_1), 0), 1)$ by rule 2
$= \delta((q_0,0) \cup \delta(q_1,0)),1)$
$= \delta((\delta(q_0, q_1) \cup \phi), 1)$
$= \delta(q_0, q_1), 1)$
$= \delta(\delta(q_1, q_2), 1), \cup \in)$ by rule 2
$= \delta(q_1, 1) \cup \delta(q_2, 1)), \in)$
$= \delta((\delta\ (q_1, q_2), \cup \phi), \in)$
$= \delta(\delta(q_1, q_2), \in)$
$= \delta(q_1, \in) \cup \delta(q_2, \in)$
$= q_1 \cup q_2$
$= (q_1, q_2)$

This set of states contains the final state $q_2$. Hence the string is accepted by this NFA machine.

The sequence of states corresponding to the input symbol is given by

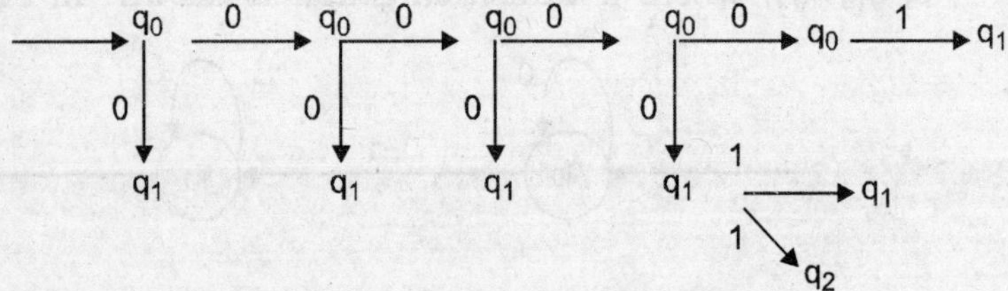

**Example 3.29:** Find the sequence of state corresponding to the input symbol 000011 for the transition digraph shown in Fig. 3.32.

**Solution:** The sequence of states of input symbol 000011 corresponding to the given transition digraph is given below

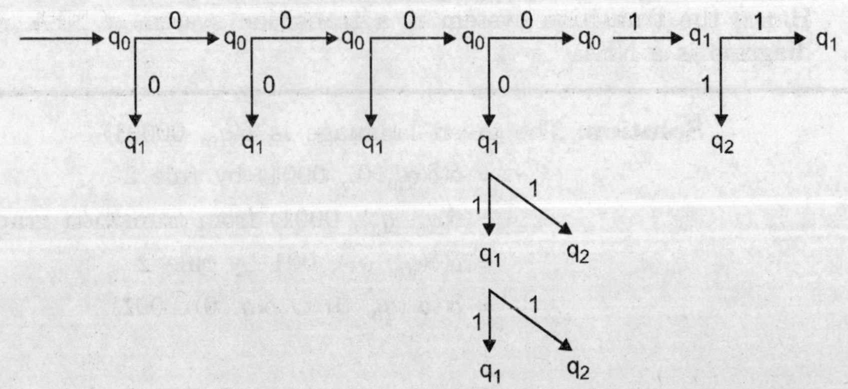

The highest length from starting symbol is 6 and the states are of 6 length from initial state $q_0$ are $\{q_1, q_2\}$. Since in the states $\{q_1, q_2\}$, $q_2$ is a final state, so the language 000011 is accepted by a NFA machine.

**Example 3.30:** Design a NFA machine that accept all strings ending with aa over input symbol $\Sigma = \{a, b\}$.

**Solution:** The transition diagram of NFA machine δ is shown in Fig. 3.33

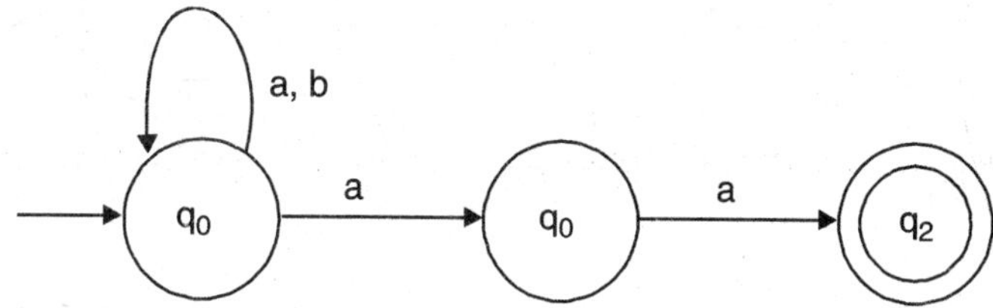


***Fig. 3.33***

Hence the NFA machine $M = (\{q_0, q_1, q_2\}, \{a, b\}, \delta, q_0, q_2)$

**Example 3.31:** Design a NFA machine that accept all strings beginning with ab and ending with bb over input symbol $\Sigma = \{a, b\}$.

**Solution:** The transition diagram of NFA machine d is shown in Fig. 3.34.

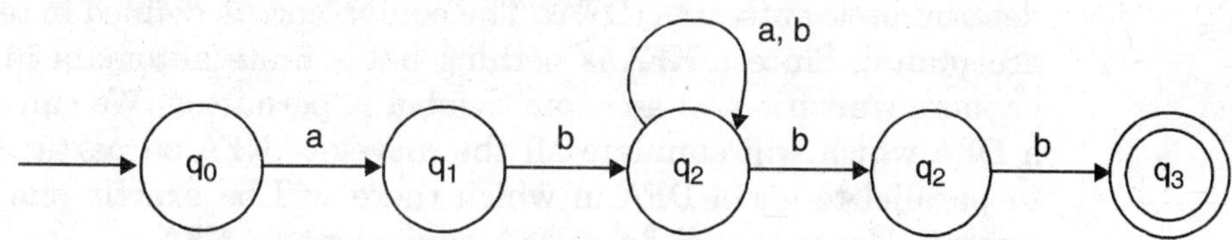


***Fig. 3.34***

**Example 3.32:** Design a NFA machine that accept all strings with exactly two *a's* over input symbol $\Sigma = \{a, b]$.

**Solution:** The transition diagram of NFA machine δ is shown in Fig. 3.35.

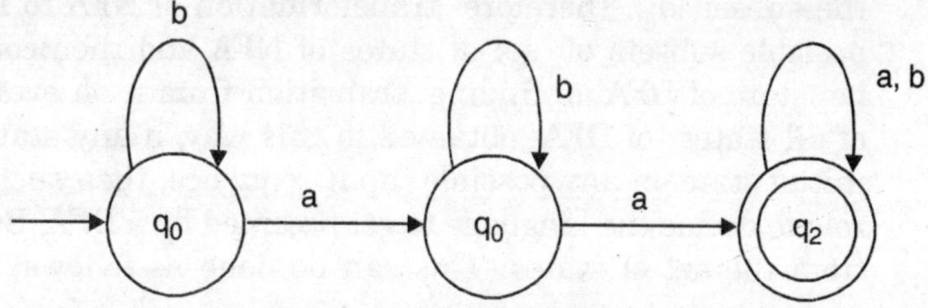


***Fig. 3.35***

**Example 3.33:** Design a NFA machine that accept all strings with exactly two *b's* and at least one a over input symbol $\Sigma = \{a, b]$.

**Solution:** The transition diagram of NFA machine δ is shown in Fig. 3.36

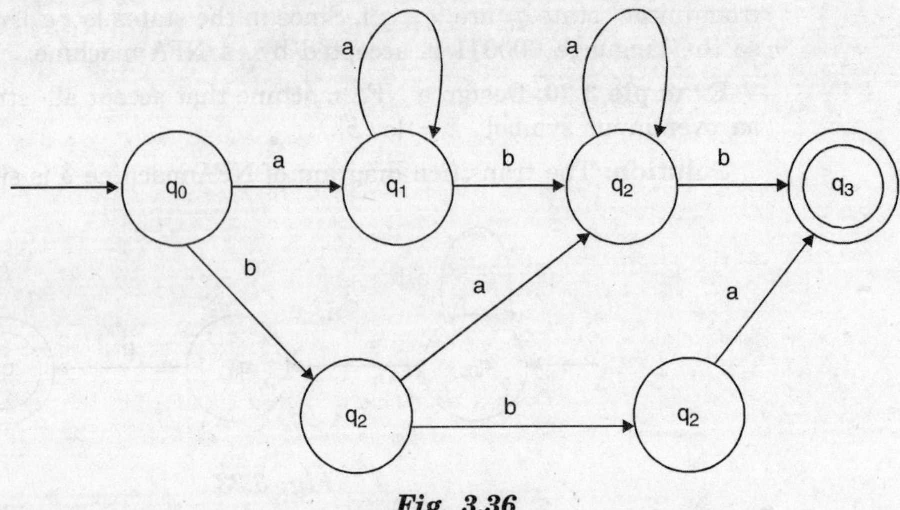


***Fig. 3.36***

## 3.7 EQUIVALENCE OF NFA AND DFA

For every non-deterministic finite automata (NFA) there exists an equivalent deterministic automata (DFA). The equivalence is defined in terms of language acceptance. Since a NFA is nothing but a finite automata in which zero, one or more transition on an input symbol is permitted. We can always construct a DFA which will simulate all the moves of NFA on particular input symbol in parallel to get a DFA in which there will be exactly one transition input symbol. Hence it will be a DFA equivalent to NFA.

Since the DFA equivalent to NFA is to simulate the moves of NFA in parallel, every state of DFA will be a combination of one or more states of NFA. Hence every state of DFA will be represented by some subset of set of states of NFA and therefore transformation of NFA to DFA is normally called as **subset construction.** Therefore if subset have n sates then the number of states of DFA will be equivalent to $2^n$, with initial state corresponding to the subset $\{q_0\}$. therefore transformation of NFA to DFA involves, finding all possible subsets of set of states of NFA and then considering each subset to be state of DFA an finding transition from it on every input symbol. But out of all states of DFA obtained in this way, if any states is not reachable form initial state on any possible input sequence, then such state does not play nay role to decide the language to get accepted by a DFA. Such states are eliminated from the set of states. This can be done as follows

Let $M = (Q, \Sigma, \delta, q_0, F)$ be a NFA accepting language $L$. We construct a DFA $M'$ that can also accept the same language $L$. Then a DFA $M'$ is defined as follows

$$M' = (Q', \Sigma, \delta', q'_0, F')$$

where

$Q'$ = $2^Q$ (Power set of $Q$ or all subset of $Q$) and all states of $Q'$ are denoted by $[q_1, q_2, q_3, ......, q_n]$

$\Sigma$ = Similar to NFA

$q'_0$ = $[q_0]$

$F'$ = Set of all subsets of $Q'$ containing an element of $F$ (*i.e.,* final state of NFA)

$\delta'$ = Transition system

**To define transition system, use the following steps**

**Step 1 :** Draw an initial state (or vertex) with label $[q_0]$ of transition diagram $\delta'$.

**Step 2 :** Take this state (*i.e,* $[q_0]$) and identify all next states from $Q'$ on all different given input symbols. Let us consider the next states as $[q_i, q_j, ..., q_k]$ on input symbol $0 \in \Sigma$ from state $[q_0]$

Create a state labeled $[q_i, q_j, ..., q_k]$ and add to transition digraph $\delta'$ an edge from $[q_0]$ to $[q_i, q_j, ..., q_k]$ with labeled 0.

**Step 3 :** Take any state of step 2 (or previously defined state) and find new next state (*i.e.,* it does not exist already) from $Q'$ on all different given input symbols.

Let us consider the next state as $[q_i, q_j, ..., q_k]$ on input symbol $0 \in \Sigma$ from state $[q_i, q_j, ..., q_k]$

Compute $\delta'(q_i, 0)$, $\delta'(q_j, 0)$,....., $\delta'(q_k\ 0)$ and then form a union of all $\delta'$, yielding the set of states $[q_i, q_j, ..., q_n]$.

Create a state with label $[q_i, q_j, ..., q_n]$ and add to transition digraph $\delta'$ and edge from $[q_i, q_j, ..., q_k]$ to $[q_i, q_j, ..., q_n]$ labeled 0.

**Step 4 :** Repeat the step 3 until no new states are generated

**Step 5 :** Draw all states as a final states of, if it contain the final state of NFA.

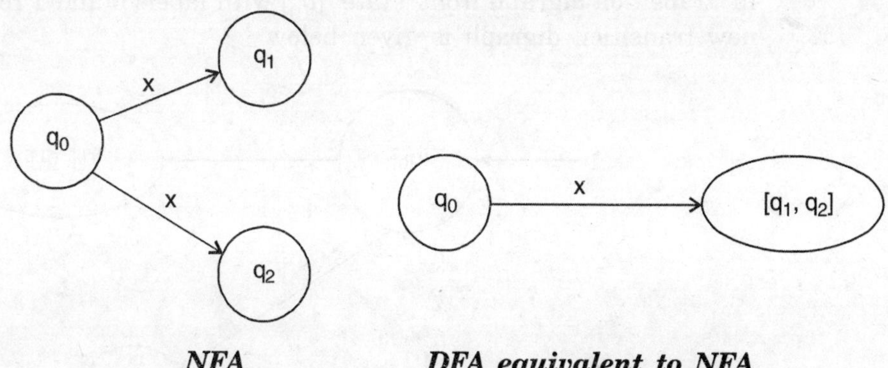


***NFA*** ***DFA equivalent to NFA***

***Fig. 3.37***

**Example 3.34:** Find a deterministic finite automata equivalent to $M(\{q_0, q_1, q_2\}, \{0, 1\}\ \delta, q_0, \{q_2\})$ where $\delta$ is defined in Fig. 3.38.

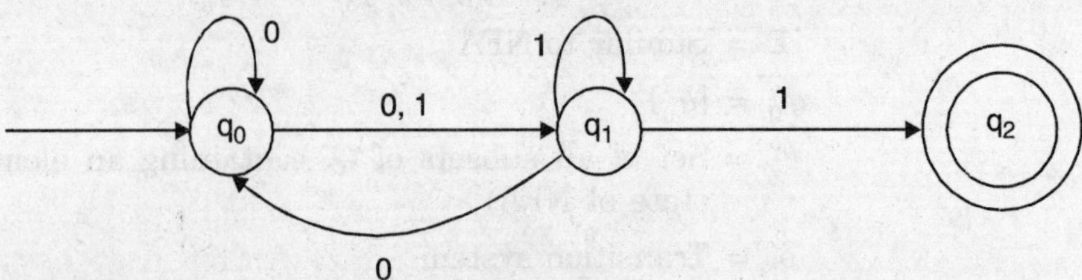


***Fig. 3.38***

**Solution:** The given NFA, $M = (\{q_0, q_1, q_2\}, \{0, 1\}\ \delta, q_0, \{q_2\})$ then its equivalent DFA $M'$ be defined by

$M' = (Q', \Sigma, \delta', q_0', F')$

where $Q' = 2^Q$(Power set $Q$)

*i.e.,* $\{\phi, [q_0], [q_1], [q_2], [q_0, q_1], [q_1, q_2], [q_0, q_1, q_2]\}$

These are the total number of states of DFA

$\Sigma =$ Similar to NFA *i.e.,* $\{0, 1\}$

$q_0' = [q_0]$. This is the initial state of DFA

$F' = [q_2], [q_0, q_2], [q_1, q_2], [q_0, q_1, q_2]\}$. These are the final states of DFA $[\subseteq Q'$ containing $q_2]$

$\delta' =$ The transition digraph determined as follows

**By step 1 :** The initial state is $[q_0]$, so transition diagram for it is shown below

**By step 2 :** The next states from $[q_0]$ are $(q_0, q_1]$ and $[q_1]$ on giving input symbol 0 and 1 respectively. Then add these new states (*i.e.,* $[q_0, q_1]$ and $[q_1]$) in transition digraph from state $[q_0]$ with labels 0 and 1 respectively. So the new transition digraph is given below.

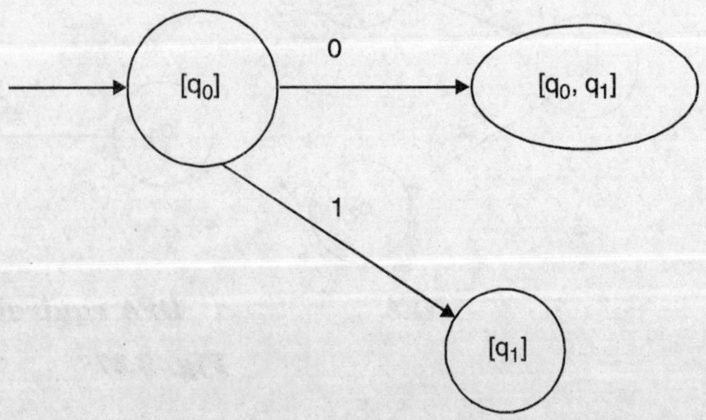

**By step 3 :** The next states from $[q_1]$ are $[q_0]$ and $[q_1, q_2]$ on input symbol 0 and 1 respectively, and from $[q_0, q_1]$ are $[q_1, q_2]$ and $[q_1, q_2]$ on giving input symbol 0 and 1 respectively as explained below.

$$\delta'(q_1, 0) = \{q_0\},$$
$$\delta'(q_1, 1) = \{q_1, q_2\},$$

Now $\delta'((q_0, q_1), 0) = \delta'(q_0, 0) \cup \delta'(q_1, 0) = \{q_0, q_1) \cup \{q_0\} = \{q_0, q_1\}$

and now $\delta'((q_0, q_1), 1) = \delta'(q_0, 1) \cup \delta'(q_1, 1) = \{q_1) \cup \{q_1, q_2\} = \{q_1, q_2\}$

Since the new state is $[q_1, q_2]$. Then add this new state (*i.e.*, $[q_1, q_2]$) in transition digraph from state $[q_0, q_1]$ with label 1. So new transition digraph is given below.

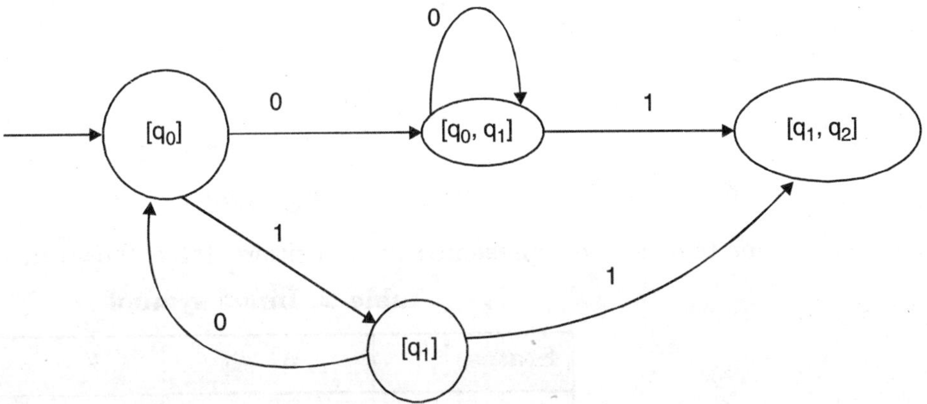


**By step 4 :** The next state from state $[q_1, q_2]$ are $[q_0]$ and $[q_1, q_2]$ on input symbol 0 and 1 respectively as explained below.

$$\delta'(q_1, 0) \cup \delta'(q_2, 0) = [q_0] \cup \phi = [q_0]$$

and $\delta'(q_1, 1) \cup \delta'(q_2, 1) = \{q_1, q_2\} \cup \phi = \{q_1, q_2\}$

Hence the transition digraph is given below

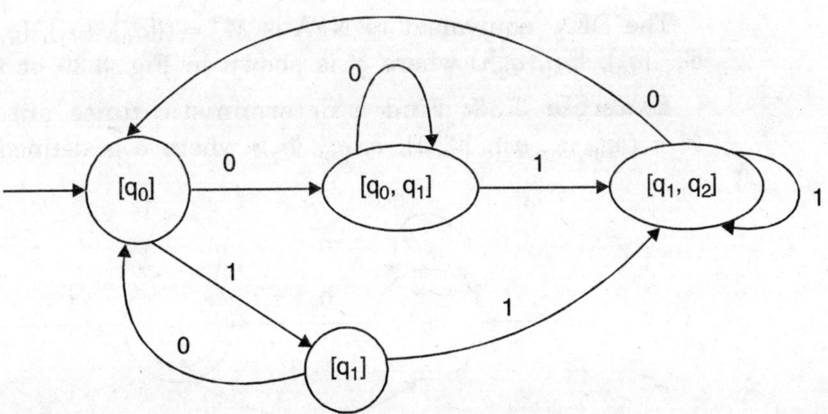


Since no new state is added in this computation so there is no need to do any more computation on any states.

**By Step 5 :** Draw all states as a final state if it contain the final state of NFA (*i.e.,* $q_2$).

Hence the final transition diagram is shown in Fig. 3.39.

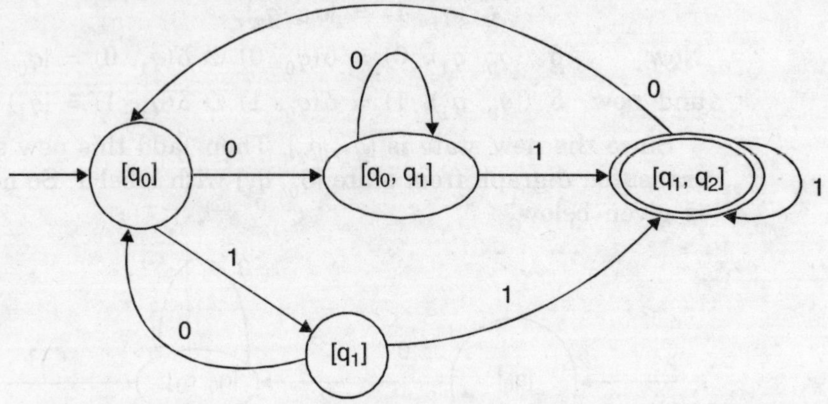


***Fig. 3.39***

or this can be represented by transition table shown in table 2.

**Table 2. Input symbol**

| States | 0 | 1 |
|---|---|---|
| $\rightarrow [q_0]$ | $[q_0, q_1]$ | $[q_1]$ |
| $[q_1]$ | $[q_0]$ | $[q_1, q_2]$ |
| $[q_0, q_1]$ | $[q_0, q_1]$ | $[q_1, q_2]$ |
| $([q_1, q_2])$ | $[q_0]$ | $[q_1, q_2]$ |

The DFA equivalent to NFA is $M' = (\{[q_0], [q_1], [q_0, q_1], [q_1, q_2]\}, \{0, 1\}, \delta', [q_0], \{[q_1, q_2]\})$ where $\delta'$ is shown in Fig. 3.39 or table 2.

**Example 3.35:** Find a deterministic finite automata equivalent to $M = (\{q_0, q_1, q_2\}, \{0, 1\}, \delta, q_0, \{q_1\})$ where $\delta$ is defined in Fig. 3.40.

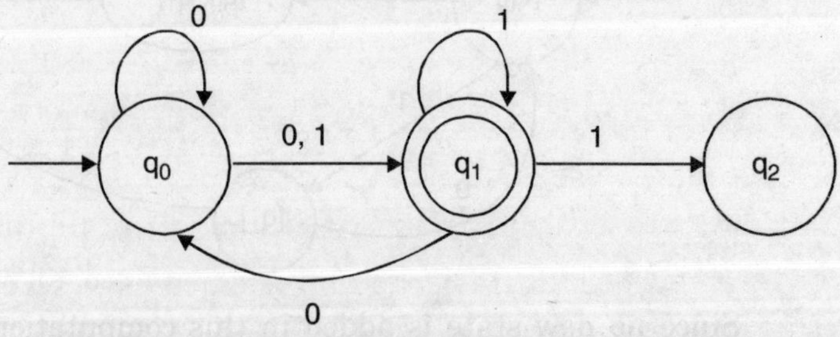


***Fig. 3.40***

**Solution.** The given NFA $M = (\{q_0, q_1, q_2\}, \{0, 1\}\ \delta, q_0, \{q_1\})$ then its equivalent DFA $M'$ is defined by

$$M' = (Q', \Sigma, \delta', q_0', F')$$

where $Q' = 2^Q$ (Power set $Q$)

*i.e.,* $\{\phi, [q_0], [q_1], [q_2], [q_0, q_1], [q_0, q_2], [q_1, q_2], [q_0, q_1, q_2]\}$

These are the total number of states of DFA

$\Sigma$ = Similar to NFA *i.e.,* $\{0, 1\}$

$q_0'$ = $[q_0]$. This is the initial state of DFA

$F'$ = $\{[q_1], [q_0, q_1], [q_1, q_2], [q_0, q_1, q_2]\}$. These are the final states of DFA

$\delta'$ = Since the final state is $q_1$, so make all states as a final state which contains the state $q_1$. Hence the transition digraph of DFA is shown in Fig. 3.41.

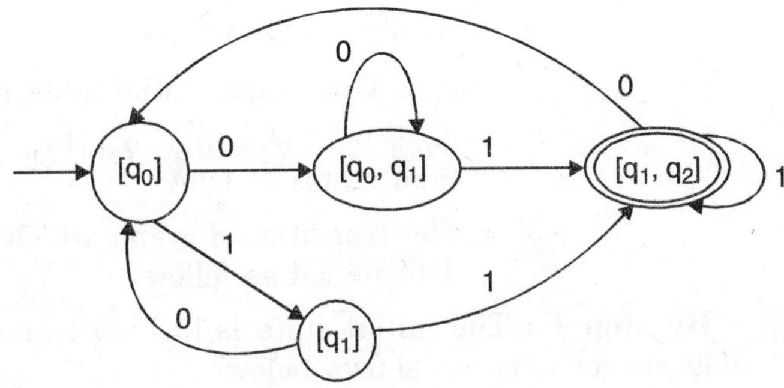


***Fig. 3.41***

or this can be represented by transition table shown in table 3.

**Table 3. Input symbol**

| **States** | **0** | **1** |
|---|---|---|
| $\rightarrow [q_0]$ | $[q_0, q_1]$ | $[q_1]$ |
| $[q_1]$ | $[q_0]$ | $[q_1, q_2]$ |
| $[q_0, q_1]$ | $[q_0, q_1]$ | $[q_1, q_2]$ |
| $[q_1, q_2]$ | $[q_0]$ | $[q_1, q_2]$ |

The DFA equivalent to NFA is $M' = (\{[q_0], [q_1]\ [q_0, q_1], [q_1, q_2], [q_1, q_2]\}, \{0, 1\}, \delta', [q_0], ([q_1], [q_0, q_1], [q_1, q_2]\}$ where $\delta'$ shown in Fig. 3.41 or table 3.

**Example 3.36:** Find a deterministic finite automata equivalent to $M = (\{q_0, q_1, q_2,\}, \{0, 1\}, \delta, q_0\{q_2\})$ were $\delta$ is defined in Fig. 2.42.

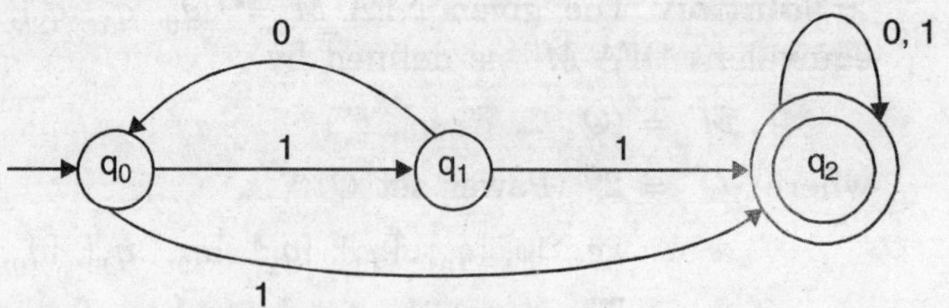


*Fig. 3.42*

**Solution:** The given NFA, $M = (\{q_0, q_1, q_2\}, (0, 1), \delta, q_0, \{q_2\})$ then its equivalent DFA $M'$ is defined by

$M' = (Q', \Sigma, \delta, q_0', F')$

Where $Q' = 2^Q$ (Power set $Q$)

*i.e.,* $\{\phi, [q_0], [q_1], [q_2], [q_0, q_1], [q_1, q_2], [q_0, q_1, q_2]\}$

These are the total number of states of DFA

$\Sigma$ = Similar to NFA *i.e.,* $\{0, 1\}$

$q_0'$ = $[q_0]$. This is the initial state of DFA

$F'$ = $\{[q_2], [q_0, q_2], [q_1, q_2], [q_0, q_1, q_2]\}$. These are the final states of DFA

$\delta'$ = The transition digraph which is determined as follows

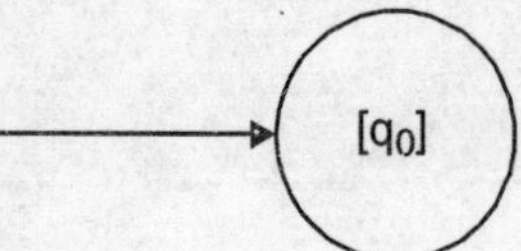


**By step 1 :** The initial state is $[q_0]$, so transition diagram for it is as shown below

**By step 2 :** The next states from $[q_0]$ are $\phi$ and $[q_1, q_2]$ on giving input symbol 0 and 1 respectively. Then add this new state (*i.e.,* $[q_1, q_2]$) in transition digraph from state $[q_0]$ with label 1. So the new transition digraph is given below.

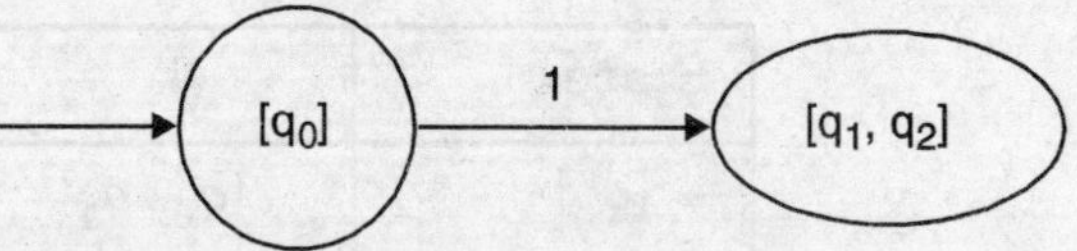


**By step 3 :** The next states from $[q_1, q_2]$ are $[q_0, q_2]$ and $[q_2]$ on giving input symbol 0 and 1 respectively a explained below.

$$\delta'([q_1, q_2), 0) = \delta'(q_1, 0) \cup \delta'(q_2, 0)$$
$$= \{q_0\} \cup \{q_2\} = \{q_0, q_2)$$

and

$$\delta'([q_1, q_2), 1) = \delta'(q_1, 1) \cup \delta'(q_2, 1)$$
$$= \{q_2\} \cup \{q_2\} = \{q_2\}$$

Since the new state is $[q_0, q_2]$ and $[q_2]$. Then add these new states (*i.e.,* $[q_0, q_2]$ and $[q_2]$) in transition digraph from state $[q_1, q_2]$ with labels 0 and respectively. The new transition digraph is as shown below.

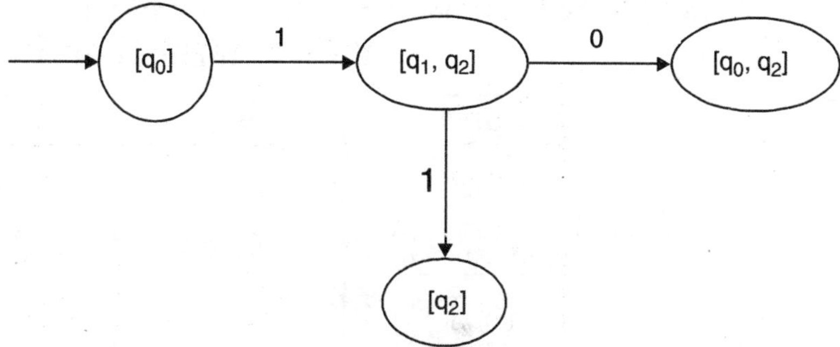


**By step 4 :** The next state from state $[q_2]$ are $[q_2]$ and $[q_2]$ on giving input symbol 0 and 1 and from $[q_0, q_2]$ and $[q_1, q_2]$ on applying symbol 0 and 1 respectively as explained below.

$$\delta'(q_2, 0) = \{q_2\},$$

$$\delta'(q_2, 1) = \{q_2\},$$

$$\delta'([q_0, q_2], 0) = \delta'(q_0, 0) \cup \delta'(q_2, 0) = \phi \cup \{q_2\} = \{q_2\}$$

and $$\delta'([q_0, q_2], 1) = \delta'(q_0, 1) \cup \delta'(q_2, 1) = \{q_1, q_2\} \cup \{q_2\} = \{q_1, q_2\}$$

Since no new state is obtained in this computation so no need to do any more computation on any states. Hence the transition diagram is shown below.

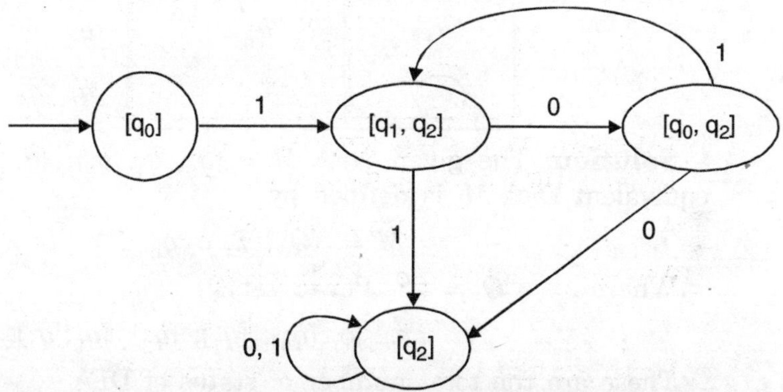


**By step 5 :** Draw all states as a final it it contains the final state of NFA (*i.e.*, $q_2$). Hence the final transition diagram is shown in Fig. 3.43.

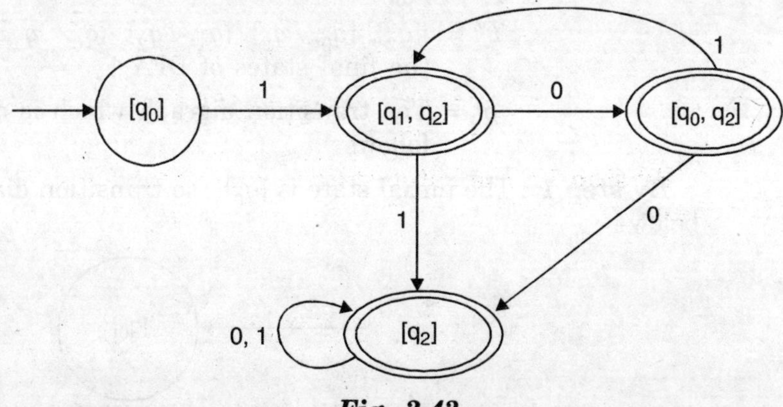


***Fig. 3.43***

or this can be transition table shown in table 4.

**Table 4. Input symbol**

| States | 0 | 1 |
|---|---|---|
| $\rightarrow [q_0]$ | $\phi$ | $[q_1, q_2]$ |
| $([q_1, q_2])$ | $[q_0, q_2]$ | $[q_2]$ |
| $([q_2])$ | $[q_2]$ | $[q_2]$ |
| $([q_0, q_2])$ | $[q_2]$ | $[q_1, q_2]$ |

**Example 3.36:** Find a Deterministic Finite Automata of a machine $M = [q_0, q_1, q_2\}, \{a, b\}, \delta, q_0 \{q_2\})$ for the table given below

**[U.P.T.U. MCA, 02, 03, B.Tech 2005]**

**Table 5. Input symbol**

| States | 0 | 1 |
|---|---|---|
| $q_0$ | $q_0, q_1$ | $q_2$ |
| $q_1$ | $q_0$ | $q_1$ |
| $(q_2)$ | – | $q_0, q_1$ |

**Solution:** The given NFA $M = [q_0, q_1, q_2\}, \{a, b\}, \delta, q_0 \{q_2\})$ then its equivalent DFA $M'$ is defined by

$$M' = (Q', \Sigma, \delta, q_0', F')$$

Where $Q' = 2^Q$ (Power set $Q$)

*i.e.*, $\{\phi, [q_0], [q_1], [q_2], [q_0, q_1], [q_1, q_2], [q_0, q_1, q_2]\}$

These are the total number of states of DFA

$\Sigma$ = Similar to NFA *i.e.*, $\{a, b\}$

$q_0'$ = $[q_0]$. This is the initial state of DFA

$F'$ = $\{[q_2], [q_0, q_2], [q_1, q_2], [q_0, q_1, q_2]\}$. These are the final states of DFA

$\delta'$ = The transition digraph which is determined as follows

**By step 1 :** The initial state is $[q_0]$, so transition diagram for it is shown below

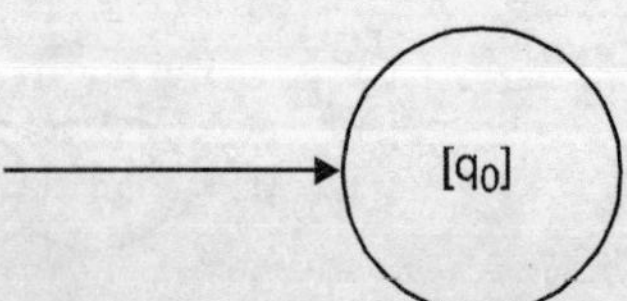

**By step 2 :** The next states from $[q_0]$ are $[q_1, q_2]$ and $[q_2]$ on giving input symbol '$a$' and '$b$' respectively. Then add this new state (*i.e.*, $[q_0, q_1]$) and $[q_2]$) in transition digraph from state $[q_0]$ with label '$a$' and '$b$' respectively. So the new transition digraph is given below.

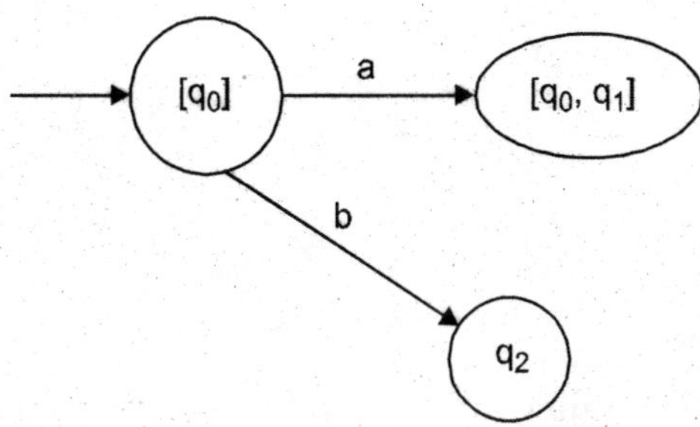


**By step 3 :** The next states from $[q_2]$ is $\phi$ are $[q_0, q_1]$ on giving input symbol '$a$' and '$b$' respectively, and from $[q_0, q_1]$ are $[q_0, q_1]$ and $[q_1, q_2]$ on giving input symbol '$a$' and '$b$' respectively as explained below.

$$\delta'(q_2, a) = \{\phi\},$$

$$\delta'(q_2, b) = \{q_2, q_1\},$$

Now $$\delta'([q_0, q_1), a) = \delta'(q_0, a) \cup \delta'(q_1, a)$$

$$= \{q_0, q_1\} \cup \{q_0\} = \{q_2, q_1)$$

and $$\delta'((q_0, q_1), b) = \delta'(q_0, b) \cup \delta'(q_1, b)$$

$$= \{q_2\} \cup \{q_1\} = \{q_1, q_2\}$$

Since the new state is $[q_1, q_2]$. The add this new state (*i.e.*, $[q_1, q_2]$ in transition digraph from state $[q_0, q_1]$ with label '$b$'. So the new transition digraph is given below.

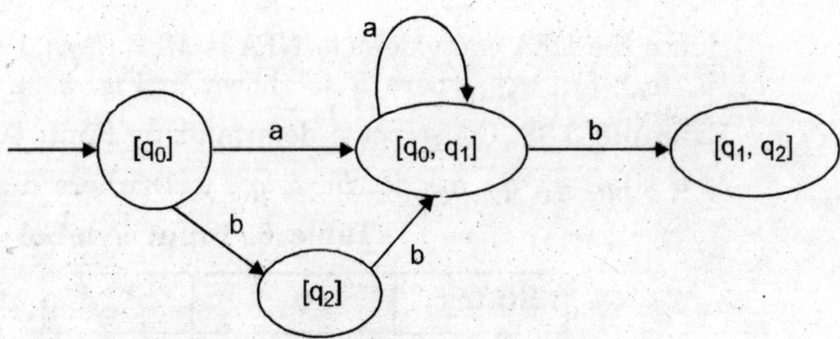


**By step 4:** The next state from state $[q_1, q_2]$ are $[q_0]$ and $[q_0, q_1]$ on input symbol '$a$' and '$b$' respectively as explained below.

$$\delta'([q_1, q_1], a) = \delta'(q_1, a) \cup \delta'(q_2, a) = \{q_0\} \cup \phi = [q_0]$$

and $$\delta'([q_1, q_2), b) = \delta'(q_1, b) \cup \delta'(q_2, b) = \{q_1] \cup \{q_0, q_1\} = \{q_0, q_1\}$$

Hence the transition digraph is given below

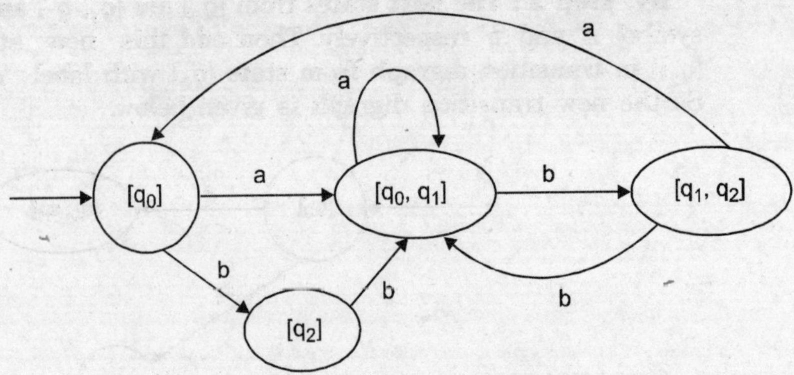


Since no new state is added in this computation so no need to do any more computation on any states

**By step 5:** Draw all states as a final it it contains the final state of NFA (*i.e.,* $q_2$). Hence the final transition diagram is shown in Fig. 3.44.

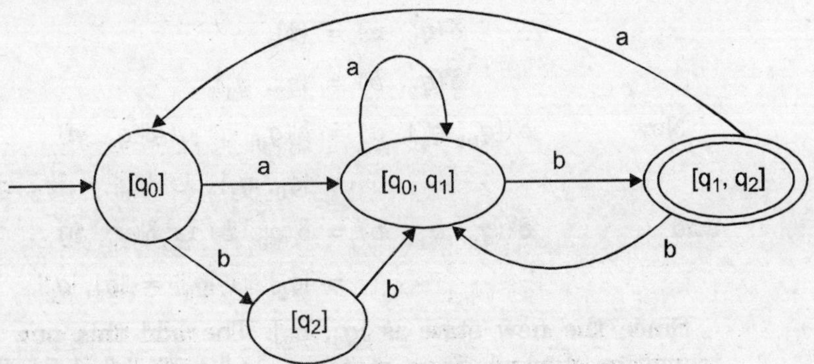


***Fig. 3.44***

Hence the DFA equivalent to NFA is $M' = (\{[q_0], [\ q_1], [q_0, q_1], [q_1, q_2]\}, \{a, b\}, \delta', [q_0], [q_1, q_2]\}$ where $\delta'$ is shown in Fig. 3.44.

**Example 3.38:** Construct a deterministic Finite Automata equivalent to $M = (\{q_0, q_1, q_2, q_3\}, \{a, b\}, \delta, q_0, \{q_3\})$ where d is given as follows

**Table 6. Input symbol**

| **States** | **0** | **1** |
|---|---|---|
| $q_0$ | $q_0, q_1$ | $q_0$ |
| $q_1$ | $q_2$ | $q_1$ |
| $q_2$ | $q_3$ | $q_3$ |
| ($q_3$) | – | $q_2$ |

**U.P.T.U. MCA (Co) 2002]**

**Solution:** The given NFA, $M = [q_0, q_1, q_{2,} q_3\}, \{a, b\}, \delta, q_0 \{q_3\})$, then its equivalent DFA $M'$, be defined by

$M' = (Q', \Sigma, \delta, q_0', F')$

Where $Q' = 2^Q$ (Power set $Q$)

*i.e.*, $\{\phi, [q_0], [q_1], [q_2], [q_3] [q_0, q_1], [q_0, q_2], [q_0, q_3], [q_1, q_2], [q_1, q_0], [q_2, q_3], [q_0, q_1, q_2], [q_0, q_1, q_3], [q_0, q_2, q_3], [q_1, q_2, q_3], [q_0, q_1, q_2, q_3]\}$

These are the total number of states of DFA

$\Sigma$ = Similar to NFA *i.e.*, $\{a, b\}$

$q_0'$ = $[q_0]$. This is the initial state of DFA

$F' = \{[q_3], [q_0, q_3], [q_1, q_3], [q_2, q_3], [q_0, q_1, q_3], [q_0, q_2, q_3], [q_1, q_2, q_3], [q_0, q_1, q_2, q_3]\}$

$\delta'$ = The transition digraph is determined follows

**By step 1 :** The initial state is $[q_0]$, so transition diagram for it is shown below

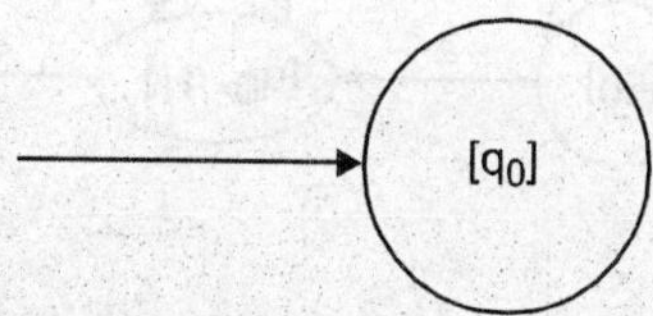


**By step 2 :** The next states from $[q_0]$ are $[q_0, q_1]$ and $[q_0]$ on giving input symbol '*a*' and '*b*' respectively. Then add $q_1$ new state (*i.e.*, $[q_0, q_1]$) in transition digraph from state $[q_0]$ with label '*a*'. So the new transition digraph is given below.

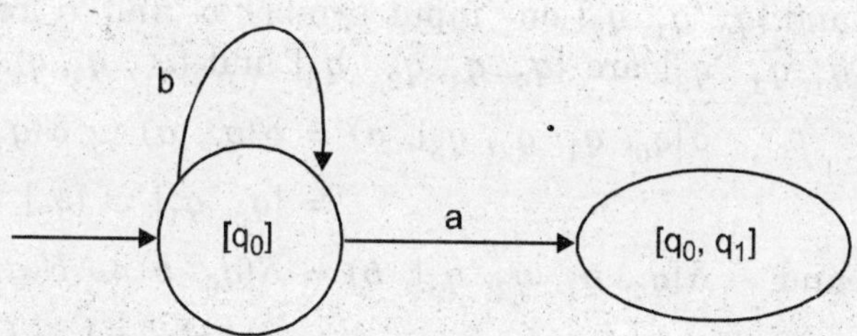


**By step 3 :** The next states from $[q_0, q_1]$ are $[q_0, q_1, q_2]$ and $[q_0, q_1]$ on giving input symbol 'a' and 'b' respectively as explained below.

$$\delta'([q_0, q_1], a) = \delta'(q_0, a) \cup \delta'(q_1, a) = \{q_{0,} q_1\} \cup \{q_2\} = \{q_0, q_1, q_2\}$$

and

$$\delta'([q_0, q_1], b) = \delta'(q_0, b) \cup \delta'(q_1, b) = \{q_0\} \cup \{q_1\} = \{q_0, q_1\}$$

Since the new state is $[q_0, q_1, q_2]$. Then add this new state (*i.e.*, $[q_0, q_1, q_2]$) in transition digraph from state $[q_0, q_1]$ with label '*a*'. So the new transtition digraph is given below.

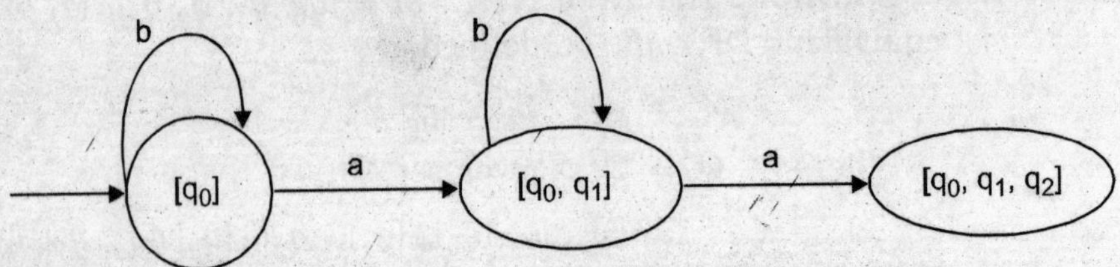


**By step 4 :** The next states from state $[q_0, q_1, q_2]$ are $[q_0, q_1, q_2, q_3]$ and $[q_0, q_1, q_3]$ on input symbol 'a' and 'b' respectively as explained below.

$$\delta'[q_0, q_1, q_2], a) = \delta'(q_0, a) \cup \delta'(q_1, a) \cup \delta'(q_2, a)$$
$$= [q_0, q_1] \cup [q_2] \cup [q_3] = [q_0, q_1, q_2, q_3]$$

and $\delta'[q_0, q_1, q_2], b) = \delta'(q_0, b) \cup \delta'(q_1, b) \cup \delta'(q_2, b) = [q_0] \cup [q_1] \cup [q_3]$
$$= [q_0, q_1, q_3]$$

Hence the transition digraph is given below

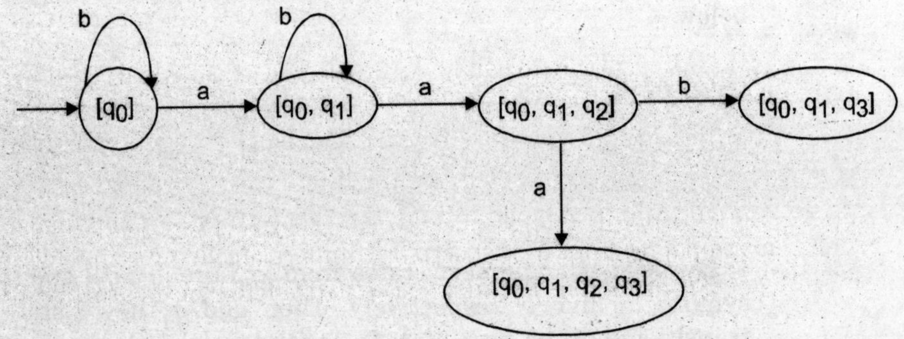


Again applying step 4 the next states from state $[q_0, q_1, q_3]$ are $[q_0, q_1, q_2]$ and $[q_0, q_1, q_2]$ on input symbol '$a$' and '$b$' respectively and from state $[q_0, q_1, q_2, q_3]$ are $[q_0, q_1, q_2, q_3]$ and $[q_0, q_1, q_2, q_3]$ as explained blow.

$$\delta'[q_0, q_1, q_2, q_3], a) = \delta'(q_0, a) \cup \delta'(q_1, a) \cup \delta'(q_3, a)$$
$$= [q_0, q_1] \cup [q_2] \cup \phi = [q_0, q_1, q_2]$$

and $\delta'[q_0, q_1, q_2, q_3], b) = \delta'(q_0, b) \cup \delta'(q_1, b) \cup \delta'(q_3, b)$
$$= [q_0] \cup [q_1] \cup [q_2]$$
$$= [q_0, q_1, q_2]$$

$$\delta'[q_0, q_1, q_2, q_3], a) = \delta'(q_0, a) \cup \delta'(q_1, a) \cup [q_2, a] \cup [q_3, a]$$
$$= [q_0, q_1] \cup [q_2] \cup [q_3] \cup \phi = [q_0, q_1, q_2, q_3]$$

$$\delta'[q_0, q_1, q_2, q_3], b) = \delta'(q_0, b) \cup \delta'(q_1, b) \cup \delta'[q_2, b] \cup \delta'(q_3, b)$$
$$= [q_0] \cup [q_1] \cup [q_3] \cup [q_2] = [q_0, q_1, q_2, q_3]$$

Hence the transition digraph is given below.

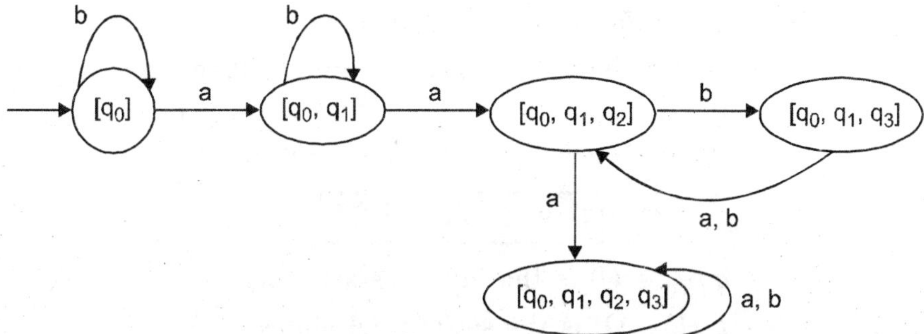


Since no new is added in this computation so no need to do any more computation on any states

**By step 5:** Draw all states as a final it it contains the final state of NFA (*i.e.,* $q_2$). Hence the final transition diagram is shown in Fig. 3.45.

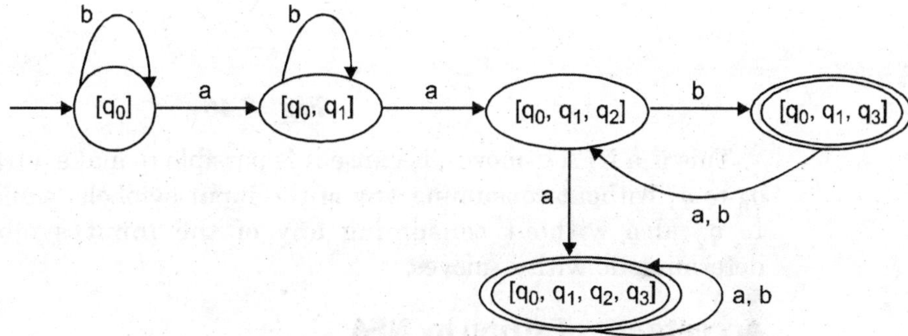


***Fig. 3.45***

Hence the DFA equivalent to NFA is $M' = (\{[q_0], [\ q_0, q_1], [q_0, q_1, q_2], [q_1, q_2, q_3]\}, \{a, b\}, \delta', [q_0], [q_0, q_1, q_3], [q_0, q_1, q_2, q_3]\})$ where $\delta'$ is shown in Fig. 3.45.

## 3.8 NFA WITH ∈-MOVES

If a non deterministic finite automata (*i.e.,* Zero, One or more transitions) is modified to allow transitions with at last one edge without input symbols (*i.e.,* ∈), then we get a NFA with ∈-move, because the transition without input symbol is called as ∈ transitons.

Or mathematically a non-deterministic finite automaton (NFA) $M$ with ∈-moves is defined by

$$M = (Q, \Sigma, \delta, q_0, F)$$

Where,

→ $Q$ is-a finite set of a states,

→ $\Sigma$ is a finite alphabet, the input alphabet.

→ $\delta$ is the transition system which represents a mapping between states with input alphabet or $\in$ to power set of states

*i.e.*, $Q \times \{\Sigma \cup \in\} \to 2^Q$ ($2^Q$ is power set of $Q$)

→ $q_0 (q_0 \in Q)$ is the initial state and

→ $F$ $(F \in Q)$ is the set of final states

For example, Consider the NFA given by following digraph:

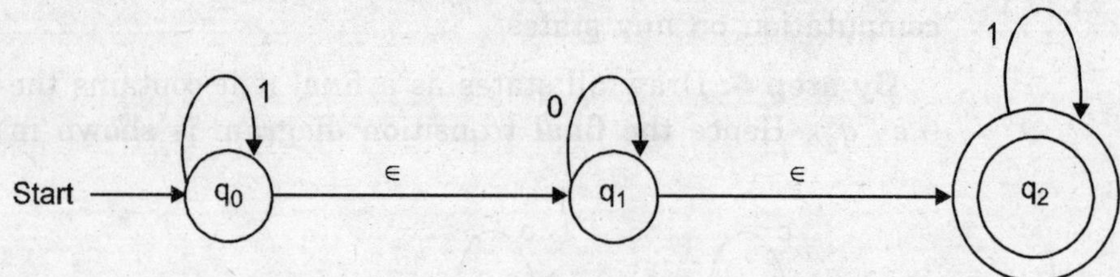


***Fig. 3.46***

This is a NFA $\in$-moves, because it is possible to make a transition from state $q_0$ to $q_1$ without consuming any of the input symbols, similarly from state $q_1$ to $q_2$ also without consuming any of the input symbols, being a non deterministic with $\in$-moves.

## Acceptance of string by NFA

A string $x$ in $\Sigma^*$ will be accepted by NFA with $\in$-moves, if there exists at least one path corresponding to $x$, which starts with an initial state and ends with one of the final states, but since path may be formed by $\in$-transition as well as non $\in$-transition; to find out whether $x$ is accepted or not by the NFA with $\in$-moves, we require to define a function $\in$-closure ($q$), where $q$ is the state of automata.

The function $\in$–closure ($q$) is defined as follows:

$\in$-closure ($q$) = Set of all states of the automata which can be reached form $q$ on a path labeled by $\in$.

$$\in\text{-closure } (q_0) = \{q_0, q_1, q_2\}$$
$$\in\text{-closure } (q_1) = \{q_1, q_2\}$$
$$\in\text{-closure } (q_2) = \{q_2\}$$

The $\in$-closure ($q$) will never be an empty set, because $q$ is always reachable from itself without consuming any input symbol, *i.e.*, on path labeled by $\in$, hence $q$ will always be there in $\in$-closure ($q$).

If P be a set of states then $\in$-closure function can be extended to find out $\in$–closure $(p)$ as follows: $\in$-closure $(P) = \cup_{\text{for every } q \text{ in } p}$ $\in$-closure $(q)$

## 3.9 EQUIVALENCE OF NFA WITH $\in$-MOVES TO NFA WITHOUT $\in$- MOVES

For every NFA with $\in$-moves there exists an equivalent NFA without $\in$-moves, accepting the same language. That is you have to find a NFA without $\in$-moves to an equivalent NFA with $\in$-moves or you can say, you have to remove $\in$-transition from a given NFA without changing its behavior, but simply removing the $\in$-transitions from a given NFA with $\in$-moves will change the language accepted by an NFA. Hence for every $\in$-transition, to be eliminated you have to add some non $\in$-transitions as substitute so as keep the language accepted by the NFA the same. Therefore transformation of NFA with $\in$-moves to NFA without $\in$-moves involve finding out the non $\in$-transitions to be added to the NFA for every $\in$-transition to be eliminated.

Use the following steps to convert the NFA with $\in$-moves to NFA without $\in$-move Let us consider we want to remove $\in$-moves from state $q_1$ to state $q_2$

**Step 1 :** Find all the edges starting from state $q_2$

**Step 2 :** Duplicate all these edges starting from state $q_1$ without changing the edge labels.

**Step 3 :** If state $q_1$ is an initial state make state $q_2$ also as initial state.

**Step 4 :** If state $q_2$ is a final state make state $q_1$ also as final state.

**Example 3.39:** We want to convert the following NFA with $\in$-moves into NFA without $\in$-moves.

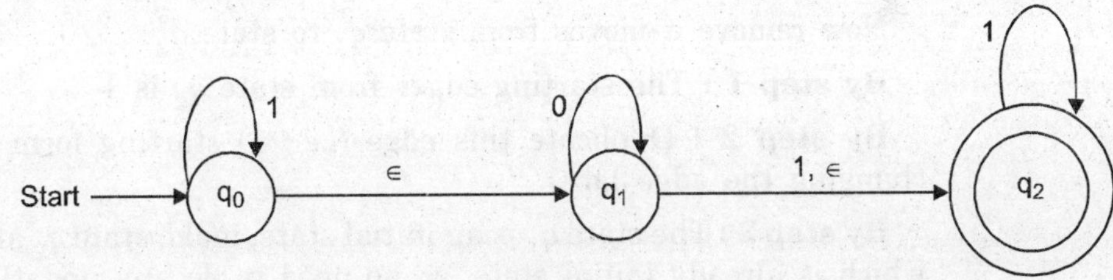


*Fig. 3.47*

**Solution:** The $\in$-move is given between state $q_0$ and $q_1$ and $q_1$ $q_2$.

So, we first remove $\in$-moves from state $q_0$ to state $q_1$

**By step 1 :** The starting edges from state $q_1$ are 0, 1 and $\in$

**By step 2 :** Duplicate all these edges (*i.e.,* 0, 1, $\in$) starting from state $q_0$ without changing the edge labels.

**By step 3 :** The state $q_0$ is an initial state, make state $q_1$ also as initial state.

**By step 4 :** The state $q_1$ is not a final state, so state $q_0$ shall not be a final state.

The transition digraph looks like a shown in Fig. below

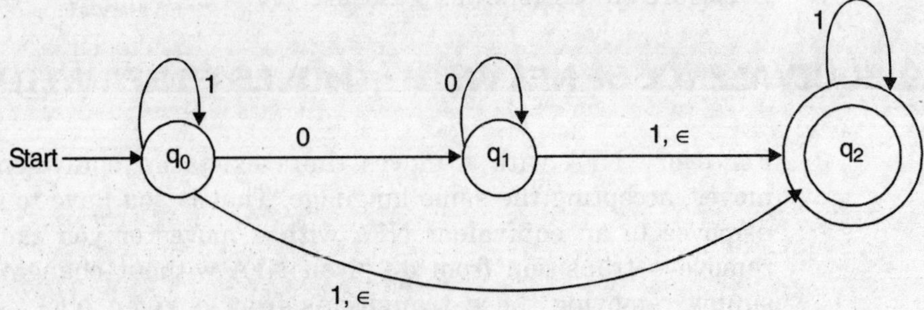


Now remove ∈-moves from state $q_0$ to state $q_2$

**By step 1 :** The starting edges from state $q_2$ is 1

**By step 2 :** Duplicate this edge (*i.e.*, 1) starting from state $q_0$ without changing the edge label.

**By step 3 :** The state $q_0$ is an initial state, make state $q_2$ also as initial state.

**By step 4 :** The state $q_2$ is a final state, so state $q_0$ also a final state.

The transition digraph looks like as shown in fig below

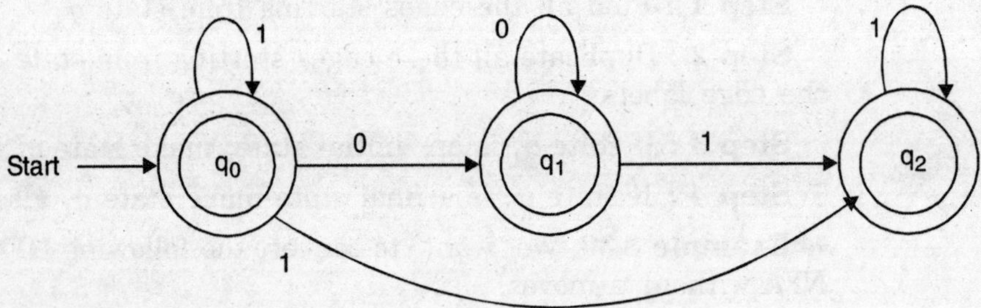


Now remove ∈-moves from state $q_1$ to state $q_2$

**By step 1 :** The starting edges from state $q_2$ is 1

**By step 2 :** Duplicate this edge (*i.e.*, 1) starting form state $q_1$ without changing the edge label.

**By step 3 :** The state $q_1$ is an initial state, make state $q_2$ also as initial state which is already initial state, so no need to do any updation.

**By step 4 :** The state $q_2$ is a final state, so state $q_1$ also a final state.

The transition digraph looks like as shown in Fig. 3.48.

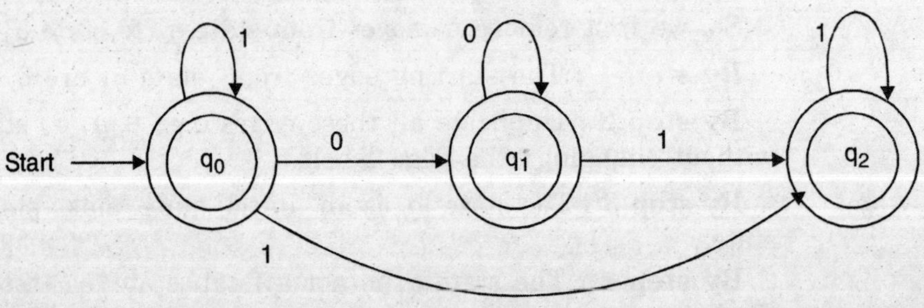


*Fig. 3.48*

This transition digraph does not contain ∈-moves, so this is the equivalent NFA to the given transition digraph without ∈-moves.

**Example 3.39:** Convert the following NFA to DFA

*[U.P.T.U. MCA 2002-2003]*

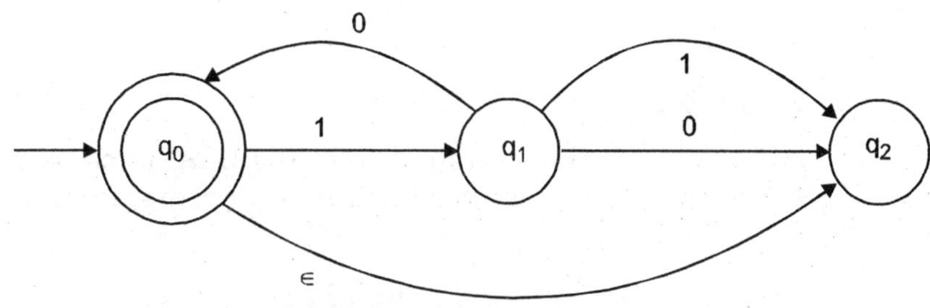


***Fig. 3.49***

**Solution:** This transition digraph contains ∈-moves, so the transition digraph without ∈-move is shown as in Fig. 3.50 using above steps.

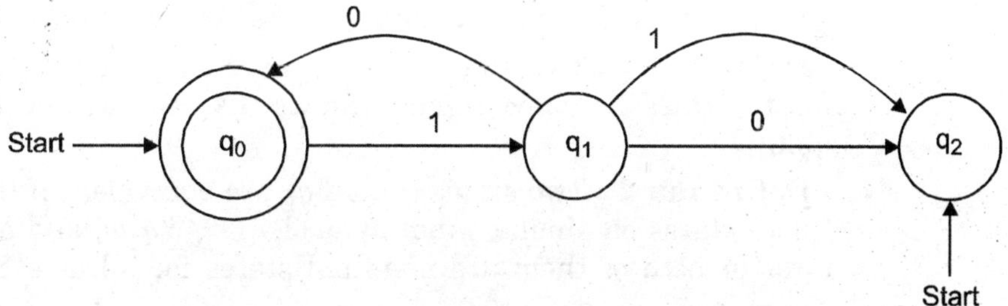


***Fig. 3.50***

Now using the procedure to convert NFA to DFA, we will get the transition digraph of an equivalent DFA machine which is shown in Fig. 3.51.

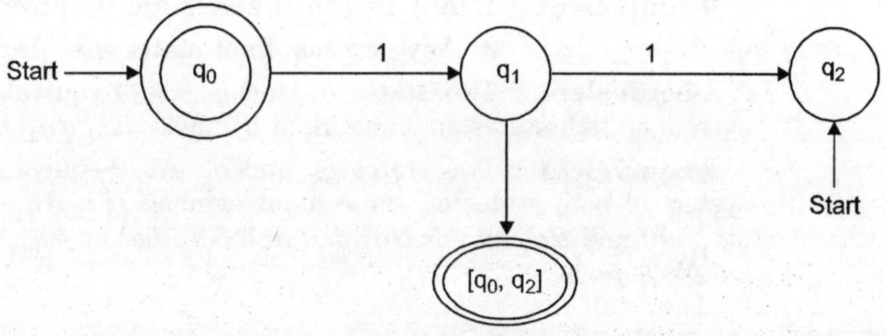


***Fig. 3.51***

## 3.10 MINIMIZATION/OPTIMIZATION OF A DFA

Minimization/optimization of a deterministic finite automata refers to detecting those states of a DFA whose presence or absence in a DFA does not affect the language accepted by the automata, hence these states can be eliminated from the automata without affecting the language accepted by the automata.

Such states are Unreachable States, Dead States and Non Distinguishable. (or equivalent) States.

### Unreachable States

These are those states of a DFA, which are not reachable from the initial state of DFA on any possible input sequence.

### Dead States

A dead state is that non-final state of a DFA, whose transitions on every input symbol terminates on itself *i.e.*, $q$ is a dead state if $q$ is non final state and $\delta(q, q) = q$ for every a in $\Sigma$.

### Equivalent or Non-distinguishable States

These are those of DFA for which there exists no distinguishing string. Hence they can not be distinguished from one another and we can replace all of them by one equivalent state.

We can find equivalent states by the following definitions.

**Definition 1 :** Two states $q_1$ and $q_2$ are equivalent if the transition system of both states on same input symbols (*i.e.*, $\delta(q_1,a)$ and $\delta(q_2, a)\}$ are exactly equal.

**Definition 2 :** Two states $q_1$ and $q_2$ are equivalent if the transition system of both states on similar input symbols (*i.e.*, $\delta(q_1w)$ and $\delta(q_2,w)$ are both final states or both of them are non-final states for all $w \in \Sigma^*$.

**Definition 3 :** Two states $q_1$ and $q_2$ are $n$-equivalent ($n \geq 0$) if the transition system of both states on similar input symbols (*i.e.*, $\delta(q_1,w)$ and $\delta(q_2,w)$ are final states or both of them are no-final states for all string w of length n or less $\in \Sigma^*$.

**0-equivalent :** 1. Any two final states are 0-equivalent state.

or 2. Any two non-final states are also 0-equivalent state.

**1-equivalent :** Two states $q_1$ and $q_2$ are 1-equivalent if the transition system of both states on same input symbols (*i.e.*, $\delta(q_1, a)$ are exactly equals.

**2-equivalent :** Two states $q_1$ and $q_2$ are 2-equivalent if the transition system of both states on same input symbols (*i.e.* $\delta(q_1, aa)$ and $\delta(q_2, aa)$ or $\delta(q_1, ab)$ and $\delta(q_2, ab)$ or $\delta(q_1, ba)$ and $\delta(q_2, ba)$ or $\delta(q_1, bb)$ and $\delta(q_2, bb)$ are exactly equals.

## 3.11 CONSTRUCTION OF MINIMUM AUTOMATON

Use the following steps to construct *a* minimum automaton

**Step 1 :** Construct $\pi_0$ by definition of 0-equivalent *i.e.*

$$\boxed{\pi_0 = (Q_1^0, Q_2^0)}$$

where $Q_1^0$ = The set of all final states

$Q_2^0$ = The set of all non-final states (*i.e.*, $Q - Q_1^0$)

**Step 2 :** Construct $\pi_1$ from $\pi_0$ by definition of 1-equivalent

**Step 3 :** Construct $\pi_{n+1}$ from $\pi_n$ by definition of $n$-equivalent

**Step 4 :** Construct $\pi_k$ for $k$ = 1, 2, 3, ...., until $\pi_k = \pi_{k+1}$ by definition of 1-equivalent

**Step 5 :** Convert all states of step 4 into equivalence classes. The equivalence classes are obtained by replacing a state $q$ by $[q]$

**Example 3.41:** Construct the minimum state automaton equivalent to the transition diagram given in Fig. 3.51

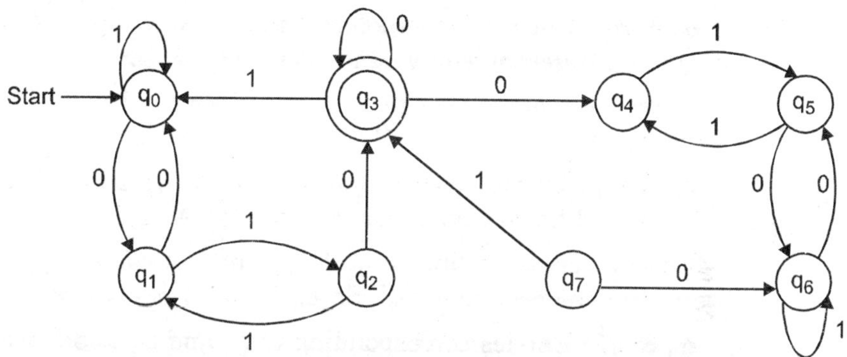


***Fig. 3.52***

**Solution:** Transition table is a given below:

**Table 7**

| State | Σ | |
|---|---|---|
| | 0 | 1 |
| $q_0$ | $q_1$ | $q_0$ |
| $q_1$ | $q_0$ | $q_2$ |
| $q_2$ | $q_3$ | $q_1$ |
| ($q_3$) | $q_3$ | $q_0$ |
| $q_4$ | $q_3$ | $q_5$ |
| $q_5$ | $q_6$ | $q_4$ |
| $q_6$ | $q_5$ | $q_6$ |
| $q_7$ | $q_6$ | $q_3$ |

$$Q_0 = \{q_0, q_1, q_2, q_3, q_4, q_5, q_6, q_7\}$$
$$Q_1 = \{q_3\}$$
$$Q_2^0 = Q - Q_1^0 = \{q_0, q_1, q_2, q_4, q_5, q_6, q_7\}$$
$$\pi_0 = \{\{q_3\}\ \{q_0, q_1, q_2, q_4, q_5, q_6, q_7\}\}$$

**Formation of $\pi_1$** is achieved by partitioning the subsets of $\pi_0$.

$Q_1^0 = \{q_3\}$ can not be partitioned further. 0S0 $Q_1^1 = \{q_3\}$

$Q_2^0 = \{q_0, q_1, q_2, q_4, q_5, q_6, q_7\}$ may be partitioned further which can be verified as given below:

**[A]** – Consider $q_0$ with every other state coming after (succeeding) it *i.e.*, $q_1, q_2, q_4, q_5, q_6, q_7$ successively as follows.

**$q_0$ & $q_1$ :** Entries corresponding to $q_0$ and $q_1$ under 0-col are $q_1 \in Q_2^0$ & $q_0 \in Q_2^0$ *i.e.*, same equivalence class $Q_2^0$

Entries corresponding to $q_0$ and $q_1$ under I-col are $q_0 \in Q_2^0$ & $q_2 \in Q_2^0$ *i.e.*, same equivalence class. So $q_0$ is 1-equivalenct to $q_1$.

**$q_0$ & $q_2$ :** Entries corresponding to $q_0$ and $q_2$ under 0-col are $q_1 \in Q_2^0$ & $q_3 \in Q_1^0$ *i.e.*, different equivalence class $Q_1^0$ & $Q_2^0$

Entries corresponding to $q_0$ & $q_2$ under 1-col are $q_0 \in Q_2^0$ & $q_1 \in Q_2^0$ *i.e.*, same equivalence classes $Q_2^0$. So $q_0$ is not 1-equivalent to $q_2$.

**$q_0$ & $q_4$ :** Entries corresponding to $q_0$ & $q_4$ under 0-col are $q_1 \in Q_2^0$ & $q_3 \in Q_1^0$ *i.e.*, different equivalence class $Q_2^0$ & $Q_1^0$

Entries corresponding to $q_0$ & $q_4$ under 1-col are $q_0 \in Q_2^0$ & $q_3 \in Q_2^0$ *i.e.*, same equivalence class $Q_2^0$. So $q_0$ is not 1-equivalent to $q_4$.

**$q_0$ & $q_5$ :** Entries corresponding to $q_0$ and $q_5$ under 0-col are $q_1 \in Q_2^0$ & $q_6 \in Q_2^0$ *i.e.*, same equivalence class $Q_2^0$

Entries corresponding to $q_0$ and $q_5$ under 1-col are $q_0 \in Q_2^0$ & $q_4 \in Q_2^0$ *i.e.*, same equivalence class. So $q_0$ is 1-equivalent to $q_5$.

**$q_0$ & $q_6$ :** Entries corresponding to $q_0$ and $q_6$ under 0-col are $q_1 \in Q_2^0$ & $q_5 \in Q_2^0$ *i.e.*, same equivalence class $Q_2^0$

Entries corresponding to $q_0$ and $q_6$ under 1-col are $q_0 \in Q_2^0$ & $q_6 \in Q_2^0$ *i.e.*, same equivalence class $Q_2^0$. So $q_0$ is 1-equivalence to $q_6$.

**$q_0$ & $q_7$ :** Entries corresponding to $q_0$ and $q_7$ under 0-col are $q_1 \in Q_2^0$ & $q_6 \in Q_2^0$ *i.e.*, same equivalence class $Q_2^0$.

Entries corresponding to $q_0$ and $q_7$ under 1-col are $q_0 \in Q_2^0$ & $q_6 \in Q_1^0$ *i.e.*, different equivalence class. So $q_0$ is not 1-equivalent to $q_7$.

Thus $q_0$-is 1-equivalent to $q_1$, $q_5$ & $q_6$.

So $Q_2^1 = \{q_0, q_1, q_5, q_6\}$ Remaining elements are $\{q_2, q_4, q_7\}$

**[B]** Consider $q_2$ with $q_4$, & $q_7$ as $q_1$, $q_5$ & $q_6$ have been included in $Q_2^1$.

**$q_2$ & $q_4$ :** Entries corresponding to $q_2$ and $q_4$ under 0-col are $q_3 \in Q_1^0$ & $q_3 \in Q_1^0$ *i.e.*, same equivalence class $Q_1^0$

Entries corresponding to $q_2$ and $q_4$ under 1-col are $q_1 \in Q_2^0$ & $q_5 \in Q_2^0$ *i.e.*, same equivalence class. So $q_2$ is 1-equivalent to $q_4$.

**$q_2$ & $q_7$ :** Entries corresponding to $q_2$ and $q_7$ under 0-col are $q_3 \in Q_1^0$ & $q_6 \in Q_2^0$ *i.e.*, different class. No need to consider-1-col now.

So $q_2$ is not 1-equivalent to $q_7$.

Therefore $Q_3^1 = \{q_2, q_4\}$. The only element left over is $q_7$. So $Q_4^1 = \{q_7\}$

| Hence | $\pi_1 = [(q_3),$ | $(q_0, q_1, q_5, q_6),$ | $(q_2, q_4),$ | $(q_7)]$ |
|---|---|---|---|---|
| | $\downarrow$ | $\downarrow$ | $\downarrow$ | $\downarrow$ |
| | $Q_1'$ | $Q_2'$ | $Q_3'$ | $Q_4'$ |

**To find $\pi_2$**

$Q_1^2 = \{q_3\}$ as $q_3$ can not be partitioned further. We shall partition other subsets.

Partitioning of $\{q_0, q_1, q_5, q_6\} = Q$

**[A]** Consider $q_0$ with $q_1$, $q_5$ & $q_6$

$q_0$ **&** $q_1$ **:** Entries corresponding to $q_0$ and $q_1$ under 0-col are $q_1 \in Q_2^1$ & $q_0 \in Q_2^1$ *i.e.*, same class.

Entries corresponding to $q_0$ and $q_5$ under 1-col are $q_0 \in Q_2^1$ & $q_2 \in Q_3^1$ different equivalence class. So $q_0$ is not 2-equivalent to $q_1$.

$q_0$ **&** $q_5$ **:** Entries corresponding to $q_0$ and $q_5$ under 0-col are $q_1 \in Q_2^1$ & $q_6 \in Q_2^1$ *i.e.*, same class.

Entries corresponding to $q_0$ and $q_5$ under 1-col are $q_0 \in Q_2^1$ & $q_4 \in Q_3^1$ different class. So $q_0$ is not equivalent to $q_5$.

$q_0$ **&** $q_6$ **:** Entries corresponding to $q_0$ and $q_6$ under 0-col are $q_1 \in Q_2^1$ & $q_5 \in Q_2^1$ same class.

Entries corresponding to $q_0$ and $q_6$ under 0-col are $q_0 \in Q_2^1$ & $q_6 \in Q_2^1$ same class. So $q_0$ is 2-equivalent to $q_6$.

$$Q_2^2 = \{q_0, q_6\}$$

Left over elements are $q_1$ & $q_5$. So see if they are 2-equivalent or not. We can see that $q_1$ is 2-equivalent to $q_5$. So $Q_3^1 = \{q_1, q_5\}$.

Again $q_2$, $q_4$ & $q_7$ remain out of which $q_2$ is 2-equivalent with $q_4$ & not with $q_7$.

So $\quad Q_4^2 = \{q_1, q_5\}$

$\quad Q_5^2 = \{q_7\}$

So $\quad \pi_2 = \{\{q_3\}, \{q_0, q_6\}' \{q_1, q_5\}, \{q_2, q_4\}, \{q_7\}\}$

**To find $\pi_3$.** $q_0$ is 3-equivalent to $q_6$ $Q_2^3 = \{q_0, q_6\}$

$Q_1^3 = \{lq_3\}$ $q_1$ is 3-equivalent to $q_5$ $Q_3^3 = \{q_1, q_5\}$

$q_2$ is 3-equivalent to $q_4$ $Q_4^3 = \{q_2, q_4\}$

$Q_5^3 = \{q_7\}$

So $\pi_3$ is same as $\pi_2$

So $\pi_2$ gives the equivalence classes.

Minimum state automation is $M' = (Q', \{0, 1\}, \delta', q_0'. F')$

where $Q' = \{\{q_3\}, \{q_0, q_6\}, \{q_1, q_5\}, \{q_2, q_4\}, \{q_7\}\}$

$q'_0 = \{q_0, q_6\}$, $F' = \{q_3\}$ and $\delta'$ is given below

**Table 8**

| State | Σ | |
|---|---|---|
| | 0 | 1 |
| $[q_0, q_6]$ | $[q_1, q_5]$ | $[q_0, q_6]$ |
| $[q_1, q_5]$ | $[q_0, q_6]$ | $[q_2, q_4]$ |
| $[q_2, q_4]$ | $[q_3]$ | $[q_1, q_5]$ |
| $[q_3]$ | $[q_3]$ | $[q_0, q_6]$ |
| $[q_7]$ | $[q_0, q_6]$ | $[q_3]$ |

This represents a transition function of a transition system. This can also be represented in the form of transition digraph. which is shown in Fig. 3.53

**Transition diagram**

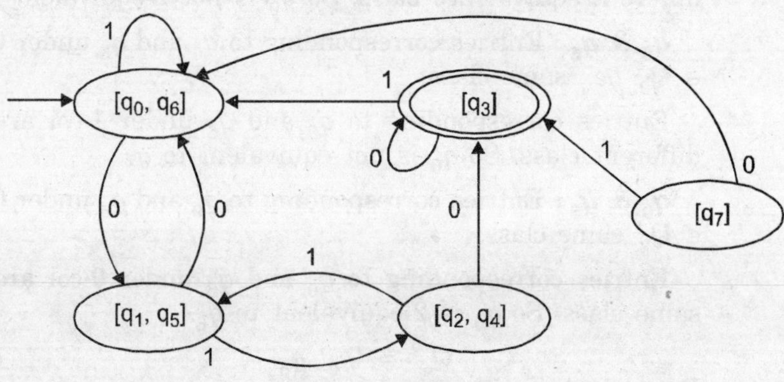


*Fig. 3.53*

**Example 3.42:** Construct a minimum state automaton equivalent to the finite automation given in Fig. 3.54.

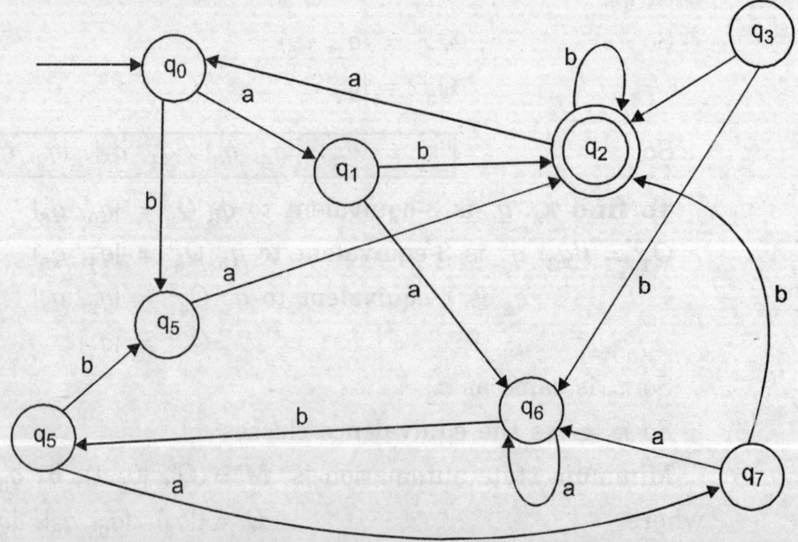


*Fig. 2.45*

**Solution:** Transition Table shall be as follows:

**Table 9**

| State | Σ | |
|---|---|---|
| | **a** | **b** |
| → $q_0$ | $q_1$ | $q_5$ |
| $q_1$ | $q_6$ | $q_2$ |
| $q_2$ | $q_0$ | $q_2$ |
| $q_3$ | $q_2$ | $q_6$ |
| $q_4$ | $q_7$ | $q_5$ |
| $q_5$ | $q_2$ | $q_6$ |
| $q_6$ | $q_6$ | $q_4$ |
| $q_7$ | $q_6$ | $q_2$ |

$$Q = \{q_0, q_1, q_2, q_3, q_4, q_5, q_6, q_7\}$$

$$Q_1^{\,0} = \{q_2\},\ Q_2^{\,0} = Q - Q_1^{\,0} = \{q_0, q_1, q_3, q_4, q_5, q_6, q_7\}$$

$$\pi_0 = \{\{q_2\}\ \{q_0, q_1, q_3, q_4, q_5, q_6, q_7\}$$

Set $\{q_2\}$ can not be partitioned further so $Q_1^1 = \{q_2\}$ is a subset in $\pi_1$

Partitioning of $Q_2^0 = \{q_0, q_1, q_3, q_4, q_5, q_6, q_7\}$ to find $\pi_1$.

**(A)** Consider $q_0$ with every other $q_i$ $i = 1, 3, 4, 6, 7$ succeeding it separately.

***(i)*** $\boldsymbol{q_0}$ **&** $\boldsymbol{q_1}$**:** Entries under $a$-column corresponding to $q_0$ & $q_1$ are $q_1$ & $q_6$ both of which belong $Q_2^0$.

Entries under b-column corresponding to $q_0$ & $q_1$ are $q_5$ & $q_2$. These both $\notin$ $Q_1^2$ & also $\notin$ $Q_2^0$.

$$\begin{cases} \text{one of them } q_5 \in Q_2^0 \\ \text{\& the other } q_2 \in Q_1^0 \end{cases}$$

So $q_0$ & $q_1$ are not 1-equivalent [Had they both belonged to either $Q_1^0$ or $Q_2^{\,0}$, the $q_0$ & $q_1$, would have been 1-equivalent.

***(ii)*** $\boldsymbol{q_0}$ **&** $\boldsymbol{q_3}$ **:** Entries corresponding to $q_0$ & $q_3$ under $a$-col are

$$\frac{q_1 \in Q_2^0 \ \& \ q_2 \in Q_1^0}{\text{Different sets}}$$

Entries corresponding to $q_0$ & $q_3$ under $b$-col are $\dfrac{q_5 \in Q_2^0 \ \& \ q_6 \in Q_2^0}{\text{Same set}}$

***(iii)*** $\boldsymbol{q_0}$ **&** $\boldsymbol{q_5}$ **:** Entries corresponding to $q_0$ & $q_5$ under $a$-col are $q_1 \in Q_2^{\,0}$ & $q_2 \in Q_1^0$

Entries corresponding to $q_0$ & $q_3$ under $a$-col are $q_5 \in Q_2^{\,0}$ & $q_6 \in Q_2^{\,0}$

(*iv*) $q_1$ **&** $q_7$ **:** Entries corresponding to $q_0$ & $q_7$ under *a*-col are $q_1 \in Q_2^0$ & $q_6 \in Q_2^0$

Entries corresponding to $q_0$ & $q_7$ under *b*-col are $\frac{q_5 \in Q_2 \ \& \ q_2 \in Q_1^0}{\text{Different}}$

(*v*) $q_0$ **&** $q_4$ **:** Entries corresponding to $q_0$ & $q_4$ under *a*-col are $q_1 \in Q_2^0$ & $q_7 \in Q_2^0$

Entries corresponding to $q_0$ & $q_4$ under *b*-col are $\frac{q_5 \in Q_2^0 \ \& \ q_5 \in Q_2^0}{\text{Same Set}}$

(*vi*) $q_1$ **&** $q_7$ **:** Entries corresponding to $q_0$ & $q_6$ under *a*-col are $q_1 \in Q_2^0$ & $q_5 \in Q_2^0$

Entries corresponding to $q_0$ & $q_6$ under *b*-col are $\frac{q_5 \in Q_2^0 \ \& \ q_4 \in Q_2^0}{\text{Same Set}}$

Therefore $Q_2^1 = \{q_1, q_4, q_6\}$ is a sub set in $\pi_1$

So $q_1$ is 1-equivalent so $q_0$ is not 1-equivalent to $q_3$, $q_5$ & $q_7$ also to $q_4$ & $q_6$.

**(B)** Now consider $q_1$ with each of the other $q_i$ ($i$ = 3, 5, 7) successding it *i.e.*, $q_3$, $q_5$, $q_7$ as $q_4$ & $q_6$ have been taken-in $Q_2'$ as in A.

(*i*) $q_1$ **&** $q_3$ **:** Entries corresponding to $q_1$ & $q_3$ under *a*-col are

$\frac{q_6 \in Q_2^0 \ \& \ q_2 \in Q_1^0}{\text{Different sets}}$

Entries corresponding to $q_1$ & $q_3$ under *b*-col are $\frac{q_2 \in Q_2^1 \ \& \ q_6 \in Q_2^0}{\text{Different}}$

(*ii*) $q_1$ **&** $q_5$ **:** Entries corresponding to $q_1$ & $q_5$ under *a*-col are $q_6 \in Q_2^0$ & $q_2 \in Q_1^0$

Entries corresponding to $q_1$ & $q_5$ under *b*-col are $q_2 \in Q_1^0$ & $q_6 \in Q_2^0$

(*iii*) $q_1$ **&** $q_7$ **:** Entries corresponding to $q_1$ & $q_7$ under *a*-col are $q_6 \in Q_2^0$ & $q_6 \in Q_2^{0d}$

Entries corresponding to $q_1$ & $q_7$ under *b*-col are $\frac{q_2 \in Q_1^0 \ \& \ q_2 \in Q_1^0}{\text{Same Set}}$

---

**Subset are $Q_2$ for *a*-col & $Q_1$ for b-col**

---

So $q_1$ is 1-equivalent to $q_7$. therefore $Q'_3 = \{q_1, q_7\}$ is also a subset in $\pi_1$ Now only $q_3$ & $q_5$ are left to be considered in $Q_2^0$.

**(C)** Consider $q_3$ with $q_5$ the only left over value

$q_3$ **&** $q_5$ **:** Entries corresponding to $q_3$ & $q_5$ under *a*-col are $q_2 \in Q_1^0$ & $q_2 \in Q_1^0$

Entries corresponding to $q_3$ & $q_5$ under *b*-col are $q_6 \in Q_2^0$ & $q_6 \in Q_0^2$

**SO $q_3$ is 1-equivalent to $q_5$**

Therefore $Q'_4 = \{q_3, q_5\}$

Hence

$$\pi_1 = \{\{q_2\}, \{q_0, q_4, q_6\}, \{q_1, q_7\}, \{q_3, q_5\}\}$$

Now we have to find $\pi_2$

$Q_1^2 = \{q_2\}$ is $\pi_2$ as it can not be partitioned further

**(D)** Consider $q_0$ with $q_4$ & $q_6$

(*i*) **$q_0$ & $q_4$ :** Entries corresponding to $q_0$ & $q_4$ under *a*-col are $q_1$ & $q_7$ lying in same equivalence class in $\pi_1$.

Entries corresponding to $q_0$ & $q_4$ under *b*-col are $q_5$ & $q_5$ lying in same equivalence class in $\pi_1$.

So, $q_0$ & $q_4$ are 2-equivalent.

Therefore $\{q_0, q_4\}$ is a subset of $\pi_2$ or $Q_2^2 = \{q_0, q_4\}$

(*ii*) **$q_0$ & $q_6$ :** Entries corresponding to $q_0$ & $q_6$ under *a*-col are $q_1$ & $q_6$ lying in different equivalence class in $\pi_1$.

Entries corresponding to $q_0$ & $q_6$ under *b*-col are $q_5$ & $q_4$ lying in different equivalence class in $\pi_1$. So $q_0$ & $q_6$ are not 2-equivalent.

Therefore $\{q_0, q_4, q_6\}$ in $\pi_1$ is partitioned into 2 classes $\{q_0, q_4\}$ & $\{q_6\}$ in $\pi_2$.

$q_1$ & $q_7$ are 2-equivlent *i.e.*, $Q_3^2 = \{q_1, q_7\}$

$q_3$ & $q_5$ are 2-equivlent *i.e.*, $Q_4^2 = \{q_3, q_5\}$

Hence $$\pi_2 = \{q_2\}, \{q_0, q_4\}, \{q_6\}, \{q_1, q_7\}, \{q_3, q_5\}\}$$

Again $q_0$ & $q_4$ are 2-equivalent

$q_1$ & $q_7$ are 2-equivalent

$q_3$ & $q_5$ are 2-equivalent

Hence $$\pi_3 = \{q_2\}, \{q_0, q_4\}, \{q_6\}, \{q_1, q_7\}, \{q_3, q_5\}\}$$

Then $\pi_3 = \pi_2$

$\pi_2$ gives the equivalence classes & the minimum state automation is

$M' = \{Q', \{a, b\}, \delta, \{q'_0, F'\})$

where $Q' = \{[q_2], [q_0, q_4], [q_6], [q_1, q_7], [q_3, q_5]\}$

$q'_0 = [q_0, q_4]$ as $q_0$ the initial state has been combined will $q_4$.

$F' = [q_2]$ & $\delta'$ is given below.

**Table 10**

| State | Σ | |
|---|---|---|
| | **a** | **b** |
| → $[q_0, q_4]$ | $[q_1, q_7]$ | $[q_3, q_5]$ |
| $[q_1, q_7]$ | $[q_6]$ | $[q_2]$ |
| $[q_2]$ | $[q_0, q_4]$ | $[q_2]$ |
| $[q_3, q_5]$ | $[q_2]$ | $[q_6]$ |
| $[q_6]$ | $[q_6]$ | $[q_0, q_4]$ |

Although corresponding $q_6$ under *b*-col in original table the state is $q_4$, but $q_4$ is now not a state. It has been maerged with $q_0$. So the state shall become $\{q_0, q_4\}$

Its transition diagram shown in Fig. 3.55

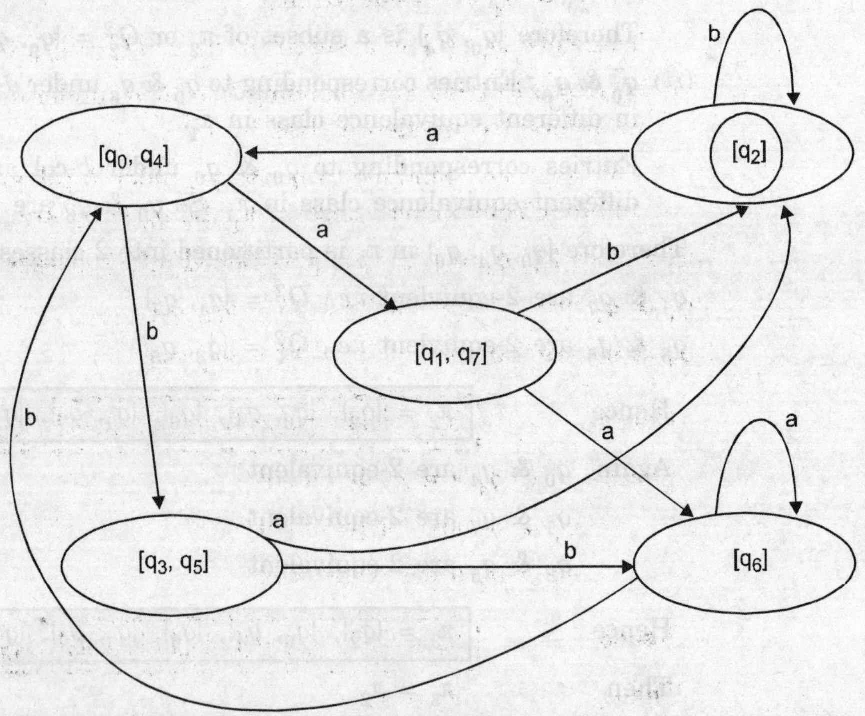


***Fig. 3.55***

## 3.12 EQUIVALENCE OF THE FINITE AUTOMATA

Two finite automata over Σ are equivalent if they accept the same strings over Σ. If they are not equivalent, then there must be some string w over Σ, such that one automaton reaches a final state on application of *w* (*i.e.*, recognize or accepts ω), while the other automaton reaches a non final state on application of ω (*i.e.*, does not recognize or accept *w*).

## Comparison Method (to test equivalence)

$M_1$ & $M_2$ are two FAs over $\Sigma$ (represented by diagram or otherwise) each consisting of $n$ input symbols say $a_1$, $a_2$, ..., $a_n$.

Construct a comparison table having $(n + 1)$ columns. Second, third......column shall correspond to first, second, ......input paths.

First row } First entry in the first column shall consist of the pair of initial states of $M_1$ & $M_2$ row *e.g.*, $q^1_0$ & $q^2_0$ ($q^1_0 \in M_1$ & $q^2_0 \in M_2$, both being initial states).

The first entry in second column ($a_1$ -col) shall consist of $a_1$-paths *i.e.*, that pair of states which are reached on application of input $a_1$ to the initial states $q^1_0$ & $q^2_0$.

The first entry is third column ($a_2$ – col) shall consist of $a_2$ – paths *i.e.*, that pair of states which are reached on application of input $a_2$ to the initial state $q^1_0$ & $q^2_0$.

This procedure is continued to the last column

Then we check all the pairs of states in this first row under each column.

**CHECK:** If any of the pair under any column is such that one element of the pair denotes the final state of $M_1$ (or $M_2$ and the other element of the same pair denotes the non final state of $M_2$ (or $M_1$), the construction is terminated and it is concluded that $M_1$ and $M_2$ are not equivalent.

If such a condition is not observed in the first row, we proceed to construct the second row as follows:

Construction Succeeding rows } The pairs of states in first row under second, third, ... of second & columns (*i.e.*, input columns) that are different from the first entry in the first column are entered as Succeeding rows succeeding entries under first column.

Corresponding to each such entry under first column, we find $a_1$- *paths*, $a_2$-paths, ... as explained earlier.

If any pair of entries (states) in any row under input column is different from all the entries under first column up to that row, then this pair is also entered as a succeeding entry under first column.

The check as explained earlier is applied at the end of row to decide whether to terminate the construction further ($M_1$ & $M_2$ being declared not equivalent) or to continue the construction of the table further.

In the latter case the construction is, continued up to that row in which no pair of states is different from all the pairs of states under first column up to that row and in this case we say that the two automata are equivalent.

**Example 3.43:** Test the equivalence of the following two deterministic finite automata $M_1$ and $M_2$ over $\{a, b\}$.

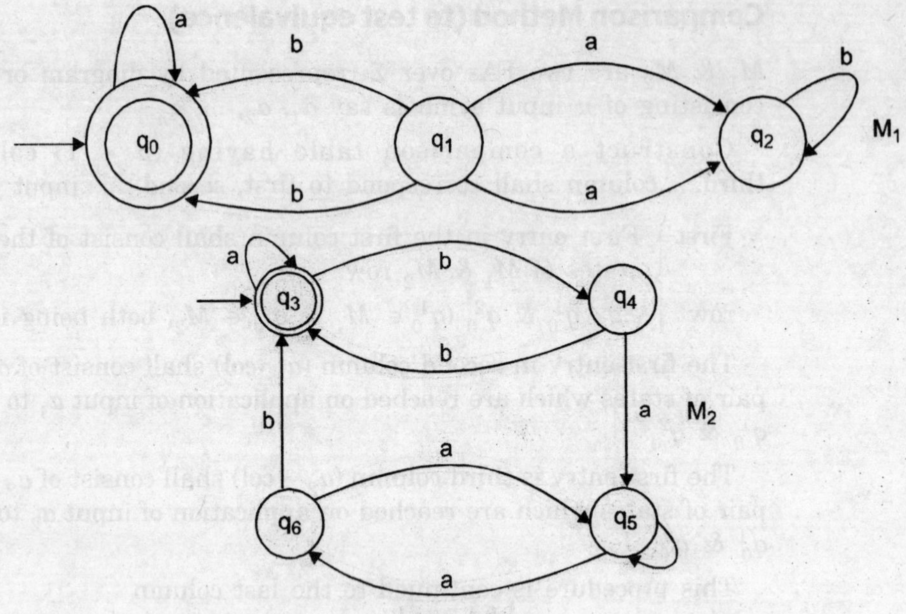


***Fig. 3.56***

**Solution:** Pair of initial states to be kept as first entry under first column is ($q_0$, $q_3$). Comparison table shall consist fo 3 columns in all as number of input symbols is 2. Input symbols are $a$ & $b$.

Ⓐ
Initial state $q_0$ of $M_1$ changes to $q_0$ on receiving input $a$
Initial state $q_3$ of $M_2$ changes to $q_3$ on receiving input $a$

Initial state $q_1$ of $M_1$ changes to $q_1$ on receiving input $b$
Initial state $q_4$ of $M_2$ changes to $q_4$ on receiving input $b$

**Check :** No pair of entry in this row contain one final state of $M_1$(or $M_2$) and one non-final state of $M_2$ (or $M_1$)

So proceed further.

Now in first row the entry different from those under col-1 upto row-1 is ($q_1$, $q_4$)

So the second entry under col-1 becomes ($q_1$, $q_4$) in second row. To find corresponding entries under $a$ & $b$ cols in second row we proved as in Ⓐ above.

State $q_1$ of $M_1$ changes to $q_2$ on receiving input $a$
State $q_4$ of $M_2$ changes to $q_5$ on receiving input $a$
Hence row-2 entry corresponding to ($q_2$, $q_5$) under $a$-col is ($q_2$, $q_5$)

State $q_1$ of $M_1$ changes to $q_0$ on receiving input $b$
State $q_4$ of $M_2$ changes to $q_3$ on receiving input $b$
under $b$-col is ($q_0$, $q_3$)

**Check :** It allows to proceed further.

In second row the entry different from all the entries under col-1 upto second row is $(q_2, q_5)$. So the third entry under col-1 becomes $(q_2, q_5)$ in third row.

To find corresponding entries in third row under $a$-col & $b$-col. (corresponding to entry $(q_2, q_5)$ under 1-col) we again proceed as in (A)

State $q_2$ of $M_1$ changes to $q_1$ on receiving input $a$
State $q_5$ of $M_2$ changes to $q_6$ on receiving input $a$
} Hence row-3 entry corresponding to $(q_1, q_6)$ under $a$-col is $(q_1, q_6)$

State $q_2$ of $M_1$ changes to $q_2$ on receiving input $b$
State $q_5$ of $M_2$ changes to $q_5$ on receiving input $b$
} under b-col is $(q_2, q_5)$

**Check:** Allows us to proved further.

In the third row, the entry different from all the entries under col-1 upto third row is $(q_1, q_6)$. So the fourth row (corresponding to entry $(q_1, q_6)$ under col-1) we again proceed as in (A)

State $q_1$ of $M_1$ changes to $q_2$ on receiving input $a$
State $q_6$ of $M_2$ changes to $q_5$ on receiving input $a$
} Hence row-4 entry corresponding to $(q_1, q_6)$ under $a$-col is $(q_1, q_5)$

State $q_1$ of $M_1$ changes to $q_0$ on receiving input $b$
State $q_6$ of $M_2$ changes to $q_3$ on receiving input $b$
} under b-col is $(q_0, q_3)$

**Check :** allows us to proceed further.

In the fourth row there is no entry different form all the entries under col-1 upto 4th row. Therefore we stop here & conclude that $M_1$ is equivalent to $M_2$.

**Table 11. Comparison table**

| col-1 $(q, q')$ | $a$-col $(q_a, q'_a)$ | $b$-col $(q_b, q'_b)$ |
|---|---|---|
| $(q_0, q_3)$ | $(q_0, q_3)$ | $(q_1, q_4)$ |
| $(q_1, q_4)$ | $(q_2, q_5)$ | $(q_0, q_3)$ |
| $(q_2, q_5)$ | $(q_1, q_6)$ | $(q_2, q_5)$ |
| $(q_1, q_6)$ | $(q_2, q_5)$ | $(q_0, q_3)$ |

As we do not have a pair $(q, q')$, where $q$ is a finial state & q' is a non final state (or vice verse) at every row, we proceed until all the elements in the second & third column are also in the first column. Therefore $M_1$ & $M_2$ are equivalent.

## 3.13 FINITE AUTOMATA WITH OUTPUT

The fnite automata is a collection of $(Q, \Sigma, \delta, q_0, F)$ where $Q$ is a set of states including $q_0$ as a start state. In *FA* after reading the input string if we get final state then the string is said to be ***'acceptable'***. If we do not get final state then it is said that stringis ***'rejected'***. That means there is noneed of output for the finite automata.

The 'accept' or 'reject' acts like 'yes' or 'no' output for the machine. But if there is a need for specifying the output other than yes or no then in such a case we require finite automata along with output.

---

An automaton that accepts input strings and translates then into output strings is called an automaton with outputs (or a sequential finite state machine, or a transducer)

---

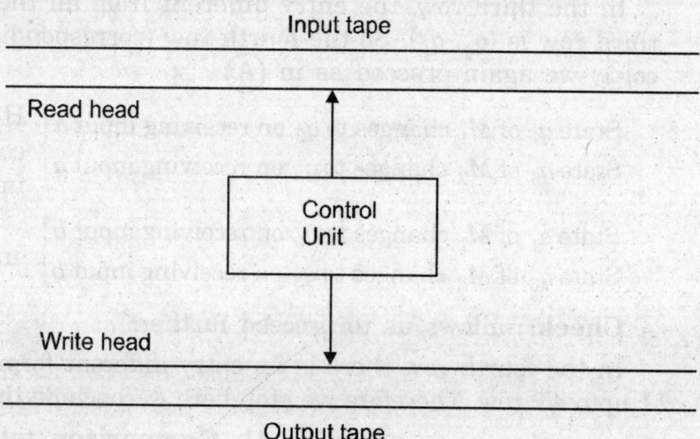


***Fig. 3.57***

This automaton is like a deterministic finite automaton except that the set of accepting states is replaced by an output set and an output function. The automaton with outputs can be used to model many kind of machines including vending machine, delay machines, binary adder etc.

There are two types of *FA* with output and those are –

(1) Moore Machine

(2) Mealy Machine

A finite automaton with output is defined in two different ways: First, a machine whose outputs are corresponding to their each state. Such type of machine is called ***Moore machine***. Second, machines whose outputs are corresponding to their input and state both. Such type of machine ins called ***Mealy machine***. If $P(t)$ be the output of these machine then

The output function of a Moore machine is defined as follows

$$P(t) = \lambda\ (q(t))$$

The output function of a Mealy machine is defined as follows

$$P(t) = \lambda\ (q(t).\ w(t))$$

Where $q(t)$ is a present state, $w(t)$ is a present input symbol and $\lambda$ is a output function.

These two machines can be defined mathematically as follows.

### 3.13.1 Moore Machine

A Moore machine $M$ consists of 6 tuples.

$$M = (Q, \Sigma, \Delta, \delta, \lambda, q_0)$$

where

1. $Q$ is a finite non empty set of states.
2. $\Sigma$ is a non empty set of input symbols
3. $\Delta$ is a output alphabet
4. $\delta$ is a transition system and $\delta \in Q \times \Sigma \rightarrow Q$
5. $\lambda$ is a output function and $\lambda \in Q \rightarrow Q$
6. $q_0$ is a initial state and $q_0 \in Q$.

Graphical representation of a Moore Machine is given below

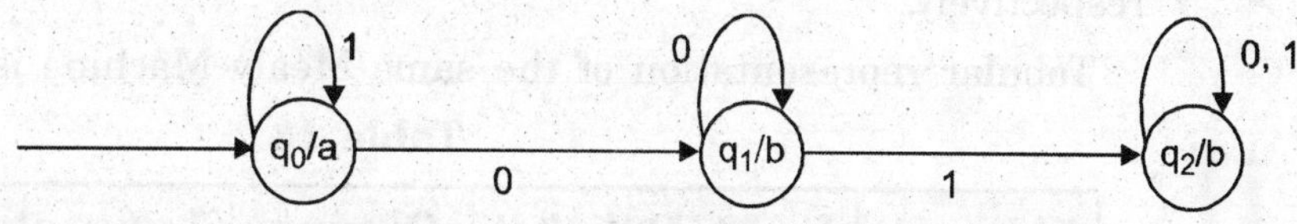


***Fig. 3.58***

Here the outputs are a and b corresponding to the non-final and final states respectively.

Tabular representation of the same Moore Machine is given below:

**Table 12**

| Current States | Input alphabet | | Outputs |
|---|---|---|---|
| | 0 | 1 | $\lambda$ |
| $q_0$ | $q_1$ | $q_0$ | $a$ |
| $q_1$ | $q_1$ | $q_2$ | $a$ |
| $q_2$ | $q_1$ | $q_2$ | $b$ |

If the length of input string is $n$ then the length of output string is $n + 1$.

## 3.13.2 Mealy Machine

A Mealy machine $M$ consists of 6 tuples.

$$M = (Q, \Sigma, \Delta, \delta. \lambda. q_0)$$

Where,

1. $Q$ is a finite non empty set of states.
2. $\Sigma$ is a non empty set of input symbols
3. $\Delta$ is a output alphabet
4. $\delta$ is a transition system and $\delta \in Q \times \Sigma \rightarrow Q$
5. $\lambda$ is a output function and $\lambda \in Q \times \Sigma \rightarrow Q$
6. $q_0$ is a initial state and $q_0 \in Q$.

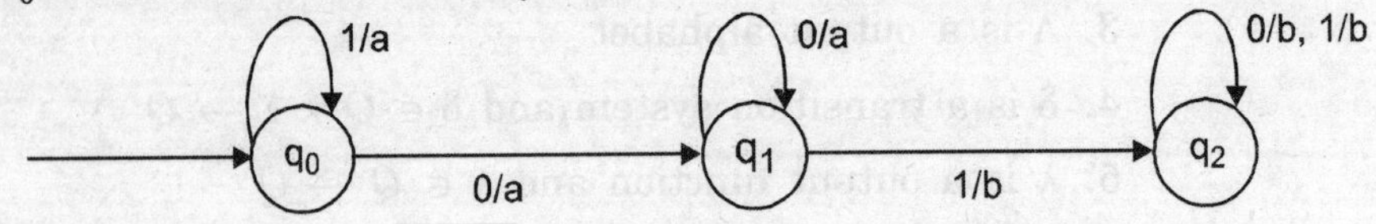


*Fig. 3.59*

Here the output are a and $b$ corresponding to the non-final and states respectively.

Tabular representation of the same Mealy Machine is as follows:

**Table 13**

| Current | Input alphabet | Outputs | Input alphabet | Outputs |
|---|---|---|---|---|
| States | 0 | $\lambda$ | 1 | $\lambda$ |
| $q_0$ | $q_1$ | $a$ | $q_0$ | $a$ |
| $q_1$ | $q_1$ | $a$ | $q_2$ | $b$ |
| $q_2$ | $q_2$ | $b$ | $q_2$ | $b$ |

If the length of input is $n$ then the length of output string is also $n$

**Example 3.44:** Design a Mealy machine to produce a I's complement of any binary string.

**Solution:** The transition digraph for a Mealy machine is shown below

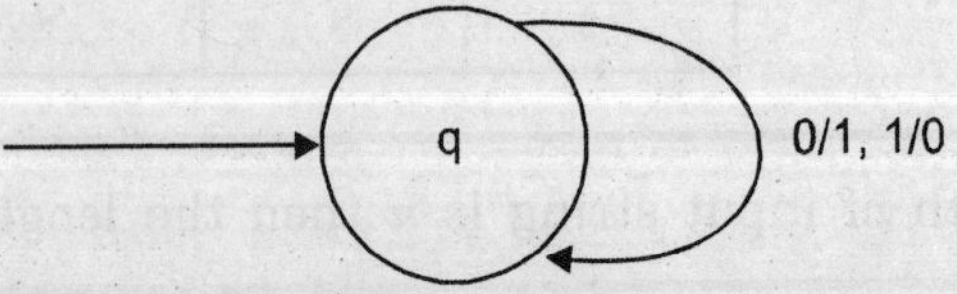


*Fig. 3.60*

**Example 3.45:** Design a Moore Machine to generate 1's complement of given binary number.

**Solution:** The generate 1's complement of given binary number the simple logic which we will apply is that if input is 0 then output will be 1 and if input is 1 then output will be 0. That means there are three state one-start state, second state is for taking 0's input and produces output as 1. Then third state is for taking 1's as input and producting output as 0.

Hence the Moore Machine will be,

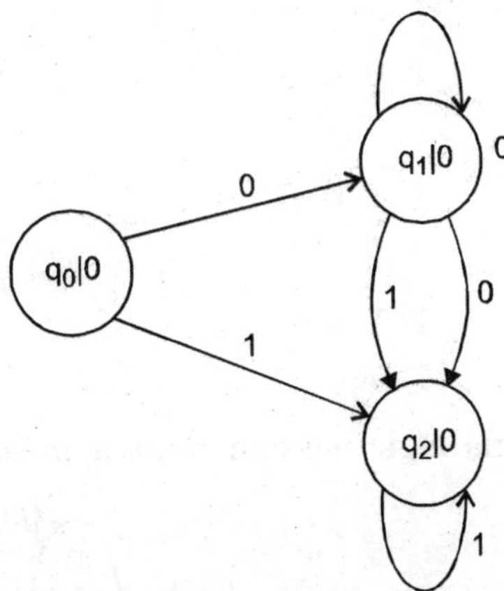


***Fig. 3.61***

The transition table can be draw as below

**Table 14**

| Current States | Input alphabet (δ) | | Outputs |
|---|---|---|---|
| | 0 | 1 | λ |
| $q_0$ | $q_1$ | $q_2$ | 0 |
| $q_1$ | $q_1$ | $q_2$ | 1 |
| $q_2$ | $q_1$ | $q_2$ | 0 |

Thus Moore Machine

$M = (Q, \Sigma, \Delta, \delta, \lambda, q_0)$ where

$a = \{q_0, q_1, q_2\}$

$\Sigma = \{0, 1\}$

$\Delta = \{0, 1\}$

The transition table shows the δ and λ functions

**Example 3.46:** Design a Moore Machine which will increse the given binary number by 1.

**Solution:** We will read the binary number for LSB one bit at a time. We will replace each 1 by 0 until we get first 0. Once we get first 0 we will replace it by 1 and then keep remaining bits as it is.

For example–

1 0 1 1
← read from LSB bit by bit

1 0 1 0
↑

1 0 0 0
↑

1 1 0 0
↑

1 1 0 0
↑

Using this logic we can built a mealy machine as follows –

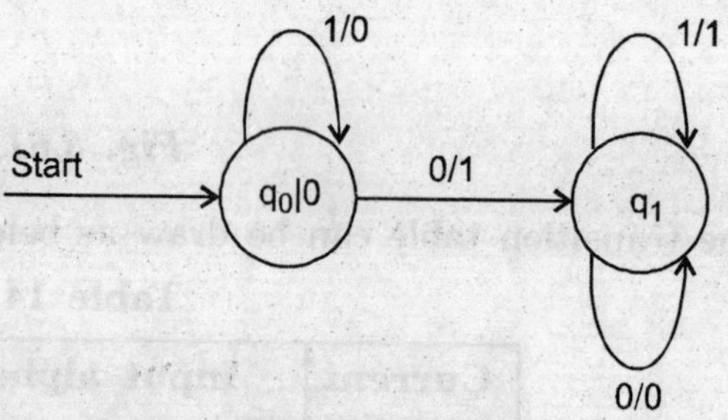


***Fig. 3.62***

**Example 3.47:** Construct a Moore Machine to determine residue mod 3 for binary number.

**Solution:** This Moore Machine is also called remainder 3 tester. In this machine we will get remander 0, remainder 1 and remainder 2. To interpret the given binary number in its decimal value we consider $n$ as a number if 0 is written after $n$ then its value becomes $2n$. If 1 is written after $n$ then it's value becomes $2n + 1$. For instance, if $n = 0$ then its decimal value is 0 then,

$$01 = 2n + 1 = 1 \times 0 + 1 = 1$$

$$011 = 2n + 1 = (1 \times 2) + 1 = 3$$

Consider $n = 1$ its decimal value is 1. After 1 if 0 comes then its value will be

$$10 = 2n = 2 \times 1 = 2$$

If 1 comes after 10 then its value becomes,

$$101 = 2n + 1 = (2 \times 2) + 1 = 5$$

With this logic we can construct a Moore Machine with 3 states. $q_0$ is the start state and is considered as remainder 0 state. $q_1$ is considered to be remainder 1 state and $q_2$ is considered as remainder 2 state.

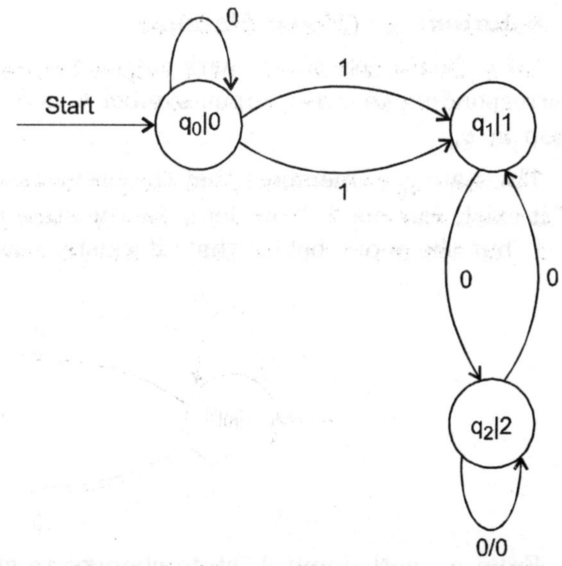


***Fig. 3.63***

**Example 3.48:** Design a Mealy Machine to find 2's complement of a given binary number.

**Solution:** For designing 2's complement of a binary number we assume that input is read from LSB to MSB. We will keep the binary number as it is until we read first 1. Keep that 1 as it is then change remaining 1's by 0's by 1's.

For example,

Let the binary number be

1011

←

read from LSB

Keep the first 1 from LSB as it is and toggle the remaining bits we will get 0101

Thus 2's complement of 1011 is 0101. The required Mealy Machine will be–

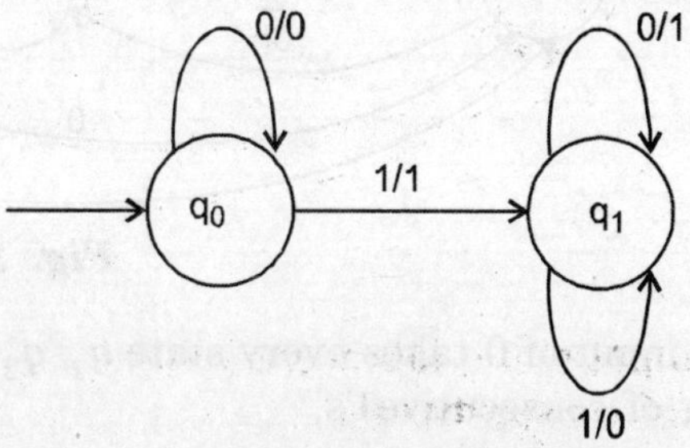


***Fig. 3.64***

**Example 3.49:** Design a transducer (Moore/Mealy Meachines) that gives a 1 as its output if and only if the least three digit are all 1's assume that $\Sigma = \{0, 1\}$

**Solution:** (*a*) (Moore Machine)

Let $q_0$ be the initial sets with output 0 since the output corresponding to every input symbol 0 is 0, we have a loop at $q_0$:

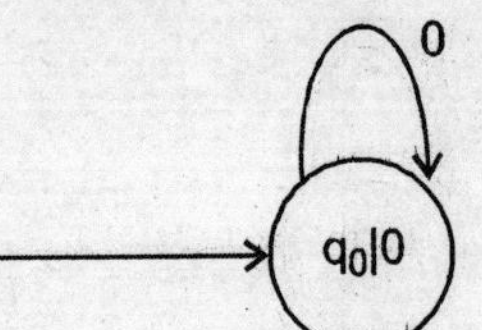


The state $q_0$ remembers that the previous input value, if it exist, was not 1. Now, let $q$, be the state that tells the previous input was *a* 1, but the input before that, if exists; was not 1, thus we have

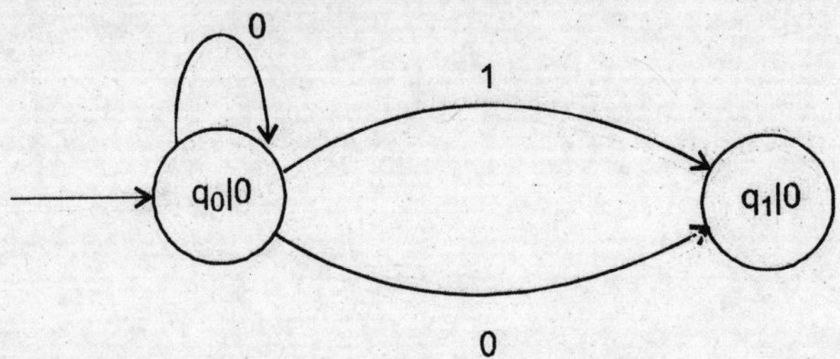


From $q_1$, with input 1, state changes to state $q_2$, where $q_2$, now, specifies that the previous two input were 1's *i.e.,*

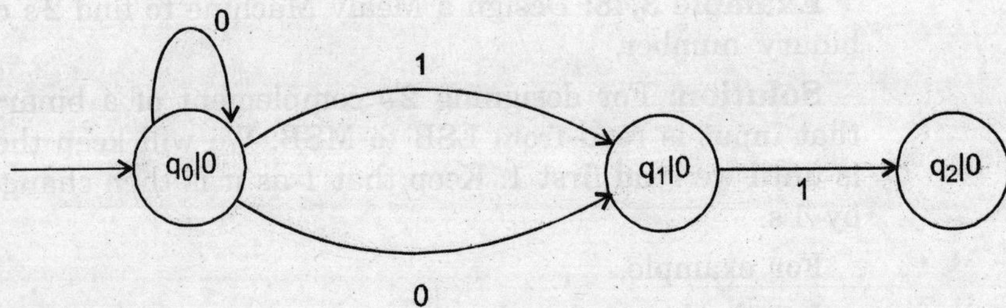


Now if the next input symbol is 1, it is the third consecutive ones, hence the corresponding output will be 1. More over, we will have a loop at this new state, $q_3$ corresponding to input 1. Thus we have

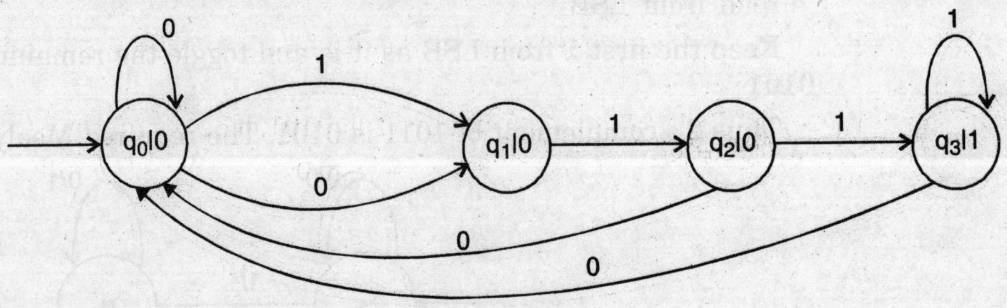


***Fig. 3.65***

An input of 0 takes every state $q_1$, $q_2$ and $q_3$ to $q_0$, since this breaks up any string of consecutive1's.

(*b*) (Mealy Machine)

There exists a Mealy Machine for the above problem with three states only, namely $q_0$, $q_1$, and $q_2$ as defined in part (*a*).

Since $q_2$ is the state that remember that the previous two input were 1's an input of 1 will takes $q_2$ to itself.

The transition diagram of this machine is as follow:

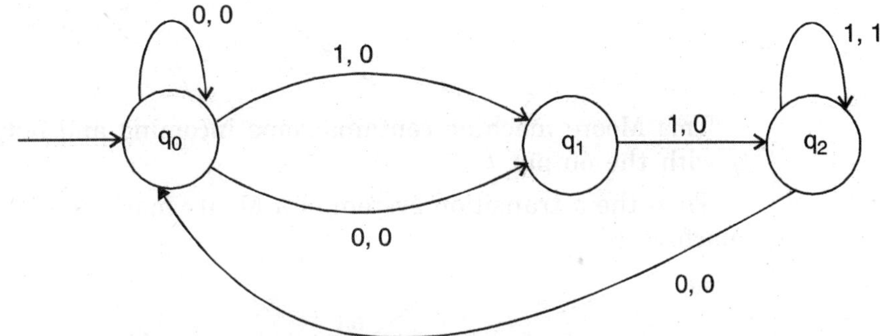


***Fig. 3.66 Mealy Meachine***

## 3.14 EQUIVALENCE OF MOORE MACHINE AND MEALY MACHINE

These two machines are equivalence to each other if they are producing the same output for any given input string. Even though if they are not equal, then you can generate equivalent Moore machine from Mealy machine or vice versa.

### 3.14.1 Conversion from Moore Machine to Mealy Machine

Let $M = (Q, \Sigma, \delta, \lambda, q_0)$ be a Moore Machine. The equivalent Mealy Machine can be represented by $M' = (Q, \Sigma, \delta, \lambda', q_0)$. The output function $\lambda'$ can be obtained as –

$$\lambda'(q, a) = \lambda(\delta(q, a))$$

**Theorem 1:** *If* $M_0 = (Q', \Sigma', \Delta', \delta', \lambda', q_0')$ *is a Moore machine then exists an equivalent Mealy machine* $M_e$.

**Proof:** Let $M_0 = (Q', \Sigma', \Delta', \delta', \lambda', q_0')$ be a Moore machine then you can define its eqivalent Mealy machine

$$M_e = (Q', \Sigma', \Delta', \delta', \lambda', q_0') \text{ where}$$

$$Q', = Q,$$

$$\Sigma' = \Sigma,$$

$$\Delta' = \Delta,$$

$$q_0' = q_0$$

and Δ' & Δ', are defined as follows

Let us consider a transition system of a Moore machine in the form of

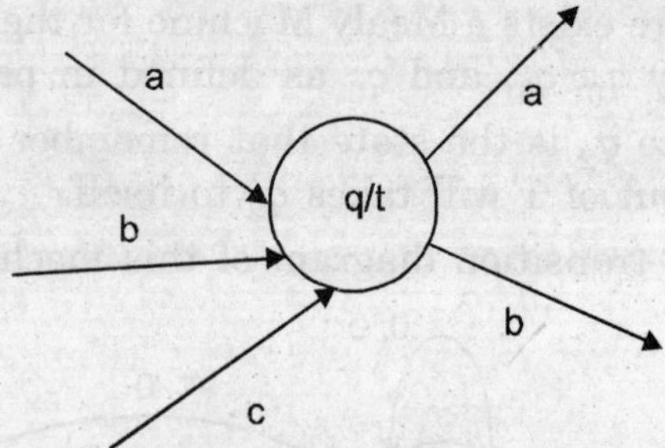


This Moore machine contains some incoming and outgoing edges on state $q$ with the output $t$.

Then the a transition system of a Mealy machine equivalent to this Moore machine is

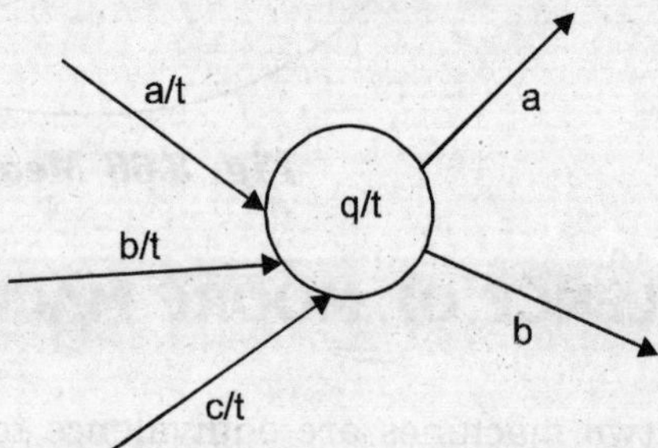


Assign output of a state $q$ to all incoming edges on state $q$, which is equivalent to a Mealy machine:

Repeat this procedure of all states of Moore machine and the resultant machine is called a Mealy machine.

**Example 3.50:** Convert the following Moore machine into its equivalent Mealy machine

***Fig. 3.67***

**Solution:** In the given Moore machine, three states $q_0$, $q_1$ and $q_2$ are given whose corresponding outputs are, $a_1$ $a$ and $b$ respectively. The incoming edge on state $q_0$ is 1 so 1 becomes as $a$, 1/$a$, similarly the incoming edges on state $q_1$ are 0 from state $q_0$ and again 0 from state $q_1$ so both zero becomes as a 0/$a$ and similarly the incoming edges on state $q_2$ are 1 from state $q_1$, 0 from state $q_2$ and 1 from state $q_2$, so 1, 0 and 1 becomes as a 1/$b$ 0/$b$ and 1/ $b$. All these are shown in below

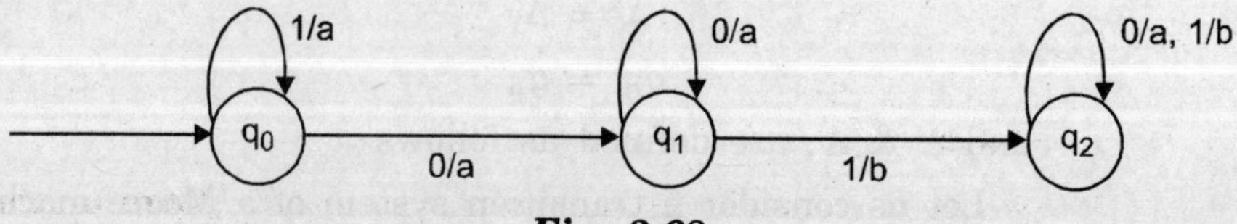


***Fig. 3.68***

Alternatively a tabular method for the above mentioned problem is as follows.

A tabular representation of a above Moore Machine is shown below

**Table 14**

| Current States | Input alphabet 0 | 1 | Outputs λ |
|---|---|---|---|
| $q_0$ | $q_1$ | $q_0$ | $a$ |
| $q_1$ | $q_1$ | $q_2$ | $a$ |
| $q_2$ | $q_2$ | $q_2$ | $b$ |

The outputs of the states $q_0$, $q_1$ and $q_2$ are $a$, $a$ and $b$ respectively. In a mealy machine the next state is similar to a Moore machine for all state and inputs. So, assign output of a Mealy machine for all inputs corresponding to their next state. For example, the next state of a state $q_0$ is $q_1$ on input symbol 0, so the output of state $q_0$ on input symbol 0 is a because a is an output of state $q_1$ in Moore machine.

A Mealy machine equivalent to given Moore machine is shown below

**Table 12**

| Current States | Input alphabet 0 | Outputs λ | Input alphabet 1 | Outputs λ |
|---|---|---|---|---|
| $q_0$ | $q_1$ | $a$ | $q_0$ | $a$ |
| $q_1$ | $q_1$ | $a$ | $q_2$ | $b$ |
| $q_2$ | $q_2$ | $b$ | $q_2$ | $b$ |

**Example 3.50:** Convert the following Moore machine into its eqivalent Mealy machine

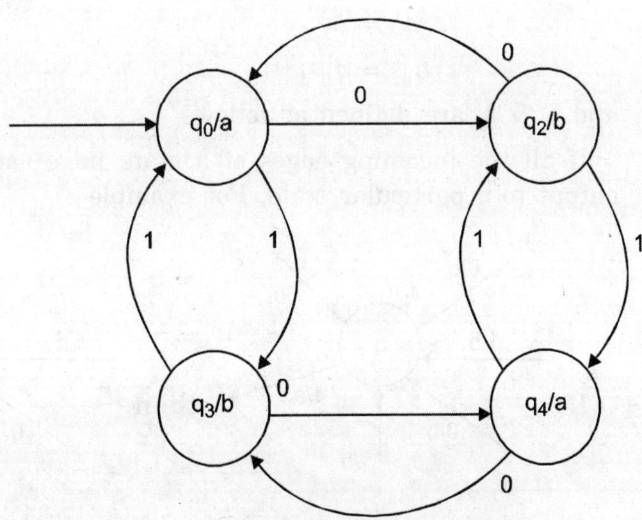


***Fig. 3.69***

**Solution:** A Mealy machine equivalent to given Moore machine is shown below

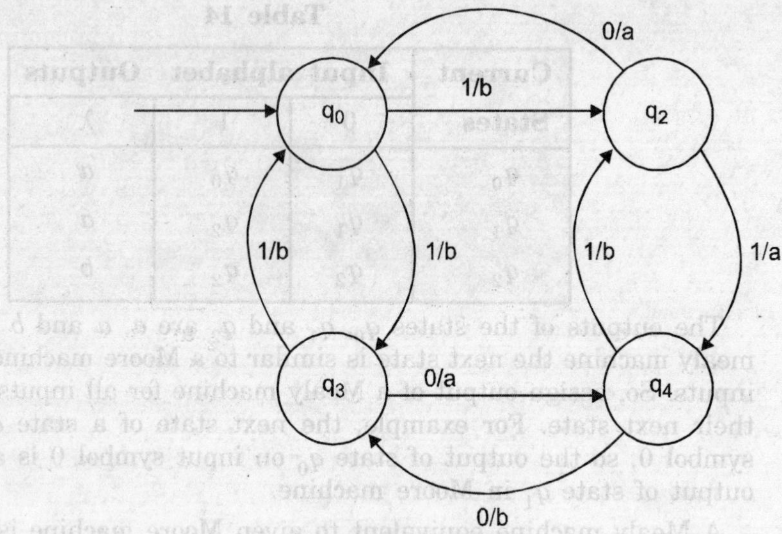


***Fig. 3.70***

## 3.14.2 Conversion from Mealy Machine to Moore Machine

**Theorem 2:** *If $M_e = (Q, \Sigma, \Delta, \delta, \lambda, q_0)$ is a Mealy machine then there exists a eqivalent Moore machine $M_0$.*

**Proof:** Let $M_e = (Q, \Sigma, \Delta, \delta, \lambda, q_0)$ be a Mealy machine then you can define its eqivalent Moore machine

$$M_0 = (Q', \Sigma', \Delta', \delta', \lambda', q_0') \text{ where}$$
$$\Sigma' = \Sigma,$$
$$\Delta' = \Delta,$$
$$q_0' = q_0$$

and δ' & λ' are defined as follows

If all the incoming edges of a state have same output then assign that output to a particular state. For example

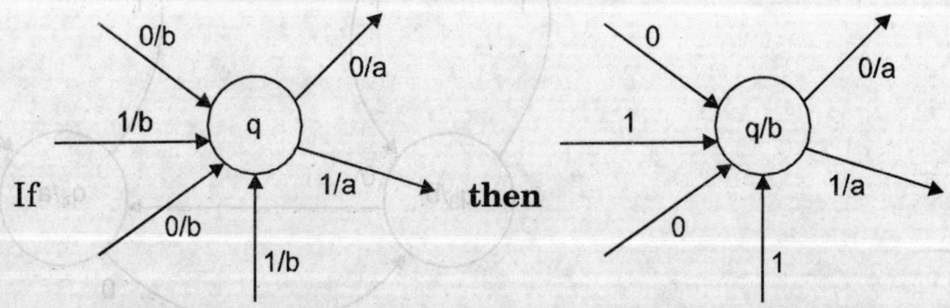

If the incoming edges of a state have different outputs the factorize that state corresponding to the different outputs. For example

A Mealy machine with different outputs on their incoming edges to state $q$ is given below:

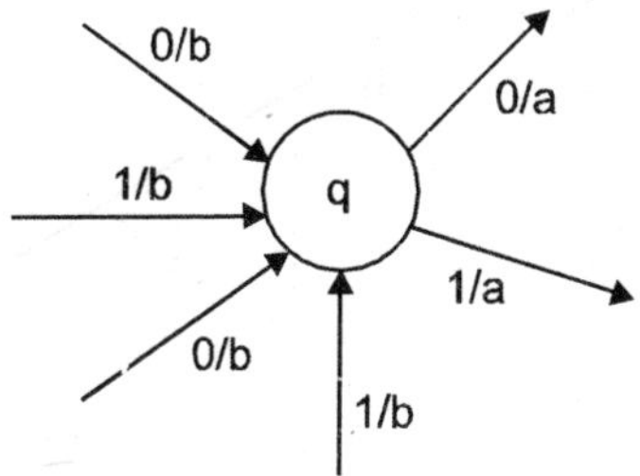


Then the transition system of a Moore machine equivalent to this machine is

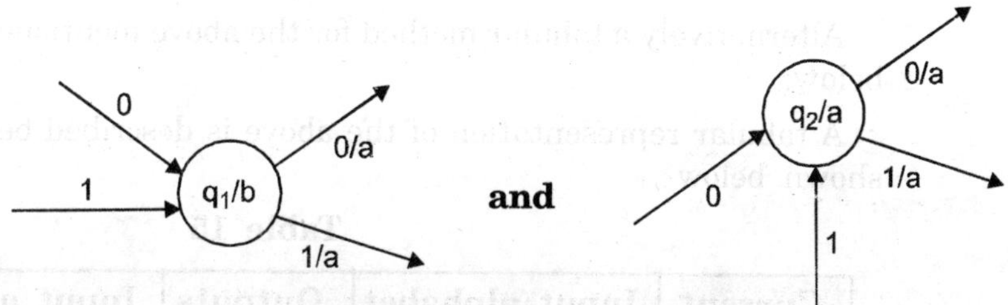


and $Q'$ is the total number of states of Moore machine

Repeat this procedure for all incoming edges of all states of Mealy machine and the resultant machine is called a Moore machine.

**Example 3.52:** Convert the following Mealy machine into its equivalent Moore machine

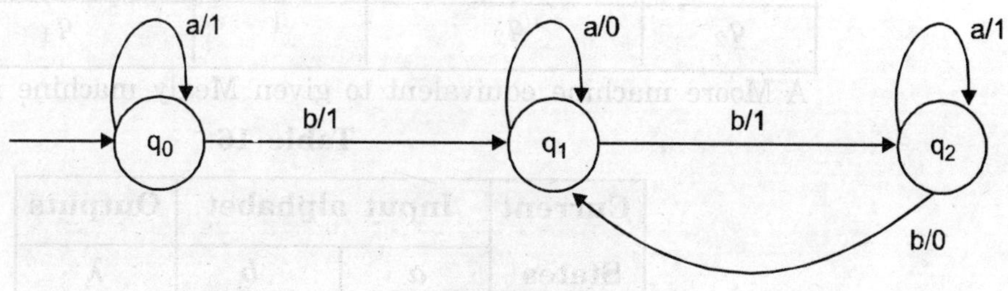


***Fig. 3.71***

**Solution:** In the given Mealy machine, three states $q_0$, $q_1$ and $q_2$ are given. On state $q_0$ there is only one output symbol corresponding to the incoming edge *i.e.*, 1. Similarly on state $q_2$ there is only one output symbol corresponding to the two incoming edges *i.e.*, again 1. But on state $q_1$, there are two output symbols corresponding to their two incoming edges. One is 0 and second is 1. So, you break the state $q_1$ into two parts corresponding to their outputs according to procedure explained above. Let us consider these two states are $q_{10}$ and $q_{11}$ corresponding to the output 0 and 1 respectively. All these are shown in below.

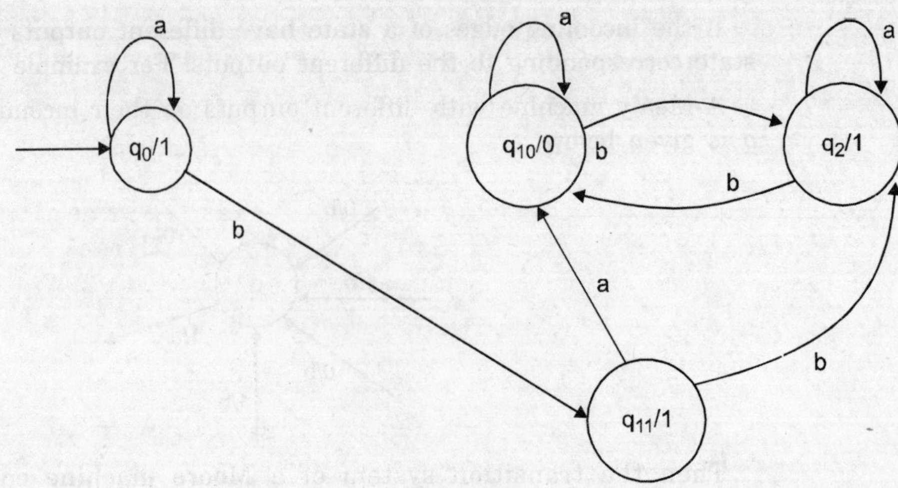


*Fig. 3.72*

Alternatively a tabular method for the above mentioned problem is described below:

A tabular representation of the above is described below Mealy Machine is shown below

**Table 15**

| Current States | Input alphabet $a$ | Outputs $\lambda$ | Input alphabet $b$ | Outputs $\lambda$ |
|---|---|---|---|---|
| $q_0$ | $q_0$ | 1 | $q_1$ | 1 |
| $q_1$ | $q_1$ | 0 | $q_2$ | 1 |
| $q_2$ | $q_2$ | 1 | $q_1$ | 0 |

A Moore machine equivalent to given Mealy machine is shown below.

**Table 16**

| Current States | Input alphabet $a$ | Input alphabet $b$ | Outputs $\lambda$ |
|---|---|---|---|
| $q_0$ | $q_0$ | $q_{11}$ | 1 |
| $q_{10}$ | $q_{10}$ | $q_2$ | 0 |
| $q_{11}$ | $q_{10}$ | $q_2$ | 1 |
| $q_2$ | $q_2$ | $q_{10}$ | 1 |

**Example 3.53:** Convert the following Mealy machine into its equivalent Moore machine

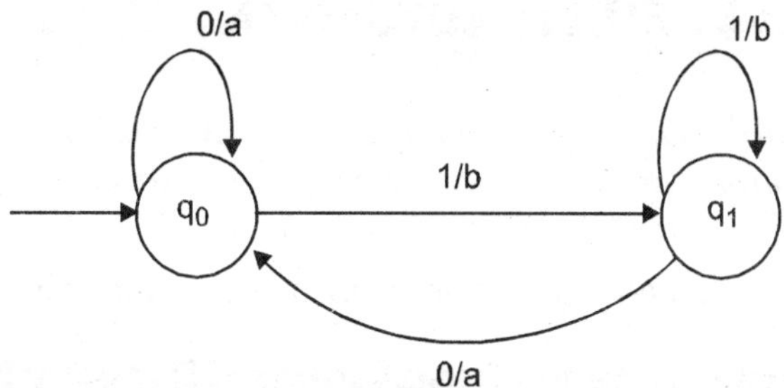


***Fig. 3.73***

**Solution:** A Moore machine equivalent to given Mealy machine is shown below

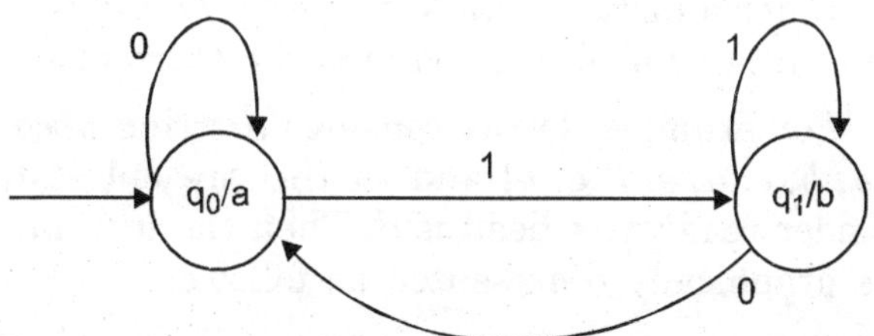


***Fig. 3.74***

Alternatively a tabular method for the above mentioned problem is also given below:

A tabular representation of the above Mealy Machine is shown below

**Table 18**

| **Current States** | **Input alphabet** 0 | **Outputs** λ | **Input alphabet** 1 | **Outputs** λ |
|---|---|---|---|---|
| $q_0$ | $q_0$ | 1 | $q_1$ | 1 |
| $q_0$ | $q_0$ | $a$ | $q_1$ | $b$ |
| $q_1$ | $q_0$ | 0 | $q_1$ | 1 |

A Moore machine equivalent to given Mealy machine is shown below

**Table 19**

| **Current States** | **Input alphabet** 0 | 1 | **Outputs** λ |
|---|---|---|---|
| $q_0$ | $q_0$ | $q_1$ | $a$ |
| $q_1$ | $q_0$ | $q_1$ | $b$ |

## 3.15 TWO-WAY FINITE AUTOMATA

Two way finite automata is a finite automata in which read/ write head fo a transition system will move in both direction (i.e., left to right or right to left) but in one direction at a time.

It is defined in the form of deterministic and non-deterministic both.

### Instantaneous Descriptions (ID) Using Move Relation

An Instantaneous Descriptions (ID) of Two-way Deterministic Finite Automation is the form of string *xyz*, where *x* is the sub-string of input string, *y* is the present state of Two-way

Deterministic Finite Automation *M* and *z* is also a sub-string of input string and first symbol of *z* contains the Current symbol of Read/Write (R/W) head,

For example, let us consider a string $abcq_2defgh$ over input alphabet $\Sigma = \{a, b, c, d, e, f, g, h\}$ and let the' present state be $q_2$ and the present symbol under read/write head is *d*. Then the instantaneous description of this string is graphically represented as follows:

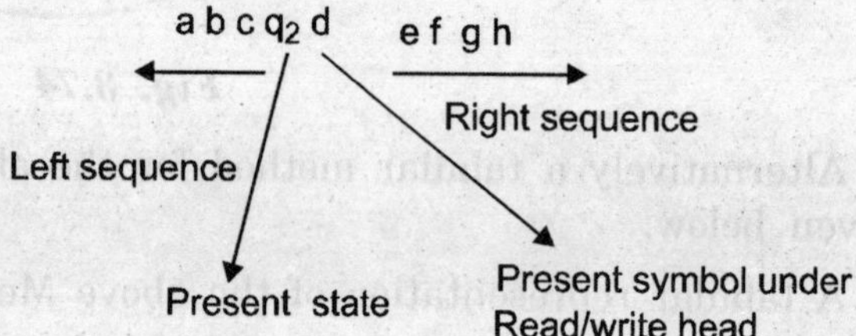


### Moves in a Two-Way Deterministic Finite Automation

Moves in a Two-way Deterministic Finite Automation occur under the following two rules:

(*i*) If the transition function $\delta(q, q_i) = (q, R)$ in the input string

$$a_1\ a_2\ a_3 \ldots\ldots\ a_{i-1}\ a_i\ a_{i+1}\ a_{i+2} \ldots\ldots\ a_n$$

and the present state is *q* and the present symbol under read/write head is $a_i$. Then the instantaneous description before processing $a_i$ is

$$a_1\ a_2\ a_3 \ldots\ldots a_{i-1}\ q_1\ a_i\ a_{i+1}\ a_{i+2} \ldots\ldots a_n$$

and after processing $a_i$ is

$$a_1\ a_2\ a_3 \ldots\ldots a_{i-1}\ b\ q_i\ a_{i+1}\ a_{i+2} \ldots\ldots a_n$$

(*ii*) If the transition function $\delta(q, q_i) = (q_1, L)$ in the input string

$$a_1\ a_2\ a_3 \ldots\ldots a_{i-1}\ a_i\ a_{i+1}\ a_{i+2} \ldots\ldots a_n$$

and the present state is *q* and the present symbol under read/write head is $a_i$. Then the instantaneous description before processing $a_i$ is

$$a_1\ a_2\ a_3 \ldots\ldots a_{i-1}\ q\ a_i\ a_{i+1}\ a_{i+2} \ldots\ldots a_n$$

and after processing $a_i$ is

$$a_1\ a_2\ a_3 \ldots\ldots a_{i-2}\ q_1\ a_{i+1}\ b\ a_{i+1} \ldots\ldots a_n$$

## Acceptability of a Language (or string) by a Two-Way Deterministic Finite Automaton

A language (string) $w$ is accepted by a two-way finite automation $M = (Q, \Sigma, \delta, q_0, F)$ if $\phi\ (q_0, w) = q$ for some $q \in F$.

**Example 3.54:** Consider the following 2DFA machine $M = (\{q_0, q_1, q_2\}, \{0,1\}, \delta, q_0, \{q_1\})$ where a transition graph is shown below

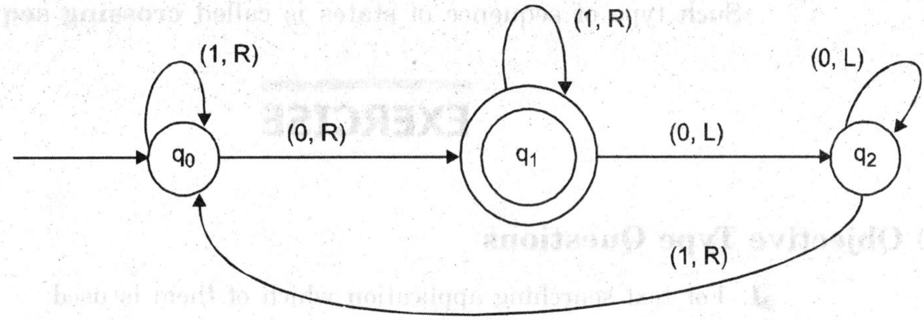


***Fig. 3.75***

Check if the string 010110 is accepted by 2DFA. Also find the sequence of states.

**Solution:** The Instantaneous Descriptions (ID) of a given input and its moves are represented as follows

$q_0 010110$

$0 q_{11} 0110$

$01 q_1 0110$

$0 q_2 10110$

$01 q_0 0110$

$010 q_1 110$

$0101 q_1 10$

$01011 q_1 0$

$0101 q_2 10$

$01011 q_0 0$

$010110 q_1 \in$

$q_1 \in F$

Hence the string is accepted by 2DFA machine.

The sequence of states corresponding to the input symbol is given by

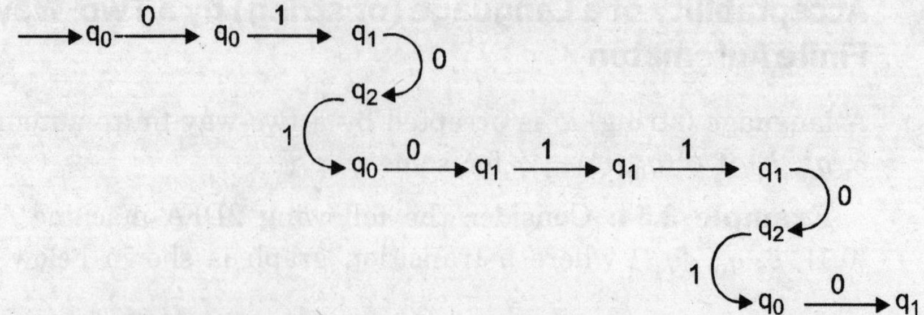


Such type of sequence of states is called **crossing sequence.**

# EXERCISE

## (A) Objective Type Questions

**1.** For text searching application which of them is used:

(*a*) nfa (*b*) dfa

(*c*) pda (*d*) npda

**2.** Consider the following two finite state machine in Fig.

(*a*) Both are equivalent

(*b*) The second finite state machine accepts e-only

(*c*) The first finite state machine accepts nothing

(*d*) none of the above

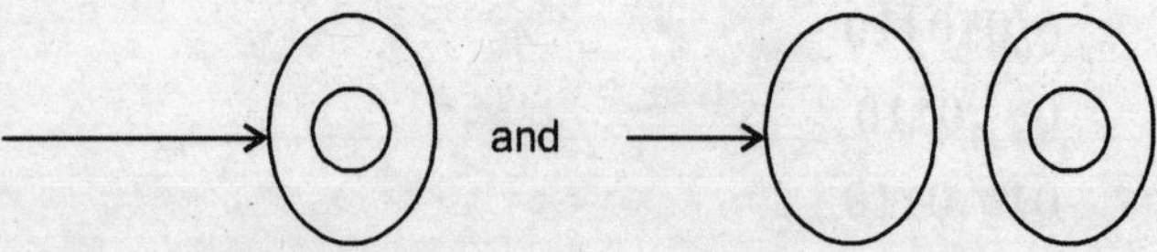


**3.** The reconizable property of dfa and ndfa

(*a*) May be different (*b*) Must be different

(*c*) Must be same (*d*) None of the above

**4.** Given an arbitary non-deterministic finite automation (nfa) with $N$ states, the maximum number of states is an equivalent minimized dfa is at least

(*a*) $N^2$ (*b*) $2^N$

(*c*) $2^N$ (*d*) $N!$

**5.** Choose the correct statements

(*a*) Moore and Mealy Machines are finite state machines with output capability

(*b*) Any given Moore Machine has an equivalent Mealy Machine

(*c*) Any given Mealy Machine has an equivalent Moore Machine

(*d*) All

**6.** The major difference between a Moore and Mealy Machine is

(*a*) Output of Moore depands on present state and input

(*b*) Output of Moore depands on state only

(*c*) Output of Moore depands on output only
(*d*) None

**7.** Choose the correct statement
(*a*) A Mealy Machine generates no language as such
(*b*) A Moore Machine genreates no language as such
(*c*) A Mealy Machine has no terminal state
(*d*) All

**8.** Choose the correct statement
(*a*) A Mealy Machine generates no language as such
(*b*) A Moore Machine generates no language as such
(*c*) A Mealy Machine has no terminal state
(*d*) All

**9.** The automata in which the output depends only on the status of the machine is called:
(*a*) Mealy Machine (*b*) Any finite automata
(*c*) Moore Machine (*d*) Both (*a*) & (*b*)

**10.** Moore Machine is
(*a*) Automaton in which the output depends only on the states
(*b*) Automaton in which the output depends only on the input
(*c*) Automaton in which the output depends only on the state and the input.
(*d*) None of the above

**11.** The finite state machine in Fig. is a
(*a*) Mealy Machine (*b*) Moore Machine
(*c*) Kleene Machine (*d*) none of the above

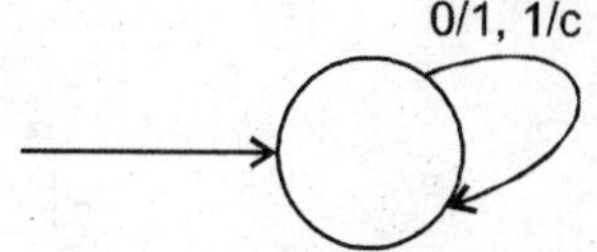


## ANSWERS

| | | | | |
|---|---|---|---|---|
| **1.** (*a*) | **2.** (*a*) | **3.** (*a*) | **4.** (*b*) | **5.** (*d*) |
| **6.** (*b*) | **7.** (*c*) | **8.** (*c*) | **9.** (*c*) | **10.** (*a*) |
| **11.** (*a*) | | | | |

## (B) Problems

**1.** Which of the following strings are accepted by the DFA machine M whose transition diagram is shown in Fig. 2.1

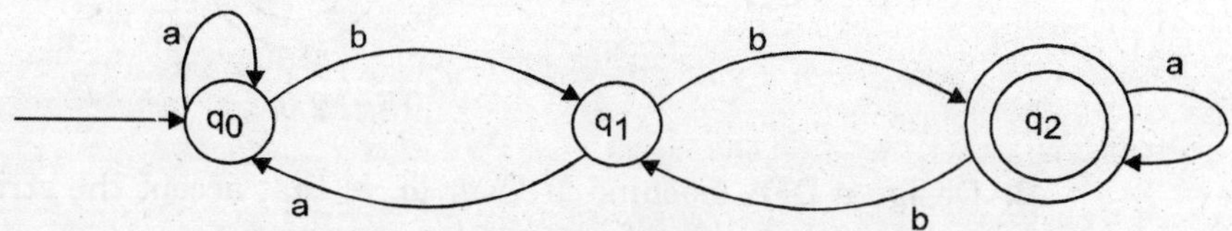


***Fig. 2.1***

(a) aaab (b) abaab

(c) aaaaba (d) ababbaa

(e) bbbb (f) bbbabb

(g) aaaababb (h) aaaaaa

(i) bbbabb

**2.** For the transition diagram M given in Fig. 1, find the sequence of states for the following inputs.

(a) aaaaabaaa (b) baaabb

(c) bbbbbb (d) bbaaabb

(e) aabbaabb

**3.** Design a DFA machine $M$ for the following language

(a) $L = \{ab^4wb^3 : w \in \{a, b\}^*\}$

(b) $L = \{awa : w \in \{a, b\}^*\}$

(c) $L = \{bw_1abw_2 : w_1, w_2 \in \{a, b\}^*\}$

(d) $L = \{w : |w| \bmod 3 = 0, w \in \{a, b\}^*\}$

(e) $L = \{w : |w| \bmod 3\ w : |w| \bmod 3 \neq 0, w \in \{a, b\}^*\}$

(f) $L = \{a^nb^m : n \geq 1, m \geq 2\}$

(g) $L = \{a^nb : n \geq 0\} \cup \{b^n a : n \geq 1\}$

(h) $L = \{a^n : n \geq 0, \neq 3\}$

**4.** Find all set of strings of DFA machine M whose transition diagram is shown in Fig. 2.2

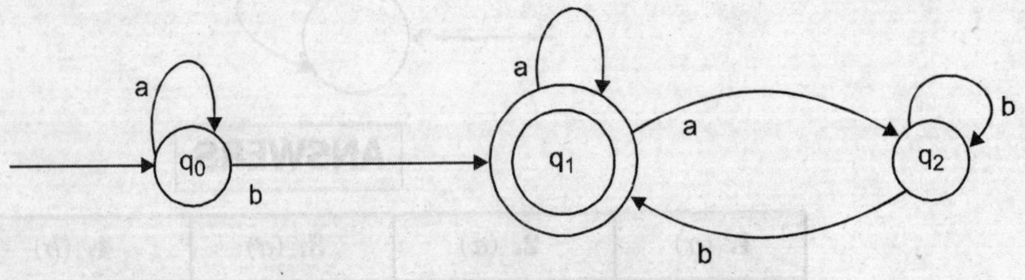


***Fig. 2.2***

**5.** Find a language $L$ accepted by the automation in the given Fig. 2.3 Also design a DFA accepts $L^2$.

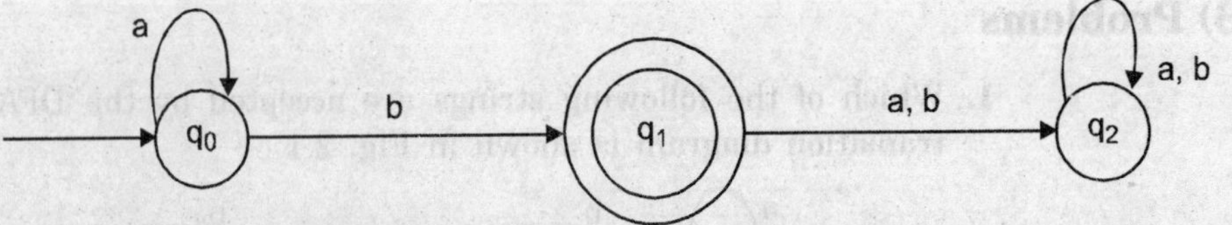


***Fig. 2.3***

**6.** Design a DFA machine $M$ Over $\{a, b\}$ that accept the strings in which the left most symbol differ from right most one.

7. Design a DFA machine over input alphabet $\Sigma = \{a, c, m, r, t\}$ that accept the strings mat, rat or cat.
8. Design a DFA with exactly six states that accepts the same language as the DFA in Fig. 2.4

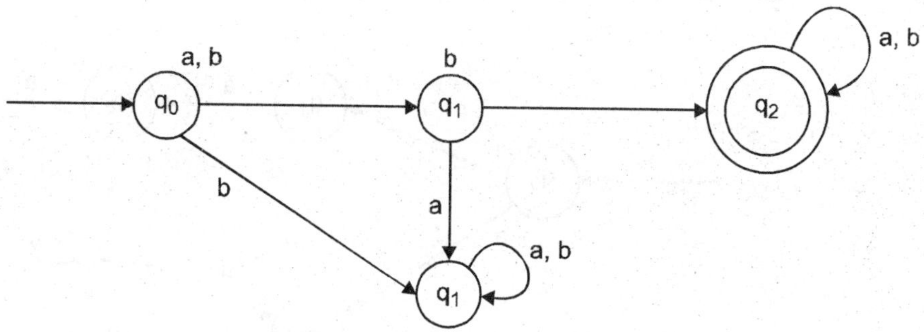


***Fig. 2.4***

9. Find the language accepted by the automata given in Fig. 2.5. If we change state $q_2$ in a non final state and $q_0$ & $q_1$ in final states, then what language is accepted by this machine

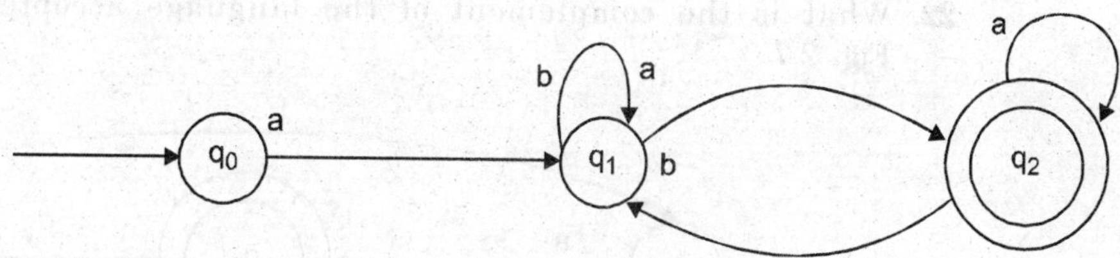


***Fig. 2.5***

10. Find a DFA that accepts only the strings *baa, ab* and *abb* and no other string longer or shorter over input symbol $\Sigma = \{a, b\}$.
11. Find a DFA that accepts only those strings that have more than four letter over input symbol $\Sigma = \{a, b\}$.
12. Find a DFA that accepts only those strings that have fewar than four letters over input symbol $\Sigma = \{a, b\}$.
13. Find a DFA that accepts only those strings with exactly four letters over input symbol $\Sigma = \{a, b\}$.
14. Find a DFA that accepts only, those strings that do not end with *ba* over input symbol $\Sigma = \{a, b\}$.
15. Find a DFA that accepts only those strings that begin and with double letters over input symbol $\Sigma = \{a, b\}$.
16. Find a DFA that accepts only those strings that have even number of sub strings *ab* over input symbol $\Sigma = \{a, b\}$.
17. Find a DFA that accepts all strings that have even length that is not divisible by 6 over input symbol $\Sigma = \{a, b\}$.

**18.** Find a NFA that accepts the language $L = (aa^* (a + b))$

**19.** Find a NFA that accepts $L(r)$ where, $r = 01^* + 01$.

**20.** Find a NFA that accepts $L = (ab^* aa + bba^* ab)$

**21.** Find a DFA that accepts language defined by the NFA in Fig. 2.6

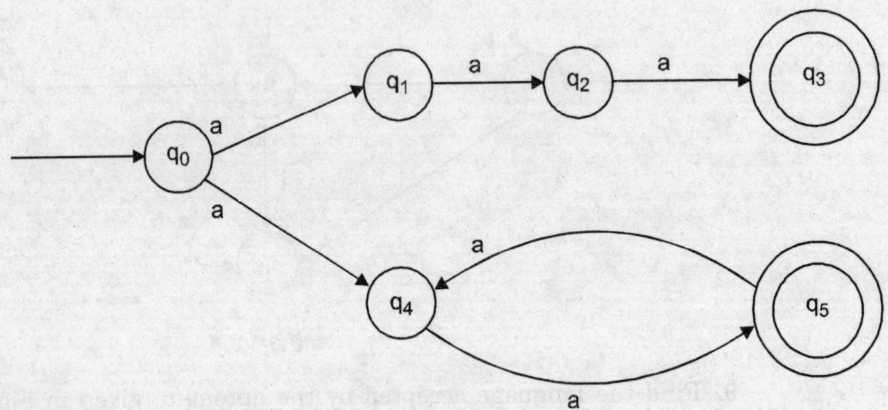


***Fig. 2.6***

**22.** What is the complement of the language accepted by the NFA in Fig. 2.7

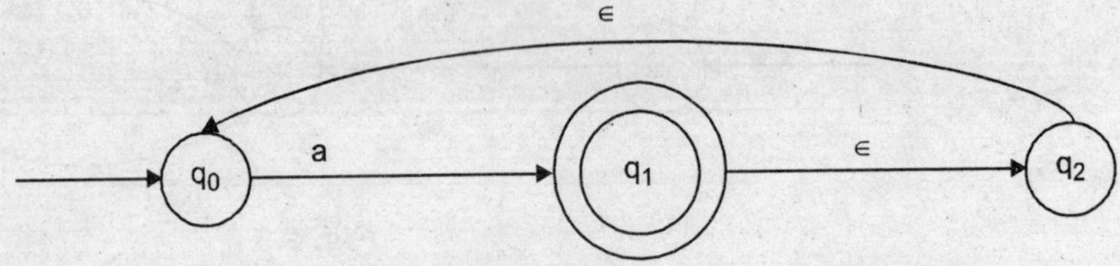


***Fig. 2.7***

□□□

C H A P T E R

# 4

# REGULAR EXPRESSIONS AND REGULARGRAMMAR

## 4.1 INTRODUCTION

We have already defined the finite automata in preveious chapter. Now we switch our attention from machine like description of language to an algebraic description: "the regular expression."

We will find that, regular expressions can define exactly the same languages that the various forms of automata describe: the regular languages.

We will answer to the question 'whether every formal language is regular or not'? And in the last we will describe another important feature of the theory of computation namely, regular grammar.

## 4.2 REGULAR EXPRESSION (R.E.)

Regular expressions are used to represent certain sets of strings in algebraic fashion. A formal recursive definition of regular expression over Σ is as follows

1. ∈ and ∅ are regular expression
2. Any terminal symbol of input alphabet S is a regular expression. It is denoted by $\{a\}$
3. If $R_1$ and $R_2$ are regular expression then
   (*a*) The union $R_1$ and $R_2$ is also a regular expression. It is denoted by $R_1 + R_2$
   (*b*) The concatenation of $R_1$ and $R_2$ is also a regular expression. It is denoted by $R_1 R_2$
4. The Kleen star (iteration) of a regular expression *R*, is also a regular expression. It is written as $R^*$.
5. If *R* is a regular expression, then (*R*) is also a regular expression,
6. Expression obtained recursively by application of rules 1 – 5 given above once or several times are also regular expression.

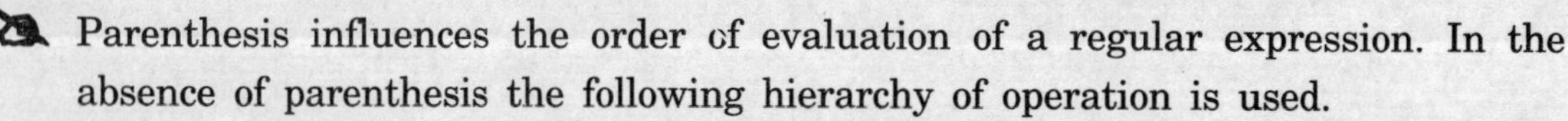

Parenthesis influences the order of evaluation of a regular expression. In the absence of parenthesis the following hierarchy of operation is used.

1. Iteration 2. Concatenation 3. Union

**Example 4.1:** Find the regular over $\Sigma = \{a, b\}$ such that all strings have at least one pair of consecutive *a's*.

**Solution:** Every string contain at least one *aa* but what comes before and what comes after is completely arbitrary. An arbitrary string on $\{a, b\}$ can be defined by $(a + b)^*$. Using these observation together, we get the solution *i.e.*, $(a + b)^* \, aa \, (a + b)^*$

Hence the regular expression is

$$(a + b)^* \, aa \, (a + b)^*$$

**Example 4.2:** Find a regular expression for the language $L = \{ab^n w : n \geq 3, w \in \{a, b\}^*\}$.

**Solution:** The regular expression of given language is defined as follows:

1. Since $n \geq 3$ so the string length of $b$ is greater than or equal to 3.
2. The substring $w$ contains an arbitrary string of $\{a, b\}^+$ *i.e.*, $\{a + b\}^+$.

So we combine these together, we get a regular expression

$$abbb^+ \, (a + b)^+$$

or

$$abbbb^+ \, (a + b)^+$$

## 4.3 REGULAR LANGUAGE

Regular language over $\Sigma$ is the language $L$, if there exists a regular expression $r$ over $\Sigma$ such that

$$L = L(r)$$

For example,

$\Sigma = \{a, b\}$, then each of the following is an expression $r$ and corresponding language $L(r)$

(*a*) Let $r = a^*$, then $L(r)$ consists of all power of a *i.e.*, all word in a including expty word $\in$.

(*b*) Let $r = aa^*$, then $L(r)$ consists of all power of a *i.e.*, all word in a excluding empty word $\in$.

(*c*) Let $r = a + b^*$, then $L(r)$ consists of a or any word in $b$ *i.e.*,

$$L(r) = \{a, \in, b, bb, bbb, ...\}$$

**Example 4.3:** Find a regular expression for the language $L = \{vwv : v, w \in (a + b)^*, |v| = 2\}$

**Solution:** In the given language every string of $v \in \{a, b\}^*$ and contains exactly of length 2 *i.e.*, the strings are *aa*, *bb*, *ab* and *ba* and the regular expression of these strings is $(aa + bb + ab + ba)$.

Every string of $w \in \{a, b\}^*$ and its equivalent regular expression is $\{a + b\}^*$. Hence the regular expression of given language is

$$(aa + bb + ab + ba) \, (a + b)^* \, (aa + bb + ab + ba)$$

**Example 4.4:** Find the regular expression over $\Sigma = \{a, b\}$ that accept the following sets (*a*) All strings that contains any order of *a* and *b*.

(*b*) All strings that contains exactly one *a*.

(*c*) All strings beginning with *a*.

(*d*) All strings ending with *a*.

(*e*) All strings beginning with *ab* and ending with *bb*.

(*f*) All strings with at least two *a's*.

(*g*) All strings with exactly two *b's* and at least one *a*.

(*h*) All strings with no more than five *a's*.

(*i*) All strings that have no *a's*.

(*j*) All strings that does not contain *aba*.

(*k*) All strings that contains all *a's* before all *b's*.

(*l*) All strings of *a's* and *b's* with at least two consecutive *a*.

**Solution:**

(*a*) The regular expression of any order of *a* and *b* is $(a + b)^*$

(*b*) The regular expression of all strings that contains exactly one a is $b^*ab^*$

(*c*) The regular expression of all strings beginning with a is $a(a + b)^*$

(*d*) The regular expression of all strings ending with *aa* is $(a + b)^* aa$

(*e*) The regular expression of all strings beginning with *ab* and ending with *bb* is $ab(a + b)^* bb$.

(*f*) The regular expression of all strings with at least two *a's* is $(a + b)^* ab^* a(a + b)^*$

(*g*) The regular expression of all strings with exactly two *b's* and at least one *a* is $((a^+b + ba)\ a^*\ ba^* + bba)a^*$

(*h*) The regular expression of all strings with no more than five *a's* is $b^*ab^*ab^*ab^*ab^* + b^*ab^*ab^*ab^*ab + b^*ab^*ab^*ab^* + ab^*ab^* + b^*ab^* + b^*$

(*i*) The regular expression of all strings that have no *a's* is $b^*$

(*j*) The regular expression of all strings that does not contain *aba* is $(a + b)^* - \{aba\}$

(*k*) The regular expression of all strings that contains all *a's* before all *b's* is $a^*b^*$

(*l*) The regular expression of all strings of *a's* and *b's* with at least two consecutive *a* is $(a + b)^* aa(a + b)^*$

**Example 4.5:** Find a regular expression for each of the following languages over $\Sigma = \{a, b\}$

(*a*) $L_1 = \{a^m b^n; m, n > 0\}$

(*b*) $L_2 = \{b^m ab^n; m, n. > 0\}$

(*c*) $L_3 = \{(ab)^m; m > 0\}$

**Solution:**

(*a*) $L_1$ consists of those word beginning with one or more *a's* followed by one or more *b's*.

Hence $r = aa^* \; bb^* = a^+ \; b^+$

(*b*) $L_2$ consists of all word beginning with one or more *b's*' followed by single a which is the followed by one or more *b's i.e.,* all words with exactly one a which is neither the first non the last letter.

Hence $r = bb^* \; abb^* = b^+ \; ab^+$

(*c*) $L_3$ consists of all words beginning with one or more *a's* followed by same number of *b's*. There exists no regular expression *r* such that $L_3 = L(r)$ *i.e.,* $L_3$ is not a regular.

Hence $r = ab(ab)^* = (ab)$

## 4.4 EQUIVALENCE BETWEEN TWO REGULAR EXPRESSIONS

Two regular expressions $R_1 = R_2$ if any only if $R_1$ represents the same set of string as $R_2$ does.

For showing the equivalence relation we need to show some identities of regular expressions.

### Some Observation of Regular Expression or Identities for Regular Expression

The following rules are useful for simplifying the regular expressions:

**Rule 1 :** $\Phi + R = R$ **Rule 2 :** $\Phi R = R\Phi = \Phi$

**Rule 3 :** $\in R = R\in = R$ **Rule 4 :** $\in^* = \in$ and $\Phi^* = \in$

**Rule 5 :** $R + R = R$ **Rule 6 :** $R^*R^* = R^*$

**Rule 7 :** $RR^* + R^*R = R$ **Rule 8 :** $(R^*)^* = R^*$

**Rule 9 :** $\in + RR^* = R^* = \in + R^*R$

**Rule 10 :** $(R_1R_2)^* R_1 = R_1 (R_2R_1)^*$

**Rule 11 :** $(R_1R_2) = (R_1{}^*R_2{}^*)^* = (R_1{}^*R_2{}^*)^*$

**Rule 12 :** $(R_1 + R_2) R_3 = R_1R_3 + R_2R_3$

and $R_1(R_2 + R_3) = R_1R_2 + R_1R_3$

1. $R$, $R_1$, $R_2$ and $R_3$ are represents a regular expression.
2. Two regular expression *P* and *Q* are equivalent or $P = Q$ if *P* and *Q* represent the same set of strings.

**Example 4.6:** Prove that the following regular expression are equivalent

(*i*) $(a + b)^* = (a + b)^* + (a + b)^*$

(*ii*) $(a + b)^* = (a + b)^* (a + b)^*$

(*iii*) $(a + b)^* = a(a + b)^* + b(a + b)^* + \in$

**Solution :**

(*i*) By rules of regular expression, we know that $R + R = R$

so R.H.S $= (a + b)^* + (a + b)^* = (a + b)^* =$ L.H.S

(*ii*) By observation of regular expression

we know that $R^*R^* = R^*$

so R.H.S $= (a + b)^* (a + b)^* = (a + b)^*$ L.H.S

(*iii*) R.H.S $= a(a + b)^* + b(a + b)^* + \in$

$= (a + b) (a + b)^* + \in$ by rules 12

$= (a + b)^* + \in$ by rules 7

$= (a + b)^*$ by rules 9

= L.H.S Hence Proved.

**Example 4.7:** Simplify the following regular expression.

$(a + bb^*a) + (a + bb^*a) (b + ab^*a)^* (b + ab^*a)$

**Solution.** $(a + bb^* a) + (\in + (b + ab^* a)^* (b + ab^* a))$ by rule 12

$= (a + bb^* a) + (e + (b + ab^* a)^+)$ by rule 7

$= (a + bb^* a) + (b + ab^* a)^*$ by rule 9

$= (\in + bb^*)a (b + ab^* a)^*$ by rule 12

$= (\in + b^+) a (b + ab^* a)^*$ by rule 7

$= b^* a(b + ab^* a)^*$ by rule 9

Which is a simplified regular expression.

**Example 4.8:** Show that $(r + s)^* \neq r^* + s^*$

**Solution:** Let us consider the L.H.S. first,

L.H.S. $= (r + s)^*$

$= \{\in, r, rr, s, ss, rs, sr, rsrs, ...\}$

$= \{\in,$ any combination of $r$ and $s\}$

R.H.S. $= \{\in, r, rr, rrr, s, ss, ...\}$

$\{\in,$ any combination of only $r$ or any combination of only $s\}$

Note that is R.H.S. there is no combination of $r$ and $s$ together. Hence

L.H.S. $\neq$ R.H.S. is proved.

## 4.5 REGULAR SETS (R.S)

Any set of word represented by a regular expression is called a regular set.

For example, let $a, b \in \Sigma$ then

(*a*) The regular set of a regular expression

$a^*$ is $\{\in, a, aa, aaa, ...\}$

(*b*) The regular set of a regular expression

$a^+$ is $\{a, aa, aaa, ...\}$

(*c*) The regular set of regular expression $(a + b)$ is $\{a, b\}$

(*d*) The regular set of a regular expression $(a + b)^*$ is $\{\in, a, b, aa, bb, ab, ba, ...\}$

*i.e.*, any order of *a's* and *b's* including $\in$

(*e*) The regular set of a regular expression $(ab + ba)$ is $\{ab, ba\}$

(*f*) The regular set of a regular expression $a(ab + b)b$ is $\{aabb, abb\}$

(*g*) The regular set of a regular set $(a + b)^* (a + bb)$ is $\{a, bb, aa, abb, ba, bbb, aaa, aabb, ...\}$

*i.e.*, any strings on $\{a, b\}$ terminated by either an *a* or *bb*. Because first part $(a + b)^*$ represents any strings of *a's* and *b's*. The second part represents $(a + bb)$ either *a* or double *bb*. So concatenation of these two expression represents the set of all strings on $\{a, b\}$ terminated by either *a* or *bb*.

(*h*) The regular set of a regular expression $(aa)^* (bb)^* b$ is $\{b, aab, abbbb, aaaab, aaaabbb, ...\}$

*i.e.*, the set of all strings with an even number of *a's* and odd number or *b's*.

**Example 4.9:** For the two regular expressions given below:

(*a*) Find a string corresponding to $r_2$ but not to $r_1$ and

(*b*) Find a string corresponding to both *r1 and* $r_2$.

$$r_1 = a^* + b^* \quad r_2 = ab^* + ba^* + b^* a + (a^* b)^*$$

**Solution:** (*a*) Any string consisting of only *a's* or only *b's* and the empty strings are in $r_1$. So we need to find strings of $r_2$ which contain at least one *a* and at least one *b*. For example, *ab* and *ba* are such strings.

(*b*) A string corresponding to $r_1$ consists of only *a's* or only *b's* or the empty string. The only strings corresponding to $r_2$ which consists of only *a's* or *b's* are *a*, *b* and the strings consisting of only *b's* (from $((a^* b)^*)$). $r_2$ does not contain the empty string.

**Example 4.10:** Find a regular expression corresponding to the language of all strings over the alphabet $\{a, b\}$ that contain at least two *a's*.

**Solution:** A string in this language must have at least two *a's*. Since any string can be in front of the first *a*, behind the second *a* and between the two

$a$'s, and since arbitrary string can be represented by the regular expression $(a + b)^*$. So, $(a + b)^* a(a + b)^* a(a + b)^*$ is a regular expression for this language.

**Example 4.11:** Find a regular expression corresponding to the language of all strings over the alphabet $\{a, b\}$ that do not end with $ab$.

**Solution:** Any string in a language over $\{a, b\}$ must end in $a$ or $b$. Hence if a string does not end with $ab$ then it ends with $a$ or if it ends with $b$ the last $b$ must be preceded by a symbol $b$. Since it can have any string in front of the last $a$ or $bb$, $(a + b)^* (a + bb)$ is a regular expression for the language.

**Example 4.12:** Find a regular expression corresponding to the language of strings of even length over the alphabet of $\{a, b\}$.

**Solution:** Since any string of even length can be expressed as the concatenation of strings of length 2 and since the string of length 2 are $aa$, $ab$, $ba$, $bb$ a regular expression corresponding to the languages is $(aa + ab + ba + bb)^*$. Note that 0 is an even number. Hence the string $\wedge$ is in this language.

**Example 4.13:** Describe as simply as possible in English the language corresponding to the regular expression $a^* b(a^* ba^* b)^* a^*$.

**Solution:** A string in the language can start and end with $a$ or $b$, it has at least one $b$, and after the first $b$ all the $b$'s in the string appear in pairs. Any number of $a$'s can appear any place in the string. Thus simply put, it is the set of strings over the alphabet $\{a, b\}$ that contain an odd number of $b$'s.

**Example 4.14:** Find the regular expressions for the languages defined by

(i) $L_1 = \{a^n b^m : n \geq 1\ m \geq 1\ mm \geq 3\}$

(ii) $L_2 = \{ab^n w : n \geq 3\ w \in \{a, b\}^+\}$

(iii) $L_3 = \{vwv : v, w \in \{a, b\}^*, |v| = 2\}$

(iv) $L^4 = \{w : |w| \bmod 3 = 0\}$

**Solution:**

(i) $L_1 = \{a^n b^m : n \geq 1, m \geq 1, nm \geq 3\}$

The regular expression is given by

$$r = aa(a^*)\ b(b^*) + a(a^*)\ bb(b)^*$$

(ii) $L_2 = \{ab^n w : n \geq 3, w \in \{a, b\}^+\}$

The regular expression for $L_2$ is given by

$$r = abbb(b^*)\ (a + b)\ (a + b)^*$$

(iii) $L_3 = \{vwv : v, w \in \{a, b\}^*, |v| = 2\}$

The regular expression for $L_3$ is given by

$$r = (a + b)\ (a + b)\ (a + b)^*\ (a + b)\ (a + b)$$

(iv) $L_4 = \{w: |w| \bmod 3 = 0$

The regular expression for $L_4$ is given by

$$r = (aaa + bbb + ccc + aab + aba + abb + bab + bba + cab + cba + caa)^*.$$

**Example 4.15:** Write the regular expression for the language $L = \{a^n b^m$: $(n + m)$ is even$\}$.

**Solution:** We know $(n + m)$ is even when

**1.** Both $n$ and $m$ are even. **2.** Both $n$ and $m$ are odd.

For case 1. Let regular expression is $r_1$ then $r_1 = (aa)^* (bb)^*$

For case 2. Let regular expression is $r_2$, then $r_2 = (aa)^* a(bb)^* b$.

Suppose the final regular expression for given language $L$ is $r$, the

$$r = r_1 + r_2 = (aa)^* (bb)^* + (aa)^* a(bb)^* b.$$

**Example 4.16:** Represent the following sets by regular expressions:

(*i*) {0, 1, 2} (*ii*) {101} (*iii*) {10, 01}

(*iv*) $\{1^{2n+1} : n \geq 0\}$ (*v*) $\{a^2, a^5, a^8, ...\}$ (*vi*) {1, 11, 111, ...}

**Solution:**

(*i*) {0, 1, 2} is the union of {0}, {1} and {2}. So this is represented by 0 + 1 + 2.

(*ii*) {101} is obtained by concatenating 1, 0 and 1. So {101} is represented by 101.

(*iii*) {10, 01} is union of {10} and {01} and {10} and {01} is represented by 10 and 01. So {10, 01} is represented by 10 + 01.

(*iv*) $1(11)^*$

(*v*) $aa(aaa)^*$

(*vi*) $1(1)^*$ because {1, 11, 111, ...} can be obtained by concatenating 1 and any element of $\{1\}^*$.

**Example 4.17:** Describe as simply as possible in English the language corresponding to the regular expression $(b + ab)^* (a + ab)^*$

**Solution:** $(b + ab)^*$ represents strings which do not contain any substring *aa* and which and in *b*, and $(a + ab)^*$ represents strings which do not contain any substring *bb*. Hence altogether it represents any string consisting on a substring with no *aa* followed by one *b* followed by a substring with no *bb*.

**Example 4.18:** Find the shortest strings that is not in the language represented by the regular expression $a^* (ab)^* b^*$.

**Solution:** It can easily be seen that $\wedge$, *a*, *b* which are strings in the language with length 1 or less. Of the strings with length 2*aa*, *bb* and *ab* are in the language. However,

*ba* is not in it. Thus the answer is *ba*.

## 4.6 ARDEN'S THEOREM

Used in simplifying regular expressions.

(Replacing a given regular expression by an equivalent simpler expression.)

**Statement:** Let $P$ and $Q$ be two regular expressions over input alphabet S. If $P$ does not contain Î, then the equation in $R$.

$$R = Q + RP$$

has a Unique solution given by $R = QP^*$

**Solution:** The given equation is

$$R = Q + RP \qquad ...(1)$$

If we replace $R$ in R.H.S of equation (1) by $QP^*$ we have

R.H.S if (1) $= Q + (QP^*) \quad P = Q\,(\in + P^*P)$

$= Q(\in + P^+)$, by $PP^* = P^*$

$= QP^*$ by $\in + P^+ = P^*$

$= R$ (by supposition)

$=$ L.H.S of (1)

Thus $QP^*$ satisfies (1) or $R = QP^*$ is a solution of equation (1).

Again we prove uniqueness as follows:

Consider R.H.S of (1) as given below

$R = Q + RP = Q\,(Q + RP)\,P$ on putting $R = Q + RP$ from ...(1)

$= Q + QP + RP^2 = Q + QP + (Q + RP)P^2$

Again putting

$R = Q + RP$

$= Q + QP + QP^2 + RP^3$

$= Q + QP + QP^2 + ... + QP^i + RP^{i+1}$ repeating the same $i$ times

Thus $R = QP + QP^2 + ... + QP^i + RP^{i+1}$

or $\quad R = Q(\varepsilon + P + P^2 + ... + P^i) + RP^{i+1}$ for $1 \geq 0$ ...(2)

If $R$ satisfies equation (1), then it must satisfy equation (2). Let $w$ be a string of length $i$ in the set $R$, then $w$ also belongs to the set $Q\,(\in + P + P^2 + ... + P^i) + RP^{i+1}$. As $P$ does not contain $\in$ (given), therefore $RP^{i+1}$ has no string of length $(i + 1)$ and hence $w$ is not in the set $RP^{i+1}$ which means that $w$ belongs to the set $Q\,(\in + P + P^2 + ... + P^i)$ & therefore to the set $QP^*$.

Now consider a string $w$ in $QP^*$. So $w$ is in the set $QP^k$ for some $k \geq 0$ and hence in the set $Q\,(\in + P + P^2 + ... + P^k)$

So $w$ is in R.H.S of equation (2).

Thus $R$ & $QP^*$ represents the same set which proves the uniqueness of sol. (1)

## 4.6.1 Application or Use of Arden's Theorem

**Example 4.19:** Find a regular expression to represent the set $L$ of strings in which every 0 is immediately followed by at least two 1s.

Also prove that $R = \in + 1^* (0\ 11)^* (1^* (011)^*)^*$ and describe the same set of strings.

**Solution:** Let $w \in L$, then either $w$ does not contain any 0 or $w$ contains a 0 preceded by 1 and followed by 11. Thus $w$ can be written as $w_1\ w_2\ ...\ w_n$ where each $w_i$ is either or 011. So $L$ is represented by regular expression. $(1 + 011)^*$ ...(1)

Again $R = \in + 1^* (011)^* (1^* (011)^*)^*$, given

$= \in + P_1P_1^*$ where $P_1 = 1^* (011)^*$

$= P^*$ (by rule 9)

$= (1^* (011)^*)^*$ on putting value of $P_1$

$= (P_2^*P_3^*)^*$ on putting $P_2 = 1$, $P_3 = 011$

$= (1 + 011)^*$ which is the same regular expression as in equation (1) above

---

$R$ & $P$, $P_1$, $P_2$ are regular expression.
Also 011, 1 etc. are regular expression.

---

**Example 4.20:** Prove that

$(1 + 00^*1) + (1 + 00^*1)\ (0 + 10^*1)^*\ (0 + 10^*1) = 0^*1\ (0 + 10^*1)^*$

***[U.P.T.U. MCA (co) 2004]***

**Solution:** L.H.S. $= (1 + 00^*1)\ (\in + (0 + 10^*1)^*\ (0 + 10^*1))$

(by taking $1 + 00^*1$ common or using rule 12)

$= (1 + 00^*1)\ (0 + 10^*1)^*$ (by rule 9)

$= (\in + 00^*)1\ (0 + 10^*1)^*$

applying rule 12 on $1 + 00^*1$ [$= (\in + 00^*)1$]

$= 0^*\ 1\ (0 + 10^*\ 1)^*$

[applying rule 9 on $\in + 00^* = 0^*$]

= R.H.S.

**Example 4.21:** Show that $(0^*\ 1^*)^* = (0 + 1)^*$

**Solution:** L.H.S $(0^*\ 1^*) = \{\in, 0, 00, 1, 11, 111, 01, 10, ...\}$

$= \{\in$, any combination of 0's any combination of 1's and any combination of 0 and 1$\}$

R.H.S. $(0 + 1)^* = \{\in, 0, 00, 000, 1, 11, 111, 01, 10, ...\}$

$= \{\in$, any combination of 0's any combination of 1's and any combination of 0 and 1$\}$

Hence, we can say

L.H.S. = R.H.S.

**Example 4.22:** Show that $(ab)^* \neq (a^* b^*)$

**Solution:** L.H.S. $(ab)^* = \{\in, ab, abab, ababab, ...\}$

R.H.S. $(a^* b^*) = \{\in, a, aa, aaa, b, bb, bbb, ab, ...\}$

Hence, we can say

L.H.S. ≠ R.H.S.

## 4.7 REGULAR EXPRESSION AND FINITE AUTOMATA

There is a close relationship between a finite automata and the regular expression. We can show this relation by following figure. These two notations turn out to represent exactly the same set of languages, which we have termed the "regular languages".

We have already shown that deterministic finite automata, and two kinds of non deterministic finite automata with and without ∈-transitions-accept the same class of languages. In order to show that the regular expressions define the same class, we must show that.

- Every language defined by one of these automata is also defined by a regular expression.
- Every language defined by a regular expression is defined by one of these automata.

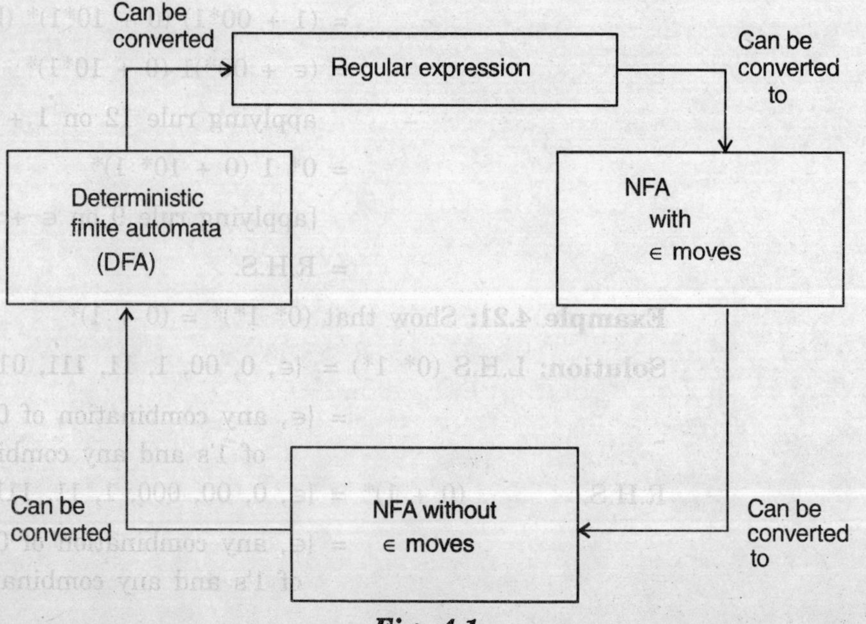


*Fig. 4.1*

### 4.7.1. Relation Between Regular Expression and Transition System

**Theorem 1:** *Every regular expression can be recognized by a transition system which mean that for every string w in the set R, there exists a path from the initial state to a final state with path value w.*

**Proof:** (by principle of Induction)

#### Characters

**Definition:** Elements of Σ, ∈, ∅, *, &, + are known as characters. If $R = \in + 10^*11^*0$, then the characters are ∈, +, 1, 0, *, 1, 1, *, 0 whose number is Nine.

[*R* is a regular expression ∈, 1, 0 etc. are regular expressions]

If the number of characters in *R* is 1, then $R = \in$ or $R = \varnothing$ or $R = a_i$ ($a_i \in \Sigma$) and the following transition system shall recognize it.

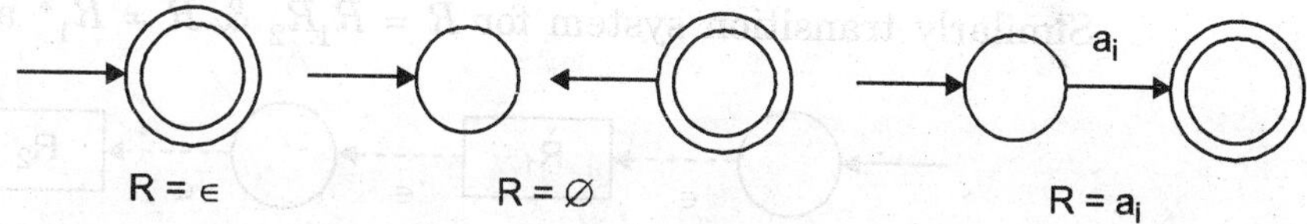


***Fig. 4.2***

Thus the theorem is true for 1 character. Now assume the theorem to be true for *n* or less characters. Then we shall prove it to be true for (*n* + 1) characters.

Suppose the r.e. *R* has (*n* + 1) characters. Then we can write

$$R = R_1 + R_2 \text{ or } R = R_1R_2 \text{ or } R = R_1^*$$

Where $R_1$ and $R_2$ are *r.e.* each having *n* or less characters $R_1$ as well as $R_1$ each having *n* or less characters can be recognized by transition system $R_i$ and $R_j$ respectively as shown below.

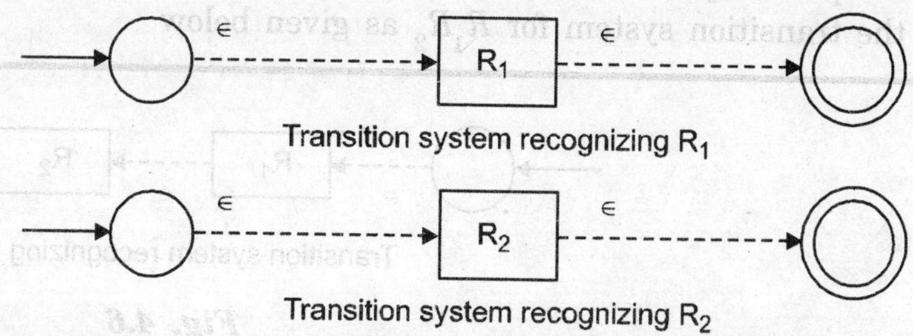


***Fig. 4.3***

The transition system $R = R_1 + R_2$ can be recognized by the transition system formed using $R_1$ and $R_2$ as follows. We introduce a new initial state $q_0$ and a new unique final state $q_f$.

$q_0$ is connected to the initial states of $R_1$ and $R_2$ by ∈ moves final states of $R_1$ and $R_2$ are connected to $q_f$ by ∈ moves and then the transition system so formed shall recognize $R_1 + R_2$.

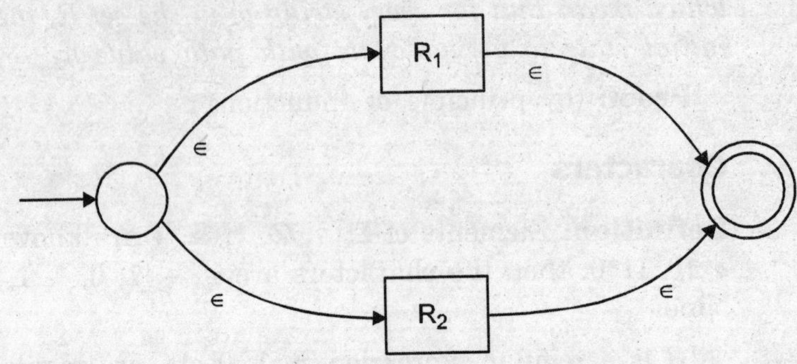


Transition system recognizing R2 + R1

*Fig. 4.4*

Similarly transition system for $R = R_1R_2$ & $R = R_1{}^*$ are given below

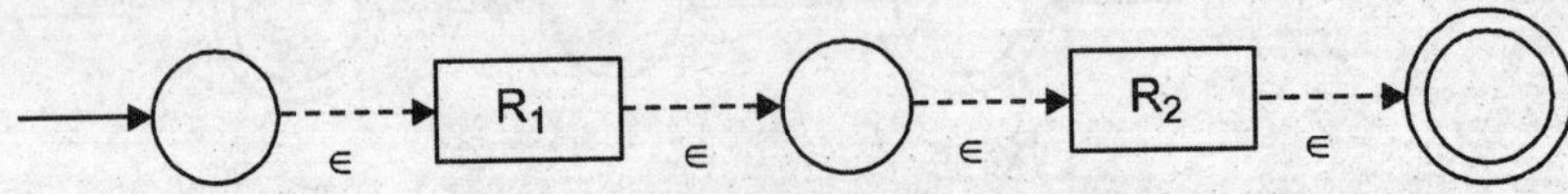


Transition system recognizing R1R2

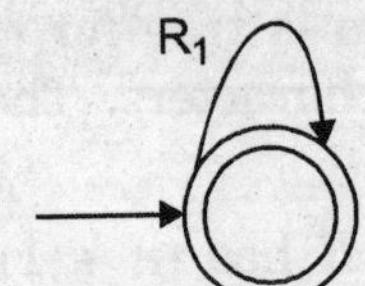


Transition system recognizing R1*

*Fig. 4.5*

---

If $R_1$ and $R_2$ are contains only a word and not a set of words then we can write the transition system for $R_1R_2$ as given below

---

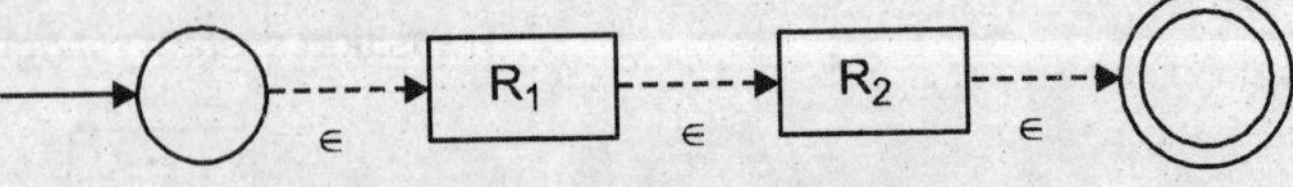


Transition system recognizing R1R2

*Fig. 4.6*

**Example 4.23:** Construct NFA with e moves for the regular expression (0 + 1)*.

**Solution:** The NFA will be constructed step by step by breaking regular expression into small regular expressions.

$$r_3 = (r_1 + r_2)$$
$$r = r^*_3$$

where $r_1 = 0$, $r_2 = 1$

NFA for $r_1$ will be

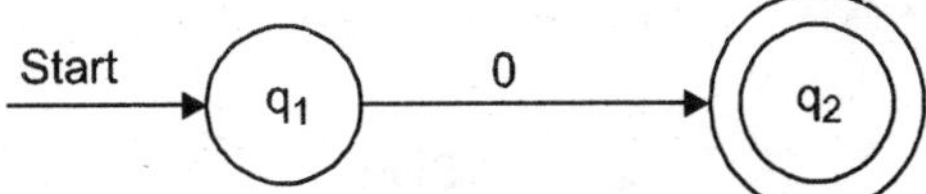


NFA for $r_2$ will be

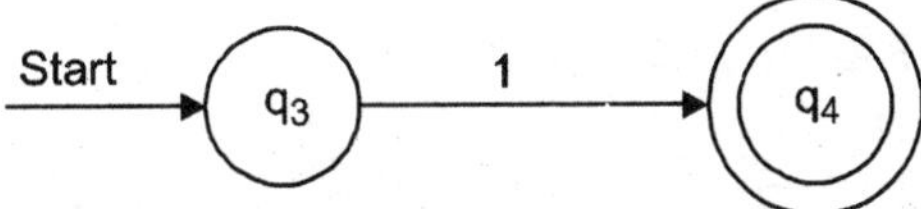


NFA for $r_3$ will be

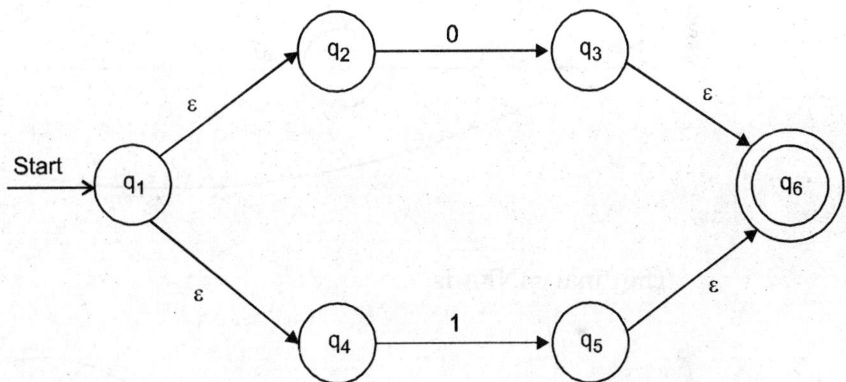


And finally

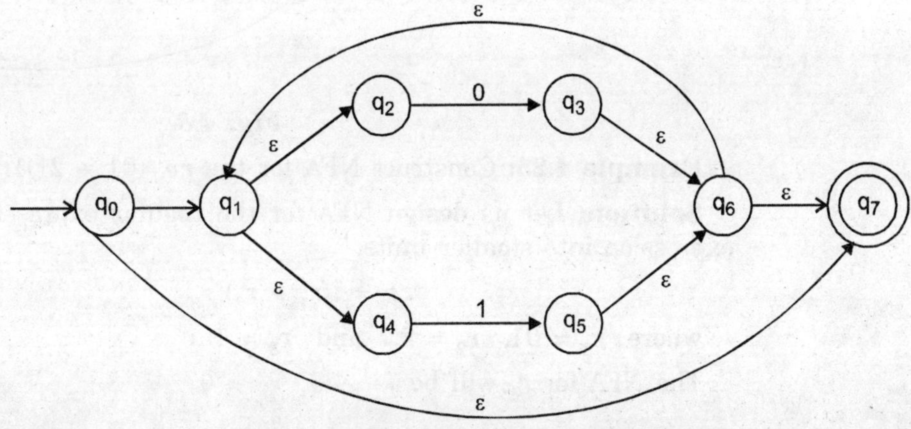


*Fig. 4.7*

**Example 4.24:** Construct the NFA for the language having odd number of zero's over the set S = {0}.

**Solution:** In this problem language $L$ is given, we have to first convert it to regular expression. The *r.e.* for this $L$ is written as *r.e.* = 0(00)*.

The $r$ is now written as

$$r = r_1 \, r_2$$

NFA for $r_1 = 0$ is

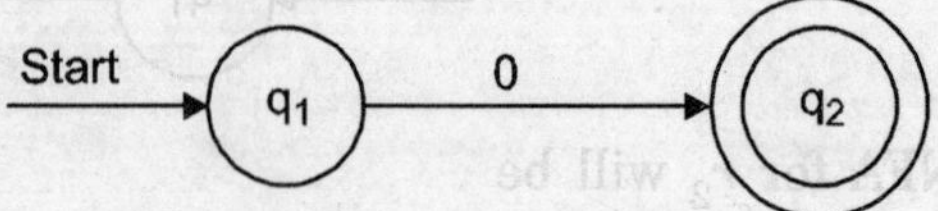


NFA for $r_2 = (00)^*$

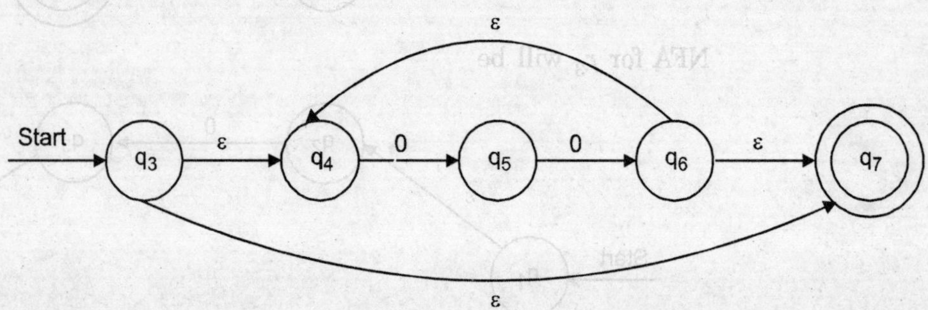


The final mNFA is,

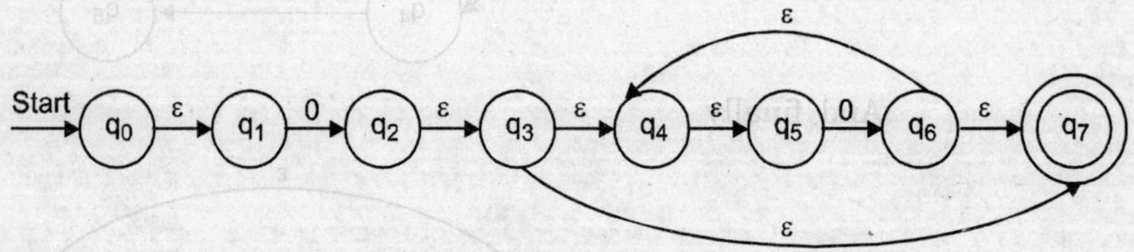


*Fig. 4.8*

**Example 4.25:** Construct NFA for the *r.e.* (01 + 2*)1.

**Solution:** Let us design NFA for the regular expression by dividing the expression into smaller units.

$$r = (r_1 + r_2) \, r_3$$

where $r_1 = 01$, $r_2 = 2^*$ and $r_3 = 1$

The NFA for $r_1$ will be

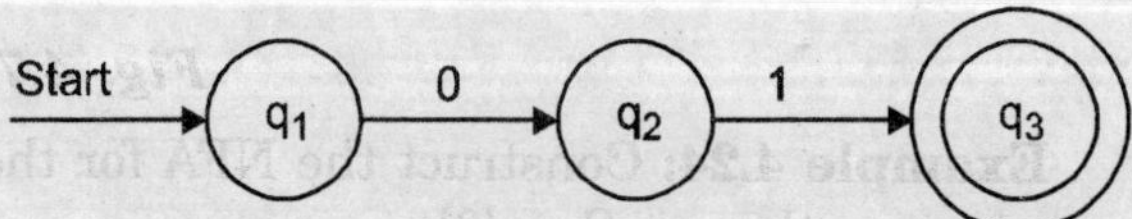

The NFA for $r_2$ will be

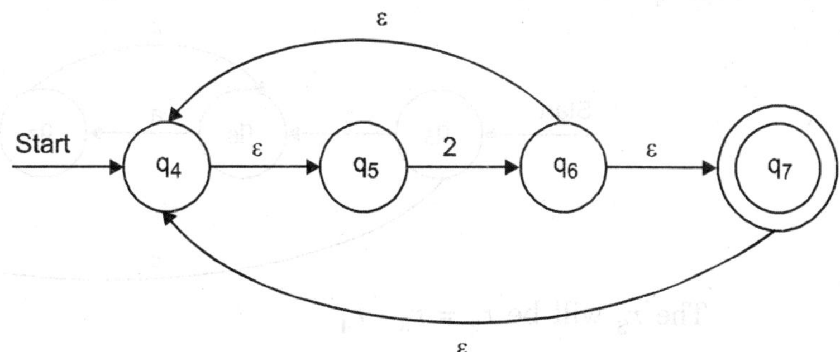


The NFA for $r_3$ will be

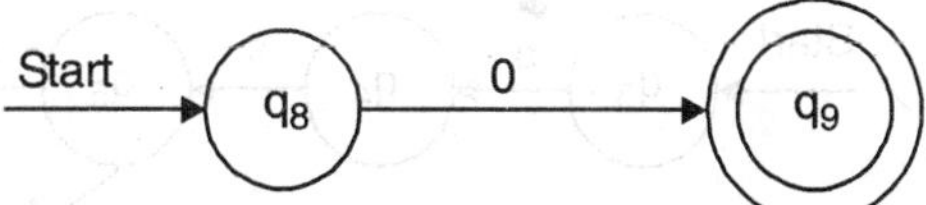


The final NFA will be

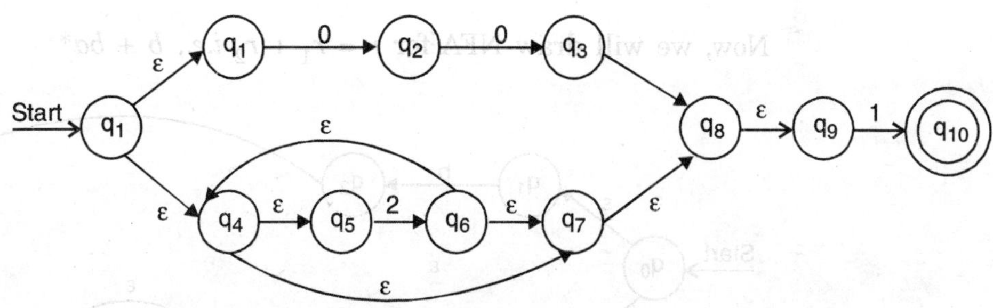


***Fig. 4.9***

**Example 4.26:** Construct NFA for the regular expression $b + ba^*$.

**Solution:** The regular expression

$r = b + ba^*$ can be broken into $r_1$ and $r_2$ as

$r_1 = b$

$r_2 = ba^*$

Let us draw the NFA for $r_1$, which is every simple.

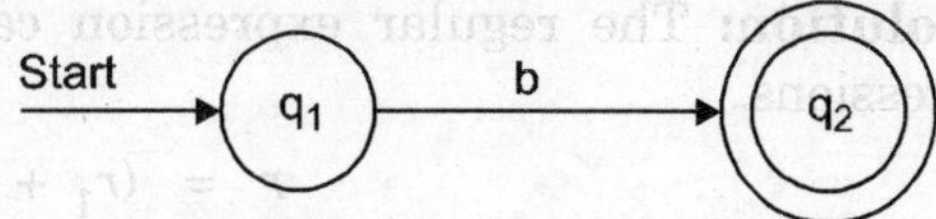


Now, we will go for $r_2 = ba^*$, this can be broken into $r_3$ and $r_4$ where $r_3 = b$ and $r_4 = a^*$. Now the case for concatenation will be applied. The NFA will look like this $r_3$ will be shown as below,

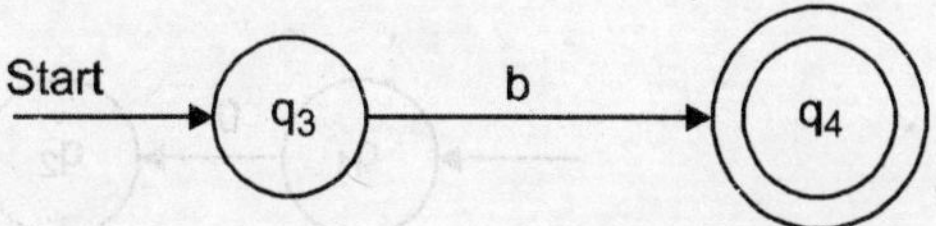

and $r_4$ will be shown as

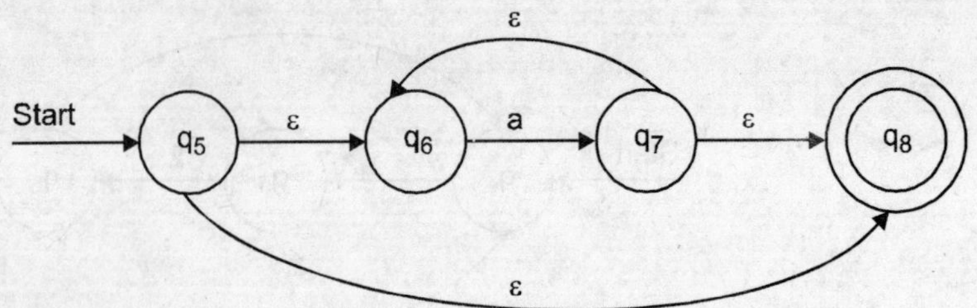


The $r_2$ will be $r_2 = r_3 \cdot r_4$

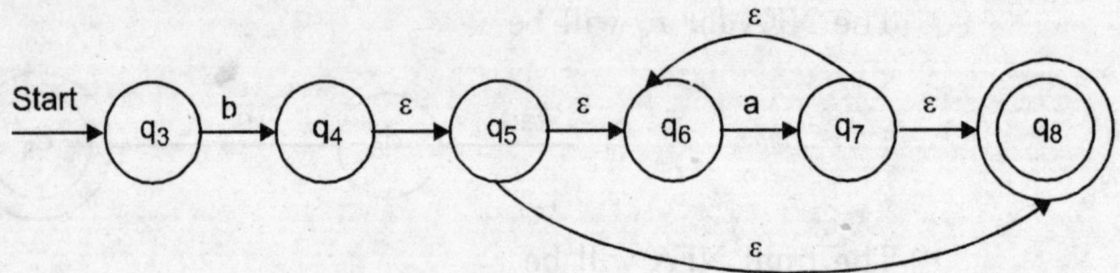


Now, we will draw NFA for $r = r_1 + r_2$ *i.e.*, $b + ba^*$

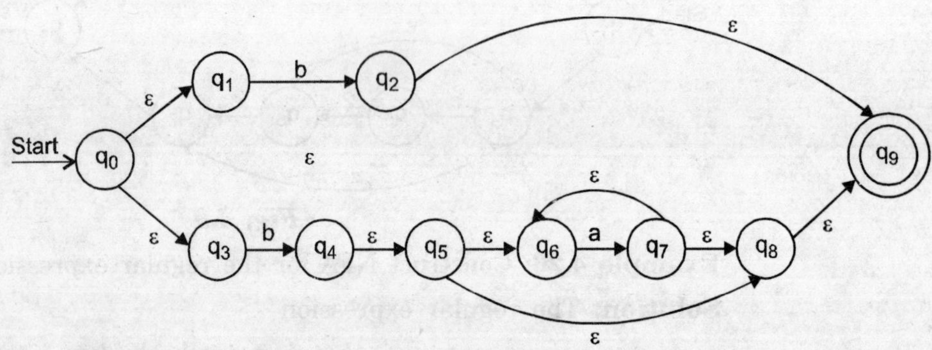


*Fig. 4.10*

**Example 4.27:** Construct NFA for the regular expression given below.

$$r = (01 + 10)^+$$

**Solution:** The regular expression can be split into two small regular expressions.

$$r = (r_1 + r_2)^+$$

where $r_1 = 01$

$r_2 = 10$

The NFA for $r_1$ is

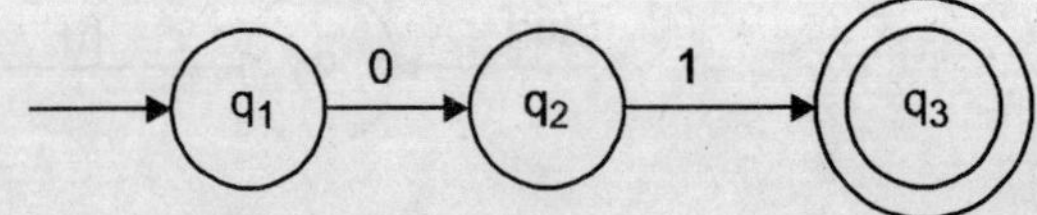

The NFA for $r_2$ is

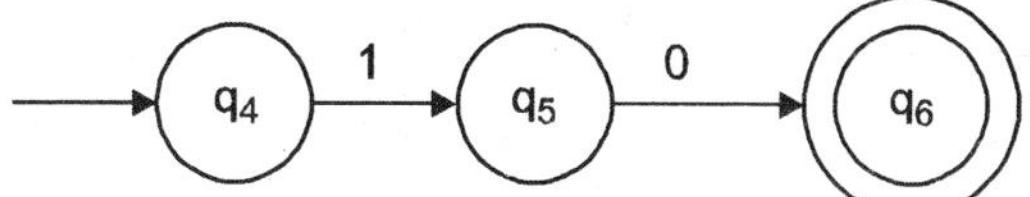


$r_3$ = 01 + 10 is drawn as

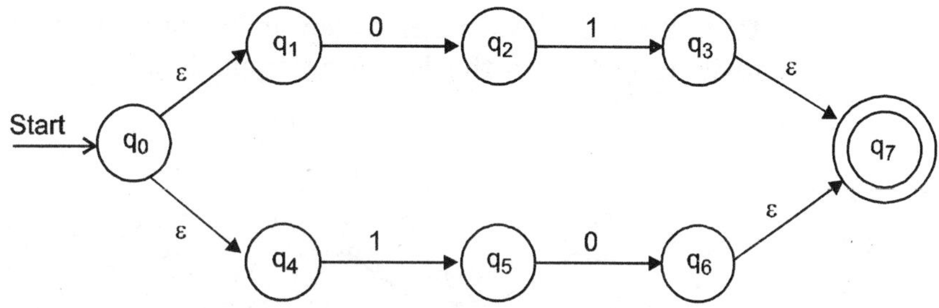


Now let us draw NFA with ∈ moves for (01 + 10)⁺.

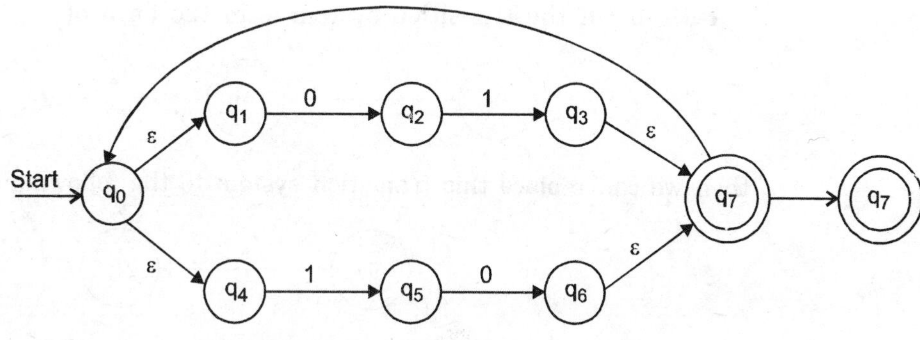


***Fig. 4.11***

Note the difference as of if $r$ = (01 + 10)*, we would have added the edge from $q_0$ to $q_8$ with ∈ transition.

---

Arden's Theorem gives a method of constructing a transition system recognizing or accepting a regular set

---

## 4.7.2 Construction of Regular Expression From Transition System

**Method 1 :** *This method gives us direct regular expression from a transition digraph by following equivalence rules.*

**Rule 1 :** If the transition system is in the form given in the figure then we can replace this transition system to the following equivalent transition digraph

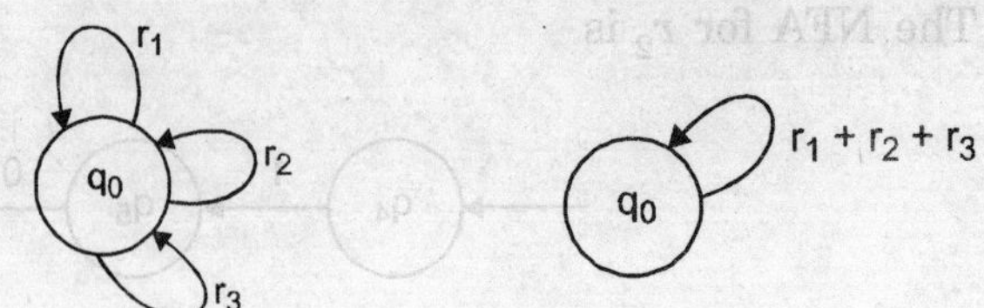


*Fig. 4.12*

**Rule 2 :** If the transition system is in the form of then we can replace this transition system to the following equivalent form

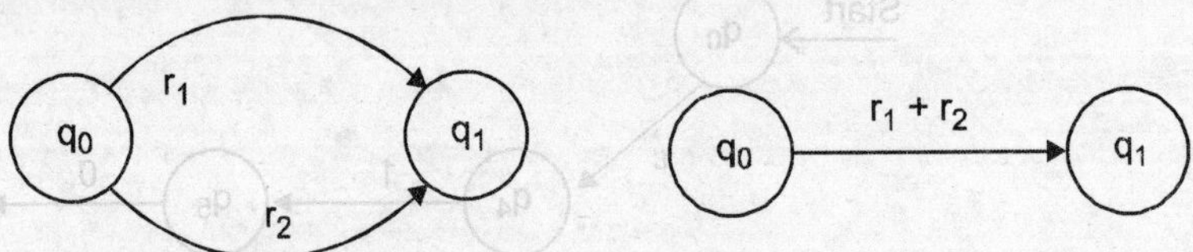


*Fig. 4.13*

**Rule 3 :** If the transition system is in the form of

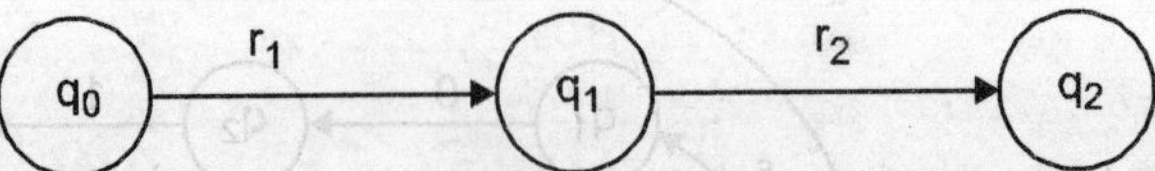


then we can replace this transition system to the following equivalent form

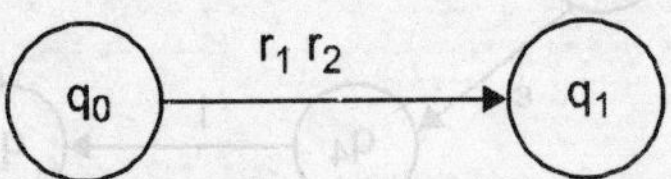


*Fig. 4.14*

**Rule 4 :** If the transition system is in the form of

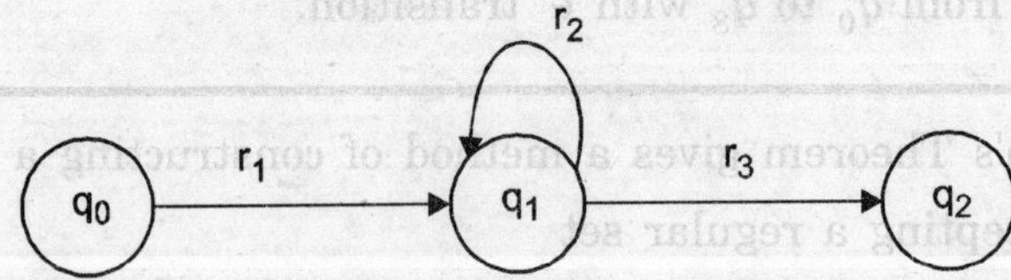


then we can replace this transition system to the following equivalent form

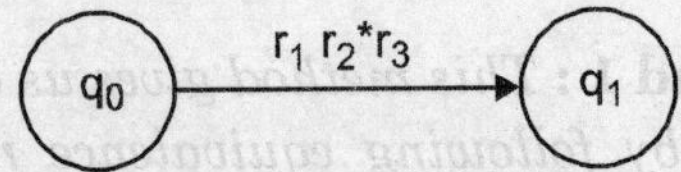


*Fig. 4.15*

**Rule 5 :** If the transition system is in the form of

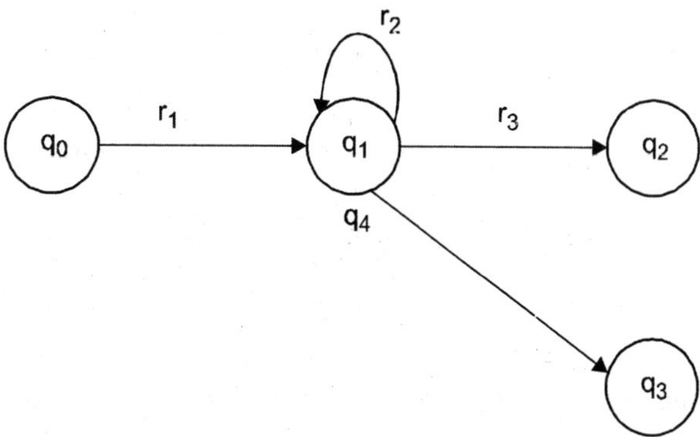


*Fig. 4.16*

then we can replace this transition system to the following equivalent form

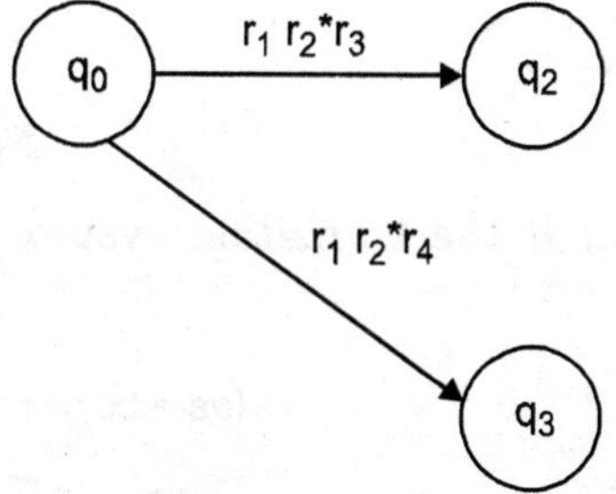


*Fig. 4.17*

**Rule 6 :** If the transition system is in the form of

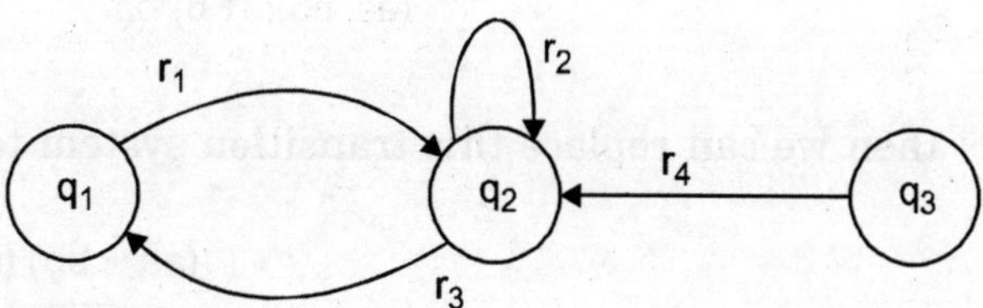


then we can replace this transition system to the following equivalent form

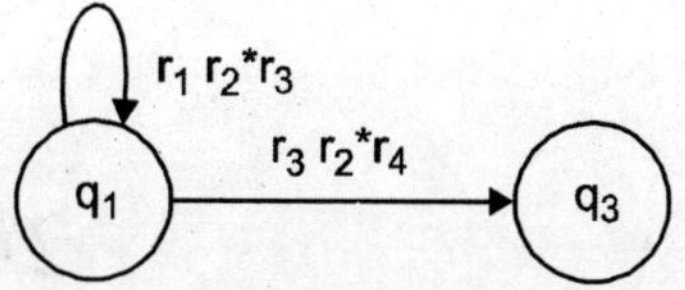


*Fig. 4.18*

**Rule 7 :** If the transition system is in the form of

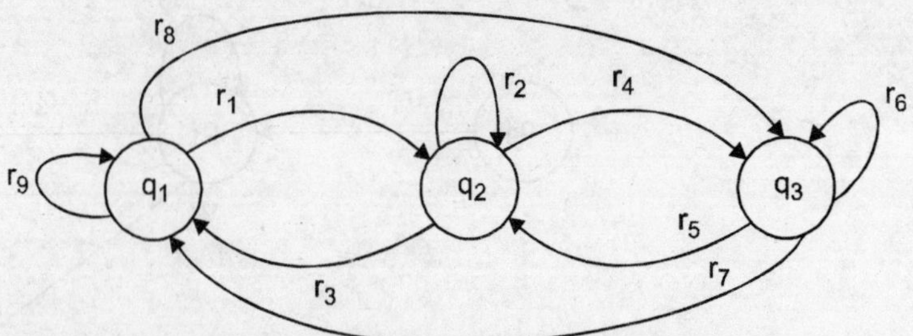


then we can replace this transition system to the following equivalent form

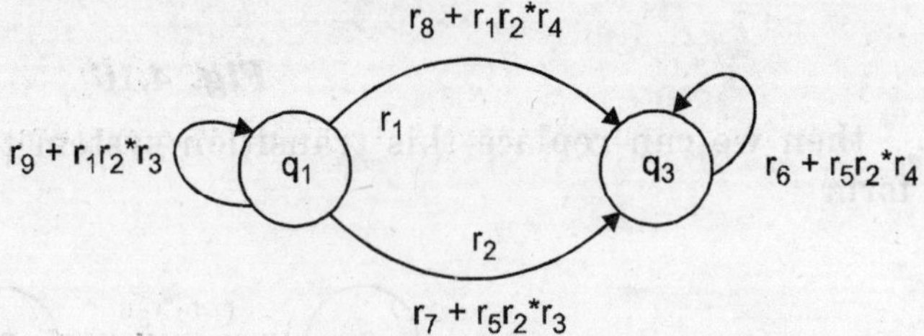


*Fig. 4.19*

**Rule 8 :** If the transition system is in the form of

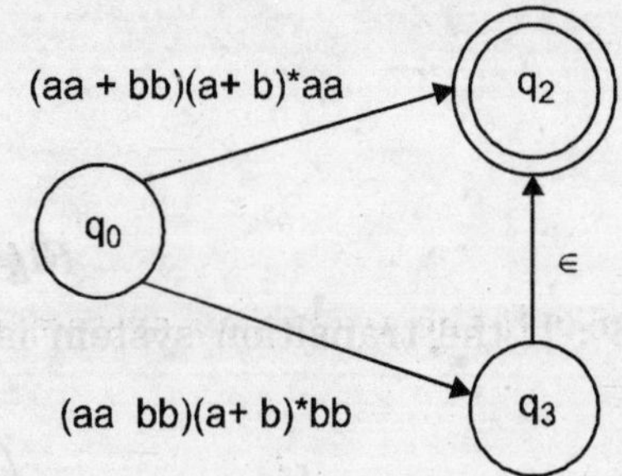


then we can replace this transition system to the following equivalent form

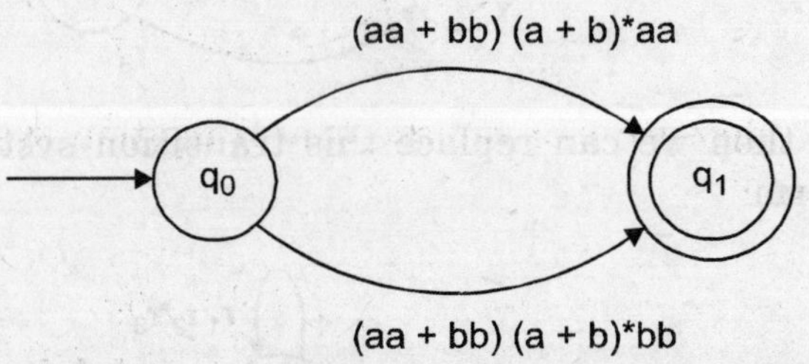


*Fig. 4.20*

The regular expression is $(aa + bb)(a + b)^*aa + (aa + bb)(a + b)^*bb$

**Example 4.28:** A transitive system is given below:

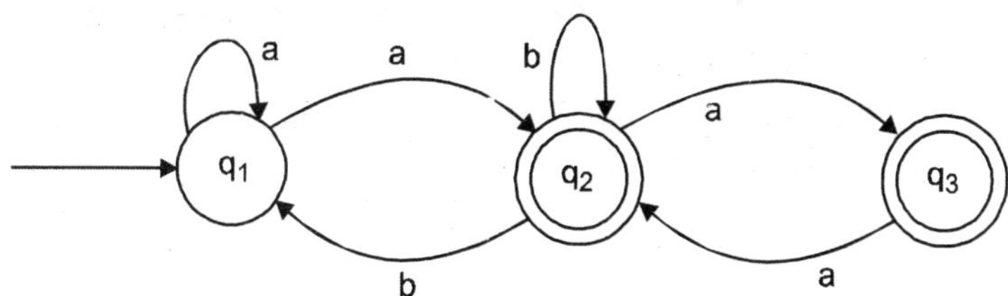


***Fig. 4.21***

prove that the strings recognized are $(a + a\,(b + aa)^*\,b)^*\,a(b + aa)^*a$

**Solution:** From the given system we see that the state $q_1$ is obtained.

either by applying input $a$ to the state $q_1$

or by applying input $b$ to the state $q_2$

or by applying input e to the state no state as it is initial state.

Therefore we can write

$$q_1 = q_1a + q_2b + e \qquad ...(1)$$

Similarly we can write

$$q_2 = q_1a + q_2b + q_3a \qquad ...(2)$$

$$q_3 = q_2a \qquad ...(3)$$

[All $a$ and $b$ denote *r.e.* given by $a$ & $b$]

Our aim is to reduce the number of unknown quantities. Putting value of $q_3$ from (3) in (2), we have

$$q_2 = q_1a + q_2b + q_2aa$$

$$= q_1a + q_2\,(b + aa)$$

$$= q_1a\,(b + aa)^* \qquad ...(4) \text{ by Arden's Theorem}$$

Now putting value of $q_2$ from (4) in (1) we get

$$q_1 = q_1a + q_1a\,(b + aa)^*b + e$$

$$= q_1\,(a + a(b + aa)^*b) + e$$

or $$q_1 = e + q_1\,(a + a\,(b + aa)^*\,b)$$

or $$q_1 = e\,(a + a\,(b + aa)^*\,b)^*$$

again by Arden's Theorem, and therefore from (4), we have

$q_2 = (a + a\,(b + aa)^*b)^*\,a\,(b + aa)^*$ & from (3), we have

$$q_3 = (a + a\,(b + aa)^*b)^*a\,(b + aa)^*a \qquad ...(5)$$

$q_2$ and $q_3$ being the final states, so the string recognized by the system is the union of state $q_2$ and $q_3$

*i.e.,* $q_2 + q_3 = (a + a\,(b + aa)^*b)^*\,a(b + aa)^* + (a + a\,(b + aa)^*\,b)^*\,a(b + aa)^*a$

$(a + a\ (b + aa)^*b)^*\ a\ (b + aa)^*\ (\varepsilon + a)$ This is the recognize language for the grammar.

**Example 4.29:** Find regular expression corresponding to the following transition digraph

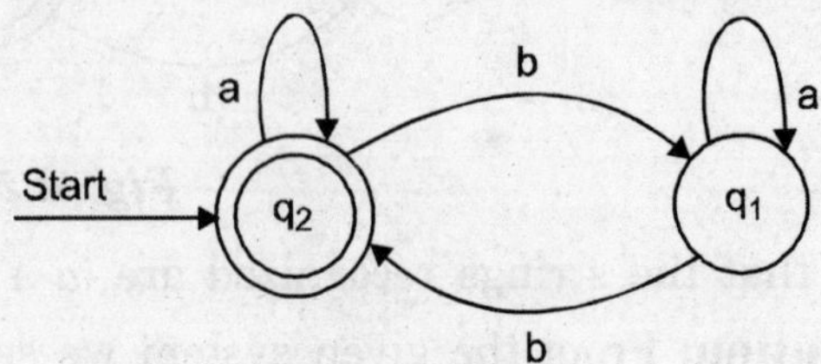


***Fig. 4.20***

**Solution:**

$$q_1 = \varepsilon + q_1a + q_2b$$
$$q_2 = q_2a + q_1b$$
$$q_2 = q_1ba^*\ (R = Q + RP \Rightarrow R = QP^*)$$
$$q_1 = \varepsilon + q_1a + q_1ba^*b$$
$$q_1 = \varepsilon + q_1\ (a + ba^*b)$$
$$q_1 = \varepsilon\ (a + ba^*b)^*$$
$$q_1 = (a + ba^*b)^*$$

So

$$q_2 = (a + ba^*b)^*b + q_2a$$
$$q_2 = (a + ba^*b)^*\ ba^*$$

Since the final state is $q_1$. So, required regular expression is $(a + ba^*b)^*$

**Example 4.30:** Find the regular expression corresponding to given digraph

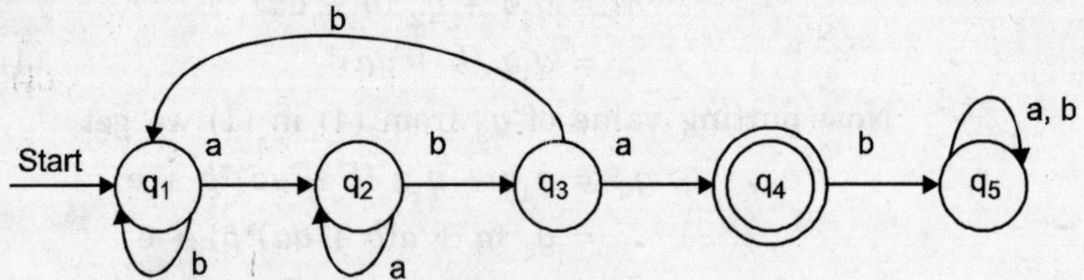


***Fig. 4.21***

**Solution:**

$$q_1 = \varepsilon + q_1b + q_3b \quad ...(1)$$
$$q_2 = q_1a + q_2a \quad ...(2)$$
$$q_3 = q_2b \quad ...(3)$$
$$q_4 = q_3a \quad ...(4)$$
$$q_5 = q_4b + q_5\ (a + b) \quad ...(5)$$

Applying Arden's theorem in equation (2), we get

$$q_2 = q_1aa^* \quad ...(6)$$

Substitute the value of $q_2$ in equation (1), we get

$$q_1 = \varepsilon + q_1b + q_2bb$$

$$q_1 = \varepsilon + q_1b + q_1aa^*bb$$

$$q_1 = \varepsilon + q_1(b + aa^*bb)$$

$$q_1 = \varepsilon + q_1 (b + aa^*bb) \quad ...(7)$$

Applying Arden's theorem in equation (7), we get

$$q_1 = \varepsilon (b + aa^*bb)^*$$

$$q_1 = (b + aa^*bb)^*$$

So $$q_2 = (b + aa^*bb)^*aa^*$$

Substitute the value of $q_2$ in equation (3), we get

$$q_3 = (b + aa^*bb)^*aa^*b$$

Substitute the value of $q_3$ in equation (4), we get

$$q_4 = (b + aa^*bb)^*aa^*ba$$

Since the final state is $q_4$, so, the required regular expression is $((b + aa^*bb)^*aa^*ba$

**Example 4.31:** Transition diagram of a finite automation is given below:

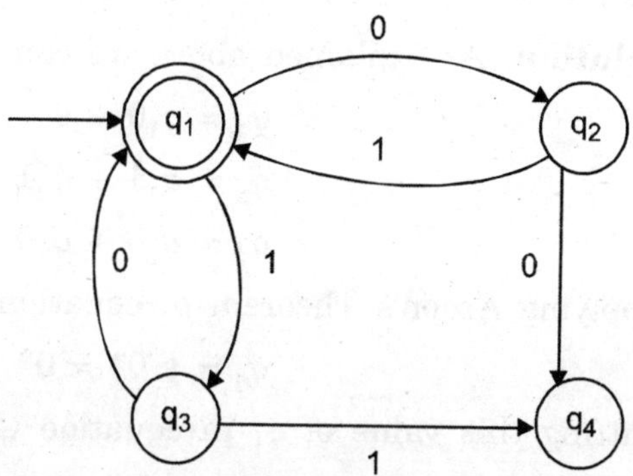


***Fig. 4.22***

Prove that it accept the set of all strings over the alphabet {0, 1} with an equal number of 0's and 1's such that each prefix has at most one more 0 then 1's and at most one more 1 then 0's.

**Solution:** As explained in the previous example we can write

$$q_1 = q_21 + q_30 + e \quad ...(1)$$

$$q_2 = q_10 \quad ...(2)$$

$$q_3 = q_11 \quad ...(3)$$

$$q_4 = q_20 + q_31 \quad ...(4)$$

$q_1$ is the final state & involves only $q_2$ & $q_3$, we shall use eqs. (2) & (3). equation (4) is redundant. Putting values of $q_2$ & $q_3$ from (2) & (3) in (1), we get

$$q_1 = q_1 01 + q_1 10 + \varepsilon = q_1 (01 + 10) + \varepsilon$$

or $q_1 = \varepsilon + q_1 (01 + 10)$

$= \varepsilon (01 + 10)^*$ by Arden's theorem

$= (01 + 10)^*$ the string which will be accepted as $q_1$ is the final state.

This string satisfies the condition given in the question

**Example 4.32:** Transition diagram or system or graph off Finite automation is given below.

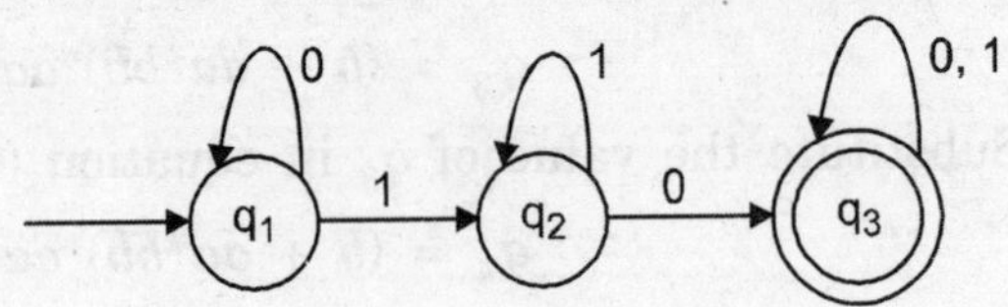


***Fig. 4.23***

Describe in English (words or language) the set of strings accepted by this system.

**Solution:** As explained above we can write

$$q_1 = q_1 0 + e \quad ...(1)$$

$$q_2 = q_1 1 + q_2 1 \quad ...(2)$$

$$q_3 = q_2 0 + q_3 0 + q_3 1 = q_2 0 + q_3 () + 1) \quad ...(3)$$

Applying Arden's Theorem to equation (1), we have

$$q_1 = \varepsilon\, 0^* = 0^* \quad ...(4)$$

Putting this value of $q_1$ in equation (2)., we have

$$q_2 = 0^*1 + q_2 1 \quad ...(5)$$

or $q_2 = (0^*1)1^*$ ...(6)

applying Arden's theorem to equation (5)

Putting the value of $q_1$ and $q_2$ in equation (3)., we have

$$q_3 = (0^*1)1^*0 + q_3\ (0 + 7) \quad ...(7)$$

Applying Arden's theorem to equation (7), we have

$$q_3 = (0^*1)1^*0(0 + 1)^*$$

Hence the string that will be accepted by the system is $(0^*1)\ 1^*0\ (0 + 1)^*$

**Example 4.33:** Transition diagram of a finite automaton (*F.A.*) is given below. Construct a regular expression corresponding to this diagram.

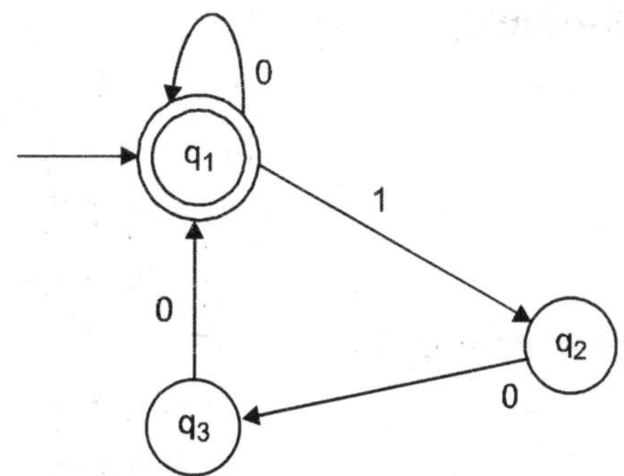


***Fig. 4.24***

**Solution:** There is no ε-moves and a single initial state. So we can write as above as follows:

$$q_1 = q_1 0 + q_3 0 + \varepsilon \qquad ...(1)$$

$$q_2 = q_1 1 \qquad ...(2)$$

$$q_3 = q_2 0 \qquad ...(3)$$

Putting value of $q_3$ from (3) in (1) we have

$$q_1 = q_1 0 + q_2 00 + \varepsilon \qquad ...(4)$$

Putting value of $q_2$ from (2) in (4) we have

$$q_1 = q_0 0 + q_1\ 100 + \varepsilon$$

$$q_1 = q_1\ (0 + 100) + \varepsilon \qquad ...(5)$$

Applying Arden's Theorem to eq. (5), we have

$$q_1 = \varepsilon\ (0 + 10\ 0)^*$$

or $$q_1 = (0 + 10\ 0)^*$$

Which is the required *r.e.* accepted by the system as $q_1$ is the only final state.

**Example 3.34:** Construct *r.e.*, for the DFA given below–

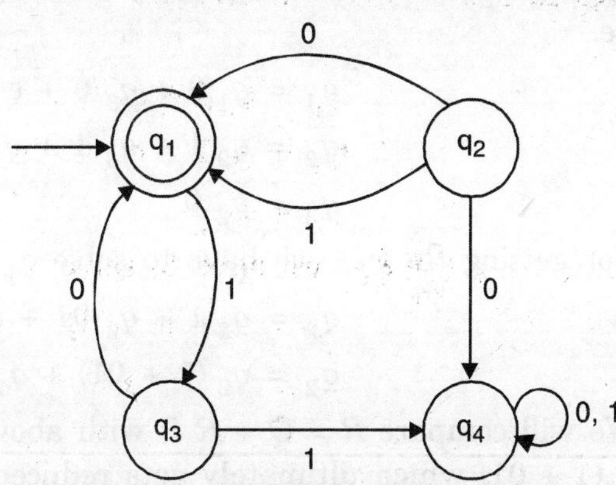


***Fig. 4.25***

**Solution:** Let us see the equations

$$q_1 = q_2\, 1 + q_3\, 0 + \varepsilon$$
$$q_2 = q_1\, 0$$
$$q_3 = q_1\, 1$$
$$q_4 = q_2\, 0 + q_3\, 1 + q_4\, (0 + 1)$$

Let us solve $q_1$ first,

$$q_1 = q_2\, 1 + q_3\, 0 + \varepsilon$$
$$q_1 = q_1\, (01 + 10) + \varepsilon \qquad \because R = Q + RP$$
$$q_1 = \varepsilon \cdot (01 + 10)^* \qquad \Rightarrow Q\, P^* \text{ where}$$
$$q_1 = (01 + 10)^* \qquad R = q_1,\, Q = \varepsilon,\, P = (01 + 10)$$

Thus the regular expression will be

$$r = (01 + 10)^*$$

Since $q_1$ is a final state, we are interested in $q_1$ only.

**Example 4.35:** Find out the regular expression from given DFA.

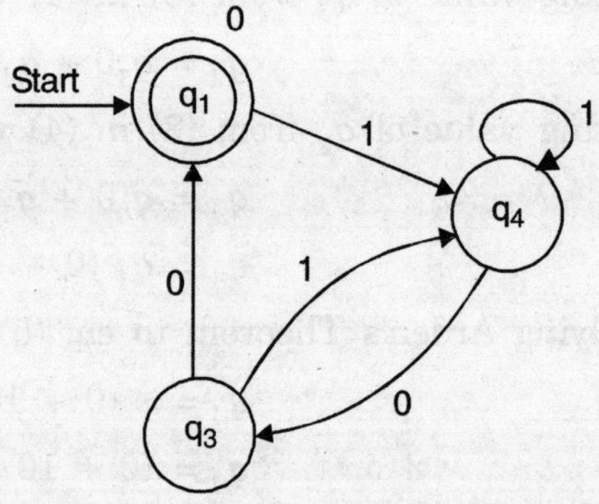


***Fig. 4.26***

**Solution:** Let us solve the DFA by writting the regular expression, for each state.

$$q_1 = q_1\, 0 + q_3\, 0 + \varepsilon \qquad \therefore \text{ initial state}$$
$$q_2 = q_2\, 1 + q_3\, 1 + q_1\, 1$$
$$q_3 = q_2\, 0$$

For getting the *r.e.*, we have to solve $q_1$ the final state.

$$q_2 = q_2\, 1 + q_2\, 01 + q_1\, 1$$
$$q_2 = q_2\, (1 + 01) + q_1\, 1$$

We will compare $R = Q + R\, P$ with above equation, so $R = q_2$, $Q = q_1$, 1, $P = (1 + 01)$ which ultimately gets reduced to $QP^*$.

$$q_2 = q_1\, 1(1 + 01)^*$$

Substituting this value to $q_1$

$$q_1 = q_1 0 + q_3 0 + \varepsilon$$
$$= q_1 0 + q_2 00 + \varepsilon$$
$$= q_1 0 + q_1 (1(1 + 01)^*) 00 + \varepsilon$$
$$q_1 = q_1 (0 + 1(1 + 01)^* 00) + \varepsilon$$

Again $R = Q + R P$

Where $R = q_1$

$Q = \varepsilon$

$P = 0 1(1 + 01)^* 00$

Hence $q_1 = \varepsilon \cdot [0 + p(1 + 01)^* \times 00]^*$

$q_1 = [0 + 1(1 + 01)^* \times 00]^*$ $\therefore \varepsilon \cdot R = R$

**Example 4.36:** Construct *r.e.,* for the given DFA.

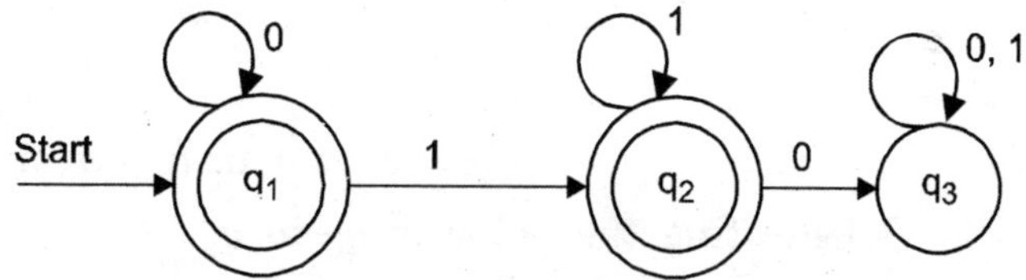


***Fig. 4.27***

**Solution:** Let us build the regular expression for each state.

$$q_1 = q_1 0 + \varepsilon$$
$$q_2 = q_1 1 + q_2 1$$
$$q_3 = q_2 0 + q_3 (0 + 1)$$

Since final states are $q_1$ and $q_2$, we are interested in solving $q_1$ and $q_2$ only. Let us see $q_1$ first

$$q_1 = \varepsilon + q_1 0$$

Which is $R = Q + R P$ equivalent so we can write

$$q_1 = \varepsilon \times (0)^*$$

$q_1 = 0^*$ $\therefore \varepsilon \times R = R$

Substituting this value into $q_2$, we will get

$$q_2 = 0^*1 + q_2 1$$

$q_2 = 0^* 1 (1)^*$ $\therefore R = Q + RP \Rightarrow Q P^*$

The regular expression is given by

$$r = q_1 + q_2$$
$$r = 0^* + 0^* 1 \times 1^*$$

$r = 0^* + 0^* 1^+$ $\therefore 1 \times 1^* = 1^+$

**Example 3.37:** Represent the language given by following DFA.

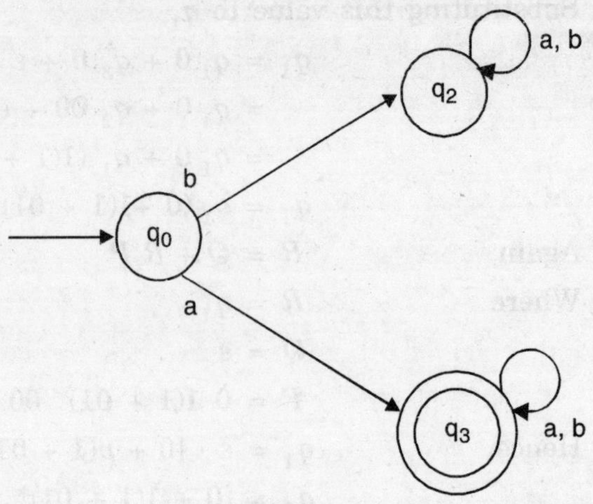


*Fig. 4.28*

**Solution:** To find the language, we will solve for regular expression,

$$q_0 = \varepsilon$$

$$q_3 = q_3\, a + q_3\, b + q_0\, a$$

Substituting the value of $q_0$ in $q_3$

$$q_3 = q_3\,(a + b)\;\varepsilon \times a$$

$$q_3 = q_3\,(a + b) + a \qquad \therefore R = Q + R\,P \Rightarrow QP^*$$

$$q_3 = a\,(a + b)^* \qquad \text{where } q = a,\ p = (a + b),\ R = q_3$$

This is a final regular expression, which represents the language containing all the strings which start with letter $a$.

**Example 3.48:** Construct the regular expression for following DFA.

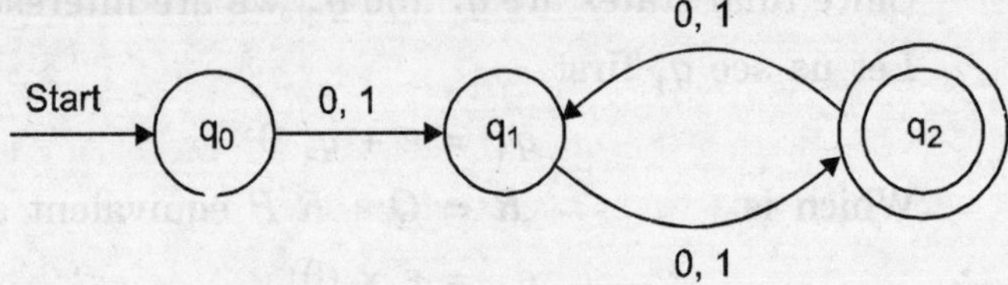


*Fig. 4.29*

**Solution:** We can get the regular expression from state $q_2$. Let us see the equation of each state.

$$q_0 = \varepsilon$$

$$q_1 = q_0\, 1 + q_0\, 0 + q_2\, 1 + q_2\, 0$$

$$q_2 = q_1\, 1 + q_1\, 0$$

Putting value of $q_0$ in $q_1$

$$q_1 = \varepsilon \cdot 1 + \varepsilon \cdot 0 + q_2\,(0 + 1)$$

$$q_1 = (1 + 0) + q_2\,(0 + 1)$$

Now solve $q_2$ $\quad q_2 = (1 + 0)\ q_1$

$$q_2 = (1 + 0)\ [(1 + 0) + q_2\ (1 + 0)]$$

$$q_2 = (1 + 0) \times (1 + 0) + q_2\ (1 + 0)\ (1 + 0)$$

Here $R = q_2$, $\quad Q = (1 + 0)\ (1 + 0),\ P = (1 + 0)\ (1 + 0)$

$$q_2 = (1 + 0)\ (1 + 0)\ [(1 + 0)\ (1 + 0)]^*$$

is a regular expression.

**Example 4.39:** Find a regular expression corresponding to the transition diagram given below: (or *F.A.* whose graph is given below).

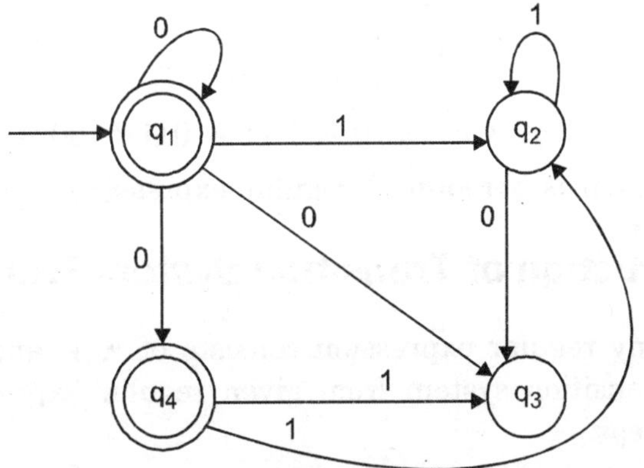


***Fig. 4.30***

**Solution:** There is only initial state and no e-moves. We can have following equations as explained in

*Example,* $\quad q_1 = q_10 + q_30 + q_40 + \varepsilon \quad$ ...(1)

$$q_2 = q_11 + q_21 + q_41 \quad \text{...(2)}$$

$$q_3 = q_20 \quad \text{...(3)}$$

$$q_4 = q_31 \quad \text{...(4)}$$

From equation (3) and (4)

$$q_4 = q_201 \quad \text{...(5)}$$

From equation (2) $\quad q_2 = q_11 + q_21 + q_2011$ (using (5))

$$= q_11 + q_2\ (1 + 011)$$

$$= q_11\ (1 + 011)^* \quad \text{(applying Arden's theorem)}$$

$$= q_1\ (1\ (1 + 011)^* \quad \text{...(6)}$$

From equation (1) $q_1 = q_10 + q_200 + q_2010 + \varepsilon$ $\quad$ using (3) and (5)

$$= q_10 + q_2(00 + 010) + \varepsilon$$

$$= q_10 + q_11\ (1 + 011)^*\ (00 + 010) + \varepsilon \quad \text{using (6)}$$

$$= \varepsilon + q_1\ (0 + 1(1 + 011)^*(00 + 010) \quad \text{...(7)}$$

Applying Arden's Theorem on (7), we have

$$q_1 = \varepsilon\ (0 + 1\ (1 + 011)^*\ (00 + 010))^*$$

$$q_1 = (0 + 1\ (1 + 011)^*\ (00 + 011))^* \quad ...(8)$$

Again from (5) $q_4 = q_2 01 = q_1 1\ (1 + 011)^* 01$ (putting value of $q_2$ from (6)

$$= (0 + 1)\ (1 + 011)^*\ (00 + 010)^*\ (1\ (1 + 011)^*\ 01)$$

on putting value of $q_1$ from (8).

Since the final states are $q_1$ and $q_4$, so the required regular expression is equivalent to $q_1 + q_4$

$$q_1 + q_4 = (0 + 1\ (1 + 011)^*\ (00 + 010)^* + (0 + 1\ (1 + 011)^*\ (00 + 010))^*\ (1\ (1 + 011)^*\ 01)$$

$$q_1 + q_4 = (0 + 1\ (1 + 011)^*\ (00 + 010))^*\ (\varepsilon + 1\ (1 + 011)^* 01)$$

which is a required regular expression.

## 4.7.3 Construction of Transition System From Regular Expression

Any regular expression consists of *, +, and alphabets from $\Sigma$. To construct transition system from given regular expression we consider following four steps:

→ Take two states one initial state and other one the final state and write the regular expression as path value from initial state to final state.

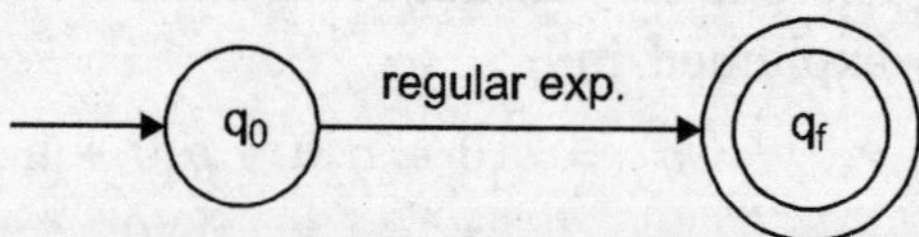


→ Now divide regular expression in two or more sub-expressions (if possible).

→ Introduce new intermediate states between initial state and final state. If there are $n$ sub-regular expressions then there will be $n - 1$ inserted intermediate states.

→ Now consider following table for construction of transition diagram for each sub-regular expression:

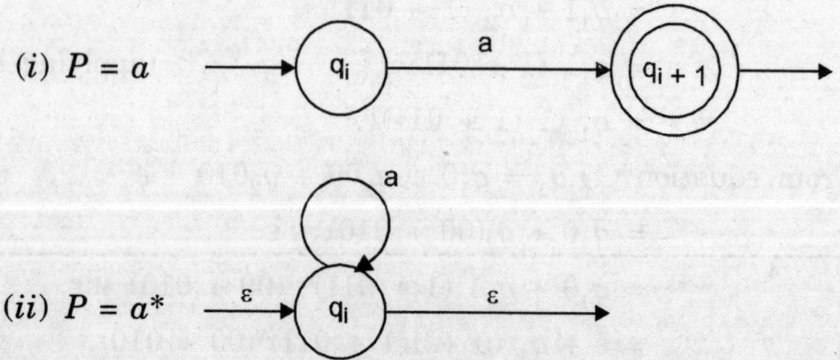

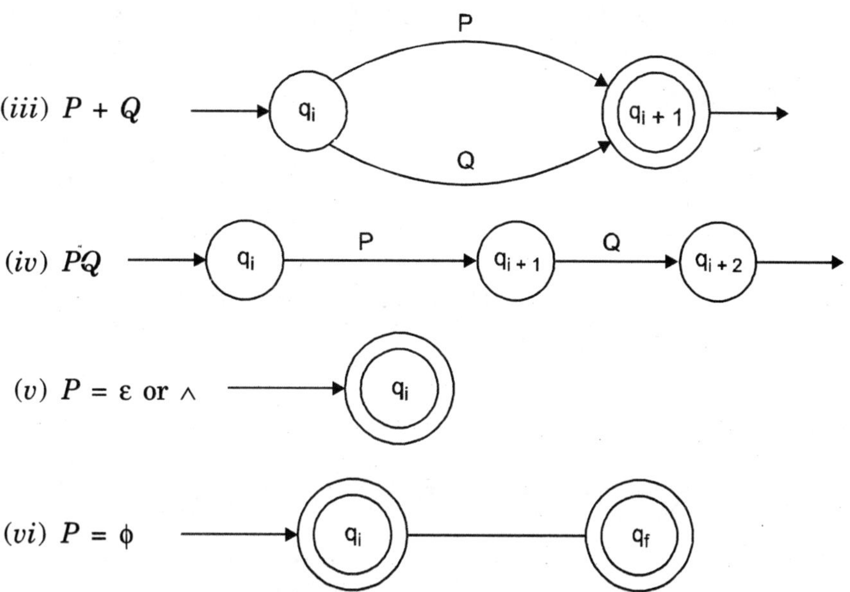


**Example 4.40:** Construct transition diagram for the regular expression $R = (ab^*)\ (a + b)^*\ (b + ab)$.

**Solution:**

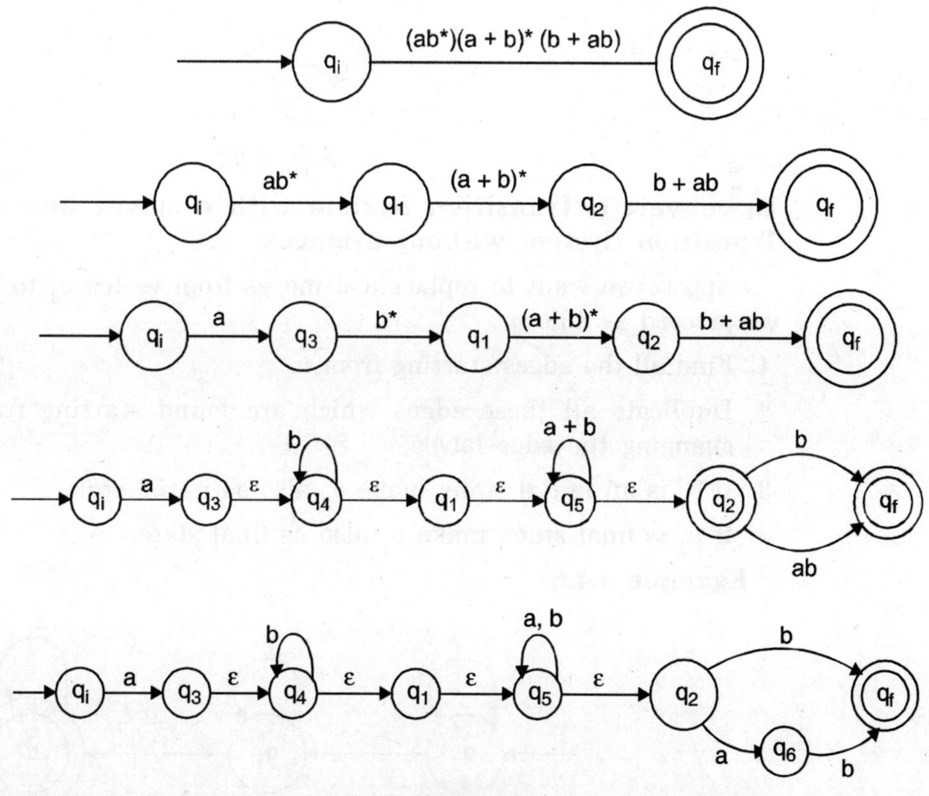


*Fig. 4.31*

**Example 4.41:** Construct an NFA equivalent to the regular expression (0 +1)* (00 + 11) (0 + 1)*.

**Solution:**

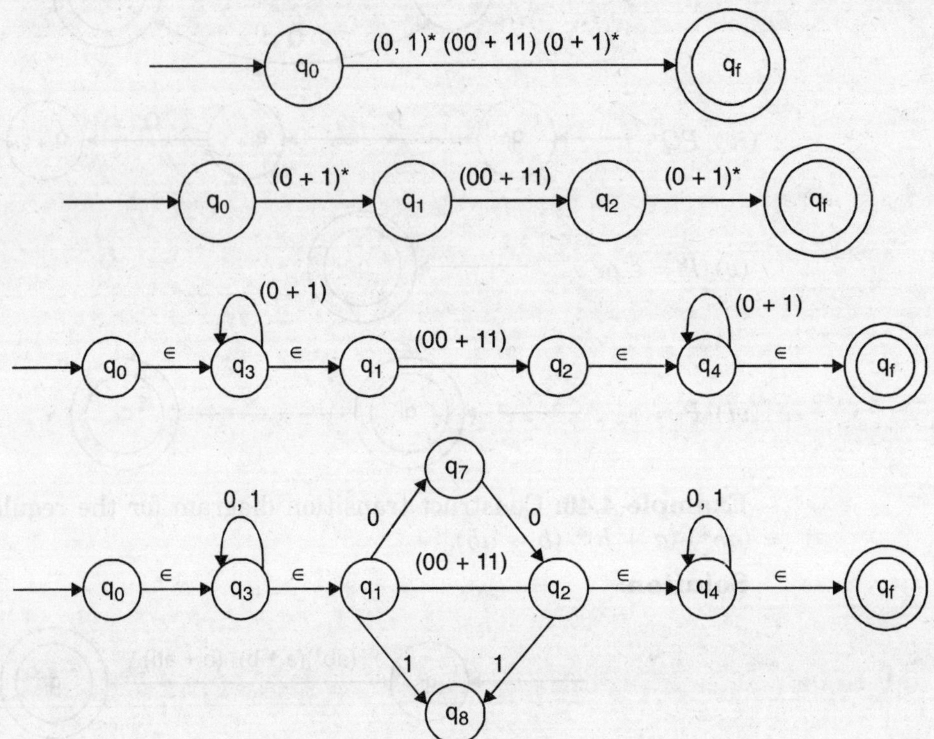


*Fig. 4.32*

**To convert a Transition System with ∈-moves into an equivalent Transition System without ∈-moves.**

Suppose we want to replace a ∈-moves from vertex $v_1$ to vertex $v_2$. Then we proceed as follows:

1. Find all the edges starting from $v$.
2. Duplicate all these edges which are found starting from $v_1$, without changing the edge labels.
3. If $v_1$ is an initial state, make $v_2$ also as initial state.
4. If $v_2$ is final state, make $v_1$ also as final state.

**Example 4.42:**

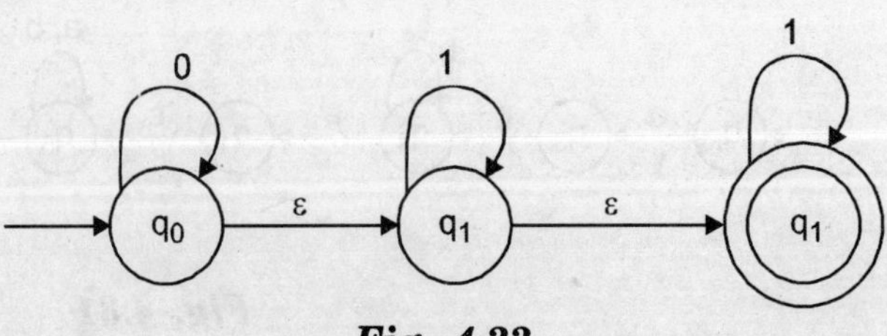


*Fig. 4.33*

Obtain an equivalent automaton without $\in$-moves.

**Solution: 1.** We first eliminate the $\in$-moves from $q_0$ to $q_1$.

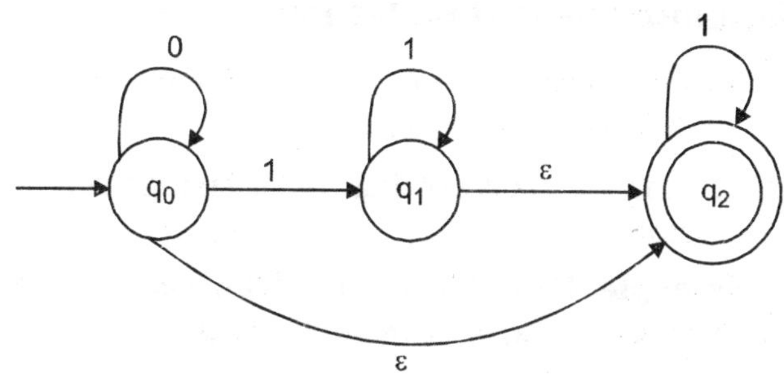


**2.** Then eliminate the $\in$-moves.

from $q_0$ to $q_2$.

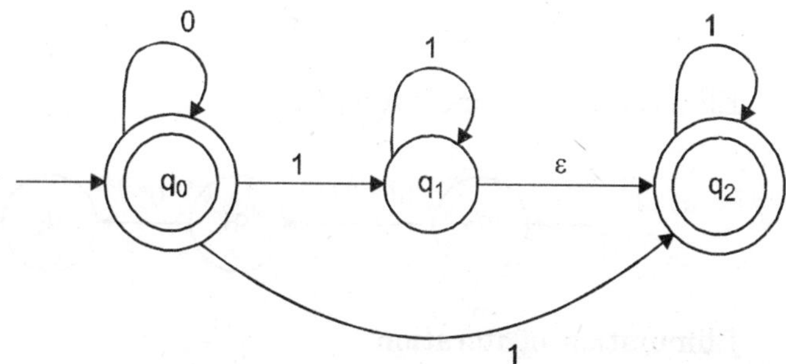


**3.** Now eliminate the $\in$-move from $q_1$ to $q_2$.

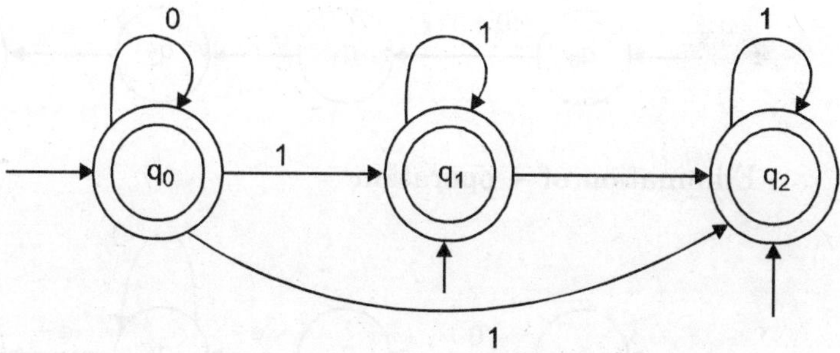


## 4.7.4 Construction of DFA Equivalent to Regular Expression

To construct a finite automaton from a regular expression use the following steps

**Step 1 :** Construct a transition diagraph equivalent to given regular expression with ε-moves

**Step 2 :** Remove the ε-moves from a transition system using procedure of ε-moves from NFA.

**Step 3 :** Construct an equivalent DFA for the transition diagraph obtained in step 2 with reduced states.

## Assumptions in this Method

1. Transition graph has no ε moves if ε-moves then remove ε from transition diagraph by algorithm.
2. $q_i$ is *r.e.* representing set of strings accepted by system as if $q_i$ is final state.

**Example 4.43:** Construct a DFA machine with reduced states equivalent to the regular expression (0 + 11) 0* 1

**Solution:** By step 1

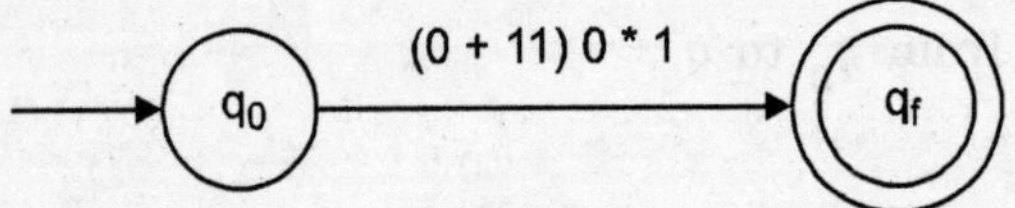


Elimination of concatenation

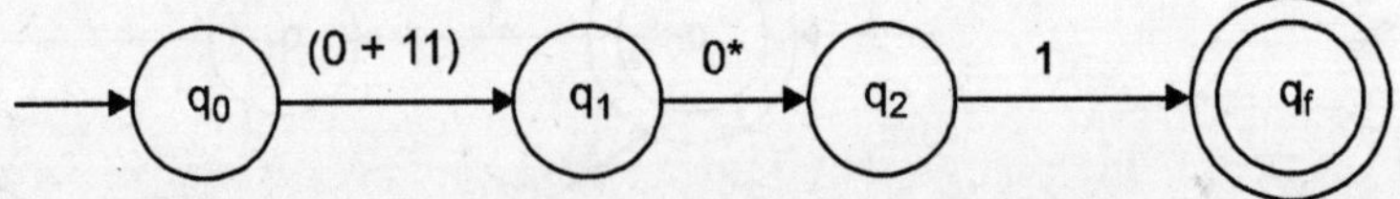


Elimination of iteration

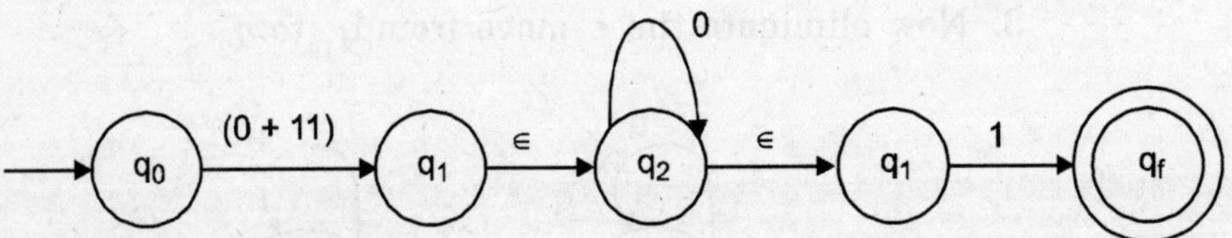


Elimination of + operation

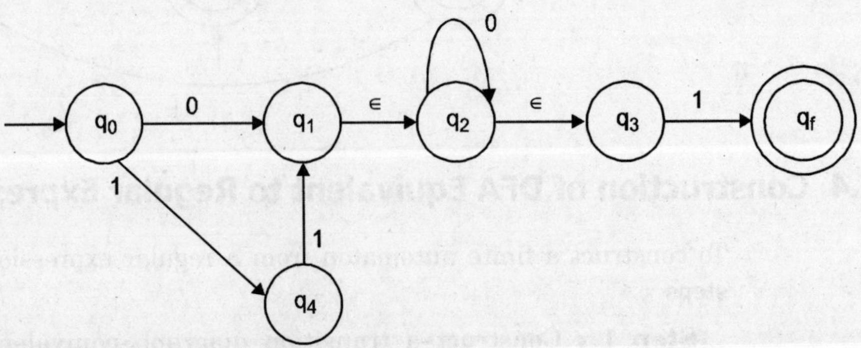


This is a transition system of ε-moves.

Applying step 2 *i.e.,* remove ε-moves from above transition system, we get

Remove ε-moves from state $q_1$ to $q_2$

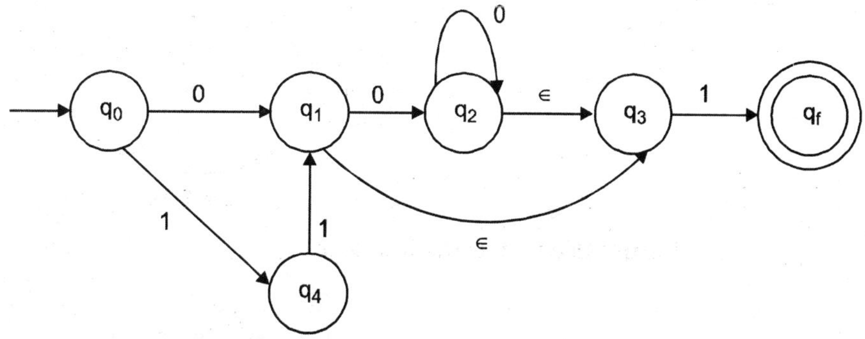


Remove ε-moves from state $q_2$ to $q_3$

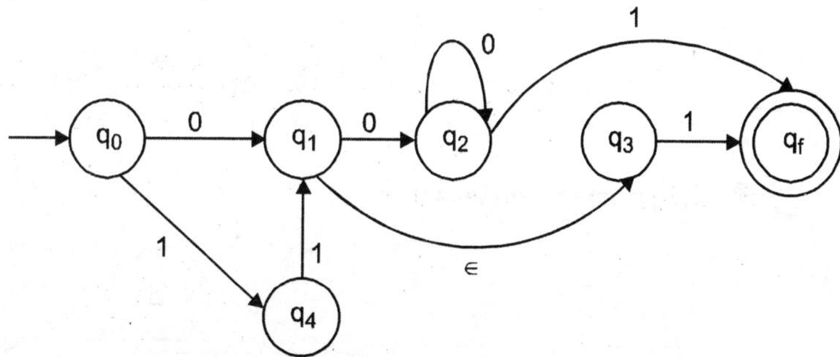


Remove ε-moves from state $q_1$ to $q_3$

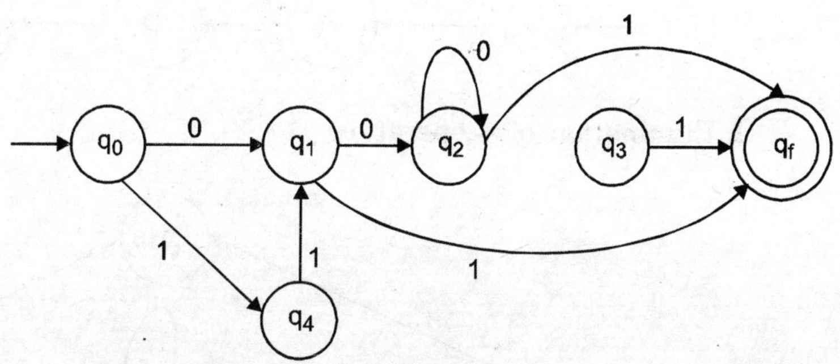


***Fig. 4.33***

This is a reduced DFA machine.

**Example 4.44:** Construct a DFA machine with reduced states equivalent to the regular expression 10 + (0 + 11) 0*1

**Solution:** By step 1

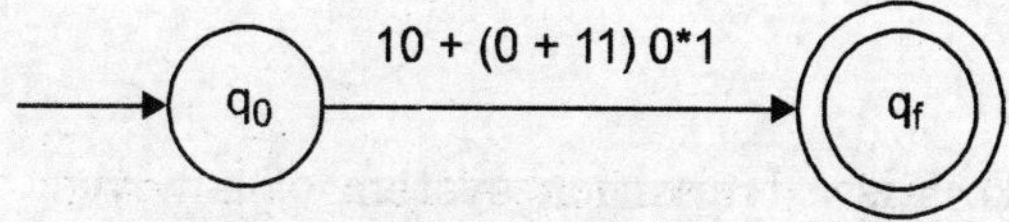


Elimination of first + operation

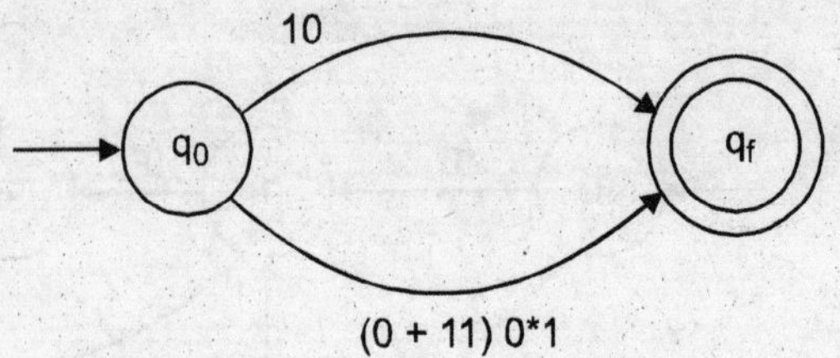


Elimination of concatenation

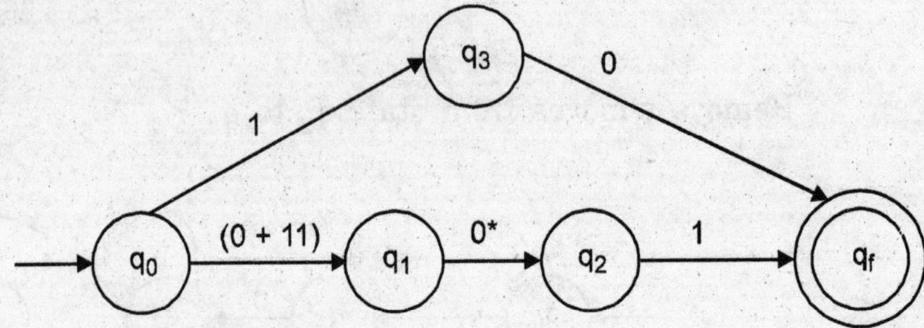


Elimination of iteration

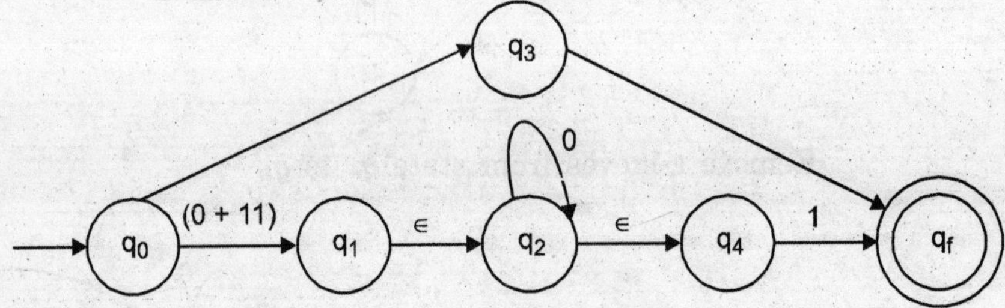


Elimination of + operation

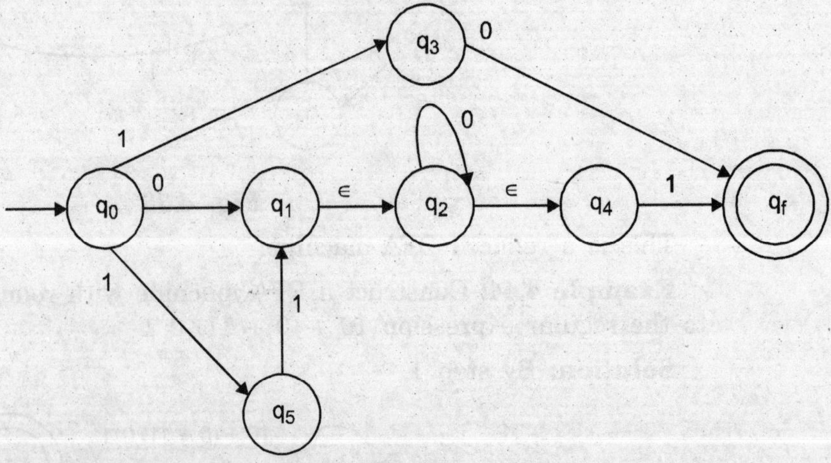


This is a transition system of ε-moves.

Applying step 2 *i.e.,* remove ε-moves from above transition system, we get

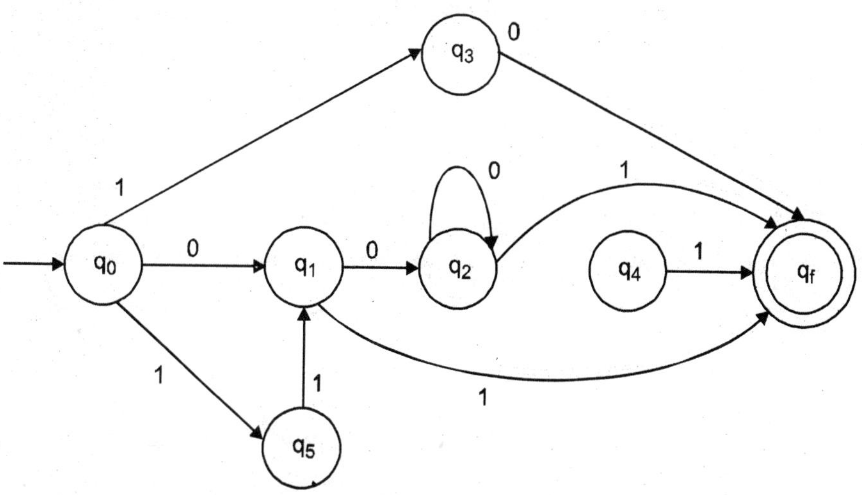


This is a transition system of without ε-moves. This transition system contains a transition system of NFA machine because on present state $q_0$ over input symbol 1, the next states are $q_3$ and $q_4$.

Applying step 3 *i.e.,* convert it into its equivalent DFA, which shows below

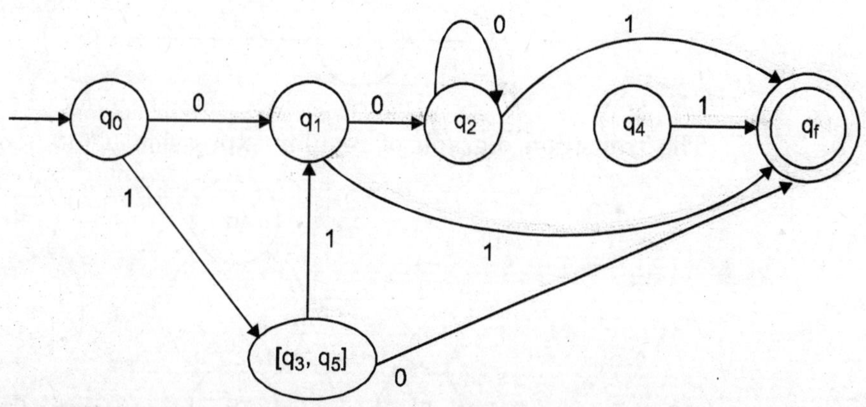


***Fig. 4.34***

**Example 4.45:** Write a regular expression that accept all strings without double $b$ over input symbol $\Sigma = \{a, b\}$. Also find its equivalent transition diagraph.

**Solution:** The regular expression for this given string $R = a^*(ab + a)^* (b + \varepsilon)a^*$

Using Arden's theorem

The transition digraph of regular expression $a^*$

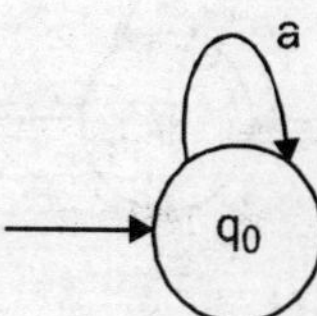

The transition digraph of regular expression $(ab + a)^*$

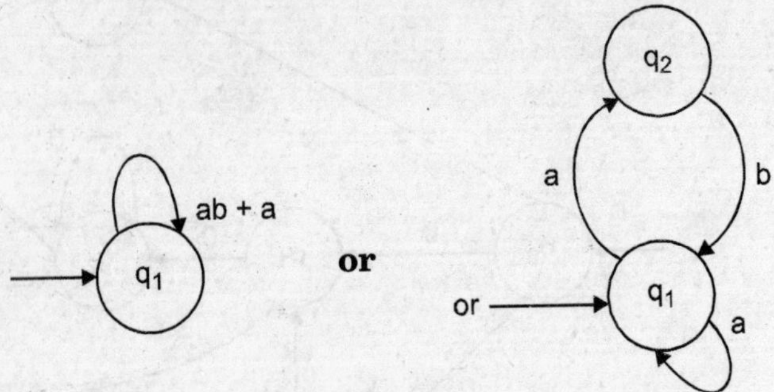


The transition digraph of regular expression $a^*(ab + a)^*$

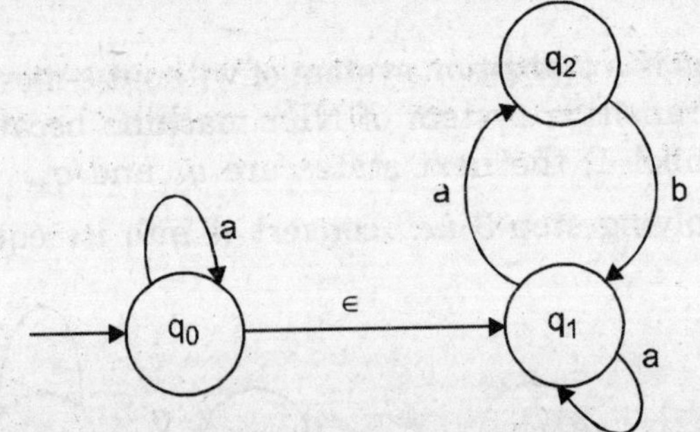


The transition digraph of regular expression $a^*(ab + a)^* (b + \varepsilon)$

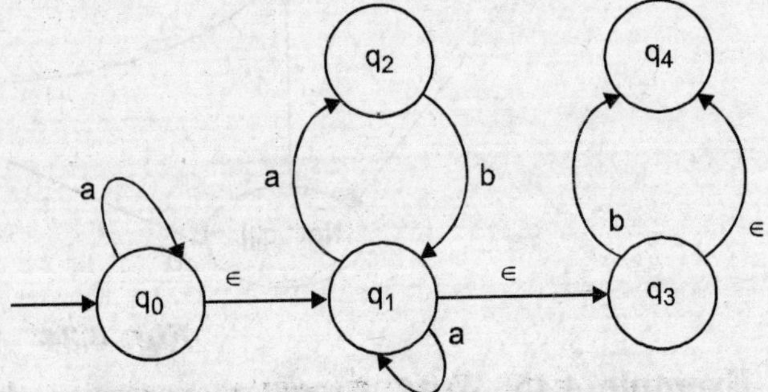


The transition diagraph of regular expression $a^*(ab + a)^* (b + \varepsilon) a^*$

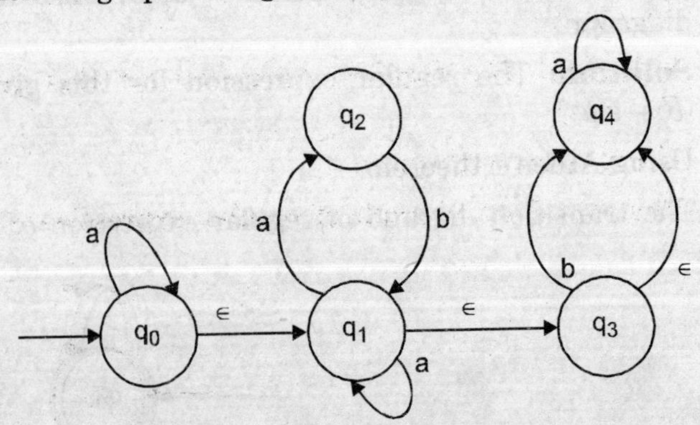

When you remove ε-moves from this transition digraph you set the following transition digraph

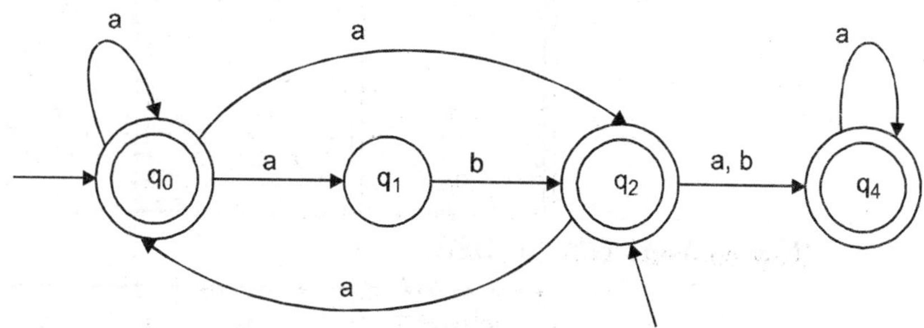


***Fig. 4.35***

**Example 4.46:** Construct a finite automation equivalent to regular expression $(a + b)^* (abb)$.

**Solution:**

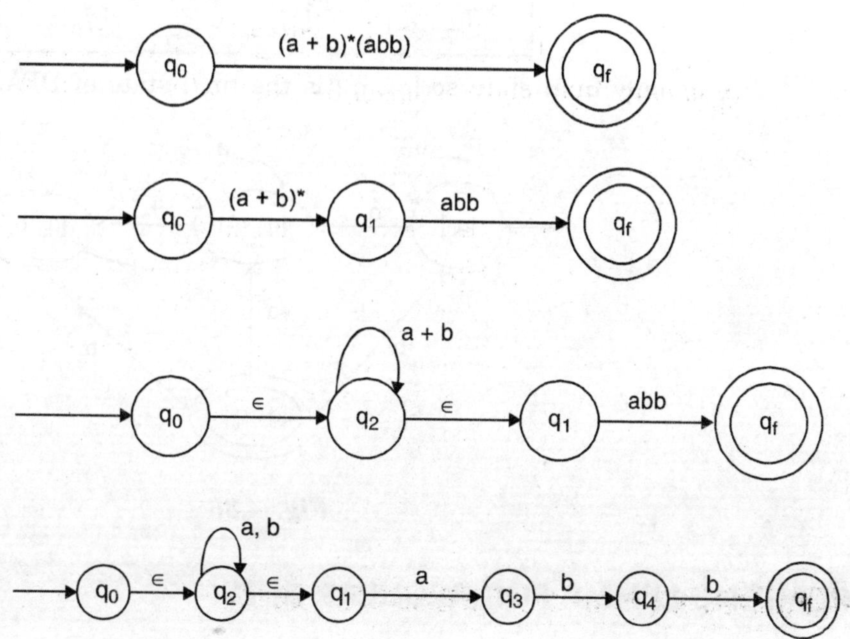


Now, we eliminate ∈-moves and we get NFA equivalent to given regular expression.

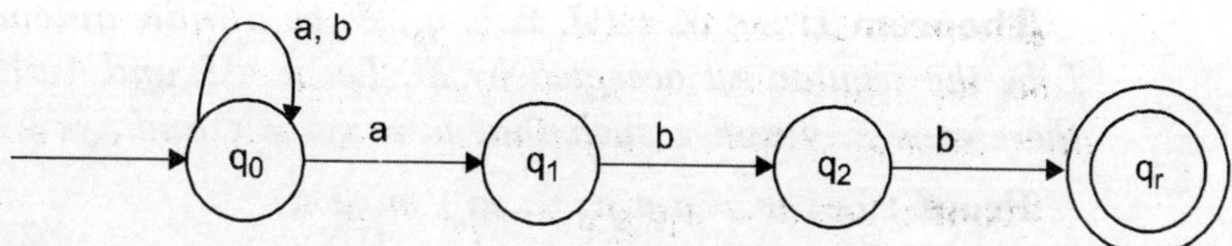


Now construct the transition tables.

| State/Σ | $a$ | $b$ |
|---|---|---|
| $\rightarrow q_0$ | $q_0, q_1$ | $q_0$ |
| $q_1$ | | $q_2$ |
| $q_2$ | | $q_f$ |
| $q_f$ | | |

Now convert NFA to DFA.

| State/Σ | $a$ | $b$ |
|---|---|---|
| $\rightarrow [q_0]$ | $[q_0, q_1]$ | $[q_0]$ |
| $[q_0, q_1]$ | $[q_0, q_1]$ | $[q_0, q_2]$ |
| $[q_0, q_2]$ | $[q_0, q_1]$ | $[q_0, q_f]$ |
| $[q_0, q_f]$ | $[q_0, q_1]$ | $[q_0]$ |

$q_f$ is only final state so $[q_0, q_f]$ is the final state of DFA.

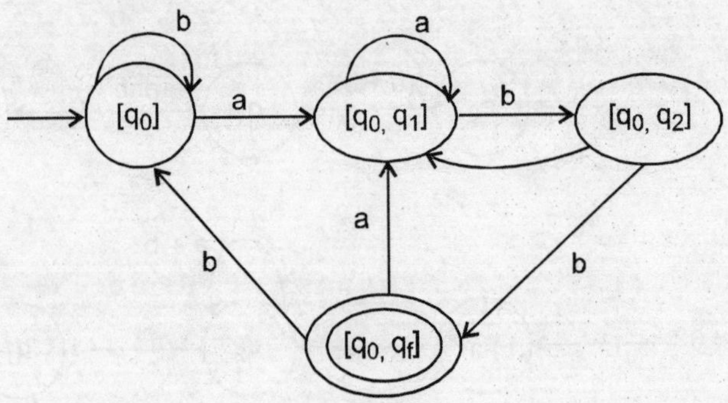


***Fig. 4.36***

## 4.8 PUMPING LEMMA FOR REGULAR SETS

This lemma is used to prove certain sets of languages (or strings) are regular or not regualr.

**Theorem 1:** *Let $M = (Q, \Sigma, \delta, q_0, F)$ be a finite automata with n state. Let L be the regular set accepted by M. Let $w \in L$ and $|w| \geq m$. If $m \geq n$, then there exist x, y and z such that $w = xyz \neq \varepsilon$ and $xyz \in L$ for each $i \geq 0$.*

**Proof :** Let $w = a_1 a_2 a_3 \ldots\ldots a_m$, $m \geq n$

and $\delta (q_0, a_1, a_2, a_3 \ldots, a_i) = q_i$ for $i = 1, 2, \ldots m$.

Since the number of different input alphabet are $m$ in sequence, so number of states in DFA is $m + 1$, *i.e.*, $\{q_0, q_1, q_2, .......q_m\}$. These sequence of states represent continuous sequence of states with input value $w = a_1\ a_2\ a_3\ ......a_n$ corresponding to these states. Consider the DFA machine, there are only $n$ distinct states & $m \geq n$. It means at least two states in sequence of states (*i.e.*, $\{q_0, q_1, q_2, ......\ q_m\}$) must coincide. Among various pairs of states in sequence of states (*i.e.*, $\{q_0, q_1, q_2, .......q_m\}$) must coincide. Among various pairs of states, we take the first pair. Let the pair be $q_j$ and $q_k$ ($q_j = q_k$) then $j$ and $k$ satisfy the condition $0 \leq j < \leq n$.

The string can be decomposed into three substring $a_1a_2......a_j$, $a_{j+1}$, $a_{j+2}$ $......a_k$ and $a_{k+1}\ a_{k+2}\ ......\ a_m$. Let $x$, $y$ and $z$ denote these string $a_1a_2\ ......a_j$, $a_{j+1}a_{j+2}\ ......\ a_k$ and $a_{k+1}\ a_{k+2}\ ...\ a_m$ respectively. As $k \leq n$, $|xy| \leq n$ and $w = xyz$. The sequence of states with input value $w$ in the transition diagram of $M$ is as shown in the figure given here

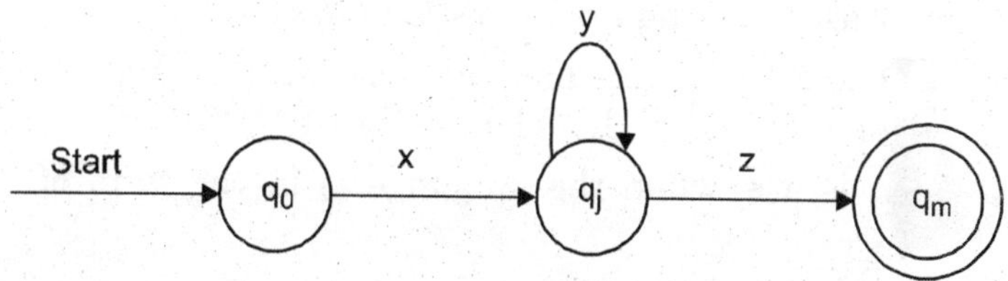


***Fig. 4.37***

Here $q_0$ is the initial state and $q_m$ is a final state. On applying input value $x$ with state label $q_0$ the next state is $q_j$ and on input values $y$ and $z$ with state label $q_j$ the next states $q_j$ and $q_m$ respectively. It shows an input value $y$ on state label $q_j$, the state will not change (*i.e.*, $y^i \mid i \geq 0$). Hence $xyz \in L$ since every state in sequence of states is obtained by applying an input symbol $y \neq \in$.

## 4.8.1 Application of Pumping Lemma

The pumping lemma gives the steps in proving if a given set is not a regular.

**Step 1 :** Assume $L$ is regular set and $n$ be the number of states in corresponding finite automata.

**Step 2 :** Choose a string $w$ such that $|w| \geq n$. Use pumping lemma to write $w = xyz$ with $|xy| \leq n$ and $> 0$.

**Step 3 :** Find a suitable integer $i$ such that $xy^iz \notin L$ *i.e.*, we have to decompose the language in the form of three string $x$, $y$ & $z$ and for each value of $i$, $y$ must exist.

If it is not possible, $L$ is not regular.

**Example 4.47:** Using pumping lemma, show that the following set is not regular:

$$L = \{a^n\ b^{2n}\ /\ n > 0\}$$ ***[U.P.T.U MCA 2003, B-Tech 05]***

**Solution:** By step 1: Assume $L$ is regular set and $n$ be the number of states $m$ corresponding finite automata accepting $L$.

By step 2: Let $w = a^n b^{2n}$

Then $|w| \geq n$

*i.e.,* $|3n| \geq n$

By pumping lemma

$$w = xyz \text{ with } |xy| \leq n \text{ and } |y| > 0 (i.e., |y| \neq 0)$$

By step 3 : We have to find for what value of $i$, the language $xy^iz, \in L$. The given language $a^nb^{2n}$ can be decomposed in the form of $xy^iz \; \forall \; i \leq 0$. Then the string $y$ can be in any of the following forms

Case 1 : $y$ has only '$a$'s' *i.e.,* $y = a^k$ for $k > 0$.

Case 2 : $y$ has only '$b$'s' *i.e.,* $y = b^1$ for $1 > 0$.

Case 3 : $y$ has both '$a$'s' and '$b$'s'.

**Case 1 :** Since $y$ has only $a$'s *i.e.,* $y = a^k$ for $k > 0$. Then $x$ should be either $\in$ or $a^{n-k}$ and $z$ should be either $a^{n-k\;k}b^{2n}$ as explained below

$x$ is a $\in$ when the language is in the form of $(\in)$ $(a^k)$ $(a^{n-k}b^{2n})$

$$\begin{array}{ccc} (\in) & (a^k) & (a^{n-k}b^{2n}) \\ \downarrow & \downarrow & \downarrow \\ x & y & z \end{array}$$

if $x$ is $a^{(n-k)}$ then the language in the form of $(a^{n-k})$ $(a^k)$ $(b^{2n})$

$$\begin{array}{ccc} (a^{n-k}) & (a^k) & (b^{2n}) \\ \downarrow & \downarrow & \downarrow \\ x & y & z \end{array}$$

Now when $i = 0$ then the string $xyz$ becomes $xz$ *i.e.,* $a^{n-k}b^{2n}$. In each of above cases the number $b$'s are not twice to number $a$'s.

Hence $xy^1z \notin L$ for $i = 0$.

**Case 2 :** Since $y$ has only $b$'s *i.e.,* $y = b^1$ for $1 > 0$. Then $x$ should be either $a^nb^{2n-1}$, or $\notin$ and $z$ should be either $\in$ or $b^{2n-1}$ as explained below

$x$ is a $a^nb^{2n-1}$ when the language in the form of $(a^nb^{2n-1})(b^1)(\in)$ and $x$ is a $a^n$ when the language in the form of $(a^n)(b^1)\,b^{2n-1}$. Now again when $i = 0$ the string $xy^iz$ is only $xz$ *i.e.,* $a^nb^{2n-1}$ in the above each cases of both $x$ and $z$ for $1 \geq 1$ (or $1 > 0$), show that the number $b$'s are not twice to the number $a$'s.

Hence $xy^iz \in L$ for $i = 0$.

**Case 3 :** $y$ has both $a$'s and $b$'s *i.e.,* $y = a^kb^1$ for $k$, $1 > 0$. Then the string $w$ in the form of

$$\begin{array}{ccc} (a^{n-k}) & (a^kb^1) & (b^{2n-1}) \\ \downarrow & \downarrow & \downarrow \\ x & y & z \end{array}$$

when $i = 2$ then string $w = xy^2z$ or $w = xyz$.

*i.e.,* $a^{n-k}a^kb^1a^kb^1b^{2n-1}$

In given language a will never come after $b's$, so $xyz \notin L$ for $i = 2$. That is $xy^2z \notin L$.

In the above all cases we got the contradiction. Therefore language $L$ is not a regular.

**Example 4.48:** Prove that $0^n1^n$ is not a regular.

**[*UPTU MCA 2002*]**

**Solution:** By step 1 : Assume $L$ is regular set and $n$ be the number of states in corresponding finite automata accepting $L$.

By step 2 : Let $w = 0^n \; 1^n$

Then $|w| \geq n$

*i.e.*, $|2n| \geq n$

By pumping lemma

$$w = xyz \text{ with } |xy| \leq n \text{ and } |y| > 0 \; (i.e., \; |y| \neq 0)$$

By step 3 : We have to find for what value of $i$, the language $xy^iz \notin L$.

The given language $0^n1^n$ can be decomposed in the form of $xy^iz$, $\forall \; i \geq 0$. Then the string $y$ can be in any of the following forms

Case 1 : $y$ has only $0's$ *i.e.*, $y = 0^k$ for $k > 0$.

Case 2 : $y$ has only $1's$ 3 *i.e.*, $y = 1^1$ for $i > 0$.

Case 3 : $y$ has both $0's$ and $1's$.

**Case 1 :** Since $y$ has only $0's$ *i.e.*, $y = 0^k$ for $k > 0$. Then $x$ should be either $\in$ or $0^{n-k}$ and $z$ should be either $0^{n-k}1^n$ or $1^n$ as explained below

if $x$ is $\in$, then the language is in the form of $\underset{x}{\underset{\downarrow}{(\in)}} \; \underset{y}{\underset{\downarrow}{(0^k)}} \; \underset{z}{\underset{\downarrow}{(0^{n-k}1^n)}}$

if $x$ is $a^{(n-k)}$, then the language is in the form of $\underset{x}{\underset{\downarrow}{(0^{n-k})}} \; \underset{y}{\underset{\downarrow}{(0^k)}} \; \underset{z}{\underset{\downarrow}{(1^n)}}$

Now when $i = 0$ then the string $xy^iz$ is only $xz$ *i.e.*, $0^{n-k} \; 1^n$, in both the cases for $k \geq 1$, which show $n - k \neq n$. *i.e.*, the number $0's$ and $1's$ are not equal.

Hence $xy^iz \notin L$ for $i = 0$.

**Case 2 :** Since $y$ has only $1's$ *i.e.*, $y = 1^1$ for $1 > 0$. Then $x$ should be either $0^n1^{n-1}$ or $\in$ and $z$ should be either $\in$ or $1^{n-1}$ as explained below

If $x$ is a $0^n1^{n-1}$, then the language is in the of $\underset{x}{\underset{\downarrow}{(0^n1^{n-1})}} \; \underset{y}{\underset{\downarrow}{(0^1)}} \; \underset{z}{\underset{\downarrow}{(\in)}}$

and if $x$ is $0^n$, then the language is in the form of $\underset{x}{\underset{\downarrow}{(0^n)}} \; \underset{y}{\underset{\downarrow}{(1^1)}} \; \underset{z}{\underset{\downarrow}{(1^{n-1})}}$

Now again when $i = 0$ the string $xy^iz$ is only $xz$ *i.e.,* $0^n1^{n-1}$ in both cases for $1 \geq 1$ (or $1 > 0$) which shows $n \neq n - 1$ *i.e.,* the number 0's and 1's are not equal.

Hence $xy^iz \in L$ for$i = 0$

**Case 3:** $y$ has both 0's and 1's *i.e.,* $y = 0^k\ 1^l$ for $k$, $1 > 0$.

Then the string ω in the form of $\underset{x}{(0^{n-k})}\ \underset{y}{(0^k i)}\ \underset{z}{(1^{n-1})}$

when $i = 2$ then string $w = xy^2z$ or $w = xyyz$.

*i.e.,* $0^{n-k}0^k1^10^k1^1\ 1^{n-1}$

In given language 0's will never come after 1's, so $xy^iz \notin L$ for $i = 2$. That is $xy^2z \notin L$.

In the above all cases we got the contradiction. Therefore language $L$ is not a regular.

**Example 4.49:** Show that the set $L = \{a^{n^2} / n \geq 1\}$ is not a regular.

**Solution:** By step 1 : Assume $L$ be a regular set and $n$ be the number of states in corresponding to finite automation accepting $L$.

By step 2 : Let $w = a^{n^2}$

Then $|w| = n^2$

and $|n^2| > n$.

By pumping lemma $w = xyz$

with $|xy| \leq n$

and $|y| > 0$.

By step 3 : we have to find the integer value of $i$ such that $xy^iz \notin L$.

Now consider $i = 1$.

Then $w = xyz$

$= a^{n^2} \in L$.

Now again consider $i = 2$

Then $w = xy^2z = xyyz = |x| + |y| + |y| + |z|$

$= |x + 2|y| + |z|$

We know $|xyz| = n^2$

So $|x| + 2|y| + |z| = n^2 + |y|$

Since $|y| \geq 1$ and $|y|\ n$.

So $n^2 + |y| \leq n^2 + n$

This is not a perfect seqare so $xyz \notin L$ for $i = 2$ *i.e.,* $xy^2z \notin L$.

This is a contradiction.

Hence given language $L$ is not a regular.

**Example 4.50:** Show that the set $L = \{a^n / n \geq 1\}$ is not regular.

**Solution:** By step 1 : Assume $L$ to be a regular set and $n$ be the number of states corresponding to finite automation accepting $L$.

By step 2 : Let $w = a^{n!}$

Then $|w| = n!$

and $|n!| > n$.

By pumping lemma

$$w = xyz$$

with $|xy| \leq n$.

and $|y| > 0$.

By step 3 : We have to find the integer value of $i$ such that $xy^iz \notin L$.

Now consider $i = 0$

Then $w = xz = n! - j$

where $j > 0$ because the length of $y$ is greater than 0

When you subtract positive length of a string from any string whose length is equivalent to factorial number, then string length will never remain a string length of factorial number. That is $n! - j \neq m!$ where $m$ is any positive number.

So $xy^iz \notin L$

for $i = 0$

This is a contradiction.

Hence given language $L$ is not a regular.

## 4.9 REGULAR GRAMMAR

### 4.9.1 Construction of DFA from Regular Grammar

Use the following procedures to convert a regular grammar to DFA (*i.e.,* Finite State Machine)

Let $G$ be a regular grammar accepting language $L(G)$.

Let $G = (\{A_0, A_1, A_2, ...A_n\}, \Sigma, P, A_0)$. We construct a DFA corresponding to the following steps

**Step 1 :** The states corresponding to the given variables $A_0$, $A_1$, $A_2$, ...$A_n$ are $q_0$, $q_1$, $q_2$, ....$q_n$

**Step 2 :** The input symbols of DFA will be the corresponding terminal symbols of regular grammar $G$.

**Step 3 :** Make initial state corresponding to the starting symbol (*i.e.,* if starting symbol is $A_0$ then initial states is $q_0$)

**Step 4 :** The transition system (*i.e.,* δ) of a DFA machine $M$ is defined corresponding to the production rules (*i.e., P*) of the grammar as follows.

(*i*) A production rule in the form of $A_i \rightarrow aAj$ includes a transition from $q_i$ to $q_j$ with label *a. i.e.,*

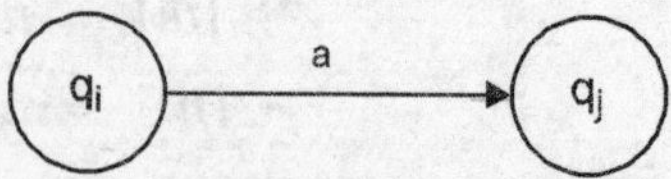


(*ii*) A production rule in the form of $A_k \rightarrow a$ induce a transition from $q_k$ to $q_f$ with label a where $q_f$ is a final state.

*ie.,*

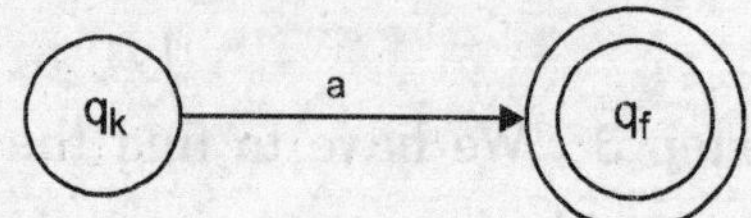


---

If $S \rightarrow \in$ is in $P$ the corresponding transition is from $q_0$ to $q_j$ with label $\in$.

---

**Example 4.51:** Let $G = (\{A_0, A_1\}, \{a, b\}, P, A_0)$ where $P$ consists of $A_0 \rightarrow aA_1, A_1 \rightarrow bA_1, A_1 \rightarrow a, A_1 \rightarrow bA_0$ construct a DFA accepting $L(G)$.

**Solution:** The given grammar $G$ is

$$G = (\{A_0, A_1\}, \{a, b\}, P, A_0)$$

Where the production rules $P$ consists of

$$A_0 \rightarrow aA_1,\ A_1 \rightarrow bA_1,\ A_1 \rightarrow bA_0,\ A_1 \rightarrow a$$

Now we construct a DFA corresponding to the following steps

**Step 1 :** The states corresponding to the given variables (*i.e.,* $A_0, A_1$) are $\{q_0, q_1\}$

**Step 2 :** The input symbols of DFA is $\{a, b\}$ corresponding to the terminal symbols $\{a, b\}$ of regular grammar $G$.

**Step 3 :** Make the initial state $q_0$ corresponding to the starting symbol $A_0$

**Step 4 :** The transition system $\{i.e., \delta\}$ of a DFA machine $M$ is define corresponding to the production rules (*i.e., P*) of a grammar as follows.

(*i*) The transition system corresponding to the production rule

$A_0 \rightarrow aA_1, A_1 \rightarrow bA_1\ A_1 \rightarrow bA_0$ are

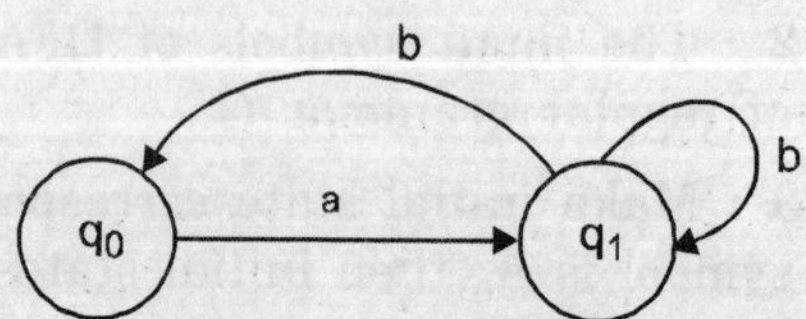

(*ii*) The transition system corresponding to the production rule $A_1 \to a$

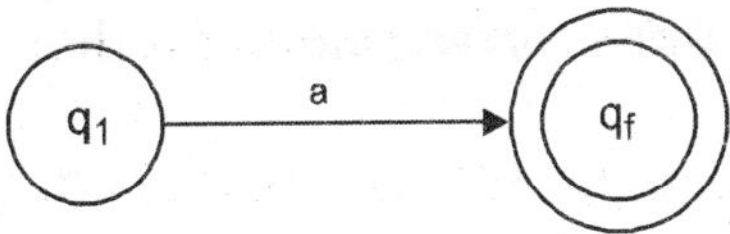


Hence the transition digraph corresponding to the production rules $A_0 \to aA_1$, $A_1 \to bA_1$, $A_1 \to bA_0$, $A_1 \to a$ is as follows

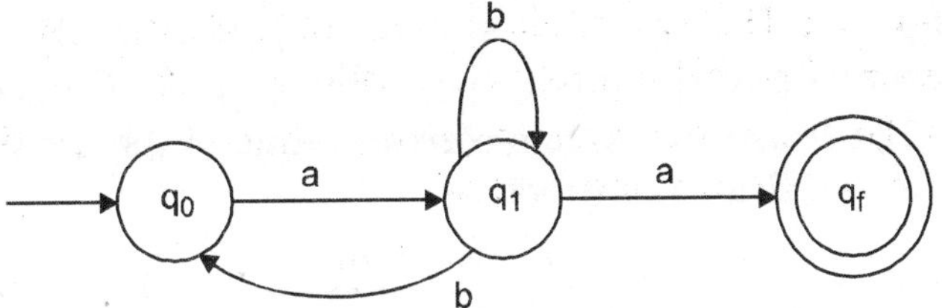


Since this transition system does not contains a transition system of DFA machine, so convert this transition system into equivalent transition system of DFA machine. We shall get the following transition diagraph of the equivalent DFA.

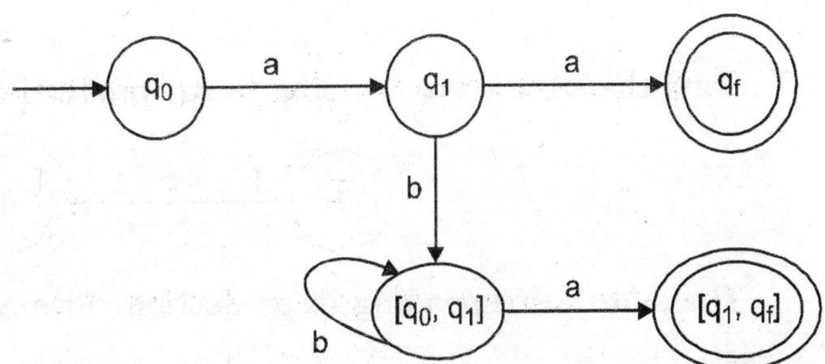


***Fig. 4.38***

Hence the minimized DFA machine $M = (\{q_0, q_1, q_f, [q_0, q_f]\}, \{a, b], \delta, q_0, \{q_f, [q_1, q_r]\})$ where δ is shown in Fig. 4.38.

**Example 4.52:** Consider the following grammar *G*

$$G = (\{S, A, B\}, \{0, 1\}, P, S)$$

where *P* is defined as follows

$$S \to 0A/1B/0/1$$

$$A \to 0S/1B/1$$

$$B \to 0A/1S$$

construct a DFA accepting *L*(*G*).

**Solution:** The given grammar *G*

$$G = (\{S, A, B\}, \{0, 1\}, P, S)$$

where *P* is defined as follows

$$S \to 0A/1B/0/1$$

$$A \to 0S/1B/1$$

$$B \to 0A/1S$$

Now we construct a DFA corresponding to the following steps

**Step 1 :** The states corresponding to the given variables (*i.e.*, $S$, $A$, $B$) are $\{q_0, q_1, q_2\}$

**Step 2 :** The input symbols of DFA is {0, 1} corresponding to the terminal symbols {0, 1} of regular grammar $G$.

**Step 3 :** Make the initial state $q_0$ corresponding to the starting symbol $S$

**Step 4 :** The transition system (*i.e.*, $\delta$) of a DFA machine $M$ is defined corresponding to the production rules (*i.e.*, $P$) of a grammar as follows.

(*i*) The transition system corresponding to the production rule $S \to 0A$ and $S \to 1B$ is shown below

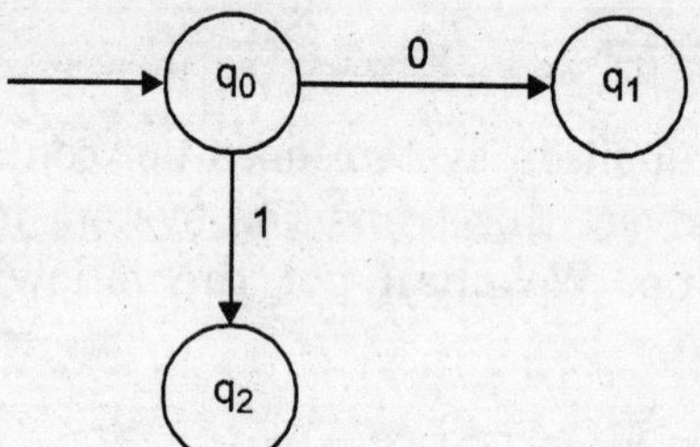


and the state corresponding to the production rule $S \to 0 \mid 1$ is as follows

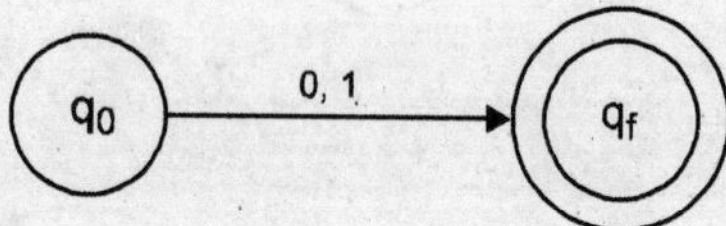


The state corresponding to production rules $S \to 0A/1B \mid 0 \mid 1$ is as follows

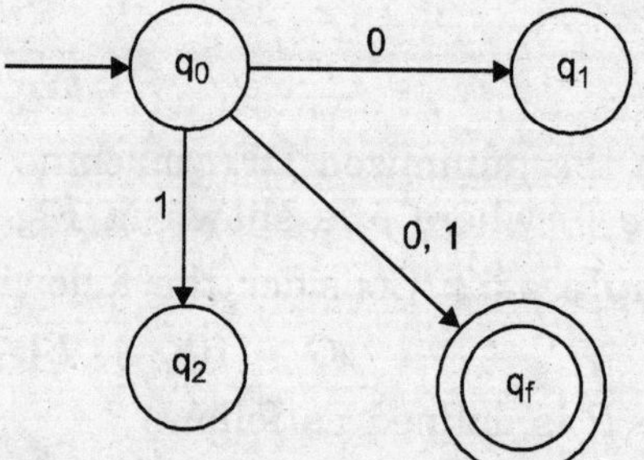


The state corresponding to production rules $S \to 0A \mid 1B \mid 0 \mid 1$ and $A \to 0S$ is as follows

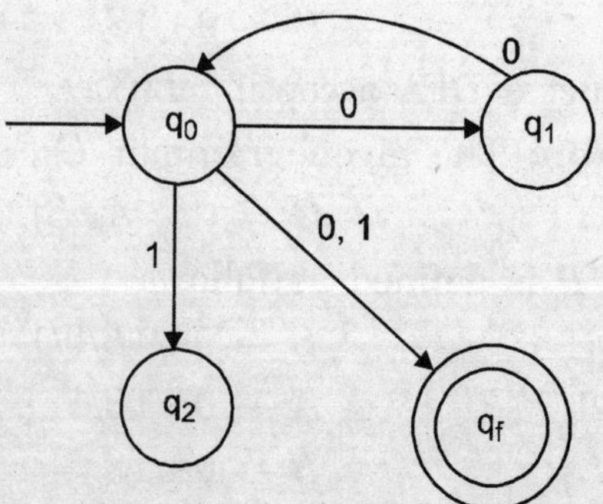

The state corresponding to production rules $S \rightarrow 0A \mid 1B \mid 0 \mid 1$ and $A \rightarrow 0S$ is as follows

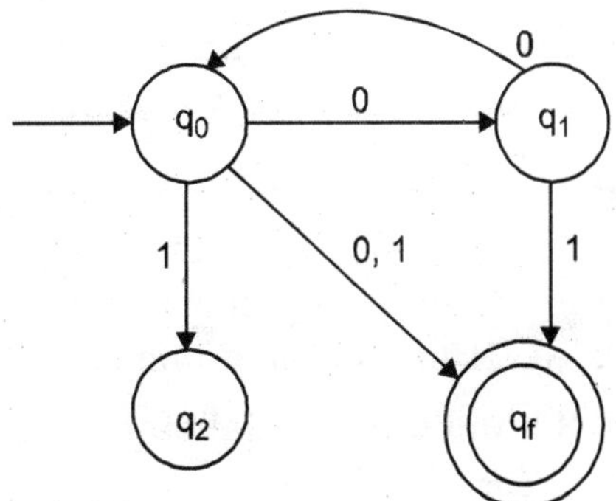


Hence the state corresponding to production rules $S \rightarrow 0A \mid 1B \mid 0 \mid 1$, $A \rightarrow 0S1$ and $B \rightarrow 0A \mid 1S$ is as follows

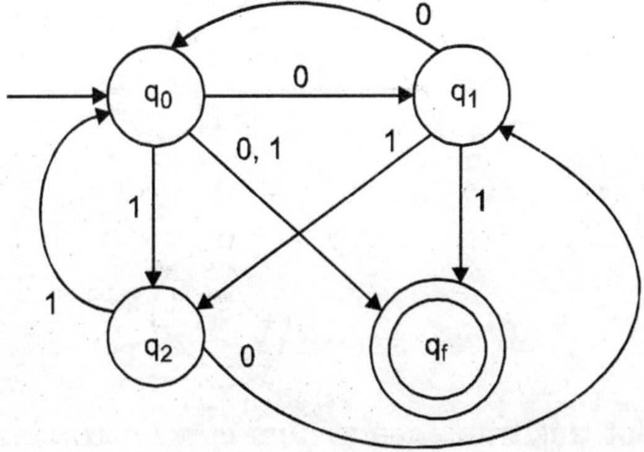


Since this transition system does not contains a transition system of DFA machine, so convert this transition system into equivalent transition system of DFA machine which gives the transition digraph of the equivalent DFA as shown below.

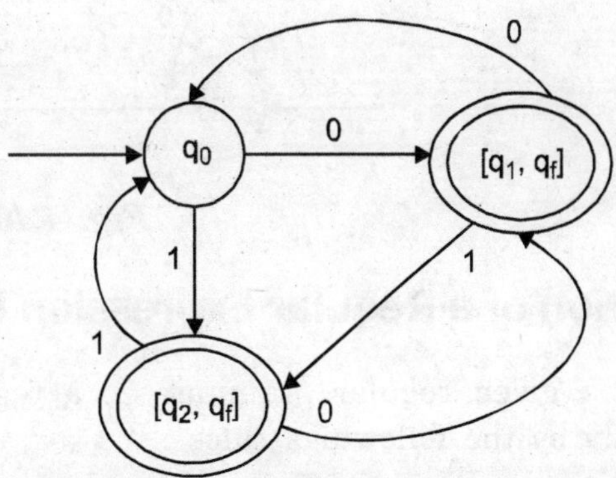


***Fig. 4.39***

**Example 4.53:** Consider the following grammar:

$$S \rightarrow 0S/1A/1$$
$$A \rightarrow 0A/1A0/1$$

**Solution:** The given production rules corresponding to the grammar are

$$S \to 0S/1A/1$$

$$A \to 0A/1A/0/1$$

Now we construct a DFA corresponding to the following steps

**Step 1 :** The states corresponding to the given variables (*i.e., S, A*) are $\{q_0, q_1\}$

**Step 2 :** The input symbols of DFA is {0, 1} corresponding to the terminal symbols {0, 1} of regular grammar *G*.

**Step 3 :** Make the initial state $q_0$ corresponding to the starting symbol *S*.

**Step 4 :** The transition system (*i.e.,* δ) of a DFA machine *M* is defined corresponding to the production rules (*i.e., P*) of a grammar is as follows.

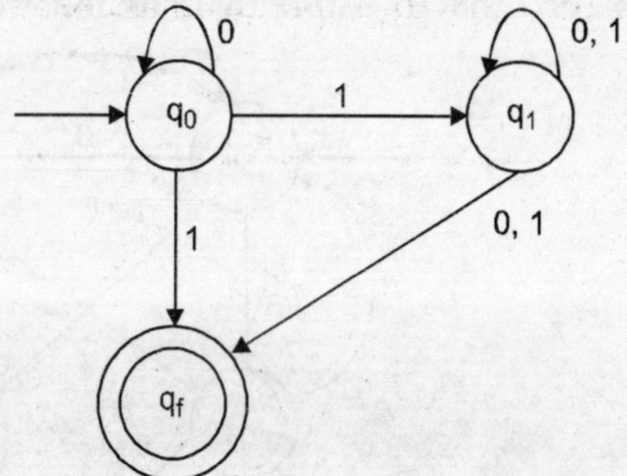


But this transition system is not a transition system of DFA machine. It is a NFA machine. Now convert this NDA machine into its equivalent DFA machine. Then we get a DFA machine whose transition digraph shall be as follows

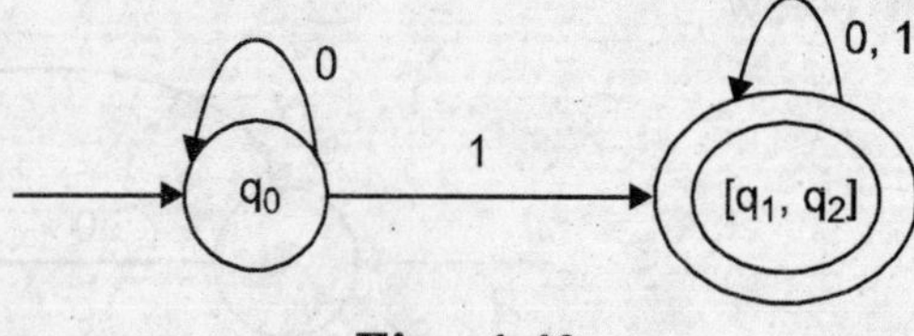


*Fig. 4.40*

## 4.9.2 Construction of a Regular Expression From a Regular Grammar

From a given regular grammar *G*, a regualr expression can be obtained directly by the followings rules :

**Rule 1 :** Replace all the symbol '→' by '=' in the production rules of a given regular grammar, to get a set of equations

**Rule 2 :** Solve the set of equations obtained above to obtain the value of the starting symbol *S* of the grammar, by following rules (*i*) If the set of equation is in the form of $A = aA \mid b$ (where $a$ and $b$ are the terminal symbols and $A$ is the non -terminal symbol), then the solution of the equation is $A = a^*b$.

(*ii*) If the set of equation is in the form of $A = aA \mid b \mid a$ (where $a$ and $b$ are the terminal symbols and $A$ is the non-terminal symbol), then the solution of the equation is $A = a^*(b + a)$.

(*iii*) If the set of equation is in the form of $A = Aa \mid b$ (where $a$ and $b$ are the terminal symbols and $A$ is the non-terminal symbol), then the solution of the equation is $A = ba^*$.

(*iv*) If the set of equation is in the form of $A = Aa \mid b \mid \in$ (where $a$ and $b$ are the terminal symbols and $A$ is the non-terminal symbol), then the solution of the equation is $A = (b + \in)\, a^*$.

**Example 5.54:** Consider the regular grammar $G = (\{S, A, B\}, \{0, 1\}, P, S)$ where production rule $P$ is defined as follows

$$S \to 0A/1B/0/1$$

$$A \to 1A/1$$

$$B \to 0B/1S$$

**Solution:** Applying rule 1, we get the following set of equation

$$S = 0A \mid 1B \mid 0 \qquad \text{...(1)}$$

$$A = 1A \mid 1 \qquad \text{...(2)}$$

$$B = 0B \mid 1S \qquad \text{...(3)}$$

Applying rule 2 (*i*) in the equation (2) and (3), we get the following equation

$$A = 1^*1 = 1^+$$

$$B = 0^*1S$$

Now substituting the value of $A$ and $B$ in equation (1), we get

$$S = 01^+ \mid 10^*1S \mid 0$$

$$S = 10^*1S \mid 01^+ \mid 0 \qquad \text{...(4)}$$

Applying rule 2 (*i*) in the equation (4)), we get the following equation

$$S = (10^*1)^*\ (01^+ + 0)$$

Hence the required regular expression is $(10^*1)^*\ (01^+ + 0)$

## 4.9.3 Construction of a Regular Grammar From a Regular Expression

To construct a regular grammar from regular expression use the following method

**Method I :** Construct a DFA from a given regular expression using the method of construction of a DFA from regular expression

Construct a regular grammar from a DFA using the method of construction of a regular grammar from DFA machine.

**Method II :** Use the following steps to write a regular grammar

**Step 1 :** Factorize the regular expression in the form of sub regular expression.

**Step 2 :** Write production rules of all its sub regular expression.

**Step 3 :** Combine all the production rules of step 2 with given order of regular expression.

There shall be the production rules of regular grammar.

---

The first method is lengthy grammar so try to write grammar from second method.

---

**Example 4.55:** Write a regular grammar for the language $(a + b)^* + a^*b$

**Solution:** By second method

By step 1 : Factorize this regular expression in the form of two sub regular expression *i..e,* $(a + b)^*$ and $a^* b$

By step 2 : The production rules for its sub regular expression $(a + b)^*$ are

$$A \rightarrow aA \mid bA \mid Î$$

The production rules for its sub regular expression $a^*b$ are

$$B \rightarrow aB \mid b$$

By step 3 : Combine all these production rules of step 2 with given order of regular expression, we get

$$S \rightarrow A \mid B$$

$$A \rightarrow aA \mid bA \mid \in$$

$$B \rightarrow aB \mid b$$

Hence the regular grammar $G = (\{S\}, \{a, b\}, \{S \rightarrow A \mid B, A \rightarrow aA \mid bA \mid A, B \rightarrow ab|b\} S)$

**Example 4.56:** Write a regular grammar for the language $a^*b(a + b)^*$.

**Solution:** By second method

By step 1 : Factorize this regular expression in the form of two sub regular expression *i..e,* $a^*b$ and $(a + b)^*$

By step 2 : The production rules for its sub regular expression $a^*b$ are

$$S \rightarrow aS \mid b$$

The production rules for its sub regular expression $(a + b)^*$ are

$$A \rightarrow aA \mid bA \mid b \mid a$$

By step 3 : Combine all these production rule of step 2 with given order of regular expression, we get

$$S \rightarrow aS \mid b$$

$$S \rightarrow bA$$

$$A \rightarrow aA \mid bA \mid b \mid a$$

Hence the regular grammar $G = (\{S, A\}, \{a, b\}, \{S \rightarrow aS \mid b, S \rightarrow bA, A\ aA \mid bA \mid b \mid a\}, S)$

### 4.9.4 Construction of a Regular Grammar From a DFA

Let $M = (\{q_0, q_1, ......q_n\}, \Sigma, \delta, q_0, F)$ then we can construct a regular grammar according to the following rules.

(*a*) The set of variables correspond to the set of states.

(*b*) The set of terminals correspond to the set of alphabets.

(*c*) The starting symbol corresponding to the initial states.

(*d*) The production rules $P$ is defined by the following

(*i*) $A_i \rightarrow aA_j$ is included in $P$ $\delta(q_i, a) = q_j \notin F$.

(*ii*) $A_i \rightarrow aA_j$ and $A_i \rightarrow a$ are included in $P$ if $\delta(q_i, a) = q_j \in F$.

**Example 4.57:** Let us consider a DFA whose transition digraph is shown in below.

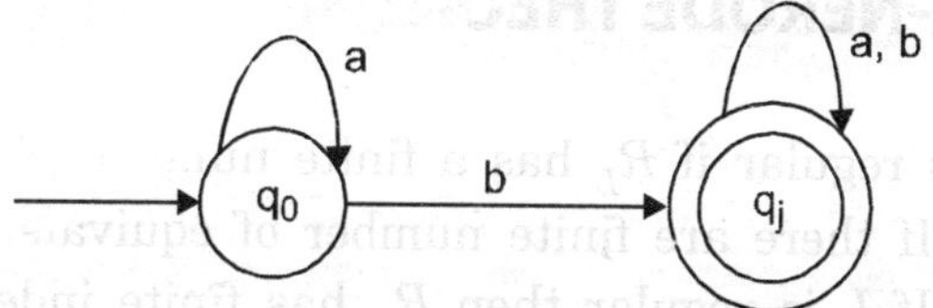


***Fig. 4.41***

Find a regular grammar equivalent to the DFA machine.

**Solution:**

(*a*) The set of variable $\{A_0, A_1\}$ corresponding to the set of states $\{q_0, q_1\}$.

(*b*) The set of terminals $\{a, b\}$ corresponding to the set of alphabets $\{a, b\}$.

(*c*) The starting symbol corresponding to the initial states.

(*d*) The production rules $P$ is defined by the following

$A_0 \rightarrow aA_0$ by rule $d(i)$

$$\left.\begin{array}{l} A_0 \rightarrow bA_1 \\ A_1 \rightarrow aA_1 \\ A_1 \rightarrow bA_1 \\ A_0 \rightarrow b \\ A_1 \rightarrow a \\ A_1 \rightarrow b \end{array}\right\} \text{by rule } d\ (ii)$$

$G = (\{A_0, A_1\}, \{a, b\}, \{A_0 \rightarrow aA_0, A_0 \rightarrow bA_1, A_1 \rightarrow aA_1A_1 \rightarrow aA_1, A_0 \rightarrow b, A_1\ a, A_1 \rightarrow a, A_1 \rightarrow b\}, A_0)$

Here $G$ is a required grammar.

**Example 4.58:** Let us consider a DFA whose transition digraph is shown in below

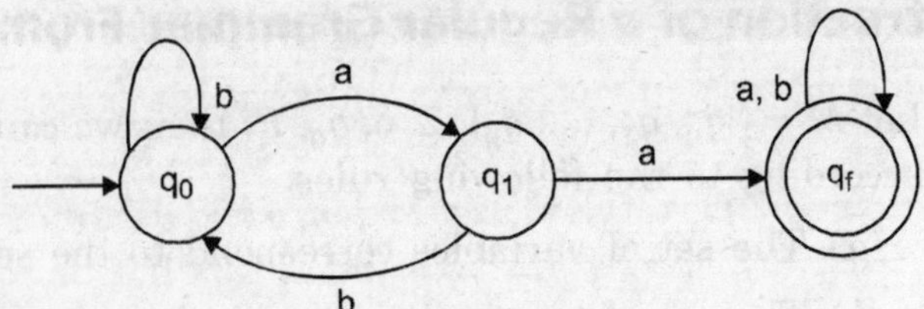


*Fig. 4.42*

Find a regular grammar equivalent to the DFA machine.

**Solution:** The regular grammar equivalent to the DFA machine, whose production rules are given shall be given below

$$A_0 \rightarrow bA_0 \mid aA_1,$$
$$A_1 \rightarrow aA_2 \mid bA_0 \mid a$$
$$A_2 \rightarrow bA_2 \mid aA_2 \mid a \mid b$$

## 4.10 MYHILL-NERODE THEOREM

$L$ is regular if $R_L$ has a finite number of equivalence classes.

- If there are finite number of equivalence classes then $L$ is regular.
- If $L$ is regular then $R_L$ has finite index.

**Theorem:** If there are finite number of equivalence classes then $L$ is regular.

**Proof:** Let each equivalence class be a state.

Start state will be $\in$.

Transition function $\delta([x],a) = [xa]$

Final states will be those equivalence classes which are subsets of $L$.

Now, $\delta([\in],w) \in F$ if $w \in L$ $[xa]$

This is a finite automata accepting $L$.

*e.g.,* $[\in] = \{\in\}$

$[a] = a\ (aa)^*$

$L_1 = (aa)^*$ $[b] = (a + b)^*\ b(a + b)^*$

$[aa] = (aa)^+$

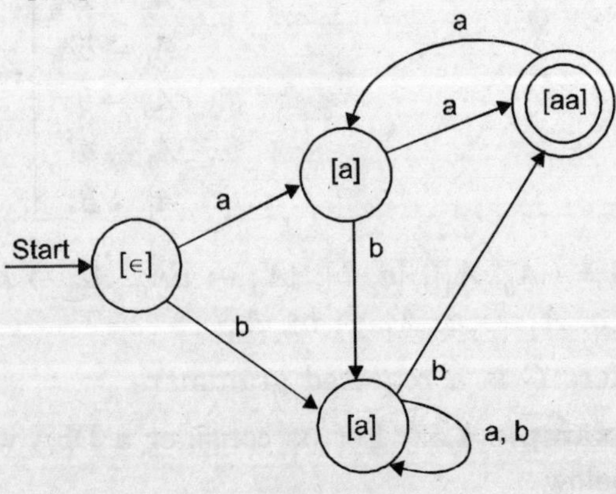


*Fig. 4.43*

This construction yields the minimum *FA*

The number of states can not be fewer, because strings belonging to different equivalence classes must take the *FA* to different states.

**Theorem:** If $L$ is regular then $R_L$ has finite index.

If $R_L$ has infinite index (number of equivalence classes), then $L$ is not regular.

**Proof:** If $x$ and $y$ are distinguishable, they must take an *FA* for $L$ to two different states. Therefore, infinite number of equivalence classes implies infinite number of states.

## 4.11 APPLICATION OF REGULAR EXPRESSION

The regular expressions can be modelled by finite automata. As we have solved many examples and experienced that regular expressions are effective representation of languages. The smaller unit of regualr expression can express the given language over certain input set.

There are following application of regular expressions and finite automata.

1. **Text Editors:** Text editors are some programs which are used for processing the text. For example UNIX text editor uses the regular expressions for substituting the string such as

   S/*bbb**/*b*/

   gives that substitute a single blank for the first string of two or more blanks found in a given line. In the UNIX text editors any regular expression is converted to an NFA with $\in$ transitions, thus NFA is then simulated directly.

2. **Lexical Analyzers:** Compiler uses this program of lexical analyses in the process of compilation. The task of lexical analyzer is to scan the input program and separate out the "tokens".

   For example: Identifiers a category of token in the source language and it can be identified by regular expression as

   (letter) (letter + digit) $\leftarrow$

   If anything in the source language matches with this regular expression then it is recognized as identifier.

   The letter is nothing bit a set {*A, B,... Z, a, b,... Z*}* and digit is {0, 1, 2, ... 9}*

   The regular expression is effective way for identifying token from a language.

# EXERCISE

## (A) Objective Type Questions

**1.** Choose the correct statements

(*a*) all languages can be generated by CFG

(*b*) any regular language has not an equivalent CFG

(*c*) some non regular languages can't be generated by an CFG

(*d*) some regular languages can't be generated by an CFG.

**2.** The set $L = \{a^n b^n c^n\}$ is an example of grammar that is

(*a*) regular (*b*) context free

(*c*) not context free (*d*) none

**3.** The productions: $E \to E + E$, $E \to E - E$, $E \to E * E$, $E \to id$

(*a*) Generated an inherently language

(*b*) Generate an ambiguous language

(*c*) Are unambiguous

(*d*) None

**4.** What is the highest type number to grammar given by these production rules $S \to ASB / d$, $A \to aA$.

(*a*) Zero (*b*) One

(*c*) Two (*d*) Three

**5.** A production of the form $A \to \alpha$ where $A \in V_N$ and $\alpha \in (V_N \cup \Sigma)^*$ represents which type of grammar?

(*a*) Zero (*b*) One

(*c*) Two (*d*) Three

**6.** If we have an algorithm to determine whether a given element belongs to a set $X$ or not, then this set is called

(*a*) Recursive (*b*) Recursively Enumerable

(*c*) Complete (*d*) Context-sensitive

**7.** Which of the following is true for the language generated by $S \to AB$, $A \to BB \mid a$, $B \to AB \mid b$

(*a*) *aabbb* doesn't belongs to this language

(*b*) *aabb* belongs to this language

(*c*) *ab* doesn't belongs to this language

(*d*) *aab* belongs to this language

**8.** Which of the following grammars can generate $\omega = aabbb$

(*a*) $S \to AB$, $A \to aA \mid a$, $B \to bB \mid b$

(*b*) $S \to AB$, $A \to BB \mid a$, $B \to AB \mid b$

(*c*) Both

(*d*) None

**9.** A recursive language is also:

(*a*) regular (*b*) recursive enumerable

(*c*) CFL (*d*) deterministic

**10.** Which of the following pairs are not equivalent

(a) $1(01)^*$ and $(10)^*1$ (b) $x(xx)^*$ and $(xx)^*x$

(c) $(ab)^*$ and $a^*b^*$ (d) $x^+$ and $x^*x^+$

**11.** The language of all words with at least 2 *a's* can be described as

(a) $(a + b)^* a(a + b)^* (a + b)^*$ (b) $(a + b)^* ab^* (a + b)^*$

(c) $b^* ab^*a(a + b)^*$ (d) all

**12.** Which of the following pairs are equivalent

(a) $(ab)^* a$ and $a (ba)^*$ (b) $(a + b)^*$ and $(a^* + b^*)$

(c) $(a^* + b)$ and $(a + b)^*$ (d) none

**13.** The set of regular languages over a given alphabet set is not closed under

(a) union (b) complement

(c) intersection (d) none

**14.** Which one is false

(a) $(r^*)^* = r^*$ (b) $r_1^* (r_1 + r_2)^* = (r_1 + r_2)^*$

(c) $(r_1 + r_2)^* = (r_1^* r_2^*)^*$ (d) none

**15.** The intersection of $(a + b)^* a$ and $b (a + b)^*$ is given by

(a) $b (a + b)^*a$ (b) $(a + b)^* ab(a + b)^*$

(c) $a (a + b)^*b$ (d) $ab (a + b)^*$

**16.** How many strings of length $t$ are in $\Sigma^*$ if $\Sigma$ is an alphabet of cardinality $r$.

(a) $rt$ (b) $rt$

(c) $tr$ (d) $r + t$

**17.** The regular expression representing the set of all strings over $\{x, y\}$ ending with $xx$ beginning with $y$–

(a) $xx (x + y)^* y$ (b) $yy (x + y)^* x$

(c) $y (x + y)^* xx$ (d) $x (x + y)^* yy$

**18.** For the following conditions find all the strings over the alphabet $\{a,\}$ that satisfy the condition, (*i*) no symbol is represented in the string and (*ii*) the length of string is 3.

(a) All possible strings of length 3

(b) Only single string *ab*

(c) No such string is possible

(d) None of the above

**19.** The regular expression representing the set of all strings over $\{a, b\}$ with three consecutive *b's*–

(a) $(a + b)^*bbb (a + b)^*$ (b) $(a + b) bbb (a + b)^*$

(c) $(a + b)^*bb (a + b)^*$ (d) $(a + b)^*bbb (a + b)$

**20.** In English language the set represented by $a^*b + b^*a$ is:

(*a*) String containing single *a* or single *b*

(*b*) String of *a's* followed by one *b* or strings or *b's* followed by one *a*.

(*c*) String containing angle *a* and single *b*

(*d*) String of *a's* followed by one *b* and strings of *b's* followed by one *a*.

**21.** The *R.E.* = $(10 + 01 + 11 + 00)^*$ represents

(*a*) all strings over 0 and 1

(*b*) set of strings with equal 0 and 1's

(*c*) set of strings with even length

(*d*) set of strings with at least one 0 and at least one 1.

**22.** Which one is TRUE

(*a*) $(10)^* = 1^*0^*$ (*b*) $(10)^* = (1^*0^*)$

(*c*) $(10)^* = 1^* + 0^*$ (*d*) {1010} belongs to $(10)^*$

**23.** $(1 + 0)^*$ represents

(*a*) Set of strings with even number of 1's and 0's

(*b*) Set of strings with equal number of 1's and 0's

(*c*) Set of strings starting with 1 and ending with 0

(*d*) Set of strings over 1 and 0

## ANSWERS

| | | | | |
|---|---|---|---|---|
| **1.** (*c*) | **2.** (*b*) | **3.** (*c*) | **4.** (*c*) | **5.** (*c*) |
| **6.** (*a*) | **7.** (*d*) | **8.** (*c*) | **9.** (*b*) | **10.** (*c*) |
| **11.** (*a*) | **12.** (*b*) | **13.** (*d*) | **14.** (*c*) | **15.** (*a*) |
| **16.** (*b*) | **17.** (*c*) | **18.** (*c*) | **19.** (*a*) | **20.** (*b*) |
| **21.** (*c*) | **22.** (*d*) | **23.** (*d*) | | |

## (B) Problems

**1.** Find the all strings of regular expression $((a + b)^* b(a + ab)^*)$ of length less than four. Also simplify this regular expression.

**2.** Find the all strings of regular expression $(a + ba)^* (b + a^*)$ of length less than three. Also find two regular expressions of its equivalent.

**3.** Find a regular expression for $L = \{a^n b^m : n \geq 1, nm \geq 3\}$

**4.** Find a regular expression for $L = \{ab^n w : n \geq 3, w \in \{a, b\}^+\}$

**5.** Find a regular expression for $L = \{v, w \in \{a, b\}^*, |v| = 2\}$

**6.** Prove that

(*a*) $(a^*)^* = a^*$

(*b*) $a^*(a + b)^* = (a + b)^*$

(*c*) $(a + b) = (a^* b^*)^*$

**7.** Find a regular expression that denotes all bit strings whose value, when interpreted as a binary integer, is greater than or equal to 40.

**8.** Give regular expression for the following languages on $\Sigma = \{a, b, c\}$

(*a*) All strings containing exactly one $a$

(*b*) All strings containing no more than three $a$'s

(*c*) All strings which contain at least one occurrence of each symbol in $\Sigma$

(*d*) All strings which contain no run of $a$'s lengths greater than two

(*e*) All strings in which all runs of $a$'s have lengths that are multiple of three

**9.** Find the language $L = (a^*(a + b))$ in the form of set of notation.

**10.** For $\Sigma = \{a, b\}$, is the expression $r = (a + b)^* \, ^*(a + bb)$ regular

**11.** Give the language of the expression

$$r = (aa)^* (bb)^* b$$

**12.** For $\Sigma = \{0, 1\}$, give a regular expression $r$ such that $L(r) = \{w \in \Sigma^* : w$ has at least one pair of consecutive zeros)

**13.** Find a regular expression for the language $L = \{w \in \{0, 1\}^* : w$ has no pair of consecutive zeros}

**14.** Simplify the expression $((0 + 1)(0 + 1)^*)^* \, 00(0 + 1)^*$

**15.** Find a regular expression for the set $\{a^n \, b^m : (n + m)$ is even}.

**16.** Give a regular expression for

(*a*) $L = \{a^n b^m, n > 4, m < = 3\}$,

(*b*) The complement of the preceding, language.

**17.** Simplify the language

$$L = ((aa)^* \, b(aa)^* + a(aa)^* \, (ba(aa)^*)$$

**18.** Give a regular expression for $L = \{a^n b^m : n > 1, m > = 1\}$

**19.** Give a regular expression for $L^R$, where $L = ((a + b)^* \, b(a + ab)^*\}$.

**20.** Give a regular expression for $L = \{ab^n \, w : n > = 3, w \in \{a, b\}^*\}$.

**21.** Give a regular expression for $L = \{vwv\text{: } v, w \in \{a, b\}^*, |v| = 2\}$.

**22.** Give a regular expression for $L = \{w \; \Sigma \; \{0, 1\}^* : w$ has exactly one pair of consecutive zeros}.

**23.** Write regualr expression for the following languages on {0, 1}:

(*a*) All strings ending in 01

(*b*) All strings not ending in 01

(*c*) All strings containing an even number of 0's

(*d*) All strings having at least two occurrences of the sub-strings 00 (Note that with the usual interpretation of a sub-string, 00 contains two such occurrences).

**24.** Show that the set $L = \{a^i \mid i \geq 1\}$ is not regular.

**25.** Show that $L = \{a^P \mid P$ is a prime$\}$ is not regular}.

**26.** Show that $L = \{0^{2n}1^{2n}, n \geq 1\}$ is not regular.

**27.** Show that $L = \{ww \mid w \in \{a, b\}^*\}$ is not regular.

**28.** Is $L = \{a^{2n} \mid n \geq 1\}$ regular.

**29.** Using pumping lemma show that the following sets are not regular:

(*a*) $\{a^n b^{2n} \mid n > 0\}$

(*b*) $\{a^n b^m \mid 0 < n < m\}$

**30.** Show that $\{0^m 1^n \mid \text{g.c.d } (m, n) = 1\}$ is not regular.

❑❑❑

# CHAPTER 5

# Context-Free Grammar

## 5.1 INTRODUCTION

Before defining the context free grammar let us consider the notion of a grammar. A grammar is a set of rules by which the valid sentences in a language are constructed.

For example, a grammar for the English language tell us whether a particular sentence is well formed or not. Our ability to understand what a sentence means is based on our ability to understand how it could be formed from the rules of grammar.

To study languages mathematically, we need the mechanism to describe then. Noam Chomsky in 1995 gave a mathematical model of a grammar. Although it was not useful for describing natural languages, it turn out to be useful for computer languages.

Context free grammars (CFG) have important paractical applications in defining the syntactic structures of programming languages and in the theory of lexical analysis of compiler construction.

## 5.2 CONTEXT FREE GRAMMAR

Context-free grammar is a type of grammar in which all the production rules are different from other types of grammar, In this grammar the following conditions accomplishes the production rule

(*i*) The left hand side of the production rule must be single non-terminal (or variable)

(*ii*) The right hand side of the production rule shall be either terminal or non-terminal or combination of terminal and non-terminal of any order and of any length.

Or mathematically, it is already defined in chapter 2.

*For example,* consider a grammar $G = (\{S, A\}, \{0\}, P, S)$

where $P$ consists of following production rules

$$S \to 0A$$
$$A \to 00A$$
$$A \to 0$$

All the production rules of this grammar contain in the left hand side only one non-terminal symbol. So, this grammar is a context free grammar (or Type 2) and the language generated by this grammar is $0^{2n} \mid n \geq 1$. That is

$$\boxed{L(G) = \{0^{2n} \mid n \geq 1\}}$$

*For example,* consider a grammar $G = (\{S, A\}, \{a, b\}, P, S)$,

where $P$ consists of following production rules

$S \to A$

$A \to aAb$

$A \to ab$

All the production rules of this grammar contain in the left hand side only one non-terminal symbol. So this grammar is a context free grammar (or Type 2) and the language generated by this grammar is $a^nb^n \mid n^3$ 1. That is

$$L(G) = \{a^nb^n \mid n \geq 1\}$$

*For example,* consider a grammar $G = (S, A, B\}, \{0, 1, 2\}, P, S)$ where $P$ consists of following production rules

$S \to AB$

$A \to 0A1$

$A \to 01$

$B \to 1B2$

$B \to 12$

All the production rules of this grammar contain in the left hand side only one non-terminal symbol. So this grammar is a context free grammar (or Type 2) and the language generated by this grammar is $0^n\ 1^{n+m}\ 2^m \mid n, m \geq 1$. That is

$$L(G) = \{0^n1^{n+m}\ 2^m \mid n, m \geq 1\}$$

*For example,* Consider a grammar $G = (\{S, A, B, C\}, \{0, 1, 2, 3\}, P, S)$ where $P$ consists of following production rules

$S \to ABC$

$A \to 0A1$

$A \to 01$

$B \to 1B2$

$B \to 12$

$C \to 2C3$

$C \to 23$

All the production rules of this grammar contain in the left hand side only one non-terminal symbol. So this grammar is a context free grammar (or Type 2) and the language generated by this grammar is

$0^n1^{n+m}\ 2^{m+p}\ 3^p \mid n, m, p \geq 1$. That is

$$L(G) = \{0^n1^{n+m}\ 2^{m+p}\ 3^p \mid n, m, p \geq 1\}$$

*For example,* consider a grammar $G = (\{E, T, F, I\}, \{id, +, -, *, /, (,)\}, \{a, b, c\})$ where $P$ consists of following production rules

$E \rightarrow E + T | E - T | T$

$A \rightarrow T * F \ | T / F / F$

$A \rightarrow (E)$

$B \rightarrow a | b | c$

All the production rules of this grammar contain in the left hand side only one non-terminal symbol. So this grammar is a context free grammar (or Type 2) and the language generated by this grammar is

$$L(G) = \text{An arithmetic expression.}$$

## 5.3 DERIVATION

A derivation refers to replacement of an instance of a non-terminal in a given by the right hand side of that production rule, whose left hand is the non-terminal to be replaced.

The derivation produces a new string to the given string, therefore *a* derivation can be used repeatedly to obtain a new string to form a given string. If *a* string obtained as a result of derivation contains only terminal symbol then no further derivation is possible.

**Example 5.1:** Consider a grammar $G = (\{S\}, \{a, b\}, P, S)$

where $P$ contains the following production rules

$S \rightarrow aSa$

$S \rightarrow \text{bSb}$

$S \rightarrow \in$

Find the derivation string for the following languages

(a) $a^3b^3 \ b^3a^3$

(b) $a^3a^3$

(c) $b^4b^4$

(d) $b^5a^5 \ a^5b^5$

**Solution:** (*a*) Since the string is $a^3b^3 \ b^3a^3$, so the derivation for the given language is

$S \rightarrow aSa$

$S \rightarrow a \ aSaa$

$S \rightarrow a \ a \ aSa \ a \ a$ by $S \rightarrow aSa$

$S \rightarrow a \ a \ a \ bSb \ a \ a \ a$ by $S \rightarrow aSa$

$S \rightarrow a \ a \ a \ b \ bSb \ b \ a \ a \ a$ by $S \rightarrow bSb$

$S \rightarrow a \ a \ a \ b \ b \ bSb \ b \ a \ a \ a$ by $S \rightarrow bSb$

$S \rightarrow a \ a \ a \ b \ b \ bSb \ b \ b \ a \ a \ a$ by $S \rightarrow bSb$

$S \rightarrow a \ a \ a \ b \ b \ b{\in}b \ b \ b \ a \ a \ a$ by $S \rightarrow \in$

$S \rightarrow a\ a\ a\ b\ b\ b\ b\ b\ b\ a\ a\ a$

$S \rightarrow a^3\ b^3\ b^3\ a^3$

(*b*) Since the string is $a^3a^3$, so the derivation for the given language is

$S \rightarrow aSa$

$S \rightarrow aaSaa$ by $S \rightarrow aSa$

$S \rightarrow aaaSaaa$ by $S \rightarrow aSa$

$S \rightarrow aaa\in Saaa$ by $S \rightarrow \in$

$S \rightarrow aaaaaa$

(c) Since the string is $b^4b^4$, so derivation for the given language is

$S \rightarrow bSb$

$S \rightarrow bbSbb$ by $S \rightarrow bSb$

$S \rightarrow bbbSbbb$ by $S \rightarrow bSb$

$S \rightarrow bbbbSbbbb$ by $S \rightarrow bSb$

$S \rightarrow bbbb\in bbbb$ by $S \rightarrow \in$

$S \rightarrow bbbbbbb$

(*d*) Since the string is $b^5a^5a^5b^5$, so the derivation for the given language is

$S \rightarrow bSb$

$S \rightarrow bbSbb$

$S \rightarrow bbbSbbb$ by $S \rightarrow bSb$

$S \rightarrow bbbbSbbbb$ by $S \rightarrow bSb$

$S \rightarrow bbbbbSbbbbb$ by $S \rightarrow bSb$

$S \rightarrow bbbbbaSabbbbb$ by $S \rightarrow bSb$

$S \rightarrow bbbbbaaSaabbbbb$ by $S \rightarrow aSa$

$S \rightarrow bbbbaaaSaaabbbb$ by $S \rightarrow aSa$

$S \rightarrow bbbbbaaaaSaaaabbbbb$ by $S \rightarrow aSa$

$S \rightarrow bbbbbaaaaa\in aaaaabbbbb$ by $S \rightarrow aSa$

$S \rightarrow bbbbbaaaaaaaaaabbbb$ by $S \rightarrow \in$

**Example 5.3:** Construct a CFG for the language

$L = \{a^nb^n : n \geq 1\}$

**Solution:** Let $G$ be CFG for language $L = [a^nb^n : \geq 1]$

$G = (\{s\}, \{a, b\}, P, S)$

where $P$ contains the following production rules

$S \rightarrow aSb$

$S \rightarrow ab$

**Example 5.4:** Construct a CFG, which generates strings having equal number of *a's* and *b's*.

**Solution:** Let CFG be $G = (\{s\}, \{a, b\}, P, S)$

where $P$ contains the following production rules

$$S \rightarrow aSbS$$

$$S \rightarrow bSaS$$

$$S \rightarrow \in$$

**Example 5.5:** Construct the CFG for the language having any number of $a's$ over the set $\Sigma = \{a\}$

**Solution:** As we know the regular expression for above mentioned language is $a^*$.

Let CFG be $G = (\{s\}, \{a, b\}, P, S)$

where $P$ contains the following production rules

$$S \rightarrow aS$$

$$S \rightarrow \in$$

Now if want *"aaaa"* string to be derived we can start with start symbols.

$S$

$a \ S$

$a \ a \ S$

$a \ a \ a \ S$

$a \ a \ a \ a \ S$

$a \ a \ a \ a \ \in$

$= aaaa$

The *r.e.*, $= a^*$ suggest a set of $\{\in, a, aa, aaa, ...\}$.

We can have a null string simply because $S$ is a start symbol, and gives $S \rightarrow \in$.

**Example 5.6:** The CFG is given as $S \rightarrow aSb \mid ab$. Find the CFL generated by the above grammar.

**Solution:** Let CFG be $G = (\{s\}, \{a, b\}, P, S)$

where $P$ contains following production rules

$$S \rightarrow aSb$$

$$S \rightarrow ab$$

Let us start with minimal length string. From production second, we can get string $ab$ in one step as $S \rightarrow ab$

To start with new derivation, we can have

| | | |
|---|---|---|
| $S \Rightarrow aSb$ | $S \Rightarrow aSb$ | $S \Rightarrow aSb$ |
| $\Rightarrow aabb$ | $\Rightarrow aaSbb$ | $\Rightarrow aaSbb$ |
| | $\Rightarrow aaabbb$ | $\Rightarrow aaaSbbb$ |
| | | $\Rightarrow aaaabbbb$ |

Thus, the language can be listed in the form of set as

$$L = \{ab, aabb, aaabbb, ......\}$$

*i.e.,* $$L = \{a^n b^n : n \geq 1\}$$

**Example 5.7:** Construct a CFG for each of the languages defined by the following regular expressions:

(*i*) $ab^*$ (*ii*) $a^*b^*$ (*iii*) $(baa + abb)^*$

**Solution:** (*i*) The required CFG for $ab^*$ is

$$S \to aB$$
$$B \to bB \mid \in$$

(*ii*) The required CFG for $a^*b^*$ is

$$S \to AB$$
$$A \to aA \mid \in$$
$$B \to bB \mid \in$$

(*iii*) The required CFG for $(baa + abb)^*$ is

$$S \to AS \mid BS \mid \in$$
$$A \to baa$$
$$B \to abb$$

**Example 5.8:** Construct CFG for the language containing all the string of different first and last symbol over $\Sigma = \{0, 1\}$.

**Solution:** In this, if the string starts 0 it should each end with 1 or if the string starts with 1 it should end with 0.

Let CFG be $G = (\{S, A\}, \{a, b\}, P, S)$

where $P$ contains the following production rules

$$S \to 0A1 \mid 1A0$$
$$A \to 0A \mid 1A \mid \in$$

The non-terminal $A \to 0A \mid 1A \mid \in$ indicates $(0 + 1)^*$

Thus the given CFG is equivalent to the regular expression

$$\{0\ (0 + 1)^*\ 1 + 1\ (0 + 1)^*\ 0\}$$

**Example 5.9:** Construct CFG for the language containing at least one occurrence of a double $a$.

**Solution:** The equivalent regular expression of given CFG is

$$\{(a + b)^*\ ab\ (a + b)^*\}$$

*i.e.,* the production rules are:

$$S \to BAB$$
$$A \to aa$$
$$B \to aB \mid bB \mid \in$$

### 5.3.1 Left Most Derivation (LMD)

A derivation $S \xrightarrow{*} w$ is called left most derivation if we apply a production only to the left most variable (or non-terminal) at every step.

### 5.3.2 Right Most Derivation (RMD)

A derivation $S \xrightarrow{*} w$ is called left most derivation if we apply a production only to the left most variable (or non-terminal) at every step.

**Example 5.10:** Consider a grammar $G$, whose production rules are son below

$$S \to 0AS \mid 0$$
$$A \to S1A \mid SS \mid 10$$

Find the Left Most Derivation and Right Most Derivation for the language 00110000.

**Solution:** The left most derivative for the language 00110000 is

| | |
|---|---|
| $S \to 0AS$ | |
| $S \to 0S1AS$ | by production rule $A \to S1A$ |
| $S \to 001AS$ | by production rule $S \to 0$ |
| $S \to 00110S$ | by production rule $A \to 10$ |
| $S \to 00110SS$ | by production rule $S \to SS$ |
| $S \to 00110SSS$ | by production rule $S \to SS$ |
| $S \to 001100SS$ | by production rule $S \to 0$ |
| $S \to 0011000S$ | by production rule $S \to 0$ |
| $S \to 00110000$ | by production rule $S \to 0$ |

And the right most derivative for the language 00110000 is

| | |
|---|---|
| $S \to 0AS$ | |
| $S \to 0ASS$ | by production rule $A \to SS$ |
| $S \to 0ASSS$ | by production rule $S \to SS$ |
| $S \to 0ASS0$ | by production rule $A \to 0$ |
| $S \to 0AS00$ | by production rule $S \to 0$ |
| $S \to 0A000$ | by production rule $S \to 0$ |
| $S \to 0S1A000$ | by production rule $S \to S1A$ |
| $S \to 0S110000$ | by production rule $S \to 10$ |
| $S \to 00110000$ | by production rule $S \to 0$ |

**Example 5.11:** Derive the string *"aabbabba"* for left most derivation and right most derivation using a CFG given by

$$S \to aB \mid bA$$
$$A \to a \mid aS \mid bAA$$
$$B \to b \mid bS \mid aBB$$

**Solution:** Let us see the left most derivation first,

| | |
|---|---|
| $S$ | |
| $a\ B$ | by production rule $S \to aB$ |
| $a\ a\ B\ B$ | by production rule $B \to aBB$ |
| $a\ a\ b\ B$ | by production rule $B \to b$ |
| $a\ a\ b\ b\ S$ | by production rule $B \to bS$ |
| $a\ a\ b\ b\ a\ B$ | by production rule $S \to aB$ |
| $a\ a\ b\ b\ a\ b\ S$ | by production rule $B \to bS$ |
| $a\ a\ b\ b\ a\ b\ b\ A$ | by production rule $S \to bA$ |
| $a\ a\ b\ b\ a\ b\ b\ a$ | by production rule $A \to a$ |

is derived. Now let us solve using right most derivation

| | |
|---|---|
| $S$ | |
| $a\ B$ | by production rule$S \to aB$ |
| $a\ a\ B\ B$ | by production rule$B \to aBB$ |
| $a\ a\ B\ b\ S$ | by production rule$B \to bS$ |
| $a\ a\ B\ b\ b\ A$ | by production rule$S \to bA$ |
| $a\ a\ B\ b\ b\ a$ | by production rule$A \to a$ |
| $a\ a\ b\ S\ b\ b\ a$ | by production rule$B \to bS$ |
| $a\ a\ b\ b\ A\ b\ b\ a$ | by production rule$S \to bA$ |
| $a\ a\ b\ b\ a\ b\ b\ a$ | by production rule$A \to a$ |

is a derivation.

## 5.4 DERIVATION TREE OR PARSE TREE

A derivation tree is a graphical representation of derivation, while deriving a string from a starting symbol $S$. This graphical representation called the derivation tree or parse tree.

The following are the observation about Derivation Tree (or Parse Tree)

(i) The root node of the tree is labeled by the starting symbol of a grammar.

(ii) The interior nodes are labeled by the non-terminals symbols.

(iii) The leaf nodes are labeled by the terminal symbols.

(iv) If an interior node has a label $X$ and has $n$ children with labels $X_1$, $X_2$, $X_3$,.........,$X_n$ *from* left to right, then there must exist production rule X $\to X_1, X_2, X_3$.........$X_n$ *in* the grammar.

The rule of information is that non-terminal A can be replaced *'ba'* if there is a production

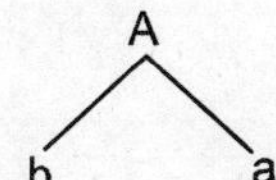

$A \rightarrow ba$ then the three is

---

There is no need to draw arrow on the edges because the direction of production is always downward.

---

**Example 5.12:** Let the grammar $G = \{\{S, A\}, \{a, b\}, P, \{S\}\}$ where $P$ as follows

$$S \rightarrow aAS \mid a$$

$$A \rightarrow SbA \mid SS \mid ba$$

Find the derivation tree for the language (or string) aabbaa.

**Solution:** The derivation for the language aabbaa is explained below from starting symbol $S$

| | |
|---|---|
| $S \rightarrow aAS$ | |
| $S \rightarrow aSbAS$ | by production rule $A \rightarrow SbA$ |
| $S \rightarrow aabAS$ | by production rule $S \rightarrow Sa$ |
| $S \rightarrow aabbaS$ | by production rule $S \rightarrow ba$ |
| $S \rightarrow aabbaa$ | by production rule $S \rightarrow a$ |

The parse tree (or derivation tree) for the given language is shown as below.

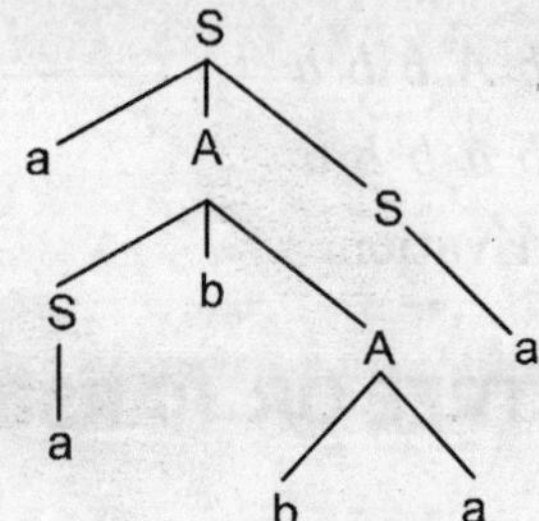


**Example 5.13:** Consider a grammar $G$, production rules are shown below

$$S \rightarrow aAS \mid a$$

$$A \rightarrow SbA \mid Ss \mid ba$$

Find the Left Most Derivation and Right Most Derivation for the language aabbaa. Also find its parse tree.

**Solution:** The derivation for the language *aabbaa* are

| **Left most** | **Right most** |
|---|---|
| $S \rightarrow$ a$AS$ | $S \rightarrow aAS$ |
| $S \rightarrow aSbAS$ | $S \rightarrow aAa$ |
| $S \rightarrow aabAS$ | $S \rightarrow aSbAa$ |
| $S \rightarrow aabbas$ | $S \rightarrow aSbbaa$ |
| $S \rightarrow aabbaa$ | $S \rightarrow aabbaa$ |

The parse tree for the derivatives are shown below

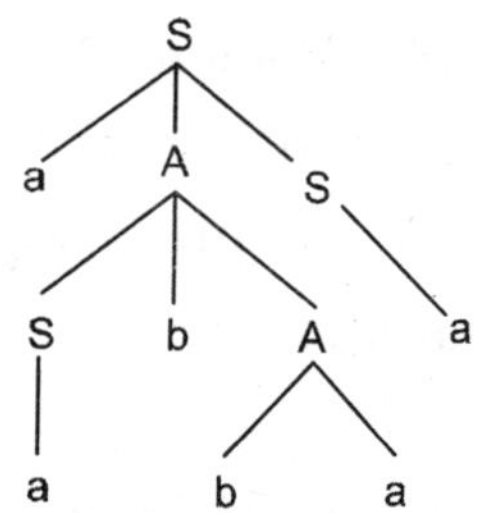


***Left most derivative***

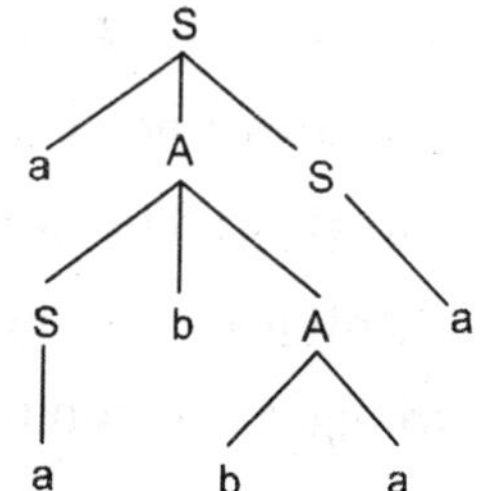


***Right most derivative***

***Fig. 5.13***

**Example 5.14:** Consider the grammar $G$ = ({$S$}, {+, *,(,), 2, 3,4}, $P$, $S$), where the production rules are defined as follows

$$S \rightarrow S + S \mid S*S \mid (S)$$

$$A \rightarrow 2 \mid 3 \mid 4$$

Find the derivation tree for the language (or string) 2 + ((3 * 4) * 2)

**Solution:** The derivation for the language 2 + ((3 * 4) * 2) is shown below from starting symbol $S$

| | |
|---|---|
| $S \rightarrow S + S$ | |
| $S \rightarrow S + (S)$ | by $S \rightarrow (S)$ |
| $S \rightarrow S + (S*S)$ | by $S \rightarrow S*S$ |
| $S \rightarrow S + ((S) *S)$ | by $S \rightarrow (S)$ |
| $S \rightarrow S + ((S*S) *S)$ | by $S \rightarrow S*S$ |
| $S \rightarrow S + ((S*S) *2)$ | by $S \rightarrow 2$ |
| $S \rightarrow S + ((S*4) *2)$ | by $S \rightarrow 4$ |
| $S \rightarrow S + (((3*4) *2)$ | by $S \rightarrow 3$ |
| $S \rightarrow S + ((3*4) *2)$ | by $S \rightarrow 2$ |

and the derivation tree for the language is shown below:

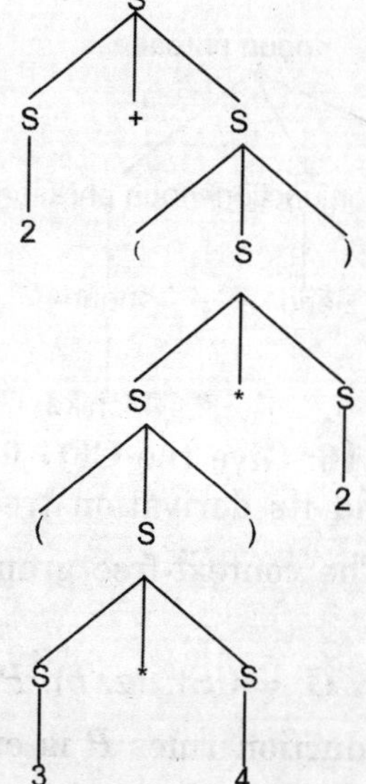

**Example 5.15:** Construct a grammar for the language

$L$ = Ashutosh and Monika ran up the hill

And also find a derivation parse tree for this language.

**Solution:** The production rules for this language are shown below

<Sentence> → <subject><predicate>

<Subject → <noun phrase>

<noun phrase> → <noun>conjunction><noun>

<conjuction> → and

<noun> → Ashutosh

<noun> → Monika

<predicate> → <verb><prepositonal phrase>

<verb> → ran

<preposition phrase> → <preposition><article><nount>

<preposition> → up

<article> → the

<noun> → hill

And the derivation tree is as shown below

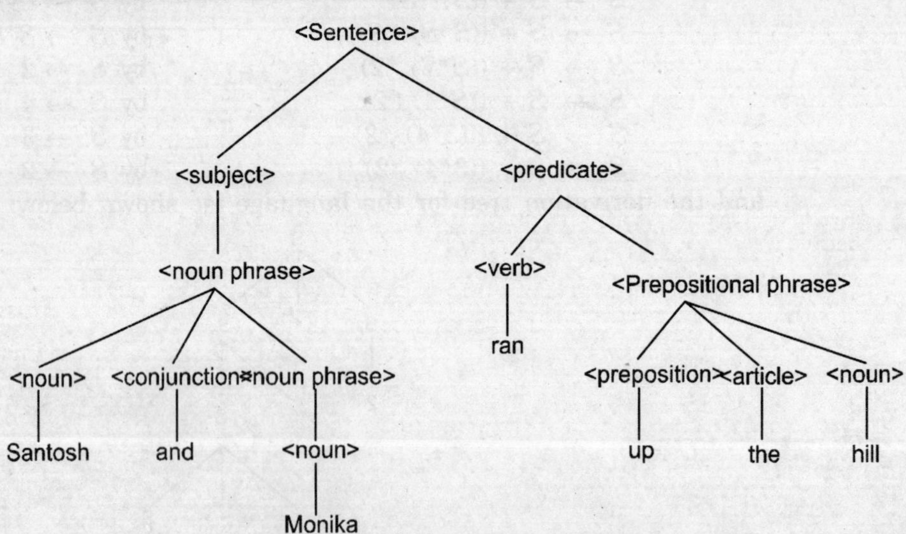


**Example 5.16:** Give the CFG for set of all palindromes over alphabet $\{a, b\}$ and also find its derivation tree for the language aabaa.

**Solution:** The context-free grammar G for the palindromes is defined as follows

$$G = (\{S\}, \{a, b\}, P, S)$$

where the production rules $P$ is explained below

$$S \to aSa \mid bSb \mid a \mid b \mid \hat{I}$$

The derivation tree for the language aabaa is explained below

$S \to aSa$

$S \to$ a aSa a by production rule $A \to aSa$

$S \to$ a a ba a by production rule $S \to b$

and the parse tree is shown below

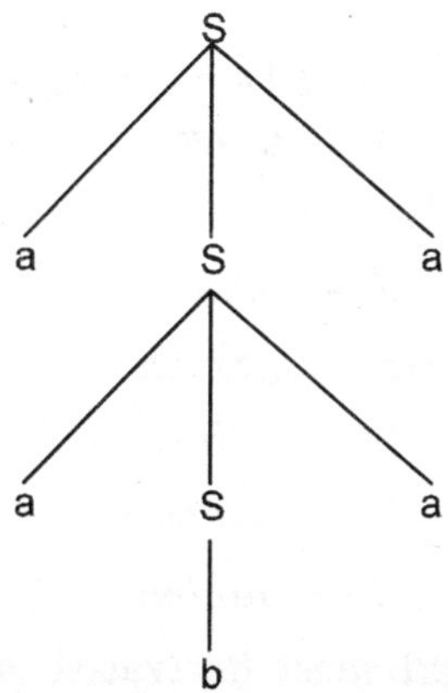


**Example 5.17:** Show the derivation steps and construct derivation tree for string *aabbbb* by using left most derivation with the grammar defined as

$S \to AB \mid \in$

$A \to aB$

$B \to Sb$

**Solution:** We start with the start symbol and the production.

$S \Rightarrow AB$

$\Rightarrow aBB$

$\Rightarrow aSbB$

$\Rightarrow aABbB$

$\Rightarrow aaBBbB$

$\Rightarrow aaSbBbB$

$\Rightarrow aa\in bBbB$

$\Rightarrow aabSbbB$

$\Rightarrow aab\in bbB$

$\Rightarrow aabbbSb$

$\Rightarrow aabbb\in b$

$\Rightarrow aabbbb$

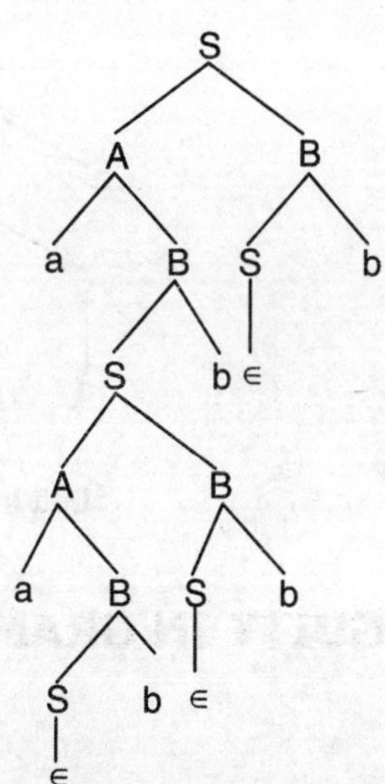


***Left-most derivation tree***

**Example 5.18:** Consider a grammar $G$, whose production rules are shown below

$$S \rightarrow aAS$$
$$s \rightarrow a$$
$$A \rightarrow SbA$$
$$S \rightarrow SS$$
$$S \rightarrow ba$$

Find the Left Most Derivation and Right Most Derivation for the language aabbaa. Also find its parse

**Solution:** The left most derivative for the language *aabbaa* is

$S \rightarrow aAS$
$S \rightarrow aSbAS$ by production rule $A \rightarrow SbA$
$S \rightarrow aabAS$ by production rule $S \rightarrow a$
$S \rightarrow aabbaS$ by production rule $S \rightarrow ba$
$S \rightarrow aabbaa$ by production rule $S \rightarrow a$

And the right most derivative for the language *aabbaa* is

$S \rightarrow aAS$
$S \rightarrow aAa$ by production rule $S \rightarrow a$
$S \rightarrow aSbAa$ by production rule $A \rightarrow SbA$
$S \rightarrow aSbbaa$ by production rule $A \rightarrow ba$
$S \rightarrow aabbaa$ by production rule $S \rightarrow a$

The parse tree for the derivatives are shown below

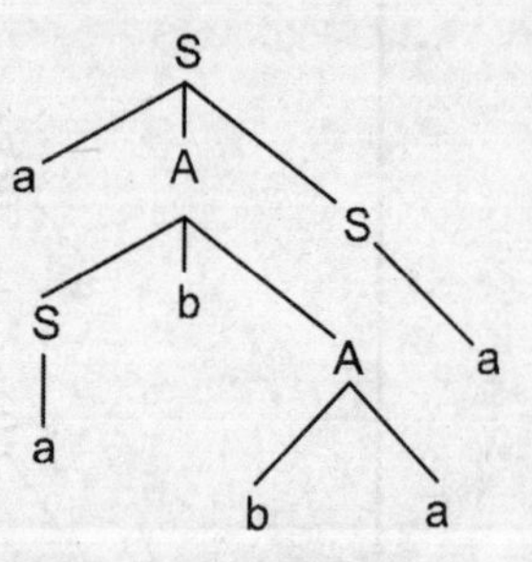

Left most derivative

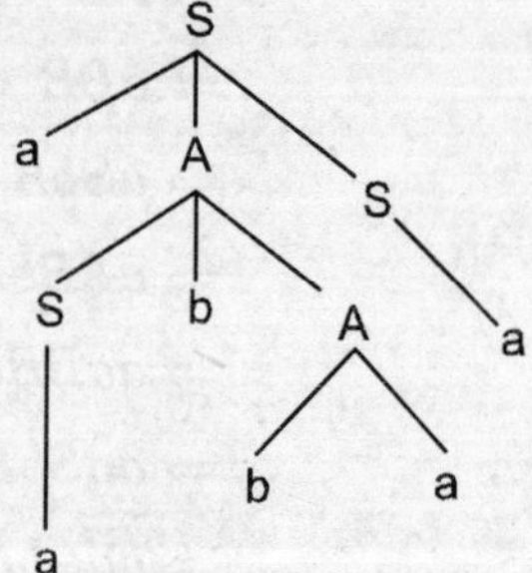

Right most derivative

## 5.5 AMBIGUITY IN GRAMMAR AND LANGUAGE

***[U.P.T.U. B-Tech 2003]***

A context-free grammar $G$ is said to be ambiguous if there exist more than one parse tree for some language (or string) $w \in L(G)$. Alternatively, ambiguity, ambiguity implies the existence of two or more left most or right most derivations.

**Example 5.19:** Check whether the given grammar is ambiguous or not.

$S \rightarrow iCtS$ $\quad\quad$ $S \rightarrow a$

$S \rightarrow iCtSeS$ $\quad\quad$ $C \rightarrow b$

**Solution:** To check whether given grammar is ambiguous or not we will have string derivation tree such as *ibtibtibtaea.*

Let us draw the derivation tree.

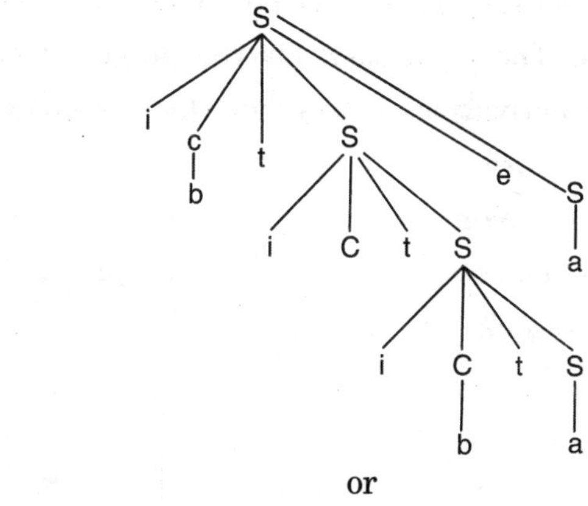

or

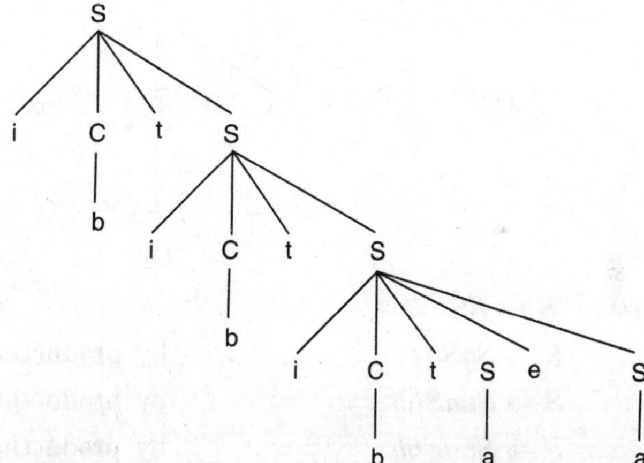

Thus we have got more than two parse trees. Hence the given grammar is ambiguous.

**Example 5.20:** Show that the grammar $G$ with production

$S \rightarrow a \mid a\ Ab \mid ab\ Sb$

$A \rightarrow aAA\ b \mid bS$

is ambiguous.

**Solution:** $S \Rightarrow absb$ $\quad\quad$ $S \rightarrow absb$

$\Rightarrow abab$ $\quad\quad$ $S \rightarrow a$

Similarly, $S \Rightarrow aAb$ $\quad\quad$ $S \rightarrow aAb$

$\Rightarrow absb$ $\quad\quad$ $S \rightarrow bS$

$\Rightarrow abab$

Since *'abab'* has more than one derivations. So the grammar $G$ is ambiguous.

**Example 5.21:** Consider a grammar $G$, whose production rules are shown below

$$S \rightarrow aSb$$
$$S \rightarrow SS$$
$$S \rightarrow \in$$

Find the derivation for the language aabb. Also find its parse tree.

**Solution:** The derivation for the language *aabb*.

Different derivatives exists for this language as shown below:

(i) $S \rightarrow aSb$

$S \rightarrow aaSbb$ by production rule $S \rightarrow aSb$

$S \rightarrow aa\in bb$ by production rule $S \rightarrow \in$

$S \rightarrow aabb$

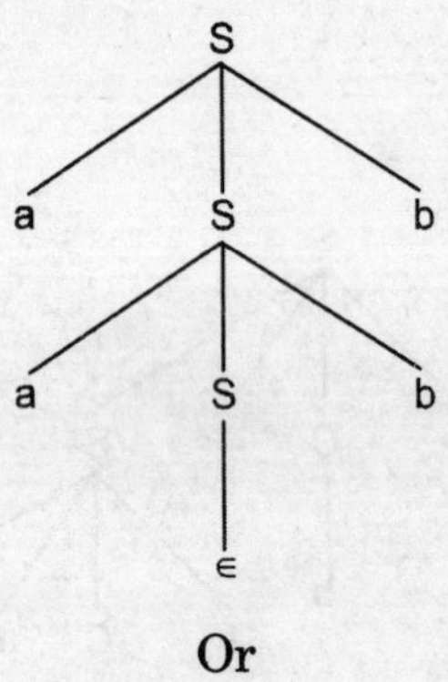


Or

(*ii*) $S \rightarrow SS$

$S \rightarrow SaSb$ by production rule $S \rightarrow aSb$

$S \rightarrow SaaSbb$ by production rule $S \rightarrow aSb$

$S \rightarrow Saa\in bb$ by production rule $S \rightarrow \in$

$S \rightarrow \in aabb$ by production rule $S \rightarrow \in$

$S \rightarrow aabb$

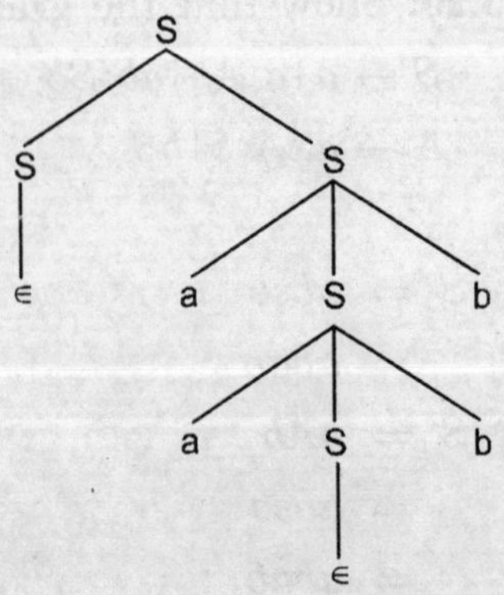

**Example 5.22:** Let $L$ be the set of all palindromes over $\{a, b\}$. Construct grammar $G$ generating $L$.

**Solution:** In the given question, we have to find a grammar but not a particular type of grammar. It means we can define any type of grammar. Here we define a context-free grammar fora given language, whose production rules are explained below

$$S \rightarrow \in$$

$$S \rightarrow a$$

$$S \rightarrow b$$

$$S \rightarrow aSa$$

$$S \rightarrow bSb$$

## 5.6 PUMPING LEMMA FOR CONTEXT FREE LANGUAGE

Let $L$ be an finite context free language. Then there exists some positive integer $m$ such that any $w \in L$ with $|w| \geq$ m can be decomposed as

$$w = uvxyz$$

and $\quad |vxy| \geq m$

such that $uv^ixy^iz \in L \; \forall \; i \geq 0$

**Proof:** Consider the language $L \neq \in$ and assume that we have equivalent grammar $G$ without unit production or null-production. Since the length of the string on the right hand side of any production is bounded, say by $k$, then length of derivation of any $w \in L$ must be at least

$|w| = k$. Since $L$ is infinite, there exists an arbitral long derivation.

Now see the LMD of a sufficiently long string. Since the number or variables of $G$ is bounded but length of derivation is not bounded in means any variable any variable say A reoccur in the left most position. Thus $a$ derivation.

$$\text{S} \xrightarrow{*} uAy_1$$

$$\xrightarrow{*} uvAy_2\, y_1$$

$$\xrightarrow{*} uvxy_2y_1 \qquad \text{....}(i)$$

with $u, v, x \in \Sigma^*$ and $y_1, y_2 \in (v \cup \Sigma)^*$.

This shows that

$$\text{S} \xrightarrow{*} x\,A \xrightarrow{*} vAy_2$$

*i.e.,*

$$\text{S} \xrightarrow{*} x\,A \xrightarrow{*} uv^ixy_2^iy_1 \forall \geq 1 \qquad \text{....}(ii)$$

Since $G$ has no unit production or null production. It means each step in the derivation creates either terminal on increase the length of the sentential form. this implies that

$$|Vy_2| \geq 1$$

Since $y_2$ and $y_1$ are $\in (V \cup \Sigma)$ then the sentential form (1) must reduce to the terminal string $w$, so that

$$y_2 \xrightarrow{*} y$$

$$y_2 \xrightarrow{*} z \text{ with } y, z \in \Sigma^*$$

Therefore $w = uvxyz$ and (2) implies that $w = uv^ixy^iz$ in $L$.

Since $|vy_2| \geq 1$

So $|vy| \geq 1$ is satisfied.

It shows that $|vxy| \geq$ m must be satisfied because $A \xrightarrow{*} x$.

## Procedure for Proving the Pumping Lemma for C.F.G.

1. Let $L$ be $a$ CFL and $m$ be the natural number obtained by using pumping lemma.
2. Choose $w \in L$ so that $|w| \geq m$, write $w = uvxyz$
3. Using $PL$ find a suitable $i$ so that $uv^ix^iyz \notin L$. This contradiction shows that $L$ is not a CFL.

*For example,* show that $L = \{a^nb^nc^n \mid n$ ³ $1|$ is not context free but context sensitive.

**Proof:**

**Step 1:** Let $L$ is a context free language and $n$ be the natural number obtained by using pumping lemma.

**Step 2:** Let $w = a^nb^nc^n$

Then $|w| \geq m$ or $n$, write $w = uvxyz$ where $|vy| \geq 1$ *i.e.,* at least one $v$ or $y$ is not null.

**Step 3:** $uvxyz = a^nb^nc^n$. As $1 \leq vy \leq n$, $v$ or $y$ can not contain all the three symbol $a$, $b$, $c$. So (*i*) $v$ or $y$ has only $a^ib^i$ or $b^ic^i$ for some $i$ and $j$ such that $i + j \leq n$

(*ii*) $v$ or $y$ has only one symbol among $a$, $b$ and $c$. Since $v$ and $y$ is the is the form of $a^ib^i$.

$$v^2 = a^ib^ja^ib^j \text{ (or } y^2 = a^ib^ja^ib^j)$$

$v^2$ is a substring of $uv^2xy^2z$ cannot be formed $a^nb^nc^n$.

So $uv^2xy^2z \notin L$. Proved.

If $v = a^i$ and $y = b^j$ for some $i$ and $j$, $i$, $\leq n$, $j \leq n$. The string $uxz$ contain remaining symbol say $a_1$ Also $a_1^n$ is substring of $uxz$ where $a_1 \notin v$ or $y$ and $a_1 < n$. So $uv^0xy^0z = uxz \notin L$. Therefore $L$ is not CFL.

## 5.7 NORMAL FORMS OF CFG

The grammar can be simplified by reducing the $\in$ production, removing useless symbols, unit production. (see 5.9). There is also a need to have grammar in some specific form.

In CFG at the R.H.S. of the production there are any number of terminal or non terminal symbols in any combination. We need to normalize such a grammar. That means we want the grammar in some specific format. That means there should be fixed number of terminals and non-terminals, in the context free grammar.

In a CFG, the right hand of a production can be any string of variable and terminals. When the productions in $G$ satisfy certain restriction then $G$ is said to be in **"normal form".**

There are two important normal forms are:

(1) Chomsky's Normal Form (CNF)

(2) Greibach Normal Form (GNF)

## 5.8 CHOMSKY NORMAL FORM (CNF)

***[U.P.T.U. B-Tech 2002, MCA 2003]***

A context-free grammar $G$ is in Chomsky Normal Form if every production is in the form of $A \to a$ or $A \to BC$ and $\Sigma \to \in$ is in grammar $G$ if $\in \in L(G)$. When $\in$ is in $L(G)$. We assume that $S^*$ does not appear on the $R.H.S$ of any production.

**Example 5.23:** Consider a grammar $G$ whose production rules are in the following forms

$$S \to AB \mid \in$$

$$S \to \in$$

$$S \to a$$

$$S \to b$$

Since every production is in the form of $A \to$ a or $A \to BC$ and $S \to \in$ (*i.e.,* either contain exactly one terminal symbol or exactly tow non-terminal symbols. Hence $G$ is in Chomsky Normal Form (CNF).

**Example 5.24 (a):** A given context-free grammar $G$ is

$$S \to ABC/ac$$

$$A \to a,\ B \to b$$

$$S \to d$$

*Convert it into Normal Form.*

**Solution:** Since $S \to aC$ which is not in $CNF$ then the terminal a can be replace by a new variable D by adding a new production rule $D \to$ a, so the CNF equivalent to $S \to aC$ is equivalent to $S \to DC$

and $D \to a$

again $S \to ABC$ which is not in *CNF*

Now $S \to AE$

$S \to BC$

Thus the given *CFG* is equivalent to the following *CNF.*

$S \to AE/DC$

$E \to BC$

$A \to a$

$B \to b$

$C \to d$

$D \to a$

**Example 5.25:** Reduce the following grammar to chomsky Normal Form

$S \to 1A/OB$

$A \to 1AA/0S|0$

$S \to 0BB|1$

**Solution:** The Chomsky normal form of given grammar is

$S \to S_1A \mid S_2B$

$S_1 \to 1$

$S_2 \to 0$

$A \to S_1S_3 \mid S_2S \mid 0$

$S_3 \to AA$

$B \to S_2S_4 \mid 1$

$S_4 \to BB$

**Example 5.26:** Change the following grammars in CNF.

$S \to 1A \mid OB$

$A \to AA \mid 0S \mid 0$

$B \to aBB \mid 1$

**Solution:** (a) In *CNF*, productions are in the form of

$A \to BC \mid a$

*i.e.,* either two non-terminals or one terminal is one the right side of production rules.

Therefore replace *AA* by $C_a$ and BB by $C_b$, 1 by $C_1$, 0 by $C_0$, a by *K,* we get

$S \to C_1A \mid C_0B$

$A \to C_1C_a \mid C_0S \mid 0$

$B \to KC_b \mid 1$

$C_1 \to 1$

$C_0 \to 0$

$C_a \to AA,$

$C_b \to BB$

$K \to a.$ Which are in *CNF.*

**Example 5.27:** Convert the following CFG into CNF.

$S \to aaaaS$

$S \to aaaa$

**Solution:** As we know the rule for Chomsky's Normal Form is

Non terminal → Non terminal. Non terminal

Non terminal → terminal

But the CFG given is

$S \to aaaaS$ rule 1

$S \to aaaa$ rule 2

If we add a rule $A \to a$ which is in CNF.

Then out rule 1 and 2 becomes,

$A \to AAAAS$

$S \to AAAA$

Let us take $S \to A$ $\boxed{AAAS}$ can be replaced by $P_1$

If we define $P_1 \to AAAS$ then the rule becomes

$S \to A\ P_1$ which is in CNF

But the new rule $P_1$ is not CNF, so let us convert it

$P_1 \to A$ $\boxed{AAS}$ can be replaced by $P_2$

then $P_1 \to A\ \ P_2$ which is in CNF

and $P_2 \to AAS$ which is not in CNF so let us convert it to CNF

$P_2 \to A$ $\boxed{As}$ can be replaced by $P_3$

$P_2 \to A\ P_3$ where $P_3 \to AS$

Now both $P_2$ and $P_3$ are in CNF.

Collectively rewrite these rules (these all indicate rule 1 of the given CFG).

$$\boxed{\begin{aligned} S &\to A\ P_1 \\ P &\to A\ P_2 \\ P_2 &\to A\ P_3 \\ P_3 &\to A\ S \end{aligned}}$$

Now consider rule 2

$$S \to AAAA$$

if we break the rule 2 as

$$S \to \boxed{AA}\ \boxed{AA}$$

$\downarrow$ $\downarrow$ indicated by

$P_4$ $P_5$

The rule becomes$S \to P_4\ P_5$ which is in CNF.

But $P_4$ and $P_5$ indicate the same rule. So we can eliminate either of then.

Hence rule 2 becomes

$$S \to P_4\ P_5$$

But $P_4$ and $P_5$ indicate the same rule. So we can eliminate either of them.

Hence rule 2 becomes

$$S \to P_4\ P_4$$

Finally we can collectively show the CFG converted to CNF as

$$S \to A\ P_1$$
$$P_1 \to A\ P_2$$
$$P_2 \to A\ P_3$$
$$P_3 \to A\ S$$
$$S \to P_4\ P_4$$
$$P_4 \to A\ A$$
$$A \to a$$

**Example 5.28:** Consider $a = (\{S, A\}, \{a, b\}, P, S)$

Where $P$ consists of

$$S \to aAS \mid a$$
$$A \to SbA \mid SS \mid ba$$

Convert it to its equivalent CNF.

**Solution:** Let us consider,

$$S \to aAS$$
$$R_1 \to a$$

then $\quad S \to R_1AS$

and if $\quad R_2 \to AS$

then $S$ becomes $\quad S \to R_1\ R_2$ is now in CNF

$S \to a$ is already in CNF

$$A \to SbA$$

Let $\quad R_3 \to b$

Hence $A \to S\,R_3\,A$

Add $R_4 \to R_3\,A$

then $A \to S\,R_4$

$A \to SS$ is already in CNF

Now as we have defined $R_1 \to a$ and $R_3 \to b$.

$A \to R_1\,R_3$ will be a conversion in CNF of $A \to ab$.

Finally, we can write

$S \to R_1\,R_2$

$S \to a$

$R_1 \to a\ R_3 \to b$

$R_2 \to AS$

$A_4 \to S\,R_4$

$R_4 \to R_3A$

$A \to SS$

$A \to R_1\,R_3$

**Example 5.29:** Convert the given CFG to CNF.

Consider $G = (V, T, P, S)$

Where $V = \{S, A, B\}$

$T = \{a, b\}$

$P$ consists of

$S \to aB$

$S \to bA$

$A \to a$

$A \to aS$

$A \to bAA$

$B \to b$

$B \to aS$

$B \to aBB$

**Solution:** Let us start with first rule.

$R_1 \to a$

$S \to R_1B$ is in CNF for $S \to aB$

$R_2 \to b$

$S \to R_2A$ is in CNF for $S \to bA$

$A \to a$

$A \to a\ S$ can be written as

$A \to R_1S$

Now $A \to bAA$ can be written as

$A \to R_2\ AA$ replace it by $R_3$

*i.e.,* $R_3 \to AA$

then $A \to R_2R_3$

$B \to a$

$B \to bS$ can be written as

$B \to R_2S$ is in CNF

Now, $B \to aBB$

*i.e.,* $B \to R_1\ BB$ $\because\ R_1 \to a$

Let $R_4 \to BB$

then $B \to R_1\ R_4$

Finally we can write,

$$S \to R_1B$$
$$S \to R_2\ A$$
$$A \to R_1S$$
$$A \to R_2\ R_3$$
$$B \to b$$
$$B \to R_2\ S$$
$$B \to R_1\ R_4$$
$$R_1 \to a$$
$$R_2 \to b$$
$$R_3 \to AA$$
$$R_4 \to BB$$

is a Chomsky's normal form.

**Example 5.30:** Convert the following CFG to CNF

$$S \to ABA$$
$$A \to aA \mid \in$$
$$B \to bB \mid \in$$

**Solution:** In the Chomsky's normal from the ε production is not allowed. So first we will eliminate e productions.

$$A \to \in \quad \text{and} \quad B \to \in$$

if put $\in$ instead of $A$ and $B$

We can get $S \to ABA \mid AB \mid BA \mid AA \mid A \mid B$

Similarly $A \to aA \mid a$

$B \to bB \mid b$

Now $S \to A$ and $S \to B$ is unit productiion getting introduced in the grammar after removal of ε production. So we will remove unit production also,

$$S \to ABA \mid AB \mid BA \mid AA \mid aA \mid a \mid bB \mid b$$
$$A \to aA \mid a$$
$$B \to bB \mid b$$

Now let us convert this grammar to Chomsky's normal form.

Let $S \to ABA$

$$S \rightarrow ABA$$

$$R_1 \rightarrow BA$$

then $S \rightarrow AR_1$

Now

| $S \rightarrow AB$ | $S \rightarrow BA$ | $S \rightarrow AA$ |
|---|---|---|

already in CNF

Let $S \rightarrow aA$

We will define $R_2 \rightarrow a$

$$S \rightarrow R_2A$$
$$R_2 \rightarrow a$$

$S \rightarrow a$ already in CNF

$$S \rightarrow bB$$

Let

$$R_3 \rightarrow b$$

then

$$S \rightarrow R_3\ B$$

$S \rightarrow b$ already in CNF

Now consider the rules,

$$A \rightarrow aA$$

We can rewrite it as

$$A \rightarrow R_2A$$
$$A \rightarrow a$$

Also, $B \rightarrow bB$ can be rewritten as

$$B \rightarrow R_3\ B$$
$$B \rightarrow b$$

Collect all the CNF s to integrate and we will get

$$S \rightarrow A\ R_1 \mid AB \mid BA \mid AA \mid R_2A \mid R_3B \mid a \mid b$$
$$A \rightarrow R_2A \mid a$$
$$B \rightarrow R_3\ B \mid b$$
$$R_1 \rightarrow BA$$
$$R_2 \rightarrow a$$
$$R_3 \rightarrow b$$

is done.

## 5.9 GREIBACH NORMAL FORM (GNF)

**[U.P.T.U. B-Tech 2002, 2005, 2007(co)]**

A CFG is said to be in GNF if very production is of the form $A \to a\alpha$, where $\alpha \in V^*$($\alpha$ may be $\in$) and $a \in S$ and $S \to \in$ is in $G$ if $\in L(G)$ when $\in L(G)$ then we assume that $S$ does not appear on the $R.H.S$ of any production.

For example, $\in$ given by

$$\left.\begin{array}{r} S \to aAB. \\ S \to \in \\ A \to bC \\ B \to b \\ C \to c \end{array}\right) \text{is in GNF}$$

**Lemma 1:** Let $G = (V, S, P, S)$ be a *CFG* and its production rules are in the form of

$X \to Xa_1 | Xa_2 \mid Xa_3 \| Xa_n$ (First symbol of RHS is similar to a LHS)

$X \to \beta_1 \mid \beta 2_2 \mid \beta_3 \mid ...........|\beta_m$

where $X, Y \in V$, $a_i \in S$ and $i \in \{1, 2, 3,............n\}$ and $b_j \in Sj \in \{1,2, 3,.......m\}$

The grammar $G_1 = (\{V \cup Y\}, S, P_1, S)$ is in the form of GNF if adding a new variable $Y$ to $V$ and replacing all the $X$-production by the following productions.

$$X \to \beta_1 \mid \beta_2 \mid \beta_3 \mid ...............|\beta_m$$
$$X \to \beta_1\, Y \mid \beta_2\, Y \mid \beta_3\, Y \mid ..............|\beta_m\, Y$$
$$Y \to \alpha_1 \mid \alpha_2 \mid \alpha_3 \mid ..............|\alpha_n$$
$$Y \to \alpha_1\, Y \mid \alpha_2\, Y \mid \alpha_3\, Y \mid ..............|\alpha_n\, Y$$

Then $\quad L(G) = L(G_1)$

**Proof:** In a given grammar $G$, all the productions are in the form of left linear, whose derivations are always representing a Left Most Derivation (LMD) and terminated with the productions

$$X \to \beta_1 \mid \beta_2 \mid \beta_3 \mid ..............|\beta_m$$

The left most derivation is

$X \to X\alpha_i \to X\alpha_i\alpha_i \to X\alpha_i\alpha_i\alpha_i \to ...... \to X\alpha_i ....... \alpha_i\alpha_i\alpha_i\alpha_i \to \beta_i\alpha_i..... \alpha_i\alpha_i\alpha_i\alpha_i$ where $i \in \{1, 2, 3,.........n\}$ and $j \in \{1,2,3,.....m\}$

This can be replaced in $G_1$ by

$X \to \beta_i Y \to \beta_i\alpha_i \to \beta_i\alpha_i\alpha_i \to ...... \to \beta_i\alpha_i ....... \alpha_i\alpha_i\alpha_i\alpha_i \to \beta_i\alpha_i..... \alpha_i\alpha_i\alpha_i\alpha_i\alpha_i$ where $i \in \{1, 2, 3,.........n\}$ and $j \in \{1,2,3,.....m\}$

This is representing a right most derivation.

Thus $\quad L(G) = L(G_1)$

**Example 5.31:** Change the following grammars in GNF

$$X \to Xa \mid Xb$$
$$X \to c \mid d$$

**Solution:** By Lemma 1, A GNF is as follows

$$X \to c \mid d$$
$$X \to cY \mid dY$$
$$Y \to a \mid b$$
$$Y \to aY \mid bY$$

**Lemma 2:** Let $G = (V, S, P, S)$ be a CFG and its production rules are in the form of

$$X \to \alpha_1 Y \alpha_2$$
$$X \to \beta_1 \mid \beta_2 \mid \beta_3 \mid \ldots\ldots\ldots\ldots\ldots \mid \beta_m$$

where $X, Y, \in V$, $\alpha_1, \alpha_2, \beta_j \in S \cup V$ but $\alpha_1$ does not contain same symbol of its left hand side production. The grammar $G_1 = (V, S, P_1, S)$ is in the forms of GNF if deleting the production $X \to \alpha_1 Y \alpha_2$ from $P$ and adding the following productions.

$$X \to \alpha_1\beta_1\alpha_2 \mid \alpha_1\beta_1\alpha_2 \mid \alpha_1\beta_1\alpha_2 \mid \ldots\ldots\ldots \mid \alpha_1\beta_m\alpha_2 \mid$$

Then $\quad L(G) = L(G_J)$

**Proof:** To derive any string $w \in L(G)$ from a given context free grammar $G$, apply the following derivation steps for the string $w$

$$X \to \alpha_1 Y \alpha_2$$
$$X \to \alpha_1\beta_j\alpha_2 \text{ where } j \in \{1, 2, 3, \ldots\ldots m\}$$

Hence $\quad L(G) \subseteq L(G_1)$

Again instead of applying derivation step, you can direct apply $X \to \alpha_1\beta_j\alpha_2$ where $j \in \{1, 2, 3, \ldots\ldots\ldots, m\}$ from $G_1$. That is $L(G_1) \subseteq L(G)$

Thus $\quad L(G) = L(G_1)$

**Example 5.32:** Change the following grammars in GNF

$$X \to bYa \mid aYb$$
$$X \to cY \mid dA$$

**Solution:** By Lemma 2, A GNF is as follows

$$X \to b\ cY\ a \mid b\ dA\ a \mid a\ cY\ b \mid a\ dA\ b$$

As the production rules are not still in GNF, so apply normal conversions rules

$$X \to b\ CY\ D \mid b\ dA\ D \mid a\ CYB \mid a\ dAB$$

$C \rightarrow c$

$D \rightarrow a$

$B \rightarrow b$

**Example 5.33:** Convert the given CFG to CNF.

$S \rightarrow CA$

$A \rightarrow a$

$C \rightarrow aB \mid b$

**Solution:** If you observe the given grammar $A$ and $C$ are in Greibach Normal Form. But $S$ is not in GNF.

Let us apply lemma 1 for $S$

$S \rightarrow CA$ can be written as

$S \rightarrow aBA \mid bA$

Thus we can write equivalent GNF as

$S \rightarrow aBA \mid bA$

$A \rightarrow a$

$C \rightarrow aB \mid b$

**Example 5.34:** Convert the given CFG to CNF

$S \rightarrow ABA$

$A \rightarrow aA \mid \in$

$B \rightarrow bB \mid \in$

**Solution:** As before converting the CFG to its normal form we usually reduce the grammar *i.e.,* we first eliminate $\in$ production, unit production and useless symbols.

As $A \rightarrow \in$ and $B \rightarrow \in$

Let us simplify the given CFG by removing $\in$ productions, and the CFG will look like this,

$S \rightarrow ABA \mid AB \mid BA \mid AA \mid A \mid B$

$A \rightarrow aA \mid a$

$B \rightarrow bB \mid b$

[We can even remove the unit productions]

Let us replace $A$ by $aA$ or $a$ in $S$

$S \rightarrow aABA \mid aAB \mid aBA \mid aB \mid aAA \mid aA \mid a$

which is GNF

similarly $S \rightarrow BA \mid B$ can be written as

$S \rightarrow bBA \mid bA \mid bB \mid b$

is also in GNF.

Finally equivalent GNF will be

$$S \rightarrow aABA \mid aAB \mid aBA \mid aB \mid aAA \mid aA \mid a$$
$$S \rightarrow bBA \mid bA \mid bB \mid b$$
$$A \rightarrow aA \mid a$$
$$B \rightarrow bB \mid b$$

**Example 5.35:** Convert given CFG to CNF

where $V = \{S, A\}$, $T = \{0, 1\}$ and $P$ is

$$S \rightarrow AA \mid 0$$
$$A \rightarrow SS \mid 1$$

**Solution:** Let us rename $S$ as $A_1$ and $A$ as $A_2$ then the CFG becomes

$$A_1 \rightarrow A_2\ A_2 \mid 0$$
$$A_2 \rightarrow A_1\ A_1 \mid 1$$

Let us start with $A_1$

As $A_1 \rightarrow A_2\ A_2$ and we need to convert this production to GNF we will reduce $A_2$ first

$$A_2 \rightarrow A_1\ A_1 \mid 1$$

Let us keep $A_2 \rightarrow 1$ as it is, since it is already in GNF.

Now $A_2 \rightarrow A_1\ A_1 \mid 1$

Here if we place $A_1$ by its productions the rule

$$A_2 \rightarrow A_2\ A_2\ A_1 \mid 0A_1 \mid 1$$

Here $\alpha = A_2\ A_1$ and $\beta_1 = 0\ A_1$ $\beta_2 = 1$

$$A \rightarrow \beta_1 \mid \beta_2$$
$$A \rightarrow \beta_1 z \mid \beta_2 Z$$
$$Z \rightarrow a$$
$$Z \rightarrow a\ Z$$

So now, $A_2 \rightarrow 0\ A_1 \mid 1$

$$A_2 \rightarrow 0\ A_1\ Z \mid 1\ Z$$
$$Z \rightarrow A_2\ A_1$$
$$Z \rightarrow A_2\ A_1\ Z$$

Note that $A_2$ is in GNF form.

Now modify $A_1$ as

$$A_1 \rightarrow A_2\ A_2 \mid 0$$

That is $A_1 \rightarrow 0\ A_1\ A_2 \mid 1\ A_2$

$$A_1 \rightarrow 0\ A_1\ Z\ A_2 \mid 1\ Z\ A_2 \mid 0$$

is in GNF

Now let us modify $Z$

$$Z \to A_2\ A_1 \mid A_2\ A_1\ Z$$

By using lemma we can substitute value of $A_2$ at right hand side of $Z$ rule. Take $Z$ production and convert to GNF as

$$Z \to 0\ A_1\ A_1 \mid 1A_1 \mid 0A_1\ ZA_1 \mid 1ZA_1$$
$$Z \to 0\ A_1\ A_1 Z \mid 1\ A_1\ Z \mid 0\ A_1\ Z\ A_1\ Z \mid 1\ Z\ A_1\ Z$$

Collectively we can rewrite the given CFG to its GNF as

$$A_1 \to 0\ A_1\ A_2 \mid 1\ A_2 \mid 0\ A_1\ Z\ A_2 \mid 1\ Z\ A_2 \mid 0$$
$$A_2 \to 0\ A_1 \mid 1 \mid 0\ A_1\ Z\ \mid 1\ Z$$
$$Z \to 0\ A_1\ A_1 \mid 1\ A_1 \mid 0\ A_1\ Z\ A_1 \mid ZA_1 \mid 0\ A_1\ A_1\ Z \mid 1\ A_1\ Z$$
$$0A_1\ Z\ A_1\ Z \mid 1Z\ A_1\ Z$$

## 5.10 SIMPLIFICATION OF CONTEXT-FREE GRAMMARS

In a CFG $G$, it may not be necessary to use all the symbols in $V'\ S$ or all the production in $P$ for deriving sentences. So, we try to eliminate symbols and productions in $G$ which are not useful for derivation of sentences.

Consider for example,

$$X \to (\{S,\ A,\ B,\ C,\ E\},\ \{a,\ b,\ c\},\ P,\ s),$$
$$C \to \{S \to AB,\ B \to C$$
$$A \to aE \to C \mid \in$$
$$B \to b$$
$$L(G) \to \{ab\}$$

In the above, grammar the symbol $C$, $E$ and $\in$ and production $B \to CE \to C|\in$ are not used to derive language $L(G) = \{a,\ b\}$. So we can eliminate these production rule.

The properties of reduced grammar are given below–

→ Each variable (*i.e.*, non termial) and each terminal of $G$ appears in the derivation of some word in $L$.

→ There should not be any production as $X \to Y$ where $X$ and $Y$ are non-terminals.

→ If $\in$ is not in the language $L$ then there need not be production $X \to \in$

We see the reduction of grammar as below–

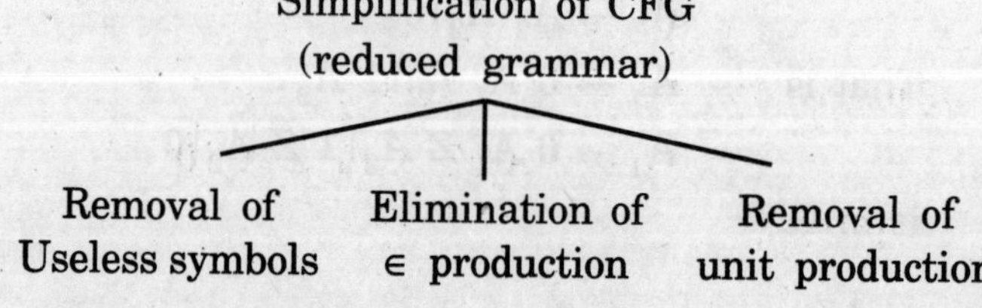

## 5.10.1 Construction of Reduced Grammar

If $G$ is a CFG such that $L(G) \neq \phi$, we can find an equivalent grammar $G'$ such that each variable in $G'$ derives some terminal string.

**Proof:** Let $G = (V, S, P, S)$ we define $G' = (V', S, P', S)$ $w_1 = \{a \in V \mid \exists$ $a$ production $A \rightarrow w$ where $w \in \Sigma^*\}$. $w_{i+1} = w_i \cup \{A \in V | \exists$ some production $A \rightarrow \alpha$ till $w_k = w_{k+1}$ for some $k \leq |V|$ therefore $V' = w_1'$ (b) Construction of $P'$

$$P' = \{A \rightarrow a \mid A, a \in (V' \cup S)^*\}$$

we can define $G' = (V', S, P', S)$. $S$ is in $V$.

**Example 5.36:** Let $G = (V, S, P, S)$ be given by the production $S \rightarrow AB$, $A \rightarrow a$, $B \rightarrow b$, $B \rightarrow C$, $E \rightarrow C$. Find $G'$ such that every variable in $G'$ derives some terminal string.

**Solution:** $G' = (V', S, P', S)$ where $V'$ is defined as follows

$w_1 = \{A, B, E\}$ because $A \rightarrow a$, $B \rightarrow b$, $E \rightarrow c$ are productions with $a$ terminal string on the $R.H.S.$

$$w_2 = w_1 \cup \{A \in V \mid A_1 \in \text{ for some } a \in (S \cup \{A, B, E\})\}$$
$$= w_1 \cup \{S\} = \{AB, E, S\}$$
$$w_3 = \{w_2 \cup \{A_1 \in V\} \, A_1 \in \text{a for some } \alpha \in (\Sigma \cup \{A, B, E, S)\}\}$$
$$= w_2 \cup \phi$$

Therefore $V' = \{S, A, B, E\}$ and $P'$ is defined as follows.

$$P' = \{A_1 \rightarrow a | \, A_1, a \in (V' \cup \Sigma)^*\}$$
$$= \{\delta \rightarrow AB, A \rightarrow a, B \rightarrow b, E \rightarrow c\}$$

Therefore $G' = (\{S, A, B, E\}, \{a, b, c\}, P', S)$

**Example 5.37:** Find CFG with no useless symbols equivalent to

$S \rightarrow AB \mid CA$ $\qquad$ $B \rightarrow BC \mid AB$

$A \rightarrow a$ $\qquad$ $C \rightarrow aB \mid b$

**Solution:** Consider, the rule

$S \rightarrow AB$ $\qquad$ 1

$S \rightarrow CA$ $\qquad$ 2

In the rule 2, $C$ and $A$ can be replaced by some terminating string but in rule 1, $B$ can not be replaced by terminating string. It tends to form a never ending loop.

*e.g.,* $\quad S \rightarrow AB \rightarrow aAB \rightarrow aaAB \rightarrow aaaAB$ and so on.

Thus we come to know as $B$ is an useless symbol. Removing $B$ the rules are now,

$S \to CA$

$A \to a$

$C \to b$

**Example 5.38:** Consider the following CFG

$G = (V, \Sigma, R, S)$

where $V = \{S, X, Y\}$

$\Sigma = (0, 1)$

$R = \{S \to XY | 0$

$X \to 1\}$

Remove the useless symbols from it.

**Solution:** As $S \to XY$

$S \to 0$

$X \to 1$

It is easy to recognize that there is no derivation for $Y$. Hence we can eliminate the production with $Y$, and the rules are

$S \to 0$

$X \to 1$

## 5.10.2 Elimination of Null Production

A context-free grammar may have production of the form $A \to \in$. The production $A \to \in$ is just used to erase $A$. So a production of the form $A \to \in$, where $A$ is a variable is called *Null production.*

*For example,* Consider a grammar whose productions are

$S \to as \mid aA \mid \in$

$A \to \in$

In This case two productions are null production *i.e.*, $S \to \in$ and $A \in \in$.

**Theorem 5.1.** *If $G = (V, S, P, S)$ is a CFG, then we can find a context-free grammar $G_1$ having no null production such that $L(G,) = L(G)$ 0b $\{\in\}$.*

**Proof:** We constant $G_1 = (V, S, P', S)$ as follows:

**Step 1:** Construction of the set of nullable variable : we find the nullable variables recursively

(*i*) $w_1 = \{A \in V \mid A \to \in \text{ is in } P\}$,

(*ii*) $w_{i+1} = w_i \cup \{A \in V \mid \exists\ a$ production $A \to a$ with a $\in w_i\}$, repeat the procedure till $w_k = w_{k+1}$ this is a set of all nullable variable.

**Step 2:** Construction of $P'$:

(*i*) Any production whose *R.H.S.* does not have any nullable variable is induded in $P'$.

(*ii*) If $A \to X_1X_2.....X_k$ is in $P$, the production of the form $A \to \alpha_1\alpha_2.......\alpha_k$ ar included in $P'$, where $\alpha_i = X_i$ if $X_i \notin w$. $a_i = X_i$ or $\in$ if $X_i \in$ wand $\alpha_1$, $\alpha_2.......\alpha_k \neq \in$.

The production are obtained either by not erasing any nullable variable on the *R.H.S* of $A \to X_1, X_2,......., X_k$ or by erasing some or all nullable variable s provided some symbol appears *R.H.S.* after erasing.

Let $G_1 = (V, S, P', S)$ has not null production.

**Example 5.39:** Remove the $\in$ production from following CFG by preserving meaning of it.

$$S \to XYX$$
$$X \to 0X | \in$$
$$Y \to 1\ Y | \in$$

**Solution:** Now, while removing $\in$ production we are deleting the rules $X \to \in$ and $Y \to \in$. To preserve the meaning of CFG we are actually placing $\varepsilon$ at right hand side where ever $X$ and $Y$ have appeared.

Let us take $\quad S \to XYX$

if first $X$ at right hand side is $\in$.

then $\quad S \to YX$

Similarly if last $X$ in R.H.S. = $\in$.

then $\quad S \to XY$

if $\quad Y \to \varepsilon$ then

$$S \to XX$$

if $Y$ and $X$ are $\in$ then

$S \to X$ also

$S \to Y$ when both $X$ are replaced by $\in$

$\therefore \quad S \to XY | YX | XX | X | Y$

Now let us consider

$$X \to 0X$$

if we place $\in$ at right hand side for $X$ then

$$X \to 0$$
$$X \to 0X | 0$$

Similarly $\quad Y \to 1\ Y | 1$

Collectively we can rewrite the CFG with removed $\in$ productions as

$$S \to XY | YX | XX | X | Y$$
$$X \to 0X | 0$$
$$Y \to 1Y | 1$$

**Example 5.40:** Eliminate the $\in$ productions from the CFG given below

$$A \to 0\ B\ 1 | 1\ B\ 1$$

$$B \to 0\ B | 1\ B | \in$$

**Solution:** Now the $\in$ production is $B \to \in$ we will delete this production. And then add the productions having $B$ replaced by $\in$.

$A \to 0\ B\ 1$

if $B \to \in$

$A \to 0\ 1$

Similarly $A \to 1\ B\ 1\ \ 11$

$\therefore$ $A \to 0\ B\ 1 | 1\ B\ 1 | 01 | 11$

Similarly, $B \to 0\ B$

if $B \to \in$

$B \to 0$

as well as $B \to 1$

$B \to 0\ B | 1\ B | 0 | 1$

$B \to 0\ B | 1\ B | 0 | 1$

Collectively, we can write

$$A \to 0\ B\ 1 | 1\ B\ 1 | 01 | 11$$

$$B \to 0\ B | 1\ B | 0 | 1$$

**Example 5.41:** For the CFG given below remove the $\in$ production.

$$S \to aSa$$

$$S \to bSb$$

$$S \to \in$$

**Solution:** According to the replacement procedure, we will place $\in$ at $S$ in the sentential form.

$S \to a\ S\ a$ if $S = \in$

$S \to a\ a$

Similarly if $S \to b\ S\ b$ if $S = \in$

$S \to b\ b$

Thus finally the rules are

$$S \to a\ S\ a | b\ S\ b | a\ a | b\ b$$

**Example 5.42:** Consider the CFG given below,

For eliminating $\in$ productions

$$S \to P\ 0\ Q | Q\ Q | 0\ R | R\ Q\ P$$

$$P \to R\ 0 | 1\ R | R\ R | R\ Q\ P$$

$$Q \to Q\ 0 | P\ Q | \in$$

$$R \to 0\ P | Q\ Q\ Q$$

**Solution:** As we can see that $Q \to \in$.

Similarly $\quad R \to QQQ \to \in$.

Hence we will replace $Q$ and $R$ by $\in$ and according add the production rules.

Similarly $\quad P \to R\ R \to \in$

Let us modify the rules if $P$ or $Q$ or $R$ becomes $\in$

$$S \to P\ 0\ Q | 0 | 0\ R | Q\ Q | R\ Q\ P$$

$$P \to R\ 0 | 0 | 1 | 1\ R | RR | RQP$$

$$Q \to Q\ 0 | 0 | PQ$$

$$R \to 0\ P | 0 | Q\ Q\ Q$$

Note that with $P$, $Q$, $R$ other meanings are associated, they are not purely giving $\in$ to us. Therefore we can not remove $P$, $Q$ and $R$ symbols.

**Example 5.43:** Construct CFG without ε production from the one which is given below.

$$S \to a | Ab | aBa$$

$$A \to b | \in$$

$$B \to b | A$$

**Solution:** If you observe carefully, then not only $A$ have $\in$ production but even $B$ also indicates ε production *i.e.,* $A \to \in$ straight forward but $B \to A \to \in$. Let us aply the method of replacement.

$$S \to A\ b$$

if $\quad A = \in$ then

$$S \to b$$

if $\quad B = \in$

$$S \to a\ a$$

$$S \to a | A\ b | b | a\ a | a\ B\ a$$

$$A \to b$$

$$B \to b$$

Finally the rules are

$$S \to a | A\ b | b | a\ a | a\ B\ a$$

$$A \to b$$

$$B \to b$$

## 5.10.3 Removing Unit Productions

The unit productions are the productions in which one nonterminal gives another non terminal.

For example if

$$X \to Y$$

$$Y \to Z \qquad Z \to X$$

then $X$, $Y$ and $Z$ are unit productions. To optimize the grammar we need to remove the unit productions.

If $A^* \Rightarrow B$ is a unit production and $B \to X_1\ X_2\ X_3$ ...... $X_n$ then while removing $A \to B$ production we should add a rule $A \to X_1\ X_2\ X_3$ ...... $X_n$.

**Example 5.44:** If the CFG is as below

$$S \to 0A \mid 1B \mid C$$
$$A \to 0S \mid 00$$
$$B \to 1 \mid A$$
$$C \to 01$$

then remove the unit productions.

**Solution:** Clearly $S \to C$ is a unit production. But while removing $S \to C$ we have to consider what $C$ gives. So, we can add a rule to $S$.

$$S \to 0A \mid 1B \mid 01$$

Similarly $B \to A$ is also a unit production so we can modify it as

$$B \to 1 \mid 0S \mid 00$$

Thus finally we can write CFG without unit production as

$$S \to 0A \mid 1B \mid 01$$
$$A \to 0S \mid 00$$
$$B \to 1 \mid 0S \mid 00$$
$$C \to 01$$

**Example 5.45:** Optimize the CFG given below by reducing the grammar. $S$ is a start symbol.

$$S \to A \mid 0C1$$
$$A \to B \mid 01 \mid 10$$
$$C \to \epsilon \mid CD$$

**Solution:** $S \to A \to B$ is a unit production

$C \to \epsilon$ is a null production.

$C \to CD$ $B$ and $D$ are useless symbol.

Reducing a grammar we have to avoid all the above conditions.

Let $\quad S \to A$

*i.e.,* $A$ $B$ is a useless symbol because $B$ is not defined further more.

$$S \to 01 \mid 10$$

*i.e.,* $\quad S \to 01 \mid 10 \mid 0C1$

But $\quad C \to \epsilon$

Hence ulitmately $S \to 01 \mid 10$

$A \to B$ but we can remove this production since $B$ is a useless symbol.

Hence $A \to 01 \mid 10$

But the start symbol

$$S \to 01 \mid 10$$

There is no $A$ in the derivation of $A$ so by considering $A$ also as a useless symbol we get final CFG as

$$S \to 01 \mid 10$$

## 5.11 CLOSURE PROPERTIES OF CFL

Like regular language, the context-free languages are closed under the operators such as union, concatenation and star-closure but there are exceptions also like complement and intersections.

Thus, closure properties that hold for regular language need not always hold for context free languages.

After performing that particular operation on those CFLs the resultant language is context free language.

These properties are as follow–

1. The context free languages are closed under union.
2. The context free languages are closed under concatenation.
3. The context free languages a are closed under kleen closure.
4. The context free languages are not closed under intersection.
5. The context free languages are not closed under complement.

**Theorem 5.2:** If $L_1$ and $L_2$ are context free languages then $L = L_1 \cup L_2$ is also context free. That is, the CFLs are closed under union.

**Proof:** We will consider two languages $L_1$ and $L_2$ which are context free languages. We can give these languages using context free grammars $G_1$ and $G_2$ such that $G_1$ and $G_2$ such that $G_1 \in L_1$ and $G_2 \in L_2$. The $G_1$ can be given as $G_1 = \{V_1, \Sigma, P_1, S_1\}$ where $P_1$ can be given as

$$P_1 = \{\ S_1 \to A_1\ S_1\ A_1 \mid B_1\ S\ B_1 \mid \in$$

$$A_1 \to a$$

$$B_1 \to b$$

$$\}$$

Here $V_1 = \{S_1, A_1, B_1\}$ and $S_1$ is a start symbol.

Similarly, we can write $G_2 = \{V_2, \Sigma, P_2, S_2\}$

$N_2 = \{S_2, A_2, B_2\}$ and $S_2$ is a start symbol.

$P_2$ can be given as :

$$P_2 = \{ S_2 \to a\, A_2\, A_2 \mid b\, B_2\, B_2$$
$$A_2 \to b$$
$$B_2 \to a$$
$$\}$$

Now $L = L_1 \cup L_2$ gives $G \in L$. This $G$ can be written as

$$G = \{V, \Sigma, P, S\}$$
$$V = \{S_1, A_1, B_1, S_2, A_2, B_2\}$$
$$P = \{P_1 \cup P_2\}$$

$S$ is a start symbol

$$P = \{ S \to S_1 \mid S_2$$
$$S_1 \to A_1\, S_1\, A_1 \mid B_1\, S\, B_1 \mid \in$$
$$A_1 \to a$$
$$B_1 \to b$$
$$S_2 \to aA_2A_2 \mid bB_2B_2$$
$$A_2 \to b$$
$$B_2 \to a$$
$$\}$$

Thus grammar $G$ is a context free grammar which produces languages $L$ which is context sensitive language.

**Theorem 5.3:** If $L_1$ and $L_2$ are two context sensitive. That means context sensitive languages are closed under concatenation.

**Proof:** Let $L_1$ is a context sensitive language which can be represented by a context free grammar $G_1$, such that $G_1 \in L_1$ and

$$G_1 = \{V_1\ \Sigma, P_1, S_1\}$$
$$V_1 = \{S_1, A_1, B_1\}$$
$$\text{S} = \{a, b\}$$

$S_1$ is a start symbol, and $P_1$ is a set of production rules,

$$P_1 = \{S_1 \to A_1\, S_1\, A_1 \mid B_1\, S_1\, B_1 \mid \in$$
$$A_1 \to a$$
$$B_1 \to b$$
$$\}$$

Similarly, $L_2$ is a context sensitive language which can be represented by a context free grammar $G_2$, such that $G_2$, such that $G_2 \in L_2$ and

$$G_2 = \{V_2, \Sigma, P_2, S_2\}$$
$$V_2 = \{S_2, A_2, B_2\}$$
$$\Sigma = \{a, b\}$$

$S_2$ is a start and $P_2$ is a set of production rules,

$$P_2 = \{S_2 \to a\ A_2\ A_2 \mid b\ B_2\ B_2$$
$$A_2 \to b$$
$$B_2 \to a$$
$$\}$$

Now $L = L_1\ L_2$ can be obtained by $G$ such that $G = G_1 \cdot G_2$. Therefore

$$G = \{V, \Sigma, P, S\}$$
$$V = \{S, S_1, A_1, B_1, S_2, A_2, B_2\}$$

where $S$ is a start symbol. The production rules, $P$ can be given as

$$P = \{S \to S_1 \mid S_2$$
$$S_1 \to A_1\ S_1\ A_1 \mid B_1\ S_1\ B_1 \mid \in$$
$$A_1 \to a$$
$$B_1 \to b$$
$$S_2 \to a\ A_2\ A_2 \mid b\ B_2\ B_2$$
$$A_2 \to b$$
$$B_2 \to a$$
$$\}$$

As grammar $G$ is context free grammar the language $L$ produced by $G$ is also context free language. Hence context free languages are closed under concatenation.

**Proof:** Let, $L_1$ be a context free language represented by $G_1$ such that $G_1 \in L_1$.

The CFG $G_1$ can be given as

$$G_1 = \{V_1, \Sigma, P_1, S_1\} \text{ where } S_1 \text{ is a start symbol}$$
$$P_1 = \{S_1\quad A_1S_1A_1 \mid B_1S_1B_1 \mid \in$$
$$A_1 \to a$$
$$B_1 \to b$$
$$\}$$

Now $L = L_1^*$ can be represented by a grammar $G$ such that

$$G = \{V, \Sigma, P, S\}$$
$$V = \{S, S_1, A_1, B_1\}$$

and

$$P = S \to S_1\ S \mid \in$$
$$S_1 \to A_1\ S_1\ A_1 \mid B_1\ S_1\ B_1$$
$$A_1 \to a$$
$$B_1 \to b$$
$$\}$$

Thus grammar $G$ is a context free grammar and language $L$ produced by $G$ is also context free language. Hence context free language are closed under kleen closure.

**Theorem 5.4 :** If $L_1$ and $L_2$ are two CFLs then $L = L_1 \cap L_2$ may be CFL or may not be CFL. That means $L$ is not closed under intersection.

**[*U.P.T.U. B-Tech 2003*]**

**Proof:** Let, $L_1 = \{0^n 1^n 2^i \mid n \geq 1, i \geq 1\}$

$L_2 = \{0^n 1^n 2^n \mid n \geq , i \geq 1\}$

The grammar for $L_1$ is

$$S \to AB$$
$$A \to 0A_1 \mid 01$$
$$B \to 2B \mid 2$$

Similarly $L_2$ can be represented by grammar

$$S \to AB$$
$$A \to 0A \mid 0$$
$$B \to \mid B^2 \mid 1^2$$

Now if we try to obtain

$L = L_1 \cap L_2$ then we get sometimes context free languages and sometimes non context free languages. Thus we can say that CFLs are not closed under intersection.

**Theorem 5.5:** If $L_1$ is a CFL then $L_1'$ may or may not be CFL. That means CFL is not closed under complement. **[*U.P.T.U. B-Tech 2002, MCA(co) 2001*]**

**Proof:** Let $L_1$ and $L_2$ are two CFLs. We will assume that complement of a context free language is a CFL itself. Hence $L_1'$ and $L_2'$ both are CFLs. We can also state that $(L_1' \cup L_2')$ is context free (since CFLs are closed under union). But $(L_1' \cup L_2') = L_1 \cap L_2$ *i.e.,* $L = L_1 \cap L_2$ may or may not be CFL. The $L_1$ and $L_2$ are arbitrary CFLs, there may exist $L_1'$ and $L_2'$ which are not be. Therefore we can say that CFL is not closed under complement operation.

## 5.12 DECIDABILITY OF CFGS

There are many questions about context free grammar that determine whether the given grammar is context free or not. Hence we can categorize the context free languages as deterministic or non-deterministic. There are many questions about context free languages that are undecidable, that means there does not exist any algorithm to answer these questions. Such questions are called the questions about undecidable context free languages–

(1) Whether or not two different context free languages define the same language.

(2) Whether given CFL is ambiguous or not?

(3) Whether complement of given CFL is context free language?

(4) Whether the intersection of two context free languages is context free?

There is no algoithm to answer these questions. But there is a certain set of questions for which the answers can be obtained such questions. Such questions are about context free languages that are decidable. Following is a list of those questions–

(1) Does the CFG $G$ generates any string. (emptiness).

(2) Is the language generated by $G$ is finite or not? (finiteness).

(3) Suppose $G$ is a grammar and $W$ is a string does $G$ generates $W$? (membership).

Now these above questions can be considered in detail.

## Emptiness

**Theorem 5.6:** There exists and algorithm which can determine whether or not the given context free grammar can generate any word at all.

**Proof:** The algorithm to determine whether or not a grammar generates any word is given below–

(*i*) Put the dot (•) above every terminal symbol. If there is any null string $\in$ then put dot over $\in$ as well. These symbols occur at right hand side of production rule.

(*ii*) If all the symbols of right hand side of the production rule are dotted then dot the corresponding non terminal (which is at left hand side of production rule) throughout the grammar. Repeat this step as long as possible.

(*iii*) If the stating symbol gets dotted then answer is yes otherwise answer is no.

Let us apply this algorithm on some grammar.

Let,

$$S \rightarrow PQ$$
$$P \rightarrow AP \mid AA$$
$$A \rightarrow a$$
$$Q \rightarrow BQ \mid BB$$
$$B \rightarrow b$$

Now if we want to put dots we will put over terminals at RHS of rule.

**Step 1:**

(1) $S \rightarrow PQ$

(2) $P \rightarrow AP \mid AA$

(3) $A \rightarrow \dot{a}$

(4) $Q \rightarrow BQ \mid BB$

(5) $B \rightarrow \dot{b}$

**Step 2:** As we RHS of rule (3) and RHS of rule (5) is dotted we will dot $A$ and $B$ throughout the grammar.

(1) $S \rightarrow PQ$

(2) $P \rightarrow \dot{A}P \mid \dot{A}\dot{A}$

(3) $\dot{A} \rightarrow a$

(4) $Q \rightarrow \dot{B}Q \mid \dot{B}\dot{B}$

(5) $\dot{B} \rightarrow \dot{b}$

Now, in rule (2) the alternate production at RHS is dotted $\left(\dot{A}\dot{A}\right)$. Hence dot $P$.

Similarly dot $Q$

Hence,

(1) $S \rightarrow \dot{P}\dot{Q}$

(2) $\dot{P} \rightarrow \dot{A}\dot{P} \mid \dot{A}\dot{A}$

(3) $\dot{A} \rightarrow a$

(4) $\dot{Q} \rightarrow \dot{B}\dot{Q} \mid \dot{B}\dot{B}$

(5) $\dot{B} \rightarrow \dot{b}$

Thus in rule (1) the RHS is dotted. Hence dot $S$. But since $S$ being dotted is a start symbol, the algorithm generates answer yes. Hence we can prove that an algorithm exists which determines whether or not the given grammar generates any string.

## Finiteness

**Theorem 5.7:** There exists an algorithm to determine whether the given context free grammar generates a finite or infinite language.

**Proof:** We will write following algorithm –

1. Make the grammar simplified by removing unit productions and useless symbols.

2. Check whether there is any self-embedded non terminal or not by following steps.
   (a) Underline some non terminal say $X$ which is at LHS of production rule.
   (b) Then put dot over all the $X$ which are at RHS throughout the grammar. The dotted $X$ and underlined $X$ are treated as two different symbols.
   (c) Put dot over any non terminal at LHS whose RHS contains any dotted symbols. Dot this non terminal throughout the grammar.
   (d) If underlined $X$ gets dotted then $X$ is called self embedded otherwise it is not self embedded.
3. If the grammar contains any self embedded non terminal then it generates infinite languages otherwise it generates finite languages.

To support this algorithm, let us take one grammar.

$$S \rightarrow PQa \mid bpz \mid b$$
$$P \rightarrow Xb \mid bZa$$
$$Q \rightarrow bPP$$
$$X \rightarrow aZa \mid aaa$$
$$Z \rightarrow ZPbP$$

The above grammar has $Z$ as useless symbol. Hence by removing it we get,

(1) $S \rightarrow PQa \mid b$

(2) $P \rightarrow Xb$

(3) $Q \rightarrow bPP$

(4) $X \rightarrow aaa$

Now we will mark $X$ of rule (4) underlined and put dot over $x$ in rule (2)

(1) $S \rightarrow PQa \mid b$

(2) $P \rightarrow \dot{X}b$

(3) $Q \rightarrow bPP$

(4) $\underline{X} \rightarrow aaa$

As RHS of rule (2) contains one dotted symbol dot $P$ throughout the grammar

$$S \rightarrow \dot{P}Qa \mid b$$
$$\dot{P} \rightarrow \dot{X}b$$
$$Q \rightarrow b\dot{P}\dot{P}$$
$$\underline{X} \rightarrow aaa$$

The $S$ gets dotted

$$\dot{S} \rightarrow \dot{P}\dot{Q}a \mid b$$

$$\dot{P} \rightarrow \dot{X} b$$

$$\dot{Q} \rightarrow b\dot{P}\dot{P}$$

$$\underline{X} \rightarrow aaa$$

Now all the non terminals are dotted but $X$ is not. That means $X$ is not self embedded symbol. Hence the grammar generates finite language.

**Membership:** There exists an algorithm which tells whether given string belongs to given grammar.

To check whether the given grammar generates desired string the derivation tree can be drawn.

Consider the grammar,

$$S \rightarrow PQ\ a \mid b$$

$$P \rightarrow X\ b$$

$$Q \rightarrow bPP$$

$$X \rightarrow aaa$$

Check whether it generates string *aaabbaaabaaaba.*

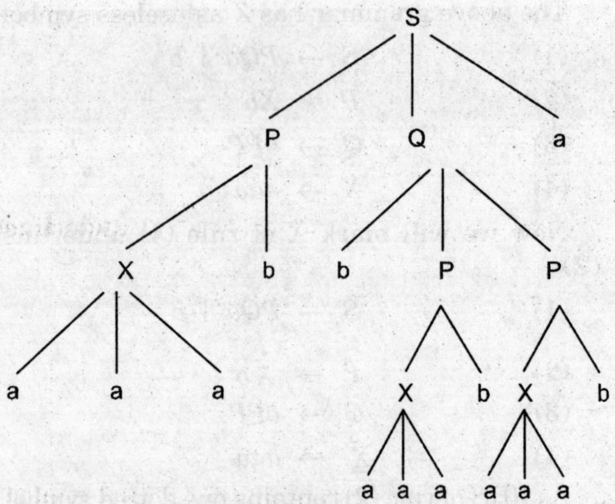


***Fig. 5.15***

The leaves generated string *aaabbaaabaaaba.*

## 5.13 APPLICATIONS OF CONTEXT FREE GRAMMAR

When any high level program like $C$ or Pascal is compiled, the compiler checks the syntax of every programming statement by constructing syntax tree. And for building the syntax tree, it is necessary to write context free grammar for each statement in the program.

Context Free Grammar (CFG) is a powerful tool used in compilers for syntax analysis and useful for document type definition (DTD) in XML.

## Important Solved Questions

**Example 5.46:** Consider the grammar $G$ whose productions ar $S \to aS \mid AB, A \to \in, B \to \in, D \to b$, Construct a grammar $G_1$ without null production generating $L(G) - \{\in\}$.

**Solution: Step 1:** Construction of the set $w$ of all nullable variables

$$w_1 = \{A_1 \in V \mid A_1 \to \in \text{ is a production in } G\}$$
$$= \{A, B\}$$
$$w_2 = \{A, B\} \cup \{S\} \text{ as } S \to AB \text{ is a production with } AB \in w_1^*.$$
$$= \{A, B, S\}$$
$$w_2 = w_2 \cup \phi = w_2$$

Thus $\quad w = w_2 = \{S, A, B\}$

**Step 2:** Construction of $P'$:

(*i*) $D \to b$ is included in $P'$.

(*ii*) $S \to aS$ gives rise to $S \to aS$ and $S \to a$.

(*iii*) $S \to AB$ gives rise to $S \to AB$, $S \to A$ and $S \to B$

Hence the required grammar without null production is $G_1 = (\{S, A, B, D\}, \{a, b\},, P', S\}$ where $P'$ consist of $D \to b$, $S \to aS$, $S \to AB$, $S \to A$, $S \to B$.

**Example 5.47:** Let $L$ be the set of all palindromes over $\{a, b\}$. Construct grammar $G$ generating $L$.

**Solution:** In the given question, you have to find a grammar but not a particular type of grammar. It means we can define any type of grammar. Here we define a context-free grammar for a given language, whose production rules are explained below

$$S \to \in$$
$$S \to \text{a}$$
$$S \to b$$
$$S \to aSa$$
$$S \to bSb$$

**Example 5.48:** Construct a grammar generating $L = \{wcw^R \mid w \in (a, b)^+\}$

**Solution:** Again in this question, you have to find a grammar but not a particular type of grammar. It means we can define any type of grammar. Here we define a context-free grammar for a given language, whose production rules are explained below

$$S \to aAa$$
$$S \to bAb$$
$$A \to aAa$$
$$A \to bAb$$
$$A \to c$$

**Useless Symbols:** Let $G = (V, S, P, S)$ be a grammar. A symbol $A$ is useful if there is $a$ derivation $A \to aAB \to w$ where w is in $\Sigma^*$ otherwise $A$ is useless symbol.

*For example,* $S \to aaS$
$S \to bBb$
$A \to Ab$

**Example 5.49:** If $G$ is the grammar $S \to SbS \mid a$ shown that $G$ is ambiguous. Consider $w = abababa \in L(G)$. Then we get the derivative trees for $w$.

$S \to SbS \to abS \to abSbS \to ababS \to ababSba \to abababa$

$S \to SbS \to SbSbS \to abSbS \to ababS \to ababSbS \to abababS \to abababa$

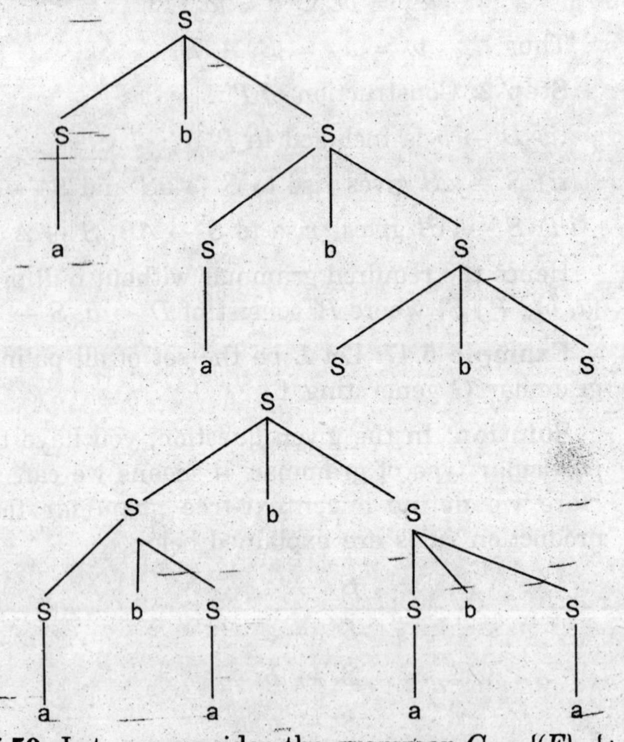

**Example 5.50:** Let us consider the grammar $G = \{(E\}, \{+, *, (,), id\}, P, \{E, \}\}$ where production rules $P$ are defined as follows:

$$E \to E + E$$
$$E \to E * E$$
$$E \to (E)$$
$$E \to id$$

Find the sentence $(id + id) * (id + id)$ and $(id * id) + (id * id)$ ar accepted by the given grammar $G$

**Solution:** The derivation of given languages are explained below

| | |
|---|---|
| $E \rightarrow E * E$ | $E \rightarrow E + E$ |
| $E \rightarrow E * (E)$ | $\rightarrow E + (E)$ |
| $\rightarrow E * (E + E)$ | $\rightarrow E + (E * E)$ |
| $\rightarrow E * (E + id)$ | $\rightarrow E + (E * id)$ |
| $\rightarrow (E) * (id + id)$ | $\rightarrow (E) + (id * id)$ |
| $\rightarrow (E + E) * (id + id)$ | $\rightarrow (E * E) + (id * id)$ |
| $\rightarrow (E + id) * (id + id)$ | $\rightarrow (E * id) + (id * id)$ |
| $\rightarrow (id + id) * (id + id)$ | $\rightarrow (id * id) + (id * id)$ |

This derivation shows that the given sentences are accepted by the given grammar.

**Example 5.51:** Give a grammar that specifies each of the following language:

(*i*) $L = \{aaa, aabb, abbaa, bbbb\}$

(ii) $L = \{x \mid x \in \{a, b\}^*$, the number $a$'s in $x$ is a multiple of 3$\}$

**[*U.P.T.U. MCA 2002*]**

**Solution:**

(*i*) The given language $L$ is $L = \{aaaa, aabb, bbaa, bbbb\}$ and the grammar for this language $G$ is $G = (\{S, A, B\}, \{a, b\}, \{S \rightarrow AB \mid AA \mid BA \mid BB, A \rightarrow aa, B \rightarrow bb\}, S)$

(*ii*) The given language $L = \{x \mid x \in \{a, b\}^*$, the number of $a$'s in $x$ is $a$ multiple of 3$\}$ and its equivalent grammar $G$ whose production rules $P$ is' shown as follows

$$S \rightarrow BAB$$

$$B \rightarrow bB \in$$

$$A \rightarrow aBaBaA \mid \in$$

**Example 5.52 (a):** Construct a grammar for the following language

$$L = \{a^i b^j \mid i, j, \leq i \neq j\}$$

(*b*) If $G = (\{S\}, \{0, 1\}, \{S \rightarrow 0S1, S \rightarrow \in S\})$, Find $L(G)$.

(*c*) *Find the language generated by the grammar*

$S \rightarrow AB, A \rightarrow A1 \mid 0, B \rightarrow 2B \mid 3$. Can the above language be generated by a grammar of higher type? **[*U.P.T.U. MCA 2003*]**

**Solution:** (*a*) The given $L = \{a^i b^j \mid i, j \geq 1, i \neq j\}$. Then the production rules $P$ of grammar $G$ is shown below:

$$S \rightarrow A$$

$$A \rightarrow aBb \mid a \mid b \mid aB \mid Cb$$

$$B \rightarrow aB \mid a$$

$$C \rightarrow Cb \mid b$$

Hence, $G \rightarrow (\{S, A, B, C\}, \{S \rightarrow 0S\ 1, S \rightarrow \in, S\}$

(*b*) The given grammar *G* is

$$G = (\{S\}, \{0, 1\}, \{S \rightarrow 0S\ 1, S \rightarrow \in, S)$$

The starting symbol *S* of a production rules contains either an equal number of 0's and 1's or $\in$ recursively. So the language generated by this grammar is

$$L(G) = \{0^n 1^n | \ n \geq 0\}$$

(*c*) The language generated by grammar $L(G) = 01^*32^*$. Yes, this language is generated by higher type.

**Example 5.53:** Show that

$$S \rightarrow aS$$

$$S \rightarrow Sa$$

$$S \rightarrow a$$

is an ambiguous grammar. **[*U.P.T.U. B-Tech 2003*]**

**Solution:** Let $S \rightarrow aS \mid Sa \mid a$

be given CFG then we can derive the string *aaaa* as follows.

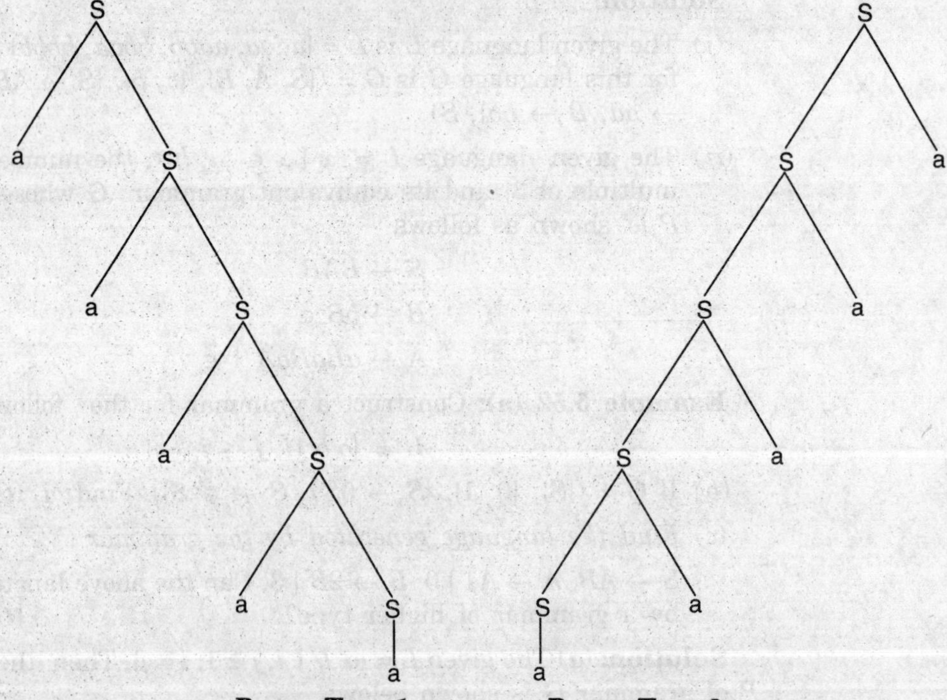

***Parse Tree 1*** ***Parse Tree 2***

Thus we have two parse tree for that grammar. So we can say that given grammar is called ambiguous grammar.

**Example 5.54:** Show the derivation tree for string *'aabbbb'* with the following grammar.

$$S \rightarrow AB \mid \in$$
$$S \rightarrow aB$$
$$B \rightarrow Sb$$

**[U.P.T.U. B-Tech 2003, 05]**

**Solution:** The derivation tree can be drawn for *"aabbbb"* as follows –

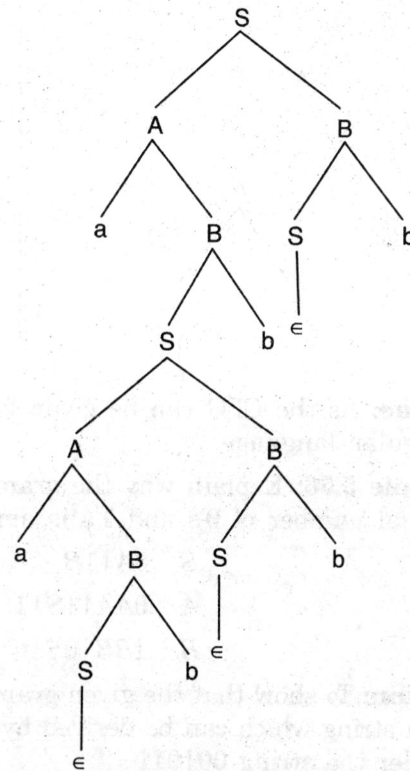


**Example 5.54:** Consider the context free grammar

$$G = \begin{Bmatrix} S \rightarrow ASb \mid AS \mid \in \\ A \rightarrow aA \mid \in \end{Bmatrix}$$

State True/False for the following

(*i*) The string *ababb* is generated by the grammar *G*.

(*ii*) Every string of the form

$a^n b^m \quad [m \geq n \geq 0]$

(*iii*) The grammar is ambiguous

(*iv*) The grammar generated by *G* is regular. **[U.P.T.U. B-Tech 2005]**

**Solution:**

**(*i*) False:** The string *ababb* can not derived from given grammar.

**(*ii*) False:** The string such a *aaab* can be derived from given grammar.

(*iii*) **True:** Consider string *aaab,* for two derivation tree can be drawn so we can say grammar is ambiguous.

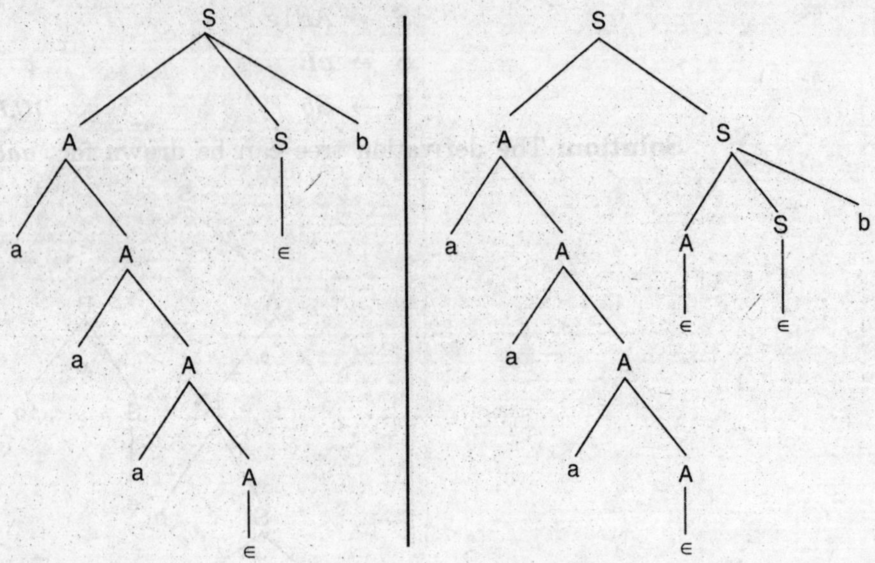


(*iv*) **True:** As the CFG can be given for this language is accepted. This is a regular language.

**Example 5.56:** Explain why the grammar below that generates string with an equal number of 0's and 1's is ambiguous.

$S \quad 0A \mid 1B$

$A \quad 0AA \mid 1S \mid 1$

$B \quad 1BB \mid 0S \mid 0$ **[*U.P.T.U. B-Tech 2004, 06*]**

**Solution:** To show that the given grammar is ambiguous we have to consider such a string which can be derived by using more than one derivation trees. Consider the string 00 | 011

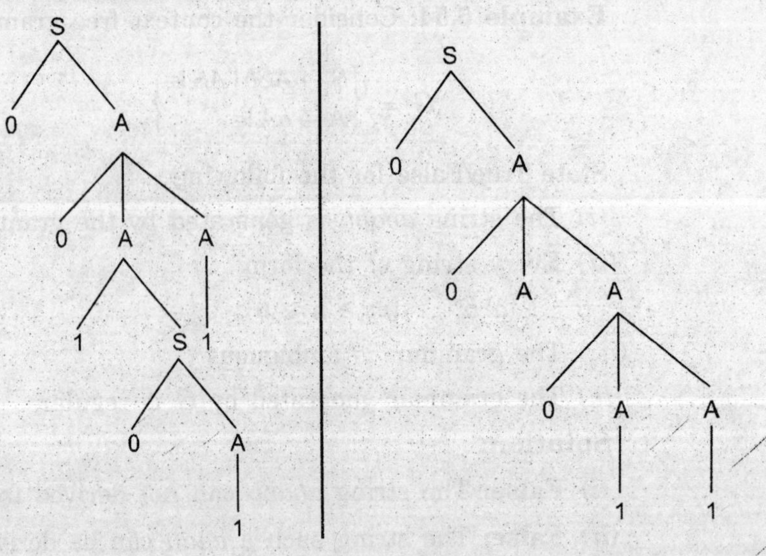

# EXERCISE

## (A) Objective Type Questions

**1.** The grammar $\{S \rightarrow aS \mid bS \mid a \mid b\}$ is not equivalent to

(a) $(a^* + b)^*$ (b) $(a^* + b)^*$

(c) $(a + b)(a + b)^*$ (d) $(a + b)^*(a + b)$

**2.** Any string of terminals that can be generated by the following CFG

$$S \rightarrow XY$$
$$X \rightarrow aX \mid bX \mid a$$
$$Y \rightarrow Ya \mid Yb \mid a$$

(a) Has at least one $b$ (b) Should end in $a$

(c) Has no consecutive $a$ or $b$ (d) Has atleast two $a$

**3.** To prove set $A = L(G)$

(a) it is enough to prove that an arbitrary member of $A$ can be generated by grammar

(b) it is enough to prove that an arbitrary string generated by $G$, belongs to $A$

(c) both the above are to be proved

(d) either of first two can be proved

**4.** Choose the correct statements:

(a) all languages can be generated by CFG

(b) any regular language has not an equivalent CFG

(c) some non regular languages can't be generated by an CFG

(d) some regular languages can't be generated by an CFG

**5.** The grammar generated by productiion rules $S \rightarrow aSBc \mid abc$, $cB \rightarrow Bc$, $aB \rightarrow aa$ is

(a) $a^n b^n c^n, n > 1$ (b) $a^n b^n c^n, n \geq 0$

(c) $a^n b^n c^n, n > 0$ (d) $a^n b^n c^n, n \leq 0$

**6.** The grammar having production as $A \rightarrow B$, where $A \in V_{n'}$, $B \in (V_n \cup \Sigma)^+$ is

(a) Type 0 (b) Type 1

(c) Type 2 (d) Type 3

**7.** A CFL is in CNF if every production is of form $S \rightarrow A$ or $S \rightarrow C$ where $S$ is in $V_{n'}$

(a) $A$ is in $\Sigma^*$ & $B$, $C$ are in $V_n$

(b) $A$ is in $\Sigma$ & $B$, $C$ are in $V_n^*$

(c) $A$ is in $\Sigma$ & $B$, $C$ are in $V_n$

(d) $A$ is in $\Sigma^*$ & $B$, $C$ are in $V_n^*$

**8.** Which of the following grammars can generate $w = aabbb$

(a) $S \to AB,\ A \to aA \mid a,\ B \to bB \mid b$

(b) $S \to AB,\ A \to BB \mid a,\ B \to AB \mid b$

(c) Both

(d) None

**9.** The language $L = \{a^n b^m c^n d^m / n \geq 1,\ m \geq 1\}$

(a) is context free

(b) is not context free

(c) abstracts the problem of checking number of formal and external parameters

(d) (b) and (c)

**10.** A grammar $G$ has productions of type

$A \to aB\ A \to Ba\ A \to a$ then $G$ is

(a) regular (b) CF

(c) both (d) none

**11.** $L = \{ww^R$ where $w$ belongs to $\{0, 1\}^*\}$ is

(a) Context sensitive (b) Context Free

(c) Both (d) None

**12.** A grammar $G$ is known to have GNF representation then

(a) we can write $G$ as left linear or right linear

(b) $G$ may be written as eft linear or right linear

(c) $G$ can't be written left or right linear

(d) None of these

**13.** Consider the language $L = \{a^p : p$ is prime$\}$

(a) RL (b) CFL

(c) Both (d) None

**14.** Every CFG is ambiguous

(a) true (b) false

(c) some times true (d) some times false

**15.** Which of the following languages cannot be produced by a Context Free Grammar?

(a) $L = \{a^n b^n : n \geq 0\}$ (b) $L = \{a^n b^k : k > n \geq 0\}$

(c) $L = \{ww^R : w \in \{a, b\}^*\}$ (d) $L = \{a^n b^n c^n : n \geq 0\}$

**16.** The intersection of a CFL and regular language

(*a*) need not be regular (*b*) need not be context free

(*c*) Is always regular (*d*) Is always context free

**17.** CFG is not closed under

(*a*) Union (*b*) Kleene star

(*c*) complementation (*d*) product

## ANSWERS

| | | | | |
|---|---|---|---|---|
| **1.** (*b*) | **2.** (*d*) | **3.** (*c*) | **4.** (*c*) | **5.** (*c*) |
| **6.** (*c*) | **7.** (*c*) | **8.** (*c*) | **9.** (*d*) | **10.** (*c*) |
| **11.** (*c*) | **12.** (*b*) | **13.** (*d*) | **14.** (*b*) | **15.** (*c*) |
| **16.** (*d*) | **17.** (*c*) | | | |

## (B) Problems

**1.** Find context-free grammars for the following languages (with $n \geq 0$, $m \geq 0$)

(*a*) $L = \{a^n b^m : n \geq m + 3\}$

(*b*) $L = \{a^n b^m : n \neq m - 3\}$

(*c*) $L = \{a^n b^m : n \neq 2m\}$

(*d*) $L = \{a^n b^m : 2n \geq m \leq 3\}$

(*e*) $L = \{w \in \{a, b\}^* : n_a(w) \neq n_b(w)\}$

(*f*) $L = \{w \in \{a, b\}^* : n_a(v) \neq n_b(v)\}$, where $v$ is any prefix of $w\}$

(*g*) $L = \{a^n b^m c^k : n = m \text{ or } + m \leq k\}$

h) $L = \{a^n b^m c^k : n = m \text{ or } + m \neq k\}$

(*i*) $L = \{a^n b^m c^k : k = n + m\}$

(*j*) $L = \{a^n b^m c^k : n + 2m = k\}$

(*k*) $L = \{a^n b^m c^k : k = [n - m]\}$

(*l*) $L = \{w \in \{a, b, c\}^* : n_a(w) + n_b(w) \neq n_c(w)\}$

(*m*) $L = \{a^n b^m v^k : k \neq n + m\}$

(*n*) $L = \{a^n b^m : n \neq m\}$

**2.** Find a context-free grammar for $S = \{a, b\}$ for the language $L = [a^n w w^R b^n : w \in S^*, n \geq 1\}$.

**3.** Let $G$ be the grammar

$$S \rightarrow aB \mid bA$$
$$A \rightarrow a \mid aS \mid bAA$$
$$B \rightarrow b \mid bS \mid aBB$$

For the string aaabbabbba find a

(a) Left most derivation

(b) Right most derivation

(c) Parse tree.

Show a derivation tree for the string aabbbb with the grammar

$$S \rightarrow AB \mid \lambda.$$
$$A \rightarrow aB$$
$$B \rightarrow sb$$

Give a verbal description of the language generated by this grammar.

**5.** Consider the grammar with productions

$$S \rightarrow aaB$$
$$A \rightarrow bBb \mid \lambda.$$
$$B \rightarrow Aa$$

Show that the string aabbabba is not in the language generated by this grammar.

**6.** Show that the grammar **S** $\rightarrow a|abSb|aAb$, $A \rightarrow bS|aaAAB$ is ambiguous.

**7.** Show that the grammar $S \rightarrow aB|ab$, $A \rightarrow aAB|a$, $B \rightarrow AB\ b|b$ is ambiguous.

**8.** A context-free grammar $G$ has the following productions $S \rightarrow 0s0|1S1|A$, $A \rightarrow 2VB3$, $B \rightarrow 2B3|3$. Describe the language granted by the parameters.

**9.** Reduce the following grammar to Chomsky normal from:

(a) $S \rightarrow 1A|0B\ A \rightarrow 1AA\ |0S|0\ B \rightarrow 0BB\ |1S|1$

(b) $G = (\{S\}, \{a, b, c\}, \{S \rightarrow a\ |b|cSS\}, S)$

(c) $S \rightarrow abSb\ |a|aAb$, $a \rightarrow bS\ |aAAb$

**10.** Reduce the following grammar to Greibach normal form:

(a) $S \rightarrow SS$ $\quad S \rightarrow 0S1|01$

(b) $S \rightarrow AB$, $\quad A \rightarrow BSB|BB|b$ $\quad B \rightarrow aAb|a$

(c) $S \rightarrow A0$, $\quad A \rightarrow 0B$ $\quad B \rightarrow A0\ \ B \rightarrow 1$

**11.** If $G = (\{S\}, \{0, 1\}, \{S \rightarrow 0S11, S \rightarrow \ \wedge\}, S)$ find $L(G)$.

**12.** If $G = (\{S\}, \{a\}, \{S \rightarrow \{s\}, S\})$, find the language generated by $G$.

**13.** Let $G = (\{S, C\}, \{a, b\}, P, S\}$, where $P$ consists of $S \rightarrow aa$, $C \rightarrow aCa\ |b$, find $L(G$.

**14.** Find $a$ grammar generating $L = \{a^n b^n c^i \mid n \geq 1, i \geq 0\}$.

**15.** Find a grammar generating $\{a^n b^n c^n \mid n \geq 1, j \geq 0\}$.

❑❑❑

C H A P T E R

# 6

# PUSHDOWN AUTOMATA

## 6.1 INTRODUCTION

A pushdown automaton (PDA) is finite state machine with a memory device. A pushdown automaton is used to design an equivalent context-free (or type-2) grammar. It is Deterministic (DPDA) and Non-deterministic (NPDA) both. Basically a pushdown automaton consists of three components:

1. An input tape
2. A pushdown store and
3. A control unit

1. An input tape consists of a linear configuration of cells each of which contains a character from an alphabet. This tape can be moved one cell at a time to the left.
2. A pushdown store is also a sequential structure that has first element and grows in either direction from the other end. Contrary to the tape head associated with the input tape, the head positioned over the current pushdown store element can read and write special pushdown store character from that position. The current pushdown store element is always the top element of the pushdown store, hence we call pushdown store is a ***"stack"***.
3. A control unit contains both tape heads and finds itself at any moment in a particular state

All these can be shown graphically as follows

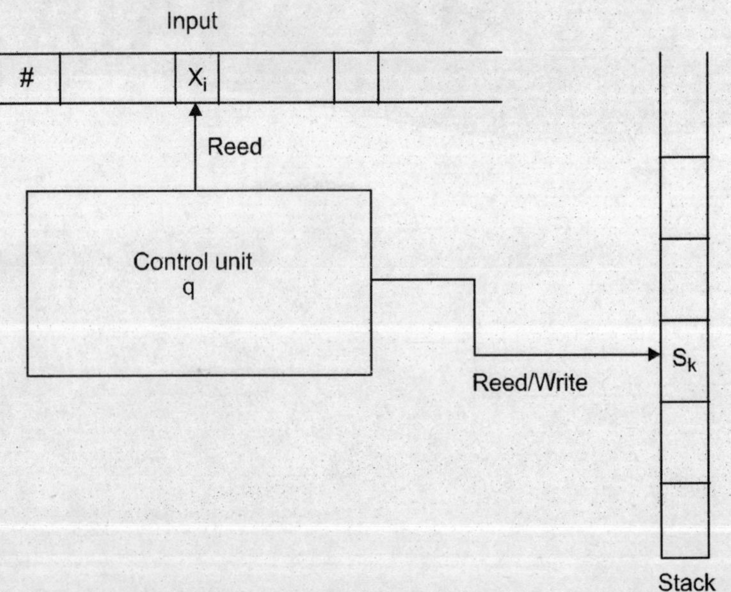


***Fig. 6.1***

## 6.2 FORMAL DEFINITION OF A PDA [UPTU B-Tech 2005, 03]

A DFA (or NDFA) is not powerful enough to recognize many context-free languages because a DFA can't count. But counting is not enough: Consider a language of palindromes, containing strings of the from ww. Such a language requires more than an ability to count; it requires a memory device called a stack. A pushdown automaton (PDA) is basically a DFA with a stack added to it.

We start with formal definition of a DFA, which is a 5-tuple, and two things added to it.

Γ is a finite set of symbols called the stack alphabet and

$Z_0$ is a initial symbols of stack

Or Mathematically a PDA is given by

$$M = (Q, \Sigma, \Gamma, \delta, q_0, Z_0, F)$$

→ $Q$ is a finite non empty set of states.

→ Σ is a finite non empty set of input symbols

→ Γ is a finite non empty set of pushdown symbols

→ δ is a transition system and $\delta \in Q \times (\Sigma \cup \{\in\}) \rightarrow Q\ x\ \Gamma^*$

→ $q_0$ is an initial state and $q_0 \in Q$.

→ $Z_0$ is an initial symbol of pushdown store

→ $F$ is a set of accepting states (or final states) and $F \subseteq Q$.

Pushdown automaton can be represented by following two different techniques.

1. Transition Function
2. Transition Digraph

### (1) Transition Function

A transition system of pushdown automata can be represented as follows

$$\delta\ (q_i, x, y) = (q_j, z)$$

where $q_i \in Q$, $x \in \Sigma$, $y \in \{\Gamma \cup \in\}$ and $z \in \Gamma^*$

Here $\Gamma^*$ represents zero, one and more symbol of a pushdown store. That is a transition system $\delta(q_i, x, y) = (q_j, z)$ is in the following form

$\delta\ (q_i, x, y) = (q_i, \in)$ For erasing a symbol from stack

$\delta\ (q_i, x, y) = (q_j, y)$ No changes in stack

$\delta\ (q_i, x, y) = (q_j, ay)$ Inserting an element in a stack and $a \in \Gamma$.

Any transition of a push down automata can be explained

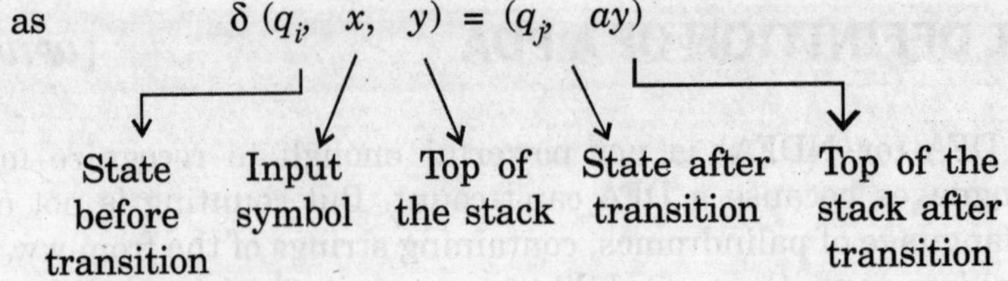


## (2) Transition Digraph

In this representation the states are represented by vertices and transition of states is represented by directed edges. These directed edges with labels are in the form of $(x/y, z)$, where $x \in \Sigma$, $y \in \Gamma$ and $z \in \Gamma^*$

For example, if there is a function $\delta(q_i, x, y) = (q_j, \in)$ then this function can be graphically represented as follows:

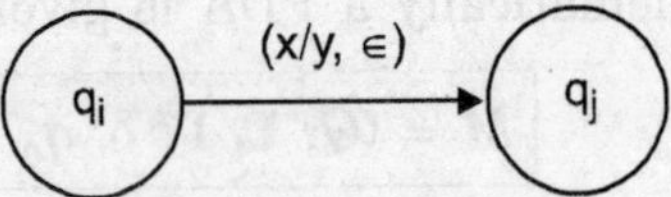


If there is a function $\delta(q_i, x, y) = (q_j, y)$ then this function can be graphically represented as follow:

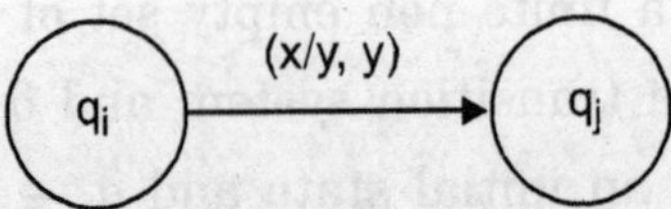


If there is a function $\delta(q_i, x, y) = (q_j, ay)$ then this function can be graphically represented as follows:

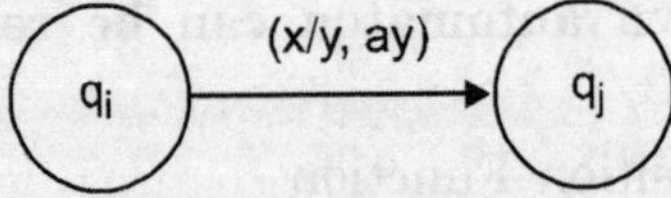


**Example 6.1:** A PDA machine for language $L = \{a^n b^n \mid n \geq 1\}$

**Solution:**

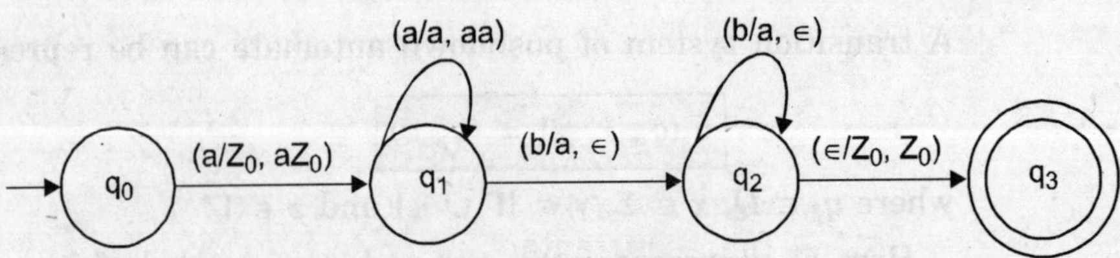


*Fig. 6.2*

## Some More Definition

**Instantaneous Description (ID):** Let $M = (Q, \Sigma, \Gamma, \delta, q_0, Z_0, F)$ be PDA then the ID is $(q, w, Z)$, where $q \in Q$ and $q$ is current state of automation.

$w \in \Sigma^*$ and unread part of an input string and

$Z \in \Gamma^*$ and stack content.

**Initial Instantaneous Description (IID):** An ID $(q_0, w, Z_0)$ is called IID if $q_0$ is initial state of PDA, $w$ is the input string to be processed and $Z_0$ is a first symbol of PDS.

**Move Relation:** If a transition function $\delta(q_i, q_1, Z_1) = (q_j, x_1)$ then move relation (denoted by) between ID is defined as

$$(q_i,\ a_1a_2a_3\ \ldots\ldots\ a_n,\ Z_1\ Z_2\ \ldots\ldots\ Z_m)\ (q_i,\ a_2a_3\ \ldots\ldots\ a_n,\ x_1Z_2\ \ldots\ldots\ Z_m)$$

## 6.3 ACCEPTANCE OF PDA

Acceptance of PDA can be defined in two different ways:

(1) Acceptance of PDA by final state (*i.e.*, $L$ ($M$))

(1) Acceptance of PDA by empty store or empty stack (*i.e.*, $L$ ($N$))

### (1) Acceptance of PDA by final state (*i.e.*, *L*(*M*))

$L(M)$ = Set of all string $w$ such that starting from Initial Instantaneous Description (IID), machine consumes all string $w$ and enters an accepting states (*i.e.*, on final states). In this case the content of stack is irrelevant.

Or in other word if $M = (Q, \Sigma, \Gamma, \delta, q_0, Z_0, q_f)$ be a PDA machine and $L(M)$ be the language accepted by its final states then the acceptability of the language from Initial Instantaneous Description (IID) is written as

$$\{w \mid (q_0, w, Z_0)\ ^*\ (q_f, \in, a)\} \text{ where } w \in \Sigma^* \text{ and } a \in \Gamma^*$$

In this case. You try to define machine through either transition digraph or transition function.

**Example 6.2:** Check if a string *aabb* is accepted by a PDA defined in example 6.1 by its final state

**Solution:** The transition digraph is similar to example 1 and an Initial Instantaneous Description of a given string w is $(q_0, aabb, Z_0)$ and its move from an Initial Instantaneous Description (IID) is shown below

$$\begin{aligned}(q_0, aabb, Z_0)\quad & (q_1, abb, aZ_0)\\ & (q_1, bb, aaZ_0)\\ & (q_2, b, aZ_0)\\ & (q_0, \in, Z_0)\\ & (q_3, \in, Z_0)\end{aligned}$$

Here the terminating state is $q_3$, which is final state. Hence the string *aabb* is accepted by a PDA by its final state. Here it does not matter what the behavior of stack is.

## (2) Acceptance of PDA by Empty Store or Empty Stack (*i.e., L(N)*)

$L(N)$ = Set of all string $w$ such that machine can consumes all string $w$ and at the same time empties its stack. In this case, we do not care whether terminating state $q$ is a final state or non-final state. That is terminating state is irrelevant.

Or in other word if $M = (Q, \Sigma, \Gamma, \delta, q_0, Z_0, \phi)$ be a PDA machine and $L(N)$ be the language accepted by its empty stack (or empty store) then the acceptability of the language from Initial Instantaneous Description (IID) is written as

$$\{w \mid (q_0, w, Z_0) * (q', \in, \in)\} \text{ where } w \in \Sigma^* \text{ and } q' \subseteq Q$$

---

In this case, you try to define machine through Context free grammar.

---

**Example 6.3:** A PDA machine for language $L = \{a^n b^n \mid n \geq 1\}$ accepted by its empty stack.

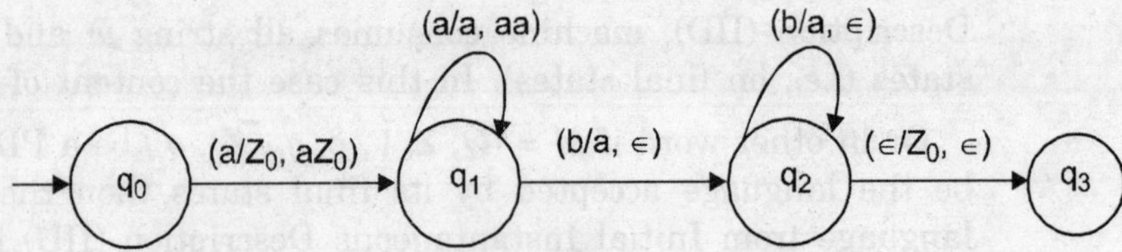


*Fig. 6.3*

Check if a string *aabb* is accepted by a PDA by its empty store.

**Solution:** An initial Instantaneous Description of a given string $w$ is $(q_0, aabb, Z_0)$ and its move from an initial Instantaneous Description is shown below

$(q_0, aabb, Z_0)$ $(q_1, abb, aZ_0)$

$(q_1, bb, aaZ_0)$

$(q_2, b, aZ_0)$

$(q_0, \in, Z_0)$

$(q_3, \in, Z_0)$

Here the stack is empty. So the string *aabb* is accepted by a PDA by its empty store. Here it does not matter what the terminating state is.

---

A PDA of example 61 is accepted by both procedures.

---

## 6.4 DETERMINISTIC AND NON-DETERMINISTIC PDA

***[U.P.T.U. B tech 2003, 04, MCA 2003]***

Pushdown automata can also manipulate the stack, as part of performing a transition. Finite state machines choose a new state, the result of following the transition. The manipulation can be to push a particular symbol to the top of the stack, or to pop off the top of the stack. The automaton can alternatively ignore the stack, and leave it as it is. The choice of manipulation (or no manipulation) is determined by the transition table.

**Put together:** Given an input signal, current state, and stack symbol, the automaton can follow a transition to another state, and optionally manipulate (push or pop) the stack.

In general pushdown automata may have several computations on a given input string, some of which may be halting in accepting configurations while others are not. Thus we have a model which is technically known as a ***"nondeterministic pushdown automaton (NPDA)".*** Non determinism means that there may be more than just one transition available to follow, given an input signal, state, and stack symbol.

If in every situation only one transition is available as continuation of the computation, then the result is a ***"deterministic pushdown automaton (DPDA)",*** a strictly weaker device.

NPDA is a similar to PDA except their transition system. A deterministic PDA is one in which every input string has a unique path through the machine. A non deterministic PDA is one in which we may have to choose among several paths for an input string. We say that an input string is accepted if there is at least one path that leads to an accept state. We shall see that a non deterministic PDA (NPDA) is more powerful than a deterministic one (DPDA), unlike the situation with FAs and NFAs. In other words, there are languages that can be accepted by an NPDA that cannot be accepted by a DPDA

### Some Important Points

- For FA's non determinism (*i.e.,* NFA's) did not increase the power of the machine to accept new language.
- DFA and NFA have equal powers
- For every NFA there exists an equivalent DFA accepting the same language as accepted by NFA.

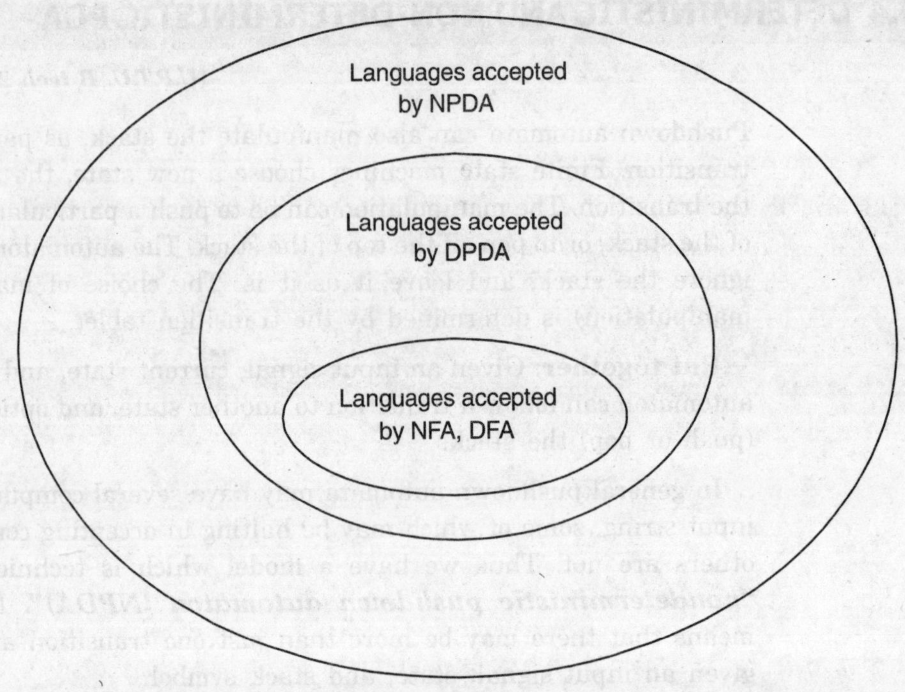


*Fig. 6.4*

- A language accepted by a NPDA may not be accepted by DPDA
- Thus for every NPDA there may not exist an equivalent DPDA
- From the above fig. DFA and NFA have equal powers. NPDA and DPDA have different capability. NPDA can accept any CFL but DPDA is a special case of CFL NPDA accepts.
- The PDA's that are equivalent to CFG's is the class of NPDA's.

DPDA is less powerful than NPDA.

**Example 6.4:** A NPDA machine for language l = {w | w is a even palindrome over input alphabet {*a*, *b*}}

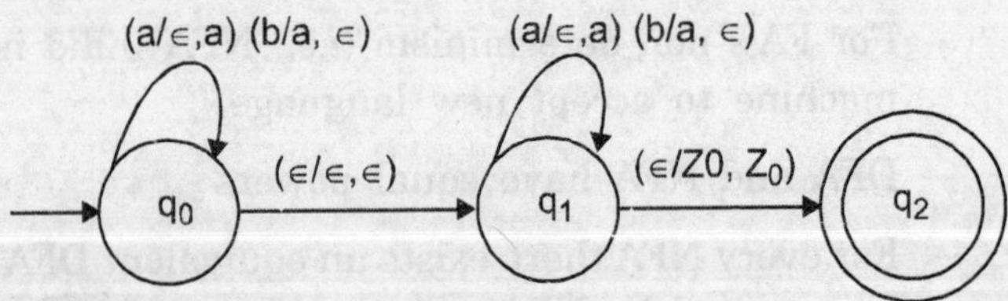


*Fig. 6.5*

Find the acceptability for a string *aabbaa*.

**Solution:**

$$
\begin{aligned}
(q_0,\ aabbaa,\ Z_0) &\vdash (q_0,\ abbaa,\ aZ_0)\\
&\vdash (q_0,\ bbaa,\ aaZ_0)\\
&\vdash (q_0,\ baa,\ baaZ_0)\\
&\vdash (q_1,\ baa,\ baaZ_0)\\
&\vdash (q_1,\ aa,\ aaZ_0)\\
&\vdash (q_1,\ a,\ a\ Z_0)\\
&\vdash (q_1,\ \in,\ Z_0)\\
&\vdash (q_2,\ \in,\ Z_0)
\end{aligned}
$$

Since $q_2$ is a final state. Hence the string *aabbaa* is accepted by a NPDA by a NPDA by its final state

## 6.5 PICTORIAL REPRESENTATION OF PDA

As we have discussed earlier PDA is more powerful than FA. Any language which can be accepted by FA can also be accepted by PDA. Not even this, PDA accepts a class of languages which even can not be accepted by FA. Thus PDA is much more superior to FA.

PDA can b represented by some flow-chart like nonations. All these pictorial representations for different types of states of PDA are given in fig. 6.6.

→ **'Start'** should be the initial state for every PDA and either 'accept' or 'reject' would be the final halt state depending on the input, whether machine has accepteditor rejected it.

→ **'Read'** state is a conditional block and represented like that because depending on what symbol read, the machine could go to different states.

→ Similarly, the **'Pop'** state is also represented by conditional block. **'Push'** state is an intermediate state and a symbol has to be provided to it which we want to push.

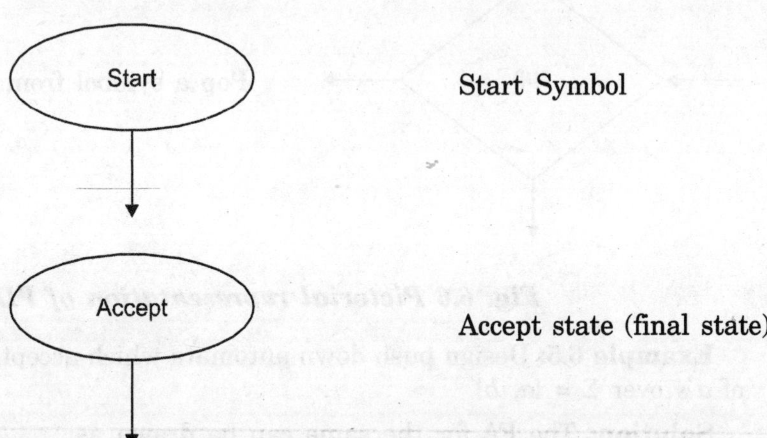

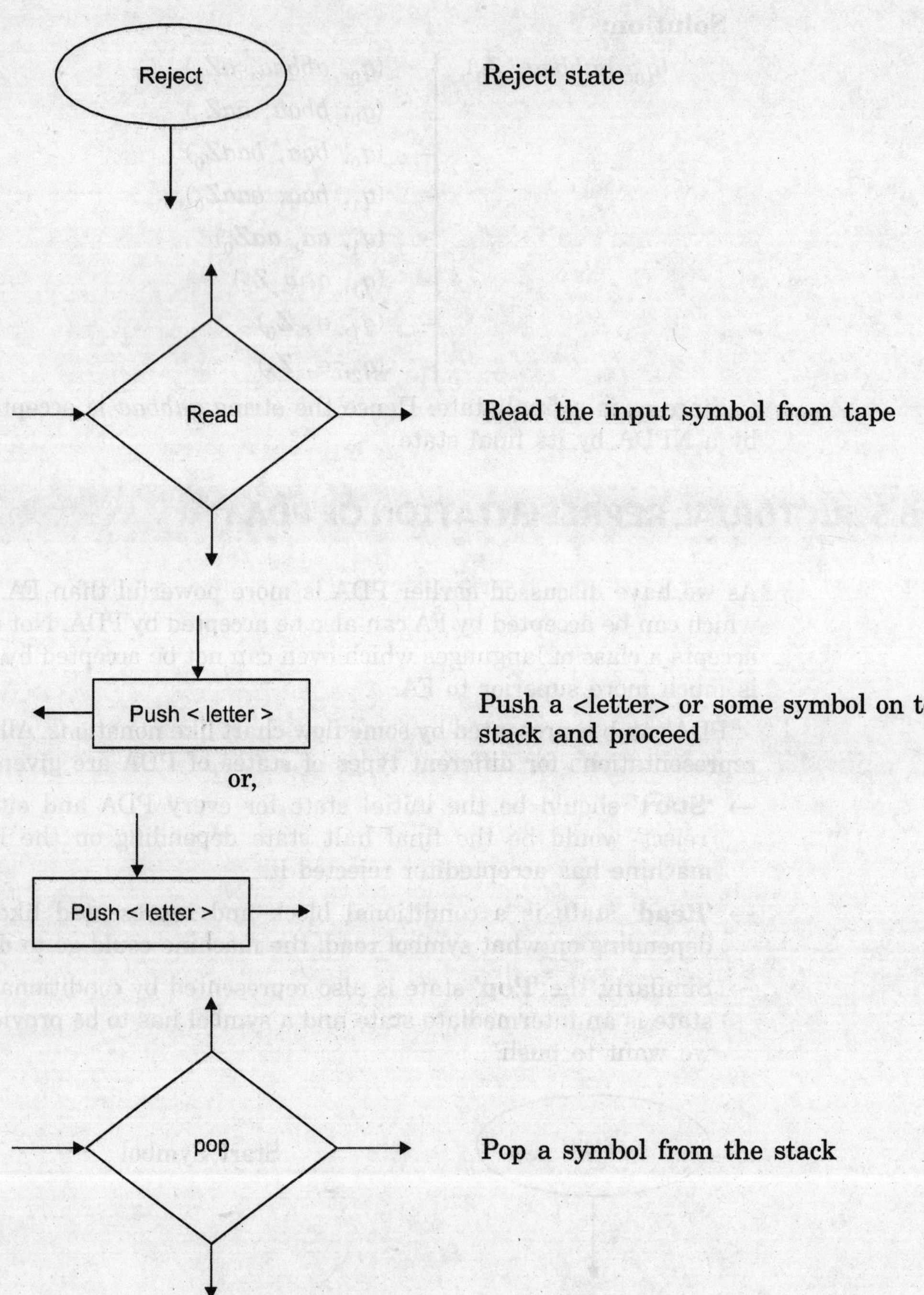


***Fig. 6.6 Pictorial representation of PDA***

**Example 6.5:** Design push down automata which accepts only odd number of *a's* over $\Sigma = \{a, b\}$

**Solution:** The FA for the same can be drawn as:

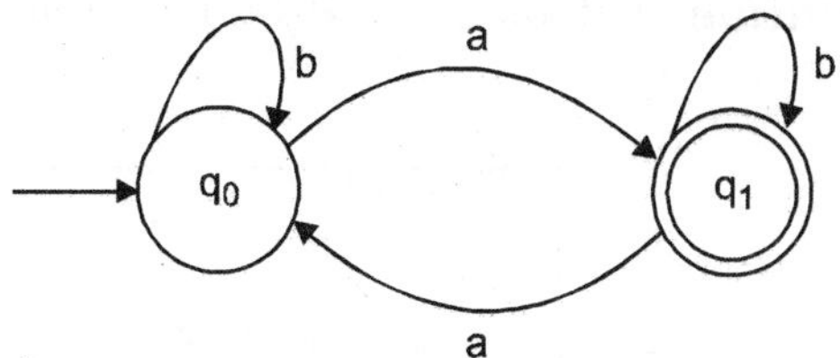


***Fig. 6.7***

We can draw the PDA similar to this

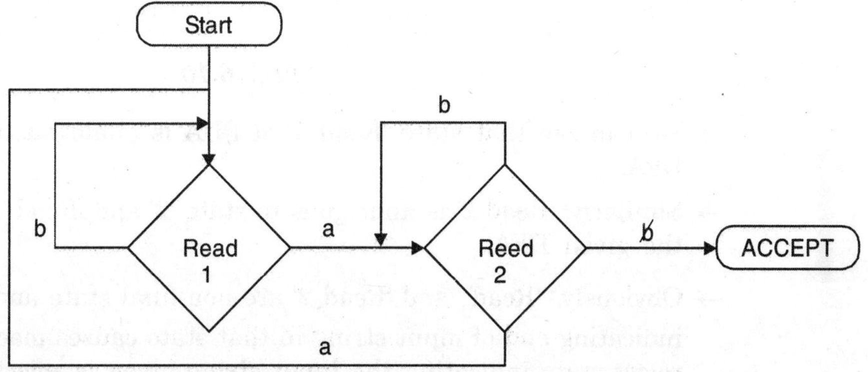


***Fig. 6.8***

→ We can see that 'Read 1' state is analogous to initial state for given DFA and 'Read 2' state is analogous to final state of the given DFA.

→ If read out '*b*' the self loop will be applied and if we read out '*a*' then it will move to next 'Read' state.

→ If on the input tape only single '*a*' is placed then that means it will read out $\not{b}$ **– the blank character.**

**Example 6.6:** Construct PDA recognizing the language accepted by the DFA given in Fig. 6.9.

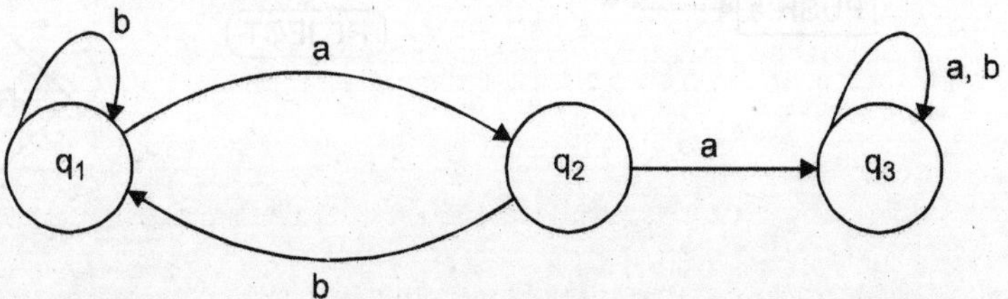


***Fig. 6.9***

**Solution:** Let us draw PDA for same using memory *i.e.,* stack.

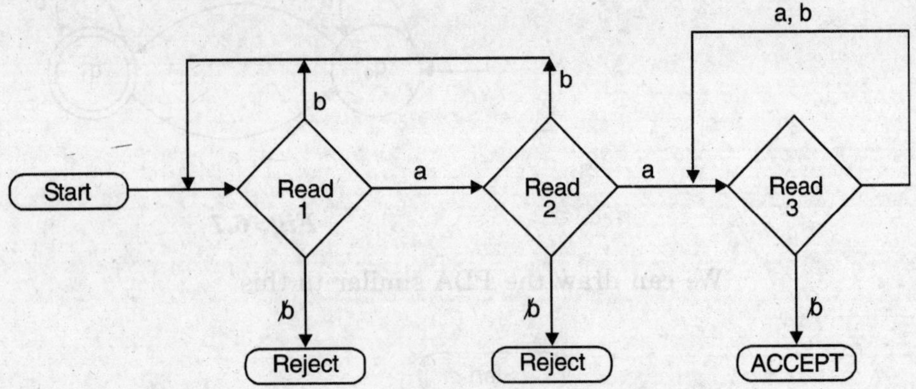


***Fig. 6.10***

→ We can see that state 'Read 1' of PDA is analogous to state '1' at given DFA.

→ Similarly, 'Read 2' is analogous to state '2' and 'Read 3' is with state '3' of the given DFA.

→ Obviously, "Read', and 'Read 2' are non-final state and reading blank 'ƀ' indicating end of input string in that state causes machine to move to the reject state indicating the input string given is rejected by the PDA.

**Example 6.6:** Design a PDA for the language

$L = \{a^n b^n\}$ where $n \geq 1$

**Solution:** Let us draw PDA for same using memory *i.e.,* stack.

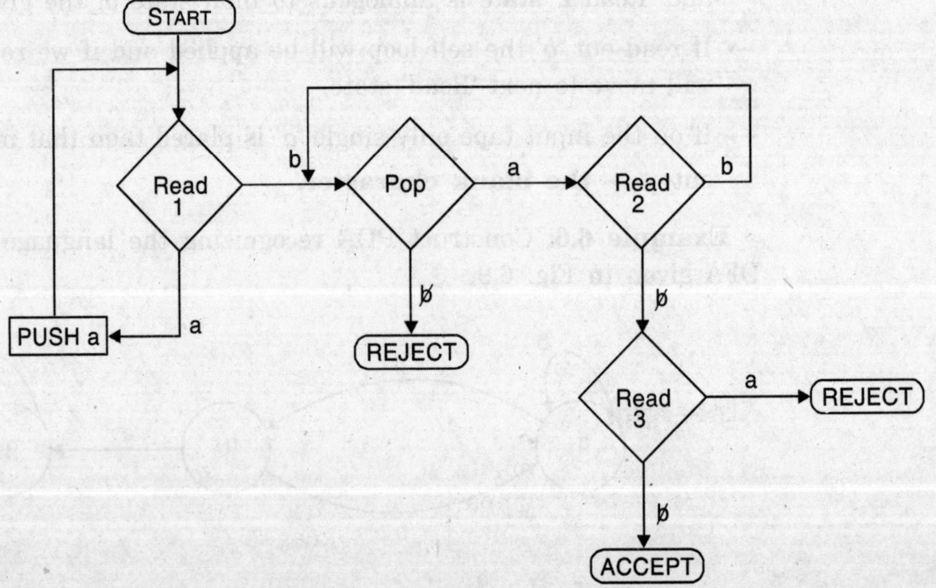


***Fig. 6.11***

→ In state 'Read 1' if we read $a$, we push that a on to the stack. This will be repeated by applying a self loop to this read statement. By this all the $a$'s will be pushed onto the stack.

→ Now when we will read one $b$ we will pop one $a$.

→ This process will be repeated till the end of input. The end marker is '$\not{b}$'.

→ After reading '$\not{b}$' from input tape, we pop the contents from the stack. If we pop '$a$' that means number of '$a$'s are move than total number of $b$'s. So we go to reject state.

**Example 6.7:** Design PDA that checks the well formedness of parenthesis.

**Solution:** The well formedness of parenthesis means that the input should start with '('opening parenthesis and it should be followed by')' closing parenthesis. The number of '('and')' should be equal. The input should not start with')'.

Thus we will design PDA which will check a valid string.

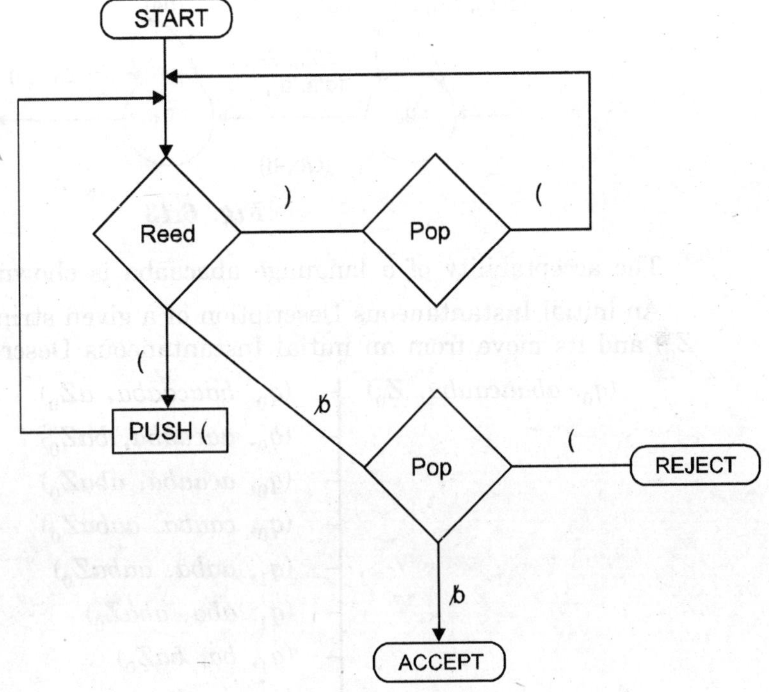


***Fig. 6.12***

## Other Approach

(*i*) Pushdown automata are used to design for a languages whose elements are perform comparison between exactly two element at a time. It is equivalent to context-free language or its subset languages.

(*ii*) The number of states must be minimized.

**Example 6.8:** Design a PDA machine that accept the following language

$$L = \{wcw^R \mid w \in \{a, b\}^*\}$$

**Solution:** The following steps are used to design a PDA machine for the given language $L$.

**Step 1 :** Push all the given elements a of string $w$ in stack (or pushdown store).

**Step 2 :** Read a symbol $c$ from a given string without any changes in a stack.

**Step 3 :** Read one symbol from given $w^R$ and remove top element of a stack.

**Step 4 :** Repeat step 3 while a given string is empty and the terminating state is final state.

A transition digraph is 0 shown below

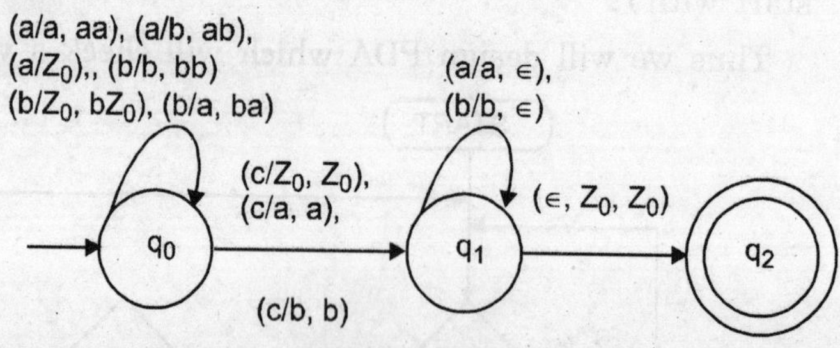


***Fig. 6.13***

The acceptability of a language abacaaba is shown below

An initial Instantaneous Description of a given string $w$ is $(q_0, abaacaaba, Z_0)$ and its move from an initial Instantaneous Description is shown below

$$\begin{aligned}(q_0, abaacaaba, Z_0) &\vdash (q_0, baacaaba, aZ_0)\\ &\vdash (q_0, aacaaba, baZ_0)\\ &\vdash (q_0, acaaba, abaZ_0)\\ &\vdash (q_0, caaba, aabaZ_0)\\ &\vdash (q_1, aaba, aabaZ_0)\\ &\vdash (q_1, aba, abaZ_0)\\ &\vdash (q_1, ba, baZ_0)\\ &\vdash (q_1, a, aZ_0)\\ &\vdash (q_1, \in, Z_0)\\ &\vdash (q_2, \in, Z_0)\end{aligned}$$

Here the terminating state is $q_2$, which is final state. Hence the string *abaacaaba* is accepted by a PDA by its final state.

**Example 6.9:** Design an empty store PDA machine that accepts the following language

$$L = \{wcw^R \mid w \in \{a, b\}^+\}$$

**Solution:** The following steps are used to design a PDA machine for a given language *L*.

**Step 1 :** Push all the given elements a of $w$ in a stack (or pushdown store).

**Step 2 :** Read a symbol $c$ from a given string without any changes in a stack.

**Step 3 :** Read one symbol from given $w^R$ and remove top element of a stack.

**Step 4 :** Repeat step 3 while a given string and stack are empty.

A transition digraph is shown below

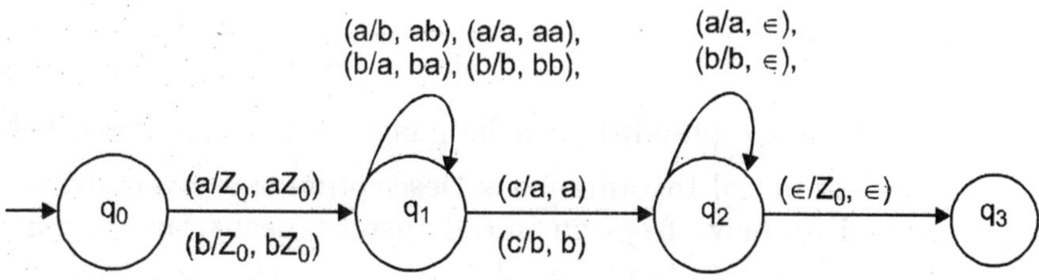


***Fig. 6.14***

The acceptability of a language abcba is shown below

An initial Instantaneous Description of a given string $w$ is ($q_0$, *abcba*, $Z_0$) and its move from an initial Instantaneous Description is shown below

$$\begin{aligned}(q_0, abcba, aZ_0) &\vdash (q_1, bcba, aZ_0)\\ &\vdash (q_1, cba, baZ_0)\\ &\vdash (q_2, ba, baZ_0)\\ &\vdash (q_2, a, aZ_0)\\ &\vdash (q_2, \in, Z_0)\\ &\vdash (q_3, \in, \in)\end{aligned}$$

Here the terminating state is $q_3$, which is non-final state but stack is empty. Hence the string *abcba* is accepted by a PDA by its empty store.

**Example 6.10:** Design an empty store PDA for a context-free language

$$L = \{a^m b^n | \ n < m\}$$ **[*U.P.T.U. B. Tech (Co) 2006*]**

**Solution:** The following steps are used to design a PDA machine for the given language *L*.

**Step 1 :** Push all *a's* of the given language *L* in a stack (or pushdown store).

**Step 2 :** Read a symbol *b* from given language *L* and remove top element of a stack.

**Step 3 :** Repeat step 3 while a given string is empty.

**Step 4 :** After step 3 at least one element is present in a stack. So remove all element from a stack on input symbol $\in$.

A transition digraph is shown below

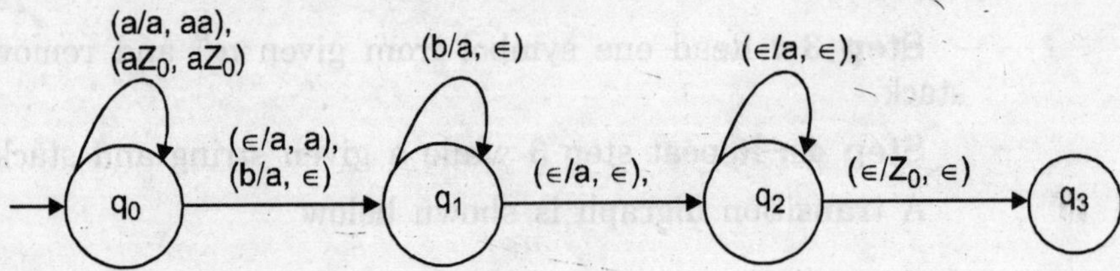


***Fig. 6.15***

The acceptability of a language *aaaabb* is shown below

An initial Instantaneous Description of a given string $w$ is ($q_0$, *aaaabb*, $Z_0$) and its move from an initial Instantaneous Description is shown below

$$
\begin{aligned}
(q_0, aaaabb, Z_0) &\vdash (q_0, aaaabb, aZ_0) \\
&\vdash (q_0, aabb, aaZ_0) \\
&\vdash (q_0, aabb, aaaZ_0) \\
&\vdash (q_0, bb, aaaaZ_0) \\
&\vdash (q_1, b, aaaZ_0) \\
&\vdash (q_1, \in, aaZ_0) \\
&\vdash (q_2, \in, Z_0) \\
&\vdash (q_2, \in, Z_0) \\
&\vdash (q_3, \in, \in)
\end{aligned}
$$

Here the terminating state is $q_3$, which is non-final state but stack is empty. Hence the string *aaaabb* is accepted by a PDA by its empty store.

**Example 6.11:** Design a PDA machine for language

$$L = \{0^n 1^{2n} | \; n \geq 1\}$$ ***[U.P.T.U. B-Tech 2006]***

**Solution:** The following steps are used to design a PDA machine for a given language $L$.

**Step 1 :** Read one 0 from given string and Push two 0's in a stack (or pushdown store).

**Step 2 :** Repeat step 1 while a next input symbol is 1.

**Step 3 :** Read one symbol 1 from a given string and remove single 0 form a stack.

**Step 4 :** Repeat step 3 while a given string is empty.

A transition digraph is shown below

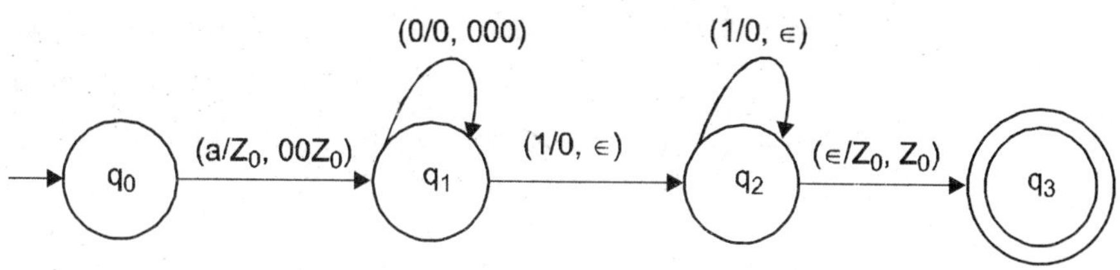


***Fig. 6.16***

**Alternative Method**

**Step 1 :** Read single 0 from given string and Push two 0 in a stack (or pushdown store).

**Step 2 :** Repeat step 1 while a next input symbol is 1.

**Step 3 :** Read two 1's from given string and remove single 0 form stack.

**Step 4 :** Repeat step 3 while a given string is empty.

A transition digraph is shown below

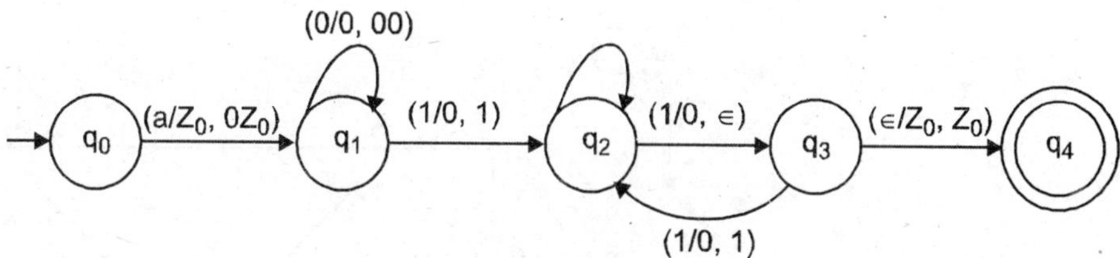


***Fig.6.17***

## 6.6 INSTANTANEOUS DESCRIPTION

As we have seen in pictorial representation of PDA, we can not represent certain problems for FA sufficiently. We need PDA wherein there is an effective use of stack as a memory.

We can describe this behavious of PDA by means of instatenous description. It is given by 1*D*. The moves of 1 *D's* are as shown below.

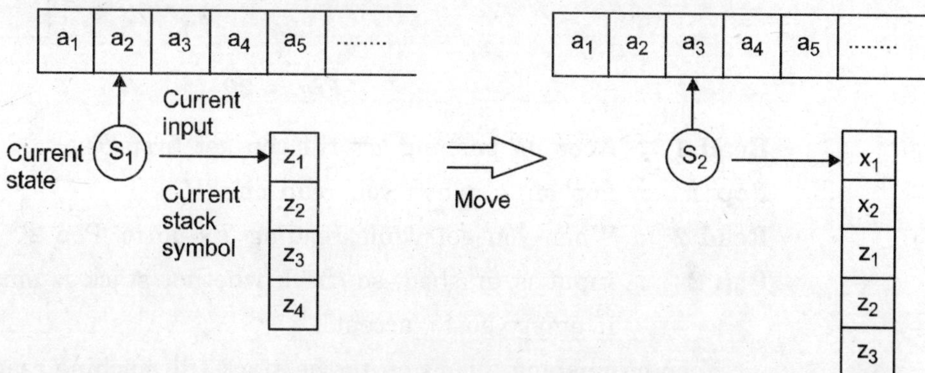


***Fig. 6.18***

**Example 6.12:** Construct a PDA accepting the following language

$$L = \{a^n b^n \mid n \geq 0\}$$ **[U.P.T.O. B.Tech 2005, 2006]**

**Solution:** As the language says it should contain same number of '*a's* followed by the same number of '*b's*. And it may contain string '∈' also if $n = 0$

If we try to design transition diagram for the above PDA it will be

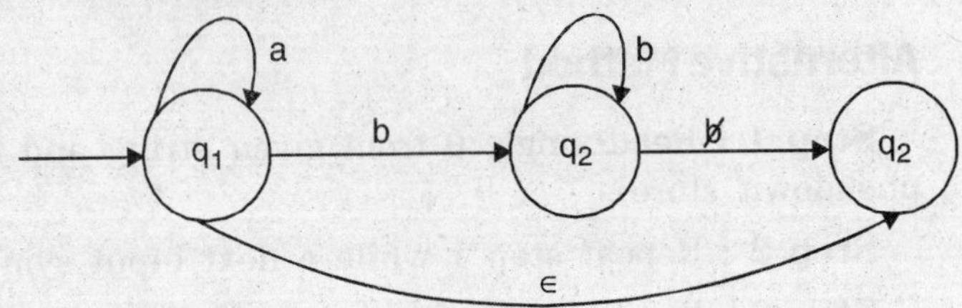


***Fig. 6.19***

Let us draw PDa for the same using memory *i.e.,* stack.

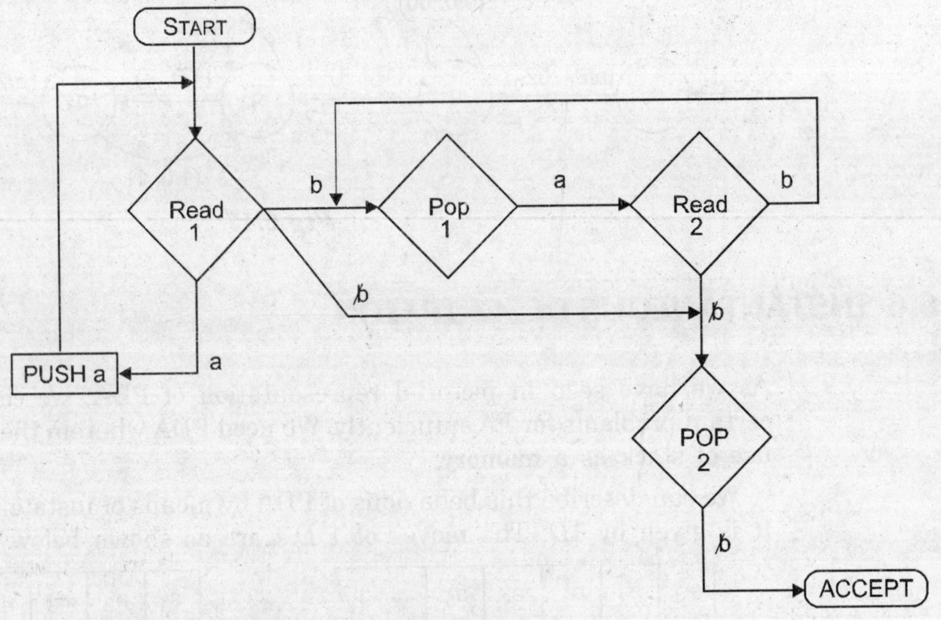


***Fig. 6.20***

**Read 1** : Keep on pushing '*a's* till you get first '*b*'.

**Pop 1** : Pop an '*a*' when you read one '*b*'.

**Read 2** : When you get while reading '*b's* go to 'Pop 2'.

**Pop 2** : Input is finished, so check whether stack is empty or not. If empty go to 'accept".

→ Keep on pushing all '*a's* on to the stack till machine reads '*b*'. Each time it reads '*b*' it pops one '*a*' from the stack.

→ If number of '*a's* equal to number of '*b*' then when input string ends. *i.e.,* blank is read from the tape, the stack top should also contain the '$\not{b}$' indicating stack empty. The only the string is accepted.

→ Read 1 is doing the job of pushing all '*a's* to the stack and on getting first '*b*' it moves to 'Pop 1' state; which along with "Read 2" will check for whether same number of '*b's* are following '*a's* or not.

**Example 6.13:** Construct PDA accepting language consisting of even palindromes strings of '*a's* and '*b's*.

**Solution:** The language can be

$$L = \{\in, aa, bb, aaaa, abba, baab...]$$

No middle letter is there, therefore, after pushing half string, the machine pops one input symbol at a time and checks that with the currently read symbol.

Let us draw PDA

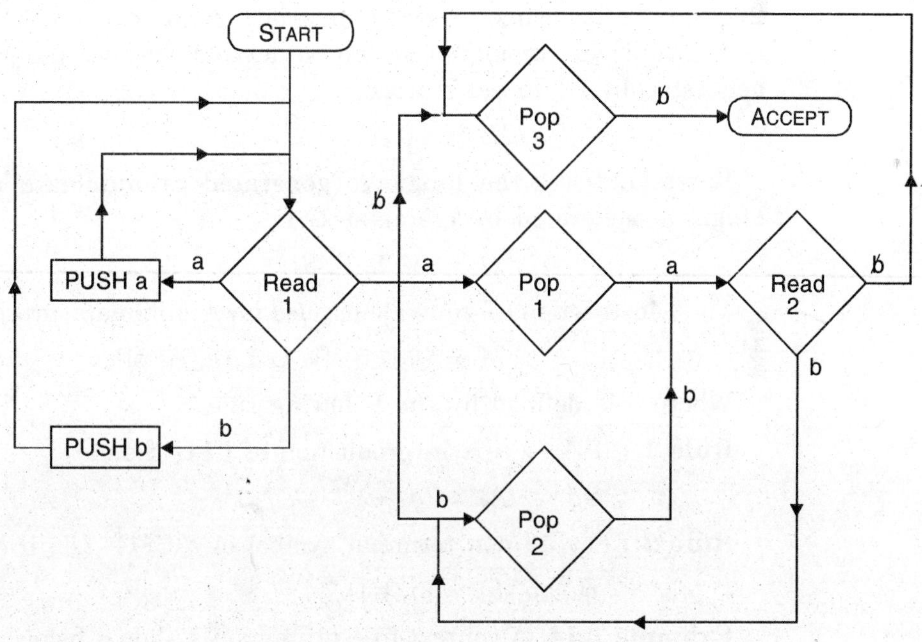


*Fig. 6.21*

## 6.7 CONTEXT FREE LANGUAGES AND PDA

Instead of deciding the algorithm for accepting the strings from a given language and then constructing PDA, which is fairly a complicated job and might not yield each time a minimized PDA; we can write a CFG generating the given language and by direct method we can convert that to PDA.

The languages defined by PDA's are exactly the context free languages.

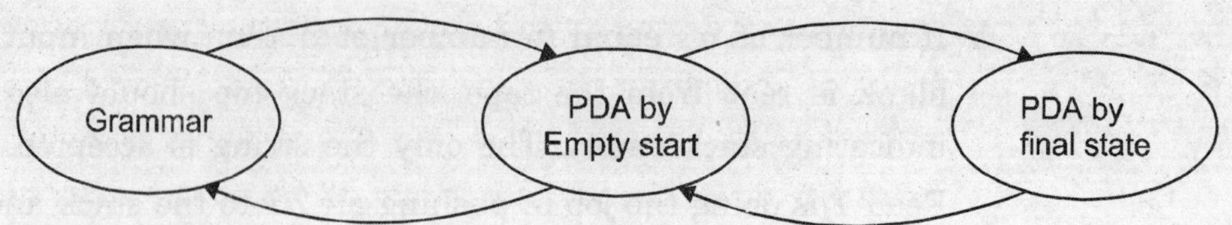


*Fig. 6.22*

The goal is to prove that the following three classes of languages:

→ The CFL, *i.e.,* the languages defined by CFG's

→ The languages that are accepted by final state by some PDA.

→ The languages that are accepted by empty stack by some PDA.

## 6.7.1 Construction of PDA from CFG

A pushdown automaton is used to design an equivalent context-free (or type-2) grammar. It means that given an arbitrary context-free (or type-2) grammar $G$, a pushdown automaton $M$ can be devised that accepts just the sentences generated by $G$. In other word

$$L(M) = L(G)$$

Where $L(M)$ is the language generated by automata and $L(G)$ is the language generated by grammar $G$ *i.e.,*

$$G = (V, \Sigma, P, S)$$

The construction of equivalent pushdown automata proceeds as follows

$$M = (\{q\}, \text{S}, \{V \cup \Sigma, q, S, \phi\})$$

Where $\delta$ is defined by the following rules:

**Rule 1 :** if $A \to \alpha$ is in production of CFG then

$$\delta(q, \in, A) = (q, \alpha)$$

**Rule 2 :** For all non terminal symbol of a CFG *i.e.,* if $b \in \Sigma$ then

$$\delta(q, b, b) = (q, \in)$$

**Example 6.14:** A context-free grammar is shown below

$$G = (\{S, A\}, \{0, 1\}, P, S)$$

where $P$ is defined as follows $S \to 0S1 \mid A$

$$A \to 1A0 \mid S \mid E$$

Construct a PDA equivalent to $G$ by an empty stack.

**[*U.P.T.U., B. Tech. 2004-2005*]**

**Solution:** A PDA machine $M$ is defined as follows

$$M = (\{q\}, \{0, 1\}, \{S, A, E, 0, 1\}, \delta, q, S, \phi)$$

where $\delta$ is defined as follows

$$\delta(q, \in, S) = (q, 0S1), (q, A)$$
$$\delta(q, \in, A) = (q, 1A0), (q, S), (q, E) \text{ By rule 1}$$
$$\delta(q, 1, 1) = (q, \in)$$
$$\delta(q, 0, 0) = (q, \in) \text{ By rule 2}$$

**Example 6.15:** Construct an empty store PDA for a language $L$ where

$$L = \{a^n b^m c^n \mid n, m \geq 1\}$$

**Solution:** A context-free grammar $G$ for a language in given below

$$G = (\{S, A\}, \{a, b, c\}, P, S)$$

where $P$ is defined as follows

$$S \to aSc \mid aAc$$
$$A \to bA \mid b$$

A PDA equivalent to a context-free grammar $G$ by empty stack is shown as follows

$$M = (\{q\}, \{0, 1\}, \{S, A, E, 0, 1\}, \delta, q, S, \phi)$$

where $\delta$ is defined as follows

$$\delta(q, \in, S) = (q, aSc), (q, aAc)$$
$$\delta(q, \in, A) = (q, bA), (q, b) \text{ By rule 1}$$
$$\delta(q, 1, 1) = (q, \in)$$
$$\delta(q, 0, 0) = (q, \in) \text{ By rule 2}$$

**Example 6.16:** Construct an empty store PDA for a language $L$ where

$$L = \{w \mid w \in \{a, b\}^+ \text{ and } n_a(w) = n_b(w)\}$$

**Solution:** A context-free grammar $G$ for a language in given below

$$G = (\{S, A\}, \{a, b\}, P, S)$$

where $P$ is defined as follows

$$S \to aSb \mid bSa \mid ab \mid ba$$

A PDA equivalent to a context-free grammar $G$ by empty stack is shown as follows

$$M = (\{q\}, \{a, b\}, \{S, a, b\}, \delta, q, S, \phi)$$

where $\delta$ is defined as follows

$$\delta(q, \in, S) = (q, aSb), (q, bSa), (q, ab), (q, ba) \} \text{ By rule 1}$$

$$\left.\begin{array}{l}\delta(q,a,a) = (q,\in)\\ \delta(q,b,b) = (q,\in)\end{array}\right\} \text{By rule 2}$$

**Example 6.17:** Construct an empty store PDA for a language $L$ where

$$L = \{w \mid n_a(w) \geq n_b(w)\}$$

**Solution:** A context-free grammar $G$ for a language in given below

$$G = (\{S\}, \{a, b\}, P, S)$$

where $P$ is defined as follows

$$S \rightarrow aSb \mid bSa \mid A$$
$$A \rightarrow a\,A \mid \in$$

A PDA equivalent to a context-free grammar $G$ by empty stack is shown as follows

$$M = (\{q\}, \{a, b\}, \{S, A, a, b\}, \delta, q, S, \phi)$$

where $\delta$ is defined as follows

$$\left.\begin{aligned}\delta(q,\in,S) &= (q,aSb),(q,bSa),(q,A)\\ \delta(q,\in,A) &= (q,aA),(q,\in)\end{aligned}\right\}\text{By rule 1}$$

$$\left.\begin{aligned}\delta(q,a,a) &= (q,\in)\\ \delta(q,b,b) &= (q,\in)\end{aligned}\right\}\text{By rule 2}$$

**Example 6.18:** Construct an empty store PDA for a language $L$ where

$$L = \{a^n b^n \mid n \geq 1 \cup b^{2m}\, a^n \mid n \geq 1\}$$

**Solution:** A context-free grammar $G$ for a language in given below

$$G = G_1 \cup G_2$$

where $\quad G_1 = (\{A\}, \{a, b\}, P_2, B)$

where $P_1$ is defined as follows

$$A \rightarrow aAb \mid ab$$

and $\quad G_2 = (\{B\}, \{a, b,\}, P_2\ B)$

where $P_2$ is defined as follows

$$B \rightarrow b\ b\ B\ a \mid b\ b\ a$$

Since $\quad G = G_1 \cup G_2$

Hence $\quad G = (\{S, A, B\}, \{a, b\}, \{S \rightarrow A \mid B \cup P_1 \cup P_2\}, S)$

A PDA equivalent to a context-free grammar $G$ by empty stack is shown as follows

$$M = (\{q\}, \{a, b\}, \{a, b\}\ \{S, A, B, a, b\}, \delta, q, S, \phi)$$

where $\delta$ is defined as follows

$$\left.\begin{aligned}\delta(q,\in,S) &= (q,A),(q,B)\\ \delta(q,\in,A) &= (q,aAb),(q,ab)\\ \delta(q,\in,B) &= (q,bbBa),(q,bba)\end{aligned}\right\}\text{By rule 1}$$

$$\left.\begin{aligned}\delta(q,a,a) &= (q,\in)\\ \delta(q,b,b) &= (q,\in)\end{aligned}\right\}\text{By rule 2}$$

**Example 6.19:** Construct an empty store PDA for a language $L$ where

$$L = \{a^n b^n \mid n \geq 1 \cup b^{2m}\, a^n \mid n \geq 1 \cup a^n b^m c^n \mid n,\ m \geq 1\}$$

**Solution:** A context-free grammar $G$ for a language in given below

$$G = G_1 \cup G_2 \cup G_3$$

where $\quad G_1 = (\{A\},\ \{a,\ b\},\ P_i,\ A)$

where $P_1$ is defined as follows

$$A \to aAb \mid ab$$

$$G_2 = (\{B\},\ \{a,\ b,\},\ P_2\ B)$$

where $P_2$ is defined as follows

$$B \to b\ b\ B\ a \mid b\ b\ a$$

and $\quad G_3 = (\{C,\ D\},\ \{a,\ b,\ c\},\ P\ B)$

where $P$ is defined as follows

$$C \to aCc \mid aDc$$

$$D \to bD \mid b$$

Since $\quad G = G_1 \cup G_2 \cup G_3$

Hence $\quad G = (\{S, A, B, C, D\},\ \{a, b, c\},\ \{S \to A \mid B \mid C) \cup P_1 \cup P_2 \cup P_3\},\ S)$

A PDA equivalent to a context-free grammar $G$ by empty stack is shown as follows

$$M = (\{q\},\ \{a,\ b\}\ \{S,\ A,\ C,\ D,\ a,\ b,\ c\},\ \delta,\ q,\ S,\ \phi)$$

where $\delta$ is defined as follows

$$\left.\begin{aligned} \delta(q,\in,S) &= (q,A),(q,B),(q,C) \\ \delta(q,\in,A) &= (q,aAb),(q,ab) \\ \delta(q,\in,B) &= (q,bbBa),(q,bba) \\ \delta(q,\in,C) &= (q,aCc),(q,aDc) \\ \delta(q,\in,D) &= (q,bD),(q,b) \end{aligned}\right\} \text{By rule 1}$$

$$\left.\begin{aligned} \delta(q,a,a) &= (q,\in) \\ \delta(q,b,b) &= (q,\in) \\ \delta(q,c,c) &= (q,\in) \end{aligned}\right\} \text{By rule 2}$$

**Example 6.20:** Construct an empty store PDA for a language $L$ where

$$L = \{a^n b^m \mid n \neq m\}$$

**Solution:** A context-free grammar $G$ for a language in given below

$$G = (\{S,\ A,\ B\},\ \{a,\ b\},\ P,\ S)$$

where $P$ is defined as follows

$$S \to aSb \mid aA \mid Bb$$

$$A \to a\ A \mid \in$$

$$B \to Bb \mid \in$$

A PDA equivalent to a context-free grammar $G$ by empty stack is shown as follows

$$M = (\{q\}, \{a, b\} \{S, A, B, a, b\}, \delta, q, S, \phi)$$

where $\delta$ is defined as follows

$$\left.\begin{array}{l}\delta(q,\in,S) = (q,aSb),(q,aA),(q,Bb)\\ \delta(q,\in,A) = (q,aA),(q,\in)\\ \delta(q,\in,B) = (q,Bb),(q,\in)\end{array}\right\}\text{By rule 1}$$

$$\left.\begin{array}{l}\delta(q,a,a) = (q,\in)\\ \delta(q,b,b) = (q,\in)\end{array}\right\}\text{By rule 2}$$

**Example 6.21:** Construct an empty store PDA for a language $L$ where

$$L = \{a^n\ b^{2n}\ a^m \mid n \geq 0,\ m \geq 1\}$$

**Solution:** A context-free grammar $G$ for a language in given below

$$G = (\{S, A, B\}, \{a, b\}, P, S)$$

where $P$ is defined as follows

$$S \rightarrow AB$$

$$A \rightarrow aAbb \mid \in$$

$$B \rightarrow aB \mid a$$

A PDA equivalent to a context-free grammar $G$ by empty stack is shown as follows

$$M = (\{q\}, \{a, b\} \{S, A, B, a, b\}, \delta, q, S, \phi)$$

where $\delta$ is defined as follows

$$\left.\begin{array}{l}\delta(q,\in,S) = (q,AB)\\ \delta(q,\in,S) = (q,aAbb),(q,\in)\\ \delta(q,\in,B) = (q,Ba),(q,a)\end{array}\right\}\text{By rule 1}$$

$$\left.\begin{array}{l}\delta(q,a,a) = (q,\in)\\ \delta(q,b,b) = (q,\in)\end{array}\right\}\text{By rule 2}$$

**Example 6.22:** Construct an empty store PDA for a language $L$ where

$$L = \{a^n\ b^m\ c^k \mid n = m \text{ or } m = k\}$$

**Solution:** A context-free grammar $G$ for a language in given below

$$G = (\{S, A, B\}, \{a, b\}, P, S)$$

where $P$ is defined as follows

$$S \rightarrow A \mid B$$

$$A \rightarrow CD$$

$$C \rightarrow aCb \mid \in$$

$$D \to DC \mid \in$$
$$B \to EF$$
$$E \to aE \mid \in$$
$$F \to bFc \mid \in$$

A PDA equivalent to a context-free grammar $G$ by empty stack is shown as follows

$$M = (\{q\}, \{a, b\} \{S, A, B, a, b\}, d, q, S, f)$$

where δ is defined as follows

$$\left.\begin{array}{l} \delta(q,\in,S) = (q,A),(q,B) \\ \delta(q,\in,A) = (q,CD) \\ \delta(q,\in,C) = (q,aCb),(q,\in) \\ \delta(q,\in,D) = (q,Dc),(q,\in) \\ \delta(q,\in,B) = (q,EF) \\ \delta(q,\in,E) = (q,aE),(q,\in) \\ \delta(q,\in,F) = (q,bFc),(q,\in) \end{array}\right\} \text{By rule 1}$$

$$\left.\begin{array}{l} \delta(q,a,a) = (q,aCb),(q,\in) \\ \delta(q,b,b) = (q,aCb),(q,\in) \\ \delta(q,c,c) = (q,aCb),(q,\in) \end{array}\right\} \text{By rule 2}$$

## Other Approach

The steps to convert CFG to PDA are as follows.

**Step 1:** Convert the given CFG to Chomsky's normal form.

**Step 2:** The PDA should start by pushing start symbol onto the stack. To derive further production rules for the start symbol, we immediately perform the pop operation. It is as shown below.

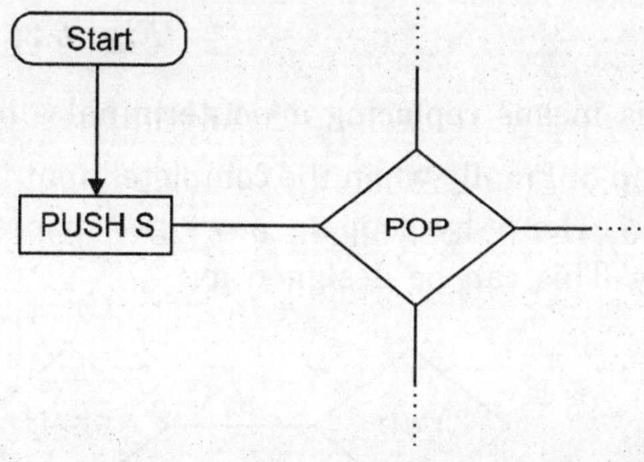


***Fig. 6.23***

**Step 3:** If the production is of the form $S \to AB$, we push $A$ and $B$ onto the stack in reverse order. (since we get after popping the reverse order is straight ∵ reverse. reverse = straight).

So $S \rightarrow AB$

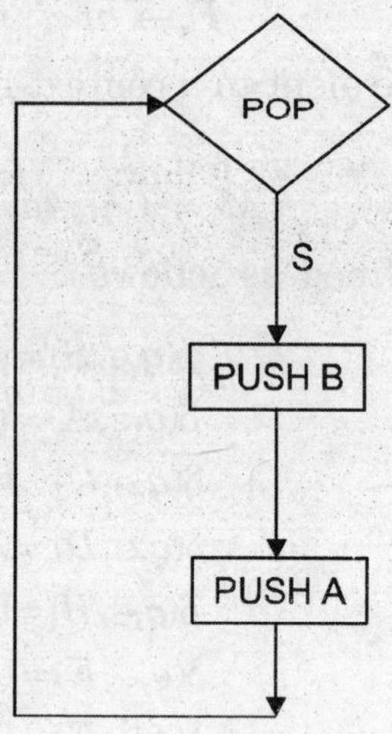


*Fig. 6.24*

**Step 4:** If the production is of the form

$S \rightarrow a$ we design as

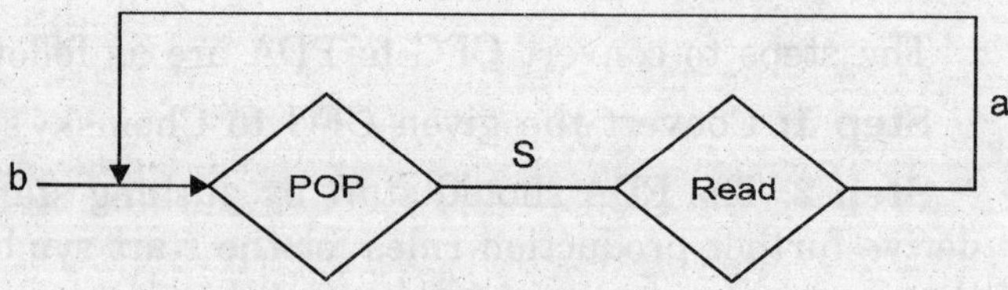


*Fig. 6.25*

This means replacing a nonterminal $s$ by $a$.

**Step 5:** Finally when the complete input is read from the tape, we encounter with $b\!\!\!/$. Hence by popping $b\!\!\!/$ we get ensured with the fact that stack is also empty. This can be designed as

*Fig. 6.26*

**Example 6.23:** Construct PDA for following grammar

$$S \rightarrow AB$$
$$A \rightarrow CD$$
$$B \rightarrow b$$
$$C \rightarrow a$$
$$D \rightarrow a$$

**Solution:** The above grammar is already in Chomsky's normal form. So we will take the grammar as it is

The PDA for rule 1 is

$$S \rightarrow AB$$

Start
PUSH S
POP
S
PUSH B
PUSH A

***Fig. 6.21***

$S \rightarrow CD$ can be

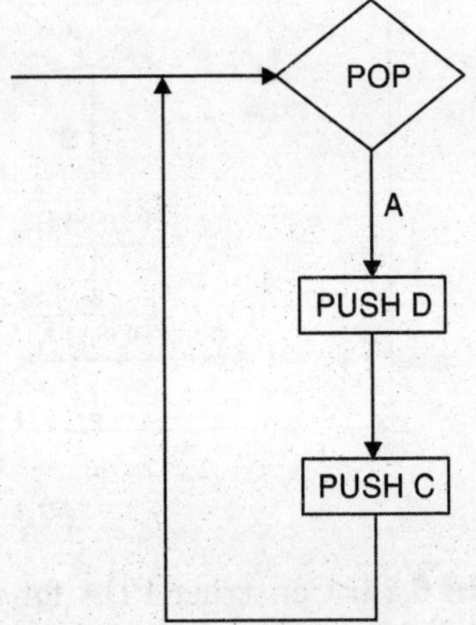


***Fig. 6.28***

$B \to b, \quad C \to a, \quad D \to a,$ can be

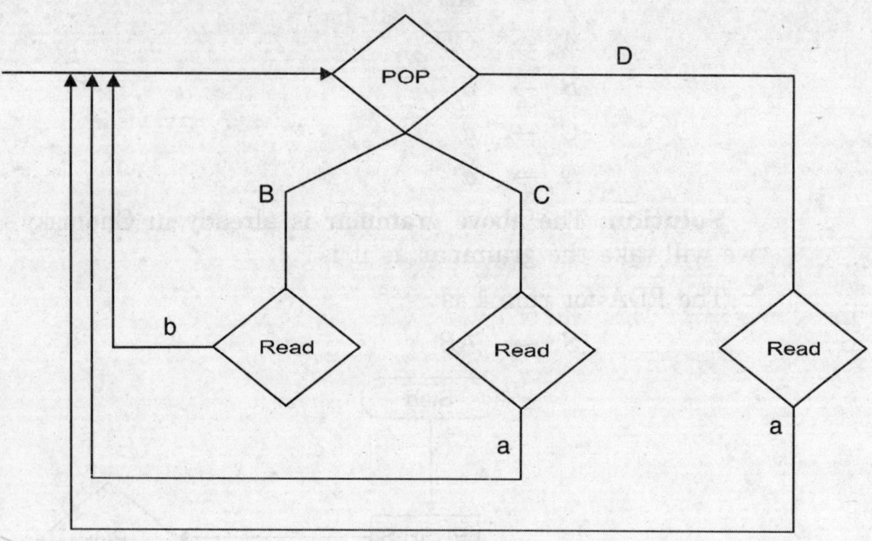


*Fig. 6.29*

Finally we could draw the complete PDA as

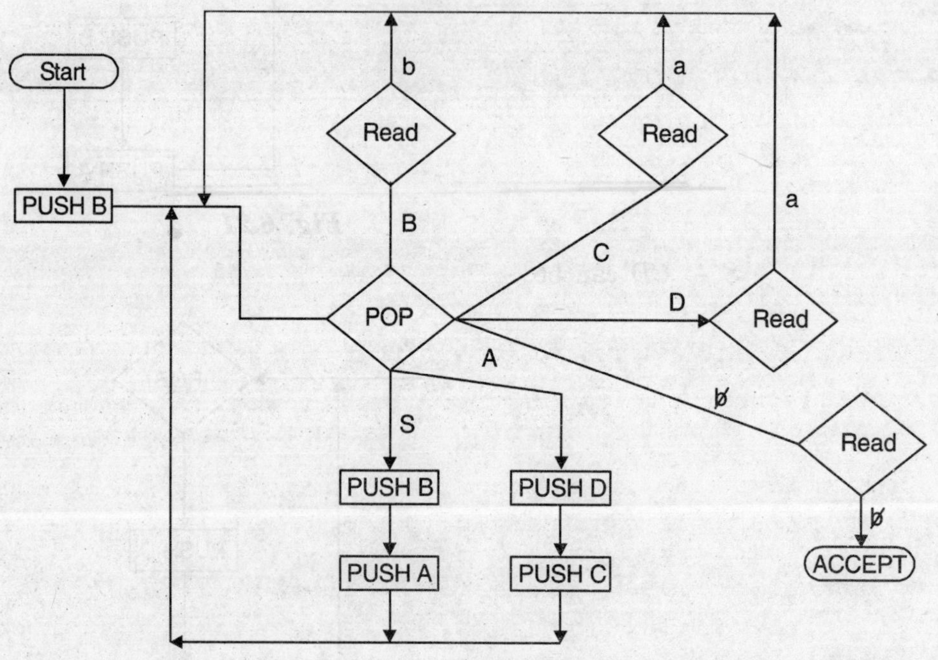


*Fig. 6.30*

**Example 6.24:** Construct PDA for the language of any combination of 0's and 1's.

**Solution:** First of all we will construct regular expression from this $L$.

$$r.e. = (0 + 1)^*$$

In the next step we will build the CFG for this

$$S \rightarrow 0S \mid 1S \mid \varepsilon$$

Now let us convert this CFG to CNF as

$$S \rightarrow 0S$$

$$A \rightarrow 0$$

Thus $S$ becomes $\quad S \rightarrow AS$

$$S \rightarrow 1S$$

$$S \rightarrow 1$$

Then, $\quad S \rightarrow BS$

Now, $\quad S \rightarrow \in$ is now allowed in CNF but we will take care of this rule by simply pushing and popping $S$. This indicates $S$ have $\varepsilon$ value. The rules in CNF are

$$S \rightarrow AS$$

$$S \rightarrow BS$$

$$A \rightarrow 0$$

$$B \rightarrow 1$$

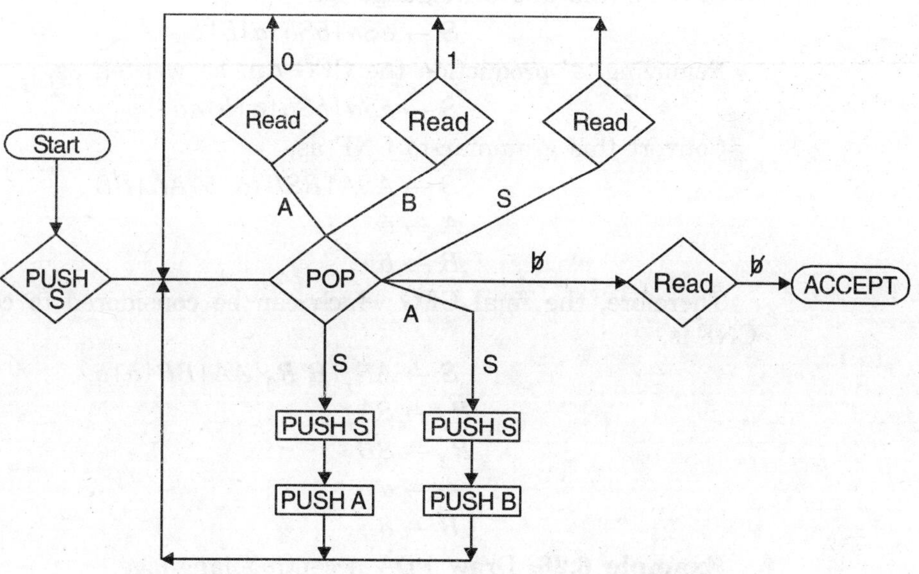


***Fig. 6.31***

As per given PDA one $S$ after popping can be replaced by $AS$ and another $S$ is simply popped to have a effect of $S \rightarrow \in$. Thus you can try out the simulation of this PDA for any string of 0's and 1's.

**Example 6.25:** Construct PDA accepting all (even and odd both) palindrome strings of '*a's* and '*b's*.

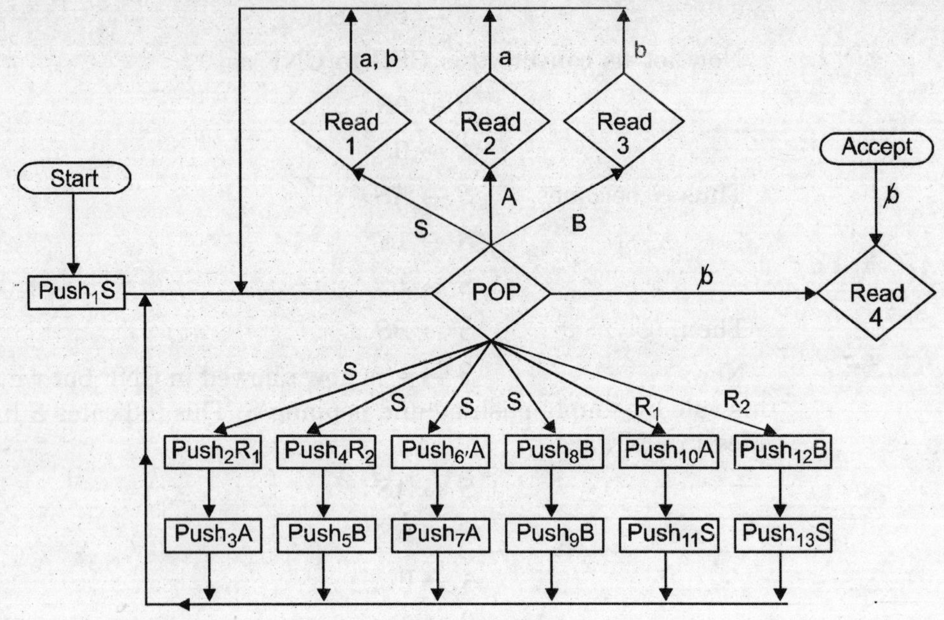


***Fig. 6.32***

CFG for the above language is,

$$S \rightarrow aSa \mid bSb \mid a \mid b \mid \in$$

Removing '∈' production the CFG can be written as,

$$S \rightarrow aSa \mid bSb \mid a \mid b \mid aa \mid bb$$

Convert this grammar to CNF as,

$$S \rightarrow ASA \mid BSB \mid a \mid b \mid AA \mid BB$$

$$A \rightarrow a$$

$$B \rightarrow b$$

Therefore, the final CFG which can be considered to construct PDA, in CNF is,

$$S \rightarrow AR_1 \mid B\ R_2 \mid AA \mid BB \mid a \mid b$$

$$R_1 \rightarrow SA$$

$$R_2 \rightarrow SB$$

$$A \rightarrow a$$

$$B \rightarrow b$$

**Example 6.26:** Draw PDA accepting language,

$$L = \{a^{2n} \mid n > 0\}$$

**Solution:** We can write CFG for the above language as,

$$S \rightarrow SS \mid aa$$

Above grammar using CNF can be written as,

$$S \rightarrow SS \mid AA$$

$$S \rightarrow a$$

Using this convert CFG in CNF, we can draw NPDA as shown in Fig. 6.33. We can trace the acceptance of any string we want, similarly as in previous problems.

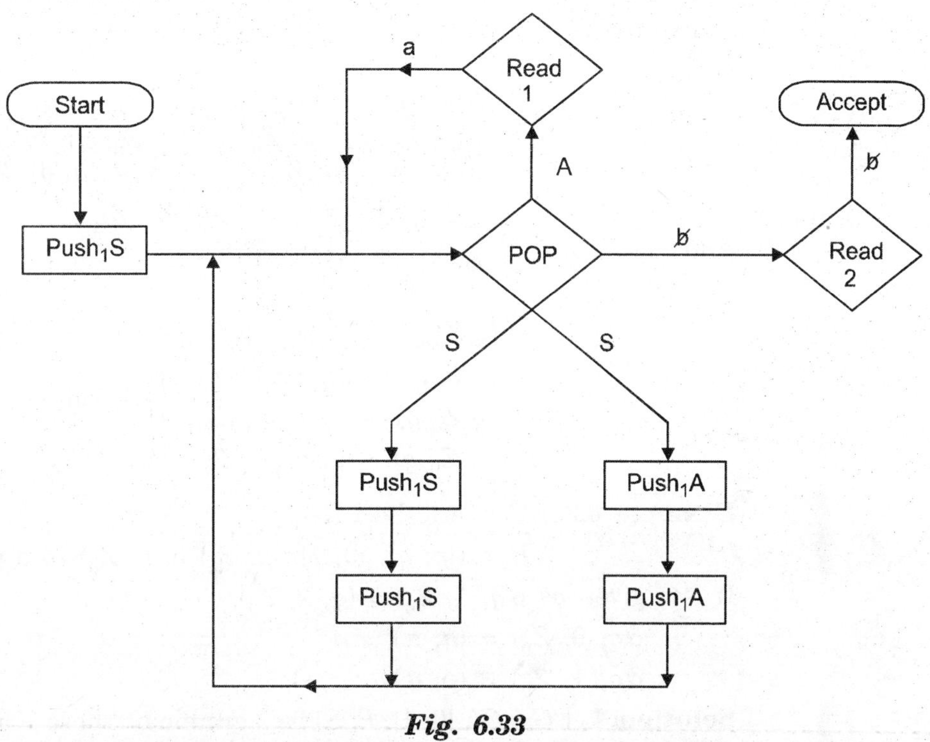


***Fig. 6.33***

## 6.7.2 Construction of CFG from PDA

Let $M = (Q, \Sigma, \Gamma, \delta, q_0, Z_0, F)$ be PDA then there exists a context-free grammar $G$ such that $L(G) = L(M)$. That is if $M$ is given than can construct its equivalent $G = (V, \Sigma, P, S)$.

Construction of $V$ : $V = \{S \cup [q, Z, q'] \mid q, q' \in Q, Z \text{ e } \Gamma\}$

Construction of $P$ : Production rules are defined according to the transition system of a PDA by the following rules:

**Rule 1:** Starting productions are given by $S \to [q_0, Z_0, q] \mid q \in Q$

**Rule 2:** Each transition function erasing a PDS symbol *i.e.*, $\delta(q, a, Z) = (q', \in)$ then add a following production in a set of production rules

$$[q, Z, q'] \to a$$

**Rule 3:** Each transition function not erasing a PDS symbol *i.e.*, $\delta(q, a, Z) = (q', Z_1, Z_2....Z_n)$ then add the following production rules in a set of production rules.

$$[q, Z, q'] \to a[q, Z_1, q_1]\ [q_1, Z_2, q_2]\ [q_2, Z_3, q_3]....[q_n, Z_n, q'].$$

where each state $q', q_1, q_2, q_3, \ldots q_n$ can be any state of $Q$

**Example 6.27:** Convert the PDA

$$P = (\{p, q\}, \{0, 1\}, \{x, Z_0\}, \delta, q, Z_0) \text{ to a CFG}$$

If δ is given as $\delta(q, 1, Z_0) = (q, x\, Z_0)$ **[*U.P.T.U., B. Tech. 2004-2005*]**

**Solution:** Let $G = (V, \{0, 1\}, P, S)$ be a grammar whose $V$ and $P$ are defined as follows

$$V = \{S, [p, x, p], [p, x, q], [q, x, p], [q, x, q], [p, Z_0, p], [p, Z_0, q], [q, Z_0, p], [q, Z_0, q]\}$$

Or $\{S \cup [q, Z, q'] \mid q, q' \in \{p, q\}, Z \in \{x, Z_0\}\}$

And $$\left.\begin{array}{l} S \to [q, Z_0, p] \\ S \to [q, Z_0, q] \end{array}\right\} \text{By rule 1}$$

$$\left.\begin{array}{l} [q,Z_0,p] \to 1[q,x,p][p,Z_0,p] \\ [q,Z_0,p] \to 1[q,x,p][q,Z_0,p] \\ [q,Z_0,q] \to 1[q,x,p][p,Z_0,q] \\ [q,Z_0,q] \to 1[q,x,q][q,Z_0,q] \end{array}\right\} \text{By rule 3}$$

**Example 6.28:** Convert the PDA

$$P = (\{p, q\}, \{0, 1\}, \{x, Z_0\}\ \delta, q, Z_0) \text{ to a CFG}$$

If δ is given as $\delta(q, 1, Z_0) = (q, x, Z_0)$,

$\delta(q, 0, Z_0) = (q, \in)$

$\delta(q, 1, Z_0) = (p, \in)$

**Solution:** Let $G = (V, \{0, 1\}, P, S)$ be a grammar whose $V$ and $P$ are defined as follows

$$V = \{S, [p, x, p], [p, x, q], [q, x, p], [q, x, q], [p, Z_0, p], [p, Z_0, q], [q, Z_0, p], [q, Z_0, q]\}$$

Or $\{S \cup [q, Z, q'] \mid q, q', \in \{p, q\}, Z \in \{x, Z_0\}\}$

And $$\left.\begin{array}{l} S \to [q, Z_0, p] \\ S \to [q, Z_0, q] \end{array}\right\} \text{By rule 1}$$

$$\left.\begin{array}{l} [q,Z_0,p] \to 1[q,x,p][p,Z_0,p] \\ [q,Z_0,p] \to 1[q,x,q][q,Z_0,p] \\ [q,Z_0,q] \to 1[q,x,p][p,Z_0,q] \\ [q,Z_0,q] \to 1[q,x,q][q,Z_0,q] \end{array}\right\} \text{By rule 3}$$

$$\left.\begin{array}{l} [q,Z,q] \to 0 \\ [q,Z,p] \to 0 \end{array}\right\} \text{By rule 2}$$

**Example 6.29:** Contruct PDA for the following

$$L = \{a^n c b^{2n}\}\ n > 1$$

Over the alphabet

$$S = \{a, b, c\}$$ **[*U.P.T.U. B-Tech 2003, 04*]**

**Solution:** The PDA has input set $\{a, b, c\}$ and the number of $b's$ following total number of $a's$ is double. And the $a's$ and $b's$ are separated by single $C$. The PDA can be as shown below:

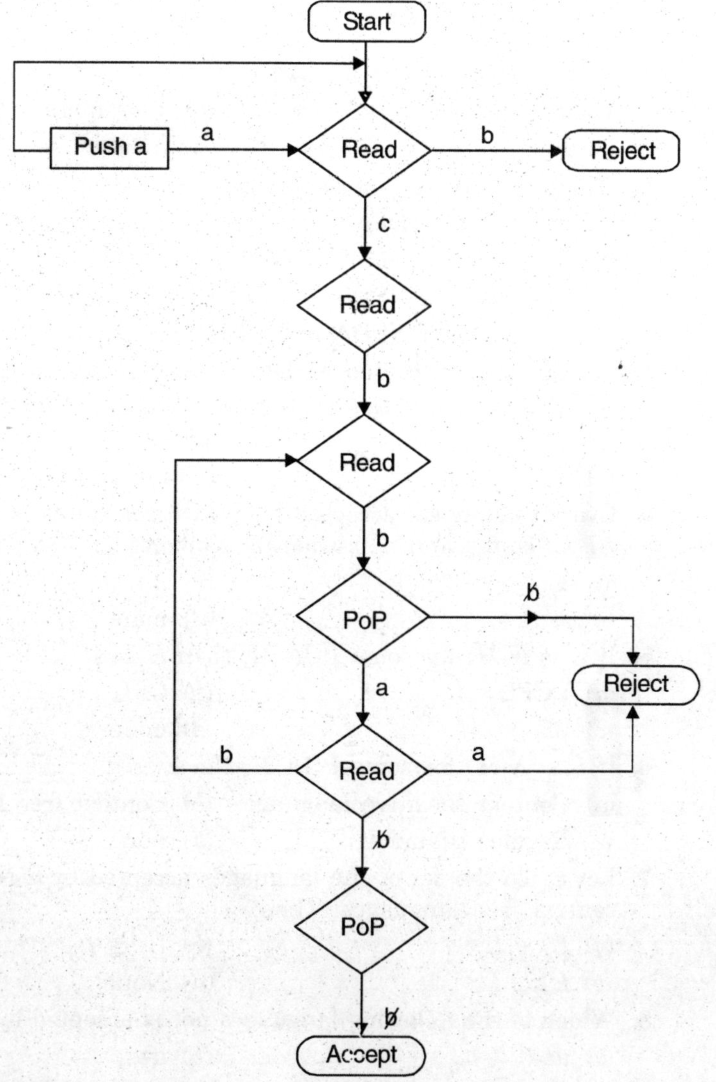


***Fig. 6.34***

The above given PDA is deterministic in nature because for every specific input there is a unique path. Initially we expect to read $a's$. And when we read $a$, we push each $a$ on to the stack. Then we read $c$ and two times $b$ and there after pop single $b$.

The logic is that on reading two $b's$ single a should be popped. This makes a check on $a^n$ and $b^{2n}$. Finally after reading $\not{b}$ the stack should also be empty. Then we will reach to accept state.

# EXERCISE

## (A) Objective Type Questions

1. A PDA behaves like an FA when the number of auxiliary memory it has is
   (*a*) 0 (*b*) 1 or more
   (*c*) 1 or more (*d*) none
2. Choose the correct statements:
   (*a*) the power of DFA and NDFA are almost same
   (*b*) the power of DFA and NDFA are different
   (*c*) the power of NPDA and DPDA are same
   (*d*) the power of NPDA and DPDA are same
3. A regular set accepted by DFA with $n$ states is accepted to final state by a DPDA with $n$ states and at least .......... pushdown symbols:
   (*a*) 1 (*b*) 2
   (*c*) 3 (*d*) none
4. Every regular set accepted by FA with $n$ states is accepted by a DPDA with .......... states and $n$ pushdown symbols
   (*a*) 1 (*b*) 2
   (*c*) $n$ (*d*) none
5. If $L$ is $N(M)$ for some PDA $M$, then $L$ is a
   (*a*) DCFL (*b*) CFL
   (*c*) RE (*d*) none
6. If $L$ is $N(M)$ for some PDA $M$, the $L$ is a
   (*a*) Context sensitive language (*b*) Context free language
   (*c*) Regular grammar (*d*) none
7. Let $L_1$ be the set of the languages accepted by a NPDA and $L_2$ be the set of context free languages. Then:
   (*a*) $L_1 = L_2$ (*b*) $L_1 \subseteq L_2$
   (*c*) $L_2 \subseteq L_1$ (*d*) None
8. Which of the following languages not is accepted by a NPDA $w$ *:
   (*a*) $ww^r$ (*b*) $ww$
   (*c*) $wcw^r$ (*d*) $a^nb^{2n}$
9. Which of the following is false:
   (*a*) Every NPDA corresponds to a CFL
   (*b*) Every CFL corresponds to a NPDA
   (*c*) None
   (*d*) Both (*a*) and (*b*)
10. Running time of a finite automata (like NPDA) for an input string of length $n$ is
    (*a*) Linear in $n$
    (*b*) Polynomial in $n$

(*c*) Exponential in $n$
(*d*) Can be anything depending on the automata

**11.** If for a language $L$ we can find a *RE* then definitely (choose most appropriate):
(*a*) we can draw NPDA for $L$ (*b*) we can's draw NPDA for $L$
(*c*) we can draw DPDA for $L$ (*d*) None

**12.** Which one of the following is true about PDA's
(*a*) PDA has an auxiliary memory in the form of a stack.
(*b*) PDA is represented by 7-tuple $(S, \Sigma, \Gamma, \delta, q_0, Z_0, F)$
(*c*) $\delta : S \times (\Sigma \cup \{\lambda\}) \times \Gamma \to S \times \Gamma^*$
(*d*) all of the above

**13.** Which of the following statements is false?
(*a*) A language is LR iff it can be accepted by a Deterministic PDA.
(*b*) A language is CFL iff it can be accepted by a Non Deterministic PDA.
(*c*) Inherently ambiguous languages can be modeled by LR grammars.
(*d*) The class of sets accepted by pushdown automata properly includes the regular sets.

**14.** The grammar given by

$$G : S \to aSb \mid SS \mid \Lambda$$

(*a*) Is LR (1) (*b*) Is LR (0)
(*c*) Is LR (2) (*d*) Is not LR ($k$) for any $k$

**15.** Which of the following can not be accepted by deterministic PDA
(*a*) $wcw^t$ (*b*) $a^nb^n \; n \geq 1$
(*c*) $a^nb^n \; n \geq 1 \; U \; a^mb^{2m} \; m \geq 1$ (*d*) none

**16.** The language $\{ww^r\}$ is
(*a*) Accepted by a DPDA not by a NPDA
(*b*) Accepted by a NPDA not by a DPDA
(*c*) None
(*d*) Cannot say

**17.** Which of the following is accepted by an NPDA and not DPDA:
(*a*) All strings in which a given symbol is present atleast twice
(*b*) Even palindromes (*i.e.*, palindromes made up if even no of symbols)
(*c*) String ending with a particular alphabet
(*d*) None

## ANSWERS

| | | | | |
|---|---|---|---|---|
| **1.** (*a*) | **2.** (*a*) | **3.** (*a*) | **4.** (*a*) | **5.** (*b*) |
| **6.** (*b*) | **7.** (*a*) | **8.** (*b*) | **9.** (*d*) | **10.** (*a*) |
| **11.** (*c*) | **12.** (*d*) | **13.** (*b*) | **14.** (*d*) | **15.** (*c*) |
| **16.** (*b*) | **17.** (*b*) | | | |

## (B) Problems

1. Design a PDA machine for the following languages
   (a) $L(G) = a^n b^m : n \leq m + 2$
   (b) $L(G) = a^n b^m : n \neq m$
   (c) $L(G) = a^n b^m : n \neq 2m$
   (d) $L(G) = a^n b^m : 2n \leq m \leq 3n$ and $n \geq 1$
   (e) $L(G) = w : n_a(w) \neq n_b(w)$
   (f) $L(G) = \{a^n b^m c^k \mid n, m \geq 1$ and $k = n + m$
   (g) $L(G) = \{a^n b^m c^k \mid n \geq 1$ and $m \leq k\}$
   (h) $L(G) = \{a^n b^m c^k \mid m,k \geq 0$ and $n = m + k]$
   or $L(G) = \{a^n b^m c^k \mid k = |n - m|\}$
   or $L(G) = \{a^n b^m c^k \mid n = k + m$ and $m = k + n\}$
   $L(G) = \{w \mid w \in \{a, b\}^*$
2. Design a PDA machine for the following context-free grammar whose production rules are given below
   (a) $S \rightarrow aA \mid aaA \mid \in$
   $A \rightarrow aAb \mid B$
   $A \rightarrow Bb \mid \in$
   (b) $S \rightarrow aSb \mid aA \mid$ Bb
   $A \rightarrow aA \mid \in$
   $B \rightarrow Bb \mid \in$
   (c) $S \rightarrow aSbb \mid aA \mid Bb$
   $A \rightarrow aA \mid \in$
   $B \rightarrow Bbb \mid \in$
   (d) $S \rightarrow aSbb \mid aSbbb \mid abb \mid abbb$
   (e) $S \rightarrow aSb \mid bSa \mid aA \mid Bb$
   $A \rightarrow aA \mid \in$
   $B \rightarrow Bb \mid \in$
   (f) $S \rightarrow aSc \mid aAc$
   $A \rightarrow bAc \mid bc$
   (g) $S \rightarrow AB$
   $A \rightarrow aA \mid \in$
   $B \rightarrow bBc \mid Cc$
   $C \rightarrow Cc \mid \in$
   (h) $S \rightarrow aSc \mid A \mid \in$
   (i) $S \rightarrow SS \mid aSb \mid bSa \mid bSb \mid \in$
   (j) $S \rightarrow aA \mid aaA \mid \in$
   $A \rightarrow aAb \mid \in$
   $B \rightarrow cBb \mid \in$
   (k) $S \rightarrow aAb \mid B$
   $A \rightarrow aAb \mid \in$
   $B \rightarrow bBa \mid \in$

❑❑❑

CHAPTER

# 7

# TURING MACHINE

## 7.1 INTRODUCTION

As we have discussed in the earlier chapter-PDA is having their own strengths and limitations. The limitation of FSM is memory, which is overcome in model pushdown Automata (PDA). The PDA uses a stack which is helping the automata to remember any arbitrary long input sequence. And thus accepts as larger class af languages than that at FA does. But still the model has certain limitations and those are removed by a new model called Turing machine. The basic limitation at pushdown automata is that it has a limited computational capability.

Turing machine is a very powerful machine, which is used to perform any calculation that can be logical designed by human beings. That means if you are able to design a step by step solution of any problem (*i.e.*, algorithm) then you are able to design its equivalent Turing Machine (TM). TM is basically used to design a type-0 (Unrestricted) grammar but it can also be used to design other types of grammar. It is designed as a Deterministic Turing Machine (DTM) and Non-Deterministic Turing Machine (NDTM) both.

## 7.2 TURING MACHINE MODEL

The turing machine was invented by ***Alan M Turing*** in 1935. This concept at turing mchine had given rise to the concept at algorithm and finite procedures: Since the basis at the Turing (TM) is to divide the process into primitive operations such that they cannot be further divisible and then does the job.

A basic model at a TM consists at a TM at Tape, Read/write (R/W) head and finite control, which is shown in the Fig. 7.1.

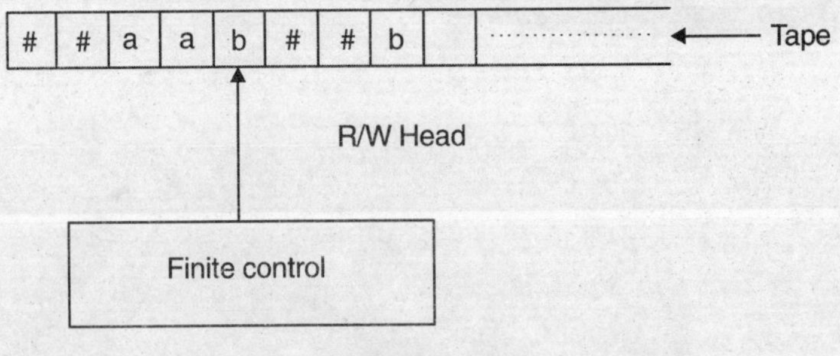


*Fig. 7.1*

**Tm consists of:**

→ The input tape is divided into cells, which are infinite at the both ends Each cell contraining one input symbol, and thus the input string can be placed on a tape,. The empty tape is filled by blank characters.

→ A head which can read or write a symbol and move left or right or stay in position: Corresponding to the square cell read, marked-off on a tape.

→ A finite set af states through which machine has to undergo.

→ Finite set af symbols, called as an external alphabet set, which are used in building the logic af turing machine.

---

A turing machine (TM) is said to be in half state it if is not able to move further.

---

### Features af TM:

→ It has unlimited memory capability

→ It has external memory which remembers arbitrarily long sequence af input.

→ The mode has a facility by which the input at left or right on the tape can be read easily.

→ The machine can produce certain output based on its input. Sometimes it may be required that the same input has to be used to generate the output. So in this machine the distinction between input and output has been removed. Thus a common set af alphabets can be used for the turing machine.

## 7.3 DETERMINISTIC TURING MACHINE (DTM)

**[UPTU B.Tech 2002, 05, 07(co)]**

Mathematically this Turing Machine $M$ consists of 7 tuples.

$$M = (Q, \Sigma, \Gamma, \delta, q_0. \#, F)$$

where

1. $Q$ is a finite non empty set of states.
2. $\Sigma$ is a non empty set of input symbols and does not contain black symbol *i.e.*, #.
3. $\Gamma$ is a finite non empty set of tape symbols and have black symbol *i.e.*, # or $(\Sigma \cup \#)$ or input symbols with #.
4. $\delta$ is a transition system mapping state with tape symbol to tape symbol with movement of the head *i.e.*, $Q \times \Gamma \rightarrow 2^Q \times \Gamma \times (L, R)$.
5. $q_0$ is the initial state, $q_0 \in Q$.
6. # is a blank symbol.
7. $F$ is the set of final states, $F \subseteq Q$.

## 7.4 REPRESENTATION OF TURING MACHINE

The Turing machine can be represented by following three different techniques.

(1) Instantaneous Descriptions (ID) using move relation

(2) Transition Table

(3) Transition Diagram

### (1) Instantaneous Descriptions (ID) using move relation

An Instantaneous Descriptions (ID) of turing machine is in the form af string *xyz,* where *x* is the sub-string at input string *y* is the present state of Turing machine *M* and *z* is also a sub-string of input string and first symbol of *z* contains the current symbol of Read/Write (R/W) head,

For example, let us consider a string *abc defgh* over input alphabet $\Sigma = \{a, b, c, d, e, f, g, h\}$ and let the present state be $q_2$ and the present symbol under read/write head is *d*. Then the instantaneous description of this string is graphically represented as follows:

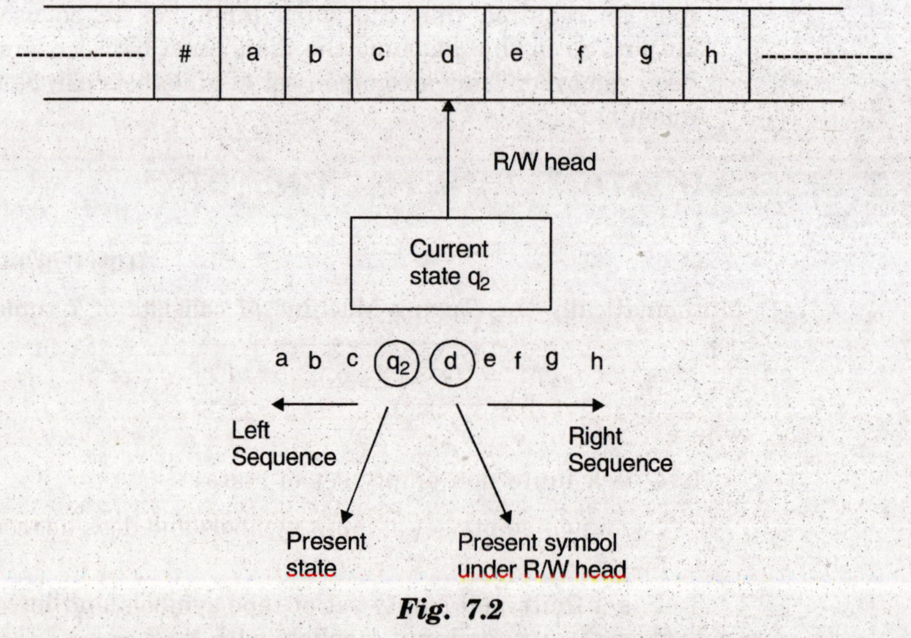


***Fig. 7.2***

The blank symbol may occur as part af the left or right substring.

**Moves in a Turing Machine:** Moves in a Turing Machine occurs under the following two rules:

(*i*) If the transition function $\delta\ (q, a_i) = (q_1, b, R)$ in the input string

$$a_1\, a_2\, a_3\, \ldots\, a_{i-1}\, a_i\, a_{i+1}\, a_{i+2}\, \ldots\, a_n$$

and the present state is $q$ and the present symbol under read/write head is $a_i$. Then the instantaneous description before processing $a_i$ is

$$a_1\, a_2\, a_3\, \dots\, a_{i-1}\, a_i\, a_{i+1}\, a_{i+2}\, \dots\, a_n$$

and after processing $a_i$ is

$$a_1\, a_2\, a_3\, \dots\, a_{i-1}\, b\, q_1\, a_i a_{i+1}\, a_{i+2}\, \dots\, a_n$$

(*ii*) If the transition function $\delta(q, a_i) = (q_1, b, L)$ in the input string

$$a_1\, a_2\, a_3\, \dots\, a_{i-1}\, a_i\, a_{i+1}\, a_{i+2}\, \dots\, a_n$$

and the present state is $q$ and the present symbol under read/write head is $a_i$. Then the instantaneous description before processing $a_i$ is

$$a_1\, a_2\, a_3\, \dots\, a_{i-1}\, qa_i\, a_{i+1}\, a_{i+2}\, \dots\, a_n$$

and after processing $a_i$ is

$$a_1 a_2 a_3\, \dots\, a_{i-2}\, q_1 a_{i-1}\, b\, a_{i+1}\, a_{i+2}\, \dots\, a_n$$

## (2) Transition Table

If we define a transition system $\delta$ is form of table, then that representation is called a transition table.

If $\delta(q, a) = (z, x, y)$, we write *xyz* under column and $q$ row. So if we get *xyz* in the table, if means that $x$ is written in the current cell, $y$ gives the movement of the head ($L$ or $R$) and $z$ denotes the new state into the turina machine enters.

For example; Let us consider a TM with five states $q_0$, $q_1$, $q_2$, $q_3$, $q_4$ where $q_0$ is as initial as well as final state. The tape symbols are $a$, $b$ and #. Then the transition table $\delta$ is defined as follows:

| Present State | Tape Symbols | | |
|---|---|---|---|
| | $a$ | $b$ | # |
| $\to q_0$ | $bRq_1$ | $aRq_2$ | $\#Rq_0$ |
| $q_1$ | $bRq_0$ | $aRq_3$ | $\#Rq_4$ |
| $q_2$ | $bRq_3$ | $aRq_0$ | $\#Rq_4$ |
| $q_3$ | $bRq_2$ | $aRq_1$ | $\#Rq_4$ |
| ($q_4$) | — | — | $\#Rq_4$ |

**Table 7.1**

This *TM* is converting all even number of either *a's* or *b's* or both *a's* and *b's* into even number of *b's* or *a's* or *b's* and *a's* respectively.

## (3) Transition Diagram

In some sitvations, grophiclal representation of the next move partial function $\delta$ af Turing machine may given better idea af the behaviour at TM in comparsion to the tabular representation at $\delta$.

In this representation, the states are represented by vertices and transition of states are represented by directed edges. These directed edges with labels are in the form of $(x, y, z)$, where $x, y \in \Gamma$ and $z \in (L, R)$.

For example, if there is a function $\delta(q_i, x) = (q_j, y, z)$ then this function can be graphically represented as follows:

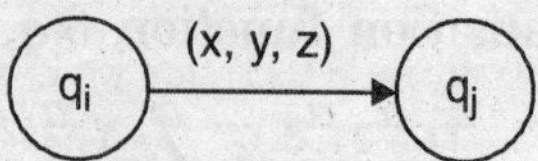


The transition system of a turing machine defined as 5-tuple $(q_i, x, y, z, q_j)$ where $q_i$ be the present state x be the current symbole under R/W head, Y be the replaced symbol, Z be the direction af head movement ad $q_j$ be the next state.

Thus each Turing machine can be described by a callection of 5-tuples repreenting all the directed edges.

For example; The transition digraph of a transition table of above is shown in Fig. 7.5

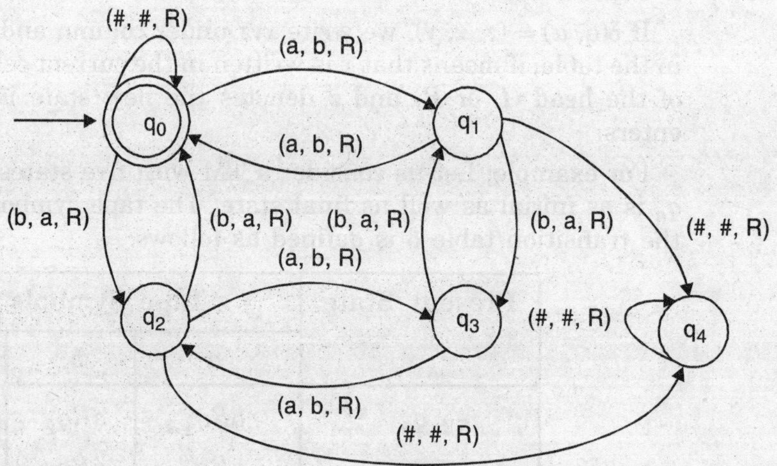


*Fig.* 7.5

**Example7.1:** Construct a Transition table and Transition diagram af Turing machine that accepts the language at the string which contain aba as a substring.

**Solution:** Let Turing machine

$$TM = (a, \Sigma, \Gamma, \delta, q_0, \#, F)$$

$$\Sigma = \{a, b\}$$

$$\Gamma = \{a, b, \#\}$$

$$Q = (q_0, q_1, q_2, q_3\}$$

$q_0$ is intal state and $q_3$ is final state.

and δ is defined as follows:

| Present state | tape symbols | | |
|---|---|---|---|
| | a | b | # |
| $\rightarrow q_0$ | $(q_1, a, L)$ | $(q_0, b, L)$ | * |
| $q_1$ | $(q_1, a, L)$ | $(q_2, b, L)$ | * |
| $q_2$ | $(q_1, a, L)$ | $(q_0, b, L)$ | $(q_3, \#, N)$ |
| $q_3$ | * | * | Accept |

**Table 7.2**

Here * is for undefined move.

Now we can construct the transition diagram as follows.

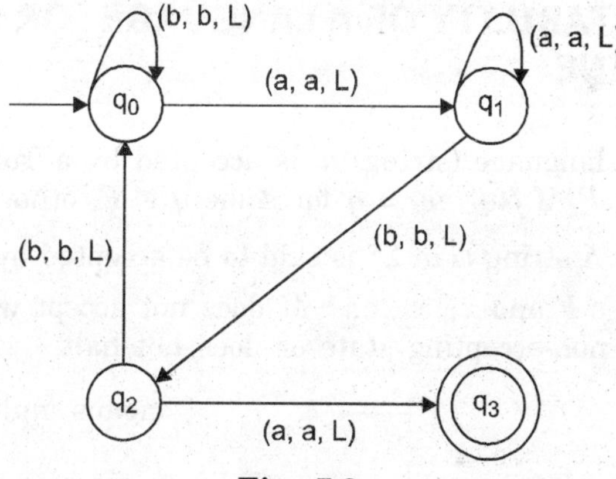


***Fig. 7.3***

**Example 7.2:** Construct a transition table and transition diagram of TM that recognized the language of all strings of even length over alphabetn {a, b}.

**Solution:** Let

$$TM = \{Q, \Sigma, \Gamma, \delta, q_0, \#, F\}$$
$$\Sigma = \{a, b\}$$
$$\Gamma = \{a, b, \#\}$$
$$Q = \{q_0, q_{10}\}$$

So, δ is define as

| Present state | tape symbols | | |
|---|---|---|---|
| | a | b | # |
| $\rightarrow q_0$ | $(q_1, a, L)$ | $(q_1, b, L)$ | (H, #, N) |
| $q_1$ | $(q_0, a, L)$ | $(q_0, b, L)$ | * |
| $H$ | * | * | Accept |

**Table 7.3**

Here H is half state when machine halfs after accepting the language $q_0$ is inifial state. We can construct the transition diagram as follows.

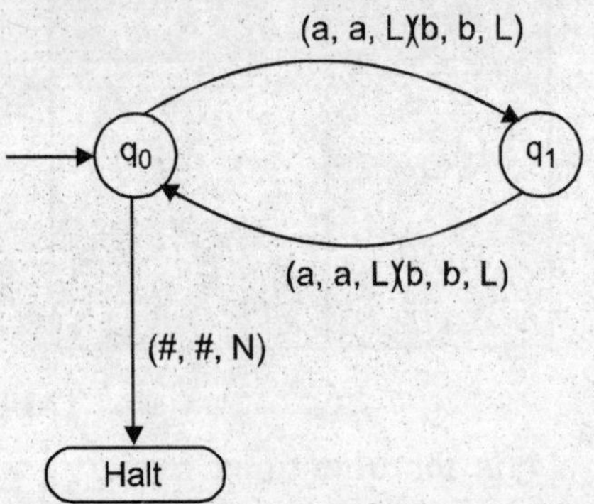


## 7.5 ACCEPTABILITY OF A LANGUAGE (OR STRING) BY TURING MACHINE

A language (string) $w$ is accepted by a Turing Machine $M = (Q, \Sigma, \Gamma, \delta, q_0, \#, F)$ if $\delta(q_0, w) = q$ for some $q \in F$, otherwise $w$ is not accepted by $TM$.

A string ω in Σ* is said to be accepted by m if $q_0\, w \overset{*}{\vdash} x_1\, P\, x_2$ for some $P \varepsilon F$ and $x_1, x_2, \varepsilon \Gamma^*$ $M$ does not accept w if the machine M either halts in a non-accepting state or does not halt.

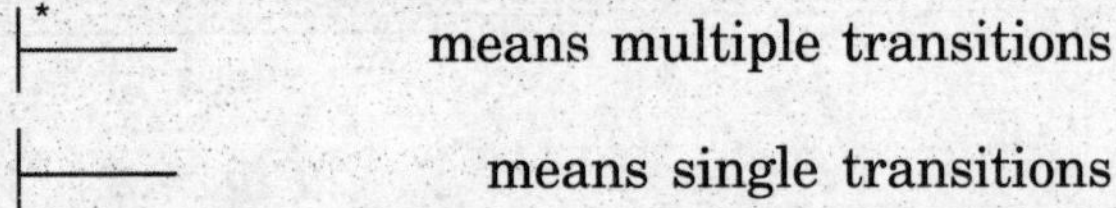

$\overset{*}{\vdash}$ means multiple transitions

$\vdash$ means single transitions

So, a turing machine is said to accept a language when it starts with initial state and input string and after processing that it reaches to the final state.

**Example 7.3:** Consider *a TM M*, whose transition digraph is shown in Fig. 6.2. Describe the acceptability of languages (*a*) 0101111, (*b*) 01011 using instantaneous description.

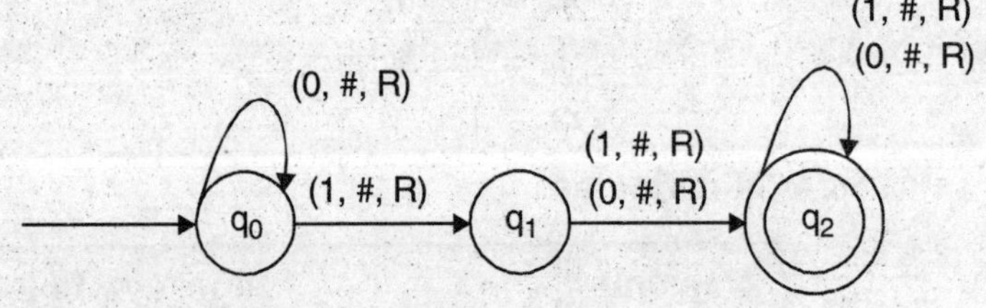


***Fig. 7.6***

**Solution:** (*a*) The initial state is $q_0$ and the current input symbol is 0 *i.e.*, the first input symbol of the given string. So, *ID* of representation is

$\# \ q_0 \ \underline{0}101111 \ \# \vdash \# \ 1 \ 0 \ 1111 \ \# \vdash \# \ \# \ q_1 \ \underline{0}1111 \ \# \vdash \# \ \# \ \#$

$q_2 \ \underline{1}111 \ \# \vdash \# \ \# \ \# \ \# \ q_2 \ \underline{1}11 \ \# \vdash \# \ \# \ \# \ \# \ \# \ q_2 \ \underline{1}1 \ \# \vdash \# \ \# \ \# \ \# \ \# \ \# \ q_2 \vdash \underline{1}$ $\# \vdash \# \ \# \ \# \ \# \ \# \ \# \ \# \ q_2 \ \#$

Since the state $q_2$ is a final state. Hence the language 01011 is accepted by a *TM*.

(*b*) The initial state is $q_0$ and the current input symbol is *i.e.*, the input symbol of the given string. So *ID* of representation is

$\# \ q_0 \ \underline{0}1011 \ \# \vdash \# \ q_0 \ \underline{1}011 \ \# \vdash \# \ \# \ q_1 \ \underline{0}11 \ \# \vdash \# \ \# \ \# \ q_2 \ \underline{1}1 \ \# \vdash \# \ \# \ \# \ \# \ \# \ q_2 \ \#$

Since the state $q_2$ is a final state. Hence the language 01011 is accepted by a *TM*.

**Example 7.4:** Consider a *TM M*, whose transition digraph is shown in Fig. 7.7. Describe the acceptability of a language (*a*) *aabb* and (*b*) *aabbb* using instantaneous description.

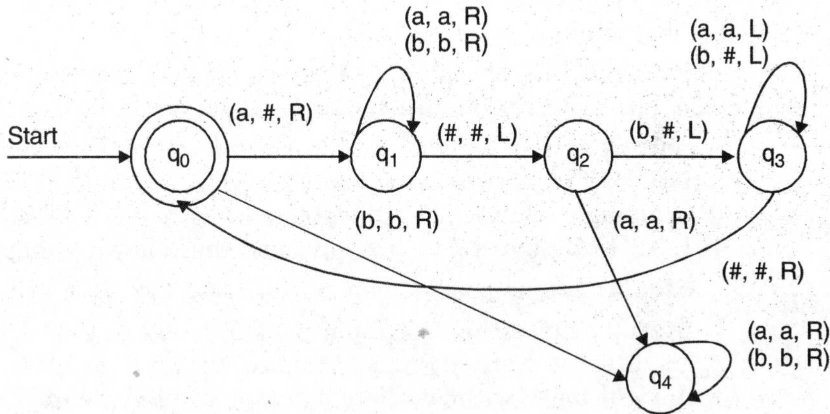


***Fig. 7.7***

**Solution:** (*a*) The initial state is $q_0$ and the current input symbol is a *i.e.*, the first input symbol of the given string. So, *ID* of representation is

$\# \ \# \ q_0 \ \underline{a} \ a \ b \ b \ \# \ \# \vdash \# \ \# \ \# \ q_1 \ \underline{a} \ b \ b \ \# \ \# \vdash \# \ \# \ \# \ a \ q_1 \ \underline{b} \ b \ \# \ \# \vdash \# \ \# \ \# \ a \ b \ q_1 \ \underline{b} \ \# \ \# \vdash \# \ \# \ \# \ a \ b \ b \ q_1 \ \underline{\#} \ \#$

$\vdash \# \ \# \ \# \ a \ b \ q_2 \ \underline{\#} \ \# \vdash \# \ \# \ \# \ a \ q_3 \ \underline{b} \ \# \ \# \ \# \vdash \# \ \# \ \# \ q_3 \ a \ b \ \# \ \# \ \# \vdash \#\#\#q_3 \_\#ab\#\#\# \vdash \# \ \# \ \# \ q_0 \ a \ b \ \# \ \# \ \#$

$\vdash \# \ \# \ \# \ \# \ q_1 \ b \ \# \ \# \ \# \vdash \# \ \# \ \# \ \# \ b \ q_1 \ \# \ \# \ \# \vdash \# \ \# \ \# \ \# \ q_2 \ b \ \# \ \# \ \# \vdash \# \ \# \ \# \ q_3 \ \# \ \# \ \# \ \# \ \# \vdash \# \ \# \ \# \ \# \ q_0 \ \# \ \# \ \# \ \#$

Here program will halt on state $q_0$. Since $q_0$ is a final state, so string is accepted by *TM*.

(*b*) The initial state is $q_0$ and the current input symbol is a *i.e.*, the first input symbol of the given string. So, *ID* of representation is

$\# \ \# \ q_0 \ \underline{a} \ a \ b \ b \ b \ \# \ \# \vdash \# \ \# \ \# \ q_1 \ \underline{a} \ b \ b \ b \ \# \ \# \vdash \# \ \# \ \# \ a \ q_1 \ b \ b \ b \ \# \ \# \vdash \# \ \# \ \# \ a \ b \ q_1 \ \underline{b} \ b \ \# \ \#$

$\vdash \# \ \# \ \# \ a \ b \ b \ q_1 \ b \ \# \ \# \vdash \# \ \# \ \# \ a \ b \ b \ b \ q_1 \ \# \ \# \vdash \# \ \# \ \# \ a \ b \ b \ q_2 \ b \ \# \ \# \vdash \# \ \# \ \# \ a \ b \ q_3 \ \underline{b} \ \# \ \# \ \#$

$\vdash \# \ \# \ \# \ a \ q_3 \ \underline{b} \ b \ \# \ \# \ \# \vdash \# \ \# \ \# \ q_3 \ \# \ a \ b \ b \ \# \ \# \ \# \vdash \# \ \# \ \# \ q_0 \ a \ b \ b \ \# \ \# \ \# \vdash \# \ \# \ \# \ \# \ q_1 \ b \ b \ \# \ \# \ \#$

$\vdash \# \# \# \# b q_1 \# \# \# \vdash \# \# \# \# b q_2 \underline{b} \# \# \# \vdash \# \# \# \# q_3 b \# \# \# \# \vdash \# \# \# q_3 \# b \# \# \# \#$

$\vdash \# \# \# \# q_0 \underline{b} \# \# \# \# \vdash \# \# \# \# b q_4 \# \# \# \#$

Here program will halt on state $q_4$. Since $q_4$ is a non-final state, so string is not accepted by *TM*.

## 7.6 TO DESIGN A TURING MACHINE

The basic guideline for designing a Turing machine are as follows:

(*i*) The read write head must know, what to do in future when they are scanning a symbol from a given string. Also machine must remember, what was the past symbol scanned.

(*ii*) The number of states must be minimized.

**Example 7.5:** Design a DTM machine that accept all language (or strings) that have exactly one 0 over input alphabet $\Sigma = \{0, 1\}$.

**Solution:** The language contains exactly one letter of 0 and the other letters may be only 1's of any order and of any length either before 0 or after 0 including $\in$. So the set of language looks like as follows {0, 10, 01, 110, 011, 101,...}. To design a TM machine use the following steps.

**Step 1:** Let us consider an initial state *i.e.*, $q_0$.

**Step 2 :** Since the first input symbol is either 0 or 1, then on initial state $q_0$ (or present state $q_0$) and on input symbol 0 consider the next state is $q_1$ with right move without changing its symbol *i.e.*, $\delta(q_0, 0) = (q_1, 0, R)$ and on initial state $q_0$ (or present state $q_0$) and on input symbol 1 the state will not change and R/W head will move right without changing its symbol *i.e.*, $\delta(q_0, 1) = (q_1, 1, R)$.

**Step 3:** On state $q_1$ the input symbol may be anyone *i.e.*, either 0 or 1. If input symbol is 1 then the next state will not change and R/W head will move right without changing its symbol *i.e.*, $\delta(q_1, 1) = (q_1, 1, R)$ which is a final state.

**Step 4:** On final state $q_1$, if input symbol is 0 the string will not be accepted by *TM* as the string to be accepted contains one 0 only. The transition digraph is shown in Fig. 6.4

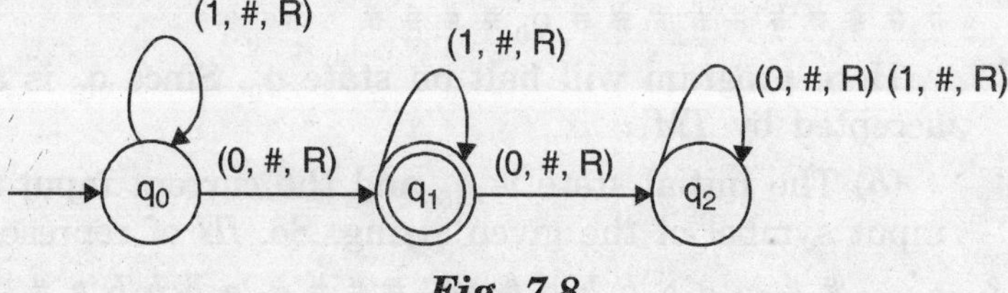


*Fig. 7.8*

This transition digraph contain all seven tuples values of a *TM* machine *i.e.*, $(Q, \Sigma, \Gamma, \delta, q_0, \#, F)$.

So a *TM* machine is $(\{q_0, q_1, q_2\}, \{0, 1\}, \{0, 1, \#\}\ \delta, q_0, \#, \{q_1\})$ where $\delta$ is shown in Fig. 7.8

**Example 7.6:** Design a *DTM* machine for the language $L = \{0w0 : w \in \{0, 1\}^*\}$.

**Solution:** The language contains first and last letter as 0 and intermediate letters may be of any order of 0's and 1's and of any length including $\in$ *i.e.*, the set of language look like as follows {00, 000, 010, 0000, 0010, 0100, 0110,...}. The design a TM machine use the following steps.

**Step 1:** Let us consider an initial state *i.e.*, $q_0$.

**Step 2:** Since the first input symbol is 0 then on initial state $q_0$ (or present state $q_0$) and on input symbol 0 the next state is $q_1$ with right move with changing its symbol 0 to # *i.e.*, $\delta(q_0, 0) = (q_1, \#, R)$.

**Step 3:** On state $q_1$ the input symbol may be anyone *i.e.*, either 0 or 1 of any order and of any length. If input symbol is 0 then the next state is $q_2$ with right move with changing its symbol 0 to # *i.e.*, $\delta(q_1, 0) = (q_2, \#, R)$ which is a final state and if input symbol is 1 the next state is $q_1$ with right move by changing its symbol 1 to # because 1 may be of any length.

It is written as $\delta(q_1, 1) = (q_1, \#, R)$.

**Step 4:** On state $q_2$ if input symbol is 0 then the next state will not change by right move with changing its symbol 0 to #, but if input symbol is 1 then next state is $q_1$ by right move with changing its symbol 1 to #.

**Step 5:** On initial state $q_0$ if input symbol is 1 the string will not be accepted by TM.

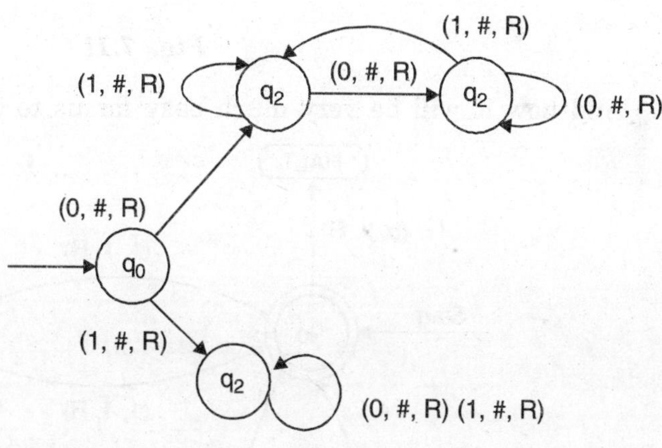


***Fig. 7.9***

The transition digraph is shown in Fig. 7.9. This transition digraph contain all seven tuples value of a *TM* machine *i.e.*, $(Q, \Sigma, \Gamma, \delta, q_0, \#, F)$. So a TM machine is $(\{q_0, q_1, q_2, q_3\}, \{0, 1\}, \{0, 1, \#\}, \delta, q_0, \#, \{q_3\})$ where $\delta$ is shown in Fig. 7.9.

**Example 7.7:** Design a *NDTM* machine that accepts all strings ending with *aa* over input symbol $\Sigma = \{a, b\}$.

**Solution:** The transition diagram of *NDTM* machine $\delta$ is shown in Fig. 7.10.

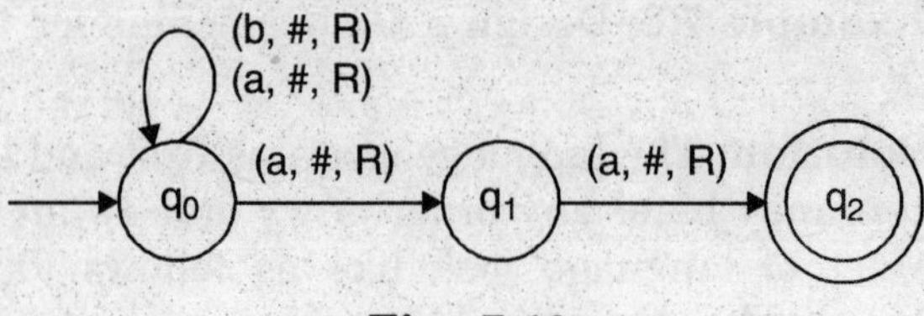


*Fig. 7.10*

**Example 7.8:** Construct a TM for the language of even number of 1's and even number of 0's over $\Sigma = \{0, 1\}$.**[UPTU B.Tech 2004 (co)]**

**Solution:** For this type of problem given we have drawn FSM.

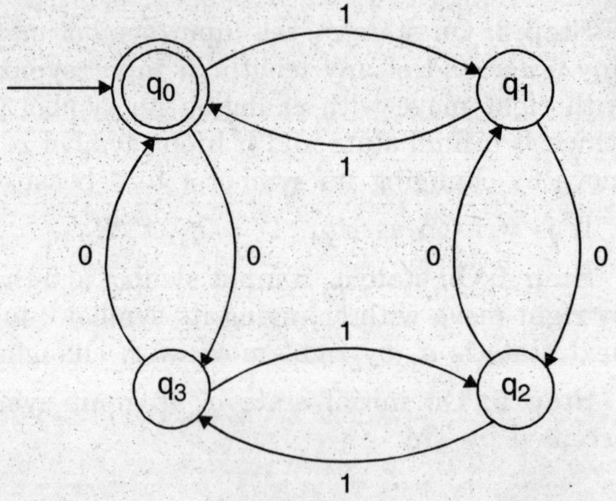


*Fig. 7.11*

And now it will be very much easy for us to convert this FSM to TM.

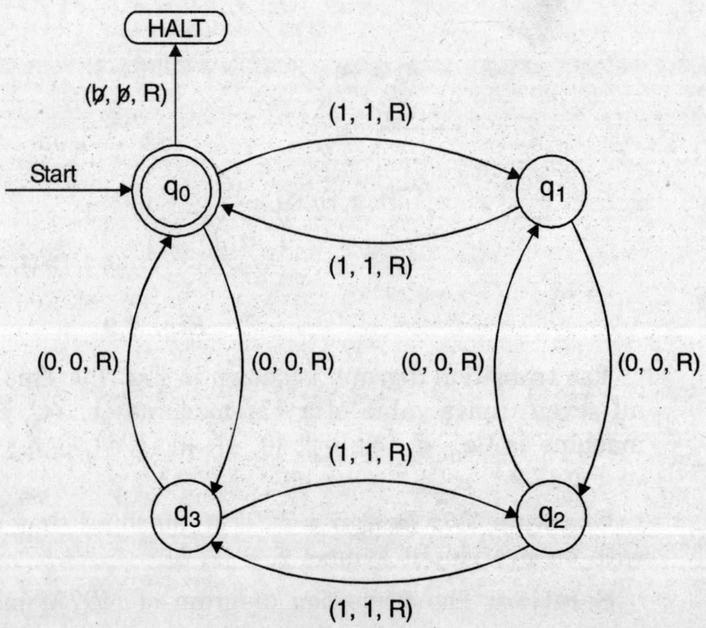


*Fig. 7.12*

**Example 7.9:** Construct TM for language consisting of trings having any number of 0's and only even number of 1's over the input set S = {0, 1}.

**Solution:** The number of zero's can be but the even number of 1's but the even number of 1's are to be allowed.

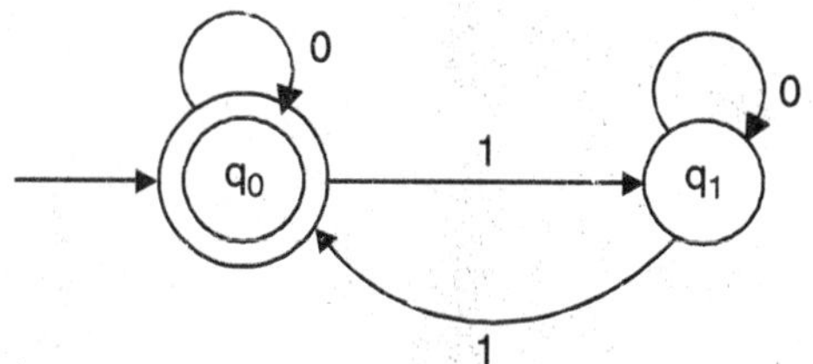


***Fig. 7.13 FSM for even number of 1's***

The same idea can be used to draw TM. We always assume that at the end at input # is placed.

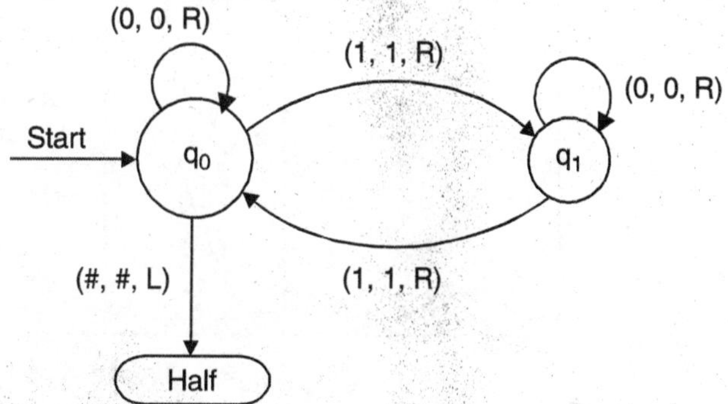


***Fig. 7.14***

**Example 7.10:** Design a *TM* that accept the language

$$\{1^n\ 2^n\ 3^n \mid n \geq 1\}.$$

**Solution:** Before designing the required Turing machine *M*, let us evolve a procedure for processing the input string 112233. After processing, we require the *ID* to be of the form $bbbbbbq_7$. The processing is done by using five steps:

**Step 1:** $q_1$ is the initial state. The $R/W$ head scans the left most 1, replaces 1 by *b*, and moves to the right. *M* enters $q_2$.

**Step 2:** On scanning the left most 2, the $R/W$ head replaces 2 by *b* and moves to the right. *M* enters $q_3$.

**Step 3:** On scanning the left most 3, the $R/W$ heads replaces 3 by *b*, and moves to the right. *M* enters $q_4$.

**Step 4:** After scanning the right most 3, the $R/W$ head moves to the left until it finds the left most 1. As a result, the left most 1, 2 and 3 are replaces by *b*.

**Step 5:** Steps 1 – 4 are repeated until all 1's, 2's and 3's are replaced by blanks.

The change of *IDs* due to processing of 112233 is given as

$q_1 111133 \vdash bq_2 12233 \vdash b1q_2 2233 \vdash b1bq_3 233 \vdash b1b2q_3 33$
$\vdash b1b2bq_4 3 \vdash b1b2q_5 b_3 \vdash b1q_5 2b3 \vdash b1q_5 b2b3 \vdash bq_5 1b2b3$
$\vdash q_6 b1b2b3 \vdash bq_1 1b2b3 \vdash bbq_2 b3b3 \vdash bbbq_2 2b3$
$\vdash bbbbq_3 b3 \vdash bbbbq_3 3 \vdash bbbbbbq_4 b \vdash bbbbbq_7 bb$

Thus,

$$q_1 112233 \overset{*}{\vdash} q_7 bbbbbb$$

As $q_7$ is an accepting state, the input string 1122233 is accepted.

Now we can construct the transition table for *M*. It is given in Table 7.4

| Present | Input tape symbols | | | |
|---|---|---|---|---|
| | 1 | 2 | 3 | 4 |
| $\to q_1$ | $bRq_2$ | | | $bRq_1$ |
| $q_2$ | $IRq_2$ | $bRq_3$ | | $bRq_2$ |
| $q_3$ | | $2Rq_3$ | $bRq_4$ | $bRq_3$ |
| $q_4$ | | | $3Lq_5$ | $bLq_7$ |
| $q_5$ | $1Lq_6$ | $2Lq_5$ | | $bLq_5$ |
| $q_6$ | $1Lq_6$ | | | $bLq_1$ |
| $q_7$ | | | | |

**Table 7.4**

It canbe seen from the table that steingsother than those of the form $0^n$ $1^n$ $2^n$ are not accepted. It is advisable to compute the computation sequence for strings like 1223, 1123, 1233 and then see that these strings are rejected by *M*.

**Example 7.11:** Design a TM to recognise all strings cousisting at even number of 1's.

**Solution:** The construction is made by defining moves in the following manner:

(i) $q_1$ is the initial state. M enters state $q_2$ on scanning 1 and writes b.

(ii) If M is in state $q_2$ and scans 1, it enters $q_1$ and writes b.

(iii) $q_1$ is the only accepting state.

So M accepts a string if it exhausts all input symbols ans finally in stae $q_1$ Symbolically,

$$M = (\{q_1, q_2\}, \{1, b\}, \{1, b\}, d, q_1, b, \{q_1\})$$

Where d is defined by Table 7.5

| Present state | 1 |
|---|---|
| $\to (q_1)$ | $bq_2R$ |
| $q_2$ | $bq_1R$ |

**Table 7.5**

Let us obtain the computation sequence of 11. Thus, $q_1 11 \vdash bq_2 \vdash bbq_1$. As $q_1$ is an accepting state, 11 is accepted. $q_1 111 \vdash bq_2 11 \vdash bbq_1 1 \vdash bbbq_2$. M halts and as $q_2$ is not an accepting state, 111 is not accepted by M.

$$L = \{a^n b^n \{n^2\ 1\}$$

**Example 7.12:** Design a TM that accept the language

$$L = \{a^n b^n c^n \mid n \geq 1\}$$ **[UPTU MCA 2002, B.Tech (co) 2005]**

**Solution:** The transition digraph for this *TM* is shown in Fig. 7.15.

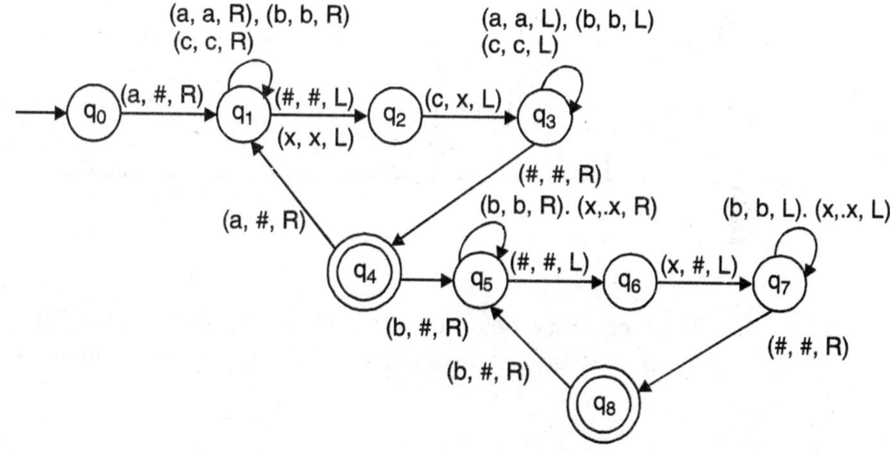


***Fig. 7.15***

**Example 7.13:** Design a *DTM* that concatenates the two strings over input alphabet $\Sigma = \{1\}$. That is, if pair of words $(w_1, w_2)$ is the input string, then the output string is $w_1\ w_2$.

**Solution:** The transition digraph is shown in Fig. 7.16.

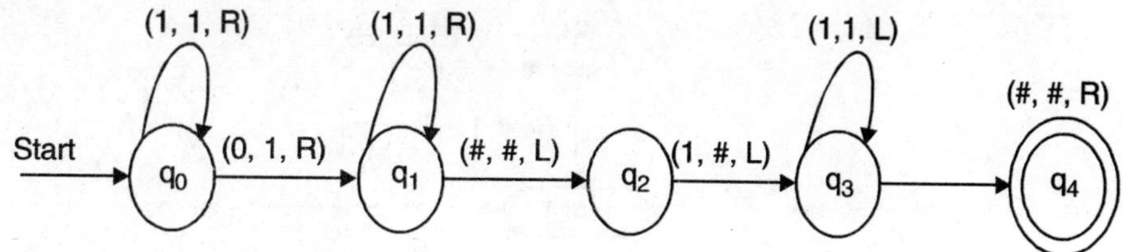


***Fig. 7.16***

**Example 7.14:** Contract TM for the langvage L = {$a^n$ $b^n$} where n £ 1.

**[UPTU B-Tech 2006]**

**Solution:** The construction is made by defining moves in the following manner:

Read out each a mark it by A and then move a head along the input tape and find out the *b* convert it to *B*. Repeat this process for all *a*'as and b's.. If there is some kind of unequality in number of a's and b's the TM will not end up in HALT state.

Let us design the transition table of the same.

| | *a* | *b* | *A* | *B* | # |
|---|---|---|---|---|---|
| $q_0$ | $(q_1, A, R)$ | – | – | $(q_3, B, R)$ | – |
| $q_1$ | $(q_1, a, R)$ | $(q_2, B, L)$ | – | $(q_1, B, R)$ | – |
| $q_2$ | $(q_2, a, L)$ | – | $(q_0, A, R)$ | $(q_2, B, L)$ | – |
| $q_3$ | – | – | – | $(q_3, B, R)$ | $(H, \#, L)$ |
| *H* | – | – | – | – | – |

**Table 7.6**

Thus equality between a's and b's can be checked by moving tape head to and fro. Let us try to design a TM using above logic.

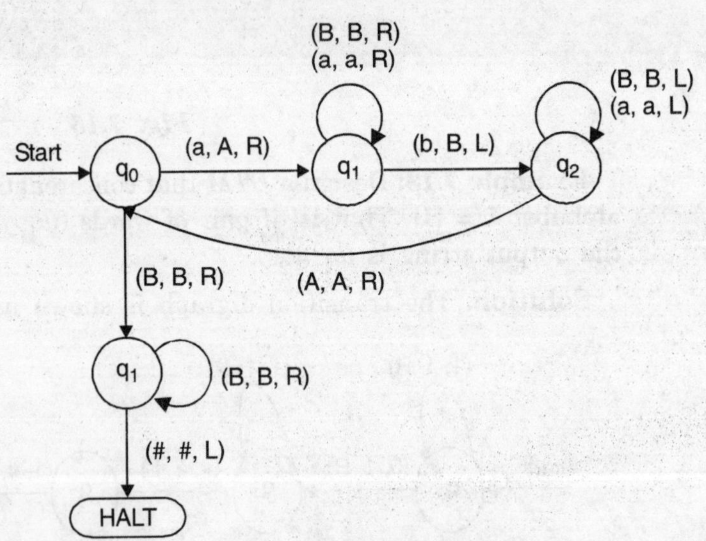


***Fig. 7.17***

**Example 7.15:** Design a *TM* that accept all the language starting with either an even number of 0's or even number of 1'*s* or even number of 0'*s* and 1'*s* both.

**Solution:** The transition digraph for this *TM* is shown in Fig. 7.18.

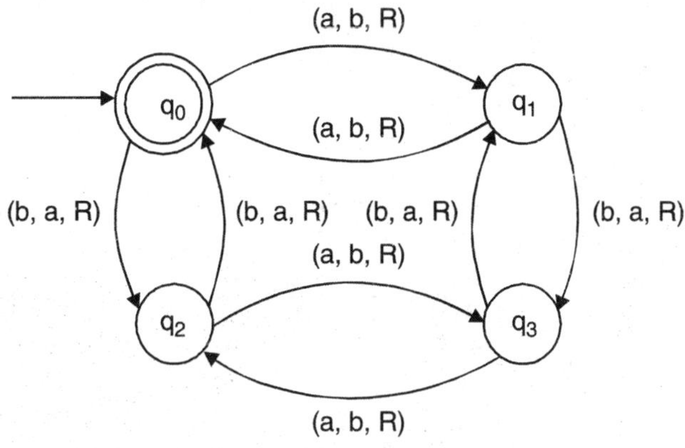


***Fig. 7.18***

**Example 7.16:** Design a *TM* that accept the language

$$L = \{w : w \in \{a, b\}^* \text{ and } n_a(w) = n_b(w)\}$$

**Solution:** The transition digraph for this *TM* is shown in Fig. 7.19

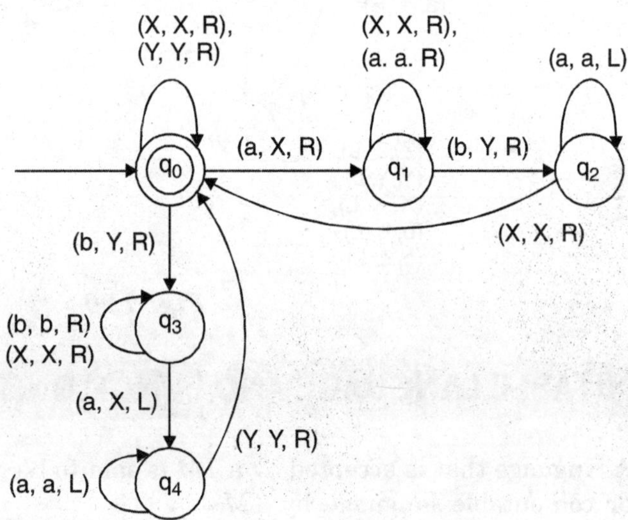


***Fig. 719***

**Example 7.17:** Design a *TM* that accept the language

$$L = \{w : w \in \{a, b, c\}^*$$

and $$n_a(w) = n_b(w) = n_c(w)\}$$

**Solution:** The transition digraph for this *TM* is shown in Fig. 7.20.

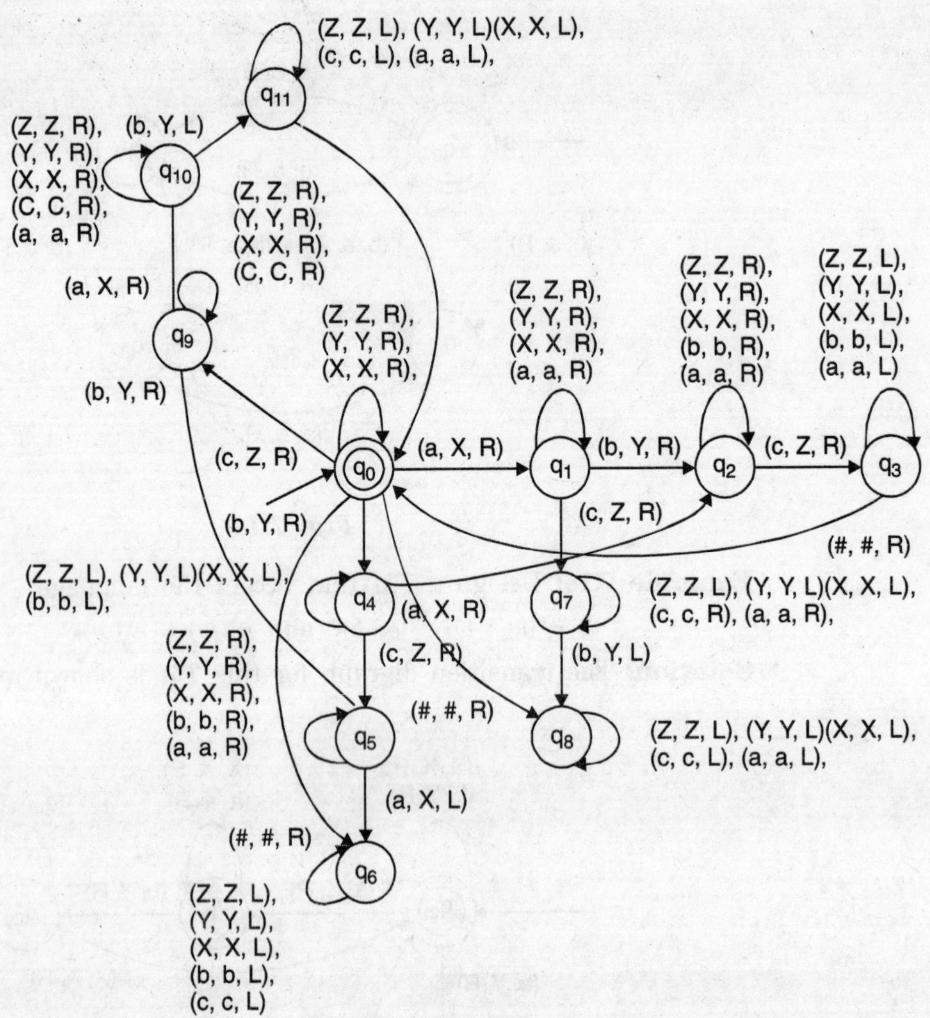


***Fig. 7.20***

## 7.7 COMPUTABLE LANGUAGE AND FUNCTIONS

A language that is accepted by a *TM* is said to be recursively enumerable (*r.e.*) or computable language by *TM*.

**Function:** *TM* may compute different function like one argument function or different functions with two arguments and so on. Also note that if *TM* computes function $f$ of $n$ arguments, then $f$ need not have values for all different $n$ argument for all $i_1, i_2, ..., i_n$.

If $f(i_1, i_2, ... i_n)$ is defined for all $i_1, i_2, ... i_n$ then $f$ is a total recursive function otherwise it is partial recursive function. All the common arithmetic function on integers, such as multiplication, $n!$ etc. are total recursive functions:

**Example 7.18:** Design a Turing machine for function $f(m, n) = m + n$

**Solution:** The given function $f(m, n) = m + n$ where $m$ and $n$ are positive integers over input alphabet $\Sigma$. Here $m$ and $n$ are representing the length of string over input symbols and $m + n$ represent the total length of function.

Since the input symbol of a function is not given, so consider input symbol $\Sigma = \{1, 0\}$ then that function can be explained as follows, where 0 is representing partition of two different strings.

***Fig. 7.21***

In means, if the first string length is m and the second string length is n then the resultant string length of a given function is $m + n$.

The transition digraph is shown in Fig. 7.16

**Example 7.19:** Design a Turing machine for **monus** function *i.e.*,

$$f(m,n) = m - n \quad \text{if } m \geq n. \qquad \text{[UPTU B.Tech (co) 2004]}$$
$$= 0 \quad \text{otherwise}$$

**Solution:** The transition digraph is shown in Fig. 7.22.

We will assume m and n as unary numbers. if $m > n$ then we will have the result of $m–n$ on the input tape. But if $m < n$ then the input tape will contain 0.

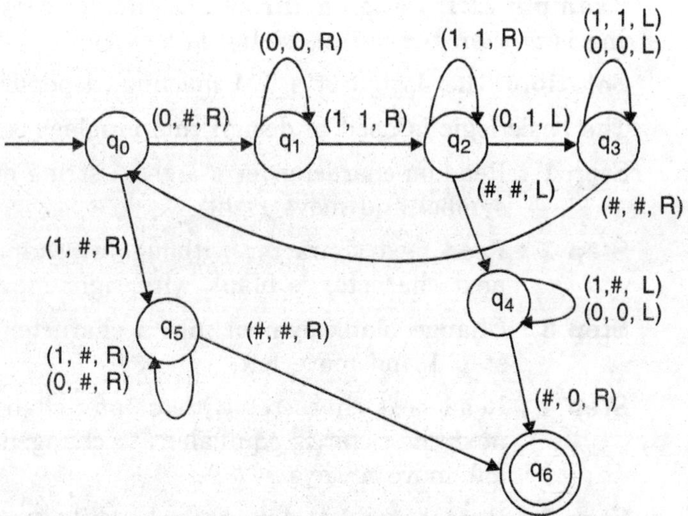


***Fig. 7.22***

**Example 7.20:** Design a *TM* for a language $L = ww^R$ where $w \in \{0, 1\}+$.

**Solution:**

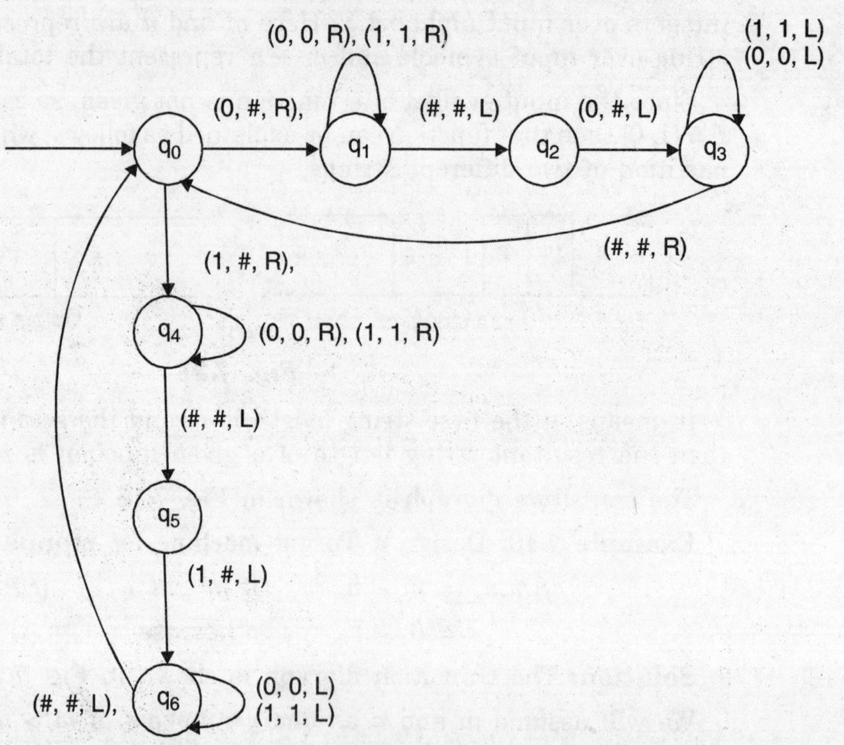


***Fig. 7.23***

**Example 7.21:** Design a Turing machine for copying a string (*i.e.*, if input string is $w$ then the output string is $w\#w$)

**Solution:** The design of a TM machine depends on input symbols $\Sigma$.

The basic logic is used to design this problem is as follows:

**Step 1 :** Read on character form a given string and change it into another symbol and move right.

**Step 2 :** Read next character without any changes recursively while the next character is blank with right move always.

**Step 3 :** Change blank symbol into a character which has been read in step 1 and move left.

**Step 4 :** Read next character without any changes recursively while the next character is equivalent to changed character in step 1 with left move always.

**Step 5 :** Repeat step 1 to 4 recursively while the given string converts into changed symbol.

**Step 6 :** Finally replace all changed symbols into original symbols, which is the final output string. Let us consider the input symbol $\Sigma = \{1\}$ then the transition digraph is shown in Fig. 7.24

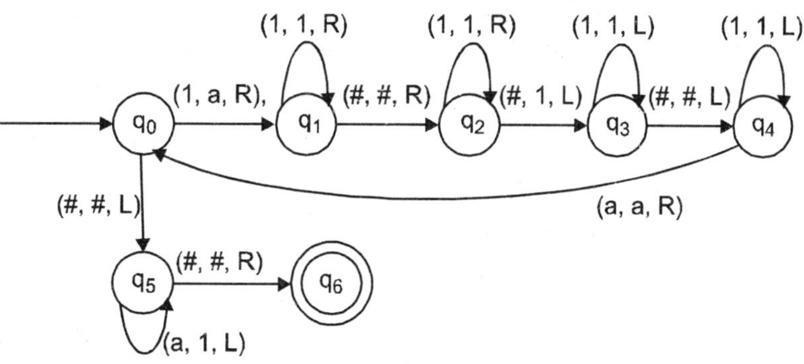


***Fig. 7.24***

The acceptability for $n = 3$ (*i.e.*, 111) is as follows

$\#q_0 111\#\# \vdash \#aq_1 11\#\# \vdash \#a1q_1 1\#\# \vdash \#a11q_1 \#\#$
$\vdash \#a11\#q_2 \# \vdash \#a11q_3 1\#1 \vdash \#a1q_4 1\#1 \vdash \#aq_4 11\#1$
$\vdash \#q_4 a11\#1 \vdash \#aq_0 11\#1 \vdash \#aa1q_1 1\#1 \vdash \#aa1q_1 \#1$
$\vdash \#aa1\#q_2 1\# \vdash \#aa1\#1q_2 \# \vdash \#aa1\#q_3 11 \vdash \#aa1q_3 \#\#$
$\vdash \#aaq_4 1\#11 \vdash \#aq_4 a1\#11 \vdash \#aaq_0 1\#11 \vdash \#aaa1q_1 \#11$
$\vdash \#aaa\#q_2 11 \vdash \#aaa\#1q_2 1 \vdash \#a1q_1 1\#\# \vdash \#aaa\#1q_3 11$
$\vdash \#aaa\#q_3 111 \vdash \#aaaq_3 \#111 \vdash \#aaq_4 a\#111 \vdash \#aaaq_0 \#111$
$\vdash \#aaq_5 a\#111 \vdash \#aq_5 a1\#111 \vdash \#q_5 a11\#111 \vdash q_5 \#111\#111$
$\vdash \#q_6 111\#111$

Let us consider the input symbol $\Sigma = \{0, 1\}$ then the transition digraph is shown in. Fig. 7.25

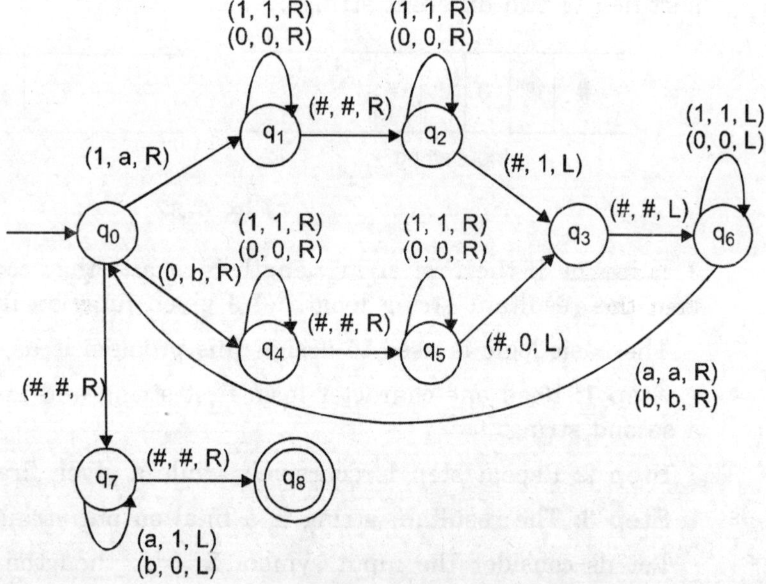


***Fig. 7.25***

Similarly you can design for any number of input symbol.

**Example 7.22:** Construct a *TM* to compute the function $f(w) = w^c$. where $w \in \{0, 1\}^+$ and $w^c$ is complement of $w$. **[UPTU B-Tech 2004]**

**Solution:** To design a *TM* for this function is very simple as shown below.

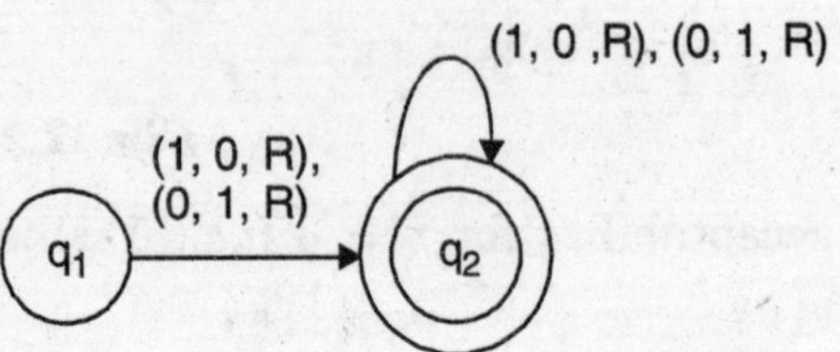


*Fig. 7.26*

**Example 7.23:** Design a Turing machine for multiplication function of two number *i.e.*,

$$f(m, n) = m*n \qquad \text{if } m, n \geq 1.$$

**Solution:** The given function $f(m, n) = m * n$ where $m$ and $n$ are positive integers over input alphabet $\Sigma$.

Here $m$ and $n$ are presenting the length of string over input symbols and $m + n$ represent the total length of function.

Since the input symbol of a function is not given, so consider input symbol $\Sigma = \{1, 0\}$ then that function can be explained as follows, where 0 is representing partition of two different strings.

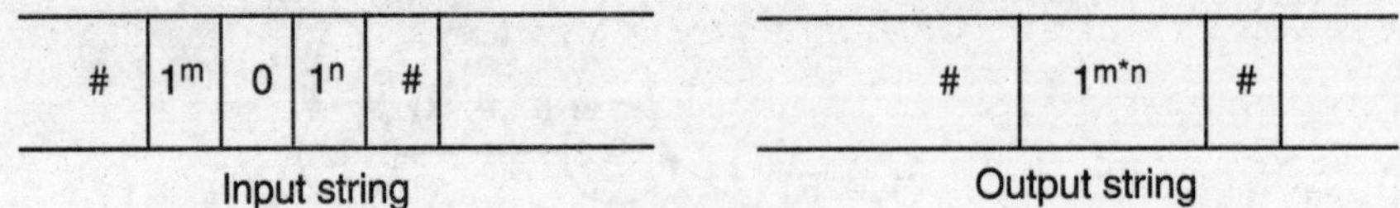


*Fig. 7.27*

It means If the first string length is $m$ and the second string length is $n$ then the resultant string length of a given function is $m * n$.

The basic logic is used to design this problem is as follows

**Step 1:** Read one character form first string and make it blank and copy a second string.

**Step 2:** Repeat step 1 recursively while a given first string is blank.

**Step 3:** The resultant string is a final output string.

Let us consider the input symbol $\Sigma = \{1\}$ then the transition digraph is shown as follows:

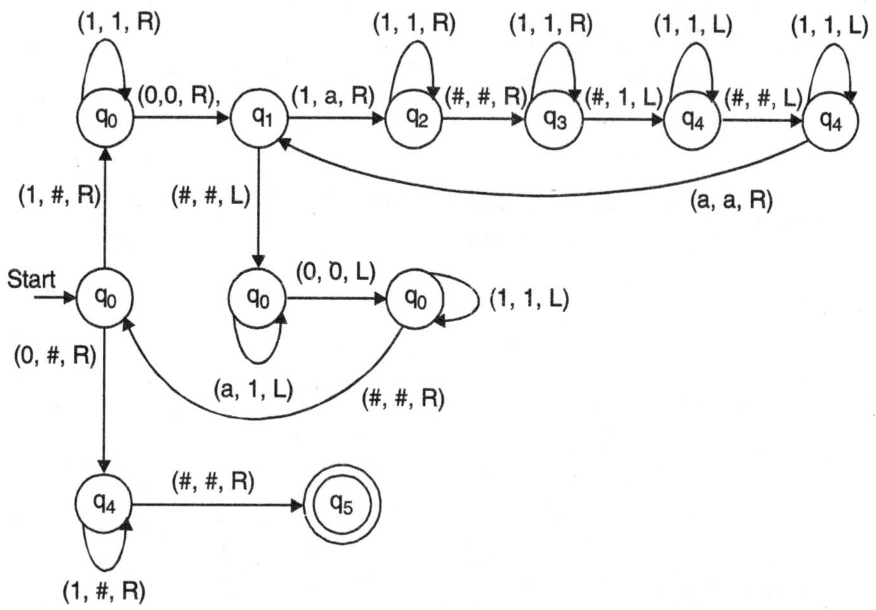


*Fig. 7.28*

**Example 7.24:** Design a Turing machine for multiplication function of any number *i.e.*,

$$f(m, n, k) = m^* \ n^* \ k^* \qquad \text{if } m, n, k \geq 1$$

**Solution:** The given function $f(m, n, k) = m^* \ n^* \ k$ where $m$, $n$ and $k$ are are positive integers over input alphabet $\Sigma$

Here $m$, $n$ and $k$ are representing the length of string over input symbols and $m^* \ n^* \ k$ represent the total length of function.

Since the input symbol of a function is not given, so consider input symbol $\Sigma = \{1, 0\}$ then that function can be explained as follows, where 0 is representing partition of two different strings.

*Fig. 7.29*

It means if the first string length is $m$, the second string length is $n$ and the third string length is $n$ then the resultant string length of a given function is $m^* \ n^* \ k$.

The basic logic is used to design this problem is as follows

**Step 1:** Move the pointer to the first symbol of the second variable from last.

**Step 2:** Use normal multiplication method defined in the previous question.

**Step 3:** Remove the blank between the lengths of two numbers.

**Step 4:** Repeat step 2 and 3 recursively until all zero are removed between the numbers.

**Step 5:** The resultant string is a final output string.

Let us consider the input symbol Σ = {1} then the transition digraph is shown as follows.

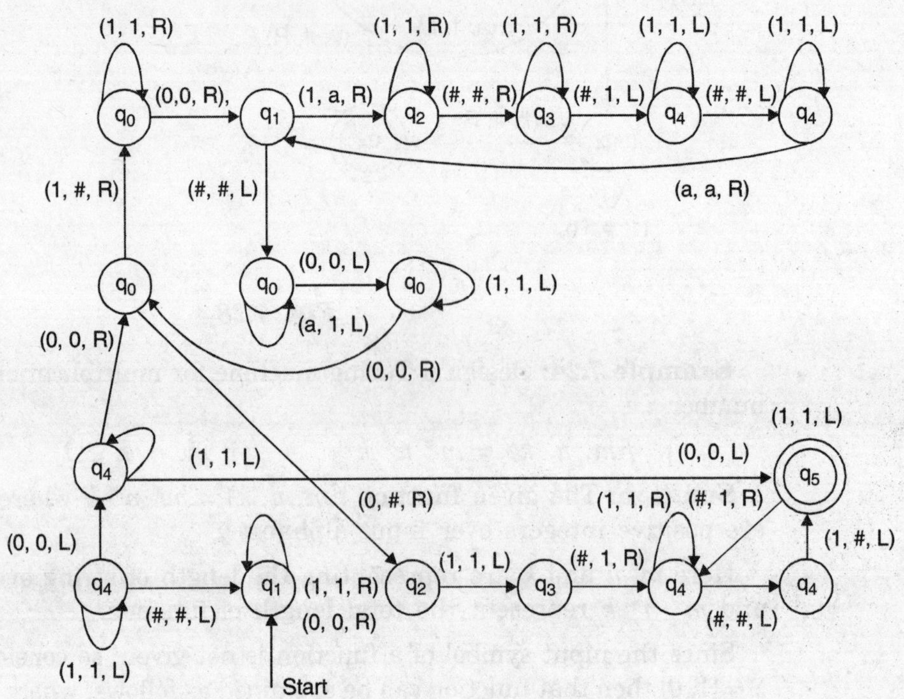


***Fig. 7.30***

---

Since the tape is finite at the left end so it will terminate at left end *i.e.*, on state $q_{17}$

---

**Example 7.25:** Design a Turing machine for perform the following function factorial $(n) = n^*(n - 1)^*(n - 2)^* \ \ldots\ ^*3^*2^*1 \ n \geq 1$.

**Solution:** The given function is factorial ($n$) where $n$ is positive integer over input alphabet Σ.

Here $n$ is representing the length of string over input symbols and factorial $(n)$ is representing the total length of the all multiplication from 1 to $n$.

Since the input symbol of a function is not given, so consider input symbol $\Sigma = \{1\}$ then that function can be explaind as follows, where 0 is representing separation of two different strings.

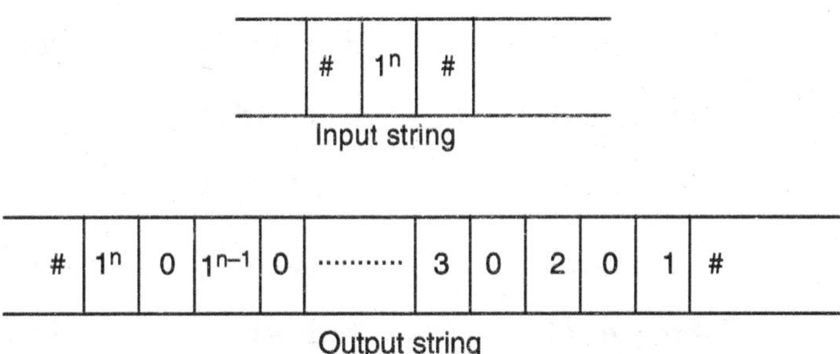


***Fig. 7.31***

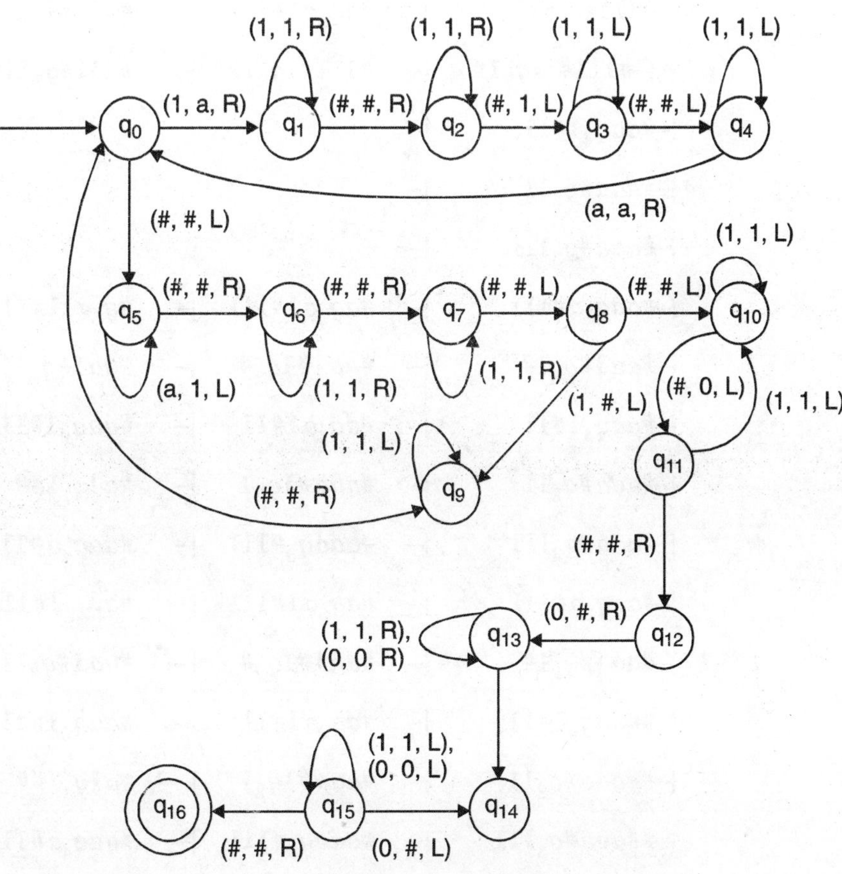


***Fig. 7.32***

Let us consider $n = 3$ then their execution for the string of length 3 (*i.e.*,111) is as follows

$\#q_0 11\#\# \vdash \#aq_1 11\#\# \vdash \#a1q_{11}\#\# \vdash \#a11q_1\#\#$

$\vdash \#a11\#q_2\# \vdash \#a11q_3\#1 \vdash \#a1q_4 1\#1 \vdash \#aq_4 1\#1$

$\vdash \#q_4 a11\#1 \vdash \#aq_0 11\#1 \vdash \#aaq_1 1\#1 \vdash \#aa1q_1\#1$

$\vdash \#aa1\#q_2 1\# \vdash \#aa1\#1q_2\# \vdash \#aa1\#q_3 11 \vdash \#aa1q_3\#11$

$\vdash \#aaq_4 1\#11 \vdash \#aq_4 a1\#11 \vdash \#aaq_0 1\#11 \vdash \#aaaq_1\#11$

$\vdash \#aaa\#q_2 11 \vdash \#aa1\#1q_2\# \vdash \#aa1\#q_3 11 \vdash \#aaa\#1q_3 11$

$\vdash \#aaa\#q_3 111 \vdash \#aq_4 a1\#11 \vdash \#aaq_0 1\#11 \vdash \#aaaq_0\#111$

$\vdash \#aaq_5 a\#111 \vdash \#aaa\#1q_2 1 \vdash \#a1q_1 1\#\# \vdash q_5\#111\#111$

$\vdash \#q_6 111\#111 \vdash \#aaaq_3\#111 \vdash \#11q_6 1\#111 \vdash \#111q_6\#111$

$\vdash \#111\#q_7 111 \vdash \#aq_5 a1\#111 \vdash \#111\#11q_7 1 \vdash \#111\#111q_7\#$

$-.\vdash \#111\#11q_8 1\# \vdash \#111\#1q_9 1\#\# \vdash \#111\#q_9 11\#\# \vdash \#111q_9\#11\#\#$

$\vdash \#aaq_4 1\#11 \vdash$

$\vdash \#aaa\#q_2 11 \vdash$

$\vdash \#aaa\#q_3 111 \vdash$

$\vdash \#aaq_5 a\#111 \vdash \#aq_5 a1\#111 \vdash \#q_5 a11\#111 \vdash q_5\#111\#111$

$\vdash \#aa1\#q_2 1\# \vdash \#aa1\#1q_2\# \vdash \#aa1\#q_3 11 \vdash \#aa1q_3\#\#$

$\vdash \#aaq_4 1\#11 \vdash \#aq_4 a1\#11 \vdash \#aaq_0 1\#11 \vdash \#aaa1q_1\#11$

$\vdash \#aaa\#q_2 11 \vdash \#aaa\#1q_2 1 \vdash \#a1q_1 1\#\# \vdash \#aaa\#1q_3 11$

$\vdash \#aaa\#q_3 111 \vdash \#aaaq_3\#111 \vdash \#aaq_4 a\#111 \vdash \#aaaq_0\#111$

$\vdash \#aaq_5 a\#111 \vdash \#aq_5 a1\#111 \vdash \#q_5 a11\#111 \vdash q_5\#111\#111$

$\vdash \#aa1\#q_2 1\# \vdash \#aa1\#1q_2\# \vdash \#aa1\#q_3 11 \vdash \#aa1q_3\#\#$

$\vdash \#\#aaq_4 1\#11 \vdash \#aq_4 a1\#11 \vdash \#aaq_0 1\#11 \vdash$

$\vdash \#\#aaa\#q_2 11 \vdash \#aaa\#1q_2 1 \vdash \#a1q_1 1\#\# \vdash$

$\vdash \#\#aaa\#q_3 111 \vdash \#aaaq_3\#111 \vdash \#aaq_4 a\#111 \vdash$

$\vdash \#\#q_{16} 11101101\#\#\# \vdash$

**Example 7.26:** Design a Turing machine to calculate the following function

factorial $(n) = n*(n-1)*(n-2)*$ .... $*3*2*1$ $n \geq 1$.

**Solution:** The given factorial $(n)$ function where $n$ is positive integer over input alphabet $\Sigma$.

Here $n$ is representing the length of string over input symbols and factorial $(n)$ is representing the total length of the all multiplication from 1 to $n$.

Since the input symbol of a function is not given, so consider input symbol $\Sigma = \{1\}$ then that function can be explaind as follows, where 0 is representing separation of two different strings.

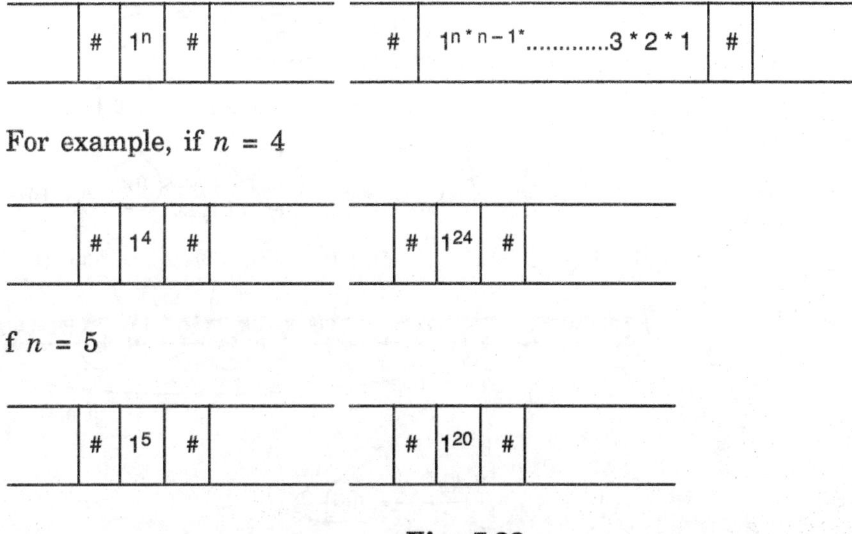


***Fig. 7.33***

The basic logic is used to design this problem is as follows

**Step 1:** Factorize the problem (Explained in Example 7.22

**Step 2:** Multiply the problem (Explained in Example 7.21

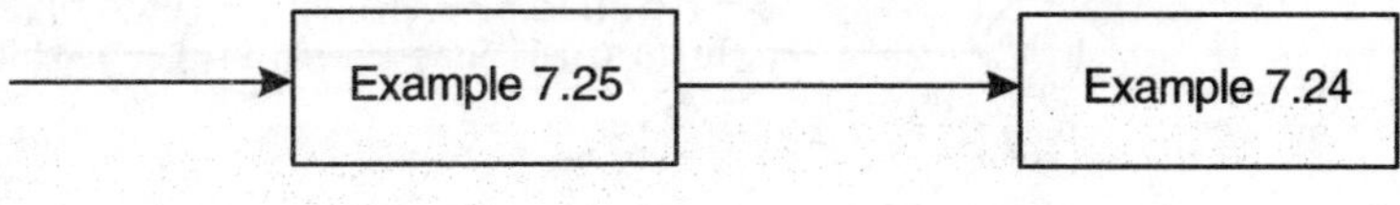


***Fig. 7.34***

The output state of a example 7.25 is used as a input state of a example 7.24.

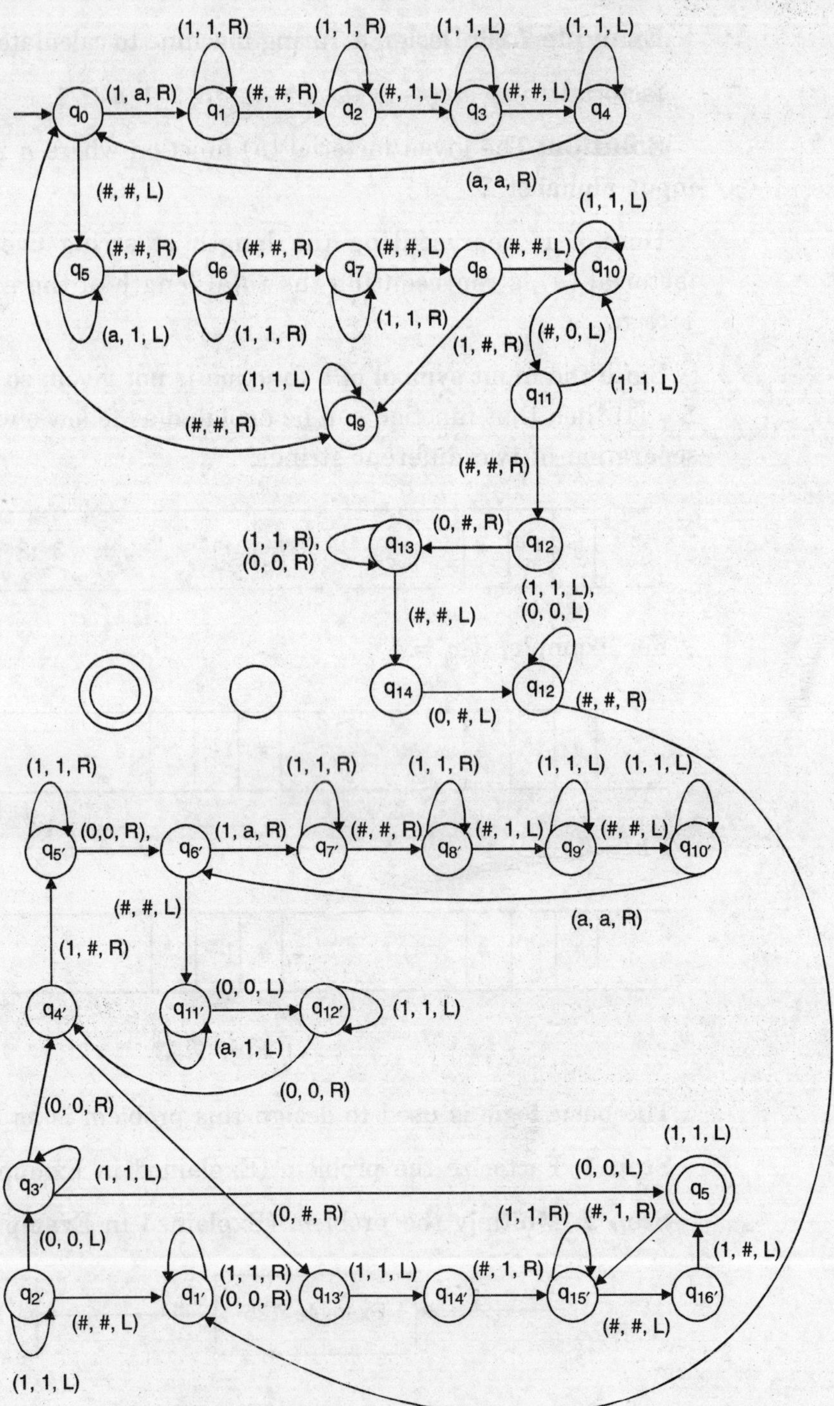


***Fig. 7.35***

**Example 7.27:** Design a Turing to calculate the following function

$$\text{Max } (m, n) = \begin{cases} m & \text{if } m > n \\ n & \text{otherwise} \end{cases}$$

**Solution:** The transition digraph is shown is Fig. 7.36

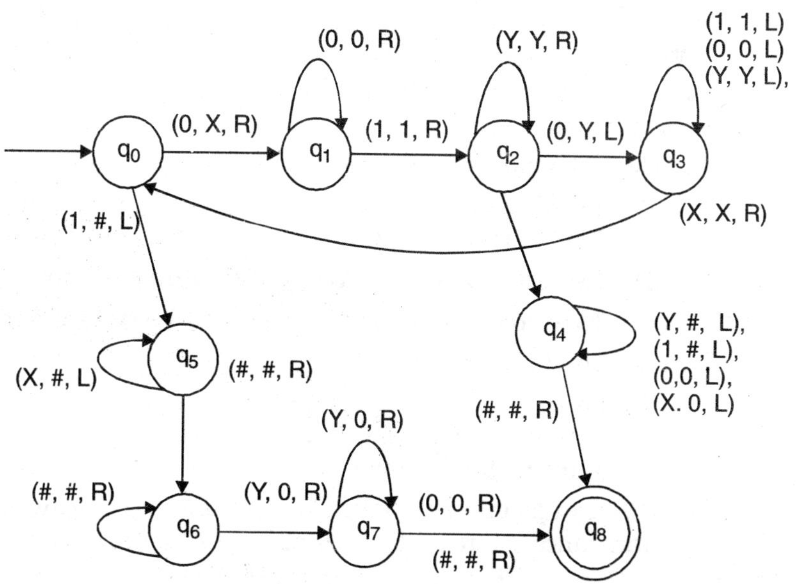


*Fig. 7.36*

**Example 7.28:** Design a Turing to machine to increase binary numbers by one

**Solution:** The transition digraph is shown is Fig. 7.37

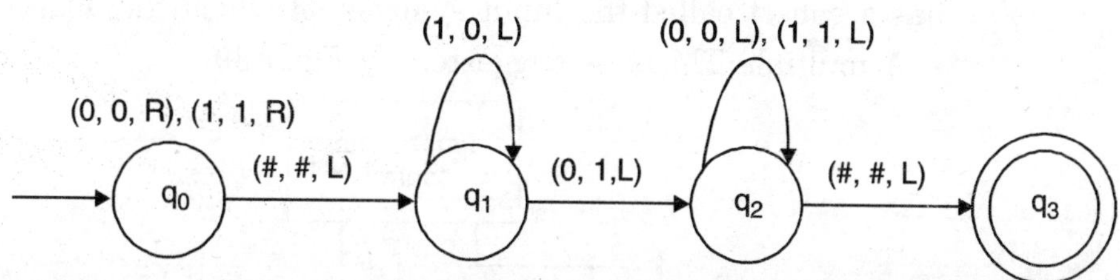


*Fig. 7.37*

**Example 7.29:** Design a Turing to machine to decrease binary numbers by one

**Solution:** The transition digraph is shown is Fig. 7.38

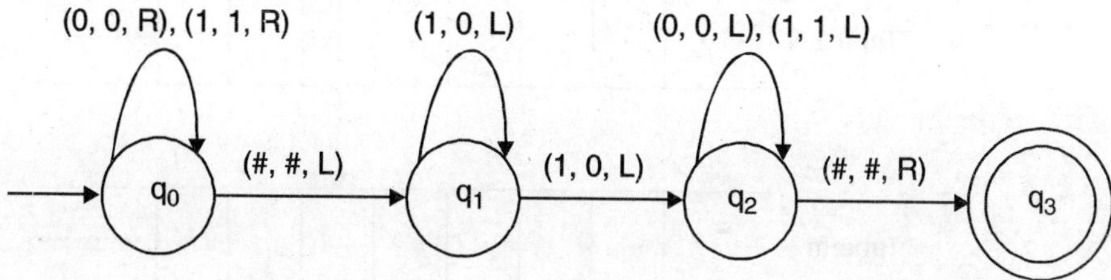


*Fig. 7.38*

## 7.8 EXTENSION TO THE TURING MACHINE

We will now show that there are various ways in which th basic definition of Turing machine can be modified without reducing its power of language recognizing.

The extension of trying machine considered are:

(1) There may be various tapes instead of one only, each tape having its own independent head.

(2) The tap may be allowed to be infinite in both the direction.

(3) There may be more than one head scanning various calls of the tape.

(4) The tape may be m-dimensional, $m \geq 2$, instead of only one-diemension.

(5) For a given pair of current state and symbol, under the head, instead of almost one possible move, there may be any finite, possible zero, number, of next moves.

This extension also makes "Programming" Turing machine easier in some circumstances, but adds no language defining power to the basic model.

### 7.8.1 Multitape Turing Machines

The device has a finite control, and some finite number of tapes. Each tape is divided into cells, and each cell can hold any symbol of the finite tape alphabet.

As in the single tape TM, the set as tape symbols includes a blank (#), and has a subset called the input symbols, of which the; blank is not a member.

A multiple TM is as suggested by Fig 7.39.

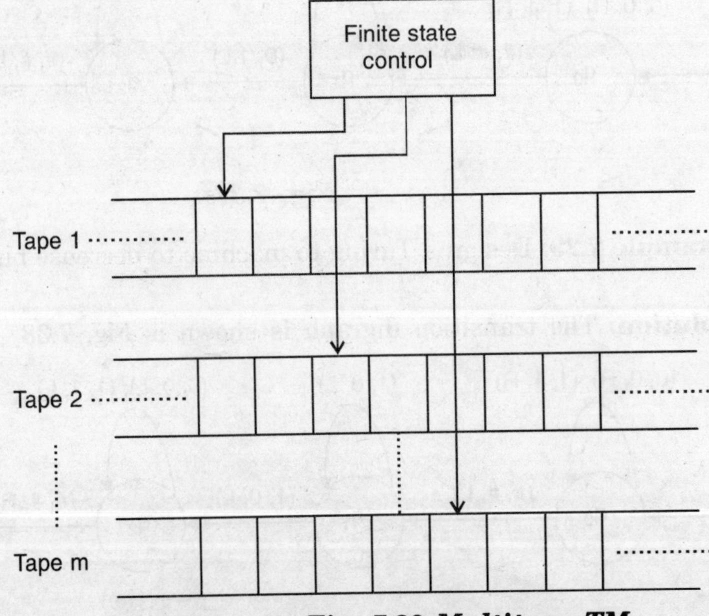


*Fig. 7.39 Multitape TM*

The set of states includes an initial state and some accepting states initially;

→ The input, a finite sequence of input symbols is placed on the first tape.

→ All others calls of all the tapes hold the blank.

→ The finite control is in the initial state.

→ The head of the first tape is at the left end of the input.

→ All other tape heads are at some arbitrary cell.

A move of the multiple TM depends on the state and the symbol scanned by each of the tape heads. In one move, the multitape TM does the followings:

→ The control enters a new state ,which could be the same as the previous state.

→ On each of new tape heads makes a move, which can be either left, right or stationary.

→ On each, a new tape symbol is written on the cell scanned. Any of these symbols may be the same as the symbol previously there.

---

The heads move independently ,so different heads may move in different directions ,and some may not move at all .

---

## 7.8.2 Eqivalence of Turing Machines

Eqivalances of TM of different units with the same input alphabet $M_1$ and $M_2$ are possible. If

$$f_{m1} = f_{m2}$$

That is $M_1$ and $M_2$ compute the same function *i.e.,* same input-output function .

We show that two kinds of TM are eqivalances by showing that for any machine of one kind there is an equivalent machine of other kind and vice versa.

## 7.8.3 Two-way. Infinite Tape

The TM is widely accepted as a model of computation because of its versatality in the power of computation.

A TM with a two-way infinite tape is denoted by

$$M = \{Q, \Sigma, \Gamma, \delta, q_0, \#, F\}$$

same as in the original model.

---

The tape head can move in forward and forward direction.

---

Here the tape is infinite to the left as well as to the right. A two way infinite tape can be easily simulated by a 2-tape machine -one tape away contains the part of the tape to the right of the square containing the first input symbols and the other contains the part of the tape to the left of the in reverse.

## 7.8.4 Non-Deterministic Turing Machine

We know that when finite automata are allowed to act non-deterministic no increase in the computational power, but that non-deterministic in push down automata are more powerful than deterministic ones.

A non-deterministic turing machine is not more powerful than a deterministic one.

A non-deterministic machine can be seen as a machine that has the ability to replicate itself whenever necessary

When more than one move is possible, the machine produces as many replicas as needed and gives each replica the task of carrying out one of the alternatives.

A string $W$ in $\Sigma^*$ is said to ne accepted by a non-deterministic TM if there exists a sequens of moves staring from the initial *ID* to an accepting condition.

It can be shown that the set of language accepted by non-deterministic TM is subset of the set of language accepted by deterministic TMs. Actually thesetwo sets of language are equal.

A non-deterministic TM is a 7 tuple $(Q, \Sigma, \Gamma, \delta, q_0, \#, F)$ Where $Q$ , $\Sigma$, $\Gamma$, $q_0$, $F$) have same meaning as in basic *TM* but transition function defined as

$$\delta : Q \times \Gamma \to \text{Power set of } Q \times \Gamma \times \{L, R\}$$

or

$$Q \times \Gamma \to 2^{Q \times \Gamma \times \{L, R\}}$$

## 7.8.5 Multidimensional Turing Machine

The multi dimensional TM has finite control tape head and a tape with more than one diemension, say $k$ diemensions infinite in all $2k$ directions.

The moves of multidimensional TM is defined as follow

Depending on the current state and the current input scanned under head, the machine change the state, change the symbol by overwriting its current cell, and moves its head in one of the $2k$ directions along one of the $k$-axes.

**For example:** Let us consider a two dimensional TM. The tape of a two dimensional TM is a square.

The moves are formally defined as

$$\delta : Q \times \Gamma \to Q \times \Gamma \{L, R, U, D\}$$

Where $L$, $R$, $U$ and $D$ specify the movement of heads left, right, up and down respectively.

Adding the multidimensional tape does not enhance computing power of TM. To prove this first we prove for a two dimensional T*M*. Further we can generalize for $k$ dimensions.

## 7.8.6 Multi Head Turing Machine

In multi head TM, we have $k$ ($k > 0$) numbers of heads on the same tape and a move of the TM depends on the state and on all the symbol scanned by each head. In one move the machine, can change state, print a symbol on each of the square scanned by take heads.

The use of multiple heads can sometimes drastically simplify the construction of *TM*. For example, if we construct a *TM* to copy a staring with the help as two heads then it can function in a way that is much more simple and natural than the one head *TM*.

## 7.8.7 Off-Line Turing Machine

An off line Turing machine is a special case of multitape Turing machine in which the input tape is made read only, input string is surrounded by end markers ¢ on the left and \$ on the right , so that the input tape head is not allowed to move off the region between end markers.

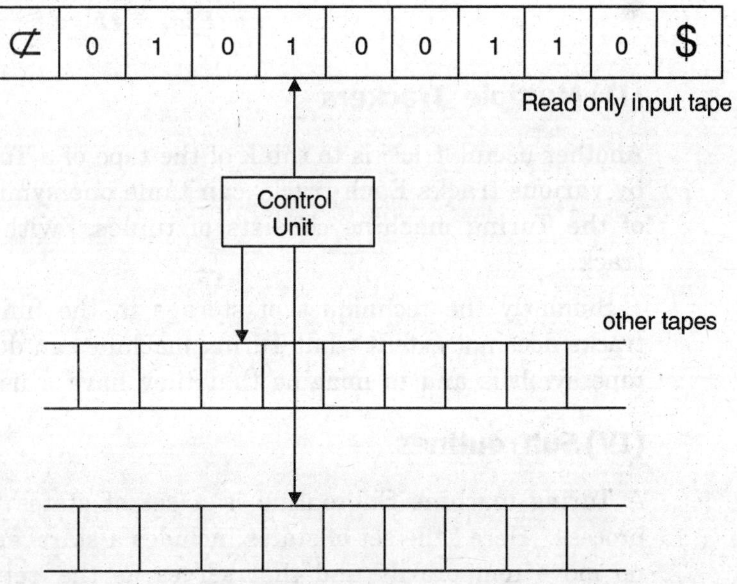


*fig. 7.40*

## 7.9 PROGRAMMING TECHNIQUES FOR TURING MACHINE

A Turing machine can be used to compute in a manner not unlike that of conventional, Eventually, we want convince you that a TM is exactly as powerful as a conventional computer. In particular we shall learn that the Turing machine can perform the sort of calculations.

### (I) Storage in the State

Finite control canbe used not only to represent the position in the program of Turing machine ,but to hold a finite amount of data.

In the Fig 7.41, we see that the finite control consisting of not only a 'control' state $q$ but three data element $A$, $B$ and $C$. Regarding states this way allows us to describe transition in a more systematic way, often making a strategy behind the Turing machine program more transparent.

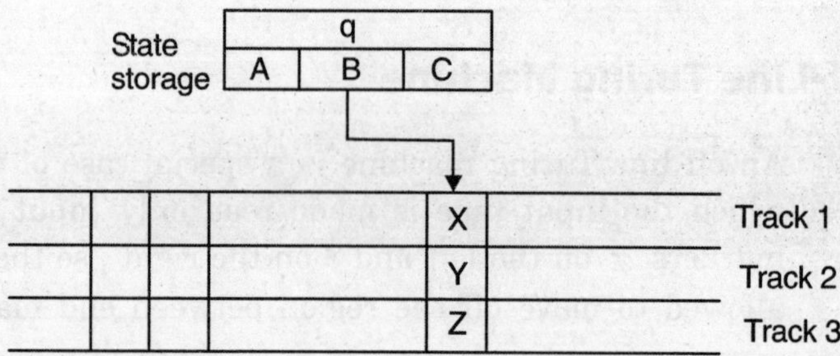


*Fig. 7.41*

### (II) Multiple Trackers

Another useful 'trick' is to think of the tape of a Turing machine as composed by various tracks Each track can tame one symbol and the tape alphabet of the Turing machine consists of tuples, with one component for each track.

Similarly the techniques of storage in the finite control, using multiple tracks does not extent what Turing machine can do. It is simply a way to see tape symbols and to imagine that they have a useful structure.

### (IV) Sub routines

A Turing machine Subroutine is a set of states that perform some useful process. Here , the set of states includes a start and another state that have no move temporarily and that serves as the 'return' state to pass control whatever other set of states called the subroutines.

## 7.10 UNIVERSAL TURING MACHINE

**[*UPTU B-Tech 2005*]**

Universal Turing machine is used to simulate the behaviour of an arbitrary TM over input alphabet *S*. *i.e,* Universal Turing machine is a machine , which is designed for general purpose.

The machine is too difficult design but it is more powerful to simulate behaviour of any computes including any Turing machine itself.

A universal machine can accept two inputs:

→ The input data

→ An algorithm for computation

"A Universal Turing machine (*U T M*) is a *TM* whose input consists of two parts. The first is the encoded Turing machine followed by a marker, the second part is a string that is interpreted as the input of the Turing machine encoded first part. The UTM then simulates the processing of second part by the encoded Turing machine in the first part of input.

### Working of Universal Turing Machine

Let Mv be the *UTM* and input of *Mv* is the encoded Turing machine $M_1$ followed by input ω. The operation of Mv is that no matter what machine $M_1$ is, and no matter what *w* is, the *Mv* will operate on the data as if it were $M_1$. If $M_1$ would have crash on this input, *Mv* will crash, if $M_1$ would accept the *wv* it will accept and if $M_1$ will loop forever, *Mv* will loop forever. The *Mv* will leave on its tape the encoded $M_1$ the marker and contents of what $M_1$would leave on its tape when it accepts *w*.

## 7.11 LINEAR BOUNDED AUTOMATA (LBA)

The model of liear bonded automata is important because:

(1) The set of context sensitive language is accepts by the model and.

(2) The inifinite storage is restricted in size but not in accessibility to the storage in comparison with the Turing machine model. It is called linear bounded automation.

A linear bounded automation is non-deterministic Turing machine which has a single tape whose length is not inifinite but bounded by a linear function of the length of the input string.

This model can be described as follows.

$$M = (Q, \Sigma, \Gamma, \delta, q_0, \#, \in, \$, F)$$

Where δ is defined as

$$Q \times \Gamma \rightarrow Q \times \Gamma \times \{R, L\}$$

Here, all the symbols have the same meaning as in the basic model of Turing machines with the difference that the input alphabet contain two special symbol ⊄ and \$, ⊄ is known as left end marker which is entered in the left most cell of the input tape and prevent the read write head from getting off left end of the tape. \$ is called right end marker which is entered in the right most cell of the input tape and percent and read-write head from getting off the right end of the tape

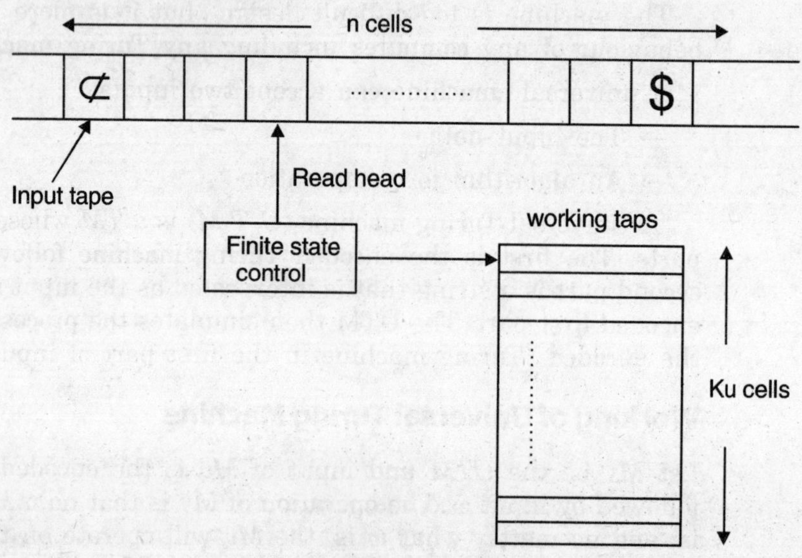


*Fig. 7.42*

The above definition of linear bounded automation is assumed to be non-deterministic. This is not a metter of convenience but essential for linear bounded autonata's. While one can define deterministic linear bounded automata's it is not known whether they are equivalent to the non-deterministic version.

**Example 7.30:** Design a Turing machine, which Computes

$L = \{a^n, b^{n+1}; n \geq 1\}$ ***[U.P.T.U. B-Tech 2003,07,08]***

**Solution:** It this input string is of the tape *aabbbB*

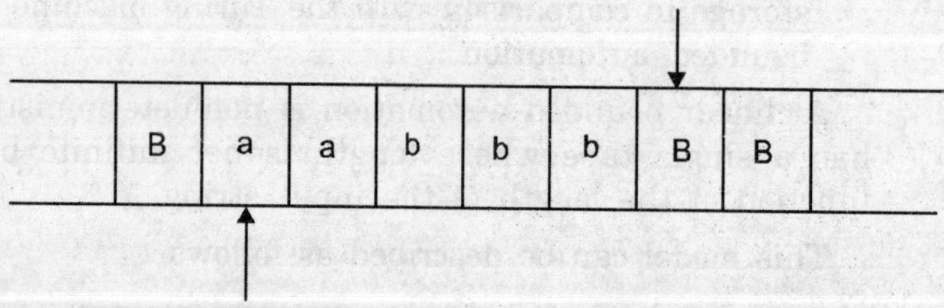


- $\delta(q_0, a) = (B, q, R)$
- $\delta(q_1, a) = (a, q_1, R)$
- $\delta(q_1, b) = (b, q_1, R)$

- $\delta(q_1, B) = (B, q_2, L)$
- $\delta(q_2, b) = (B, q_3, L)$
- $\delta(q_3, b) = (b, q_3, L)$
- $\delta(q_3, a) = (a, q_3, L)$
- $\delta(q_3, B) = (B, q_0, R)$
- $\delta(q_0, b) = (q_f, B, R)$
- $\delta(q_0, B) = (B, q_0, R)$

Transccition Table

| State | a | b | B |
|---|---|---|---|
| $\rightarrow q_0$ | $Bq_1R$ | $Bq_fR$ | $Bq_0R$ |
| $q_1$ | $aq_1R$ | $bq_1R$ | $Bq_2R$ |
| $q_2$ | – | $Bq_3L$ | – |
| $q_3$ | $aq_3L$ | $bq_3L$ | $Bq_0R$ |
| $(q_f)$ | – | – | – |

## EXERCISE

### (A) Objective Type Questions

**1.** Which automata is associated with Context Sensitive Language? (Give the best answer)

(*a*) Turing Machine (*b*) Finite Automata

(*c*) Pushdown Automata (d) Linear Bounded Automata

**2.** LBA is

(*a*) unrestricted T.M.

(*b*) restricted T.M. From one side

(*c*) restricted T.M. From both sides

(d) none

**3.** Which of the following is true: Read Write head can move

(*a*) to the left of left endmarker in LBA

(*b*) to the right of left endmarker in LBA

(*c*) to the right of right endamarker in LBA

(d) to the left of right endmarker in LBA

4. Find the false statement
   (*a*) Standard Turing machine (TM) is equivalent to multi tape TM
   (*b*) Standard TM is equivalent to non dedterministic TM
   (*c*) Standard TM is equivalent to linear bounded automata
   (d) None
5. The statement "Standard TM accepts the same languages as are accepted by a stay TM" is
   (*a*) True only if languages is a CFL
   (*b*) True only if languages is regular
   (*c*) True for all languages
   (d) Always false.
6. Non-Deterministic Turing Machine are more powerful than deterministic Turing Machine
   (*a*) Absolutely True (*b*) May be True
   (*c*) May not be True (d) Absolutely False
7. An Finite state machine can be considered to be a TM
   (*a*) a finite tape length, with rewinding and unidirectional movement
   (*b*) a finite tape length, without rewinding capability and unidirectional tape movement
   (*c*) a finite tape length, without rewinding and bi-directional movement
   (d) a finite tape length, rewinding capability and bi-directional tape movement
8. A TM is more powerful than Finite state machine because
   (*a*) tape movement is confined to one direction
   (*b*) it has no finite state control
   (*c*) it has the capability to remember arbitrary long input symbols
   (d) none
9. Choose the correct statements
   (*a*) $L$ [$a^n$ $b^n$ $c^n$} is recursively enumerable
   (*b*) Recursive languages are closed under union
   (*c*) Every recursive language is recursively enumerable
   (d) All
10. The class of TMs is equivalent to the class of
    (*a*) Type 0 Grammars (*b*) Type 1 Grammars
    (*c*) Type 2 Grammars (d) Type 3 Grammars
11. Comparing TM and computers we find
    (*a*) Computers have more computational power
    (*b*) TM have more computational power
    (*c*) Both are Equivalent
    (d) They cannot be compared

**12.** Turing machines are similar to finite automaton but have.......

(*a*) finite and read-only memory.

(*b*) unlimited and read-only memory.

(*c*) finite and read-write memory.

(d) unlimited and read-write memory.

**13.** Turing machines can do.......

(*a*) everything that a real computer can do.

(*b*) more than a real computer can do.

(*c*) less than a real computer can do.

(d) Nothing.

**14.** Turing machines use what as their memory?

(*a*) ROM (*b*) RAM

(*c*) finite tape (d) infinite tape

**15.** Turing machines can move how in memory?

(*a*) forward (*b*) backward

(*c*) forward and backward (d) It cannot move.

**16.** Turing machines output accept if they enter an accept state. When do Turing machine output reject?

(*a*) When they are not in an accept state and halts.

(*b*) When they never end.

(*c*) When they enter a reject state.

(d) Never.

## ANSWERS

| | | | | |
|---|---|---|---|---|
| **1.** (*d*) | **2.** (*c*) | **3.** (*b*) | **4.** (*c*) | **5.** (*c*) |
| **6.** (*d*) | **7.** (*d*) | **8.** (*c*) | **9.** (*a*) | **10.** (*a*) |
| **11.** (*a*) | **12.** (*c*) | **13.** (*d*) | **14.** (*a*) | **15.** (*d*) |
| **16.** (*c*) | | | | |

## (B) Problems

**1.** Design Turing machines to recognize the following languages.

(*a*) $\{0^n1^n0^n \mid n \geq 1\}$

(*b*) $\{ww^R|w \text{ is in } (0 + 1)^*\}$

(*c*) The set of strings with an equal number of 0's and 1's.

**2.** Design Turing machines to commute the following functions:

(*a*) [$\log 2^n$] (*b*) $n$ ! (*c*) $n^2$

**3.** Give recursive definition for

(*a*) $n + m$ (*b*) $b/m$ (*c*) $nm$ (*d*) $n$ !

**4.** Show that the class of recursive function is identical to the class of partial recursive functions.

**5.** Design a Turing machine to enumerate $\{0^n1^n \mid n^3n\}$.

**6.** Show that every r.e. set is accepted by a TM with only two non accpting states and one accepting state.

**7.** Design a Turing Machines (TM) that converts a binary string into its equivalent unary string.

**8.** Construct a Turing machine that can accept the strings over {0, 1} containing even number of 1's.

**9.** Design a Turing machine to recognize the language $\{a^nb^nc^m \mid n, m \geq 1\}$

**10.** Prove that the recursiveness problem of type 0 grammars is unsolvable.

**11.** Design a Turing machine with no more than three states that accepts the languages $L\ (a(a + b)^*)$. Assume that $\Sigma = (a, b)$

**12.** Design a Turing machine that accepts the language $L = \{ww : w \in \{a, b\}^+\}$

**13.** Construct a Turing machine to compute the function

$$f(w) = w^*, \text{ where } w \in \{0, 1\}^+.$$

**14.** Design a Turing machine to compute the following functions for $X$ and $Y$ positive integers represented unary.

(*a*) $f(X) = 3X$

(*b*) $f(X, Y) = x - y, x > y$.

(*c*) $f(X, Y) = 2x + 3y$

(*d*) $f(X) = \begin{cases} X/2, & \text{if } X \text{ is even} \\ (X+1)/2 & \text{if } X \text{ is odd} \end{cases}$

❑❑❑

CHAPTER

# 8

# Decidability and Indecisiveness (Undecidability)

## 8.1 INTRODUCTION

In this chapter we will discuss about a question arising from the last chapter that whether *TMs* can compute all functions. We divide the class of problems that can be solved by a *TM* as follows:

1. The first class is of those problems that have a *TM* halts whether or not it accepts its input.
2. The second class consists of these problems that are only solved by *TMs*, however, *TMs* may not half at all if they do not accept its input.

The second class raises a fundamental issue "whether the *TM T* applied to input $x$ halts or does not half"?

This problem is known as halting problem of *TMs* and undecidability (or unsolvability), *i.e.*, there exists no algorithm that can correctly answers this questions.

The existence of undecidable problems or non-computable functions have played a role of revolutionary beginning in under standing the foundations of logic and computation.

The undecidability of the halting problem has its applications in the area of CFLs. However, we find another intermediate result, known as post Correspondence Problem (*PCP*) whose undecidability follows from the undecidability of halting problems, plays an intermediate role in proving the undecidable problems about CFLs.

We exploit this undecidability result to exhibit a number of other undecidable problems. For instance, we show that all nontrivial problems about the language accepted by a Turing machine are undecidable, as are a number of problems that have nothing at all to do with Turing machine, program or computers.

---

A problem whose language is recursive is said to be decidable. Otherwise the problem is undecidable. That is, a problem is undecidable if there is no algorithm that takes as input an instance of the problem and determines whether the answers to that instance is "true" or "false"

---

## 8.2 RECURSIVE AND RECURSIVELY ENUMERABLE LANGUAGES

The language accepted by finite automata is called a regular language, the language accepted by *PDA* is a context-free language. But *Tm* defines two classes of languages such as

→ Recursive language

→ Recursirely Enumerable languages

When a string belonging to Σ runs on *Tm* then it results in three states–

(*i*) Acceptance of string

(*ii*) Loops for ever on receiving string

(*iii*) Rejects the given string

Now we can define recursively enumerable language and recursive language.

## 8.2.1 Recursively Enumerable (*RE*) Language

The set of languages recognized by a *Tm* to be the set of strings for which *Tm* halts in a final state we assumed that a *Tm* accepts an input string if it enters a halt state, else *Tm* rejects the input string. The set of languages which are accepted by a *Tm* is called the recursively enumerable languages.

"A language *L* is said to be recursively enumerable language if there exists a *Tm*." such that

$$L = L\ (M)$$

we observe that if a string $x$ is rejected by *Tm*, than one can have two options

(*i*) The *Tm* may halts in a non-accepting state.

(*ii*) The *Tm* may not halts at all and may go into an infinite loop.

This definition implies only that there exists a *Tm* *M* such that for every $\omega \in L$,

$$q_0\omega \left|\frac{*}{M}\right. x_1 q_f x_2$$

where $q_0$ is an initial state and $q_f$ is a final state. The definition says nothing about what happens for ω not in *L*.

## 8.2.2 Recursive Language

A language *L* is said to be recursive language if *L* = *L*(*M*) for some turing machine such that:

1. If ω is in *L*, then *M* accepts (and therefore halts *i.e.* rejects every word in *L*')
2. If ω is not in *L*, then *M* eventually halts, although it never enters an accepting state.

If we think of the language $L$ as a "problem". then problem $L$ is sad decidable if it is a recursive language, and it is called undecidable if it is not a recursive language.

### 8.2.3 Relationship between Recursive and RE Language

The set of recursively enumerable languages are those languages that can be enumerated by a turing machine. Basically, if a *Tm* can generate all the strings in a language, another *Tm* can accept all the strings that are in the given language.

A language is recursive if there exists a *Tm* that accepts every string of the language and rejects every string that is not in the language. So, we are sure about the rejection of the strings with not in the given recursive language.

A language $L$ is recursively enumerable if there is a *Tm* that accepts $L$ and recursive if there is a *Tm* that recognizes $L$.

Figure 8.1 suggests the relationship among two classes of languages.

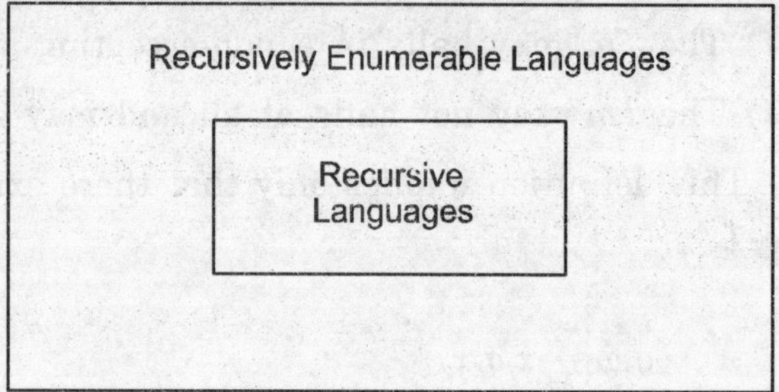


***Fig. 8.1***

From these two languages following observations are made:

(*i*) Every recursive language is recursively enumerable language.

(*ii*) Not all recursively language are recursive. That means every Tm which accepts the recursively enumerable language must have some words for which it loops forever.

The important fact about recursive and recursively enumerable languages can be seen the help of following theorem.

**Theorem 8.1:** If $L$ is recursive language then $L'$ is also a recursive language.

**Proof:** Let there will be some $L$ that can be accepted by Truing Machine $M$. Hence we can denote language $L$ by $L(M)$. On acceptance of $L(M)$ the machine $M$ always halts. Now, we construct a $Tm$ $M'$ such that $L' = (M')$. For construction of $M'$ following steps are followed–

1. The accepting steps of $M$ are made non-accepting states of $M'$ and there is no transition from $M'$. That means we have created the states such that $M'$ will halt without accepting.
2. Now create a new accepting state for $M'$ say $r$ and there is no transition from $r$.
3. In machine $M$, for each of the transition with combination of non accepting state and input tape symbol, make the same transition having the combination of accepting state and input tape symbol for machine $M'$.

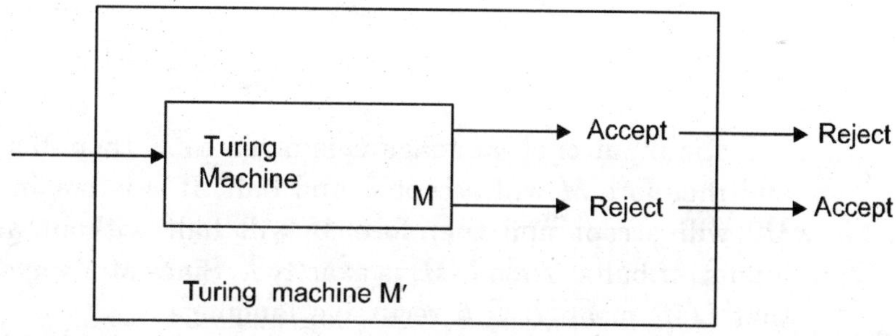


***Fig. 8.2***

Since $M$ is to halt $M'$ is also to halt. In fact, $M'$ accepts exactly those strings that $M$ does not accept. Thus we can say that $M'$ accepts $L'$.

**Theorem 8.2:** If a language $L$ is recursive, then It is recursively enumerable languages.

**Proof:** A languages is recursively enumerable if there exists a turing machine that accepts every string at the language and a language is recursive if there is a $Tm$ that accepts every string of the language and does not accept strings that are not in the language.

So, every recursive language is also recursively enumerable. Hence, statement of the theorem is true.

**Theorem 8.3:** If a language $L$ and its complement $L'$ both are *RE* then $L$ is a recursive language. **[U.P.T.U B-Tech (co) 2003]**

**Proof:** Consider a Turing machine $M$ made up of two Turing machines $M1$ and $M2$. The machine $M2$ is complement of machine $M1$. We can also denote that $L(M) = L(M1)$ and $L(M2)$. Both $M1$ and $M2$ are simulated in parallel by machine $M$. Machine $M$ is a two tape $Tm$, which can be made one tape $Tm$ for the ease of simulation. This One tape then will consist of tape of machine

$M1$ and machine $M2$. The states of $M$ consists of all the states of machine $M1$ and all the states of machine $M2$. The machine $M$ made up of $M1$ and $M2$ is as shown below.

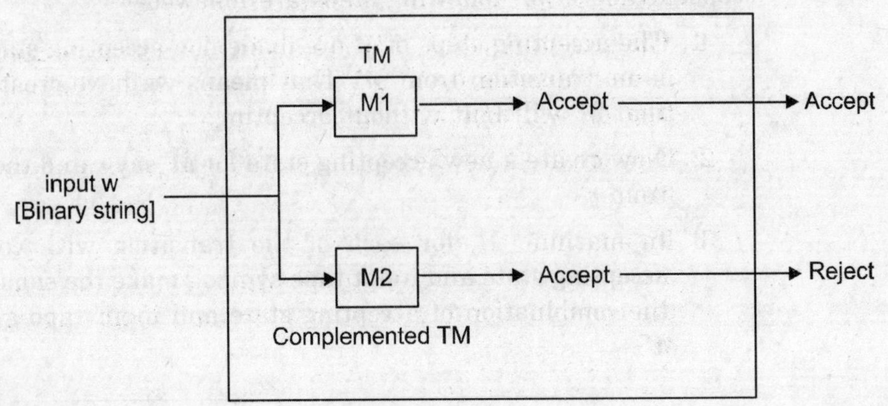


***Fig. 8.3***

If the input ω of language L is given to $M$ then $M1$ will eventually accept and therefore $M$ will accept $L$ and halt. If ω is not in $L$, then it is in $L'$. So $M2$ will accept and therefore $M$ will half without accepting. Thus on all inputs, $M$ halts. Thus $L(M)$ is exactly $L$. Since $M$ always halts we can conclude that $L(M)$ mean $L$ is a recursive language.

---

Thus a recursive language can be recursively enumerable but a recursively enumerable language is not necessarily be recursive.

---

**Theorem 8.4:** If $L_1$ and $L_2$ are two recursive languages. Then $L_1 \cup L_2$ (Union) and $L_1 \cap L_2$ (Intersection) are recursive.

**Proof:** Let $M_1$ and $M_2$ are two *Tms* and $L_1$ and $L_2$ be two recursive languages respectively.

we construct a machine $M_1$ which first simulates $M_1$.

→ If $M_1$ has output 1 then $M$ has also output 1.

→ If $M_1$ has output 0 then $M$ simulates $M_2$ and have output 1 if and only if $M_2$ has output 1.

Thus, it is clear that $M$ has output 1 if any one of $M_1$ or $M_2$ accepts input and produces 1.

The $M$ has output 0 if both $M_1$ and $M_2$ have output 0.

Hence, $M$ decides $L_1 \cup L_2$. It is also clear that both $M_1$ and $M_2$ halts for any input string, it shows that $M$ certainly halts.

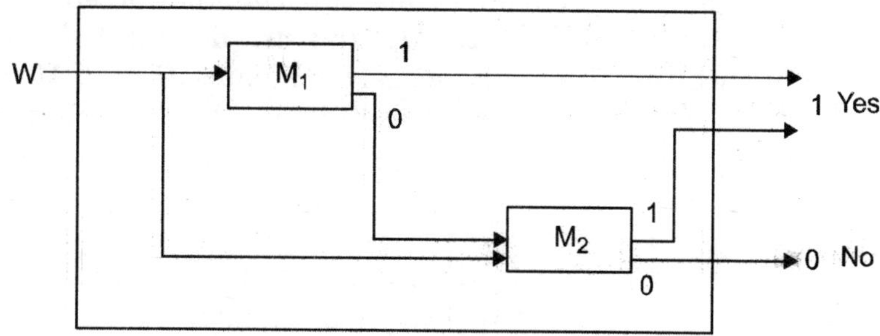


***Fig. 8.4***

**Proof:** $L_1 \cap L_2$ is similar except that $M$ accept if both $M_1$ and $M_2$.

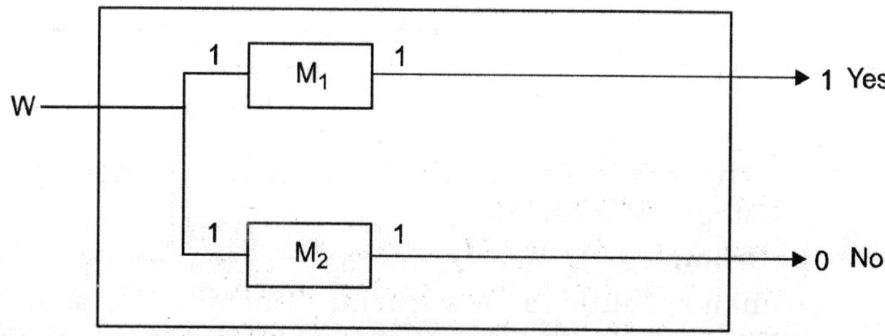


***Fig. 8.5***

**Theorems 8.5:** If the language $L$ is recursive, then its complement $\bar{L}$ is also recursive.

**Proof:** If $L$ is a recursive language then there exists a *Tm* which decides whether any string ω is in $L$ or not and produces output as 1 or 0. we can make a new *Tm M'*, which decides $\bar{L}$ by interchanging both outputs as shown in Fig.

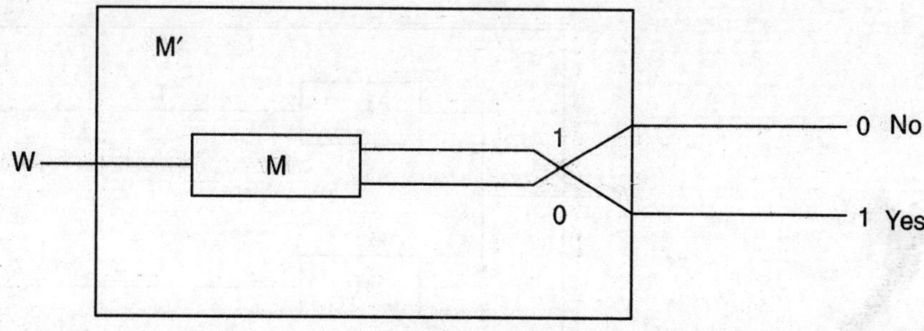


***Fig. 8.6***

Clearly *M'* is a *Tm* which decides $\bar{L}$. Hence, $\bar{L}$ is a recursive language.

**Theorem 8.6:** If $L_1$ and $L_2$ are two recursive enumerable languages then $L_1 \cup L_2$ is also recursive enumerable.

**Proof:** Let $M_1$ and $M_2$ are two *Tms* that accepts $L_1$ and $L_2$ respectively. It may be possible both $M_1$ and $M_2$ do not halt. Let us contruct a *Tm* $M$ such that $M$ simultaneously simulates $M_1$ and $M_2$ on two tapes. If any one of $L_1$ and $L_2$ is accepted, this is also accepted by $M$. *i.e.*, $L(M) = L_1 \cup L_2$.

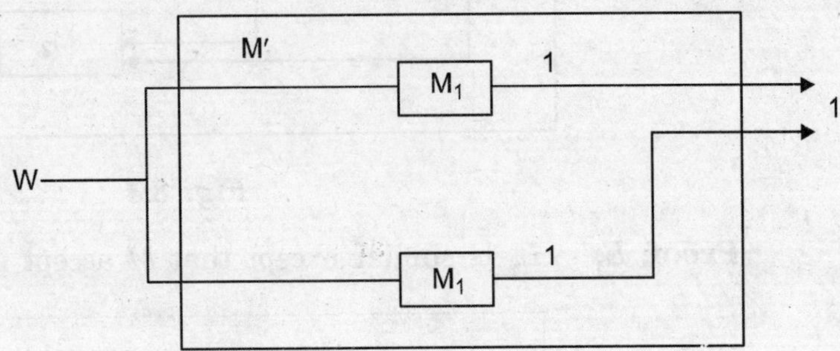


***Fig. 8.7***

**Theorem 8.7:** If $L_1$ and $L_2$ are recursive enumerable then $L_1 \cap L_2$ is also recursive enumerable.

**Proof:** Let $M_1$ and $M_2$ are the *Tm*'s that accepts $L_1$ and $L_2$ respectively. We can now build a new turing machine $M$, that first runs the input string ω on $M$, and then if string is accepted it runs the same input ω on $M_2$.

The acceptance at $M$ is analogous to the $M_2$, but it is reached only when input has accepted on both $M_1$ and $M_2$. Therefore, $M$ accepts $L_1 \cap L_2$ and hence $L_1 \cap L_2$ is also recursive enumerable.

**Theorem 8.8:** If $L$ is a recursive enumerable language whose complement $\bar{L}$ is also recursive enumerable, then $L$ is recursive.

**Proof:** Let $M_1$ and $M_2$ be *Tms* accepting $L$ and $\bar{L}$ respectively. We construct a *Tm M* for union of these two language that recognized $L$ in the manner shown is given Fig.

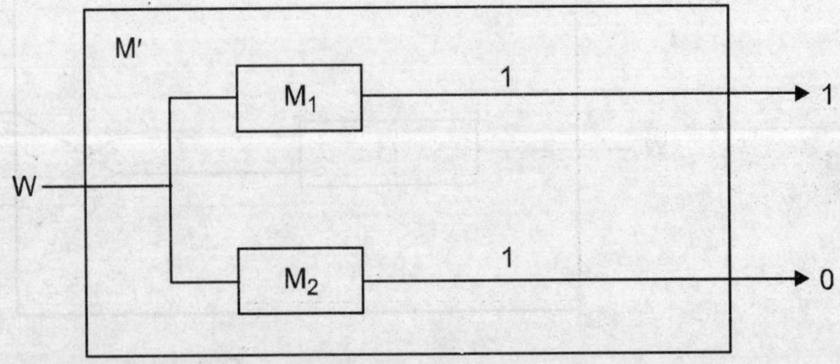


***Fig. 8.8***

The machine $M$ has output 1 for an input string ω if $M_1$ accepts ω and output o when $M_2$ accepts ω.

Since ω is in either $L$ or $\bar{L}$ is accepted by $M_1$ and $\bar{L}$ is accepted by $M_2$. It shows that $M$ will always halt with output 0 or 1 but not both.

Therefore, $L$ is recursive.

## 8.3 UNDECIDABLE PROBLEMS

By a problem we will refer a set of related statement, each at which must be true or false.

For example, "For a grammar $G$, whether $\omega \in L(G)$" or "$G$ is ambiguous". For some grammars this is true, where as for some other this is false.

---

Any problem that can be stated as a question and has a yes or no answer is called a **decision problem** we also call a problem to be **decidable** if it is solvable and similarly a problem is said to be **undecidable** if it is unsolvable.

---

A problem is undecidable if there is no algorithm that takes as input an instance of the problem and determines whether the answer to that instance is yes or one. This type of problem is also known as unsolvable problem.

If there exists any such algorithm then problem is decidable or solvable.

### 8.3.1 Reduction

A reduction is a way of converging one problem into another problem in such a way that a solution to the second problem can be used to solve first problem. Such "reducibilities" come up often in everyday life.

→ Suppose you want to find a way for a city. You know this would be easy if you a map. Thus you can reduce the problem of finding a way of the city to the problem of obtaining a map of the city.

---

Reduction is a technique in which if a problem $P_1$ is reduced to a problem $P_2$ then any solution of $P_2$ solves $P_1$.

---

If we have an algorithm to convert and instance of a problem $P_1$ to instance of a problem $P_2$ that have the same answer then it is called as $P_1$ reduces $P_2$.

Hence If $P_1$ is not recurise then $P_2$ is also not recursive. Similarly, if $P_1$ is not recursively enumerable then $P_2$ also is not recursively enumerable.

**Theorem 8.9:** If there is a reduction from $P_1$ to $P_2$ then if $P_1$ is undecidable then $P_2$ is also undecidable.

**Proof:** Let $P_1$ is undecidable and $P_2$ is decidable. Since we know that if there is reduction from $P_1$ to $P_2$ there is an algorithm to find reduction. If $P_2$ is decidable which means there is an algorithm to decide $P_2$. If we combine both algorithm as show is Fig.

The combines also shows that $P_1$ is decidable which contradict our assumption.

Hence, If $P_1$ is undecidable then so is $P_2$.

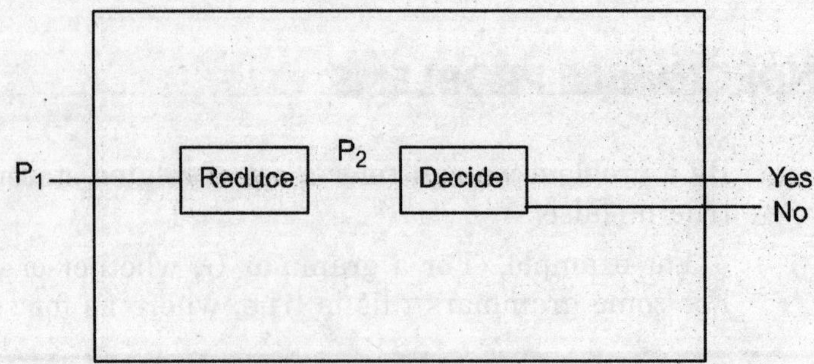


*Fig. 8.9*

Use of Reducibility to show that a problem is unsolvable–

Reducibility is the primary method for proving that a problem is computationally unsolvable. Here is how it works:

→ Reduce an unsolvable problem *x* to a more difficult or general problem, *Y*.

→ *X* is known to be unsolvable, and the solution of *X* would also solve problem *Y* then *Y* must be unsolvable too.

---

✍ Reducibility says nothing about solving *X* or *Y* alone, only about the solvability of *X* in the presence or context of *Y*.

---

Reducibility also plays an important role in classifying problem as decidable or undecidable, and later on in complexity there too.

→ When *X* is reducible to *Y*, solving *X* cannot be harder than solving *Y*, because the solution to *Y* can also be used to solve *X*.

→ In terms of the decidability/computability questions then.

(*a*) If *X* is reducible to *Y* and *Y* is decidable then *X* is also decidable.

(*b*) If *X* is undecidable/unsolvable and *X* reduces to *Y*, then *Y* is also undecidable. This is the key to proving that problem are undecidable or unsolvable.

## 8.4 EMPTY AND NON EMPTY LANGUAGE

There are two types of languages empty and non empty. Let $L_e$ denotes an empty language and $L_{ne}$ denotes non empty language. Let *w* be a binary string and $M_i$ be a *Tm*. If $L(M_j) = \phi$ then $M_i$ does not accept any input then *w* is $L_e$. Similarly if $L(M_i)$ is not the empty language then w is in $L_{ne}$. Thus we can say that

$$L_e = \{M|\ L(M) = \phi\}$$
$$L_{ne} = \{M|\ L(M) \neq \phi\}$$

Both $L_e$ and $L_{ne}$ are complement of one another.

**Theorem 8.10:** $L_{ne}$ is recursively enumerable

**Proof:** To prove this, we simply need to prove that there exists some *Tm* which accepts $L_{ne}$. To do this we need to construct Non deterministic Turing machine *M* that can be converted to deterministic Turing machine.

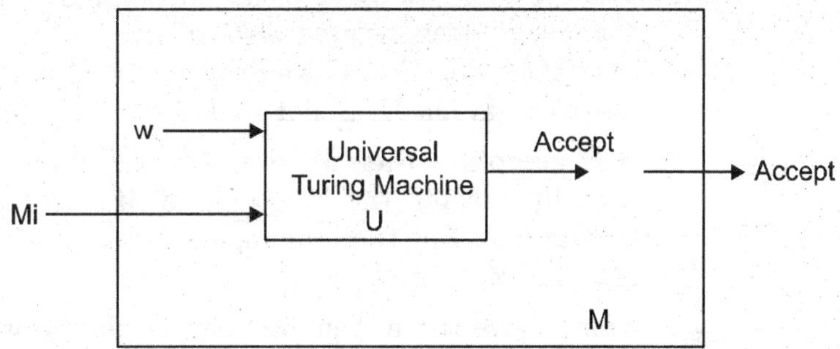


***Fig. 8.10***

The Turing machine *M* accepts another Turing Machine $M_i$ as input. With the non deterministic capability *M* can guess the input *w* that can be accepted by $M_i$ if $M_i$ accepts *w* then *M* also accepts the input $M_i$.

Thus if at all $M_i$ accepts even one input, the *M* will guess that string and will accept $M_i$. But if $L(M_i) = \phi$ that means *M* can make no guess about the input string and therefore can not accept $M_i$. This proves that there should be such a Turing machine whose language $L(M) \neq \phi$, thus $L(M) = L_{ne}$.

## 8.5 RICE'S THEOREM

Every non trivial property of *RE* language is Undecidable

**Proof:** Property of a language is a set of strings for which the Turing Machines can be drawn which ultimately represents certain class. For example a property of "context free language" in *Tm* contains all the codes for the Turing machine *M* such that all the *L*(*M*) are context free languages. Let *P* be any non trivial property of *RE* languages. That means at least one language has the property and at least one language does not. Initially we will assume $\phi$ an empty language is not having the property *P*. As *P* is the nontrivial, there should be some language *L* having property *P i.e.* $L = L_p$ and therefore there exists a coded *Tm* accepting language *L*. Let us call such *Tm* as $M_L$. Let us reduce a universal language $L_u$ to $L_p$ and as $L_u$ is undecidable $L_p$ is also undecidable. The Turing Machine *M'* can be produced on reduction. For the reduction algorithm the pair (*M*,*w*) can be given as input. Basically *M'* is a two-tape Turing machine such that

- One tape is used to simulate *Tm M* for input *w*. Then input (*M*,*w*) is used for designing the transitions of *M'*.
- The second tape is used to simulate $M_L$ on input *x*. Again a pair (*M'*,*x*) is used to build the transitions of *M'*.

The *Tm M'* does the following things

1. The Turing machine *M* is simulated for the input *w*. The *Tm M'* acts as a universal Turing machine by accepting the pair (*M*, *w*).
2. There exists two cases either *M* accepts *w* or *M* does not. If *M* accepts *w* then *M'* does nothing else. *M'* can not have its own input *x*, in such case $L(M') = \phi$. But as we have assumed $\phi$ is not in property *P* that also means code for *M'* is not in $L_p$.
3. If *M* accepts *w* then *M'* simulates $M_L$ for its own input *x* and hence *M'* actually accepts the language of $M_L$. In other words, *M'* accepts the language *L*. But the language *L* is having the property *P*, therefore the code for *M'* is in $L_p$.
4. From above three steps we can not decide whether code for *M'* is in $L_p$.

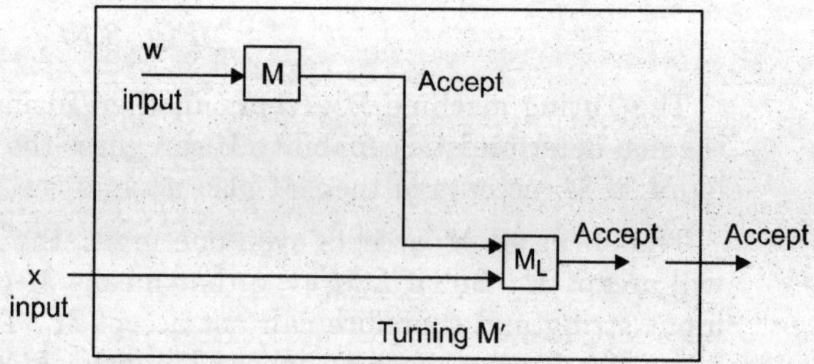


***Fig. 8.11***

This proves that property *P* is undecidable. Now there exists another possibility that if $\phi$ is in *P* then *P'* is a set of languages not having property *P*. As *P* is Undecidable *P'* is also Undecidable. But there is Turing machine which accepts a recursively enumerable language $L_{p1}$. The language $L_{p1}$. is actually a set of turing machine code. These codes actually accept the language having property *P*. Even such set of languages is same as the set of *Tm* codes that accept a set of languages having property *P'*. If at all $L_p$ is decidable then $L'_p$ is also decidable.

## 8.6 HALTING PROBLEM

We known from chapter 7 that to show a given function is computable, we need to construct a *Tm* that computes the function. The question arises that "is every well–defined function computable?"

We will now define the problem that asserts the existence of a non-computable function, known as the ***halting problem of turing machine***.

This problem is stated as follows:

"Does there exists a *Tm* which for a given a description of an arbitrary *Tm*, *T* and the representation of its input string *x*, can decide whether or not machine, *T*, halts when given *x* as its input string."

This can be expressed in the form of computability as follows:

"Does there exists a total function

$$f : N \times N \to \{0, 1\} \text{ defined as}$$

$$f(x, y) = 1 \text{ If } T_y \text{ comes to a halt state on reading } x.$$

$$= 0 \text{ If } T_y \text{ does not halt on reaching } x\text{''}.$$

In above statement, $T_y$ denotes the $y^{th}$ *Tm* according to the enumeration of the set of *Tm's*.

To state halting problem we will consider the given configuration of a turing machine. The output of *Tm* can be

(*i*) **Halt:** The machine starting at this configuration will halt after a finite number of states.

(*i*) **No Halt:** The machine starting at this configuration never reaches a halt state, no matter how long it runs.

Now the question arises based on these two observation: Given any functional matrix, input data tape and initial configuration, then is it possible to determine whether the process will ever halt? This is called halting problem. That means we are asking for a procedure which enable us to solve the halting problem for every pair (machine, tape). The answer is "no." That is the halting problem is unsolvable. Now we will prove why it is unsolvable. Let, there exists a *Tm* $M_1$ which decides whether or not any computation by a *Tm* *T* will ever halt when a description $d_T$ of *T* and tape *t* of *T* is given [That means the input to machine $M_1$ will be (machine, tape) pair]. Then for every input $(t, d_T)$ to $M_1$ if *T* halt for input *t*, $M_1$ also halts which is called accept halt. Similarly if *T* does not halt for input *t*, $M_1$ also halts which is called accept halt. Similarly if *T* does not halt for input *t* then the $M_1$ will halt which is called reject halt. This is shown by following Figure.

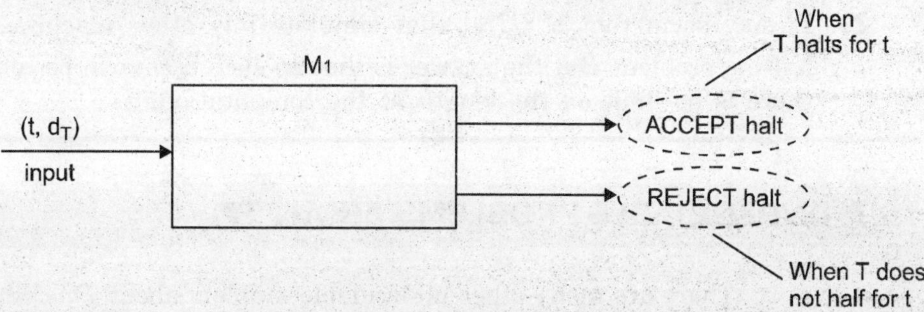


***Fig. 8.12***

Now we will consider another Turing Machine $M_2$ which takes an input $d_T$. It first copies $d_T$ and duplicates $d_T$ on its tape and then this duplicated tape information is given as input to machine $M_1$. But machine $M_1$ is a modified machine with the modification that whenever $M_1$ is supposed to reach an accepts halt, $M_2$ loops forever. Hence behavior of $M_2$ is as given. It loops if $T$ halts for input $t = d_T$ and halts if $T$ does not halt for $T = d_T$. The $T$ is any arbitrary turing machine.

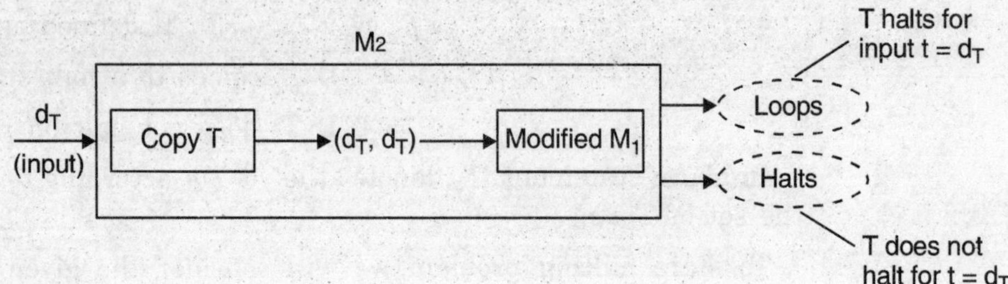


***Fig. 8.13***

As $M_2$ itself is one Turing Machine we will take $M_2 = T$. That means we will replace $T$ by $M_2$ from above given machine.

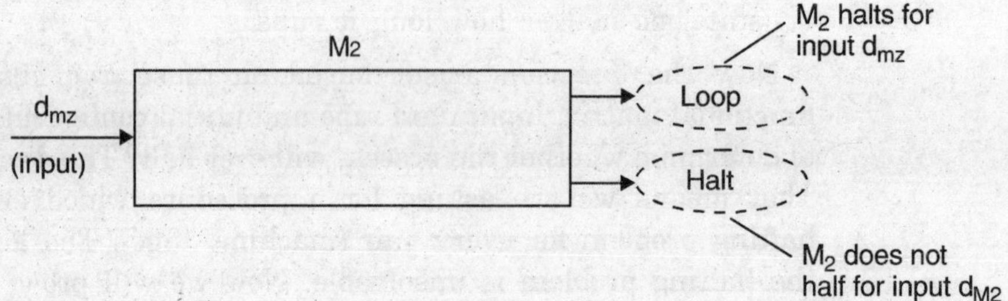


***Fig. 8.14***

Thus machine $M_2$ halts for input $d_{M2}$ if $M_2$ does not halt for input $d_{mz}$. This is a contradication. That means a machine $M_1$ which can tell whether any other *Tm* will halt on particular input does not exist. ***Hence halting problem is unsolvable.***

---

It may seem that a *UTm*, that simulate any other machine, would solve the halting problem. But the answer is that no such *UTm* can be constructed, because there is no limit on the length at the computation.

---

## 8.7 UNDECIDABLE PROBLEMS ABOUT TM

There are many other undecidable problem about *Tms* which are reducible to teh one at other undecidable problems with the help at reduction we can prove that certain problems are also undecidable.

**Theorem 8.11:** The following problems about Turing machine are undecidable.

Given a Turing machine $M_1$ does $M$ halt on the empty tape?

**Proof:** we can reduce the halting problem of Turing machine to this one. We will show that the blank tape halting problem is reducible to the halting problem, that is we shall show that for evers input pair $\{M_1, x\}$ of the halting problem, there is a *Tm, M*, such that

" $Tm_1$ halt over a blank stape iff $Tm_1$ halts over $x$".

In fact we construct a *Tm*, $M_1$ as follows:

- It first start copying string $x$ in a blank tape with a series at configurations.
- After writing the string $x$, it positions itself where $M$ would and.
- Finally, it calls $M$.

Assuming $x$ is finite of length $n$, we note that $M_1$ will require $(n + 1)$ states more than *Tm*.

The whole scheme is shown in Fig. Clearly $M_1$ will halt on blank tape if and only if $M$ halt on $x$.

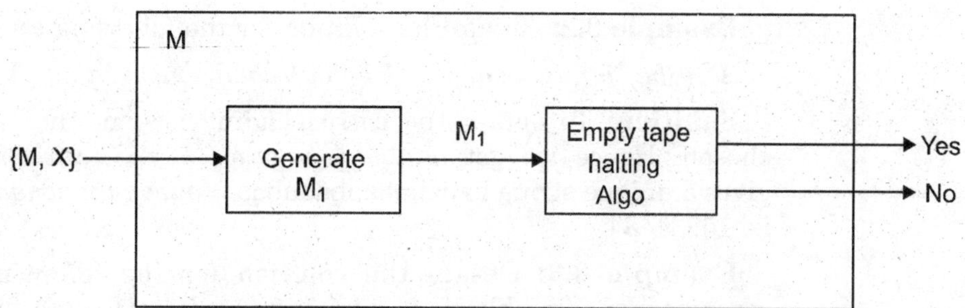


***Fig. 8.15***

Let the problem "Does $M$ halt on the empty tape" is decidable for any given $M$ and $x$. We first construct $M$, then apply the empty tape halting algorithm $T$ to it. The combined machine shown in Fig. is equivalent to the halting problem is undecidable and it is easy to contruct the algorithm "generate $M_1$". This shows that empty tape halting problem is undecidable.

## 8.8 POST CORRESPONDENCE PROBLEM (PCP)

The post correspondence problem was first formulated by ***Emit post*** in the 1945. The undecidability of strings is determined with the help of *PCP*.

Let us define the *PCP*–

The *PCP* consists of two lists of strings that are of equal length over the input $\Sigma$.

The two lists are

$A = w_1, w_2, w_3 ... w_n$ and $B = x_1, x_2, x_3 ... x_n$

then there exists a non empty set of integers $i$, $i_z$, $i_3 ... i_n$ such that

$$W_1, W_2, W_3, .... W_n = X_1, X_2, X_3 ... X_n$$

To solve the post correspondence problem we try the combinations of $i_1$, $i_2$, $i_3 ... i_n$ such that $n \geq 1$ to find the

$$W_i = X_i$$

then we say that *PCP* has a solution.

**Example 8.1:** Let $\Sigma = \{a, b, c\}$ and $P = (X, Y)$ where $X = \{b, c, ab, bca\}$ and $Y = \{bc, ab, b, a\}$. Does the *PCP P* have solution.

**Solution:** Let $X_1 = b$, $X_2 = C$, $X_3 = ab$, $X_4 = bca$

$Y_1 = bc$, $Y_2 = ab$, $Y_3 = b$, $Y_4 = a$

For the sequence {1, 2, 3, 1, 4}, the *PCP* have solution as shown below:

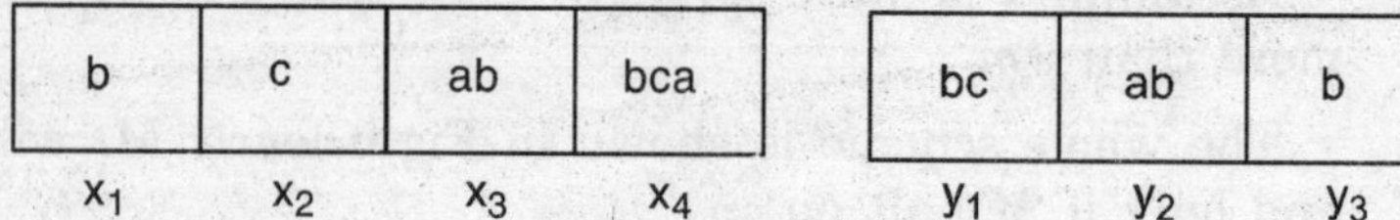


**Example 8.2:** Obtain the solution for the following correspondence system. $A = \{ba, ab, a, baa, b\}$, $B = \{bab, baa, ba, a, aba\}$. The input set $\{a, b\}$.

**Solution:** To obtain the corresponding system the one sequence can be chosen. Hence we get $w_1 w_5 w_3 w_4 w_4 w_3 w_4 = x_1 x_5 x_2 x_3 x_4 x_4 w_3 w_4$. This solution gives a unique string babababaabaaabaa = *babababaabaaabaa*. Hence solution is 15234434.

**Example 8.3:** Obtain the solution for the following system fo Posts correspondence problem. $A = \{100, 0, 1\}$, $B = \{1, 100, 00\}$

**Solution:** The solution is 1311322. The string is

$A1A3A1A1A1A3A2A2$ = 100 + 1 + 100 + 100 + 1 + 0 + 0 = 1001100100100

$B1B3B1B1B3B2B2$ = 1 + 00 + 1 + 1 + 00 + 100 + 100 = 1001100100100

**Example 8.4:** Obtain the solution for the following system of Posts correspondence problem $A = \{ba, abb, bab\}$ $B = \{bab, bb, abb\}$.

**Solution:** Now to consider 1, 3, 2 the string *bababab*b from set A and *bababbbb* from set *B* thus the two strings obtained are not equal. As we can try various combinations from both the sets to find the unique sequence but we could not get such a sequence. Hence there is no solution for this system.

**Example 8.5:** Does *PCP* with two lists $x = (b, bab^3)$ and $y = (b^3, ba, a)$ have a solution? **[UPTU B-Tech 2003]**

**Solution:** Now we have to find out such a sequence that strings formed by $x$ and $y$ are identical. Such a sequence is 2, 1, 1, 3. Hence from $x$ and $y$ list

| 2 | 1 | 1 | 3 | | 2 | 1 | 1 | 3 |
|---|---|---|---|---|---|---|---|---|
| $bab^3$ | $b$ | $b$ | $ba$ | = | $ba$ | $b^3$ | $b^3$ | $a$ |

which forms $bab^3b^3a$. Thus *PCP* has a solution.

**Example 8.6:** Explain how post correspondence problem can be treated as a game of dominoes.

**Solution:** As in the game of dominoes, the upper half corresponds to some strings and lower half corresponds to some strings.

| $A_i$ | Upper half |
|---|---|
| $B_l$ | Lower half |

To win a game, the same string appear in upper and lower half. winning of a game is equivalent to getting solution for post correspondence problem.

**Example 8.7:** Let $\Sigma = \{0, 1\}$ and $X = \{01, 110010, 1, 11\}$ and

$Y = \{0, 0, 1, 111, 01\}$. Does the *PCP* have solution.

**Solution:** Let $X_1 = 01$, $X_2 = 110010$, $X_3 = 1$, $X_4 = 11$

and $Y_1 = 0$, $Y_2 = 0$, $Y_3 = 1111$, $Y_4 = 01$

The *PCP* have solution for the sequence (1, 3, 2, 4, 4, 3).

The *PCP* have not only one solution. There may be more solution for a *PCP*. The sequence (1, 3, 2, 4, 4, 3, 1, 3, 2, 4, 4, 3) and (1, 3, 2, 4, 4, 3, 1, 3, 2, 4, 4, 3, 1, 3, 2, 4, 4, 3) have also solution.

**Example 8.8:** Let $\Sigma = \{0, 1\}$ and take two lists $X$ and $Y$ as

$X = \{010^3, 0, 01\}$ and $Y = \{01, 0^3, 1\}$. Does the *PCP* have a solution.

**[UPTU B.Tech 2004 (co)]**

**Solution:** We have $X_1 = 101^3$, $X_2 = 0$, $X_3 = 01$

and $Y_1 = 01$, $Y_2 = 0^3$ and $Y_3 = 1$.

Now, we have to determine whether or not there exists a sequence. Such that the string formed by this sequence for $x$ and $y$ are identical.

The required sequence is given (1, 2, 2, 3) *i.e.*

$x_1x_2x_2x_3 = y_1y_2y_2y_3$ are shown belows:

| 01000 | 0 | 0 | 01 |
|---|---|---|---|
| $x_1$ | $x_2$ | $x_2$ | $x_4$ |

| 01 | 000 | 000 | 01 |
|---|---|---|---|
| $y_1$ | $y_2$ | $y_2$ | $y_4$ |

Thus, the *PCP* has solution.

**Example 8.9:** Explain post correspondence problem [*PCP*]. Find atleast three solution to PCP defined by Dominoes.

| 1 | 10 | 10111 |
|---|---|---|
| 111 | 0 | 10 |

***[UPTU B.Tech 2002]***

**Solution:** The *PCP* consists two lists of equal length over the input Σ. The two list are

$$A = W_1 W_2 W_3 ... W_n$$
$$B = X_1 X_2 X_3 ... X_n$$

Then there exists a non empty set at intgers $i_1$, $i_2$, $i_3 ... i_n$ such that

$$w_1 w_2 w_3 ... w_n = x_1 x_2 x_3 ... x_n$$

Let

| The set A consist of | The set B consist of |
|---|---|
| $W_1 = 1$ | $X_1 = 111$ |
| $W_2 = 10$ | $X_2 = 0$ |
| $W_3 = 10111$ | $X_3 = 10$ |

From these dominoes we can define the *PCP* solution as

*i.e.* 101111110 = 101111110

Thus *PCP* has a solution (3, 1, 1, 2)

Repeating the sequence (3, 1, 1, 2) we can get more so results.

### 8.8.1 Modified Post Correspondence Problem (*MPCP*)

Two lists of strings that are equal length over the input $\Sigma^+$

$A = w_1, w_2, w_3 ... w_n$ and $B = x_1, x_2 ... x_n$

does there exist a sequence of integers $i$, $i_2$, $i_3 ... i_n$

such that $n \geq 1$ and

$$w_1 w_{i1} w_{i2} ... w_{in} = x_1 \, x_{i1} \, x_{i2} \, x_{i3} ... x_{in}$$

---

The difference between the *MPCP* and *PCP* is that in the *MPCP*, a solution is required to start with the first string on each list.

---

## 8.9 UNDECIDABIE PROBLEMS INVOLVING CFL'S

We will show that *PCP* can be used as a tool for proving the undecidable problems about context free languages.

In order to prove we reduce those problems into *PCP*. We are presenting here some undecidable problems.

**Theorem 8.12:** It is undecidable whether a *CFL* is ambiguous.

**Proof:** Let $X = \{x_1, x_2, ... x_n\}$ and $Y = \{y_1, y_2, ... y_n\}$ are two sequence of strings over some alphabet $\Sigma$. Let $a_1, a_2, ..., a_n$ be new of distinct symbols (not in $\Sigma$).

Let us consider the two language

$$L_x = (x_{i1}, x_{i2} ... x_{ik}\ a_{ik} ... a_{i2}\ a_{i1} \mid k \geq 1)$$

and $$L_y = (y_{i1}, y_{i2} ... y_{ik}\ a_{ik} ... a_{i2}\ a_{i1} \mid k \geq 1)$$

generated by the grammar $G_x$ and $G_y$ respectively where

$$G_x = \{S_x\}, \Sigma \cup \{a_1, a_2 ... a_n\}, P_x, S_x$$

where $P_x$ consists of $S_x \rightarrow x_i S_x a_i \mid x_i\ a_i$ for $i = 1, 2, ..., n$

and $G_y = \{S_y\}, \Sigma \cup \{a_1, a_2, ..., a_n\}, P_Y, S_Y$ where $P_y$ consists of $S_y \rightarrow y_i S_y\ a_i \mid y_i\ a_i$ for $i = 1, 2, ..., n$

Now, consider the context free grammar $G$ such that

$$L\ (G) = L_x \cup L_y$$

So, $$G = (\{S, S_x, S_y\}), \cup P_x \cup P_y$$

If, any instance $I$ of $PCP$ has a solution, say

$i_1 i_2 ... i_m$ then there is a word

$y_i, y_{i2} ... y_{im}\ q_{im}, a_{im}$ - 1 $a_{i1}$ in $l_x$ that equals the word

$x_{i1}\ x_{i2} ...\ x_{im}\ a_{im}\ a_{im}$ – 1... $a_{i1}$ in $L_y$.

This word has a leftmost derivation beginning $S \rightarrow S_x$ and another beginning $S \rightarrow S_y$. Hence in this case $G$ is ambiguous.

Conversely, Let $G$ is ambiguous. It is clear that both $G_x$ and $G_y$ are unambiguous since $a_i$'s dictate the production used and no word is $L(G_x)$ or $L(G_y)$ have more than one left most derivations. Thus, there must be some string derivable from both $S_x$ and $S_y$. If this word is $Za_{ik}\ a_{ik}$ – 1... $a_{i2}\ a_{i1}$ where $Z$ is in $\Sigma^*$ then $i_1, i_2, i_k$ is a solution to *PCP*. Thus, we have reduced the *PCP* to the ambiguity problem for *CFG's*. But we know that the *PCP* is undecidable and therefore ambiguity problem for *CEG's* is also undecideable.

**Theorem 8.13:** For given two *CFGs* $G_1$ and $G_2$ it is undecidable to determine whether $L(G_1) \cap L(G_2)$ is empty.

**Proof:** Take $G_x$ and $G_y$ defined in previous theorem. If $L(G_x) \cap L(G_y)$ have some $Z$ is not empty then $L(G_x)$ and $L(G_y)$ have some common elements, *i.e.*,

$$x_{i1}, x_{i2} - x_{ik}\ a_{ik-1} ...\ a_1 = y_{i1}\ y_{i2} ... y_{ik}\ a_{ik}\ a_{ik-1}\ ...\ a_1$$

Clearly $(i_1, i_2, ... i_k)$ must be a solution of an instance of *PCP*.

Conversely, if there is a solution $i_1, i_2 ... i_k$ for the instance of *PCP*, the string, $w$ constructed previously is an element of $L(G_x) \cap L(G_y)$.

Therefore, $L(G_1) \cap L(G_2)$ is non empty if and only if an instance of *PCP* has solution.

Thus, have reduced *PCP* to empty problem of intersection of two context free language. Since *PCP* is undecidable, so is the later.

## 8.10 GREIBACH'S THEOREM

This theorem is an analog of Rice's theorem for the context-free languages. It states that

"Let σ be a class of languages that is effectively closed under concatenation with regular sets and union, and for which $L = \Sigma^*$ is undecidable for any sufficiently large fixed Σ. Let *P* be any non-trivial property that is true for all regular sets and that is preserved under a, where a is a single symbol. Then *P* is undecidable for σ."

If *P* is the property of *L* then it is preserved under symbol a means,

$$L/a = \{w/wa \in L\}$$

Greibach's theorem can be used to prove that many problems related to *CFG's* are undecidable. Let us see the problem to check whether for an arbitrary *CFG G*, *L*(*G*) is regular or not. We know that *CFL's* are closed under concatenation with regular sets and union. Let *P* be the property that *L* is regular. *P* is a non-trivial property for *CFL's* and hence from the Greibach's theorem the problem whether the *CFL* is regular is undecidable. Similarly, it can be shown that inherent ambiguity of *CFL's* is undecidable.

## 8.11 CHURCH'S HYPOTHESIS

Hypothesis means proposing certain facts. The church's hypothesis or church's Turing thesis can be stated as,

"The assumption that the intuitive notion of computable functions can be identified with partial recursive functions."

However, this hypothesis can not be proved. The computability of recursive functions is based on following assumptions –

(1) Each elementary function is computable.

(2) Let f be the computable function and *g* be the another function which can be obtained by applying an elementary operation to *f*, then *g* becomes a computable function.

(3) Any function becomes computable if it is obtained by rule 1 and 2.

# EXERCISE

## (A) Objective Type Questions

1. Set of all Turing machines is
   (a) Uncountable (b) Countable but infinite
   (c) Finite (d) Void
2. If there exists a language *L*, for which there exists a *Tm*, *T* that accepts every word in *L* and either rejects or loops for every word that is not in *L*, is said to be
   (a) recursive (b) recursively enumerable
   (c) NP-HARD (d) non of the above.
3. If we have an algorithm to determine whether a given element belongs to a set X or not, then this set is called...
   (a) Recursive (b) Recursively Enumerable
   (c) Complete (d) Context-sensitive
4. If we have a procedure to determine whether a given element belongs to a set *X* or not, then set is called...
   (a) Recursive (b) Recursively Enumerable
   (c) Complete (d) Context-sensitive
5. Find the correct statement
   (a) Recursively enumerable implies recursive
   (b) Recursive implies recursively enumerable
   (c) Recursive is same as recursively enumerable
   (d) None
6. Find the false statement
   (a) *L* is recursively enumerable then so si complement of *L*
   (b) *L* is recursive then so in complement of *L*
   (c) *L* is recursive then complemnt of *L* is recursively enumerable
   (d) If *L* and complement of *L* are recursively enumerable then both are recursive
7. Find the incorrect statement:
   (a) set fo real numbers is not enumerable
   (b) If a set *S* is infinite countable then its power set is not countable
   (c) If *L* is not recursively enumerable then its complement cannot be recursive
   (d) family of recursive is a equivalent to family of recursively enumerable.

**8.** Which of the following statements is true?

(a) A set $X$ is recursive if we have a algorithm to decide whether a given element belongs to $X$ or not.

(b) A recursive set is recursively enumerable.

(c) A context sensitive language is recursive

(d) All of the above

**9.** Let $A$ = set fo recursive languages $B$ = set of recursively enumerable languages. Then

(a) $A$ is subset of $B$ (b) $B$ is a subset of $A$

(c) $A$ and $B$ are the same set (d) $A$ and $B$ are disjoint sets.

**10.** Any language generated by an unrestricted grammar is

(a) Recursive (b) Recursively enumerable

(c) Not recursively enumerable (d) None of these

**11.** The family of recursive languages is not closed under which of the following operations:

(a) Union (b) Intersection

(c) Complementation (d) None of these

**12.** A problem whose language is recursive is said to be:

(a) decidable (b) undecidable

(c) can't say (d) none

**13.** The complement of recursive is:

(a) recursive (b) non-recursive

(c) can't say (d) none

**14.** The problem of deterining that a Turing Machine would halt after giving a Yes/No output is

(a) Unsolvable (b) Solvable

(c) Decidable (d) None of the above

**15.** Which of the following statement is correct?

(a) If the emptiness problem is decidable for Type 3 grammars, then it is also decidable for Type 0 grammars.

(b) If the emptiness problem is decidable for Type 0 grammars, then it is also decidable for Type 3 grammars

(c) If the emptiness problem is undecidable for Type 0 grammars, then it is also undecidable for Type 3 grammars

(d) None of the above.

**16.** Select the false statement:

(a) The Turing Machine Halting problem is Undecidable

(b) The Turing Machine Halting problem is decidable

(c) The blank-tape halting problem is undecidable

(d) None of the above.

**17.** Decidability in Decidable and Undecidable Problems refers to

(a) Unsolvability

(b) Existence of algorithm which generates the set of solutions.

(c) Existence of algorithm which takes an instance of the problem and determines whether the answer to that instance is "yes" or "no".

(d) Those problems whose answers are only either in "yes" or "no".

**18.** Which of the folowing is decidable?

(a) The halting problem

(b) The problem of determining whether or not $L(G)$ = f where $G$ is unrestricted grammar.

(c) The question whether or not $L(M)$ is finite, where $M$ is a Turing machine.

(d) None of above.

**19.** Which of teh following is decidable?

(a) The modified Post Correspondence Problem

(b) The problem to determine whether a string is in $G$ or not, where $G$ is unrestricted grammar.

(c) The problem to decide whether *CFG* is ambiguous or not.

(d) None of the above.

**20.** Which of the following is decidable?

(a) The modified Post Correspondence Problem

(b) The problem to determine whether a string is in $G$ or not, where $G$ is unrestricted grammar.

(c) The problem to decide whether *CFG* is ambiguous or not.

(d) None of the above.

**21.** The membership problem for Type 0 grammars is?

(a) Decidable (b) Undecidable

(c) Partially decidable (d) None of the above.

## ANSWERS

| | | | | |
|---|---|---|---|---|
| **1.** (a) | **2.** (b) | **3.** (b) | **4.** (c) | **5.** (d) |
| **6.** (d) | **7.** (a) | **8.** (b) | **9.** (d) | **10.** (a) |
| **11.** (d) | **12.** (b) | **13.** (d) | **14.** (a) | **15.** (b) |
| **16.** (b) | **17.** (c) | **18.** (d) | **19.** (b) | **20.** (d) |
| **21.** (a) | | | | |

## (B) Problems

1. Find two unsolvable decision problems neither of which can be reduced to other, and prove your answer.
2. Let $M_1$ and $M_2$ are two Turing machines. Show that following problems are undecidable.
   (i) Are there any strings accepted by neither $M_1$ nor $M_2$?
   (ii) Is $L(M_1) \cap L(M_2)$ nonempty?
   (iii) Is $L(M_1) \subseteq L(M_2)$ or $L(M_2) \subseteq L(M_1)$?
3. For a given Turing machine $M_1$, for each decision problem given below, determine whether it is decidable or undecidable, and prove your answer.
   (i) Does $M$ accept the string $\in$ in even number of moves?
   (ii) Is there any string it accepts in even number of moves?
   (iii) Does $M$ loop forever on any input string $w$?
   (iv) Are there any input strings on which $M$ loop forever?
4. Show that the halting problem of *Tm* can be regarded similar to the problem of the existence of recursive enumerable language but not recursive.
5. Let $T$ be any *Tm*. Show that the problem "whether $L(T)$ = finite?" is undecidable.
6. Let $T_1$ and $T_2$ be two *Tms*. Show that the problem. "Does there exist a string on which $T_1$ and $T_2$ both halt" is undecidable.
7. Find the problem "whether an arbitrary *Tm* ever writes a non-blank symbol when started on the empty tape" is decidable or undecidable?
8. Does the *PCP* with $x = (b^3, ab^2)$ and $y = (b^3, bab^3)$ have a solution?
9. Find at least three solutions to *PCP* defined by the dominoes:

| 1 | 10 | 10111 |
|---|---|---|
| 111 | 0 | 10 |

10. Prove that *PCP* is solvable if $|\Sigma| = 1$s

❑❑❑

CHAPTER

# 9

# THEORY OF RECURSIVE FUNCTION AND INTRACTABILITY

## 9.1 INTRODUCTION

In the previous chapters, we have discussed the automata or machine models of the computational phenomenon. The automata approach to computation is operational in nature,3 i.e. automata approach is concerned with the computational aspect of "how the computation is to be performed".

In the first half of this chapter, we will concerned with Recursive Function Theory, which is a functional or declarative approach to computation. Under this approach, computation is described in terms of "what is to be accomplished" instead of "how to accomplish".

In the second half of this chapter, we will concerned with intractable problems.

---

Problems which cannot be solved in polynomial time, called intractable problems.

---

Chomsky classified the languages according to their "structural complexity" such as type 0, type 1 etc.

In the second part of this chapter, we will talk of another method, known as "Computational Complexity", method, known as "Computational Complexity", which is based on the space, time and other resources required by a languages to be accepted by a universal machine such as *TM*.

## 9.2 THEORY OF RECURSIVE FUNCTION

Recursive function is class of functions those are Turing computable. The theory of recursive functions is just converse to Church's hypothesis. Recursive function theory begins with some very elementary functions that are intuitively effective. Then it provides a few methods for building more complicated functions from simpler functions. That means the computability of given function can be proved using the initial function and some building operations which are few in number.

**Initial function:** The initial functions are the elementary functions whose values are independent of their smaller arguments. The following functions comprise the class of recursive functions.

The zero function : $z(X) = 0$

The successor function : s(X) = successor of $x$ (roughly, "$x$+1")

The identity function : $id(X) = x$

The zero functions returns zero regardless of its argument.

The successor functions returns the successor of its argument. Since successorship is a more primitive notion.

The zero and successor functions take only one argument each. But the identity functions is designed to take any number of arguments. When it takes one argument (as above) it returns its argument as its value. When it takes more one argument, it returns one of them. That means,

$$id(x,y) = x$$
$$id(x,y) = y$$

## 9.2.1 Structuring Rules

Now we are ready to consider ways to combine functions to obtain new ones. The initial functions provide an infinite set of functions from which other functions may be build by using the structuring rules.

We define three structuring rules–

(*i*) Composition

(*ii*) Primitive Recursion

(*iii*) Minimization

### (*i*) Composition

It is sometimes necessary to combine two functions so that the valves of the one becomes the arguments of the other. Such a process of combination is called composition and the resulting function is called the ***composite function.***

We will start with the successor function,

$$s(x) = x+1$$

Then we may replace its argument, $x$, with a function. If we replace the argument, $x$, with the zero function.

$z(x)$ then the result is the successor of zero,

$$s(z(x)) = 1$$
$$s(s(z(x))) = 2 \text{ and so on.}$$

In this way, with the help of the initial functions we can describe the natural numbers. It should be clear that when composition is applied to computable functions, only computable functions will result.

### (*ii*) Primitive Recursion

The second building operation is called primitive recursion. Primitive recursion is a method of defining new functions from old function. The function h is defined through functions $f$ and $g$ by primitive recursion when

$$h(x,0) = f(x)$$
$$h(x,s(y)) = g(x,h(x,y)))$$

Where f and g are known computable functions. There are two equations. When h's second argument is zero, the first equation applies; when it is not zero, we use the second. Use of successor function in second equation enforces the condition that the argument be greater than zero. Hence, the first equation applies in the minimal case and the second applied in every other case.

To solve the function by primitive recursion

(1) When the second argument of $h$ is zero, the function is equivalent to some known function $f$ and we compute it;

(2) Otherwise it is equivalent to some known function $g$ and we compute it.

Thus the function obtained will be computable in nature. For example, we can calculate the factorial function using recursion as:

Initially 1! = 1 and to calculate $n!$, if we multiply $n$ by $(n - 1)$ then it will generate a non recursive series. Instead of that we will multiply $n$ by $(n - 1)!$ We can express the calculation of factorial function by following two equations–

$$1! = 1$$

$$n! = n^*(n - 1)$$

A strict definition of the factorial function, $f(n)$ then, consists of these two equations:

$$f(n) = 1 \quad \text{when } n = 1 \quad ...(1)$$

$$f(n) = n^*(f(n - 1)) \quad \text{when } n > 1 \quad ...(2)$$

Consider $n = 5$ then using equation (2) we will get,

$$f(5) = 5^*f(4)$$

$$f(4) = 4^*f(3)$$

$$f(3) = 3^*f(2)$$

$$f(2) = 2^*f(1)$$

By putting the value of equation (1) for calculating $f(2)$ we will get,

$$f(2) = 2^*1 = 2$$

Then $f(3) = 3^*f(2)$

$= 3^*2$

$= 6$

Then $f(4) = 4^*f(3)$

$= 4^*6$

$= 24$

Then $f(5) = 5^*f(4)$

$= 5^*24$

$= 120$

Primitive recursion is like mathematical induction. The first equation defines the basis, and the second defines the induction step.

### (*iii*) Minimization

If $g(x)$ is a function that computes the least $x$ such that $f(x) = 0$, then we know that $g$ is computable. And we can say that $g$ is produced from $f$ by minimization. But we can build $g$ by minimization only if $f(x)$ is already known to be computable.

For example: Suppose we want to obtain least $x$ which makes $f(x) = 0$, then we will try the natural numbers 0,1,2,....until we reach the first value that gives $f(x) = 0$. Now if such search for x never gets terminated then it is called ***unbounded minimization***. And if we obtain such $x$ within some tests then it is called ***bounded minimization.*** While unbounded minimization has the disadvantages of a partial function which may never terminate, bounded minimization has the disadvantage of sometimes failing to minimize.

**Example 9.1:** Define $m!$ recursively. ***[GGSU B-Tech 2002]***

**Solution:** Let $g(m) = m! = m * (m - 1) * (m - 2) *....*1$

We know that $0! = 1! = 1$

So, $g(0) = 1g(m) = m * f(m - 1)$ [for $m \geq 1$]

If $h$ is a function defined by, $h(x,y) = x * y$

$$g(n+1) = h(n + 1, g(n)$$

So $m!$ is recursively.

**Example 9.2:** Define the sum of $n$ natural numbers by recursive function.

***[B-Tech 2001]***

**Solution:** We can obtain the sum of $n$ natural number by the recursive function which is defined inductively as follows:

$$f(o) = 0$$

$$f(n) = f(n - 1) + n \quad \text{for} \geq 1$$

For example,

$$\begin{aligned} f(3) &= f(2) + 3 \\ &= f(1) + 2 + 3 \\ &= f(0) + 1 + 2 + 3 \\ &= f(0) + 1 + 2 + 3 \\ &= 0 + 1 + 2 + 3 \\ &= 6 \end{aligned}$$

Let $g$ be another function on $N \times N$ defined by $g(n, m) = n + m$.

We can then write the function $f$ recursively as follows:

$$\begin{aligned} f(o) &= o = z(0) \\ f(n) &= g(n, f(n - 1)) \\ &= g(h_1(n), h_2(n)) \end{aligned}$$

where $h_1(n) = n = 5(n - 1)$, successor of $(n - 1)$ and

$h_2(n) = f(n - 1) = f(P(x))$ for all $n \geq 1$.

**Example 9.3:** Show that the function $f : N \times N \rightarrow N$ such that $f(m, n) = m^2 - n^2$ can be constructed by composition of other functions.

***[DU MCA 1998]***

**Solution:** we can write

$$m^2 - n^2 = (m + n)(m - n)$$

Let $g_1(m, n) = (m + n)$

$g_2(m, m) = (m - n)$

and, $h(m,n) = m \cdot n$

By composition we can define $f(m, n)$ in terms of $g_1$, $g_2$ and $h$ as follows:

$$f(m, n) = h(g_1\ (m, n), g_2\ (m, n))$$

**Example 9.4:** Express the function $f(n, m) = n^2 + m^2$, $(n, m) \in N^2$ in generalized composition form.

**Solution:** Let us define the function $g$ and $h$ on $N^2$ by

$g(n_1, n_2) = n_1 + n_2$ and

$h(n_1, n_2) = n_1 * n_2$ for $(n_1, n_2) \in N^2$

Then we can write $f$ is

$f(n, m) = g(h(n, n), h(m, m))$ for $(n, m) \in N^2$

## 9.3 CLASSIFICATION OF RECURSIVE FUNCTION

We can classify of recursive functions as follows:

(*i*) Partial Recursive Function

(*ii*) General Recursive Function

(*iii*) Primitive Recursive Function

The relationship among the functions are shown in the venn diagram as below:

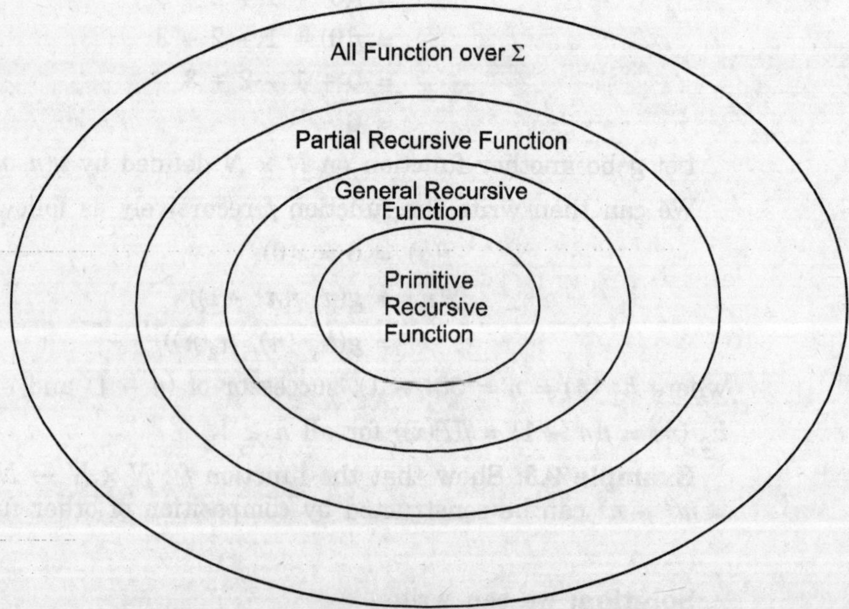


***Fig. 9.1 Hierarchy of RF***

or we say that

| Primitive $RF \subset$ General $RF \subset$ Partial $RF \subset$ all Functions |
|---|

### 9.3.1 Partial Recursive Function

**[*B-Tech 2007, 2005*]**

The function is called Partial recursive function it is can be obtained by applying composition primitive recursion and minimization as operations.

We know that partial *RF* are Turing computable, it means that there exist a Turing machine *TM* for every partial recursive function.

### 9.3.2 General Recursive Function

The function is called general recursive if it is obtained by applying composition, primitive recursive and an unbounded minimization that happen to terminate. The general recursive function is a larger class than partial recursive functions.

### 9.3.3 Primitive Recursive Function

A function is primitive if it follows the following condition:

(*i*) It is an initial function or

(*ii*) It is obtained from recursive or composition of initial functions.

or in other words,

"The function is called primitive recursive if it is obtained by applying composition, primitive and unbounded minimization that does not terminate".

---

Most popular general *RF* are primitive recursive functions, however some are not. For example, the ackermann function is general *RF* but not primitive recursive function.

---

**Example 9.5:** Show that addition function of two integers is primitive recursive.

**Solution:**

$$f(m, o) = m = P_1(m)$$

$$f(m, n+1) = f(m, n) + 1 = s(f(m, n))$$

For example, let us consider $f(8, 2)$

$$f(8, 2) = s(f(8, 1)) = f(8, 1) + 1$$

$$= s(f(8, 0)) + 1$$
$$= f(8, 0) + 1 + 1$$
$$= 8 + 1 + 1$$
$$= 10$$

Hence, $f$ is a primitive function

### Some important point of Primitive Recursive Function

According to David Hilbert. "Primitive recursion is nothing but the principle of mathematical induction process. The basic idea is that the principle of mathematical induction can be used to construct functions recursively.

For example, consider the following functions:

$$f(n, m) = n^m \; (n, m) \in N^2$$

We can obtain this function $f$ inductively as follows:

(*i*) $f(n, o) = n^o = 1$

(*ii*) $f(n, m + 1) = n^{m+1} = n \times n^m$

$$= n \times f(n, m)$$

We can thus define the class of primitive recursive function as follows:

(*i*) All base or initial functions and primitive recursive.

(*ii*) All function obtained by generalized composition or by primitive recursion from primitive recursive functions are primitive recursive.

In other words, the functions that can be constructed out of the base functions and finitely many applications of two operations generalized composition and primitive recursion are primitive recursive functions.

**Example 9.6:** Show that Fibonacci numbers 0, 1, 1, 2, 3, 5, 8, 13, 21, ..... can be defined recursively.

**Solution:** Let $f(n)$ be the $n^{\text{th}}$ Fibonacci number.

Then we can define f recursively as follows:

$$f(0) = 0$$
$$f(1) = 1$$
$$f(n) = f(n - 1) + f(n - 2) \qquad \text{for } n \geq 2$$

we can further write it as

$$f(0) = 0$$
$$f(1) = 1$$
$$f(n) = g(h_1 \; (n), \; h_2(n)) \qquad \text{for } n \geq 2$$

where, $g(n, m) = n + m \;\forall\; (n, m) \in N \times N,$

$h_1(n) = \mathrm{f}(\mathrm{n} - 1) = f\,(p\;(n))$ and

$h_2(n) = f(n - 2) = f(p(p(n))) \qquad \text{for } n \geq 2$

### Primitive *RF* over an Alphabet

It is possible to extend the notion of primitive recursive functions to functions other than those of integers. For example, to the functions defined over an alphabet set Σ (or on string of symbols).

Let $\Sigma = \{a_1, a_2, \ldots a_n\}$ be a finite alphabet also, let a set of functions be defined from $(\Sigma)^n \rightarrow \Sigma$, where $\Sigma^*$ stands for the set of all finite strings of symbols from Σ including ∈(NULL string).

## 9.4 GODEL NUMBERING

Till now we had no system that could convert a string into numbers and numbers into string for some alphabet.

The Kurt Godel used an idea to develop an encoding scheme to assign numbers to strings and formulas.

"A Godel numbering is an encoding technique which encodes a string as a number". This is also known as ***Godelelization.***

In other words,

"A Godel numbering is a function which assigns to each symbol and formula of some formal language a unique natural number called on Godel number (*GN*)."

Godel numbers are constructed as follows. First we identify the elements we are to represent, and then we assign a natural number to each one. Finally, we assign a natural to each possible sequence of the elements; these last numbers are our Godel numbers.

To number the primitive sings, they are assigned the first 7 odd numbers:

"0" (zero) = 1

"succ"(successor) = 3

"¬" (not) = 5

"⊢"(logical or) = 7

" " (for all) = 9

"(" (left parenthesis) = 11

")" (right parenthesis) = 13

Each variable of type *n* is uniquely assigned a number of the form *p n* where *p* is a prime greater than 13; each variable of a given type will have a different value of *p*.

This allows us to represent every sequence of basic signs as a sequence of natural number.

Finally, given the sequence $(n_1, n_2, \ldots\ldots n_k)$, which can be mapped to a given sequence of signs, we seek to represent this sequence as a single number. We do this by mapping $(n_1, n_2, \ldots n_k)$ to $2n_1, 3n_2, \ldots p_k n_k$ where $p_k$ prime. This product of powers of primes is the Godel number of the expression.

For example –

The expression "succ($n$)", where n is a variable of type 1, can be expressed by the sequence (1,17), where "such" is represented by 1, and "n" is represented by 17 to the power of 1. We convert this to a single number by calculating $2^1.2^{17} = 258280326$. This rather large number 258280326 is the Godel number of "succ($n$)".

**Example 9.7:** Consider $\Sigma = \{a, b, c\}$. Find Godel numbers for the strings $a$, $ab$, $abc$, $ccc$, $acb$.

**Solution:** Since $|\Sigma| = 3$, so $B = 3 + 1 = 4$

We use 4 as a base for number system corresponding to $\Sigma$, Let $a \equiv 1$, $b \equiv 2$, $c \equiv 3$ and $\epsilon \equiv 0$.

then
$$G_n(a) = 4^0 \times 1 = 4$$
$$G_n(ab) = 4^1 \times 1 + 4^0 \times 2 = 6$$
$$G_n(abc) = 4^2 \times 1 + 4^1 \times 2 + 4^0 \times 3 = 27$$
$$G_n(ccc) = 4^2 \times 3 + 4^1 \times 3 + 4^0 \times 3 = 63$$
$$G_n(acb) = 4^2 \times 1 + 4^1 \times 3 + 4^0 \times 2 = 30$$

We can find the inverse of a Godel number in order to find the string for a given number. This is called the inverse of Godel number represented as $G_n^{-1}$

**Example 9.8:** Let $\Sigma = \{a, b, c\}$. Find the string corresponding to the numbers 0, 3, 13, 63.

**Solution:** Since $|\Sigma| = 3$, $B = 3 + 1 = 4$. We convert the numbers into base 4 which shows the integer value of the characters in the string. Note that if $n = 0$, then $(0)_{10} \equiv (0)_4$

$$G^{-1}(0) = 0 = \varepsilon$$

if $n = 3, (3)_{10} = (3)_4$

$$G_n^{-1}(3) = c \qquad \{\text{since, } C \equiv 3\}$$

if $n = 13, (13)_{10} = (31)_4$

$$G_n^{-1}(31) = ca$$

if $n = 63, (63)_{10} \equiv (333)_4$

$$G_n^{-1}(63) = ccc$$

---

There are a variety of Godel numbering schemes. Some use prime numbers to factorize the number instead of base $B = n + 1$, *i.e.*, the string $a_1, a_2, ..., a_n$ can be Godelize as

$$G_n(a_1, a_2, ..., a_n) = 2^{a_1} 3^{a_2} 5^{a_3} ...(P_r N(n))^{a_n}$$

where $P_r N_{(n)}$ generates the $n^{th}$ prime number.

---

## 9.5 THEORY OF INTRACTABILITY

To analyze the problems it requires to determine what are the operations it is composed of and their relative costs. These operations may include simple arithmetic ones such as addition, subtraction, multiplication and division or may include other operations like floating point arithmetic, comparisons and so on.

Majority of these simple operations typically take no more than a fixed amount of time and can be said that their time is bounded by a constant. But this is not true for all operations.

For example, comparisons of two character strings depends on the length of the strings any may differ every time depending on that length parameter.

Let us see what are the measures used for the complexity of a problem and the classification of these problems depending on their complexity measures.

"Interactability means techniques for showing problems not to be solvable in polynomial time."

## 9.6 COMPLEXITY OF A PROBLEM

There are two kinds of computational complexity

→ Time complexity

→ space complexity

### Time complexity

If a problem can be solved by some *TM*, then we can write a computer program to solve it. If we assume the single transition of the *TM* as the unit of measure, then the total number of transitions performed by *TM* before reaching or halting state is called the time complexity.

### Space Complexity

Space complexity is defined as the maximum number of tape cells used by *T* for any input string of length '*n*'.

We note that the complexity analysis depends on the number of factors stated as follows:

→ what is the unit of measure?

→ what is the "size" of input?

→ what algorithm is chosen to solve a given problem?

→ what is the model of computation?

### Mathematical Notations for Complexity Measure

There are various mathematical notations which are very useful in the complexity analysis. The complexity analysis with the help of these notations concentractes on determining the order of magnitude of the frequency of execution of a problem rather than worrying about the machine depends.

### (*i*) O-notation

One of these notations is the O-natation. It may be define as –

$$f(n) = O(g(n))$$

read as "f of $n$ equals big oh of $g$ of $n$"

A problem for which we are determining the computing time $f(n)$ said to have computing time $O(g(n))$. We mean that for increasing values of n, the resulting time will always be less than some constant time $|g(n)|$.

That means to find out the order of magnitude of computing time $f(n)$ of a problem we try to obtain the smallest $g(n)$ such that $f(n) = 0(g(n))$.

For example, if there are two problems having computing time equals to $O(n)$ and $O(n^2)$, both working on $n$ inputs and performing the same task, then the problem having computing time $O(n)$ is superior and more faster compared to the problem with computing time $O(n^2)$.

The most common computing times for many problems are $O(1)$, $O(\text{logn})$, $O(n)$, $O(n\text{logn})$, $O(n^2)$, $O(n^3)$ and $O(2^n)$. These can be mapped against the number of inputs $n$ as show in Fig.

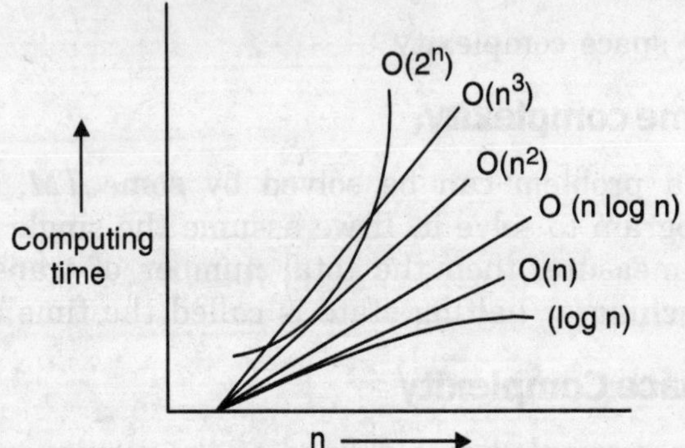


***Fig. 9.2 Computing time comparisons***

The relationships among these different computing timer can be seen as follows:

$$O(1) < O(\text{logn}) < O(n\text{logn}) < O(n^2) < O(n^3) < O(2^n)$$

### (*ii*) W-notation

If we wish to find a function which is a lower bound on the computing time there is another notation used reffered to as Ω-notation (omega).

$$f(n) = \Omega(g(n))$$

read as "$f$ of $n$ equals omega of $g(n)$"

### (*iii*) θ-notation

In some cases $g(n)$ represents both lower and upper bound on the computing time $f(n)$. In such case θ-notation is used.

$$f(n) = \theta(g(n))$$

read as "if of $n$ equals θ of $g(n)$.

## 9.7 CLASSIFICATION OF PROBLEMS

We have seen that a solvable problem is one that admits an algorithm. It this case a problem is solvable "in principle". But, in practice, the algorithm may require a lot of space (memory) and time (time to apply the steps of the algorithm). When the space and time required for implementing the algorithm are reasonable, we can say that the problem is ***tractable*** (*i.e.* solvable in practice).

A decision problem is tractable if there is an algorithm to solve the given problem and the time required is expressed as a polynomial $P(n)$, $n$ being the length of the input string. Usually problems are ***intractable*** if the time required for any of the algorithm is at least $f(n)$, where $f$ is an exponential function of $n$.

---

The problems that can be solved in polynomial time are called tractable problems and the problems that require more than any polynomial running time are called intractable.

---

Many of the problems that we know are broadly classified into main two categories–

(*i*) Polynomial time ($P$) problem

(*ii*) Non-polynomial time ($NP$) problem

### 9.7.1 The Class P Problem

**[*MCA 2001, B-Tech 2002*]**

The problem whose solution can be given by a polynomial time algorithm, which means, the function $f(n)$ representing the computing time of a problem is a polynomial; then the problem is $P$ type problem.

In other words, we can say

"A language $L$ is said to be in class $P$ if there exists a (deterministic) $TM$ $M$ such $M$ is of time complexity $P(n)$ for some polynomial $P$ and $M$ accepts $L$."

The class of problems which are solvable by deterministic *TM* in polynomial time is denoted by P. A problem is tractable if it is belongs to class *P* and a problem which is not in class *P* is called intractable.

Examples of problems belonging to the class P are many. Some of the problems are summarized below:

| S.No. | Problems | Algorithms | Time complexity |
|---|---|---|---|
| 1. | ***Sorting.*** To sort an array of $n$ numbers | Quicksor | $O(n \log n)$ –an average case running time. $O(n^2)$ –an worst case running time |
| 2. | ***Searching an element.*** To determine whether an item can be found in an $n$-element list. | Simple search | $O(n)$ |
| 3. | ***Matrix multiplications*** of order $n \times n$ | Strassen's method | $O(n^{2.81})$ |
| 4. | ***FFT.*** To compute the Forurier transform of a sequence of $n$ complex | Fast fourier transform (*FFT*) | $O(n\ h(n))$, $h(n) = a_1(p_1-1) +...+ h_k(p_k-1)$ where $n$ $p_1^{a_1} p_2^{a_2} ... p_k^{a_k}$ |
| 5. | ***Network flow problem.*** To determine the maximum net quantity of fluid that could be flowing from source to sink in a network in which every edge has integer capacity. | Ford and Fulkerson | "a finite number of steps" |
| 6. | ***MST.*** To obtain minimum spanning tree from an undire cted connected graph with $n$-vertices and $e$-edges | Prim's method Kruskal's method | $O(n^2)$ $O(e \log e)$ |
| 7. | ***Single source shortest path.*** To determine the shortest path from so- | Dijkstra's Greedy method | $O((n + e)\log n)$ |

| | | | |
|---|---|---|---|
| | urce node to all remaining vertices of a directed graph | | |
| 8. | ***Multistage graph problem.*** To find a minimum cost path from source $s$ to sink $t$ from a multistage graph with $n$-vertices and $e$ edges | Forward (or Backward) dynamic programming | $O(n + e)$ |

## 9.7.2 The Class NP Problem

**[*B-Tech 2001, 2003, 2005*]**

If there is no polynomial time algorithm to solve a problem, then the problem can be classified as *NP* type problem.

In other words, we can say

"A language $L$ is in class *NP* if there is a nondeterministic Turing machine $M$ such that $M$ is of time complexity $P(n)$ for some polynomial $P$ and $M$ accepts $L$."

---

The class of problems which are solvable by non-deterministic *TM* in polynomial time is denoted by *NP*.

---

## 9.7.3 Compare of Class *P* and *NP* problem

Although the definitions of $P$ and *NP* are worded similarly, there is a vast difference between them.

→ when $L$ is in $P$, the number of moves to test whether any input string of length $n$ is less than or equal to $P(n)$.

→ when $L$ is in *NP*, the number of moves for testing is less than or equal to $n$ only for strings accepted by $M$.

→ class *NP* consists of decision problems for which we have only to verify that an alleged solution is correct. we do not, in fact, look to find a solution fo the problem.

→ class $P$ is consists of decision problems for which we look to find a solution where as in class *NP* we only check the correctness of a claimed answer.

One of the open problems in theoretical computer science is whether

$$P = NP$$

It is obvious that $P \subseteq NP$. It is not known whether there exists some language $L$ in $NP$, which does not have a deterministic $TM$ accepting it. Many practical and important are known to be in $NP$. So for none of them admit a deterministic $TM$ accepting it.

In the next section, we shall explore this problem further by introducting two new classes-$NP$-hard and $NP$-complete. But to define these classes, we need to defined the notation of polynomial-time reductions.

**Definition:** Let $P_1$ and $P_2$ be two problems. We say that $P_1$ is polynomially reducible to $P_2$ if we can solve $P_1$ by a deterministic algorithm in a polynomial time using a deterministic algorithm that solves $P_2$ in polynomial time.

Since we use the terms problem and language interchangeable, we may also introduce the notion of reducibility between languages as follows.

**Definition:** Let $L_1 \subseteq \Sigma_1^*$ and $L_2 \subseteq \Sigma_2^*$ be two languages. we then say that $L_1$ is polynomially reducible to $L_2$ if there exists a polynomial-time algorithm that converts each input $x_1 \in \Sigma_1^*$ to another input $x_2 \in \Sigma_2^*$ such that $x_1 \in L_1$ iff $x_2 \in L_2$.

## 9.8 NP-COMPLETENESS [UPTU B-TECH 2006]

$S.A$ cook introduced the concept of $NP$-completness as a step towards solving "$P = NP$". Now a number of $NP$-complete problems exist in various areas.

### 9.8.1 NP-Hard and NP Complete Classes

There are some problems that if they are in $P$, then all of $NP$ is in $P$. We call such problems to be ***NP-complete problems***

We say that a problem $Q$ is $NP$-complete if the following hold about $Q$.

(*i*) $Q$ is in $NP$, and

(*ii*) for every problem $R$ in $NP$, $R$ is polynomially reducible to $Q$.

A problem $Q$ with the property (*ii*) is called ***NP-hard problem***

Thus, we can say that a problem $Q$ is in $NP$ and $Q$ is $NP$-hard.

---

✍ A problem $A$ is $NP$-hard if and only if satisfiability reduces to $A$. A problem $A$ is $NP$-complete if and only if $A$ is $NP$ hard and $A \in NP$.

---

To show that a $NP$-hard problem is $NP$-complete we have just to determine a polynomial time non-deterministic algorithm for that problem.

### Properties of the class of *NP*-complete problems

Once we have some *NP*-complete problems, we can prove a new problem to be *NP*-complete by reducing some know *NP*-complete problem to it, using a polynomial-time reduction.

Now let us discuss some properties of *NP* complete problems.

(*i*) No polynominal time algorithm has been found for any one of them.

(*ii*) It is not established that polynomial time algorithm for these problems do not exist.

(*iii*) If a polynomial-time algorighm is found for one at them, there will by polynomial-time algorighm for all at them.

(*iv*) If it can be proved that no polynomial time algorithm exists for any one at them, then it will not exist for every one of them.

There are various examples of *NP*-complete problems such as

→ Travelling salasman Problem

→ zero-one programming problem

→ Satisfiability problem (SAT)

→ vertex cover Problem

→ Four color Problem

→ clique Problem

→ Hamitonian circuit Problem

→ Dominating set Problem

## EXERCISE

### (A) Objective Type Questions

**1.** Which of the following is not primitive recursive:

(a) Addition (b) Division

(c) LCM (d) Ackerman's function

**2.** If $\omega \varepsilon L(G)$ and $|w| = k$ where $G$ is in Chomsky Normal Form, the number of steps in derivation of $w$ are:

(a) $2k$ (b) $2k - 1$

(c) $k - 1$ (d) $k$

**3.** If $\omega \varepsilon L(G)$ and $|w| = k$ where $G$ is Greibach Normal From, the number of steps in derivation of $\omega$ are:

(a) $2k$ (b) $2k - 1$

(c) $k - 1$ (d) $k$

**4.** Consider a language $L$ for which there exists a *TM*, $T$ that accepts every word in $L$ and either rejects or loops for every word that is not in $L$, the language $L$ is

(a) *NP*-hard (b) *NP*-complete

(c) recursive (d) recursively enumerable

**5.** Let $P_1$ be reduced to $P_2$. Let $P_2$ be undecidable. Then what can be said about $P_1$:

(a) Decidable (b) Undecidable

(c) Cannot say (d) None of these

**6.** Let $A$ = set of recursive languages

$B$ = set of recursively enumerable languages. Then

(a) $A$ is a subset of $B$ (b) $B$ is a subset of $A$

(c) $A$ and $B$ are the same set (d) $A$ and $B$ are disjoint sets.

**7.** The family of languages belonging to *NP* is closed under which of the following operations:

(a) Unoin (b) Intersection

(c) Complementation (d) All of the above.

**8.** A problem $L$ is *NP*-complete iff

(a) $L$ is *NP*-hard

(b) $L$ is in *NP*

(c) SAT is reducible to $L$ and $L$ is in *NP*

(d) $L$ is in co*NP*

**9.** Which of the following problem is not *NP*-complete:

(a) 3-coloring problem (b) Travelling Salesman problem

(c) Knapsack problem (d) 2-SAT problem

**10.** If $NP \neq coNP$ then

(a) $NP = P$ (b) $NP \neq P$

(c) $P \neq coNP$ (d) $P = coNP$

**11.** Let $L$ be an *NP*-complete problem. Then $P = NP$ iff

(a) SAT is reducible to $L$

(b) $L$ is in $P$

(c) $L$ is polynomially reducible to some *NP*-complete problem.

(d) $L$ is in co*NP*

**12.** Intractable problems are those which

(a) are not solvable (b) which are not in *NP*

(c) which are not in $P$ (d) which are in co*NP*

**13.** A *NP*-hard problem is a problem

(a) which is harder than *NP* problem

(b) which is not is *P*

(c) to which all the *NP* problems are polynomially reducible

(d) which is in *P*

**14.** A class of problems called———if there is solution of one decision problem from that family then there will be solution for each and every decision problem from that family

(a) *P* (b) *NP*

(c) *P*-complete (d) *NP*-complete

**15.** A problem is *NP* hard if

(a) It is hard to implement.

(b) It can be verified in polynomial time by a deterministic machine.

(c) Every problem in *NP* is transformable to it in polynomial time.

(d) It can not be solved in exponential time.

**16.** There is no known polynomial time algorithm for the following problem:

(a) Determine if a graph is 2-colorable

(b) Determine all the shortest paths in a weighted graph.

(c) Determine if a number is prime

(d) Find the transitive closure of a relation

**17.** If $P = NP$ then

(a) Every problem in *NP* can be solved in polynomial time

(b) No problem in *NP* can be solved in polynomial time

(c) SAT can not be solved in polynomial time

(d) It is unknown what would happen

**18.** What version of problem is used to determine if it is *NP* hard

(a) Optimal solution problem (b) Worst case solution

(c) Decision problem (d) Optimal value problem

## ANSWERS

| | | | | |
|---|---|---|---|---|
| **1.** (*d*) | **2.** (*b*) | **3.** (*d*) | **4.** (*d*) | **5.** (*b*) |
| **6.** (*a*) | **7.** (*d*) | **8.** (*c*) | **9.** (*d*) | **10.** (*b*) |
| **11.** (*b*) | **12.** (*c*) | **13.** (*c*) | **14.** (*d*) | **15.** (*a*) |
| **16.** (*a*) | **17.** (*c*) | **18.** (*c*) | | |

## (B) Problems

1. Show that the function $f(x, y) = x - y$ is partial recursive
2. Show that a constant function is primitive recursive.
3. Show that Fibonacci numbers are generated by a primitive recursive function.
4. Define $n!$ by recursion.
5. Show the $f(x, y) = x^y$ is a primitive recursive function.
6. Evalvate $A(1, 1)$, $A(2, 1)$, $A(1, 2)$, $A(2, 2)$
7. Prove that, Let $L$ be an $NP$-complete language then $P = NP$ if and only if $L$ is in $P$.
8. Prove that the function, which finds the minimum of two positive integers is primitive recursive function.

❑❑❑

CHAPTER

# 10

# Propositions and Predicates

## 10.1 INTRODUCTION

In this chapter we introduce prepositions and logical connectives. Logic is language for reasoning. It is a collection of rules we use when doing logical reasoning we also investigate the truth value of quantified state- ment, which are statements which use logical quantifiers "for every" and "there exists".

## 10.2 PROPOSITIONS

Consider the following sentences

1. Lucknow is capital of Utter pradesh
2. Kolkata is capital of Gujarat
3. $2 + 3 = 5$
4. $3 + 4 = 9$
5. $7 > 5$
6. $9 < 4$
7. $x + y > 0$ for $x > 0, y > 0$
8. $x = 3$ is a solution of $x^2 = 9$
9. Prime minister of India has to be a man.
10. $101 + 1 = 110$ (in decimal system)
11. $101 + 1 = 110$ (in binary system)
12. Women are more intelligent than men.
13. What is your name ?
14. Watch the movie,
15. Go to your school.
16. $x + y > 0$.

Here we can say that the facts mentioned in sentences 1, 3, 5, 7, 8 and 11 are true or more correctly are universally true and the facts mentioned in sentences 2, 4, 6, 9 and 10, are universally false. The sentence 12 is not universally true. Some people will say it is true while others may say that it is false. The sentences 13, 14 and 15 are not declarative. So we cannot say if these are true or false. Sentences 16 can be true or false depending upon the values of $x$ and $y$. ***Those declarative sentences that are either universally true or universally false but not both are called statements, or propositions.*** Therefore the facts given in sentences 1, 2, 3, 4, 5, 6, 7, 8, 9, 10 and 11 are propositions. We can always find out the truth values of a it can become a proposition only when values of $x$ and $y$ are given. By ***truth***

***value*** of a proposition we mean whether it is, true or false. The truth values of ***'true'*** and ***'false'*** are denoted by '*T*' and '*F*' respectively and the proposition are generally represented by lower case letters like *p*, *q*, *r* etc.

If we are represent the statement

The sun rises in the east by *p* and the statement 3 + 7 > 20 by *q*, then we can write

*p* : The sun rises in the east.

*q* : 3 + 7 > 20

and say that the truth values of *p* and *q* are *T* and *F* respectively.

## 10.3 COMPOUND PROPOSITIONS

The propositions that cannot be broken into simple propositions are called primitive propositions.

These are the propositions *P*(*p*, *q*,.....) that are composed of sub-propositions and various connectives, like and, or, not etc. Such a proposition can be broken into simpler propositions. Truth value of compound proposition is completely determined by the truth values of its sub-propositions together with the way in which it is connected to form the compound proposition or we can define a proposition *P*(*p*, *q*, ....) as an expression constructed form logical variables *p*, *q*, ........, which take on the value "True' (*T*) or 'False' (*F*) and the logical connectives ^, v, ¬, ......

**For example:**

1. The sun rises in the east and sets in the west. It has two sub-proposition viz., *p*: The sun rises in the east and *q*: The sun sets in the west and a connective 'and'.
2. 3 + 7 > 2 or 4 5 < 11 has **two sub-propositions** *p* : 3 + 7 > 2 and *q* : 4 + 5 < 11 and a connective **'or'.**

## 10.4 LOGICAL CONNECTIVES

The words **"and", "or" "if........, then..........", "if and only if"** (denoted by ^, v, ⇒, ⇔ respectively) that serve to connect two simple statements to form a third compound statement are called **logical connectives.**

The name of various logical connectives and the symbols to denote them are given below:

| **Connectives** | **Symbols** |
|---|---|
| Negation (= not) | ~ or/or ¬ |
| Conjunction (= and) | ^ |
| Disgunction (= or)* | v |

| | |
|---|---|
| Exclusive disjunction (= or)* | $\oplus$ or |
| Implication (= If......, then....) | $\Rightarrow$ or $\rightarrow$ |
| Equivalence or Biconditional (-if and only if) | $\Leftrightarrow$ |

(*). *a* n *b* means either *a* or *b* or *a b* both. *a* Å *b* means either *a* or *b* but not *a* and *b* both.

## 10.5 TRUTH VALUES OF COMPOUND STATEMENTS

The compound statement is first broken into simple or primitive statements each being represented by *p*, *q*, *r* ete., and the given compound propositions is represented in symbolic form. Then its truth value is calculated as given in the following discussion.

Suppose our compound statement is Kolkata is in East Bengal and Delhi his in India. **Its primitive propositions can be written as**

*P* : Kolkata is in East Bengal

*q* : Delhi in India.

The symbolic representation of the given compound statements is $p \wedge q$. Here truth value of *p* is *T* and that *q* is *T*.

Similarly the symbolic representation of the compound statement "4 + 3 = 9 or 7 + 3 < 15" shall be $p \vee q$ (where $p$: 4 + 3 = 9 and $q$ : 7 + 3 < 15). Here *p* is *F* and *q* is *T*.

The symbolic representation of "7 + 3 ≠ 5 and 4 + 3 = 7" shall be $\sim p \wedge q$ where $p$ : 7 + 3 = 5 and $q$ : 4 + 3 = 7. Here *p* is *F* and *q* is *T*.

The symbolic representation of "If it rains, then I shall use umbrella" is $p \Rightarrow q$ where *p*: it rains and *q*: I shall use umbrella. The symbolic representation of $x + y > 0$, if and only if $x > 0, y > 0$ shall b $p \Leftrightarrow q$ where $p$: $x + y > 0$ $q$ : $x > 0, y > 0$.

### Truth values of compound propositions using different connective have been calculated below:

### 1. Conjunction, $p \wedge q$

It is a compound proposition formed by combining two primitive propositions by the word **"and"**. It is called **conjunction** of the original propositions represented by *p* and *q* respectively and is written as $p \wedge q$.

$p \wedge q$ being a proposition has a truth value which depends only on the truth values of *p* and *q*. The following table gives the truth value of $p \wedge q$ for different combination of truth values of *p* and *q*.

**Table 1. Truth Table for $p \wedge q$**

| $p$ | $q$ | $p \wedge q$ |
|---|---|---|
| T | T | T |
| T | F | F |
| F | T | F |
| F | F | F |

$p \wedge q$ is true if $p$ is true and $q$ is true

**We give belong a few compound statements ($p \wedge q$) and their truth values (enclosed in circles).**

(*a*) Kolkata is in Bengal and Delhi is in India (*T*)

(*b*) Lucknow is capital of U.P. and 3 + 2 = 6 (*F*)

(*c*) London is in China and 4 + 3 = 7 (*F*)

(*d*) 7 + 4 = 8 and 5 + 10 = 7. (*F*)

## 2 . Disjunction, *p* n *q* :

It is a compound proposition obtained by combining two propositions by the word "Or". It is called disjunction of the original propositions and is written as $p \vee q$ and read "*p* or *q*". Its truth value depends upon the truth values of *p* and *q* as shown below:

**Table 2. Truth table $p \vee q$**

| $p$ | $q$ | $p \wedge q$ |
|---|---|---|
| T | T | T |
| T | F | T |
| F | T | T |
| F | F | F |

$p \vee q$ is false only if $p$ is false and $q$ is false.

**We give below a few compound statements and their truth values (enclosed in circles)**

(*a*) Kolkata is in Bengal or Delhi is in India (*T*)

(*b*) Lucknow is capital of U.P or 3 + 2 = 6 (*T*)

(*c*) London in China or 4 + 3 = 7 (*T*)

(*d*) 7 + 4 = 8 or 5 + 10 = 7 (*F*)

---

In place of *T* and *F* we may write I and 0 respectively.

---

**Example 10.1:** Assign truth value to each of the following statements.

(*a*) 4 < 4 or < 5

(*b*) 5 × 3 = 1 and 3 + 4 = 7

**Solution:** (*a*) Let the two primitive statements be represented as follows:

$P$ : 4 < 4, 4 < 5

Here truth value of $p$ is $F$ and that of $q$ is $T$. The symbolic representation of the given statement is $p \vee q$.

When $p$ is $F$ and $q$ is $T$, then from table 2 $p \vee q$ is $T$. Thus the require d truth value is $T$.

(*b*) Let the two primitive statements be represented as follows:

$p : 5 \times 3 = 1$

and $q : 3 + 4 = 7$

The truth values of $p$ and $q$ $F$ and $T$ respectively. The symbolic representation of the given statement is $p \wedge q$.

When $p$ is $F$ $q$ is $T$, then from table 1, $p \wedge q$ is $F$. Thus the required truth value is $F$.

## 3. $p \oplus q$

The exclusive disjunction of two propositions $p$ and $q$ is the statement "Either $p$ or $q$, but not both $p$ and $q$ is denoted by $p \oplus q$.

**Table 3. Truth table for ⊕**

| $p$ | $q$ | $p \otimes q$ |
|---|---|---|
| T | T | F |
| T | F | T |
| F | T | T |
| F | F | F |

$p \oplus$ is not true if both $p$ and $q$ are true or both $p$ & $q$ are false.

**Example 10.2:** Find truth value of the following exclusive disjunction "2 + 3 = 7" Mohan is an Engineer.

**Solution:** $p \oplus q$. As $p$ is always false, so truth value depends on the truth value of $q$. Form 3rd row → If $q$ is true then $p \oplus q$ is true.

From 4 row → If $q$ is false then $p \oplus q$ is false.

## 4. Negation, Ø p

Negation of statement $p$ can be formed by writing "It is not the case that.........." or It is false that ................" before $p$ or by inserting the word ***"not"*** and is written as $\neg p$ or $\sim p$ & read "not $p$". Its truth value depends non the truth value of $p$ as given below.

**Table 4. Truth value of $\neg$ p**

| $p$ | $\neg p$ |
|---|---|
| T | F |
| F | T |

If $p$ : Delhi is capital of India, then

$\neg p$ : Delhi is not capital of India.

$\neg p$ : It is false that Delhi is capital of India.

$\neg p$ : It is not the case that Delhi is capital of India.

If $q$ : $3 + 2 = 7$

$\neg$ : $3 + 2$ ¹ $7$

$\neg$ : It is false that $3 + 2 = 7$

Alternative notation for $p \wedge q$ are $p \bullet q$, $pq$

Alternative notation for $p \vee q \rightarrow p + q$

Alternative notation for $\neg p \rightarrow$', $\bar{p}$, $\sim p$.

**Warning :** Black and white are not logically opposites necessarily. Whit and non-white (or Not White) are logical opposites. Concept of Negation is related to complementation operation. Negation of "For an is "There exists some" *e.g.*, *p*: All people are rich, **then ~p:** All people are not rich.

## Conditional and Biconditional sentences

## 5. Implications Þ (If........then)

1. If it rains then there will be no game or "It rains" implies the game will be cancelled.
2. If *ABC* is a triangle, then $AB + BC > AC$

The connective if ........then may here placed by implies.

or

Logical symbol of an implication is $\Rightarrow$ $p \Rightarrow q$ read as "if *p*, then *q*" or "*p* implies *q*" is the symbolic representation of aconditional statement.

Other examples:

1. $x = 3 \Rightarrow x^2 = 9$
2. $A \subseteq B \Rightarrow x \in A, x \in B$

**Antecedent** is that component of a conditional statement that is expressed by the "if" clause (the variables p at the tail).

**Consequent** is that component of a conditional statement that is expressed by the "then" clause. (The variables p at the head).

For example, $\underset{\text{antecedent}}{\underline{5+4=6}}$ then $\underset{\text{consequent}}{\underline{9-4=5}}$

(1) It is difficult to decide whether or not there is some connection or relation between antecedent and consequent of a conditional.

(2) $p \Rightarrow$ does not mean that $p$ is the cause of $q$ Not does it mean that it is easy to deduce $q$ from $p$.

(3) $p \Rightarrow q$ does not mean $q \Rightarrow p$.

(4) "If" can be taken to mean "whenever".

For example, **Ordinary sentences written in the "if ... then" form.**

We will go out if the weather improves → If the weather improves, then we will go out.

I will get *A* grade if *I* work hard → If I work hard, then I will get A grade.

**Conditional statement –** is a statement of the form "If $p$ then $q$ **denoted** by $p \Rightarrow q$ and read as "$p$ implies $q$" or "$p$ only if $q$" or *A* compound sentence using the connective If ...., then is called conditional statement.

**Truth table for $p \Rightarrow q$**

| $p$ | $Q$ | $p \Rightarrow q$ |
|---|---|---|
| T | T | T |
| T | F | F |
| F | T | T |
| F | F | T |

$p \Rightarrow q$ is false only when antecedent is true and consequent is false.

### 10.5.1 $p \Rightarrow q \equiv \neg p \vee q$

Now we shall show that $p \Rightarrow q$ is logically equivalent $\neg p \vee q$ and logically equivalent to $\neg q \Rightarrow \neg p$ with the help of truth tables

| $p$ | $q$ | $\neg p$ | $\neg q$ | $\neg p \vee q$ | $\neg q \Rightarrow \neg p$ | $p \Rightarrow q$ |
|---|---|---|---|---|---|---|
| T | T | F | F | T | T | T |
| T | F | F | T | F | F | F |
| F | T | T | F | T | T | T |
| F | F | T | T | T | T | T |

As the columns for $\neg p \vee q$, $\neg q \Rightarrow \neg p$ and $p \neg q$ are identical, we conclude that

$$\neg p \vee q \equiv \neg q \Rightarrow \neg p \equiv p \Rightarrow q$$

Now we summarize the discussion made above in the following form:

## Summary of if ..., then ...

[*A*] If '*p*' then $q$ *i.e.,* $p$ implies $q$ *i.e.,* $p \Rightarrow q$

$$p \Rightarrow q \equiv \neg q \vee q \equiv q \Rightarrow \neg p \text{ (if not } q \text{ then not } p)$$

$$\equiv \text{ only if } q\text{; then } p \equiv p \text{ only if } q$$

$q$ is necessary for $p$ (*i.e.,* if not $q$ then not $p$)

$p$ is hypothesis and $q$ is conclusion.

[*B*]. If $q$, then $p$ *i.e.,* $q \Rightarrow p$

$$q \Rightarrow q \equiv \neg p \vee q \equiv \neg q \Rightarrow \neg q \text{ (i.e., if not } p \text{ then not } q)$$

$$\equiv \text{ only if } p\text{, then } q \equiv q \text{ only if } p$$

$p$ is necessary for $q$ (i.e., if not $p$ then not $q$) $q$ is hypo thes is and $p$ is conclusion.

**We given below a few conditional statements along with their symbolic representation.**

**Example 10.3:** Test if the following two statement written on two restaurants are equivalent or not

1. Good food is not cheap.
2. Cheap food is not good.

**Solution:** Let p denote "the food is good", and $q$ denote "the food is cheap"

Statement 1 is : $p \Rightarrow 7q$ { we will show below that truth table for both the statements are the same.

Statement 2 is : $q \Rightarrow 7p$

| p | q | $\neg p$ | $\neg q$ | $p \Rightarrow \neg q$ | $q \Rightarrow \neg p$ |
|---|---|---|---|---|---|
| T | T | F | F | F | F |
| T | F | F | T | T | T |
| F | T | T | F | T | T |
| F | F | T | T | T | T |

Identical columns

Hence $P \Rightarrow \rceil q \equiv q \Rightarrow \rceil p$

Both the sentences are equivalent.

## 6. Biconditional Statements ("If and only if"), Û

**Statement :** "I can go to Delhi if and only if I am cured" would mean two things viz.

1. I can go to Delhi if I am cured ($p \Rightarrow q$)
2. I am cured if I can go to Delhi ($q \Rightarrow p$)

Where $p$ represent → "If I am cured"

Where $q$ represents → "I can go to Delhi"

**Definition :** If $p$ and $q$ represents any statements, the **biconditional** $p \Leftrightarrow q$ means

$$(p \Rightarrow q) \text{ and } (q \Rightarrow p)$$

or

$$(p \Rightarrow q) \wedge (q \Rightarrow p)$$

**Equivalence may be asserted verbally in a variety of ways as follows:**

$p$ is equivalent to $q$
$p$ implies q and conversely.
If $p$, then q, and conversely
$p$ is a necessary and sufficient condition for $q$
$q$ is a necessary and sufficient condition for $p$
$p$ if and only if $q$
$q$ if and only if $q$
$q$ if and only if $p$.

} All of these convey the idea that $p \Leftrightarrow q$ $p$ and $q$ are equivalent mean $p \Rightarrow q$ and $q \Rightarrow p$.

**Truth table of $p \Leftrightarrow q$**

| $p$ | $q$ | $p \Rightarrow q$ | $q \Rightarrow p$ | $(p \Rightarrow q) \vee (q \Rightarrow p)$ | $p \Leftrightarrow q$ |
|---|---|---|---|---|---|
| T | T | T | T | T | T |
| T | F | F | T | F | F |
| F | T | T | F | F | F |
| F | F | T | T | T | T |

$p \Leftrightarrow q$ is true when both $p$ and $q$ are either true or both false (i.e., equivalent) "If and only if" is sometimes abbreviated "iff"

For example. Statement (*a*) Mohan employs Hari if and only if Hari attends interview. ($p \Leftrightarrow q$)

If means the same thing as

(1) If Mohan employs Hari, then Hari attends interview. ($p \Rightarrow q$)

(2) If Hari attends interview, then Mohan employs him. ($q \Rightarrow p$).

Statement (*b*) $5x + 2 = 17$, if find only if $x = 3$ ($p \Leftrightarrow q$)

It means the same thing as

(1) If $5x + 2 = 17$, then $x = 3$ ($p \Rightarrow q$)

(2) If $x = 3$, then $5x + 2 = 17$ ($q \Rightarrow p$).

**For example:** The biconditional $(5 + 8 = 13) \Leftrightarrow (11 - 7 = 4)$ is true, since both the statements are true.

**For example:** The biconditional (men have wings) ⇔ (Birds can fly) is false, since one statements is true and one is false.

**For example:** The biconditional $(3 - 4 = 6) \Leftrightarrow (5 \times 7 = 20)$ is true, since both statements are false.

---

1. Truth values of $p \Rightarrow q$ and $q \Rightarrow$ do not necessarily agree
2. Truth values of $p \Rightarrow q$ and $q \Rightarrow p$ always agree.

---

**Example 10.4:** Establish ~ $(\alpha \vee \beta) \Leftrightarrow (-\alpha \vee \beta)$ as a tautology.

**Solution:**

**Truth table for the given propositions as follows**

| $\alpha$ | $\beta$ | $-\alpha$ | $\sim\beta$ | $\alpha \wedge \beta$ | $\sim(\alpha \wedge \beta)$ | $\sim\alpha \vee \sim\beta$ | $\sim(\alpha \wedge \beta) \Leftrightarrow (\sim\alpha \vee \sim\beta)$ |
|---|---|---|---|---|---|---|---|
| T | T | F | F | T | F | F | T |
| T | F | F | T | F | T | T | T |
| F | T | T | F | F | T | T | T |
| F | F | T | T | F | T | T | T |

Since *T* appears everywhere (in every row) of last column, the given proposition is a tautology.

## Other Connectives (USeful in Design of Computers)

(1) NAND – Combination of Not and and denoted by ↑

$$P \uparrow Q \equiv \rceil(P \wedge Q)$$

(2) NoR – Combination of Not and OR denoted by ↓

$$P \downarrow Q \equiv \rceil(P \vee Q)$$

**Example 10.5:** Using following statements:

*p* : Anu is tall.

*q* : Anu is beautiful.

Write following statement in symbolic forms:

(*i*) Anu is tall and beautiful.

(*ii*) Anu is tall but not beautiful.

(*iii*) It is false that Anu is short and beautiful.

(*iv*) Anu is tall or Anu is short and beautiful.

**Solution:**

(*i*) $P \vee q$

(*ii*) $p \vee \sim q$

(*iii*) $\sim(\sim p \vee q) \equiv p \vee \sim q$

(iv) $p \vee (\sim p \vee q)$

**Example 10.6:** Write following statement in symbolic forms:

(*i*) Indians will win world (Cup if their fielding improves

(*ii*) I will score good marks if only if 1 study hard

(*iii*) If you know Java and. Net, then you will get a job.

(*iv*) There will be no test examination tomorrow if professor is out of town or there is transporters' strike.

(*v*) If I am not in good mood or 1 am not busy then I will go for movie.

**Solution:**

(*i*) Let $p$ : Indian fielding improves.
$q$ : Indians will win words cup

$$\boxed{p \rightarrow q}$$

(*ii*) Let $p$ : I Score good marks
$q$ : I Study hard.

$$\boxed{p \leftrightarrow q}$$

(*iii*) Let $p$ : Y know Java
$q$ : You know Net
$r$ : You will get Job

$$\boxed{(p \wedge q) \rightarrow r}$$

(*iv*) Let $p$ : There is test examination tomorrow
$q$ : Professor is out town
$r$ : There is transporters' strike.

$$\boxed{q \vee r \rightarrow r}$$

(*v*) Let $p$ : I am in good mood.
$q$ : I am busy.
$r$ : I will go for a movie.

$$\boxed{(\sim p \vee \sim q) \rightarrow r \equiv [\sim (p \wedge q) \rightarrow r]}$$

**Example 10.7:** Prepare truth tables for the following propositions: (*a*) $p \wedge (\sim q)$ (*b*) $\sim(p \wedge \sim q)$ [we may use notion $\neg$ in place of $\sim$ for negation]

**Solution.** (*a*) **Truth Table for $p \wedge (\sim q)$**

| $p$ | $q$ | $\sim p$ | $p \wedge \sim q$ |
|---|---|---|---|
| T | T | F | F |
| T | F | T | T |
| F | T | F | F |
| F | F | T | F |

(*b*) **Truth table for Proposition $\neg(p \wedge \neg q)$**

| $p$ | $q$ | $\neg q$ | $p \wedge \neg q$ | $\neg(p \wedge \neg q)$ |
|---|---|---|---|---|
| T | T | F | F | T |
| T | F | T | T | F |
| F | T | F | F | T |
| F | F | T | F | T |
| | | | ↓ | ↓ |
| | | | [Using Table 1] | [Using Table 2] |

## 10.6 TAUTOLOGY AND CONTRADICTION

Tautologies are composite the propositions $P(p, q, ...)$ which contain only T in the last column of their truth tables or that are true for any truth values of their variables.

*i.e.*, $p \vee \neg p$ ("*p* or not *p*") is a tautology as shown below:

| $p$ | $\neg q$ | $p \vee \neg q$ |
|---|---|---|
| T | F | T |
| F | T | F |

Tautology is the statement formula which is true regard less of the values of the statements which replaces the variables in it. (Also called a **Universally valid formula** or a logical truth).

If $A$ and $B$ are two tautologies then their conjunction $A \vee B$ will be tautology.

$$A \equiv B$$

if $A \Leftrightarrow B$ is a tautology.

($\equiv$ is also written as $\Leftrightarrow$ and then $\Rightarrow$ is another as $\rightleftarrows$)

A statement $A$ is said to **tautologically imply** a statement $B$ if and only if $A \Rightarrow B$ is a tautology and is denoted by $A \Leftrightarrow B$

$A \Leftrightarrow B$ means that $A \Rightarrow B$ is a tautology

$A \equiv B$ means that $A \Leftrightarrow$ is a tautology.

**Both equivalence and implications are transitive**

If $A \equiv B$ and $B \equiv C$, the $A \equiv C$ and $A \Leftrightarrow B$ and $B \Leftrightarrow C$ then $A \Rightarrow B$ and $B \Rightarrow C$ are tautologies.

Hence $(A \Rightarrow B) \wedge (B \Rightarrow C)$ is also a tautology.

**Contradictions** are those proposition ($P(p, q, .....)$ That contains only $F$ in the last column of their truth table or which are false for any truth values of it's variables.

*e.g.*, $p \vee \neg p$ ("$p$ and not $p$") is a contradiction.

| $p$ | $\neg p$ | $p \wedge \neg p$ |
|---|---|---|
| T | F | F |
| F | T | F |

Negation of tautology is a contradiction and vice versa.

**Theorem 10.1.** (*Principle of Substitution*). If $P(p, q, ...)$is a tautology, then $P(P_1, P_2, ...)$ is also a tautology for any propositions $P_1$, $P_2$, ....or $P_1(p, q, ...)$ $P_2(p, q, ...)$ because $P(p, q, .....)$ is independent of truth values of it's variables $p, q, .....$

**Example 10.8:** Prove that the sentence 'It is wet or it is not wet' is a tautology.

**Solution:** Sentence can be symbolized by $p \vee \sim p$ where $p$ symbolizes the sentence 'It is wet'. Its truth table is given as follows;

| 1 | 2 | 3 |
|---|---|---|
| $p$ | $\sim q$ | $p \vee \neg p$ |
| T | F | T |
| F | T | T |

As column 3 contains $T$ every where, therefore the given proposition is tautology. This tautology is called the **Law of the Excluded Middle.**

**Example 10.9:** Prove that the proposition $\sim[p \vee (\sim p)]$ is a tautology.

**Solution:** The truth table is given below:

| $p$ | $\sim p$ | $p \wedge (\sim p)$ | $\sim[p \wedge (\sim p)]$ |
|---|---|---|---|
| T | F | F | T |
| F | T | F | T |

Since last column contains '$T$' everywhere therefore the given proposition is a tautology.

**Example 10.10:** Prove that $(\sim p \vee q) \wedge (p \vee \sim q)$ is a contradiction.

**Solution:** Truth table for the given proposition.

| $p$ | $q$ | $\sim p$ | $\sim q$ | $\sim p \vee q$ | $p \vee \sim q$ | $(\sim p \vee q) \wedge (p \wedge \sim q)$ |
|---|---|---|---|---|---|---|
| T | T | F | F | T | F | F |
| T | F | F | T | F | T | F |
| F | T | T | F | T | F | F |
| F | F | T | T | T | F | F |

Since $F$ appears in every row of the last column, therefore the given proposition is a contradiction.

## 10.7 LOGICAL EQUIVALENCE

Two propositions $P(p, q, .....)$ and $Q(p, q, .....)$ are said to be **logically equivalent** or simply equivalent or **equal.**

If they have identical truth tables and is written as $(P(p, q,.....) \equiv Q(p, q, .....)$ as shown below truth tables of $\neg(p \wedge q)$ and $\neg p \vee \neg q$ are identical. Hence $\neg(p \vee q) \equiv \neg p \vee \neg q$

| $p$ | $q$ | $p \wedge q$ | $\sim(p \wedge p)$ |
|---|---|---|---|
| T | T | T | F |
| T | F | F | T |
| F | T | F | T |
| F | F | F | T |

$\sim(p \vee q)$

| $p$ | $q$ | $\neg p$ | $\neg q$ | $\neg p \vee \neg q$ |
|---|---|---|---|---|
| T | T | F | F | F |
| T | F | F | T | T |
| F | T | T | F | T |
| F | F | T | T | T |

$\neg p \vee \neg q$

Also when a conditional $p \Rightarrow q$ and its converse $q \Rightarrow p$ are both true, the statement $p$ and $q$ are said to be logically equivalent.

**Example 10.11:** Prove that the relation of "Logical Equivalence" is an equivalence relation.

**Solution:** Consider $p, q, r$

$P \equiv p$ is trivially true Hence $\equiv$ is reflexive.

If $P \equiv q$, then $q \equiv p$ Hence $\equiv$ is symmetric.

If $P \equiv q, q \equiv r$, then $p \equiv r$ Hence $\equiv$ is transitive.

So $\equiv$ is an equivalence relation.

## 10.8 THREE CLOSE RELATIVE OF THE CONDITIONAL STATEMENTS

1. **The converse** of a given conditional is a new conditional formed by interchanging the antecedent and consequent of the given conditional. $q \Rightarrow p$ is the converse of $p \Rightarrow q$

Truth table of the converse

| $p$ | $q$ | $p \Rightarrow q$ | $q \Rightarrow p$ |
|---|---|---|---|
| T | T | T | T |
| T | F | F | T |
| F | T | T | F |
| F | F | T | T |

**For example**

(1) If 15 is an odd number, then 3 is a factor of 15.

(2) If 3 is a factor of 15, then 15 is an odd number

(2) is converse of (1).

For Example, (*a*) The conditional if birds have wings, then trees have wings' is false because it's antecedent is true and consequent is false.

Its converse 'If trees have wings, then birds have wings' is true because its antecedent is false and consequent is true.

For example, (*b*) The conditional' If 35 is an odd number, then 7 is a factor of 35' is true and its converse 'If 7 is factor of 35, then 35' is an odd number is also true.

| $p$ | $q$ | $p \Rightarrow q$ | $q \Rightarrow p$ | $\sim p$ | $\sim q$ | $\sim p \Rightarrow \sim q$ | $\sim q \Rightarrow \sim p$ |
|---|---|---|---|---|---|---|---|
| T | T | T | T | F | F | T | T |
| T | F | F | T | F | T | T | F |
| F | T | T | F | T | F | F | T |
| F | F | T | T | T | T | T | T |

2. **The Inverse** of a given conditional is a new conditional whose antecedent is the negation it the original antecedent and whose consequent is the negation of the original consequence. The inverse of $p \Rightarrow q$ is $\neg p \Rightarrow \neg q$ read as "not $p$ implies not " "if not $p$, then not $q$".

For example, **Original:** If is rains, then I shall not go out

**Inverse:** If it does rain, then I shall go out.

**True table for inverse**

| $p$ | $q$ | $\sim p$ | $\sim q$ | $p \Rightarrow q$ | $\sim p \Rightarrow \sim q$ |
|---|---|---|---|---|---|
| T | T | F | F | T | T |
| T | F | F | T | F | T |
| F | T | T | F | T | F |
| F | F | T | T | T | T |

3. **The Contrapositive** of a given conditional is a new conditional whose antecedent is the negation of the original consequent and whose consequent is the negation of the original antecedent.

For example, **original** : $p \Rightarrow q$

**Contrapositive :** $\sim q \Rightarrow \sim p$ read as "not $q$ implies not $p$" or "if not $q$, then not $p$" It is the inverse of the converse of a given conditional or is the converse of the inverse.

For example, **original:** If it rains, then I shall not go out ($p \Rightarrow \neg q$)

**contrapositive :** If I shall go out, then it does not rain. ($q \Rightarrow \neg p$)

Contrapositive or $q \Rightarrow p$ Contrapositive of $p \Rightarrow q$

For example, **original :** If $x > 5$, then $2 + 8 = 7$

**Contrapositive :** If $2 + 7$ [1] 7, then $x \not> $ (not greater) 5

Now we summarize the above discussion, Summary

| | | |
|---|---|---|
| **Statement:** | $p \Rightarrow q$ | If $p$, then $q$. |
| **Converse:** | $q \Rightarrow p$ | If $q$, then $p$. |
| **Inverse:** | $(\sim p) \Rightarrow (-\, q)$ | If not $p$, then not $q$. |
| **Contrapositive:** | $(\sim q) \Rightarrow (\sim p)$ | If not $q$, then not $p$. |

*For example,*

(*i*) **Statement:** If it is raining, then I stay at home.

**Converse:** If I stay at home, then it is raining.

**Inverse:** If it is not raining, then I do not stay at home.

**Contrapositive:** If it do not stay at home, then it is not raining.

(*ii*) **Statement:** If $x + 3 = 8$, then $x = 6$

**Converse:** If $x = 6$, then $x + 3 = 8$

**Inverse:** If $x + 3 \neq 8$, then $x \neq 6$

**Contrapositive:** If $x \neq 6$, then $x + 3 \neq 8$

**Truth tables for the four implications**

| p | q | p ⇒ q | q ⇒ p | ~p | ~p | ~p ⇒ ~q | ~ ⇒ ~p |
|---|---|---|---|---|---|---|---|
| T | T | T | T | F | F | T | T |
| T | F | F | T | F | T | T | F |
| F | T | T | F | F | F | F | T |
| F | F | T | T | T | T | T | T |

Same

Same

## 10.9 EQUIVALENT FORMS

(1) $\neg\neg P \equiv P$

(2) $P \vee P \equiv P$

(3) $(P \wedge \neg P) \vee Q \equiv Q$

(4) $P \vee \neg P \equiv Q \vee \neg Q$

(5) $(P \rightarrow Q) \equiv (\neg P \vee Q)$

(6) $P \rightarrow (Q \rightarrow R) \equiv P \rightarrow (\neg Q \vee R)$ by (5)→ means implies or ⇒

$\equiv \neg P \vee (\neg Q \vee (\neg Q \vee R)$ again by (5)

(7) $Q \rightleftarrows R \equiv (Q \rightarrow R) \wedge (R \rightarrow Q)$ ($\rightleftarrows$ means biconditional Û)

$\equiv (\neg Q \vee R \wedge (\neg R \vee Q)$ or $(Q \vee R) \vee (\neg Q \vee \neg R)$

(8) $P \wedge Q \equiv \rceil(\rceil P \vee \rceil Q)$ De morgain's law

(9) $P \vee Q \equiv \rceil(\rceil P \wedge \rceil Q)$ These can be used to remove either Conjunction or disjunction

## 10.10 NECESSARY AND SUFFICIENT CONDITIONS

*q* is necessary Conditions for *p* means $p \Rightarrow q$ or for an object to be an element at *p*, it is necessary that it be an element of *q*, although it is not sufficient, since the object may be an element of *r* (all *p's* are *q's* but not all *q's* are *p's*) as show below.

q

P

r

$p \Rightarrow q$, or *q* is necessary condition for *p* or *p* is a sufficient condition of *q* or If *p*, then *q*.

*q* is a sufficient condition for *p* means that $q \Rightarrow p$ *i.e*, for an object to be an element could be an element of *p*, without being an element of *q* (all *q's* are *p's* but not all *p's* have to be *q's*) as shown in the figure given below:

p

q

r

$q \Rightarrow p$, *q* is a sufficient condition for *p* or *p* is a necessary condition for *q*.

If $q$ is both a necessary and a sufficient condition for $p$, it means that $p$ and $q$ are logically equivalent *i.e.,* each implies the other ($p \Leftrightarrow q$).

**For example:** A necessary condition that a given whole numbers is divisible by 9 is that it be divisible by 3. It is not a sufficient condition for 6, 15, 21, though divisible by 3 are not divisible by 9. A sufficient condition that a whole number is divisible by 9 is that it be divisible by 18.

This is not a necessary condition since 27, 45, 63 are divisible by 9 but not by 18.

A necessary and sufficient condition that a whole numbers is divisible by 9 is that the sum of its digits should be divisible by 9.

**Example 10.12:** Decide if two composite statements given below are equivalent statements.

(1) If $X$ is 21 years old, then he has a right to vote

(2) $X$ is not 21 years old, or he has a right to vote.

**Solution:** Let p denote "$X$ is 21 years old" and q denote "he has a right to vote"

**Statement** (1) can be symbolised as if $p$, then $q$ or $q$ is the necessary condition for $p$ or $p \Rightarrow q$.

**Statement** (2) can be symbolised as $\sim p \vee q$. To show the two statements as equivalent we have to show that ($a$) truth values of $p \Rightarrow q$ and $\sim p \vee q$ are the same or ($b$) the biconditional formed by two $p \Rightarrow q$ and $\sim p \vee q$ are the same or ($b$) the biconditional formed by two $p \Rightarrow q$ and $\sim p \vee q$ is a tautology. We see that both are correct as shown below in the table. Hence there are equivalent composite statements.

**Truth Table**

| p | ~p | q | p ⇒ q | ~p ∨ q | (p ⇒ q) ⇔ (~p ∨ q) |
|---|---|---|---|---|---|
| T | F | T | T | T | T |
| T | F | F | F | F | T |
| F | T | T | T | T | T |
| F | T | F | T | T | T |

same (columns $p \Rightarrow q$ and $\sim p \vee q$) — Tautology (last column)

**Example 10.13:** Given that "a man must be a citizen in order to vote, which of the following statements are true?

(*i*) A man votes if is a citizen.

(*ii*) A man votes only if he is a citizen.

(*iii*) If a man does not vote, he is not a citizen.

(*iv*) All voters are citizens.

(*v*) If a man is not a citizen, he does not vote.

(*vi*) Either Mr. *A* did not vote, or he is a citizen.

(*vii*) A man is a citizen only if he votes.

(*viii*) A man does not vote only if he is not a citizen.

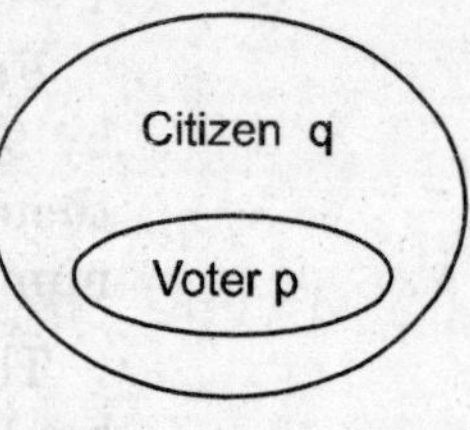


**Solution:** Let p denotes "a man (he) votes" and q denotes "a man (he) is a citizen". Given that it is necessary to be on element of q to be an elemetn of $p$ *i.e.,* $p \Rightarrow q$ or $q$ os the necessary condition for $p$ or $p$ is a sufficient condition for $q$.

**Now we change all the statements into symbolic form as:**

(*i*) If he is a citizen, then he votes i.e., $q \Rightarrow p$ which is converse. Hence **False.**

(*ii*) "$p$ only $q$" or $\sim q \Rightarrow \sim p$ or $p \Rightarrow q$ Hence **True.**

(*iii*) $\sim p \Rightarrow \sim q$ or $q \Rightarrow p$. Converse Hence **False.**

(*iv*) $p \Rightarrow q$. Hence **True.**

(*v*) $\sim q \Rightarrow \sim p$, Contrapositive of $p \Rightarrow q$. Hence **True.**

(*vi*) $\sim p \vee q$ same truth value as of $p \Rightarrow q$. Hence **True.**

(*vii*) $q$ only if $p$ or $\sim p \Rightarrow \sim q$ or $q \Rightarrow p$ converse. Hence **False.**

(*viii*) $\sim p$ only if $\sim q$ or $\sim p \Rightarrow \sim q$, the inverse Hence **False.**

## 10.11 RULE OF PRECEDENCE

Order of preference in which the connectives are applied in a formula of proposition having no brackets is as follows:

(*i*) ~ Negation

(*ii*) ^ Conjunction

(*iii*) v and ⊕ disjunction and exclusive disjunction (any one of these two can be preferred to the other).

**For example:** Truth values of $(p \oplus q) \vee r$ are the same as that of $p \oplus (q \vee r)$.

(*iv*) ⇒ and ⇔ conditional and biconditional.

**Example 10.14:** Write down the truth values (or table) of $p \rightarrow q \vee \sim r \leftrightarrow r \oplus q$.

**Solution:**

(*i*) First find truth value of $\sim r$.

(*ii*) then find truth value of $(q \vee \sim r)$

(*iii*) then find truth value of $(r \oplus q)$

(*iv*) then find truth of either $p \rightarrow (q \vee \sim r)$, $(q \vee \sim r) \downarrow (r \oplus q)$. (we chosen to apply $\rightarrow$ first)

(*v*) and finally find truth value of the remaining one as shown in the truth table given below:

**Truth Table of $p \to q \vee \sim r \leftrightarrow r \oplus q$**

| $p$ | $q$ | $r$ | $\sim r$ | $q \wedge \sim r$ | $r \oplus q$ | $p \to q \wedge \sim r$ | $p \to q \wedge \sim r \leftrightarrow r \oplus q$ |
|---|---|---|---|---|---|---|---|
| T | T | T | F | F | F | F | T |
| T | T | F | T | T | T | T | T |
| T | F | T | F | F | T | F | F |
| T | F | F | T | F | F | F | T |
| F | T | T | F | F | F | T | F |
| F | T | F | T | T | T | T | T |
| F | F | T | F | F | T | T | T |
| F | F | F | T | F | F | T | F |

Alternative symbol used in Mathematical logic

$\to$ for implies $\Rightarrow$

$\rightleftarrows$ for Biconditional $\Leftrightarrow$

$\Leftrightarrow$ equivalence $\equiv$

$\Rightarrow$ for tautology *i.e.*, $A \Rightarrow B$ states $A \to B$ is a tautology or $B$ has the truth value $T$ whenever $A$ has the truth value $T$.

| **Different versions of** | |
|---|---|
| $P \Leftrightarrow q$ **or** $p \to q$ | $p \Leftrightarrow$ **or** $p \rightleftarrows q$ **or** $p \leftrightarrow q$ |
| (*i*) $P$ implies $q$ | (*i*) $p$ and $q$ imply each other |
| (*ii*) $q$ follows from $p$ | (*ii*) $p$ and $q$ are equivalent to each |
| (*iii*) $q$ is a logical consequence | (*iii*) $p$ holds if and only if $q$ holds of $p$ |
| (*iv*) If $p$ is true then $q$ is true | (*iv*) $q$ is a characterization a of $p$ (when both $p$ or $q$ express some properties of the same object) |
| (*v*) If $q$ is false then $p$ is false | (*v*) $q$ holds if $p$ holds and conversely |
| (*vi*) $p$ is false unless $q$ holds | (*vi*) $q$ holds if $p$ holds, but not otherwise |
| (*vii*) $p$ is a sufficient condition | (*vii*) if $p$ is true, then $q$ is true and if for $q$ $p$ is false then $q$ is also false |
| (*viii*) $q$ is a necessary condition for $p$ | (*viii*) $q$ is necessary as well as sufficient condition for $q$. |
| (*ix*) $p$ is true only if $q$ is true. | |

## 10.12 EQUIVALENCE OF FORMULA

Two statement formulae $P$ and $Q$ in variables $p_1, p_2, \ldots p_n (\nu \geq 1)$ are said to be equivalent if they have the same truth value. Such formulae are considered as the same for all logical purposes.

We give below a list of such standard equivalent formulae. They serve as laws of Algebra of propositions.

Hence $T$ denotes tautology and F denotes contradiction.

### Equivalence Formula of Laws of Algebra of Propositions

**Idempotent laws**

1. (*a*) $p \vee p \equiv p$ 1. (*b*) $p \wedge p \equiv p$

**Associative laws**

2. (*a*) $(p \vee q) \vee r \equiv p \vee (q \vee r)$ 2. (*b*) $(p \wedge q) \wedge r \equiv p \wedge (q \wedge r)$

**Commutative laws**

3. (*a*) $p \vee q \equiv q \vee p$ 3. (*b*) $p \wedge q \equiv q \wedge p$

**Distributive laws**

4. (*a*) $p \vee (q \wedge r) \equiv (p \vee q) \wedge (p \vee r)$ 4. (*b*) $p \wedge (q \vee r) \equiv (p \wedge q) \vee (p \wedge r)$

**Identity laws**

5. (*a*) $p \wedge F = F$ 5. (*b*) $p \vee F \equiv p$

6. (*a*) $p \wedge T = p$ 6. (*b*) $p \vee T \equiv T$

**Complement laws**

7. (*a*) $p \vee \neg p \equiv T$ 7. (*b*) $p \wedge \neg p \equiv F$

8. (*b*) $\neg T \equiv F$ 8. (*b*) $\neg F \equiv T$

$\sim q \wedge q \equiv F$

**Involution laws**

9. $\neg \neg p \equiv p$

**De-Morgen's laws**

10. (*a*) $\neg (p \vee q) \equiv \neg P \wedge \neg q$ 10. (*b*) $\neg (p \wedge q) \equiv \neg p \wedge \neg q$

**Absorption laws**

$p \vee (p \wedge q) \equiv p,$ $p \wedge (p \vee q) p$

**Detachment laws**

$((p \Rightarrow q) \wedge p) \Rightarrow q$

**Disjunctive Addition**

$p \Rightarrow (p \vee q)$

**Conjunctive simplification**

$(p \wedge q) \Rightarrow p$

**Chain rule**

$(p \Rightarrow q) \wedge (q \Rightarrow r) \Rightarrow (p \Rightarrow r)$

**Disjunctive simplification**

$((p \vee q) \wedge (\neg p) \Rightarrow q$

**Conditional rules**

$(p \Rightarrow q) \Rightarrow ((\neg p) \vee q)$

$(p \Rightarrow q) \Leftrightarrow \neg q \Rightarrow \neg p$

**Equivalence rules**

$(p \Rightarrow q) \Rightarrow (p \Rightarrow q) \wedge (q \Rightarrow p)$

$(p \Leftrightarrow q) \Leftrightarrow (p \vee q) \vee (\neg p) \vee (\neg q))$

$(\neg (p \Leftrightarrow q)) \Leftrightarrow (p \Leftrightarrow (\Leftrightarrow q))$

**Implication rules**

$(p \Rightarrow q) \Rightarrow ((p \wedge r) \Rightarrow (q \wedge r))$

$(p \Rightarrow q) \Rightarrow ((p \vee r) \Rightarrow (q \vee r))$

**Contrapositive Inference**

$((p \Rightarrow q) \wedge (\neg q)) \Rightarrow (\neg p)$

**Duality Law :** Two formulae $A$ and $A^*$ are said to be duals of each other if either can obtained form the other by replacing ^ and v v and ^.

The two connections ^ and v are said to be dual to each other. If any formula contains $T$ and $F$, then its dual is obtained by interchanging $T$ and F in addition to the change explained above:

For example, Duals of $(P \vee Q) \vee R$ is $(P \vee Q) \vee R$.

**Example 10.15:** Use laws to prove that

$$\sim(\sim p \wedge q) \wedge (p \vee q) \equiv p$$

**Solution:** L.H.S. $\equiv (p \vee \sim q) \vee (p \vee q)$ by De'Morgan's law

$\equiv p \vee (\sim q \vee q)$ by distribution law

$\equiv p \vee F$ where $F$ denote a contradication

$\equiv p$ by identity law.

**Example 10.16:** If $P$ and $Q$ are true and $R$, $S$ are false then find the truth value of

$$[(P \Rightarrow R) \vee (R \Rightarrow Q)] \Rightarrow (P \Rightarrow S)$$

**Solution:** $P$ is true, $R$ is false, so $P \Rightarrow R$ is false, $R$ is false and $Q$ is true, so $R \Rightarrow Q$ is true

Thus $(P \Rightarrow R) \vee (R \Rightarrow Q)$ is true ...(1)

Again $P$ is true and $S$ is false, so $P \Rightarrow S$ is false ...(2)

From (1) and (2) $[(P \Rightarrow R) \vee (R \Rightarrow Q)] \Rightarrow (P \Rightarrow S)$

*i.e.*, (True) $\Rightarrow$ (false) is false.

**Example 10.17:** Prove that

$$P \Rightarrow (Q \Rightarrow R) \equiv (P \wedge Q) \Rightarrow R$$

**Solution:** L.H.S. $\equiv \neg P \vee (Q \Rightarrow R) \equiv \neg P \vee (\neg Q \vee R)$

By 10.6.1 $\equiv (\neg P \vee \neg Q) \vee R$ by associativity

$\equiv \neg(P \wedge Q) \vee R$ by De Morgan's law

$\equiv (P \wedge Q) \Rightarrow$

## 10.13 ARGUMENT

It is an assertion that a given set of proposition $p_1, p_2, \ldots\ldots, p_n$ called premises yields (has a consequence) another proposition $Q$ called the conclusion and is denoted by $P_1, P_2, \ldots, P_n$ $Q$.

That mean, "An argument is a sequence of statements. All statements except the final one are called premises ($P_1$, $P_2$, $P_3 \ldots P_n$) and the final statement is called Conclusion.

**Valid Argument :** An argument $P_1, P_2, \ldots P_n \vdash Q$ is said to be valid if $Q$ is true whenever all the premises $P_1, P_2, \ldots P_n$ are true.

**Fallacy :** It is an argument which is not valid. Now $P_1, P_2, \ldots P_n$, are true simultaneously if and only if proposition $P_1 \wedge P_2, \ldots P_n$ is true. Hence we have the following theorem:

**Theorem :** The argument $P_1, P_2, \ldots P_n \vdash Q$ is valid if and only if $Q$ is true whenever $P_1 \wedge P_2 \wedge \ldots \wedge P_n$ is true or $(P_1 \wedge P_2 \wedge \ldots \wedge P_n) \Rightarrow Q$ is a tautology.

### Procedure to prove the validity of an argument :

If $P$ and $Q$ are two statement formulae, then we say that $Q$ logically follows $P$ or $Q$ is valid conclusion or consequence of the premise $P$ if and only if $P \Rightarrow Q$ is a tautology. If we are given a set of premises $P_1, P_2, \ldots P_n$, and a conclusion $Q$, than it is possible to determine whether the conclusion $Q$ logically follows from the given premises $P_1, P_2, \ldots, P_n$ by constructing the truth table.

The conclusion $Q$ is said to logically follow from the given premises $P_1$, $P_2, \ldots, P_n$ if either of the following condition is satisfied.

(1) $Q$ is true whenever all the premises are simultaneously true.

or (2) $Q$ is true whenever the conjunction $P_1 \wedge P_2 \wedge \ldots \wedge P_n$ is true.

or (3) $(P_1 \wedge P_2 \wedge \ldots \wedge P_n) \Rightarrow Q$ is a tautology.

### 10.13.1 Logical Implication

For any propositions $P(p, q, \ldots)$ (and $Q(p, q, \ldots)$, the following three statements are equivalent.

(*i*) $P(p, q, ...)$ logically implies $(Q\ (p, q,...)$ i.e., $P(p, q, ...) \Rightarrow Q\ (p, q, ...)$

(*ii*) The argument $P(p, q, ..) \vdash Q(p, q, ...)$ is valid.

(*iii*) The proposition $P(p, q, ...) \Rightarrow Q(p, q, ...)$ is a tautology.

Anyone of the above is possible–

If $Q\ (p, q, ...)$ is true whenever $P(p, q, ...)$ is true.

For example. To prove $p \Rightarrow p \vee q$, or $p \vdash p \vee q$ we shall prove that $p \vee q$ is true whenever $p$ is true a shown below:

| | $p$ | $q$ | $p \vee q$ |
|---|---|---|---|
| → | T | T | T |
| | T | F | T |
| | F | T | T |
| | F | F | T |

$p$ is true in row 1 and 2 in which $p \vee q$ is also true. Therefore $p$ implies $p \vee q$.

**Example 10.18:** Show that $p \Leftrightarrow q$ does not logically imply $p \Rightarrow q$.

**Solution:** Truth table

| | $p$ | $Q$ | $\sim q$ | $p \Leftrightarrow \sim q$ | $p \Rightarrow q$ |
|---|---|---|---|---|---|
| | T | T | F | T | T |
| → | T | F | F | F | T |
| → | F | T | T | T | F |
| | F | F | T | T | T |

We see that $p \Leftrightarrow \sim q$ is true in rows 2 and 3 both, but $p \Rightarrow$ is not true in row 3. Thus $p \Leftrightarrow \sim q$ does not imply $p \Leftrightarrow q$.

For example (*a*). The following argument is valid: $p, p \rightarrow q \vdash q$ (law of detachment)

**Proof.** In the fallowing truth table $p$ and $p \rightarrow q$ are true simultaneously only in case of row 1 and in this case $q$ is also is true. Hence the argument is valid.

For example (*b*). The following argument is a fallacy:

$p \Rightarrow q, q \vdash$ because $p \Rightarrow q$ and $q$ are both true in row 3 but in this case $p$ is false. Hence it is a fallacy.

| $p$ | $q$ | $p \to q$ |
|---|---|---|
| T | T | T |
| T | F | F |
| F | T | T |
| F | F | T |

**Example 10.19:** Prove that the argument $p \Rightarrow q, \neg p, \vdash \neg q$ is a fallacy,. (or determine the validity of the argument).

**Solution:** Here premises are $P_1 : P \Rightarrow q$. $P_2 : \neg p$ and conclusion is $Q : \neg q$

**Truth Table**

| p | q | ¬p | ¬q | p ⇒ q | (p ⇒ q) ∧ ¬p | [(p ⇒ q) ∧ ¬p] ⇒ ¬q |
|---|---|---|---|---|---|---|
| T | T | F | F | T | F | T |
| T | F | F | T | F | F | T |
| F | T | T | F | T | T | F |
| F | F | T | T | T | T | T |

Hence the given argument is a fallacy because

(1) Conclusion $\neg q$ is not always true where all the propositions of the premises i.e., $p \Rightarrow q$ and $\neg p$ are true simultaneously (i.e., row 3)

or (2) Conclusion $\neg q$ is not away true where conjunction of the proposition of premises

or (3) $[(p \Rightarrow q) \wedge \Rightarrow p] \Rightarrow \neg q$ is not tautology.

---

We can use anyone of the above three methods – First method is preferred as it requires less number of columns.

---

**Example 10.20:** Find if the following argument is valid or not.

If it rains, he will be sick

It did not rain

He was not sick.

**Solution:** Let $p$ denote "it rains" and $q$ denote the "he is sick". The argument translated into symbolic from shall become $p \Rightarrow q, \neg p \vdash \neg q$ which has been proved to be a fallacy in example.

**Example 10.21:** Prove that the following argument is a fallacy:

If two sides of a triangle are equal, then the opposite angles are equal. Two sides of a triangle are not equal. The opposite angles of a triangle are not equal.

**Solution:** Let $p$ denote "two sides of a triangle are equal"

and $q$ denote "the opposite angles are equal."

Translating the argument into symbolic form we have $p \Rightarrow q, \neg \vdash$ which has been proved to be a fallacy.

**Example 10.22:** Check validity of:

Either Ram will or Hari will practice Karate. If hari practices Karate, the Ram studies, Ram does not study. Therefore Hari will practice Karate.

$[(p \vee q) \wedge (q \rightarrow r) \wedge \sim r] \Rightarrow q$

**Solution:** Let $p$ denote Ram will cook.

Let $q$ denote Hari will practice Karate.

Let $r$ denote Ram studies.

The symbolic form of the argument is

$$(p \vee q),\ q \rightarrow r,\ \sim r \vdash q$$

Its truth table shall be as shown here.

**Truth table**

| $p$ | $q$ | $r$ | $p \vee q$ | $q \Rightarrow r$ | $\sim r$ |
|---|---|---|---|---|---|
| T | T | T | T | T | F |
| T | T | F | T | F | T |
| T | F | T | T | T | F |
| T | F | F | T | T | T |
| F | T | T | T | T | F |
| F | T | F | T | F | T |
| F | F | T | F | T | F |
| F | F | F | F | T | T |

Last 3 columns are true simultaneously in row number 4 in which $q$ is not true. Hence the argument is not valid.

**Example 10.23:** Determine whether the following argument is valid or not:

$$p \Rightarrow \neg q$$

$$r \Rightarrow q$$

$$r$$

$$\therefore \quad \neg p$$

**Solution:** We construct a truth table:

| $p$ | $q$ | $r$ | $\neg q$ | $p \Rightarrow \neg q$ | $r \Rightarrow q$ | $\neg q$ |
|---|---|---|---|---|---|---|
| 0 | 0 | 0 | 1 | 1 | 1 | 1 |
| 0 | 0 | 1 | 1 | 1 | 0 | 1 |
| 0 | 1 | 0 | 0 | 1 | 1 | 1 |
| → 0 | 1 | 1 | 0 | 1 | 1 | 1 |
| 1 | 0 | 0 | 1 | 1 | 1 | 0 |
| 1 | 0 | 1 | 1 | 1 | 0 | 0 |
| 1 | 1 | 0 | 0 | 0 | 1 | 0 |
| 1 | 1 | 1 | 0 | 0 | 1 | 0 |

In only row 4, all the premises are true and in this row conclusion is also true.

Thus, the argument is solid.

**Example 10.23:** Show that the following argument is valid.

$P$

$p \Rightarrow q$

$q \Rightarrow r$

$r$

**Solution:** First Method: Let $f \equiv [p \wedge (p \Rightarrow q) \wedge (q \Rightarrow r)] \Rightarrow r$.

Now, construct the truth table for $f$

| $p$ | $q$ | $r$ | $p \Rightarrow q$ | $q \Rightarrow r$ | $p \wedge (p \Rightarrow q) \wedge (q \Rightarrow r)$ | $f$ |
|---|---|---|---|---|---|---|
| T | T | T | T | T | T | T |
| T | T | F | T | F | F | T |
| T | F | T | F | T | F | T |
| F | T | T | T | T | F | T |
| T | F | F | F | T | F | T |
| F | T | F | T | F | F | T |
| F | F | T | T | T | F | T |
| F | F | F | T | T | F | T |

The last column contains all the truth values T. Hence, $f$ is a tautology and hence the given argument is valied.

**Second Method:**

Let $f \equiv [p \wedge (p \Rightarrow q) \wedge (q \Rightarrow r)] \Rightarrow r$

$\equiv [p \wedge (\neg \vee q) \wedge (\neg q \vee r) \Rightarrow r \equiv \neg [p \wedge (\neg p \vee q) \wedge (\neg q \vee r)] \vee r$

$\equiv [\neg p \vee \neg (\neg p \vee q) \vee \neg (\neg q \vee r)] \vee r \equiv \neg p \vee (q \wedge \neg q) \vee (q \wedge \neg r) \vee r$

$\equiv \neg p \vee \neg q \vee \neg r \vee r$

Thus, $f \equiv \neg p \vee \neg q \vee \neg r \vee r = 1$

Since $f$ reduced to 1, reduced to 1, this also shows that the argumet is valid.

**Third Method:**

Consider the following sequences of arguments

| | |
|---|---|
| $p$ | a premine |
| $p \Rightarrow q$ | a premise |
| $q$ | by the law of detachment |
| $q \Rightarrow r$ | a premise |
| $r$ | by the law detachment |

Thus the argument is valid.

## 10.14 RULES OF INFERENCE

For checking the validity at a given argument, we were using truth tables, but as the numbers of variables in the premises gets larger, truth tables grow to 64, 128 more rows. So, in this situation, it becomes impossible to use this technique and we use some rules of entrance.

These rules at inferences are simply tautologies in the form of implications. For example.

$$P \Rightarrow (p \vee q)$$

is such a tautology and it is rule of inference. We write this in the form $\frac{p}{p \vee q}$. Here $p$ denotes a premise and $p \vee q$. denotes the conclusion.

In the following table. We give some rules of inference. Here, observe that for valid argument, we can use the rules of inference.

| Name | Rules of inference | Implication form |
|---|---|---|
| Addition | $\frac{p}{\therefore p \vee q}$ | $p \Rightarrow (p \vee q)$ |
| Conjunction | $\frac{q}{\because p \wedge q}$ | $q \Rightarrow (p \wedge q)$ |

| | | |
|---|---|---|
| Simplification | $\dfrac{p \wedge q}{\therefore p}$ | $(p \wedge q) \Rightarrow p$ |
| Modus ponens | $p \Rightarrow q$<br>$\underline{p}$<br>$\therefore\ q$ | $[(p \Rightarrow q) \wedge p] \Rightarrow q$ |
| Modus tollens | $p \Rightarrow q$<br>$\underline{\sim q}$<br>$\therefore \sim p$ | $[(p \Rightarrow q) \wedge \sim q] \Rightarrow \sim p$ |
| Hypothetical | $p \Rightarrow q$<br>$\underline{q \Rightarrow r}$<br>$\therefore p \Rightarrow r$ | $[(p \Rightarrow q) \wedge (q \Rightarrow r)] \Rightarrow (p \Rightarrow r)$ |
| Disjunction | $p \vee q$<br>$\sim p$<br>$\therefore q$ | $[(p \vee q) \vee \sim p] \Rightarrow q$ |
| Constructive | $p \Rightarrow q \wedge (r \Rightarrow s)$<br>$p \vee r$<br>$\therefore q \vee s$ | $[(p \Rightarrow q) \wedge (r \Rightarrow s)] \wedge (p \vee r) \Rightarrow$ |
| Destructive | $p \Rightarrow q \wedge (r \Rightarrow s)$<br>$\sim q \vee \sim s$<br>$\therefore \sim p \vee \sim r$ | $[(p \Rightarrow q) \wedge (r \Rightarrow s) \wedge (\sim q \vee \sim s)]$<br>$\Rightarrow (\sim p \vee \sim r)$ |

In logical reasoning, a certain number of propositions, are assumed to be true, and based on that assumption some other propositions are inferred or derived. We can to give more rules of inference and use them in valid arguments.

Important rules at inference are–

1. Law of Detachment (Modus ponens)
2. Law of Contraposition (Modus tollens)
3. Disjunctive syllogism
4. Hypothetical syllogism

**For example:**

**(1) Law of Detachment:** If Mohan can work hard he will get a job.

$[(p \rightarrow q) \wedge p] \Rightarrow q$ Mohan can work hard

Therefore he will get a job. $\rightarrow$ **Valid**

**(2) Law of Contraposition:** If Mohan can work hard he will get a job.

$[(p \rightarrow q) \wedge \sim q] \Rightarrow \sim p$ Mohan will not get a job.

Therefore Mohan cannot work hard. **Valid**

(3) **Disjunctive Syllogism:** Either the pen is white or pencil is hard

$$(p \vee q) \wedge \sim p \Rightarrow q$$

The pen is balck (not white)

Therefore pencil is hard. **Valid**

(4) **Hypothetical Syllogism:** If Mohan is a 'sarpanch' he will head of the panchayat $(p \rightarrow q) \wedge (q \rightarrow r) \Rightarrow r)$ If Mohan heads the panchyat he will decide on all disputes.

Therefore, if Mohan is a sarpanch, he will decide on all disutes.

### (1) Law of Detachment:

$$[(p \rightarrow q) \wedge p] \Rightarrow q$$

The argument $p, p \Rightarrow \vdash q$ is valid

**Proof:**

| $p$ | $Q$ | $p \Rightarrow q$ | $p \wedge (p \Leftrightarrow q)$ | $p \wedge (p \Rightarrow q) \rightarrow q$ |
|---|---|---|---|---|
| T | T | T | T | T |
| T | F | F | F | T |
| F | T | T | F | T |
| F | F | T | F | T |

Hence argument is valid because

(1) Conclusion $q$ is true when $p$ and $p \Rightarrow q$ (premises) are true simultaneously viz., in row 1.

or (2) Conclusion $q$ is true where $p \wedge (p \Rightarrow q)$ i.e., conjunction of proposition of premises is true (viz row. 1)

or (3) $[p \wedge (p \Rightarrow q)] \Rightarrow q$ is tautology.

---

For validity of an argument, the conclusion should be true where all the propositions in the premises are true.

---

**Example 10.25:** Test the validity of the following argument.

If Ram works hard, he will get a job

Ram works hard

Therefore, he will get a job.

**Solution:** Let $p$ denote "Ram works hard" and $q$ denote "he (Ram) will get a job". The given argument can be written in symbolic form as–

$$p \to q, p \vdash q$$

or $$[(p \Rightarrow q) \wedge p] \Rightarrow q$$

Here the premises are $p \Rightarrow q$, the conclusion is $q$.

If we construct the truth table as in the case of law of detachment, we will see that the argument is valid.

**Example 10.26:** Prove that argument $p \Rightarrow q, q \vdash p$ is a fallacy.

**Proof:** See truth of the law of detachment.

The given argument is fallacy because

(1) The conclusion $p$ is not true whenever both propositions $p \Rightarrow q$ and $q$ of the premises are true as can be seen from row 3 where both propositions of the premises are true but the conclusion is false. (no matter it holds for row 1)

or

(2) As may be seen from the following table conclusion $p$ is not true when $(p \Rightarrow q) \wedge q$ (i.e., row 3) i.e., conjunction of propositions of premises is true.

| $p$ | $q$ | $p \Rightarrow q$ | $(p \Rightarrow q) \wedge q$ | $[(p \Rightarrow q) \wedge q] \Rightarrow p$ |
|---|---|---|---|---|
| T | T | T | T | T |
| T | F | F | F | T |
| F | T | T | F | F |
| F | F | T | F | T |

or (3) $[(p \Rightarrow q) \vee q] \Rightarrow p$ is not a tautology.

## 2. Law of Contraposition or Modus tollens

Test whether the following argument is valid or not

$p \Rightarrow q, \neg q \vdash p$, (Law of Contraposition)

**Proof.** (in short). Truth Table

| $p$ | $q$ | $\neg p$ | $\neg q$ | $p \Rightarrow q$ | $(p \Rightarrow q) \wedge \neg q$ | $[(p \Rightarrow q) \wedge \neg q] \to \neg p$ |
|---|---|---|---|---|---|---|
| T | T | F | F | T | F | F |
| T | F | F | T | F | T | F |
| F | T | T | F | T | F | F |
| F | F | T | T | T | F | F |

$\neg p$ is true when $(p \Rightarrow q) \wedge \neg q$ is true or $[(p \Rightarrow q) \wedge \neg q] \to p$ is tautology.

Hence the given argument is valid.

**Example 10.27:** Test the validity of the argument:

If it rains, Ram will be sick

Ram was not sick

It did not rain

**Solution:** Let $p$ : it rains $q$ : Ram is sick.

Then the symbolic representation of the given argument is $p \Rightarrow q, \neg q \vdash \neg p$ or $[(p \Rightarrow q) \wedge (\neg q)] \Rightarrow \neg p$

and this has been proved to be a valid argument in the law of contraposition.

### 3. Law of Hypothetical Syllogism

Verify if the following argument is valid "If p implies q and q implies r, then p implies $r$" or $(p \Rightarrow q) \wedge (q \Rightarrow r) \Rightarrow (p \Rightarrow r)$

**[*U.P.T.U. MCA I Sem. 2002-2003*]**

**Proof.** To prove it we have to show that

Either $(a)$ $p \Rightarrow r$ is true whenever $(p \Rightarrow q) \wedge (q > r)$ is true.

or $(b)$ $[(p \Rightarrow q) \wedge (q \Rightarrow r)] \Rightarrow [p \Rightarrow r]$ is a tautology as seen below.

| $p$ | $q$ | $r$ | $p \Rightarrow q$ | $q \Rightarrow r$ | $(p \Rightarrow q) \wedge (q \Rightarrow r)$ | $p \Rightarrow r$ | $[(p \Rightarrow q) \wedge (q \Rightarrow r)] \Rightarrow (p \Rightarrow r)$ |
|---|---|---|---|---|---|---|---|
| T | T | T | T | T | T | T | T |
| T | T | F | T | F | F | F | T |
| T | F | T | F | T | F | T | T |
| T | F | F | F | T | F | F | T |
| F | T | T | T | T | T | T | T |
| F | T | F | T | F | T | T | T |
| F | F | T | T | T | T | T | T |
| F | F | F | T | T | T | T | T |

Tautology

Only columns no 1, 2, 3, 4, 5 and 7 sufficient to prove the argument as valid since col. 7 is T whenever col. 4 and 5 are simultaneously true.

**Example 10.28:** Consider the following arguments:

Premises $S_1$ : If a man is bachelors he is unhappy

$S_2$ : If a man is unhappy, he dies young.

Conclusion $S$ : Bachelors die young

Test whether the conclusion is valid

or whether $S_1, S_{2,} \vdash S$ is valid.

**Solution:** Let $p$ represent "He is a bachelor"

$q$ represent "He is unhappy"

and $r$ represent "He dies young"

So the argument is of the form:

$$S_1 \text{ is } p \Rightarrow q,\ S_2 \text{ is } q \Rightarrow r$$
$$S \text{ is } p \Rightarrow r$$
$$p \Rightarrow q,\ q \Rightarrow r \vdash p \Rightarrow r$$

or we have to prove that $p \Rightarrow r$ is true whenever $(p \quad q) \wedge (q \Rightarrow r)$ is true.

or if $[(p \Rightarrow q) \wedge (q \quad r)] \Rightarrow [p \Rightarrow r]$ is a tautology which is proved in law of Hypothetical syllogism.

## 4. Law of Disjunctive Syllogism

$$[(p \vee q) \vee (\sim p)] \Rightarrow q$$

or the argument $(p \vee q), \sim p \vdash$ is valid.

**Proof.** The truth table for the argument is given below.

| $p$ | $q$ | $\sim p$ | $p \wedge q$ |
|---|---|---|---|
| T | T | F | T |
| T | F | F | T |
| F | T | T | T |
| F | F | T | F |

Conclusion Premises

All the premises are true in the third row in which conclusion also true. Hence the argument is valid.

**Example 10.29:** Test the validity of the following argument.

Either the horse is white or the dog is brown

The horse is not white

Therefore the dog is brown.

**Solution:** Let $p$ : the horse is white

$q$ : the dog is brown

Then the argument is : $p \vee q, \sim p \vdash q$ and this being the law of disjunctive syllogism can be likewise proved to be a valid argument.

**Example 10.29:** Show that the following argument is a fallacy : If $7 < 4$, then 7 is not a prime number $7 \nless 4$; Therefore 7 is a prime number.

**Solution.** Let p denote "7 is less than 4 and $q$ denote" 7 is a prime number.

The given argument in symbolic form is $p \Rightarrow \neg q,\ P \vdash q$

**Truth Table**

| $p$ | $q$ | $\neg p$ | $\neg q$ | $p \Rightarrow \neg q$ | $(p \Rightarrow \neg q) \wedge \neg p$ |
|---|---|---|---|---|---|
| T | T | F | F | F | F |
| T | F | F | T | T | F |
| F | T | T | F | T | T |
| F | F | T | T | T | T |

Premises $p \Rightarrow \neg q$ and $\neg\, p$ are true simultaneously in rows 3 and 4, but the conclusion $q$ is not true in row 4.

Hence it is fallacy.

Or we can shown that q is not always true when conjunction of propositions $p \Rightarrow \neg\, q$ and $\neg\, p$ is true as is seen in row 4.

Hence the given argument is a fallacy.

**Example 10.31:** Test the validity of the following argument.

$$\underbrace{p \rightarrow \neg q, r \rightarrow q, r}_{\text{3 propositions of premises}} \vdash \underbrace{\neg q}_{\text{conclusion}}$$

**Proof:** **Truth Table**

| $p$ | $q$ | $\neg p$ | $\neg q$ | $r$ | $r \Rightarrow \neg q$ | $r \Rightarrow p$ |
|---|---|---|---|---|---|---|
| T | T | F | F | T | F | T |
| T | T | F | F | F | F | T |
| T | F | F | T | T | T | F |
| T | F | F | T | F | T | T |
| F | T | T | F | T | T | T |
| F | T | T | F | F | T | T |
| F | F | T | T | T | T | F |
| F | F | T | T | F | T | T |

As all the propositions $p \rightarrow \neg q$, $r \rightarrow r$ are $r$ are true simultaneously in row 5 only, in which is conclusion $\neg p$ is also true. Hence the argument is valid.

---

Here we should not make the conjunction of propositions of premise etc. That will take more time.

---

**Example 10.32:** Determine the validity of the following argaument with explanation:

"If wages increase, then there will be inflation. The cost of living will not increase if there is no inflation.

Wages will increase.

Therefore, the cost of living will increase.

***[U.P.T.U. MCA I*[st] *Sem 2001-2002].***

**Solution:** Let $p$ : the wages increase, $q$: there will be inflation $r$: the cost of living increase.

The symbolic representation of the problem is:

**Premises:** $P_1 : p \Rightarrow q$, $P_2 : \neg q \Rightarrow \neg r$, $P_3$:

$p$ Conclusion $Q : r$,

Hence $p \Rightarrow q, \neg q \Rightarrow \neg r \vdash p$

**Truth Table**

| $p$ | $q$ | $r$ | $\sim q$ | $\neg r$ | $p \Rightarrow q$ | $\neg q \Rightarrow \neg r$ |
|---|---|---|---|---|---|---|
| T | T | F | F | T | F | T |
| T | T | F | F | F | F | T |
| T | F | F | T | T | T | F |
| T | F | F | T | F | T | T |
| F | T | T | F | T | T | T |
| F | T | T | F | F | T | T |
| F | F | T | T | T | T | F |
| F | F | T | T | F | T | T |

All the premises are simultaneously true in rows 1 and 2 but the conclusion $r$ is not true in row 2. Hence the argument is not valid.

## 10.15 PROPOSITIONAL FUNCTION

A propositional function or a predicate in a varibale $x$ is a sentence $p(x)$ involving $x$ that becomes a propositio when we give $x$ a definite value from the set of values it can take. Such functions are denoted by $p(x)$ or $q(x)$ etc.

The set of values $x$ can take is called the Universe of discourse.

If $p(x)$ is '$x$' > 6', then $p(x)$ is not a proposition, but when we give $x$ particular vaues say $x = 8$ or $x = 0$, then we get propositions " > 6 (is greater than 6) is the predicate".

Hence $p(8)$ is a true proposition and $p(0)$ is a false proposition.

---

A predicate is usually not a proposition, but of course every proosition is a propositional function in the same way that every real number is a real valued function, namely the constant function.

---

## Some Propositional Function

Let $A$ be a given set (say a **set** of **positive integers** $N$) and $p(x)$ be an expression defined on $A$ (say $p(x)$ is "$x + 2 < 7$") **with the property that $p(a)$ is true or false for each $a \in A$**

Which means $p(x)$ becomes a statement (with a truth value) whenever any element $a \in A$ is substituted for the variables $x$.

*e.g.*, $p(1)$ is true as $1 + 2 < 7$

$p(2)$ is true as $1 + 2 < 7$

$p(3)$ is true as $3 + 2 < 7$, $p$ (4) is true.

$p(6)$ is false as $6 + 2 \nless 7$ etc.

Then **set** $A$ is called the **DOMAIN of $p(x)$, set $T_p$** of all elements of $A$ for which $p(a)$ is true is called the TRUTH SET of $p(x)$

$$T_p = \{1, 2, 3, 4\} = \{x : x \in A, p(x) \text{ is true}\}$$
$$= \{x : p(x)\}.$$

$p(x)$ is called a "PROPOSITIONAL FUNCTION" or an "open sentence" or "contition"

**Other example**

(*a*) Let $p(x)$ be "$x + 3 > 7$" defined on the set $N$ of positive integers then it's truth set $T_p = \{x : x \in N, x + 3 > 7\} = \{5, 6, 7, 8, ....\}$ *i.e.*, integers $\geq 5$ *i.e.*, $p(x)$ is true for all positive integers equal to or greater than 5. or

(*b*) Let $p(x)$ be "$x + 6 < 3$" defined again on $N$. Then its truth set $T_p = \{x : x \in N, x + 6 < 3\} = \varnothing$ = empty set. So $p(x)$ is not true for any positive integer in $N$.

(*c*) Let $p(x)$ be "$x + 8 > 1$" then it's truth set is $\{x : x \in N, x + 8 > 1\} = N$. Thus $p(x)$ is true for every element in $N$.

It is clear from here that propositional function p(x) defined on a set A can be true (*a*) for all $x \in A$ or (*b*) for some $x \in A$ or (c) for no $x \in A$.

**Statement Formulae** are the compound statement derived form the primitive statements like *p*, *Q* called variables by using connectives and parentheses.

$$\neg PP \wedge Q(P \wedge Q) \vee \quad (\neg P) P \wedge (\neg Q)$$

Formula has no truth value until and unless the statement variables in a formula are replaced by definite statements that have truth value. Statement formula is not a statement, however a statement can be derived from it by replacing the variables by statements. A **statement Formula** is an expression which is a string, consisting of variables (capital letters with or without subscripts), parentheses and connectives symbol.

Not every string of these symbols is a formula.

## 10.16 WELL FORMED FORMULA

A well formed formula can be generated by the following rules.

1. A statement variables standing alone is a well formed formula.
2. If *A* is a well formed formula then $\neg A$ is a well formed formula.
3. If *A* and *B* are well formed formulae then $(A \wedge B)$, $(A \vee B)$, $(A \rightarrow B)$ an $(A \Leftrightarrow B)$ are well formed formula.
4. A string of symbols containing the statement variables, connectives, and parentheses are well formed formulae. If it can be obtained by finitely many applications of the rule 1, 2, and 3.

The following are well formed formulae

$\neg(P \wedge Q)$ $\neg(P \vee Q)$ $(P \rightarrow (P \vee Q))$ $(P \rightarrow (Q \rightarrow R))$ $(((P \rightarrow R)) \Leftrightarrow (P \rightarrow R)$

The following are not well-defined formulae

1. $(P \rightarrow Q) \rightarrow (\wedge Q)$ as $\wedge Q$ is not a well formed formula
2. $(P \rightarrow Q)$
3. $((P \wedge Q) \rightarrow Q)$ one parenthesis in the beginning is missing.

**Substitution Instance:** A formula *A* is called a **substitution instance** of another formula *B* if *A* can be obtained from *B* by substituting formula for some variables of *B*, with the conditions that the same formula is substituted for the same variable each time it occurs.

For example, $B : P \Rightarrow (J \vee P)$

Substitute $R \Leftrightarrow S$ for *P* in *B* we get

$A : (R \Leftrightarrow S) \Rightarrow (J \vee (R \Leftrightarrow S))$

Then $A$ is a substitution instance of $B$. Note that $(R \Leftrightarrow S) \Rightarrow (J \wedge P)$ is not the substitution instance of $B$ because $P$ in $J \wedge P$ has not been replaced by $R \Leftrightarrow S$.

Any substituting instance of a tautology is also a tautology.

## 10.17 QUANTIFLERS

To change propositional function into statements is to assign specific valves to their variables. Another way to obtain statepents from propositional function is to add quantifiers quantifiers are words that refer to quantities such as "all", "some", "none" and indicate how frequently a certain statement is true.

### Types of Quantifiers

Quantifiers are two types:

(*i*) Universal quantifiers

(*ii*) Existential quatifiers

#### (*i*) Universal quantifiers

Let $P(x)$ be a propositional function defined on a set A. Then the universal quantifiers of a $P(x)$ is the statement "for all valves $x \in A$, $P(x)$ is true".

Symbols used for universal quantifiers

The symbol $\forall x$ which reads "for all $x$" or "for every $x$" is called the universal quantifier.

Above statement is also denoted in either of the following form:

$\forall x \in A : P(x)$   $P(x), \forall x \in A$

$\forall x\ P(x)$ $P(x)$, is true for all $x \in A$

For example,

(*i*) every whole number is equal to itself is written as:
"For all $x$ in $w_1 x = x$" or $\forall x \in w,\ x = x$,
where $w$ is set of whole numbers.

(*ii*) For all $x$, $y$, $z$ in $N$ is written as $\forall\ x, y, z \in N$
where $N$ is a set of natural numbers.

(*iii*) For all $x$ in whole numbers, $x + o = x$ is written as
$\forall\ x \in w,\ x + o = x$

#### 2 Existential Quantifiers

Let $P(x)$ be a propositional function defined on a set. Then existential quantifier of a $P(x)$ is the statement "there exists at least one value $x$ in A such that $P(x)$ is true".

Symbols used for existential quantifiers

The symbol $\exists x$ which reads "There exists an $x$" or "For somex is called the existential quantifiers.

Above statement is also denoted in either of the following form:

$(\exists\ x \in A)\ P(x)$ $(\exists\ x,\ P(x)$

There exists an $x$ such For some $x$, $P(x)$

that $P(x)$ is true

For example,

(*i*) There exists an $n$ in whole numbers such that $n\ .\ n = 1$ is written as $\exists n, \in w,\ n.n = 1$

---

An open sentence like "$x$ is a bird" is neither true nor false. The statement after quantifing an open sentence may be judged either true or false and is therefore a statement.

---

## Quantifiers Related to Propositional Functions

### [A] Universal Quantifiers

**Statement-1:** $P(x)$ is a propositional function defined on set $A(\forall x {\in} A)$, $P(x)$ or simply $\forall x P(x)$ are read as "For every $x$ in $A$, $P(x)$ is true statement" or simply "For all $x$, $P(x)$"

**Statement-1:** $Tp = \{x : x \in A,\ P(x)\} = A$

*i.e.*, truth set of $P(x)$ is the entire set A. **Both of the statements are equivalent to each other.**

**Rule:** if $\{x : x \in A,\ P(x)\} = A$, then $\forall x\ P(x)$ is true, otherwise $\forall x P(x)$ is false.

---

The expression $P(x)$ by itself is an open sentence or condition and therefore has no truth value. However $\forall x\ P(x)$, that is $P(x)$ preceded by the quantifier $\forall$, does have a truth value.

---

For example, (1) The propositon $(\forall n \in N)\ (n + 9 > 8)$ is true since $\{n : n + 9 > 8\} = \{1, 2, 3,...\} = N$.

(2) The proposition $(\forall\ n \in N)\ (n + 3 > 8)$ is false, since $\{n : n + 3 > 8\} = \{6, 7, 8,...\} \neq N$.

### (*B*) Existential Quantifier

**Statement-1:** $\boldsymbol{p(x)}$ is propositional function defined on set $A$, $(\exists x \in A)\ p(x)$ or $\exists x\ p(x)$, read as "There exist an $x$ in $A$ such that $p(x)$ is a true statement or "For some $x$, $p(x)$"

The above statement is equivalent to the following statement–2.

**Statement-2:** $T_p = \{x : x \in A, p(x) \neq \emptyset$, *i.e.*, truth set of $P(x)$ is not empty.

**Rule:** If $\{x : p(x)\}$or $\{x : x \in A, p(x)\} \neq \emptyset$, then $\exists x, p(x)$ is true, otherwise $\exists x\ p(x)$ is false.

For example, (1) The proposition $(\exists\ n \in N)\ (n + 5 < 8)$ is true since $\{n : n + 5 < 8\} = \{1, 2\} \neq \emptyset$.

(2) The proposition $(\exists n \in N)\ (n + 8 < 4)$ is false since $\{n : n + 8 < 4\} = \emptyset$.

For example,

using $M(x)$ : $x$ is man, $Q(x)$ : $x$ is a mortal

$A(x)$ : $x$ is a flower, $R(x)$ : $x$ is red.

$I\ (x)$ : $x$ is a flower, $R(x)$ : $x$ is red.

$P(x)$ : $x$ is either positive or negative the various sentences and their symbolic representation are given below:

| **Sentences and their paraphrases** | **Symbolic representation** |
|---|---|
| (1) All man are mortal. | $(\forall x)\ (M\ (x) \rightarrow Q(x))$ |
| or | |
| For all x, if x is a man, then x is a mortal. | |
| (2) Every flower is red. | |
| or | |
| For all x, if x is a flowers, then x is red. | $(\forall x)\ (A(x) \rightarrow R(x))$ |
| (3) Any integer is either positive or negative. | |
| or | |
| For all $x$, if $x$ is an integer, then $x$ is either positive or negative. | $(\forall x)\ (I(x) \rightarrow P(x))$ |

**Some other Predicate Formula**

(1) If $P(x)$ : $x$ is a person

$F(x, y)$ : $x$ is the father of $y$.

$M(x, y)$ : $x$ is the mother of $y$.

**To write the statement "$x$ is the father of the mother of $y$"** we name a person called $z$ as the mother of $y$. Now we want to say, that $x$ is the father of $z$ and $z$ is the mother of $y$, which is symbolized as:

$\exists(z)\ (P(x)) \wedge F(x, z) \wedge M(z, y))$

(2) If$P(x)$ : $x$ is a person

$L(x)$ : $x$ is a lover

$R(x, y)$ : $x$ loves $y$.

To write "All the person loves a lover"

It can be symbolised as

$(\forall x)\ (P(x)) \rightarrow \forall y\ (P(y) \wedge L(y) \rightarrow R(x, y)))$

$(\forall x)$ and $(x)$ both means the same thing.

(3) using $G(x)$ : $x$ is a tree.

$M(x)$ : $x$ is a man

Symbolic representation of the statement "**All men are trees**" shall be $(\forall x)$ $(M(x) \rightarrow G(x))$

## 10.18 NEGATION OF QUANTIFIED STATEMENTS

**Statement:** "All birds are dogs" $(\forall x \in M)$ ($x$ is a dog) ...(1)

where $M$ represent set of birds.

**Negation of this Statement** : (1) Is is not the case that all birds are dogs.

$\sim (\forall x \in M)$ ($x$ is a dog) ...(2)

or equivalently

(2) There exists at least one bird who is not a dog.

$(\exists\ x \in M)$ ($x$ is a not a dog) ...(3)

$(1) \equiv (2)$ 3

*i.e.*, $\sim(\forall x{\in}M)$ ($x$ is a dog) $\equiv (\exists\ x \in M)$ ($x$ is not a dog) ...(4)

or if $p(x)$ denotes "$x$ is a dog" we can write the above equivalence relation (4) as –

$\sim (\forall x \in M)\ p(x) \equiv (\exists\ x \in M) \sim p(x)$ ...(5)

**Negation of $\forall x\ p(x)$** is "It is not true (not the case) that for all $x$, $p(x)$ is true".

or $\sim (\forall x\ p(x)) = (\exists x) \sim p(x)$ ...(6)

or there exists at least one value of $x$ for which $p(x)$ is not true.

This is true for any propositon. We can write (6) as

$\sim (\forall x \in A)\ p(x) = (\exists\ x \in A) \sim p(x)$ ...(7)

**This is called De Morgan's law or Theorem.**

and can be written in the form of following two equivalent statements

(1) It is not true that, for all $a \in A$. $p(a)$ is true.

(2) There exists an $a \in A$ such that $p(a)$ is false.

**Similarly we have an analogous Theorem for Negation of a proposition containing existential Quantifiers.**

**Statement :** There exist an $x$ in A such that $p(x)$ is true $(\exists\ x \in A)$ $p(x)$ ...(8)

**Negation of this Statement : (1)** It is not the case that there exists an $x$ in $A$ such that $p(x)$ is true or

$$\sim (\exists\ x \in A)\ p(x)$$

or equivalently

(2) For all $x$ in $A$ $p(x)$ is not true $(\forall x \in A) \sim p(x)$

*i.e.*, $\sim (\exists x \in)\ p(x) \equiv (\forall x \in A) \sim p(x)$ – De Morgan's Law.

The following two statements are equivalent:

(1) It is not true that, for some $a \in A$, $p(a)$ is true.

(2) For all $a \in A$, $p(x)$ is false.

For example, The following statements are negative of each other:

"For all positive integers $n$ we have $n + 3 > 8$ "There exist a positive integer $n$ such that $n + 3 \not> 8$".

(1) The following statements are also negative of each other:

"There exists a living person who is 250 years old"

"Every living person is not 250 years old".

Note (1) $\sim p(x)$ or $p(x)$ has the obvious meaning that

"The statement $\sim p(a)$ is true when $p(a)$ is true when $p(a)$ is false and vice versa".

(2) The statement "$p(x) \wedge p(x)$" is defined by:

"The statement $p(a) \wedge q(a)$ is true when $p(a)$ and $q(a)$ are true"

(3) The statement "$p(x) \vee q(x)$" is defined by:

"The statement $p(a) \vee q(a)$ is true when $p(a)$ or $q(a)$ is true"

(4) (*a*) $\sim p(x)$ is the comple ment of $p(x)$<br>(*b*) $p(x) \wedge q(x)$ is the inter section of $p(x)$ and $q(x)$<br>(*c*) $p(x) \vee q(x)$ is the union of $p(x)$ and $q(x)$<br>} in terms of truth set.

(5) Laws applicable for propositions also hold for propositional function *e.g.*, De Morgan's laws :

$$\sim(p(x)) \wedge q(x)) \equiv \sim p(x) \wedge \sim q(x)$$

and $$\sim(p(x) \vee q(x)) \equiv \sim p(x) \vee \sim q(x).$$

**Example 10.33:** Write negation of $[(\forall x_1 \in U_1)\ (\exists x_2 \in U_2)\ (\exists x_3 \in U_3)\ (\forall x_4 \in U_4)\ (\exists x_n \in U_n)\ p(x)]$.

**Solution:** $[(\exists x_1 \in U_1)\ (\forall x_2 \in U_2)\ (\forall x_3 \in U_3)\ (\exists x_4 \in U_4)\ (\forall x_n \in U_n)\ (\sim p(x))]$.

**Example 10.34:** Write negation of :

(*a*) The politician can fool all the people all the time

(*b*) Every real number is the square of some real number

(*c*) There is a lawyer who never tells lies.

**Solution:** Given statement is : $(\forall t \in [0, \infty[)\ (\forall x \in H)\ p(x, t)$.

Where $p(x, t)$ is the predicate.

$p(x, t)$ = The politician can fool $x$ at time $t$ seconds. $H$ is the set of human beings

**Negation is:** $(\exists t \in [0, \infty[)\ (\exists x \in H)\ (\sim p(x, t))$

*i.e.*, there is some body who is not fooled by the politician at for one moment.

(*b*) Given **statement is :** $(\forall\ x \in R)\ (\exists y \in R)\ (x = y^2)$

Its **Negation** is : $(\exists c \in R)\ (\forall y \in y^2)$

*i.e.*, there is a real number which is not the square of any real number.

(*c*) Given **statement is :** $(\exists x \in L)\ (\forall x \in [0, \infty[)\ p(x, t)$ where L is the set of lawyers and $p(x, t)$; $x$ does not lie at time $t$.

Its **negation** is : $(\forall x \in L)\ (\exists t \in [0, \infty[)\ (\sim p)$ *i.e*, every lawyer tells a lie at sometime or at least at one time.

For example. Find truth values of

(*a*) $(x \geq 0) \Rightarrow (\exists\ y)\ (y^2 = x)$ True

(*b*) $(\forall x)\ (\exists! y)\ (xy = 0)$ True

(*c*) $(\forall x)\ (\exists!\ y)\ (y^2 = x^3)$ False *e.g.*, $x = -1$, no $y$ satisfy $y^2 = x^3$.

**Relationship of Factors with Tautology and Contradiction :**

(*a*) A necessary and sufficient condition for an elementary product to be identically false (or contradiction) is that is contain at least one pair of factors in which one is the negation of the other.

(*b*) A necessary and sufficient condition for an elementary sum to be identically true (or tautology) is that it contains at least one pair of factors in which one is trhe negatrion of the other.

## 10.19 NORMAL FORMS

The problem of finding whether a given statement is tautolog or contradiction in a finite number of steps is called a decision problem. But the process is very difficiult when the number of variables increases. We therefore consider alternate procedure known as reduction to normal forms.

There are two normal forms, which are:

→ Disjunctive normal form (*DNF*)

→ Conjunctive normal form (*CNF*)

## 10.19.1 Disjunctive Normal Form (DNF)

A formula, which has a sum of elementary products and is equivalent to the given formula, is called Disjunctive Normal Form (DNF) of the given formula.

## 10.19.2 Conjunctive Normal Form (CNF)

A formula, which has a product of elementary sums and is equivalent to the given formula, is called conjunctive Normal Form (CNF) of the given formula.

**Example 10.35:** Obtain Disjunctive normal forms of

(*a*) $P \wedge (P \to Q)$

(*b*) $\neg (P \vee Q) \Leftrightarrow (P \wedge Q)$

**Solution:** (*a*) $P \wedge (P \to Q) \equiv P \wedge (\neg P \vee Q)$

$\equiv (P \wedge \neg P) \vee (P \wedge Q)$ by distributive law

Which is the sum of variables and their negation i.e., sum of elementary products and is therefore in disjunctive normal form.

(*b*) $\neg (P \vee Q) \Leftrightarrow (P \wedge Q)$

$\equiv (\neg (P \wedge Q) \vee (P \wedge Q)) \vee ((P \vee Q) \wedge \neg (P \wedge Q))$

Since, $R \Leftrightarrow S \equiv (R \wedge S) \vee (\neg R \wedge \neg S)$ $((\neg P \wedge \neg Q) \wedge (P \wedge Q)$ $((P \vee Q) \wedge (\neg P \vee \neg Q))$

**(by De Morgan's rule)**

$\equiv ((\neg P \wedge \neg Q) \wedge (P \wedge Q) \vee ((P \vee Q) \wedge \neg P) \vee ((P \vee Q) \wedge \neg Q))$

**(by distributive law)**

$\equiv ((\neg P \wedge \neg Q) \wedge (P \wedge Q)) \vee (P \wedge \neg P) \vee (P \wedge \neg Q)$ and $(Q \wedge \neg P)$

Which is sum of variables and their negation *i.e.*, sum of elementary products and hence is in disjunctive normal form.

**Example 10.36:** Obtain a conjunctive Normal From of

(a) $P \wedge (P \to Q)$ or $P \wedge (P \Rightarrow Q)$

(*b*) $\neg (P \wedge Q)$ or $P \Leftrightarrow (P \wedge Q)$

**Solution:** (*a*) $P \wedge (P \to Q) \equiv P \wedge (\neg P \vee Q)$ (by Equivalent formula)

Which is product of sum of variables and their negation *i.e.*, product of elementary sums and is, therefore in conjunctive normal form.

(*b*) $\neg (P \vee Q) \Leftrightarrow (P \wedge Q)$ $\equiv (\neg (P \wedge Q) \to (P \wedge Q)) \wedge ((P \wedge Q) \to \neg (P \vee Q))$

$\equiv ((P \vee Q) \wedge (P \wedge Q)) \wedge (\neg (P \wedge Q) \vee (\neg P \wedge \neg Q))$

$\equiv ((P \vee Q \vee P) \wedge (P \vee Q \vee Q)) \wedge ((\neg P \vee \neg Q) \vee (\neg P \wedge \neg Q))$

(by distributive law)

$\equiv (P \vee Q \vee P) \wedge (P \vee Q \vee Q)) \wedge (\neg P \vee \neg Q \vee \neg P) \wedge (\neg P \vee \neg Q \vee \neg Q)$

Which is product of sum of variables and their negation *i.e.*, product of elementary sums and is, therefore in conjunctive normal form.

## EXERCISE

### (A) Objective Type Questions

**1.** Which of the following propositions is tautology?

(a) $(p \wedge q) \to p$ (b) $(p \wedge (q \to p)$

(c) $(p \wedge (p \to q)$ (d) $p \to (q \to p)$

**2.** The proposition is $p \wedge (\sim p \vee q)$ is

(a) A tautology

(b) A contradicition

(c) Logically equivalent to $p \wedge q$

(d) None of these

**3.** Let *P, Q* and *R* be three atomic propositional assertioons. Let *X* denote $(p \vee q) \to R$ and *Y* denote $(P \to R) \vee (Q \to R)$. Which one of the following is a tautology?

(a) $X \equiv Y$ (b) $X \to Y$

(c) $Y \to X$ (d) $\bar{Y} \to X$

**4.** Let *p* and *q* be propositions. Using only the truth table decide whether $p \Leftrightarrow q$ does not imply $p \to 7_q$.

(a) True (b) False

**5.** $(p \vee p) \wedge (p \to q \vee q)$ is equivalent to

(a) $p \to q$ (b) $p \vee q$

(c) $p \wedge q$ (d) $q \to p$

**6.** Let *a, b, c* and *d* be propositions. Assume that equivalences $a \leftrightarrow (b \vee 7b)$ and $b \leftrightarrow c$ hold. Then the truth value of the formula

$(a \wedge b) \to ((a \wedge c) \vee d)$ is always

(a) True

(b) False

(c) Same as the truth value of $b$

(d) Same as the truth value of $d$

**7.** Given that $(p \vee q) \wedge (\sim p \vee \sim q)$ is false, the truth values of $p$ and $q$ are

(a) both false (b) both true

(c) $p$ true and $q$ false (d) $p$ false and $q$ true

**8.** $(p \to q) \wedge (r \to q)$ is equivalent to

(a) $(p \vee r) \to q$ (b) $p \vee (r \to p)$

(c) $p \vee (r \to q)$ (d) $p \to (q \to r)$

**ANSWERS**

| | | | |
|---|---|---|---|
| **1.** (*c*) | **2.** (*c*) | **3.** (*b*) | **4.** (*b*) |
| **5.** (*c*) | **6.** (*a*) | **7.** (*a*) | **8.** (*a* |

## (B) Problems

**1.** Find the truth value of each ofthe following statements

(a) $3 + 5 = 8$ or $0 > 1$

(b) $1 > 0$ or $3 + 8 - 1 = 23$

(c) Delhi is in Germany and Lucknow is in U.P. [**Ans.** (*a*) T (*b*) T (*c*) F]

**2.** If $p$ denote "He is intelligent" and $q$ denotes "He is rich", then write each of the following statements in symbols form:

(a) He is intelligent but not rich.

(b) He is neither but not rich.

(c) It is not true that he is not intelligent or rich.

[**Ans.** (*a*) $p \wedge \sim q$ (*b*) $\sim P \wedge \sim q$ (*c*) $\sim(\sim p \vee q)$]

**3.** Show that $p \vee \sim (P \wedge q)$ is a tautology and $(p \wedge q) \wedge \sim (p \vee q)$ is a contradiction.

**4.** Without constructing the truthtable, provet hat

(a) $p \vee (p \wedge q) \equiv p$

(b) $\sim(p \vee q) \vee (\sim p \vee q) \equiv \sim p$

**5.** Find the truth values of each of the following propositions and prove that these are equivalent.

(a) If is not true (or not the case) that cats are sick and dogs are dangerous $[= \neg(p \wedge q)]$

(b) Cats are not sick or dogs are not dangerous.

[**Ans.** Truth table in each case is $\begin{pmatrix} F \\ T \\ T \\ T \end{pmatrix}$

**6.** Rewrite the following statements without using the conditional.

(a) If he works hard, he gets a job

(b) It price increase, demand decreases.

[**Ans.** (*a*) He does nto work hard orhegets a job

(*b*) Price does not increaseordemand decreases.]

**7.** Write $p \Leftrightarrow q$ in terms of the three connectives $\wedge$, $\vee$ and ~.

[**Ans.** $(\sim p \vee q) \wedge (\sim q \vee p)$]

❑❑❑

# APPENDIX–A

## MODEL QUESTION

## Paper – I

1. Find DFA's that recognizes the following sets:

   (a) $L = \{x \in \{a, b, c\}^* \mid |x|$ is a multiple of 2 or 3$\}$

   (b) $L = \{x \in \{a, b, c\}^* \mid abc$ is a substring of $x\}$

   (c) $L = \{x \in \{a, b\}^* \mid (|x|_a$ as odd$) \wedge (|x|_b)$ is even$)\}$

   (d) $L = \{x \in \{a, b\}^* \mid (|x|_a$ is even$) \vee (|x|_b)$ is odd$)\}$

   (e) $L = \{x \in \{a, b\}^* \mid |x|_a$ is odd$\}$

2. Construct nfa that accepts the languages:

   (a) $L = \{x \in \{a, b, c\}^* \mid x$ contains exatly one $b$ immediately following $c\}$

   (b) $L = \{x \in \{0,1\}^* \mid$ every block of five consecutive symbols in $x$ contains at least two 0's$\}$

   (c) $L = \{x \in \{0, 1\}^* \mid$ is starting with 1 and $|x|$ divisible by 3$\}$

   (d) $L = \{x \in \{a, b\}^* \mid x$ contains any number of a's followed by at least a single $b\}$

   (e) The set of all strings over {0, 1} having at most one pair of 0's or at most one pair of 1's.

3. Construct DFA from nfa's given in question (2).

4. Obtain equivalent DFA for the following NFA:

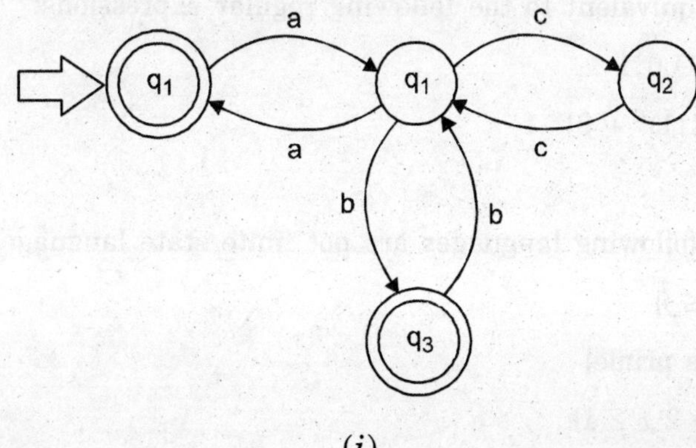


(*i*)

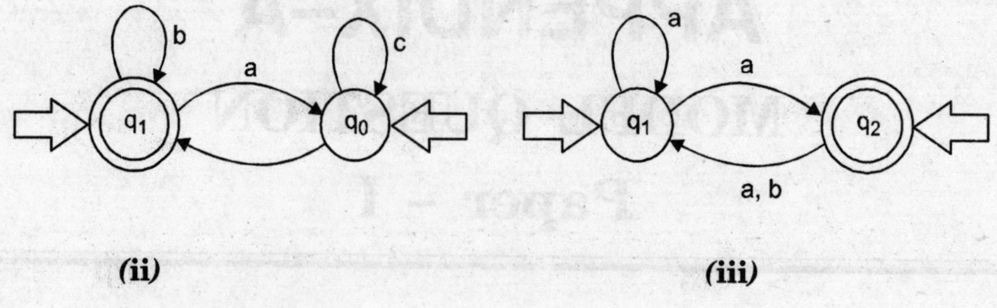


(ii) (iii)

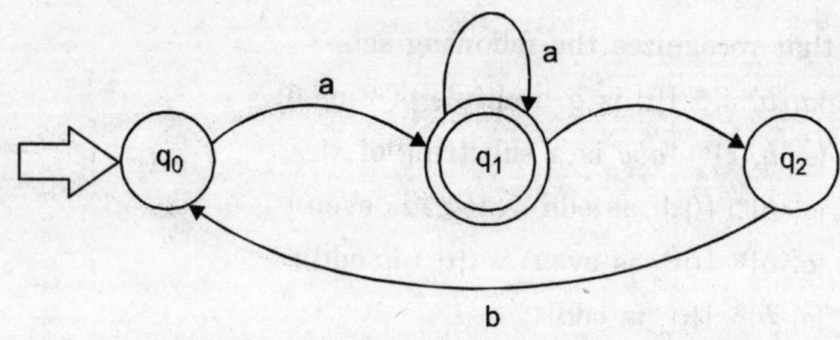


(iv)

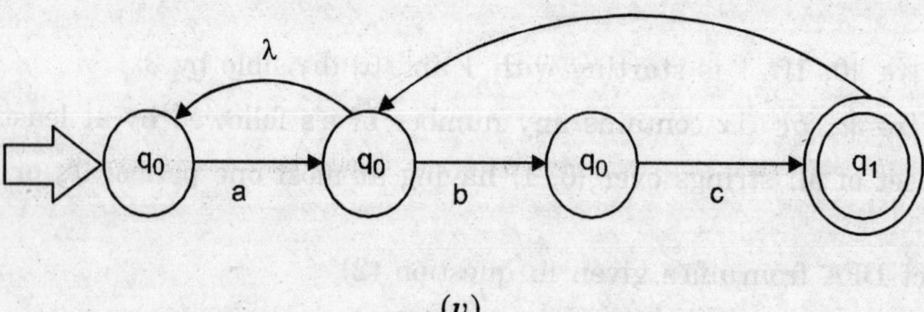


(v)

**5.** Construct dfa equivalent to the following regular expressions:

(a) 10 + (0 + 11) 0*1

(b) 01 [(10* + 111)* + 0]* 1

(c) $(aab^*\ ab)^*$

**6.** Show that the following languages are not finite state languages

(a) $L = \{a^i b^j \mid i \leq j\}$

(b) $L = \{a^n \mid n$ is prime$\}$

(c) $L = \{0^k \mid k = 2^i, i \geq 1\}$

(d) $L = \{WW^R \mid W \in \{a, b\}^*\}$

**7.** Minimize the states in the dfa's depicted in the following diagrams:

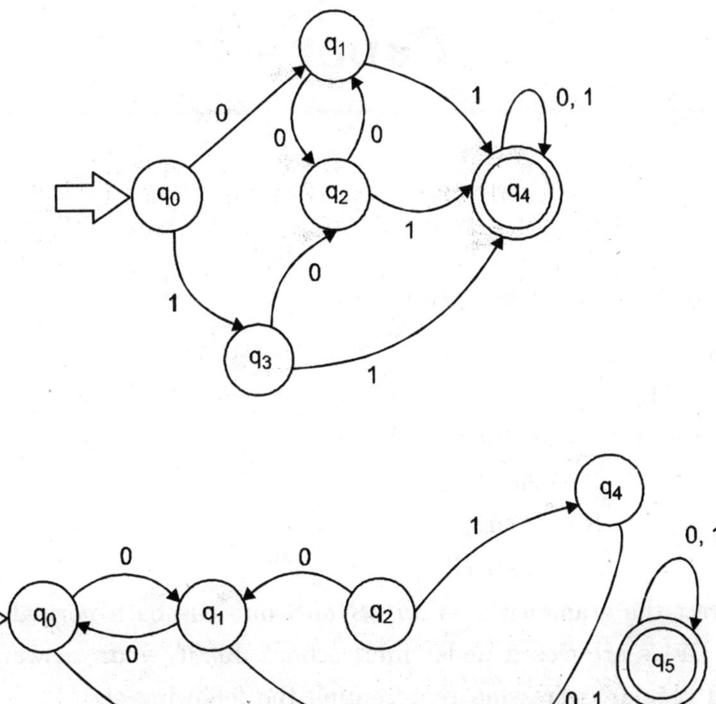


**8.** Construct regular grammars for the following languages on $\{a, b\}$:

(a) $L = \{a^n b^m \mid n \geq 2, m \geq 3\}$

(b) $L = \{W \in \{a, b\}^* \mid n_a(w)$ and $n_b(w)$ both even$\}$

**9.** Assume that *AB* is a read having very high traffic density. There is one cur *PQ* making the road as *T* (see Fig.) The traffic density in *PQ* is very low. The traffic takes place along the directed arrows. The sensor get when there is vehicle at *Q* otherwise resets. Also when vehicle passes over from *Q* it gets reset. Construct a transition diagram modelling it as Meare or Mealy machine.

# MODEL QUESTION
# Paper – II

*Time : 3 hours* *Maximum Marks : 70*

***Answer question 1 and any four from 2 to 6.***

**1.** (a) Find a grammer that generates $L = \{a^n b^{n+1} \mid n \geq 0\}$ (2)

(b) Is the following true: "If $L_1$ and $L_1.L_2$ are regular, so is $L_2$?"

(c) Remove all unit productions from

$$S \to Aa \mid B$$
$$S \to A \mid ab,$$
$$S \to a \mid bc \mid B,$$ (2)

(d) Correct the grammer $S \to ab \mid aS \mid aaS$ into Greibach normal form. (2)

(e) Are CFL's are closed under intersection? Justify your answer. (2)

(f) Find regular expression representing the following set:

"The set of all strings over $\{a, b\}$ which has almost two $a$'s". (2)

(g) Show that the grammar

$$S \to a \mid abSb \mid aAb,$$
$$S \to bS \mid aAAb,$$

is ambiguous. (2)

(h) State the Post Correspondence Problem. (2)

(i) For $\Sigma = \{0,1\}$, design a Turing machine that accept the language denoted by the regular expression 00*. (2)

**2.** (a) Obtain equivalent dfa for the following nfa defined over $\Sigma = \{a, b\}$: (8)

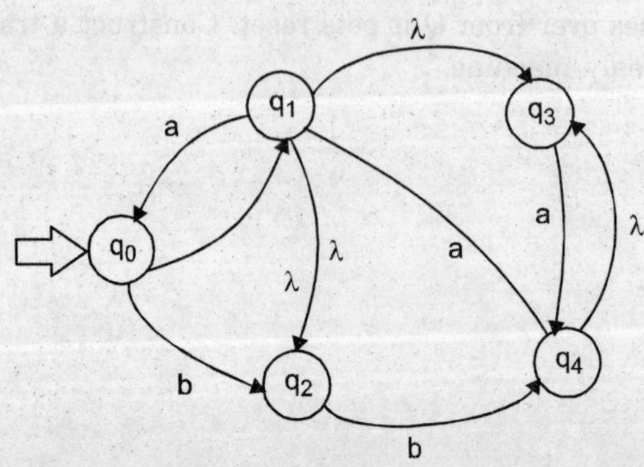

(b) Show that the language $L = \{a^i b^j \mid i \leq j\}$ is not a finite state language. (5)

**3.** (a) Convert the grammar $S \rightarrow AB, A \rightarrow BS \mid b, B \rightarrow SA \mid a$ into GNF (Greibach normal form) (5)

(b) Constant an npda accepting the language defined over $\{a, b, c\}$ as

$$L = \{wcw^R \mid w \in \{a,b\}^*\}$$

when $w^R$ is the reverse string of $w$. (8)

**4.** (a) Given a context free grammar $G$ and a string $w \in \Sigma^*$, can we determine algorithmically whether $w \in L$? Justify. (8)

(b) Given two positive integers m and n, design a Turing machine that computes $m + n$. (5)

**5.** (a) Prove that the halting problem (HP) of Turing machine over $\{0,1\}$ as unsolvable.

(b) Let $\Sigma = \{0,1\}$. Let $A$ and $B$ be lists of three strings as given below:

| $i$ | List A | List B |
|---|---|---|
| | $w_i$ | $x_i$ |
| 1 | 10 | 101 |
| 2 | 011 | 11 |
| 3 | 101 | 011 |

find, whether this instance of PCP has a solution or not. (5)

**6.** (a) What do you mean by Hierarchy (Chomsky) of grammar? Explain with the help of example. (8)

(b) Prove that the language

$$L = \{a^p \mid p \text{ is a prime}\}$$

is not a context-free language. (5)

# MODEL QUESTION
# Paper – III

**1.** Find context grammars for the following languages (with $n \geq 0$, $m \geq 0$)

(i) $L = \{a^n b^n \mid n \neq m\}$

(ii) $L = \{a^n b^m c^k \mid n = m \text{ or } m \leq k\}$

(iii) $L = \{a^m b^m c^k \mid k = n + m\}$.

**2.** Show that the following grammars are ambiguous

(i) $S \to AB \mid aaB,\ A \to a \mid Aa,\ B \to b$

(ii) $S \to aSbS \mid bSaS \mid \lambda$

**3.** Eliminate useless symbols and productions from the following grammars:

(i) $S \to aS \mid A \mid c,\ A \to a, B \to aa,\ C \to acb$

(i) $S \to a \mid aA \mid B \mid C, A \to aB\lambda,\ B \to Aa,\ C \to cCD,\ D \to ddd$

**4.** Convert the following grammars into *CNF*:

(i) $S \to abAB,\ A \to bAB \mid \lambda,\ B \to Baa\ \mid A\ \lambda$

(ii) $S \to ABa,\ A \to aab,\ B \to Ac$

**5.** Convert the following grammars into GNF:

(i) $S \to ABb \mid a,\ A \to aaA \mid B, B \to bAb$

(ii) $S \to ab \mid aS \mid aaS$

**6.** Determine whether the string $W = aabbb$ is in the language generated by the grammar

$$S \to AB,\ A \to BB \mid a,\ B \to AB \mid b$$

**7.** Construct an npda for the languages:

(i) $L = \{w \in \{a,b\}^* \mid n_a(w) = n_b\ (w)\}$

(ii) $L = \{ww^R \mid W \in \{a,\ b\}^*\}$

(iii) $L = \{a^n b^{2n}\ \mid n \geq 0\}$

(iv) $L = \{a^m b^n \mid m \leq 2m\}$

**8.** Construct an npda corresponding to the grammar:

$$S \to aABB, aAA$$

$$A \to aBB \mid a,\ B \to bBB \mid\ A$$

**9.** Find a *CFG* that generates the language accepted by the *npda*

$M = [\{q_0,\ q_1\},\ \{a,\ b\},\ \{A,\ Z\},\ S,\ F_0,\ Z,\ \{q,\ z\}]$ with transition

$$S(q_0, a, z) = \{q_0,\ AZ)\}$$

$$S(q_0, b, A) = \{q_0,\ AA)\}$$
$$S(q_0, a, A) = \{q_1,\ \lambda)\}$$

**10.** Prove that the following languages are not CFL:

(*i*) $\{a^{n!} \mid n \geq 0\}$

(*ii*) $\{ww \mid wc\{a, b\}^*\}$

(*iii*) $\{a^n b^j \mid n \leq j^2\}$

(*iv*) $\{w \in \{a, b, c\}^* \mid n_a(w) = n_b(w) = n_c(w)\}$

**11.** Show that the family of context– free languages is closed under:

(*i*) homomorphism

(*ii*) reversal

**12.** Give an example of a CFL whose complement is not context free.

**13.** Let $L = \{a^i b^j c^j d^i \mid i, j \in N\}$

(*i*) Find a *pda* (which via final state) that recognizes *L*.

(*ii*) Is there a *DPDA* that recognizes *L*.

(*iii*) Find a grammar equivalent to the *pda* in part (*b*).

**14.** Give reasons why one might conjuinctive that the following language is not deterministic:

$$L = \{a^n b^m c^k \mid n = m \text{ or } m = k\}$$

**15.** Show that the following languages are deterministic context–free languages:

(*i*) $\{a^n b^{2n} \mid n \geq 0\}$

(*ii*) $\{w \in \{a, b\}^* \mid n_a(w) \neq n_b(w))\}$

❑❑❑

# APPENDIX–B

# B. TECH

## Fourth Semester Examination

## 2002-2003

*Time : Three hours* *Total Marks : 100*

**Note :** Attempt ALL questions.

**1.** Attempt is FOUR of the following: (5 × 4= 20)

(a) What is Moore Machine? Change the given Moore machine into Mealy machine:

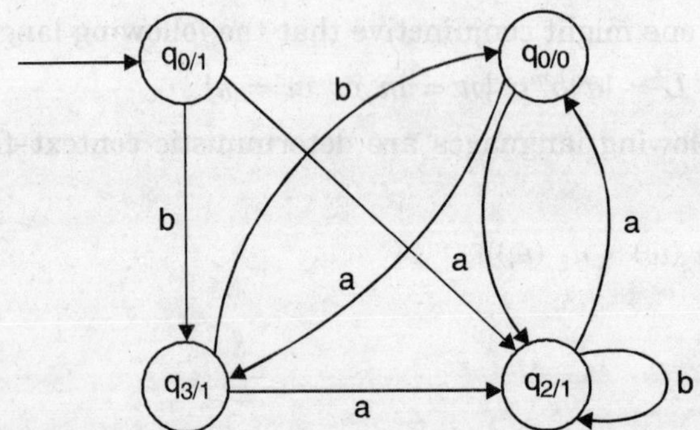


(b) Find out Regular Expression of the given diagram:

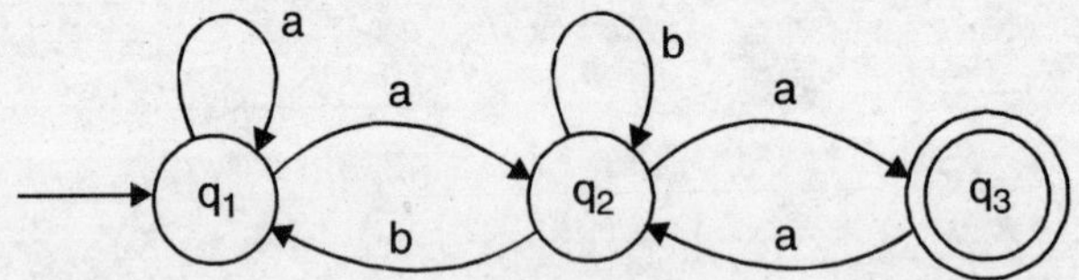


(c) Give deterministic finite automata accepting the following languages over the alphabet {0, 1}:

(*i*) The set of all strings ending in 00.

(*ii*) The set of all strings such that every block of five consecutive symbols contains at least two 0's.

(d) Construct a *DFA* equivalent to the following NDFA:

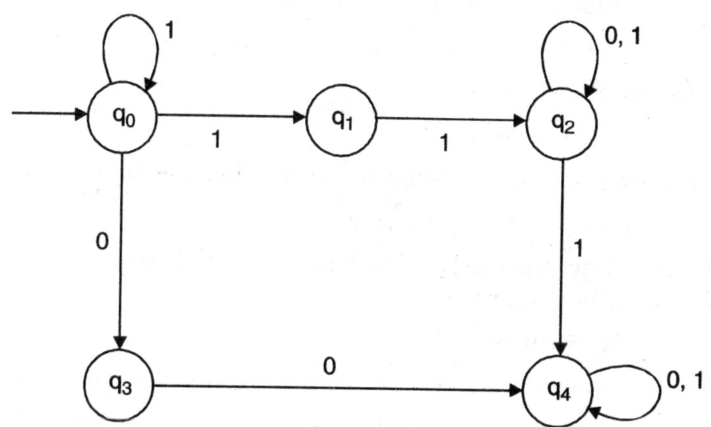


(e) What is the difference between Two-way Finite Automata (2 *DFA*) and One-way Finite Automata?

(b) Find the regular grammar for the language

$$L = \{a^n b^m \mid n + m \text{ is even}\}$$

**2.** Attempt any *FOUR* of the following: (5× 4 = 20)

(a) State Myhill-Nerode Theorem.

(b) What is Ambiguity? Show that $S \to$ as | Sa | a is an ambiguous grammar.

(c) Convert the given grammar in Chomsky Normal Form (*CNF*):

$$S \to ABa$$
$$A \to aab$$
$$B \to Ac$$

(d) Show that $L = \{ww/wt\ \{a, b\}^*\}$ is not regular set.

(e) Explain Pumping Lemma for *CFL*. Consider the following languages:

$$L = \{a^n b^n c^n \mid n \geq 1\}$$

Using pumping lemma, show that $L$ is not a *CFL*.

(f) Show the derivation tree for string 'aabbbb' with the following grammar:

$$S \to AB/\varepsilon$$
$$A \to aB$$
$$B \to Sb$$

**3.** Attempt any TWO of the following: (10 × 2 = 20)

(a) Write down the algorithm to determine whether *CFL* is

(*i*) Empty

(*ii*) Finite or

(*iii*) Infinite

(b) Explain the difference between Deterministic and Non-Deterministic Push Down Automata giving their definition. Illustrate with an example of each.

(c) Construct *PDA* for the following

$$L = \{a^n cb^n \mid n \geq 1\}$$

Over the alphabet $S = \{a, b, c\}$.

**4.** Attempt any TWO of the following: (10 × = 20)

(a) Define a Turing Machine. Design a Turing Machine that accepts the language

$$L = \{a^n\ b^{n+1} \mid n > 0\}.$$

(b) Does the Post Correspondence Problem (PCP) with two lists $x = (b, bab^3,$ ba) and $y = (b^3, ba, a)$ have a solution?

(c) State True/False with reason:

(*i*) Every language described by regular expression can be recognised by *DFA*.

(*ii*) Every recursively enumerable language can be generated by a *CFL*.

(*iii*) The halting problem of TM is decidable.

(*iv*) Complement of any recursively enumerable language is also enumerable.

(*v*) Every *CFL* can be recognised by *TM*.

**5.** Attempt any *TWO* of the following: (10 ×2= 20)

(a) Show that $L = \{a^n b^n c^n \mid n \geq 1\}$ is not context-free but context-sensitive.

(b) Give the production rule for Type 0, Type 1, Type 2 and Type 3 grammars of Chomosky hierarchy.

(c) Show that CSL are closed under:

(*i*) Union

(*ii*) Substitution

(*iii*) Concatenation

(*iv*) Intersection

# B. TECH
# Fourth Semester Examination
# 2004-2005

*Time : Three hours* *Total Marks : 100*

**Note :** (*i*) Attempt ALL questions.

(*ii*) All questions carry equal marks.

**1.** Attempt any Four parts of the following: (5 × 4 =20)

(a) Differentiate between the Mealy Machine and Moore type Machine with example.

(b) Convert the following NFA to equivalent DFA.

| | 0 | 1 |
|---|---|---|
| → p | {q, s} | {q} |
| *q | {r} | {q, r} |
| r | {s} | {p} |
| *s | f | {p} |

(c) Construct *DFA* from the graph given below.

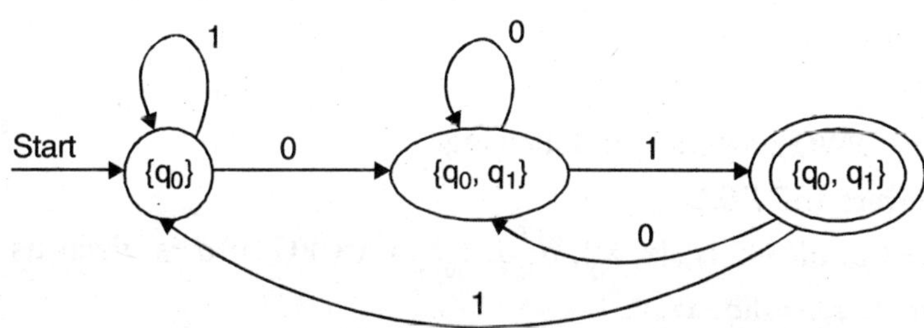


(d) Design *NFA* to recognise the following sets of string *abc*, *abd* and *aacd*. Assume the alphabet is {*a*, *b*, *c*, *d*}.

(e) Give the English description of the language of the following regular expression.

$$(1 + s)\ (00^*1)^*0^*$$

(f) Write the regular expression for the following language:

(*i*) A set of strings of 0's and 1's with at most one pair of consecutive 1's.

(*ii*) Set of all strings of 0's and 1's such that every pair of adjacent 0's appear before any pair of adjacent 1's.

**2.** Attempt any *FOUR* parts of the following: (5 × 4 = 20)

(a) Prove or disprove the following statements about regular expressions.

(*i*) $(R + S)^* = R^* + S^*$

(*ii*) $(RS + R)^*RS = (RR^*S)^*$

(b) Explain with example the algebraic laws for regular expressions.

(c) Prove that the following is not a regular language.

(*i*) $\{f^n 1^n \mid n \geq 1\}$

(*ii*) $\{0^n \mid n$ is a perfect square$\}$

(d) Prove, if $L$ is a regular language over alphabet $S$, then $\bar{L} = S^* - L$ is also a regular language.

(e) Design a context-free grammar for the following language.

(*i*) The set $\{0^n 1^n \mid n \geq 1\}$, *i.e.*, the set of all string of one or more 0's followed by an equal number of 1's.

(*ii*) A set $\{a^i b^j c^k \{ i \neq j$ or $j \neq k\}$ i.e., the set of string of *a's* followed by *b's* followed by *c's,* such that there are either a different number of *a's* and *b's* or a different number of *b's* and *c's* or both.

(f) The following grammar generates the language of regular expression $0^*1\ (0 + 1)^*$:

$S \rightarrow A1B$

$A \rightarrow OA \mid s$

$B \rightarrow OB \mid 1B \mid s$

Give the left most and right most derivation of the following strings..

(*i*) 00101

(*ii*) 1001

**3.** Attempt any TWO parts of the following:

(*a*) (*i*) Convert the *PDA*

$P = (\{p, q\}, \{0, 1\}, \{x, z_0\}, d, q, z_0)$ to a CFG, if $d$ is given as

$d(q, 1, z_0) = \{(q. xz_0)\}$.

(*ii*) Convert the grammar

$S \rightarrow OS1 \mid A$

$A \rightarrow 1AO \mid S \mid E$

to *PDA* that accepts the same language by empty stack.

(b) Show that if *P* is a *PDA*, then there is a one-state *PDA* $P_1$ such that $N(P_1) = N(P)$.

(c) Show that the language:

$L = \{0^n 1^n \mid n \geq 1 \mid \cup \{0^n 1^0 \mid n \leq 1\}$

is a context-free language that is not accepted by any *DPDA*.

**4.** Attempt any TWO of the following: (10 × 2= 20)

(a) Describe the truing machine. Design a turing machine that can accept the following language.

(*i*) $L = (a^n b^{2n} \mid n > 0\}$

(*ii*) $L = \{a^n b^n c^n \mid n > 1\}$

(b) Design the following 2-tape *TM* to accept the language of all strings of 0's and 1's with an equal number of each. The first tape contains the input and is scanned from left to with. The second tape is used to store the excess of 0's over 1's or vice-versa, in the part of the input seen so far. Specify the states, transition and the intuitive purpose of each state.

(c) (*i*) Describe the counter machine accept the following language.

$$\{0^n \ 1^m \ | n \geq m \geq 1\}$$

(*ii*) Explain how:

(*a*) A compute can simulate a turing machine.

(*b*) A turing machine can simulate a computer.

**5.** Attempt any *TWO* parts of the following: (10 × 2 = 20)

(*a*) Convert the *TM*

$M = (\{q_1, q_2, q_3\}, \{0, 1\}, \{0, 1, B\}, \delta, q_1, B, \{q_3\}$ where δ is given by:

| $q_1$ | $\delta(q_i, 0)$ | $\delta(q_i, 1)$ | $\delta(q_i, B)$ |
|---|---|---|---|
| $q_1$ | $(q_2, 1, R)$ | $(q_2, 0, L)$ | $(q_2, 1, L)$ |
| $q_2$ | $(q_3, 0, L)$ | $(q_1, 0, R)$ | $(q_2, 0, R)$ |
| $q_3$ | – | – | – |

and input string $w = 01$ to an instance of *MPCP*.

(b) Show that the following question is decidable.

(*i*) The set of codes for *TM's M* such that when started with black tape will eventually write some non-blank symbol on its tape.

(c) Show that a set of *TM* codes for *TM's* that accept all inputs that are palindrome (possibly alongwith some other inputs) in undecidable.

# B. TECH

## Fourth Semester Examination

## 2006-2007

*Time : Three hours* *Total Marks : 100*

**Note :** (*i*) Attempt ALL questions.

(*ii*) All questions carry equal marks.

**1.** Attempt any *FOUR* of the following: (5 × 4 = 20)

(a) Construct a *DFA* that accepts the strings which contains the alphabets pattern 011 (Σ = 0, 1).

(b) For the given state diagram of a *NFA*. Convert it to an equivalent *DFA*.

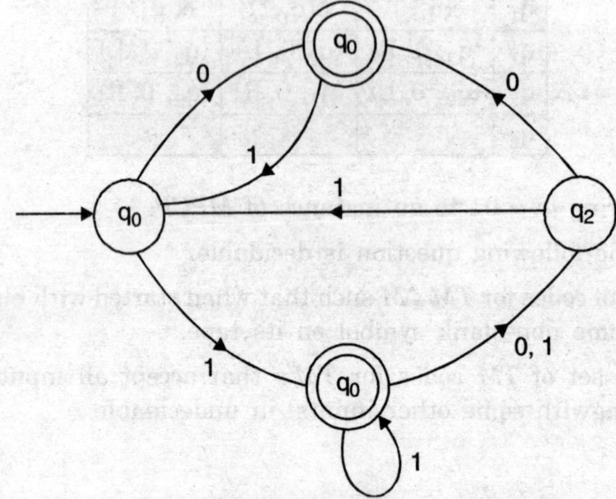


(c) Construct the *FA* for the language $L_n$ (for $n \geq 1$) i.e.

$L_n$ = {*x s* {0, 1}* | 1 × 1 ≥ *n* and $n^{th}$ symbol from the right in *x* is 1}

(d) Draw a moore or Mealy machine that generates output 'Yes' when accepts a set of strings from (0 + 1)* terminating in last two same symbols.

(e) Construct a *DFA* from the given *NFA* with s moves.

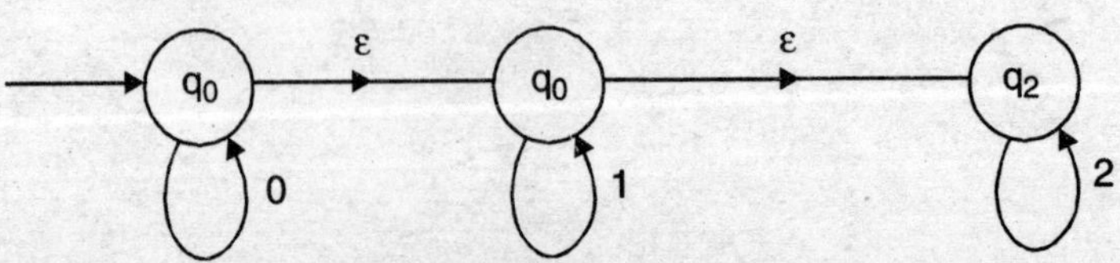


(f) Minimize the *DFA* corresponding to *NFA* of question 1(*b*).

**2.** Attempt any *TWO* of the following: (10 × 2 = 20)

(a) Illustrates the pumping lemma for regular languages. Prove that language $L = \{0^{i2} \mid i\ ^3\ 0|\}$ is not regular.

(b) Show that *CFG G* with following productions

$$S \rightarrow a \mid Sa \mid bSS \mid SSb \mid SbS$$

is an ambiguous grammar. Can you convert it to an unambiguous grammer?

(c) Convert the given grammar into GNF:

$$S \rightarrow AA \mid a$$

$$A \rightarrow SS \mid b$$

**3.** Attempt any *TWO* of the following: (10 × 2 = 20)

(a) Construct the grammer for the language $L = \{a^{n2} \mid n\ ^3\ 1\}$. Identify the type of the grammar obtain.

(b) How to make a *PDA* deterministic i.e. *DPDA*. Construct the *DPDA* for the language $L = \{x\ s\ \{a, b\}^* \mid x$ has equal of *a's* and *b's*.

(c) Give a context free grammar. How do you determine that the grammar as:

(*i*) Empty or Non-empty

(*ii*) Finite or non-finite.

(*iii*) Whether a string × belongs to the language of the grammar.

**4.** Attempt any TWO of the following: (10 × 2 = 20)

(a) State and prove that Post correspondence problem (*PCP*) is decidable.

(b) Let $f_1$ and $f_2$ are two natural functions which are computed by *TMs* $M_1$ and $M_2$ respectively. Construct a *TM* that computes max $(f_1, f_2)$.

(c) Design a turing machine that recognisers the following:

$$L = \{a^n\ b^n \mid n \geq 1\}.$$

**5.** Attempt any *TWO* parts of the following: (10 × 2 = 20)

(a) Give the complete hierarchy of grammars with their recognisers as well as the form of production rules.

(b) Write a left linear grammar for the following language. All strings of $(a + b)^*$ such that *bbb* is a substring in them.

(c) Define context sensitive grammars and Linear Bound Automata (*LBA*).

# B. TECH
# Fourth Semester Examination
# 2007-2008

*Time : Three hours* *Total Marks : 100*

**Note : (*i*) Attempt ALL questions.**

**(*ii*) All questions carry equal marks.**

**1. Attempt any *TWO* parts of the following:**

**(a) (*i*) Find the transitive closure $R^+$ and reflexive and transitive closure $R^*$ of the relation**

**$R = \{(1, 2), (2, 3), (3, 4), (5, 4)\}$** **(4)**

**(*ii*) Consider the following transition diagram. (6)**

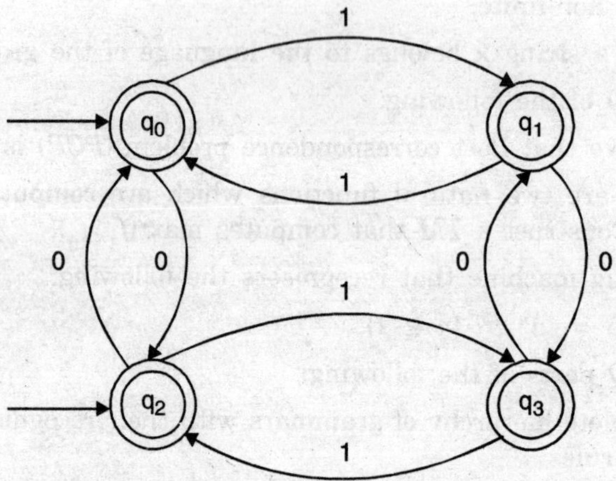


**Test whether the string 110101 is accepted by the finite automata represented by above transition diagram. Show the entire sequence of states traversed.**

**(b) Give *DFA* accepting the following languages over the alphabet {0, 1}:**

**(*i*) The set of all strings with three consecutive zeros.**

**(*ii*) The set of all string such that every block of 05 consecutive symbols contains at least two zeros.**

**(c) Find the equivalence partition and correponding reduced machine in standard form, for the following machine**

| PS | NS,Z | |
|---|---|---|
| | X = 0 | X = 1 |
| A | F, 0 | B, 1 |
| B | G, 0 | A, 1 |
| C | B, 0 | C, 1 |
| D | C, 0 | B, 1 |
| E | D, 0 | A, 1 |
| F | E, 1 | F, 1 |
| G | E, 1 | G, 1 |

Where, *PS* = Present State, *NS* = Next State, *Z* = Output, *X* = *I*/*P*.(10)

**2.** Attempt any *TWO* parts of the following:

(a) Construct DFA equivalent to the *NFA* ({*p*, *q*, *r*, *s*}, {0, 1}, *d*, *p*, {*s*}), where d is given by

| 0 | | 1 |
|---|---|---|
| *p* | *p*, *q* | *p* |
| *q* | *r* | *r* |
| *r* | *s* | – |
| *s* | *s* | *s* |

(10)

(b) Construct *NFA* for $(a/b)^+$ and derive *DFA* through subset construction algorithm. (10)

(c) Prove or disprove the following for regular expressions r, s and t

(*i*) $(r + s)^* = r^* + s^*$

(*ii*) $s(rs + s)^* = r = rr^*s(rr^*\ s)^*$

**3.** Attempt any *FOUR* parts of the following:

(a) Construct finite automata equivalent to following regular expression 10 + (0 + 11)0*1 (5)

(b) Write regular expression for the following language over the alphabet {0, 1} "The set of all strings not containing 101 as a substring." (5)

(c) Explain the procedure to convent a Moore machine into its corresponding Mealy machine, with the help of an example. (5)

(d) Find parse tree for the expression abbcde considering the productions

$$S \rightarrow a\ Ac\ Be$$

$$A \rightarrow Ab$$

$$A \rightarrow b$$

$$B \rightarrow d$$

(5)

(e) What is an ambiguous grammar? Explain with example. (5)

(f) Consider the grammar ({$S, A, B$}, {$a, b$}, $P$, $S$) that has the productions

$$S \rightarrow bA / aB$$
$$A \rightarrow bAA / aS / a$$
$$B \rightarrow aBB / bS / b$$

Find an equivalent grammar in *CNF*. (5)

**4.** Attempt any *TWO* of the following:

(a) Define concept and working of a *PDA*. (10)

(b) Construct a *PDA* equivalent to the following grammar: (5)

$$S \rightarrow aAA$$
$$A \rightarrow aS / bS / a$$

(c) Construct a *PDA* accepting the language {$a^i \ b^j \ c^k$ / $i \neq j$ or $j \neq$ } (10)

**5.** Attempt any *FOUR* parts of the following:

(a) Define the basic model of a Turing machine. (5)

(b) Explain the techniques for Turing machines construction. (5)

(c) Explain Church's thesis. (5)

(d) Design Turing machine to compute the function $f(n) = n^2$. (5)

(e) Design Turing machine to recognize the language "The set of strings with an equal number of 0's and 1's." (5)

(f) Give recursive definitions for : $n + m$. (5)

❑❑❑

# GGSIPU

## End-Term Examination
## [Paper Code : ETCS – 211]
## Fifth Semester [B.Tech.]

---

*Time : 3 Hours* *Total Marks : 70*

Attempt any five questions.

1. (a) Is the language $\{a^n ba^m ba^{n+m} \mid n,m \geq 1\}$ regular? Prove your claim. (8)

   (b) Show that if $L$ is a regular language, then the language $L^n$ is regular for all $n \geq 0$. (6)

2. Find a non-deterministic finite automaton accepting the regular expression $(ab + aab + aba)^*$. Convert the NFA thus obtained into an equivalent deterministic finite automaton. (14)

3. (a) Design a push down automaton that accepts the language $\{w \in \{a, b\}^* :$ has equal numbers of $a's$ and $b's\}$. (8)

   (b) Prove that each context free language is accepted by some push down automaton. (6)

4. (a) What is the language generated by a grammar $G$ whose only production rule is

   $$S \rightarrow as \mid aSbS \mid \lambda$$

   Prove your claim. (7)

   (b) Find the grammar that generates the following language. (7)

   (*i*) $\{a^n b^n a^n b^n \mid n \geq 0\}$

   (*ii*) $\{a^n x b^n \mid n \geq 0, x \in \{a,b\}^*\}$

5. (a) Design a Turing machine to recognize the language $\{0^n 1^n 0^n \mid n \geq 1\}$. (10)

   (b) Design a Turing machine to compute for positive integer $n$. (4)

   $$f(n) = n + 1$$

6. (a) (*i*) Show that $10^6 n^2 = \theta(2^n)$ (7)

   (*ii*) Show that $[\{\log_2(n+1)]^k = \theta(n^{\epsilon}), \forall \in, k > 0$

   (b) Prove that the Fibonacci function defined as (7)

   $$F(0) = 0, F(1) = 1$$

   $$F(n + 2) = F(n) + F(n + 1) \text{ for } n \geq 0$$

   is a primitive recursive function.

**7.** (a) Prove that

(*i*) $(a + b)^* a(a + b)^* b(a + b)^* = (a + b)^* ab (a + b)^*$ (4)

(*ii*) $(00^* 1)^* 1 = 1 + 0 (0 + 10^*)11$ (4)

(*iii*) $(111^*)^* = (11 + 111)^*$ (4)

(*iv*)$(a + b)^* = (a + b)^* + (a + b)^*$ (2)

**8.** Write short notes on any four of the following: (14)

(*a*) Church-Turing Thesis

(*b*) Turing Machine Halting Problem

(*c*) The set *P*, *NP* and *NP* complete

(*d*) Chomsky Hierarchy

(*e*) Relevance of formal grammars to programming languages.

(*f*) Pumping Lemmas

(*g*) Extension to Turing Machines.

(*i*) Church-Turing Thesis

# GGSIPU

## End-Term Examination
## [Paper Code : ETCS – 211]
## Fifth Semester [B.Tech.]

*Time : 3 Hours* *Total Marks : 70*

Attempt any five questions.

**1.** (a) What do you mean by Chomsky's normal form? Write the steps to convert any context free grammar $G = (V, T, S, P)$ with no null productions to an equivalent grammar $G^1 = (V^1, T, S, P^1)$ in Chomsky's normal form. (7

(b) Consider the following grammar: (7)

$$S \rightarrow aSa$$

$$S \rightarrow SSa$$

$$S \rightarrow a$$

Convert this grammar to Chomsky's normal form.

**2.** (a) Draw a Moore machine with alphabet $\Sigma = \{a, b\}$ and output alphabet $\Gamma = \{0, 1\}$ with the following transition and output table. (3.5)

| | $a$ | $b$ | Output |
|---|---|---|---|
| $q_0$ | $q_1$ | $q_2$ | 0 |
| $q_1$ | $q_2$ | $q_3$ | 0 |
| $q_2$ | $q_3$ | $q_4$ | 1 |
| $q_3$ | $q_4$ | $q_4$ | 0 |
| $q_4$ | $q_0$ | $q_0$ | 0 |

(b) Convert above Moore machine to a mealy machine. (3.5)

(c) Is the language $L = \{a^{n!} \mid n \geq 0\}$ regular? Justify your answer. (7)

**3.** Design a Turing machine to recognize the language $\{0^n 1^{2n} \mid n \geq 1\}$ (14)

Check your machine by tracing strings 001111 and 0001111.

**4.** (a) Prove that given any PDA, there is another PDA that accepts exactly the same language with the additional property that whenever a path leads to AC-CEPT, the STACK and Tape contain only blanks. (7)

(b) Build a deterministic Push down automaton that accepts the languages $\{a^n b^{n+1}\}$. (7)

**5.** Find a non-deterministic finite automaton accepting the regular expression $(a/b)^*$ $ab\ (b)^*$. Convert the NFA thus obtained into an equivalent deterministic finite automaton. (14)

**6.** (a) Consider the language $S^*$, where $S = \{ab, ba\}$. Write out all the words in $S^*$ that have seven or fewer letters. (3)

(b) Give a recursive definition for the set $ODD = \{1, 3, 5, 7 \ldots.\}$ (3)

(c) Write regular expression for $S = \{a, b\}$ that generates. (3)

(*i*) All strings that have exactly one double letter in them.

(*ii*) All strings with at least one a.

(d) Prove that $(a + b)^*\ ab\ (a + b)^* + b^*a^* = (a + b)^*$. (4)

**7.** (a) Suppose that $L$ is a finite language whose words are $w_1, w_2, w_3 \ldots w_{83}$. Prove that there is a transition graph that accepts exactly the language $L$. (7)

(b) Show that $[\log (n + 1)]^k = 0(n),\ \forall\ n,k > 0$ (7)

**8.** Write short notes on any three of the following: (14)

(a) The set $P$, $NP$ and $NP$ complete.

(b) Pumping Lemma for CFG.

(c) Nonregular Languages.

(d) Kleene's theorem.

(e) FA with $\lambda$ moves.

# UTTARANCHAL UNIVERSITY

## Fourth Semester Examination B.Tech

*Time : 3 Hours* *Total Marks : 100*

Attempt ALL questions.

**1.** Attempt any Four of the following: 5 × 4 = 20

(a) What is Moore Machine? Change the given Moore machine into Mealy machine:

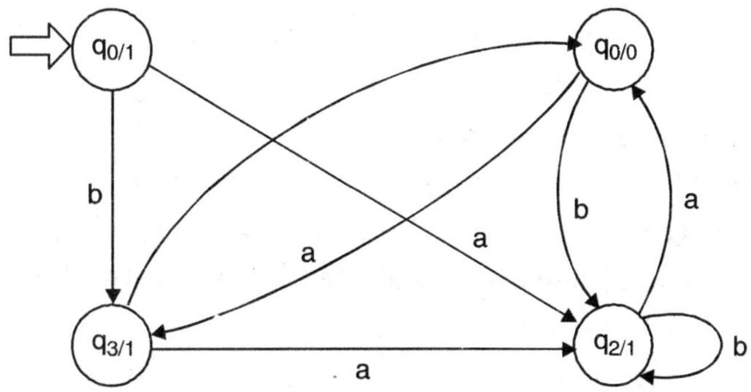


(b) Find out Regular Expression of the given diagram:

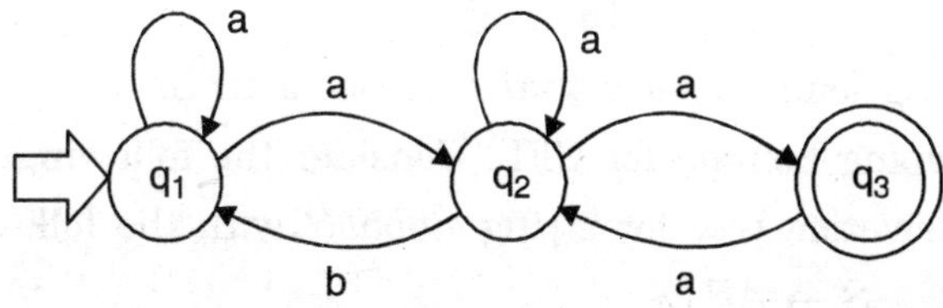


(c) Give deterministic finite automata accepting the following languages over the alphabet {0,1}:

(*i*) The set of all strings ending in 00.

(*ii*) The set of all strings such that every block of five consecutive symbols contains at least two 0's.

(d) Construct a dfa equivalent to the following ndfa:

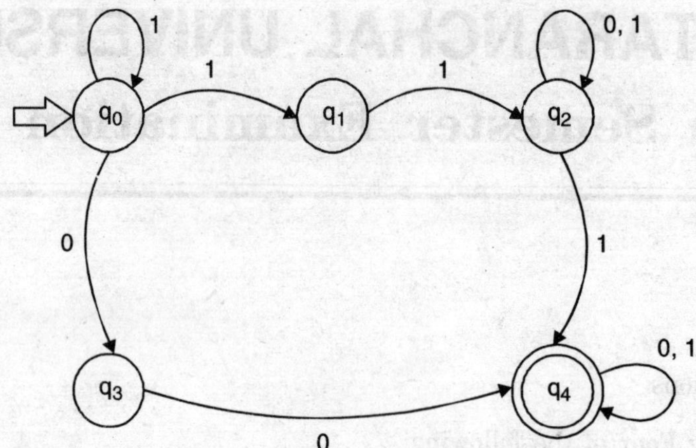


(e) What is the difference between Two-way Finite Automata (2 dfa) and One way Finite Automata?

(f) Find the regular grammar for the language

$$L = \{a^n b^m \mid n + m \text{ is even}\}$$

**2.** Attempt any Four of the following: $5 \times 4 = 20$

(a) State Myhill-Nerode Theorem.

(b) What is Ambiguity? Show that $S \to as \mid Sa \mid a$ is an ambiguous grammar.

(c) Convert the given grammar in Chomsky Normal Form (CNF):

$$S \to ABa$$
$$A \to aab$$
$$B \to Ac$$

(d) Show that $L = \{ww \mid w \varepsilon \{a,b\}^*\}$ is not regular set.

$$L = \{a^n b^n c^n \mid n \geq 0\}.$$

Using pumping lemma, show that $L$ is not a CFL.

(e) Explain Pumping Lemma for CFL. Consider the following language:

(f) Show the derivation tree for string '*aabbbb*' with the following grammar:

$$S \to AB \mid \lambda$$
$$A \to aB$$
$$B \to Sb$$

**3.** Attempt any Two of the following: $10 \times 2 = 20$

(a) Write down the algorithm to determine whether CFL is

(*i*) Empty

(*ii*) Finite or

(*iii*) Infinite.

(b) Explain the difference between Deterministic and Non-Deterministic Pushdown Automata giving their definition. Illustrate with an example of each.

(c) Construct PDA for the following $L = \{a^n c b^{2n} \mid n \geq 1\}$ over the alphabet $\Sigma = \{a, b, c\}$.

**4.** Attempt any Two of the following: 10 × 2 = 20

(a) Define a Turing Machine. Design a Turing Machine that accepts the language

$$L = \{a^n b^{n+1} \mid n > 0\}.$$

(b) Does the Post Correspondence Problem (PCP) with two lists $x = (b, bab^3, ba)$ and y = $(b^3, ba, a)$ have a solution?

(c) State True/False with reason:

(*i*) Every language described by regular expression can be recognised by dfa.

(*ii*) Every recursively enumerable language can be generated by a CFL.

(*iii*) The halting problem of *TM* is decidable.

(*iv*) Complement of any recursively enumerable language is also enumerable.

(*v*) Every CFL can be recognised by *TM*.

**5.** Attempt any Two of the following: 10 × 2 = 20

(a) Show that $L = \{a^n b^n c^n \mid n \geq 1\}$ is not context-free but context-sensitive.

(b) Give the production rules for Type 0, Type 1, Type 2 and Type 3 grammars of Chomsky hierarchy.

(c) Show that CSL are closed under:

(*i*) Union

(*ii*) Substitution

(*iii*) Concatenation

(*iv*) Intersection

# UNIVERSITY OF DELHI

# MCA (New Course) Paper – CS.303

# Theory of Computation-I

*Time : 3 Hours* *Total Marks : 100*

Write your Roll No. on the top immediately on receipt of this question paper-Answer all questions.

**1.** (a) Given two finite automata $M_1$, $M_2$ can we determine whether the languages $L(M_1)$ and $L(M_2)$ accepted by them are same? If so, how? (5)

(b) Construct a dfa which accepts the following language: (5)

$\{w \in \{a,b\}^* : w$ has an odd number of a's and an even number of $b$'s$\}$

**2.** Let $D = \{0,1\}$ and let $T = D \times D \times D$. A correct addition of two numbers in binary notation can be pictured as a string in $T^*$ if we think of symbols in $T$ as vertical columns. For example,

$$\begin{array}{cccc} 0 & 1 & 0 & 1 \\ 0 & 1 & 1 & 0 \\ \hline 1 & 0 & 1 & 1 \end{array}$$

would be pictured a the following string of four symbols:

$$\begin{bmatrix}0\\0\\1\end{bmatrix}\begin{bmatrix}1\\1\\1\end{bmatrix}\begin{bmatrix}0\\1\\1\end{bmatrix}\begin{bmatrix}1\\0\\1\end{bmatrix}$$

Show that the set of all strings in $T^*$ that represent correct addition is a regular language. (10)

**3.** Are the following languages regular? Justify your answer. (10)

(a) All odd-length words over $\{a,b\}^*$ for which the first letter matches the centre letter.

(b) $\{x \in \{0,1\}^*$ the base 2 number represented by $x$ is a power of 2$\}$.

**4.** (a) Convert the following grammar to Chomsky normal form: (5)

$S \rightarrow cBA$

$S \rightarrow B$

$A \rightarrow cB$

$A \rightarrow AbbS$

$B \rightarrow aaa$

(b) Prove that the language $\{b, b^2, b^4, b^8, \ldots\}$ is not context free. (5)

**5.** Let $K_S$ be the set of all languages (defined over $\Sigma$) that are not context free. Determine whether or not

(*i*) $K_\Sigma$ is closed under complementation.

(*ii*) $K_\Sigma$ is closed under intersection. (10)

**6.** Design a Turing machine which finds sum of two binary numbers of same length. You machine should take care of any overflow. (10)

**7.** Write a grammar for the language: $\{a^n b^n c^n : n \geq 0\}$ (10)

**8.** (a) Identify the function described below:

$$A(x,y) = \begin{cases} 0, \text{ if } x = 0 \text{ or } y = 0 \\ \mu z \leq x[\exists w \leq x[w.y + z = x]], \text{if } x \neq 0, y \neq 0 \end{cases}$$ (5)

(b) Suppose that function $g = N^k \to N^t$ is known to be primitive recursive. Show that $G : N \to N$ is primitive recursive, where for any $n \in N$, $G\ (n)$ = the maximum value of $g(n_1,...n_k)$ for $n_1,...n_k \leq n$ (5)

**9.** (a) What are thue system? State the word problem for the thue systems. (3)

(b) Show that the following problem is not solvable:

Given a Turing machine $M$, does $M$ halt on an empty tape. (7)

**10.** Show that initial functions are Turing computable. (10)

# MCA/III Sem. (New Course)
# Paper – CS.303
# Theory of Computation-I

*Time : 3 Hours* *Total Marks : 100*

Write your Roll No. on the top immediately on receipt of this question paper. Answer all questions. Parts of a question shold be answered together.

**1.** The star height $h$ (α) of a regular expression a is defined by induction as follows: (8)

$$h(\phi) = 0$$

$$h(a) = 0 \quad \forall \quad a \in S$$

$$h(\alpha \cup \beta) = h(\alpha\beta) = \max(h(\alpha), h(\beta))$$

$$h(\alpha)^* = h(\alpha) + 1$$

For each of the following cases obtain a regular expression which represents the same language and has star height as small as possible:

(i) $((abc)^*ab)^*$

(ii) $(a(ab^*c)^*)^*$

**2.** Which of the following are true? Justify. (8)

(a) $b^*a^* \cap a^*b^* = a^* \cup b^*$

(b) $a^*b^* \cap c^*d^* = \phi$

**3.** Obtain equivalent dfa for the following nfa defined over $\Sigma = \{a, b\}$ (8)

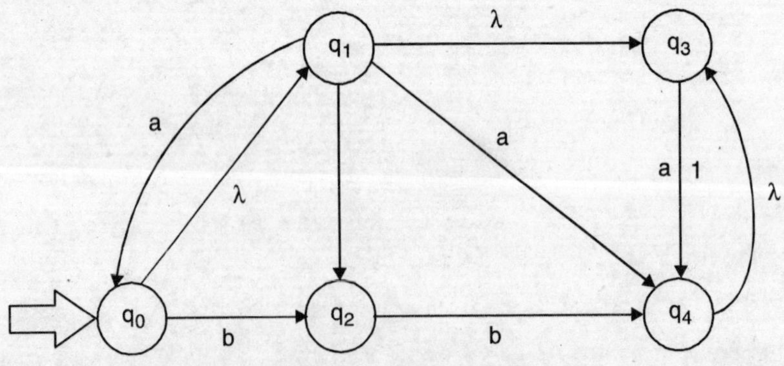


**4.** Given the finite automata $M_1$ and $M_2$, gives an algorithm to check whether $L(M_1) \subseteq L(M_2)$.

**5.** You are given that $L, L' \subseteq \Sigma^*$. If language $L$ is regular, is language

$$L/L' = \{w \in \Sigma^* : L \text{ for some } x \in L'\}$$

regular? Justify your answer. (8)

**6.** (a) If $C$ is any set of regular languages, is $\cup C$ is regular language? Justify.

(b) Is the language $\{a^n : n \text{ is prime}\}$ regular? Justify your answer. (8)

**7.** (a) Show that the context free languages are not closed under complementation.

(b) Given a context free grammar $G$ and a string $w \in \Sigma^*$, can we say determine algorithmically whether $w \in L$? Justify. (8)

**8.** (a) Construct a push down automaton for the language : $\{a^m b^n : m \leq n \geq 2m\}$.

(b) Suppose that $G = \{V, \Sigma, P, S\}$ is ac context free grammar such that each rule in $P$ is either of the form $A \to wB$ or $A \to A\ Bw$, where in each case $A, B \in V - S$ and $w \in \Sigma^*$. Is $L(G)$ necessarily regular? Prove it or give a counter example.

**9.** Formally define: (10)

(*i*) A $k$-tape Turing machine

(*ii*) Configuration of such a machine

(*iii*) The yields in one step relation between configurations for such a machine.

**10.** Write grammar for the following language: $\{a^n b^n c^n : n \geq 0\}$. (8)

**11.** Informally justify that the primitive recursive functions are Turing-computable. (8)

**12.** Show that the following problems about Turing machine are unsolvable:

(a) Given a Turing machine $M$, does halt on every input string?

(b) Given two context free grammars $G_1$ and $G_2$, determine whether $L(G_1) \cap L(G_2) = \phi$.

(10)

❑❑❑

## A



## C



## D



## E

## Q



## R



## S



## T



## U



## W



□□□